THE ROUTLEDGE HISTORY
OF SLAVERY

The Routledge History of Slavery is a landmark publication that provides an overview of the main themes surrounding the history of slavery from ancient Greece to the present day. Taking stock of the field of slave studies, the book explores the major advances that have taken place in the past few decades in this crucial subject.

Offering an unusual, transnational history of slavery, the chapters have all been specially commissioned for the collectioan. The volume begins by delineating the global nature of the institution of slavery, examining slavery in different parts of the world and over time. Topics covered here include slavery in Africa and the Indian Ocean World, as well as the transatlantic slave trade. In Part 2, the chapters explore different themes that define slavery, including slave culture, the slave economy, slave resistance and the planter class, as well as areas of life affected by slavery, such as family and work. The final part goes on to study changes and continuities over time, looking at abolition, the aftermath of emancipation and commemoration. The volume concludes with a chapter on modern slavery.

Including essays on all the key topics and issues, this important collection from a leading international group of scholars presents a comprehensive survey of the current state of the field. It will be essential reading for all those interested in the history of slavery.

Gad Heuman is Professor of History and has served as Director of the Centre for Caribbean Studies at the University of Warwick. He is author of *Between Black and White* (1981), *The Killing Time* (1994) and *The Caribbean* (2006). He is editor of the journal *Slavery & Abolition*.

Trevor Burnard is Professor of American History at the University of Warwick. He specialises in the history of plantation societies and slavery in the Americas, and is author of *Mastery, Tyranny, and Desire: Thomas Thistlewood and his Slaves in the Anglo-Jamaican World* (2004).

THE ROUTLEDGE HISTORIES

The Routledge Histories is a series of landmark books surveying some of the most important topics and themes in history today. Edited and written by an international team of world-renowned experts, they are the works against which all future books on their subjects will be judged.

THE ROUTLEDGE
HISTORY OF SLAVERY

Edited by
Gad Heuman and Trevor Burnard

Routledge
Taylor & Francis Group

LONDON AND NEW YORK

First published 2011 by Routledge
2 Park Square, Milton Park, Abingdon, Oxon OX14 4RN

Simultaneously published in the USA and Canada by Routledge
270 Madison Avenue, New York, NY 10016

Routledge is an imprint of the Taylor & Francis Group, an informa business

© 2011 Gad Heuman and Trevor Burnard for selection and editorial matter;
individual chapters, the contributors
The right of Gad Heuman and Trevor Burnard to be identified as authors of this
work has been asserted by them in accordance with sections 77 and 78 of the
Copyright, Designs and Patents Act 1988.

Typeset in Sabon by Taylor & Francis Books

British Library Cataloguing in Publication Data
A catalogue record for this book is available from the British Library

Library of Congress Catalog-in-Publication Data
The Routledge history of slavery / edited by Gad Heuman and Trevor Burnard.
p. cm. -- (The Routledge histories)
1. Slavery--History. 2. Slavery. I. Heuman, Gad J. II. Burnard, Trevor G.
(Trevor Graeme) III. Title: History of slavery.
HT861.R68 2010 2011
306.3'6209--dc22
2010017402

ISBN13: 978-0-415-46689-9 (hbk)
ISBN13: 978-0-203-84057-3 (ebk)

CONTENTS

CONTENTS

CONTRIBUTORS

Christopher Leslie Brown, Professor of History at Columbia University, works on the history of the British Empire and comparative slavery and abolition. He is author of *Moral Capital: Foundations of British Abolitionism* (2006) and co-editor of *Arming Slaves: From Classical Times to the Modern Age* (2006).

Trevor Burnard is Professor of American History, Head of the Department of History and Director of the Yesu Persaud Caribbean Centre at the University of Warwick. He works on planters and slave societies in colonial British America. He is author of numerous articles on the British West Indies and the Chesapeake, and of *Mastery, Tyranny, and Desire: Thomas Thistlewood and His Slaves in the Anglo-Jamaican World* (2004) and *Creole Gentlemen: The Maryland Elite 1691–1776* (2002).

Gwyn Campbell is Canada Research Chair in Indian Ocean World History at McGill University and author and editor of many publications, including *An Economic History of Imperial Madagascar, 1750–1895* (2005/2009); *The Structure of Slavery in Indian Ocean Africa and Asia* (2004); *Children and Slavery Through the Ages* and with Suzanne Miers and Joseph Miller *Women and Slavery*, 2 vols (2009, 2008 and 2007).

Matt D. Childs is an Associate Professor of History at the University of South Carolina. He is author of *The 1812 Aponte Rebellion in Cuba and the Struggle against Atlantic Slavery* (2006), and co-editor of *The Yoruba Diaspora in the Atlantic World* (2005) and *The Changing Worlds of Atlantic Africa* (2009). Childs has received research grants from the Social Science Research Council, the Ford Foundation, the American Council of Learned Societies, and the Fulbright-Hays Program.

Laurent Dubois is Professor of History and Romance Studies at Duke University. He is author of *Avengers of the New World* (2004), *A Colony of Citizens* (2004) and *Soccer Empire: The World Cup and the Future of France* (2010). He has also published *Origins of the Black Atlantic* (with Julius Scott, 2009) and *Slave Revolution in the Caribbean, 1789–1804: A History in Documents* (with John Garrigus, 2006).

Richard Follett is Reader in American History at the University of Sussex. He is a historian of slavery and emancipation in the United States and the Caribbean, and is author of many articles, electronic databases www.sussex.ac.uk/louisianasugar, and the prize winning *The Sugar Masters: Planters and Slaves in Louisiana's Cane World, 1820–1860* (2005).

Sylvia R. Frey is Professor of History Emerita at Tulane University. She is author of *Water from the Rock* (1991) and *The British Soldier in America* (1981), and co-author of *Come Shouting to Zion* (1997). She has edited several works including *New World, New Roles: A Documentary History of Women in Pre-Industrial America* (1986) and *From Slavery to Emancipation in the Atlantic World* (1999).

John Garrigus is Associate Professor of History at the University of Texas at Arlington. He is author of *Before Haiti: Race and Citizenship in Saint-Domingue* (2006), which won the Gilbert Chinard Prize from the Society for French Historical Studies, and co-editor (with Laurent Dubois) of *Slave Revolution in the Caribbean, 1789–1804: A Brief History with Documents* (2006).

Steven Hahn is Roy F. and Jeannette P. Nichols Professor of American History at the University of Pennsylvania. He is author of *The Roots of Southern Populism* (1983), *A Nation under Our Feet* (2003) and *The Political Worlds of Slavery and Freedom* (2009), and editor of *The Countryside in the Age of Capitalist Transformation* (1985) and *Freedom: A Documentary History of Emancipation* (2009).

Gad Heuman is Professor of History and has served as Director of the Centre for Caribbean Studies at the University of Warwick. He is author of *Between Black and White* (1981), *The Killing Time* (1994) and *The Caribbean* (2006). He has also edited and co-edited several books, including *The Slavery Reader* (2003) and *Contesting Freedom* (2005). He is editor of the journal *Slavery & Abolition*.

Timothy James Lockley is Associate Professor of History and Director of the School of Comparative American Studies at the University of Warwick. His research concentrates on slavery and white society in the colonial and antebellum American South. His publications include *Welfare and Charity in the Antebellum South* (2007) and *Lines in the Sand: Race and Class in Lowcountry Georgia, 1750–1860* (2001).

Paul E. Lovejoy FRSC is Distinguished Research Professor, Canada Research Chair in African Diaspora History, York University (Toronto) and Director of The Harriet Tubman Institute for Research on the Global Migrations of African Peoples. He has published more than 35 books and more than 80 chapters and articles on Africa and the African Diaspora. He is Editor of the *Harriet Tubman Series on the African Diaspora*.

Niall McKeown is a lecturer in Ancient History at the University of Birmingham in the Institute of Archaeology and Antiquity. He works on both ancient Greek and ancient Roman slavery, and is author of *The Invention of Ancient Slavery?* (2007).

Jennifer L. Morgan is Professor of History in the Department of Social and Cultural Analysis and the Department of History at New York University. She works on gender and slavery in the colonial Black Atlantic. She is author of *Laboring Women: Gender and Reproduction in the Making of New World Slavery* (2003). She is currently at work on a project that considers colonial numeracy, racism and the rise of the trans-Atlantic slave trade.

Joel Quirk is Deputy Director of the Wilberforce Institute for the study of Slavery and Emancipation, University of Hull. His research focuses primarily upon the relationship between historical slave systems and contemporary forms of slavery. This is reflected in two books: *Unfinished Business: A Comparative Survey of Historical and Contemporary Slavery* (2009) and *The Anti-Slavery Project: From the Slave Trade to Human Trafficking* (forthcoming).

Edward B. Rugemer is Assistant Professor of African American Studies and History at Yale University. He studies the transatlantic struggle over slavery, and has published articles in the *Journal of Southern History* and *Slavery and Abolition*. His first book, *The Problem of Emancipation: The Caribbean Roots of the American Civil War*, was published in 2008.

James Sidbury is Professor of History at the University of Texas at Austin and author of *Ploughshares into Swords: Race, Rebellion, and Identity in Gabriel's Virginia* (1997) and *Becoming African in America: Race and Nation in the Early Black Atlantic* (2007).

Lorena Walsh was for 27 years a research historian with the Colonial Williamsburg Foundation. She works on plantation agriculture, slavery and the trans-Atlantic slave trade. She is author of numerous articles on the economy and society of the colonial and early national Chesapeake, and is author of *Robert Cole's World* (1991, with Lois Green Carr and Russell R. Menard), *From Calabar to Carter's Grove* (1997) and *Motives of Honor, Pleasure, and Profit* (2010).

Betty Wood is a Reader in American History at the University of Cambridge and a Fellow at Girton College, Cambridge. She is author of several books, including *Slavery in Colonial Georgia, 1730–1775* (1984), *Women's Work, Men's Work: The Informal Slave Economies of Lowcountry Georgia, 1750–1830* (1995), *The Origins of American Slavery* (1997) and (with Sylvia R. Frey) *Come Shouting to Zion: African-American Protestantism in the American South and British Caribbean to 1830* (1998).

INTRODUCTION

Trevor Burnard and Gad Heuman

"O what a rogue and peasant slave am I", William Shakespeare has Hamlet, the doomed Prince of Denmark exclaim at the end of Act 2 of *Hamlet*.[1] Hamlet is a prince, so is almost as far removed from an actual slave as it is possible to be. Moreover, neither in Denmark, where the play is set, nor in early seventeenth-century England, where the play was performed, was slavery common. But the idea of slavery, as Shakespeare recognised, was well known even in places where a person would seldom meet a slave, let alone become a slave oneself. Shakespeare used the imagery of slavery to get at a deeper truth. To be a slave, or to feel like a slave, was to be in the pit of despair because no condition could be worse than being a slave. Slavery was a form of exploitation in which one human was owned by another person, and in which the slave hovered uncertainly between the contradictory positions of being both a piece of property and also a person. It was also, as imaginative artists since Aristophanes and thinkers beginning with Aristotle have realised, a state of mind, a status that affected how one thought of oneself, if one was a slave, and how others thought of slaves. To be a slave, as Hamlet imagined himself to be, was to experience helplessness and degradation, even if – as in this case, but not normally in actual slavery – enslavement was not accompanied by physical violence. As Betty Wood notes in Chapter 4 of this volume, for Elizabethan English people, enslavement was dehumanisation: to treat men or women as slaves was to treat them as beasts.

The 20 chapters in this volume consider not just what it felt like be a slave, but slavery in all its forms, from a means of extracting labour from unwilling people to a means whereby some people could gain status and others lose it. The essays also discuss how the existence of slavery in a society affected a variety of social, economic, political and cultural patterns. In this book, we examine slavery over both time and place: we begin with the first major slave societies developed in ancient Greece and Rome and then move on to slavery in Africa and the Indian Ocean World. We focus intently on slavery in the Americas before it ended in the late nineteenth century, and conclude with a treatment of slavery as it exists in the twenty-first century. We look at enslavement in its many different aspects. The chapters in this volume explain how slavery began, how slaves were moved from one place in the world (from the early modern period onwards mainly from West and East Africa), and how slavery was legally stopped. We look at enslaved people as workers and as members of families and cultural groupings. Other essays examine the religious and cultural beliefs of slaves and the constraints – demographic, cultural, economic, physical – that enslaved people encountered while trying to shape viable lives for themselves under extremely trying conditions.

A major theme of this volume is that slavery was a formal institution but also a negotiated relationship. Enslaved people formed their own communities, with value systems and forms of behaviour that differed from the social norms of non-enslaved people, but these communities were set within larger social groupings that exerted their own pull over enslaved people's desires. While the focus in this book is on the individual and collective experience of enslaved people, that experience was modified and influenced by their relationship with their owners and with people who were not enslaved. It was also modified in both the Atlantic and Indian Ocean Worlds by race. Gwyn Campbell (Chapter 3) makes the important point that we need to move on from a simplistic, black-and-white dichotomy that does not really work for an Atlantic World where Native Americans and people of mixed race were enslaved alongside Africans. And such a model, he argues, makes no sense for an Indian Ocean World where most slaves were of the same race as their owners and where some slaves, especially female slaves, lived better than their masters. Nevertheless, race was very important, especially in the Atlantic World, both in shaping relations between slaves and free people and in providing an intellectual justification for enslavement.

A noticeable feature of slavery in the period and place on which we concentrate most – the Americas from the time of the Columbian encounter in 1492 through to the abolition of slavery in Brazil in 1888 – is that enslaved people were differentiated from free people by virtue of race. Slaves were either Native American or else African or of African descent; free people were meant to be persons of European descent (although in practice a number of free people, as John Garrigus notes in Chapter 14, were either of mixed race or solely of African descent). Nevertheless, race is a slippery concept ideologically and an even more slippery biological construct. What happened when the "races" of African, Native American and European mixed? Several chapters describe the complications that developed in relation to slavery when a class of people emerged in the Americas who were both mixed race and also free people rather than enslaved.

How enslaved people got their freedom and what freedom meant for ex-slaves is also a major part of this volume. We are suspicious of tendencies within the historiography of slavery to treat every disagreement between enslaved people and their owners as a manifestation of slave resistance. We are also careful to stress how unsuccessful both individual and collective slave resistance normally was in the face of overwhelming owner power, buttressed usually by the power of a supportive state. Yet it is undeniable that enslaved people disliked their condition and often worked actively to try and alter what they most detested about enslavement. Sometimes, this resistance took the form of trying to reform particular abuses within the parameters of slavery. At other times, most notably in the slave rebellion that destroyed the greatest slave society of them all, Saint Domingue, enslaved people turned to violence to counter the violence that customarily governed their lives as slaves. Two chapters in this volume, by James Sidbury (Chapter 12) and Gad Heuman (Chapter 13), look explicitly at slave resistance and rebellion. Other essays focus on how slavery was weakened and then abolished by forces outside the slave system itself. Laurent Dubois (Chapter 16) stresses the importance of the Age of Revolution (American, French, Haitian and Latin American) between 1776 and 1825 in changing opinion about the morality of slavery. Christopher Brown explains in Chapter 17 the intellectual and political underpinnings of this developing abolitionist campaign, one of the more surprising and undoubtedly more important social movements in human history. We are particularly concerned in this volume to understand why social reformers focused so intently on slavery as an especial evil that needed to be eradicated. We note that these reformers, just like slaves, faced powerful opposition. As Trevor Burnard argues in Chapter 11 on the planter class in the Americas, and as Tim Lockley explores in his treatment of the many interactions that slaves had with free people (Chapter 15), there were large and powerful groups in the Americas who were as committed to maintaining slavery as a social institution as there were slaves and abolitionists who wanted to make slaves free. The strength of the supporters of slavery was considerable, even as the moral case in favour of slavery declined: slavery did not end in the nineteenth or even in the twentieth century. Indeed, slavery flourished, especially in the first half of the twentieth century, and continues to thrive, as Joel Quirk makes clear in Chapter 20, in the twenty-first century.

Nevertheless, the intellectual underpinnings that supported the subjugation and exploitation of certain groups of human beings by other humans came under unprecedented attack following the American, French, Haitian and Latin American revolutions. While the main protagonists in this intellectual tussle against slave owners were European and white North American abolitionists, slaves and ex-slaves played a significant role in their own liberation. More importantly, in their struggles against slavery, they developed understandings of freedom that were different from the ideas of freedom that abolitionists imagined for them and which their ex-owners wanted to impose upon them in the aftermath of the owners' losing battle to keep slavery intact. Edward Rugemer (Chapter 19) points out that ex-slaves did not feel any sense of gratitude or obligation to other people for their emancipation. Moreover, ex-slaves commemorated their emancipation in highly distinctive ways, in which the main focus was on the role the enslaved themselves played in their own emancipation.

The gaining of freedom for slaves did not, of course, mean the end of conflict between ex-slaves and their erstwhile helpers and antagonists. Freedom was forged, as Steven Hahn explains in Chapter 18, within a maelstrom of expectation on the part of the recently freed, bitterness on the part of those who had lost their enslaved property, and racial and class condescension on the part of people outside the slave system – people who had opposed slavery but had little affection for the people who had suffered under slavery.

The importance of slavery in the Americas

In this volume, we concentrate heavily on one kind of slavery – that experienced by enslaved people in the Americas – rather than on slavery in all its forms over place and time. At the same time, we hope readers will regard the chapters in this volume that deal with slavery in places other than the Americas both as valuable in their own right, and as important guides to a rich historiography on slavery that does not take American slavery as necessarily normative for slavery in other places and times. This volume is intended to be useful for university classes about slaves and slavery, and the great majority of these classes in the English-speaking world focus on slavery in the Americas since the Columbian encounter. Slavery was vitally important in transforming the Americas into the most economically dynamic part of the world in the early modern period. Indeed, it is hard to contemplate how the Americas could have developed as they did without slavery. As Barbara Solow argues, "It was slavery that made the empty lands of the western hemisphere valuable producers of commodities and valuable markets for Europe and North America: what moved in the Atlantic in these centuries were predominantly slaves, the outputs of slaves, the inputs to slave societies, and the goods and services purchased with the earnings on slave products." It is also undeniably correct, as David Eltis, Frank D. Lewis and David Richardson argue, that the plantation sector was the most dynamic part of the New World economy before 1800, with rates of economic growth that corresponded well to rates in industrialising Britain and the United States and with strong productivity gains, especially in the second half of the eighteenth century (Solow, 1991: 1; Eltis *et al.*, 2005: 673–74). To understand the Americas, one needs to understand slavery. Nevertheless, as we insist in this volume, if we are to understand slavery, we need to appreciate that it had a beginning that preceded the European discovery of the New World; was developed alongside other forms of slavery, such as those in Africa and in the Indian Ocean World, that may have affected considerably more people than was the case even in Atlantic slavery; and did not end just because it became illegal in the Americas. Indeed, as Joel Quirk points out in his sobering essay on the persistence of forms of enslavement into the twenty-first century, the number of people caught up in modern slavery may be as high as 27 million – well over twice the number of people who, as Trevor Burnard notes in Chapter 11, were taken from West Africa during the period of the Atlantic slave trade.

Slavery in the New World was not only economically crucial to its development; it was also different from slavery elsewhere, especially in being based upon understandings of racial difference. If we are to understand the pernicious effects of race in the making of the modern world, then we need to understand the workings of slave society in the Americas. It was in these societies that enslavement became most attached to theories of biological racism, in which people of African descent were considered biologically suitable for enslavement in ways that other "races" were not. This scientific racism reached its intellectual apogee in the US South in the second quarter of the nineteenth century. But denigration of Africans was apparent from the time when Africans were first enslaved. We can explain why Africans became enslaved as arising from a combination of African willingness to sell people overseas, as Paul Lovejoy and Trevor Burnard note (Chapters 2 and 5), and from the need to acquire labour, as Niall McKeown, Gwyn Campbell and Betty Wood explain (Chapters 1, 3 and 4). But, as Wood insists, the sixteenth-century stereotyping by the English of Africans as racially suited for hard labour on plantations provided an ideological justification for African enslavement that substantially pre-dated the development of biological racism.

In addition, understandings of gender difference were crucial to explaining the origins of enslavement and its particular evolution. Betty Wood and Jennifer Morgan (Chapters 4 and 8) both note the importance of European understandings of proper gender relations in their consideration of how English settlers came to develop forms of labour arrangement based on African chattel slavery that were unknown in England, although well established in Iberian America. Morgan insists that Europeans found it easy to conceptualise the enslavement of Africans after they had decided that black women were naturally monstrous and unfeminine, yet somehow ideally suited to labour. The importance of gender runs throughout this volume. It not only influenced the process by which slaves became enslaved; it was the most crucial determinant of how slaves worked. Whereas Europeans thought it inappropriate to use white women in agricultural work, they had no such qualms about making African women labour as plantation workers. Planters saw female slaves as workers well before they saw them as mothers. Indeed, as Lorena Walsh, Richard Follett and Jennifer Morgan argue (Chapters 6–8), motherhood was significantly devalued in favour of seeing slaves as workers. That determination to see female slaves as destined to work in the field persisted in all places and over long periods. Slave owners were prepared to revise their opinion of the proper work and social role of black men. Yet they were reluctant to do the same with black women. Nevertheless, if black women were seldom seen through the prism of motherhood, they were certainly seen through the prism of sexuality. Europeans saw black women as naturally libidinous and desired them sexually, even while denigrating them as bestial. For black women, white desire for them was generally unwelcome, especially when it led, as it often did, to sexual exploitation. But white sexual desire for black women could occasionally be turned by black women to their own advantage. As John Garrigus notes, it was no accident that the majority of slaves who were manumitted tended to be the female companions of male slave owners.

Slavery in the Americas is especially interesting as being both a highly destructive and also a highly creative force. The Atlantic slave trade and slavery in the Americas devoured people. Death was the single most important feature of the slave experience in the Americas, as Richard Follett outlines clearly in Chapter 7.[2] Most Africans who were sent to the Americas, especially those who went to the heartlands of slavery in the Caribbean and north-east Brazil, lived Hobbesian lives of quiet desperation – nasty, brutish and short, as Thomas Hobbes memorably described life in a state of nature – that resulted in an early death with few, if any, descendants to remember their travails. The demographic statistics are startling: Africans accounted for the great majority of immigrants into the Americas before 1820. However, they made up a small percentage of the total population of the Americas in 1900, their numbers swamped by the huge waves of European migrants who not only moved to the Americas in great numbers from the mid-nineteenth century, but, crucially, survived and flourished demographically. That much of the Americas is not demographically dominated by black people in the twenty-first century is testimony to the physical destructiveness of slavery. Nevertheless, out of death and despair, enslaved people created new forms of cultural expression that, as Matt Childs notes in Chapter 10, were based on their African cultural inheritances but were modified by New World experience into something new, distinctive and valuable. These new forms of cultural and political expression profoundly shaped the social, political and, especially, cultural worlds of the Americas. That American culture is different from that found in Europe, Asia and Africa is in no small measure due to the influence that enslaved people had on social forms within the regions where they unwillingly found themselves. Several essays in this volume, notably Sylvia Frey's on slave religion (Chapter 9) and Matt Childs' on slave culture, make a strong case for the enduring importance of African American enslaved people's ideas and value systems on the society and culture of dominant groups in the Americas.

Finally, our modern understandings of freedom are indelibly shaped by struggles over slavery in the Americas. In this volume, we place a considerable amount of importance on the transforming effects of the Age of Revolutions in altering not just ideas of freedom but, as Laurent Dubois insists in Chapter 16, on anchoring and institutionalising ideas of right and sovereignty that provided a foundation for future struggles over freedom. This was the case not just for slaves, but also for other subordinate groups such as women, Jews and the unpropertied. The Americas were the homes not just of slavery (which paradoxically was often strengthened as an institution as more people clamoured for an expansion of their rights), but of democratic thinking as well. In order to understand democracy and freedom, we have to understand, as Hegel first argued in the late eighteenth century, slavery and subjugation.[3]

Definitions

What is a slave? What does enslavement mean? These are crucial questions that are addressed in various ways in this volume. We know that slavery is, as Paul Lovejoy notes in his essay on slavery in Africa, a form of exploitation that is common in most societies and in most historical periods. It usually involves some form of physical coercion – not many people willingly agree to be the property of another person. It also customarily involves some form of psychological bullying, as the people who benefit from having slave property try to imprint upon their human chattels a sense of shame, inferiority and unworthiness. Historians have shied away from discussions of the psychological impact of enslavement upon the enslaved ever since adventurous but under-theorised speculations on slave psychology published in the 1950s and 1960s were put to dubious use in contemporary social policy making, notably in the United States.[4] But slavery necessarily has a psychological dimension, as scholars trying to define the principal features of slavery note in their analyses. For Igor Kopytoff and Suzanne Miers, slavery can be defined as an institution of "marginality", where people who are in some way or another considered marginal to social structures are included within such social structures on highly disadvantageous terms. Slaves are, almost by definition, political and social outsiders. They are, as Claude Meillasoux has postulated, alienated individuals, who become subordinated people within social structures with a status normally below that of any other people in those social structures. Indeed, conceptualised as property, enslaved people become similar in status to livestock, a startling equation that was often manifested in listings of property where slaves ("Negroes and other slaves") were generally detailed in ways similar to how livestock were described. The reduction of slaves to people more akin to beasts than to other people had profoundly dehumanising effects. It is for this reason that Orlando Patterson has described slavery as a form of "social death", where the social existence of slaves was supposedly extinguished by owners in order that a slave might be considered a physical and ideological extension of the owner. Patterson calls this "natal alienation" and speculates that it served to create huge psychological crises of selfhood for slaves expected to have no independent identity separate from the slave owner but who, of course, retained a considerable measure of their own selfhood (Kopytoff and Miers, 1975; Meillassoux, 1975; Patterson, 1982). It is important to note, however, that Patterson's conception of slavery as being a form of "social death" is highly contested. The contributors to this volume are divided about the continuing utility of Patterson's formulation for understanding slavery. As is clear in a number of chapters, perhaps most notably in Paul Lovejoy's and Gwyn Campbell's essays on slavery outside the Atlantic World (Chapters 2 and 3), to see slaves as socially dead, or even as categorically distinct from the least privileged categories of free people, is to take at face value some of the more outrageous assertions made by slave owners about slaves' sense of their debasement.

The primary purpose of making people slaves, however, was not to dehumanise them, but to use them to acquire wealth and greater resources. Slave owners often fantasised about slaves as being incorporated within elaborate familial hierarchies and thought about their interactions with enslaved people using familial metaphors, but slaves were workers before they were family members. Slavery is a form of labour exploitation connected to, but significantly different from, other forms of labour exploitation, such as indentured servitude, family labour, and wage labour capitalism. It is important to note that mass chattel slavery – the form of slavery that most concerns us in this volume – was a logical response to various forms of labour shortage, but was far from a universal response. Slavery has been a universal institution, found in most societies at most times, from Mesopotamia and China in the distant past to India and Pakistan in the present. But relatively few societies turned whole-heartedly to slavery as the dominant form of social and labour organisation. Niall McKeown points out, following the views put forward by Moses Finley, one of the great theorists of slavery in the ancient world, that only a few societies – ancient Greece and Rome, the tropical societies of the early modern and nineteenth-century Americas and West Indies – became what Finley called "slave societies." For Finley, slavery was seldom adopted by elites – they tended to exploit internal labour sources if they could – because the costs of acquiring and maintaining slaves were exorbitant and, even more importantly, the risks involved in having to control rebellious slaves were too great for most societies to contemplate (Finley, 1988, ch. 2). Finley makes an important distinction about slavery that has been extremely influential in slave studies for several decades. Only some societies that had slaves, he insists, became slave societies in the sense that Frank Tannenbaum meant in his theorising about slavery in the 1940s. "Slave societies", Tannenbaum argued, were societies in which the slavery could not be separated from ordinary life, but instead suffused every aspect of life. In these societies – the subject of most attention in this volume – slavery was an integral part of social, economic, cultural and political structures. In particular, slaves were essential to how the economy operated, being both expensive items of property themselves, and also integral to how wealth was produced through the hard work they did in extracting wealth and passing it on to their owners.[5]

Slaves became enslaved in a variety of ways. As Gwyn Campbell notes in his chapter on slavery in the Indian Ocean World, outside the Americas most enslaved people became slaves through debt. Generally, getting enslaved through debt was reversible, which may have been a reason why people often entered slavery willingly as a credit-securing strategy. Of course, this strategy did not always work, and what started off as a temporary condition often became an inheritable condition.

Campbell's useful caution that Atlantic slavery should not be seen as always normative is an important reminder that slavery varied considerably over space. It also varied over time. An earlier generation of scholars tended to think of slavery as a constant, with social patterns and economic imperatives that remained the same from the time when slavery was established until the time it was demolished. The extensive work that was done on American slavery in the 1950s and 1960s encouraged historians to think of slavery as an unchanging and unchangeable institution (Genovese, 1976). Recent scholarship has tended to correct that picture. Ira Berlin, in particular, has been influential in showing that slavery was an evolving, constantly changing institution in the Americas (and by implication elsewhere). The generation of slaves who were the first plantation slaves in the Americas lived quite differently from their predecessors – they were what Berlin calls Atlantic creoles (Matt Childs discusses this group extensively in Chapter 10) – and from their successors: people who helped transform the Age of Revolutions into a period where the morality of slavery, as Christopher Brown emphasises, was challenged for the first time. One of the major themes of this volume is to take up Berlin's challenge to see slavery as varied by both time and space. As James Sidbury notes in his chapter on slave resistance, cultural hybridity and adaptation by slaves of African descent to changing European cultures was a continuation of the cultural hybridity and adaptability that characterised the West African cultures from which they came. Fluidity and constant change – these were worlds in motion, not static entities – marked slavery at all times (Berlin, 1998).

Imperatives and constraints: work and demography

Slave ownership conferred many benefits, including prestige, and political and social authority within societies that thought the ownership of slaves important. But people bought slaves primarily to make them money. Does this mean that slavery was capitalist? Opinion varies, and has done so since Adam Smith and Karl Marx raised the question of slavery as an economic institution in the late eighteenth and nineteenth centuries. It is now generally accepted that slavery, if not exactly the same as industrial capitalism, was compatible with most forms of capitalist endeavour. As Richard Follett notes, planters were both slaveholders and thoroughly modern businessmen. Tim Lockley and Trevor Burnard detail, in their chapters on planters and on interactions between free people and slaves, the many ways in which relations between slaves and masters were shaped by economic imperatives, notably slave owners' desire for slaves to make them money.

The result for slaves was that they were workers above all else. The work they did, as Lorena Walsh details, was onerous, tedious and dangerous. Time and place were very important in determining slaves' work patterns. Work was particularly intense as new societies were being formed, as Betty Wood and Jennifer Morgan insist. Observers were in little doubt that slaves were terribly oppressed, and in ways that were new and different, at least in the Americas, from European experience. The employment of African slave women as field labourers was especially noticeable. Europeans had strong gender conventions about what women could and could not do. Those distinctions vanished in the Americas. Black women laboured in the fields just as men did, and were given little latitude as mothers. The needs of production took priority over the needs of reproduction, at least until abolitionist pressure made slaveholders pay some attention to trying to improve slaves' demographic performance. The demands of capitalist efficiency and quickening commerce in the eighteenth and nineteenth centuries only sharpened gender differences between the slave and free populations. In the slave community, men and women were defined above all else by work, in ways that did not happen among free people.

Work was always diverse. Slaves cleared land, ran livestock, worked in domestic service and sailed ships. But most of all, they worked in plantation agriculture. Those slaves – the great majority of slaves in the Americas – who worked as plantation labourers drew the short straw. Their work was hard and unremitting and they were subjected to extremely harsh discipline. Nutrition was poor, as Richard Follett explains, and not suited to the life cycle needs of slaves. Moreover, slaves, especially in the West Indies, often had to work not just for planters, but also for their own sustenance, since in most cases they grew their own food on provision grounds. This kind of production did allow enslaved people some entry into market relations and gave a few slaves money and agency. But the possibility of making money for oneself as a slave was always compromised by time and energy. Slaves won some small successes but masters won most work battles. In those battles, masters were guided mostly by economic concerns. As Lorena Walsh acutely comments, profit almost always won out over humanitarian impulses.

If plantation workers in general drew the short straw, the worst work and demographic experiences came to those slaves working in sugar production. Sugar was just one of many tropical crops – tobacco, rice, cotton and coffee were the principal other tropical crops produced by slaves – but sugar was the most important, the most profitable and the most debilitating for workers. Both Lorena Walsh and Richard Follett point up the centrality of sugar to enslaved people's work experience. It was also central to slaves' demographic experience. The immorality of slavery becomes immediately clear when one examines the poor demographic experience of the enslaved. Only in antebellum America did the slave population become both self-reproducing and also demographically flourishing. In this slave society, slavery was always viable, making it harder to abolish than in other areas where slaveholders relied on outsiders to get the slaves they needed to work their plantations. Everywhere except antebellum America, slaveholders relied on the Atlantic slave trade to replenish diminishing slave populations. Richard Follett's penetrating case study of the Codrington estates in Barbados and the dreadful demographic conditions experienced by the enslaved demonstrates in graphic fashion just how terrible slave demography was, especially for slaves working in sugar cultivation. The greatest slave society – eighteenth-century Saint Domingue – provides evidence of the destructive impact of slavery. Saint Dominguean planters imported 800,000 Africans to the island between 1680 and 1777, yet by the latter date had a population of only 290,000 enslaved people. Mortality was high and fertility was low. The result was not only that planters had to rely upon the slave trade to "stock" their estates, using the phrase that planters employed. It also meant that enslaved people faced ill-health and the trauma of losing children to disease and death in greater numbers than in most free populations. It made slave family formation very difficult. Yet slaves did form families, and these families provided sustenance – emotionally, physically and financially – for slaves in surprisingly vibrant slave communities. Family life was always problematic. Slave families were broken up not just by death, but also by owners selling slaves. Yet families provided the bedrock of slave life and were the means whereby slave cultural patterns were formed and transmitted to future societies. Unfortunately, it is difficult to discover how slaves themselves imagined slavery, coped with slavery, and found alternative sources of meaning outside slavery. As Niall McKeown argues for classical slavery, and as is true for virtually all slaves in any slave society, the documentation we have seldom allows the enslaved to talk in their own voices about what slavery meant for them. Many of the chapters in this volume grapple with this major evidential problem.

Creolisation, culture and the formation of new societies

One of the most intriguing issues in the study of slavery has been the debate about New World slave cultures, and the extent to which these cultures were reflections of African cultural forms. Initially, there were opposing sides to the argument, epitomised in the work of two early scholars of the Americas, E. Franklin Frazier and Melville Herskovits.

Both Matt Childs and James Sidbury (Chapters 10 and 12) discuss at length the opposing arguments of these two scholars and their legacy for our theoretical understandings of the transmission of African culture to the Americas. Frazier argued that, as a result of the horrors of the Middle Passage and enslavement, slaves had been stripped of their African culture. For Frazier slaves, especially in the United States, had no connection with Africa. On the other hand, Melville Herskovits maintained that enslaved people had managed to reconstitute their African culture in the Americas. Working extensively on the Caribbean, Herskovits believed that slave culture in the Americas was closely linked to African culture (Frazier, 1939; Herskovits, 1958).

In the past several decades, the arguments about slave culture have become more sophisticated. Two anthropologists, Sidney Mintz and Richard Price, maintained that enslaved people developed a creole culture in the Americas. Although removed forcibly from their homes in West and Central Africa, slaves shared a common underlying African culture. For Mintz and Price, however, the variety of African ethnic groups in the Americas made it impossible for the enslaved to recreate their African culture. Instead, the enslaved developed a creolised slave culture, distinct from their masters, once they arrived in the Americas (Mintz and Price, 1992).

Subsequent research has moved the argument forward. As James Sidbury suggests in Chapter 12, scholars of slave culture increasingly look to patterns of creolisation in Africa itself. He is not alone in this view. Matt Childs argues in Chapter 10 that the cultural changes among the enslaved occurred on the treks prior to the Middle Passage. Those treks of enslaved people to the West African coast were frequently longer than the Middle Passage itself. Moreover, slaves were often kept together for significant periods in the forts along the coast before being transported to the New World. The result was a diasporic culture that emerged even before Africans had to confront their new masters in the Americas.

One of the most significant aspects of this diasporic culture was religion. In Chapter 9, Sylvia Frey discusses the rich history of African Atlantic religions. As Frey points out, Christianity had a significant history in Africa that had an impact on New World cultures. Central Africans in particular not only had adopted Christianity, but also had transformed it into an Africanised version of Catholicism. This would have a significant impact on the development of New World religions such as Brazilian *Candomblé*, Cuban *Santeria* and Haitian *Vodun*.

Frey argues that Africanised Catholicism arrived largely intact in the Americas. Other scholars also believe in the cultural continuities between Africa and the Americas for the enslaved. It may therefore be possible, as both James Sidbury and Matt Childs suggest, to map the transfer of specific cultures from Africa to particular places in the Americas. This not only would reinforce Melville Herskovits' contribution to the debate about slave culture, but also would highlight further how slaves resisted the imposition of white culture.

Whether the culture of the enslaved developed independently of whites, it is clear that blacks and whites often led interconnected lives. This went far beyond master–slave relationships, although Trevor Burnard's chapter on the planter class demonstrates that long-lasting emotional bonds between white men and black women were not uncommon. There were other areas that brought whites and black together. As Tim Lockley points out in Chapter 15, whites and blacks sometimes acted as trading partners. Whites also harboured runaway slaves, and white indentured servants and enslaved people sometimes plotted to resist their joint subjugation. Moreover, the brothels and taverns of the Americas were spaces that were often shared by whites and blacks. Lockley's research suggests that the debate about creolisation and culture is far from over.

Resistance

Resistance was a feature of all slave societies, although it took different forms at different times. Although we know most about resistance in the Americas, it is important to stress that slaves resisted slavery from the moment of their enslavement. There was significant resistance in Africa itself: many slaves escaped their captors during the long marches to the coast. Imprisoned in the forts and barracoons along the West African coast, enslaved people also managed to flee. On the Middle Passage itself, there was significant resistance. David Richardson has estimated that one in 10 ships on the Middle Passage was affected by violence. As Trevor Burnard's chapter on the slave trade makes clear, most of the revolts on board these ships failed. Yet the resistance had a significant impact. The extra costs involved in securing the ships against revolt, and the fear of slave revolts in particular parts of West Africa, meant that around one million fewer slaves were shipped across the Atlantic (Rathbone, 1986; Richardson, 2001, 72, 89).

Once in the Americas, slaves continued to resist: some of them ran away from their masters and formed maroon communities. These autonomous societies, consisting initially of African-born slaves, date from the earliest European settlements in the New World. One such community was formed in Hispaniola in the early sixteenth century, not long after Columbus had established the colony. As James Sidbury notes in this volume, maroon communities were beacons of freedom: they were communities that provided an inspiration for other slaves to abandon slavery. By attacking plantations, the maroons impeded the development of plantation society. Yet, ultimately, these communities became bulwarks of the slave system. In Jamaica and Suriname, where they continue to exist today, maroons survived by becoming agents of the state, capturing runaway slaves and helping whites put down slave rebellions.

Yet when slaves ran away, they did not generally seek to join maroon communities. The overwhelming majority of runaway slaves did so for relatively short periods. Many ran away for personal reasons: they were seeking to join partners, children or other family members. Whatever their motivation, slaves who ran away were resisting their own enslavement by denying labour to their owners. The majority of runaways were young skilled males, some of whom were seeking to merge into the free black and free coloured urban communities of the Americas. While female slaves also ran away, they did so in fewer numbers than males, largely because of the difficulty of running away with children. The gendered differences in patterns of running away help to highlight the importance of slave families.

Although running away was significant, there were often more subtle types of day-to-day resistance. These could take a variety of forms. James Scott has discussed the behaviour of peasants in terms of "hidden transcripts", using "foot-dragging" or "poaching" as part of an everyday pattern of resistance. In slave societies, this could lead to tool-breaking or destruction of property; it could also mean, as James Sidbury suggests, cooperating to slow down the pace of work. Slaves were using the "weapons of the weak", as Scott has referred to them. Although it is clear that masters had ultimate power over their slaves, it is also the case that slaves' use of these "weapons of the weak" led to negotiations over such matters as work times and labour productivity (Scott, 1990, xiii).

The most dramatic form of slave resistance was rebellion. From Spartacus' rebellion in ancient Rome to the Mâle revolt in nineteenth-century Brazil, rebellions frightened masters. Only one rebellion in the Americas, the Haitian Revolution, was ultimately successful. It not only destroyed slavery in Saint Domingue, but also led to the independence of Haiti. Yet, curiously, many of the Haitian rebels were not intent on full freedom; they were seeking a gradual end to slavery and freedom for three days in the week, in the first instance. Slave rebels therefore had different aims. As Gad Heuman suggests in Chapter 13, African-led rebellions in the Americas were not necessarily seeking an end to slavery. Instead, they wanted to end their own enslavement, but envisioned the continued slavery of others. The nineteenth-century rebellions in the Americas, such as the Jamaica Christmas rebellion in 1831 and the Nat Turner revolt in Virginia in the same year, were of a different magnitude: they were seeking to abolish slavery. The amount of force used by masters in putting down rebellions suggests how worried they were by these violent outbreaks.

Freedom

Freedom was a gradual process. Across the Americas, it was often slow in coming. When slavery was abolished in the Anglophone Caribbean in 1834, for example, it was followed by an apprenticeship system. This meant that ex-slaves, although legally free, were required to work for their former masters for 45 hours per week without pay for up to six years. Nearly 50 years later in Cuba, the *patronato* system was comparable: slaves were classified as apprentices for a maximum of eight years before they could become fully free. In Brazil, the Free Womb Law of 1871 also delayed emancipation: the law freed the children of slave mothers, but not the mothers themselves. Gradual emancipation also characterised the northern states of the United States. Although most of them passed legislation ending slavery in the late eighteenth and early nineteenth centuries, these states had to pass subsequent legislation decades later declaring the end of slavery.

In Haiti, there was a different problem. Slavery came to a sudden end in 1794 as a result of the Haitian Revolution. But as Laurent Dubois suggests in Chapter 16, there were serious problems in the transition from slavery to freedom in Haiti. The leader of the Haitian Revolution, Toussaint L'Ouverture, sought to keep the plantation economy working: he wanted to rebuild the economy based on the production of sugar and coffee. In the process, he instituted a harsh labour regime that denied ex-slaves most of the rights they had sought.

The enslaved generally had clear expectations about freedom: they wanted to work for employers of their choice, to move around freely and to reconstitute their families. They also believed that freedom meant more than the ending of slavery; in the Caribbean, many of the slaves expected to be given the houses they had built and the provision grounds they had worked. Land was a particularly potent symbol of freedom but, across the Americas, ex-slaves were often denied the possibility of obtaining it. Instead, they were frequently confronted with legislation designed to restrict their movement or limit their rights (Marshall, 1993).

Across the Americas, planters and former masters sought to pass laws that would have continued the subjugation of the ex-slaves. The Black Codes in the United States, although generally annulled, made it clear that southern planters wanted slavery to continue in all but name. Similarly, in much of the Caribbean, the planters and former masters enacted legislation designed to limit the movement of free people and to force them to continue working on the plantations. In Brazil and in parts of the Caribbean, the planters imported labourers to compete with the newly freed people. In the case of Brazil it was European labour, while in the Caribbean it was primarily indentured labourers from India who were brought to the region. The aim was clear: imported labourers would have the effect of driving down wages for ex-slaves, making it difficult for them to resist the terms of emancipation.

Despite these measures, free people were able to leave plantations in significant numbers. For example, five years after the abolition of slavery in the French Caribbean, one-fifth of the ex-slaves had left the estates. In Jamaica, the figures were comparable: 60,000 people had established freeholds by 1845, seven years after emancipation (Heuman, 2006, 101). These freeholds were often small properties, which meant that many free people also needed to work part-time on the estates. Nonetheless, the flight of ex-slaves from the plantations demonstrated the desire of free people to farm the land and work for themselves. Moreover, in some colonies such as Jamaica, freed people were able to establish free villages, often with the help of European missionaries.

It was not just that many free people were able to leave the plantations; it was also the case that many women ceased working on them. This was significant, since enslaved women had often made up the majority of field workers on the plantations, as Lorena Walsh, Richard Follett and Jennifer Morgan discuss in Chapters 6–8. Rather than continue on the plantations, many women chose to work on their provision grounds and to market their produce. This made economic sense: their pay on the plantations was significantly lower than that of men, and they could earn more money working on their own account. This also gave women far more control of their lives, an important factor in light of the regimented and often harsh conditions on a plantation (Brereton, 1999).

Yet in spite of the flight from the estates and the changed conditions of many free women after emancipation, power continued to remain largely in the hands of the former slave-owning elites. In the United States, Reconstruction was followed by Redemption and nearly a century of white power in the South. In the Caribbean and in Brazil, whites continued to dominate their societies politically, socially and economically. As Steven Hahn suggests in Chapter 18, slavery ended, but race was even more significant after emancipation than it had been during slavery. For those in power, race became a central part of the armoury of control.

Conclusion

The study of slavery is a vibrant historiographical field. The annual bibliographies printed in the leading journal on slavery, *Slavery & Abolition*, not only show just how much work is being done on slavery, but also demonstrate that production is on a strong upward curve. We know more now about slavery, as well as abolition and emancipation, than we have ever known before. Doubtless we shall soon know even more, as new generations of scholars refine the conclusions so ably presented by the writers of the 20 chapters in this volume. We believe that these essays provide an excellent introduction to the major issues in the history of slavery, not just in the Americas, but also in the ancient world, in Africa and in the Indian Ocean World. Each chapter concisely lays out the major issues that have occupied historians' attention in the past few decades, while providing readers with a wealth of necessary empirical information. The chapters conclude with a helpful list of major works in the field. We hope that the general reader, students and academic specialists will all find something useful in this book.

Notes

1 For Shakespeare and his understanding of slavery, see Vaughan and Mason Vaughan (1993).
2 For a persuasive essay on this theme, see Brown (2009).
3 See the discussion of Hegel in Davis (1975), 561–63.
4 We refer here to works such as Elkins (1959) and to the controversy over the Daniel Moynihan report on the black family (US Department of Labor, 1965).
5 Tannenbaum (1946); for the continuing utility of the Tannenbaum thesis, see de la Fuente (2004).

Bibliography

Berlin, Ira, *Many Thousands Gone: The First Two Centuries of Slavery in North America* (Cambridge, MA: Harvard University Press, 1998).

Brereton, Bridget, "Family Strategies, Gender and the Shift to Wage Labour in the British Caribbean", in Bridget Brereton and Kelvin Yelvington, eds, *The Colonial Caribbean in Transition: Essays on Postemancipation Social and Cultural History* (Gainesville: University Press of Florida, 1999), 77–107.

Brown, Vincent, "Social Death and Political Life in the Study of Slavery", *American Historical Review*, 114 (2009), 1231–49.

Davis, David Brion, *The Problem of Slavery in the Age of Revolution* (Ithaca: Cornell University Press, 1975).

Elkins, Stanley, *Slavery: A Problem in American Institutional and Intellectual Life* (Chicago: University of Chicago Press, 1959).

Eltis, David, Lewis, Frank W. and Richardson, David, "Slave Prices, the African Slave Trade and Productivity in the Caribbean", *Economic History Review*, 58 (2005), 673–700.

Finley, Moses I., *Ancient Slavery and Modern Ideology* (Princeton: Marcus Weiner, 1988).

Frazier, E. Franklin, *The Negro Family in the United States* (Chicago: University of Chicago Press, 1939).

de la Fuente, Alejandro, "Slave Law and Claim Making in Cuba: The Tannenbaum Debate Revisited", with comments by Mariá Elena Diaz and Christopher Schmidt-Nowara, *Law and History Review* 22 (2004), 339–88.

Genovese, Eugene, *Roll, Jordan, Roll: The World the Slaves Made* (New York: Vintage, 1976).

Herskovits, Melville J., *The Myth of the Negro Past* (Boston: Beacon Press, 1958).

Heuman, Gad, *The Caribbean* (London: Hodder Arnold, 2006).

Kopytoff, Igor and Miers, Suzanne, "African 'Slavery' as an Institution of Marginality", in *idem*, eds, *Slavery in Africa: Historical and Anthropological Perspectives* (Madison: University of Wisconsin Press, 1975).

Marshall, Woodville, "'We be wise to many more tings': Blacks' Hopes and Expectations of Emancipation", in Hilary Beckles and Verene Shepherd, eds, *Caribbean Freedom: Society and Economy from Emancipation to the Present* (Kingston: Ian Randle, 1993), 12–20.

Meillassoux, Claude, ed., *L'esclavage en Afrique précoloniale* (Paris: Francois Maspero, 1975).

Mintz, Sidney W. and Price, Richard, *The Birth of African-American Culture: An Anthropological Perspective* (Boston: Beacon Press, 1992).

Patterson, Orlando, *Slavery and Social Death: A Comparative Study* (Cambridge, MA: Harvard University Press, 1982).

Rathbone, Richard, "Some Thoughts on Resistance to Enslavement in Africa", in Gad Heuman, ed., *Out of the House of Bondage: Runaways, Resistance and Marronage in Africa and the New World* (London: Frank Cass, 1986), 11–22.

Richardson, David, "Shipboard Revolts, African Authority, and the Atlantic Slave Trade", *William and Mary Quarterly*, 3rd ser., 58, (2001), 69–92.

Scott, James, *Domination and the Arts of Resistance: Hidden Transcripts* (New Haven: Yale University Press, 1990).

Solow, Barbara L., *Slavery and the Rise of the Atlantic System* (Cambridge: Cambridge University Press, 1991).

Tannenbaum, Frank, *Slavery and Citizen: The Negro in the Americas* (New York: Random House, 1946).

US Department of Labor, *The Negro Family: The Case for National Action* (Washington, DC: Office of Policy Planning and Research, United States Department of Labor, 1965).

Vaughan, Alden T. and Mason Vaughan, Virginia, *Shakespeare's Caliban: A Cultural History* (New York: Cambridge University Press, 1993).

Part 1

SLAVERY AS A GLOBAL INSTITUTION

1

GREEK AND ROMAN SLAVERY

Niall McKeown

Introduction

When one thinks of the Greco-Roman world, one probably thinks of Alexander the Great or Julius Caesar. It was also, however, the world of Spartacus, perhaps the most famous slave in history, and tens of millions of its other inhabitants were also slaves. There is robust disagreement as to how to reconstruct their lives. This might seem surprising. Greek and Roman slavery have been studied for over 150 years and comparatively little new evidence has been discovered in that time. Historians have an inbuilt ability to disagree with one another, but one might still have expected increasing consensus. The continuing debate is, however, largely the product of three factors that lend the study of ancient slavery its distinctiveness and help it to make a very individual contribution to the general study of slaves.

First, "Greco-Roman" actually covers a number of very different slave systems. Our evidence allows us only snapshots of some of these, such as Athens between about 450 and 300 BC, and Roman Italy between about 100 BC and AD 200. These in turn were subject to considerable change over time. In addition, slaves fulfilled a great range of different roles within Athens and Rome. All these differences make generalisations difficult, but also offer interesting comparisons.

Second, historians of Greek and Roman slavery lack the kind of bureaucratic records used in the study of more modern slave societies. They are forced to glean information from a wide range of material, including drama and poetry. Their especial sensitivity to both the possibilities and the problems of such material is perhaps their most distinctive contribution to the overall study of slavery. The great variety of potential "readings" of texts, however, provides a second explanation for continued debate.

Modern geography, curiously, provides the final reason (see McKeown, 2007, especially ch. 2–4). While there are no "national" schools of thought on ancient slavery, different areas have developed somewhat different emphases in their work. English-speaking scholars have tended to emphasise conflict between master and slave. French and Italian scholars have often taken a similar line, though with a greater willingness to apply Marxist ideas of class conflict. On the other hand, some German-speaking scholars, while recognising the inhumanity of slavery, have also asked why slavery was able to function successfully as long as it did, and have examined how slaves and ex-slaves were assimilated into the wider society.

If these differences help to explain why the past 150 years have not produced much agreement, they also explain why historians of Greek and Roman slavery provide provocative studies where one can find most of one's assumptions about slavery challenged, as well as a variety of very different, though equally sophisticated, ways of reading evidence. Antiquity, moreover, offers us relatively well documented slave societies where, unlike many modern examples, neither capitalism nor race was crucial, even if racism existed and slave owners expected to profit from their slaves.

Early Greek slaveries and slavery in Athens

Homer's *Iliad* and *Odyssey* provide us with a (fictionalised) portrait of early Greek society of around 700 BC. Chattel slaves (outsiders bought for cash) and more numerous "semi-free" dependents served local "lords" and were apparently treated similarly. It has been suggested that Homeric servitude was a quasi-contractual relationship, with an expectation of rewards for the "good" servant. While it is certainly significant that the text emphasised the idea of the "good servant" and "good lord", the servant's rewards were precarious, and slavery was a fate one wanted to avoid. For example, after Odysseus bloodily regained control of his palace after 20 years away, he hanged 12 of his maids, apparently for sleeping with other noblemen (Garlan, 1988, 29–37).[1]

The comparative unimportance of chattel slavery in Homer may represent the norm in archaic Greece (700–500 BC). For some states, however, it remained the pattern into the "classical" period (500–300 BC). The Spartans, for example, lived off the labour of *helots* (Cartledge, 1979, ch. 10). Most historians believe these were the original inhabitants of Messenia and Laconia, which were conquered by the Spartans, though they may have been the losers in a struggle within Spartan society. They heavily outnumbered the Spartans, though the traditional ratio of 7:1 may be exaggerated. Some contemporaries referred to *helots* as slaves, but modern scholars usually place them between slave and free: "communal slaves" or even "serfs". *Helots* were owned by the state rather than by the individuals whose farms they worked. They lived in family units and were allowed to keep part of their crop. Recent archaeological work suggests that there may have been sizeable, socially differentiated settlements of *helots* in Messenia (Hodkinson, 2008). Unfortunately, most of our evidence about *helots* comes from non-Spartans writing long after the events they describe and who had a tendency to sensationalise. Ancient writers clearly believed, however, that *helots* were harshly treated, humiliated and sometimes murdered. *Helots* responded with rebellions, particularly in Messenia. They had a common language and identity, and lived separately from their masters in areas that provided favourable territory for flight and resistance. There have been recent attempts to downplay the tensions between *helot* and Spartan. The weight of the evidence, however, suggests serious conflict. The Messenian *helots* were eventually able to assert their independence with the support of Sparta's Greek enemies after 370/69 BC, and helotry seems to have disappeared in Laconia some time after the Roman conquest of the second century BC.

Some states, notably Athens, chose to use chattel slaves. Little evidence survives to explain the history of the process that culminated in perhaps a third of the population of classical Athens being slaves (Finley, 1998, ch. 2; Morris, 2002). Moses Finley argued that slavery on such a scale was historically unusual because of the problems in controlling slaves and the costs in acquiring and maintaining them. He believed that the exploitation of internal labour sources (as in Sparta) was the usual choice for most elites in history. Finley suggested that three preconditions were needed before the rise of mass chattel slavery. (1) Large, privately controlled farms – if a ruler could simply appropriate a farmer's surplus, or if farmers only produced at subsistence level, there would be little incentive to buy an extra labourer. (2) The development of market exchange – this helped to ensure a constant supply of slaves. It also created opportunities to sell any surpluses they created and made it easier to provision them. (3) Crucially, a lack of internal sources of labour – Finley believed that democratic structures helped protect ordinary Athenians from exploitation, most notably when debt-bondage was abolished in 594 BC. This forced larger landowners to import external labour to fulfil their man-power needs.

Finley may have exaggerated the importance of the abolition of debt-bondage. The development of democracy and of slavery were more probably processes lasting several hundred years into the fifth century. Indeed, some historians argue that rather than democracy helping to create slavery, slavery helped the development of democracy by allowing farmers time to engage in politics. There was also clearly some demand for chattel slaves even before 594 BC, and it has been suggested that Finley underestimated the positive economic attractions of slave labour (such as its flexibility). The infrequency with which we see slave systems on the Athenian scale, however, suggests that more than economic factors are required to explain its rise. For the moment, therefore, Finley's position still represents the orthodoxy.

By the classical period Athens was the urban centre of a triangle of territory ("Attica") approximately 40 miles on each side. At its height, between about 450 and 300 BC, modern estimates suggest a free population of 150,000–250,000 with 50,000–100,000 slaves. The figure for slaves is, however, largely an educated guess. Our sources imply that most slaves came from the Balkans and from Turkey, though some were from other Greek cities. The market was the main mechanism of acquiring slaves, with warfare, kidnapping and possibly child exposure the likeliest ultimate sources of those traded. There is little surviving evidence of slave breeding (or slave families), though it may have been significant.

The debate about the spread of slave ownership in Athens indicates the problems and choices faced by historians of ancient slavery. The traditional picture suggested that the richest few thousand Athenians used slaves to produce the bulk of their wealth. Another 10,000 middling farmers, the *hoplites*, allegedly owned one or two slaves as well. It was suggested that a growing population and attendant land division forced *hoplites* to intensify production with extra labour. Hired labour was despised and undependable, and only slave labour allowed farmers the free time required to engage in democratic life. The remaining 10,000–15,000 poorer citizens also aspired to own slaves, but may not have been able to afford them.

Some historians have, however, argued that slave ownership was restricted to the rich (Jameson, 2002). Texts implying that *hoplites* owned slaves may reflect their wishes rather than reality. Even if they needed extra labour (and the evidence for a land short-age and the supposed intensification it necessitated has been questioned), it has been suggested that extra labour could have been found from family or neighbours or hired workers (ordinary Athenians may have been more willing to be hired out than aristo-cratic contemporaries suggested). Computer models of probable farm production also suggest that it is doubtful whether *hoplites* could have afforded to buy and keep slaves. Lastly, it has been argued that the democracy improved the position of smaller farmers, directly through cash payments and indirectly by preventing exploitation by the rich.

This, in turn, allegedly removed part of the need to intensify production, the supposed reason for buying a slave.

This position, however, implies a peasantry so poor that it would have been vulnerable both to periodic famine and to control by wealthy patrons, even given the benefits of democracy. Neither phenomenon is very significant in our sources. In addition, the computer modelling of *hoplite* farm production has such a wide margin of error that it cannot rule out the possibility of slave ownership. There are, then, problems with the argument that slave ownership was restricted to the rich, especially as it also requires actively arguing away all the literary evidence pointing to *hoplite* ownership of slaves. Relatively widespread slave ownership seems likelier.

Up to a third of slaves in Athens may have worked in her silver mines. We know little about their lives. It has been suggested that expensive inscriptions left behind by some, and the skilled work seen in the mines, indicate that their life may have been relatively tolerable. This seems doubtful. Mining in antiquity was often a punishment, and slave rental agreements involving the replacement of dead miners also hint at low life expectancy. The surviving inscriptions may well be the product of slave supervisors, not ordinary slaves, and the high standard of the mining work may simply show effective control.

Most slaves in Athens probably were involved in mixed agricultural and domestic work, living alongside their masters. One author described slave barracks and an overseer on the estate of a very wealthy landowner, but concentrations of more than a dozen slaves were probably quite unusual, and ownership of just one or two slaves the norm. In addition, the property of the wealthy was probably generally dotted about the countryside rather than in single units.

The remaining slaves did mostly artisan work. Some lived separately from their masters, paying a form of rent. A small number of slaves helped run businesses, including primitive banks, or acted as commercial agents. There were, finally, some state-owned slaves serving as record keepers, "civil servants", street cleaners and even policemen. A few of these may have led quite independent lives.

Apart from their job, the temperament of their master was probably the other crucial element in a slave's life. Comic sources suggest casual violence against slaves, though the interpretation of such material is problematic, as we shall see. Athenians, however, unlike the Romans, spent little time discussing abuses committed against slaves. This could be interpreted optimistically, suggesting the absence of severe abuse, but Athenian sources generally either ignore slaves altogether or adopt a cynical attitude towards them. Slaves certainly had little legal protection. A right of asylum existed, but the fate of slaves who used it is unknown. Killing one's own slave was an offence against the gods, but any religious stigma could be removed with purification rites. Killing someone else's slave was treated legally as damage to property. To the surprise of contemporaries, slaves were technically protected alongside the free from *hubris*, assault designed to humiliate. Even if it dated from a time when Athenians could be enslaved for debt, the law was certainly applied in the classical period. It may, however, have protected the owner's honour rather than the slave's, or been used to discourage misbehaviour towards slaves that might later be applied to citizens.

Slaves of both sexes were subject to sexual abuse from their master. There were few taboos against a male citizen seeking sex outside marriage, and slave prostitution was also an acceptable part of daily life. The only hint of a limitation on sexual use was an apparent distaste of the practice of castrating (Greek) slaves.[2]

Slaves were barred from pleading in courts, except in some commercial cases in the fourth century BC. When slaves testified, they typically did so under torture (Mirhady, 2000). Curiously, we have little evidence of this from surviving court speeches, and many examples of litigants refusing to surrender their slaves for torture. Some believe that torture was a legal fiction and never took place. Others have suggested that torture was common, and regarded as so effective in establishing the truth that it was unnecessary afterwards to continue with the court case, explaining the absence of references to it in court speeches. The continued demands to hand slaves over for judicial examination do indeed make little sense if torture was not a real possibility. In any case, the alleged incapacity of the slave to speak the truth without physical compulsion, and their physical vulnerability in law, helped to distinguish slave from free on an ideological level.

Athenian drama is potentially one of the most fruitful sources of evidence for general attitudes towards slaves (DuBois, 2003, 137–52). At first sight it suggests a degree of sympathy. Euripides' plays *Hecuba*, *The Trojan Women* and *Andromache* have as their heroines slaves who were captive royal women from the time of the (mythical) Trojan War. It could, however, be questioned how far Athenians associated these mythical royal characters with contemporary slaves. Indeed, it has been argued that the plays chiefly allowed Athenian male citizens to express their own fears of enslavement. When Euripides deals with ordinary non-Greek slaves, he is quite capable of portraying them as fawning cowards. Even statements that clearly appear positive towards slaves need to be examined in their dramatic context. For example, a character in Euripides' *Ion* claims there was no difference between a slave and a free man.[3] This is often quoted as an example of an author questioning the justice of slavery. The character speaking is, however, a slave who is conspiring with his mistress to murder a fellow servant who they feel is rising above his place. The passage is, therefore, rather ironic. Even where slaves are clearly depicted showing an unselfish loyalty to their owners, for example in Euripides' *Alcestis*, this may be done more to throw into relief the actions of a particularly selfish free character than to praise the slaves.

The comic plays of Aristophanes are, unlike tragedies, at least set in the contemporary world of the audience rather than a mythologised past (DuBois, 2003, 119–25). Slave characters such as Xanthias in *The Frogs* and Carion in *Wealth* are near equals of their masters. Both characters, however, largely disappear from the action as the plays reach their climax. Carion is also less noble than his master. Xanthias' character in *The Frogs* can only be understood against the political backdrop of the play. Athenians sometimes conscripted slaves into their navy and had recently offered some of them citizenship. Aristophanes appears to have disapproved, and Xanthias' ability to swap places with his cowardly master in *The Frogs* may be a bad-tempered commentary on Athens' decision.[4]

Aristophanes' comedies are, as noted, full of jokes about casual brutality towards slaves. Together with the material from the law courts and philosophers, they reinforce the association of slavery and physical vulnerability. In a grimly funny scene in *The Frogs*, Xanthias engages in a rather peculiar contest with his master: they should both be whipped until one of them shows pain. His master may be a god, but Xanthias reckons that he has more than enough experience and will hold out longer.[5] There is, admittedly, certainly trust between master and slave in Aristophanes' comedies (as well as in Menander's comedies of about 300 BC). This trust mirrors some of our evidence from non-comic sources: for example, in the use of slaves as commercial managers, mentioned above. Efforts by some historians to stress the positive elements in drama may be over-stated, however. Slaves remained secondary characters and their status was regarded as degraded and vulnerable.

Integration, resistance and anti-slavery thought

Writing around 400 BC, the "Old Oligarch" complained that Athenian slaves led relatively privileged lives, refusing to step aside in the street and indistinguishable from the free, who could not strike them.[6] Considerable independence was indeed given to a few slaves, especially those involved in commercial activities. In addition, slaves sometimes allegedly claimed to be citizens. Athenian orators even occasionally claimed their opponents had slave parentage, and Athens felt forced to make several wholesale checks on the identity of its citizens. Some ex-slaves were even granted citizenship: they included the bankers Pasio and Phormio, amongst the richest Athenians known. It has been suggested recently that the dividing line between slave and free may, therefore, have sometimes been fluid (Vlassopoulos, 2009).

There are, however, reasons to be doubtful. Firstly, the testimony of the Old Oligarch is dubious. The booklet is a vicious attack on Athenian democracy and the "rule of the poor". Its views on the privileged lives of slaves should perhaps be taken with a pinch of salt. In one law court speech, we hear of a citizen boy sent into a garden to pull up plants. The speaker's enemies allegedly hoped that the garden owner would manhandle the boy assuming him to be a slave, thereby committing assault.[7] Contrary to the Old Oligarch, this implies that one could normally differentiate slave from free (and that a slave could be beaten). Secondly, periodic scares about citizenship lists actually suggest a continuing Athenian desire to maintain barriers dividing citizen from slave or free immigrant. While isolated allegations of slaves impersonating citizens indicate that such cases were conceivable, they do not tell us how often this may have happened: defendants may have been telling the truth when they claimed they were free. Thirdly, Pasio and Phormio were probably highly atypical in gaining citizenship, which required a vote of at least 6000 citizens.

Athenians certainly did free slaves, though we cannot tell how often, or why. Freedom might repay loyalty, and sometimes acquaintances provided a loan for a slave to buy freedom. Semi-independent artisan slaves were probably more able to buy their freedom than mining or agricultural slaves, but we can see nothing like Roman *peculium*, slave pocket-money. It is possible that ex-masters had some rights to the work of their freed slaves, but the evidence for this in Athens is poor. Ex-slaves who remained in Athens became *metics* alongside free immigrants (Whitehead, 1977). They lacked political rights as well as the crucial privilege to own land. Athenian xenophobia would not have helped integration, nor would alleged contempt for the manual trades pursued by many slaves and ex-slaves. Athenian drama suggests that *metics* were best advised to remain inconspicuous.[8] When *metics* fought to help restore the democracy after a particularly bloody right-wing coup in 404/03 BC, Athenian citizens were ultimately very grudging in their thanks (Whitehead, 1977, 154–59). The social mobility of non-citizens, and particularly non-Greek slaves, should not be exaggerated.

We have no examples of slave rebellions from Athens, and few from the rest of the Greek world. They may have been under-reported, but Greek writers typically associated rebellion with *helots* rather than slaves. In truth, considerable difficulties faced would-be slave rebels in Athens. Slaves mostly lived with or near their masters and in small households. Differences in origins and occupation would also have undermined potential solidarity. Geographical conditions did not provide places of easy refuge. "Slave contentment" therefore need not explain the lack of rebellion, as has been suggested. Similarly, the willingness of Athenians and others to conscript slaves (generally as rowers rather than as infantry) probably indicates desperation in times of crisis rather than an expectation of devotion (Hunt, 1998). There are one or two stories of slaves murdering masters, but it is difficult to tell how major a problem this was perceived to be. The willingness to execute a whole household when a master was murdered betokens a horror of the possibility, though it need not imply much about its actual frequency. Some literary passages have been used to suggest that Athenian slave owners feared their slaves. Plato wondered, for example, about the fate awaiting an owner marooned with his slaves.[9] Plato's point was, however, that slave owners in Athens *were not* on the equivalent of a desert island.

Regardless of the fear of violence, owners still clearly faced other forms of resistance. While there is no suggestion that Athenians chained the bulk of their slaves, there were certainly concerns that slaves might run away, as allegedly more than 20,000 did in wartime after 413 BC. Greek writers also mention fears of slaves pilfering and gossiping, the latter of real concern in an honour-based society such as Athens. References in Aristophanes' comedies to the tortoise-like back of the slave, hardened by repeated whippings, may also indicate poor work as a form of resistance. Talking back was an option allowed fictional comic slaves, though legal and other sources defined slaves as people who could *not* say what they wanted to. Ultimately, while some recent authors have tried valiantly to rescue the story of slave resistance from the silence of our sources, slaves in Athens were notable chiefly by their incapacity to defend themselves.

Slavery was largely accepted by the free as a fact of life. The philosopher Aristotle produced a short justification of slavery (Garnsey 1996, ch. 8), suggesting that at least some criticism of the institution existed, though this was probably directed more at Spartan helotry than Athenian chattel slavery. Aristotle's defence rested on four key assumptions. (1) Racism: Aristotle believed that easterners were intelligent but soft, northerners being strong but stupid. (2) The belief that some people had to be controlled for their own good. (3) The perception that slaves looked and behaved "slavishly", probably a warped reflection of the roles they were forced to perform. (4) Someone had to do the work. Aristotle knew that some slaves, notably Greek war captives, did not fit his criteria of natural slaves, and his justification of slavery has been condemned for its inconsistencies. Contemporary Athenians, however, may not have noticed them as they shared his core assumptions. The possibility of one's own enslavement in times of war may also further have eased any pangs of conscience. Some fourth-century writers did, however, begin to question the morality of enslaving fellow Greeks. It is noteworthy that the mistreatment of a woman originally captured from the Greek town of Olynthus by Philip of Macedon in the 340s provoked scandal in Athens, a very unusual example of outrage over the abuse of a slave.[10]

Roman slavery

The Roman Empire had approximately 50–100 million inhabitants at its height, 7–14 million of them in Italy. It was, therefore, a vastly larger society than classical Athens.

It has been argued that 30–40 per cent of the population of Italy were slaves, and 10–15 per cent of the whole empire. These estimates are speculative, however, and the current trend is to revise them downwards. In general, one would expect Italy, home to the imperial elite, to have had the highest proportion of slaves in the empire, followed by wealthy areas in the east, and then the more Romanised areas in the west, especially northern Africa, southern Spain and southern France. Slavery may have been relatively restricted in other areas such as northern France.

Slaves came from the children of existing slaves, free children left exposed to die by their parents and raised as slaves, or individuals purchased or captured outside the empire. It has been argued that at least 75 per cent of Rome's slaves must have been bred, otherwise the sources outside the empire would have been denuded and improbably high numbers of exposed children would have been required from within the empire (Scheidel, 2005). Whilst criticised, this remains the most convincing picture of Roman slave sources, if 10 per cent or more of the empire's inhabitants were indeed slaves. It implies that few female slaves of child-bearing age were freed.

The orthodox explanation for the massive development of chattel slavery, particularly in Italy, comes from the work of Moses Finley (1998, ch. 2) and Keith Hopkins (1978, ch. 1–2). Both stressed the unavailability of indigenous labour. Roman peasants were vital to the army and had important political rights that discouraged their direct economic exploitation. Hopkins argued that the profits from the expansion of the empire flooded into the hands of the elite, allowing them to buy peasant farms which had been undermined by their owners' long absences on military service abroad. The elite also used their new wealth to buy slaves to work this land. The army and cities – whose populations grew as peasants left the land – also provided markets for the new slave-run estates.

Increasing doubts have been raised about this model (De Ligt, 2006). (1) Literary evidence and the results of archaeological surveys suggest that small farms may have survived on a much greater scale than Hopkins believed. (2) Rather than undermine small farmers, military service may have helped them by removing surplus labourers at points in the life cycle of farms. (3) Long-term urban growth in imperial Italy implies a continuously replenished supply of rural emigrants and therefore a continuing population of small farmers. (4) Finally, it has been argued that slavery was not well suited to grain production, and that only a few hundred thousand slaves (not the two or three million claimed) would have been required to produce other key Roman crops (notably olives and grapes).

The critics of the Finley/Hopkins model, however, themselves face difficulties. Firstly, even if we dramatically reduce our estimate of the number of slaves in Italy and accept that many small farms survived, slaves were still clearly crucial to key areas of the Roman rural and urban economy. For example, Roman agricultural writers assume large farms had permanent slave workforces. Secondly, the only alternative explanation proffered to the Finley/Hopkins model suggests that slavery developed because it offered a more flexible and profitable labour force than free workers or tenants. If this were true, one wonders, as with Athens, why mass chattel slavery has not been more common historically. Hopkins' answer at least fits with the surviving literary evidence.

Who owned the slaves? We know very little about slave ownership among poorer Romans. It was probably a common aspiration, though slaves probably typically cost the equivalent of several years of food for a family. The ownership of hundreds of slaves does not seem unusual for the elite, consisting of the richest few thousand Romans, and ownership of thousands is known.

The sheer variety of slave jobs makes generalisation difficult. Most slaves were probably active in agriculture, domestic work or urban trades, with mining less significant than in Athens. A number of Roman authors, including Cato, Varro and Columella, discuss slaves in agriculture. Individual farms might have some dozens of slaves. They lived in barracks with a slave overseer, and masters were often absent for part or all of the year. Some slaves were chained, most probably not. We have little evidence of any family life for farm labourers except for overseers, though recent work has suggested that female slaves (and their children) may have been much more significant than previously believed. Apart from arable farming, slaves were also used in herding. Here we have a little more evidence of family life and indications of a degree of independence, perhaps one reason why herders are relatively prominent in the stories of slave rebellions discussed below.

Our evidence for domestic slavery is heavily biased towards the households of the very wealthy. The degree of specialisation in such households is striking: male and female slaves ministered to every physical and mental need of their owners. Romans were happy to use slaves in jobs requiring a high degree of training, including secretaries and teachers. They were proud of their educated, especially Greek-speaking, slaves. Domestic work was not, however, the only activity of city-based slaves. Epigraphic evidence indicates slaves engaging in an extraordinary range of trades, and legal evidence shows masters operating as silent partners in businesses run by slaves or ex-slaves. Slaves and ex-slaves are particularly prominent in the inscriptions put up by urban workers. It has been suggested that these indicate a pride in work consciously opposed to the anti-labour prejudices of the slaves' masters. Little can be said of the organization of labour, apart from exceptional cases such as the factory production of pottery at Arezzo, though businesses were probably generally small-scale. It is clear, however, that many slaves and freedmen joined trade- and household-based social and funerary clubs known as *collegia*.

Slaves owned by the state, whether by local municipalities or by the emperor, form a final important group. As Rome expanded its empire in an *ad hoc* fashion, aristocrats were given short-term control of provinces and war zones, and relied on their slave households for secretarial support. The first emperors took over many of the functions of the Republican aristocracy and created something close to a professional bureaucracy staffed by slaves and ex-slaves. We shall see below that some of these could rise to positions of extraordinary influence. While many state-owned slaves had purely menial jobs, such as tending to aqueducts or making pipes, both municipal slaves and particularly the emperor's slaves seem to have enjoyed advantages compared with ordinary slaves. Slaves owned by the municipalities were sometimes given pay and independent lodging. The imperial slaves appear to have had a higher chance than ordinary slaves of forming a partnership with a free woman which could become a legitimate marriage after manumission.

There is considerable debate over the treatment of Roman slaves, partly because of the difficulty in assessing the typicality of the surviving evidence (Bradley 1987 and 1994). The letters of Pliny the Younger and of Cicero, for example, as well as much of the surviving epigraphic material, suggest a close relationship between some slaves and their masters. These slaves were, however, predominantly urban rather than rural, and also often highly trained and especially useful to their masters. They may represent only a small minority, though it may still be significant that some owners wished to appear "good" masters to "good" slaves.

On the other hand, there are also shocking stories of abuse, as in Juvenal's *Satires* or the philosophical work of Seneca. Some women, Juvenal wrote, paid an annual salary for someone to flog their slaves.[11] There is, however, a problem with such anecdotal evidence. There were indeed professional slave-floggers and torturers. On the other hand, Juvenal's text, in common with many other statements about Roman slavery, is part of a moralising discourse. Juvenal satirises the evil effects of female vanity and paranoia. Compare the story of how Vedius Pollio attempted to feed to his lampreys a slave who had broken an expensive goblet: the story is told to indicate Pollio's meanness and viciousness.[12] His guest, the first emperor Augustus, reacted with fury at his behaviour. The episode is often cited, but not always with its original moral.

The problem of interpretation is also very clear with one of our largest sources of evidence on Roman slavery: legal texts (Watson, 1987). Roman law dealt with slaves almost exclusively as property rather than as people. We should not, however, exaggerate the significance of the lack of recognition of the humanity of the slave in this material. The vast bulk of surviving Roman law concerns the adjudication of property disputes between the free, particularly disputes concerning business and inheritances. The willingness of Romans to use slaves as agents and representatives meant that quarrels concerning the consequences of slaves' actions could become very complicated. Roman law concentrates on such issues and is, therefore, a potentially rather one-sided picture of attitudes towards slaves. There are, however, passages mirroring the kinds of abuses seen in other literature: for example, the possibility that a master might starve his slaves to death. Of course, the reason we hear of this was a desire to intervene to prevent it. Roman law attempted, at least theoretically, to protect slaves from some aspects of abuse by their masters from the first century AD onwards. For example, the emperor Hadrian forbad the throwing of slaves to wild beasts in public entertainments without the permission of a magistrate. Antoninus Pius attempted to check "excessive brutality" against slaves. Killing a slave "without just cause" was to be punished as severely as killing someone else's slave.[13] The murder of a slave was, therefore, not taken as seriously as the murder of a free man. In addition, "excessive" and "just cause" were doubtless tricky concepts to define, especially as fellow slave owners made the determination, and death from "justified" whipping was never legally punishable. While we have every right to be sceptical about the reach of legislation into the lives of most slaves, we should, however, also recognise that it at least reflected either a desire to establish new norms of behaviour, or existing ideas of "the done thing".

The evidence of Roman law, however, clearly conforms to Orlando Patterson's (1982) famous definition of slaves as vulnerable, and this is true also concerning their lack of kin and of honour. Roman lawyers did not recognise any kinship relations between slaves, except for some prohibitions on incest, though we know from inscriptions that *de facto* families did exist. There were occasional qualms expressed about breaking up family groups, but separations must have been inevitable given Roman inheritance patterns. Only in the fourth century AD do we see any legislation attempting to prevent it. As for honour, protection of slaves from the actions of third parties was, as in Greece, conceived as protection of the property of the master. There was, however, potential recourse available with the master's support for serious assault, and here the honour of the slave could, at least potentially, be considered.[14]

There were no legal controls on what a master might do sexually with his slaves, apart from repeated and apparently unsuccessful attempts to prevent the trade in castrated slaves.[15] There was little discussion of what might constitute the limits of acceptable sexual behaviour towards slaves before the Christian era and, it has been suggested, even then (Bradley, 1987, 116–18; Glancy, 2002). Slave prostitution was widespread and there were no taboos against masters sleeping with their female slaves. Any child produced was a slave. Slave women were sometimes freed on the condition that they marry their ex-owner (though the practice was prevented at the very highest levels of society), and widowers (even emperors) also sometimes took slave or ex-slave concubines: new off-spring would not then threaten the inheritance of a dead wife's children. Sexual relations between masters and male slaves were probably less common than with female slaves, though poets such as Martial and Statius used erotic language to describe "pets" who were usually adolescent and pre-adolescent male slaves. Relationships between free women and slaves were, typically, not socially acceptable, and could face legal sanctions, though it is difficult to know how far they affected the lowest levels of society.

The slave in literature, particularly in drama, is again the focus of some very interesting recent work (Fitzgerald, 2000). "Cunning slaves" are often at the centre of the comedies of Plautus, usually struggling to help their master's son get the girl of his dreams by tricking other characters, including their master. Other slaves give speeches stressing their loyalty, and in one play a "noble" slave saves his master from captivity by switching places with him. On the other hand, slaves are also called "whipping posts", and threats of violence towards them are common. It is not difficult to see how different historians have used this material to argue both a negative and a positive picture of slave life.

Almost all of the arguments used can be turned on their head. The cheeky but loyal slave may depict not reality but the upside-down carnival world of comedy, representing a mechanism by which the young and powerless could mock their elders and social superiors. Slaves who give speeches about their loyalty almost immediately prove to be fools incapable of doing what their master wants. The noble slave who saves his master was, we discover, originally a free man kidnapped as a child and, fortuitously, the son of the man currently holding him prisoner. Finally, as in Athens, we cannot determine the reality of violence against slaves simply from the names they are called in comedy. "Whipping post" may be shorthand for "bad", and it clearly indicates the possibility of brutality and punishment, but it tells us little about its frequency. The threat of extreme violence in drama may be comic in itself, and some characters are criticised precisely *because* of their unreasonable violence towards slaves.

The nature of the differing types of evidence on Roman slavery, therefore, allows great latitude in general attempts to reconstruct slave life. Much is hidden from us. Our evidence is patchy and potentially unrepresentative of slaves as a whole. One should not lose sight, however, of the vulnerability of the slave and the clear desire of slaves to gain freedom. While Romans certainly discussed the point at which the acceptable treatment of slaves turned into socially reprehensible mistreatment, that *could* be seen in a negative light, suggesting higher levels of abuse: one made a son obey, but broke a slave.

Integration, resistance and anti-slavery thought

Securing one's freedom in Rome seems to have been a result of an emotional bond with one's master/mistress or else an economic exchange making use of the *peculium*

(Andreav 1993). The *peculium* consisted of money or goods that an owner allowed a slave. While it always remained the property of the owner, Romans had good reason not to take it away arbitrarily. The *peculium* allowed a form of "limited liability" insurance when slaves operated independently of their masters in business. It was also a crucial mechanism in stimulating labour as slaves saved to buy luxuries, including other slaves, or freedom. We do not know how many slaves had a *peculium*, though it appears to have been widespread among urban slaves. Nor can we calculate the chances of a slave being freed. One throwaway remark implied that slavery might typically last as little as six years. Given the demographic debate on Roman slavery, this seems an exaggeration, particularly for female slaves. This remains true even if the first Roman emperor Augustus felt the need to regulate manumission more closely. After manumission, freedmen had a duty of respect towards their masters even if some Roman writers complained that this was not always fulfilled. Masters also had considerable power over the ex-slave's right to bequeath property and over the rights of freedwomen to marry. The freed also often had to complete *operae*, days of work for their patrons. The state was prepared to protect ex-slaves from particularly demeaning or inconvenient *operae*, but it also defended the rights of the ex-master.

Ex-slaves exercised a degree in influence in at least three ways. (1) They were given citizenship, though there were political battles about how much weight their vote should carry. (2) Some were proverbially wealthy, helped by their experience as business agents, and possibly also by financial support and bequests from their patrons. They also had considerable success in fields such as medicine and literature. (3) Some wielded great influence in the imperial bureaucracy, particularly in the first century AD: the aristocrat Tacitus, for example, supposed that they effectively decided who would succeed the emperor Claudius.[16] It has been suggested that these imperial bureaucrats were still slave-like in that they were kinless and without honour, though this may over-emphasise *elite* contempt of these men. It is probably better to see such slaves and ex-slaves as examples of status dissonance: scoring high in some status indicators, low in others.

There is some evidence to suggest that at the lowest social levels, slave and free and freed socialised easily. The stigma of being an ex-slave – or even being descended from a slave – could, however, be strong in some quarters. Petronius' satire the *Satyricon* describes the fabulously wealthy fictional freedman Trimalchio. His crudity shows us how not to behave in society; he is the "parvenu who never arrived". A number of children of freedmen did gain high political office in Rome, but social advancement was apparently easier outside the city of Rome: the descendants of ex-slaves were a vital element in the social elite of Italian municipalities such as Ostia. We should not simply accept the Roman aristocratic view of such men as tasteless upstarts, but is still clear that ex-slaves faced prejudice and discrimination. They and their descendants may nonetheless have constituted a large proportion of the upwardly mobile section of Roman society.

Rebellions involving tens of thousands of slaves occurred in Sicily in the late 130s BC, again in 104–01 BC, and finally in Italy in 73–71 BC (Urbainczyk 2008). They were focused on the countryside, and initially defeated full Roman armies before ultimate failure. The Sicilian rebellions allegedly even manifested a level of proto-state organisation. Perhaps surprisingly, some of the key ancient sources on these events manifest at least a limited degree of sympathy with the plight of the slaves and qualified admiration for some of the slave leaders (especially Spartacus).

A few minor rebellions occurred at other times in Roman history, but the concentration of the major rebellions within a 60-year period requires explanation. The empire had taken massive numbers of slaves, from specific areas such as Cilicia and Syria, who cooperated more easily than slaves of more diverse origin. Rome's attention was also distracted by major foreign wars. Finally, contemporaries believed that imperial growth had brought a flood of cheap slaves and easy wealth, which encouraged some owners to treat their slaves particularly inhumanely, provoking insurrection. Some modern writers have downplayed the significance of the rebellions to the history of slavery, stressing problems with the surviving narratives, possible religious or nationalist causes, and the participation of free people in the revolts. While some of the details of the events are indeed questionable, the overall picture probably should not be rejected. There is little evidence that the religiosity of the slaves differed significantly from that of the Romans themselves, and Roman writers clearly believed that slaves, not disgruntled peasants, formed the bulk of the rebels. There is little evidence, however, that the slave rebellions prompted major change.

Some Roman politicians claimed that their opponents involved slaves in violent political struggles between citizens, using the *collegia* clubs where slaves, freed and free mixed. Such claims may simply be malicious, even if the Roman state was keen to regulate the *collegia*. Slave resistance was typically less dramatic than organised violence. Roman writers expressed horror at the killing of individual masters by slaves. Roman law declared that a slave household that failed to help a murdered master should be tortured and executed. The notion, however, that the Romans lived in fear of their slaves is highly debatable. It is difficult to tell whether murders were anything other than very exceptional. Most of our evidence implies that the obedience of slaves was expected and their loyalty hoped for. Romans did not lock their bedroom doors when they went to bed at night.

Slaves could, of course, resist their owners in non-violent ways. It is impossible to determine to what degree, though the strong association of slavery and discipline via the whip is suggestive. Roman law indicates many ways in which a slave could defraud or cause loss to a master, but such texts again inform us more about the possibility of such actions than their commonness. Concerns about runaways appear often. Those who wished to disappear were helped by the sheer size of the empire and the looseness of bureaucratic control, the relative independence of some slaves, and the difficulties of differentiating slave and free. Laws from the fourth century AD indicate that free men might help fugitives, possibly in order to gain labourers. Overall, however, effective opposition, including flight, would have been very dangerous and may have been less of a problem for slave owners than is sometimes implied.

Unlike Greece, Rome saw significant discussion of the morality of slavery (Bradley, 1994, ch. 7; Garnsey, 1996, ch. 9–14). The Stoic Seneca complained about the inhuman treatment of slaves, most famously in his *Moral Letters* 47. Stoics argued that men should be judged by their morality, not their legal status; masters addicted to luxury might be the "true" slaves, not those who served them. Stoics taught, however, that the troubles of the world such as slavery were to be endured, not resisted: the test of a man was how he dealt with his lot. Some early Christian thought was very similar. St Paul argued that in the eyes of God there was neither Jew nor Gentile, slave nor free, male nor female.[17] He was not thereby implying that slavery be abolished (any more than gender), though he did suggest that masters should not treat their slaves harshly. Both the early Christians and the Stoics have been criticised for reinforcing slavery by undermining resistance among slaves, especially as Christians quickly moved to tell slaves that they should obey their masters. The Christian empire of the fourth century onwards certainly fully accepted slavery. Stoicism and Christianity may nonetheless have had *some* positive impact. The legislation protecting slaves in the early empire cannot be traced directly to Stoic thought, but it is possible that it was prompted by the kind of moralising debates we saw earlier in Roman literature, and they almost certainly *were* affected by such thinking. The legislation was limited, but the social values expressed were nonetheless significant. Christianity may have brought *a little* change regarding sexual behaviour, and perhaps a more positive attitude towards manual work. And if Christians told slaves to obey their masters, there were at least some injunctions for masters to behave properly too. Overall, however, Christianity quickly adapted itself to slave society and may have had less influence on slave life than Stoic-influenced pagan moralising.

The end of ancient slavery

At some point in the later Roman Empire, villa-based direct exploitation of agricultural slaves in Italy declined in favour of free- and slave-tenant farming. Slaves became increasingly like the rest of the rural poor as they were given a degree of autonomy and allowed to live in family units. There has been considerable debate as to why this change happened. It has been suggested that traditional slave exploitation simply became uneconomic at some point after 100 AD. Arguments that the end of Roman expansion at that time made captives more costly rest, however, on the questionable assumption that war was the main source of slaves and that breeding was uneconomic. Nor is there clear evidence, as some have claimed, that increasing supervision costs made slavery unprofitable. There is at least some archaeological support for the idea that the export markets of slave-run farms in Italy were undermined by the development of non-slave production centres elsewhere in the empire. Slave-run villas may also have been compromised by the decline of market production in favour of barter in the later empire. One feels slightly nervous, however, of such an economic explanation of the decline of Roman slavery when economic theories, as we saw, fail to clarify why slavery in Roman Italy reached such an unusual magnitude in the first place.

This, of course, brings us back to Moses Finley's emphasis on the availability of exploitable indigenous "free" labour, his "default" historical system of exploitation (Finley, 1998, ch. 4). We saw that Italian peasants initially had important roles as voters and soldiers. They lost these as the empire first removed their voting rights and then recruited armies from outside Italy. Increasing economic pressure could therefore be placed upon them, making tenancy more profitable than directly supervised slaves: the remaining slaves could simply be converted into tenants. In addition, the decline in the market economy removed another of Finley's preconditions for mass slavery.

A third position is possible, however. It could be argued that slavery never actually declined (Whittaker, 1993, ch. 5). Slaves appear often in our texts up to the end of the Western Empire in 476 AD, and also in sixth-century Byzantine law codes. Some medievalists argue for relatively high percentages of slaves in post-Roman societies such as Anglo-Saxon England, where slaves may have comprised ten per cent or more of the population. Historians of Roman slavery are, therefore, able to push the "decline" of the institution beyond the point they themselves study. It should be noted, however, that the move from direct agricultural exploitation of slaves to a tenant system requires explanation. Finley's argument certainly appears the most attractive explanation in terms of its simplicity. It fails, however, to explain why Roman peasants had originally managed to gain such military and political influence in the first place and it is therefore difficult to prove or disprove. As such, it remains symbolic of much of the rest of the debate about Greek and Roman slavery.

Notes

1 Maidservants: Homer, *Odyssey*, 22.457ff, in A. T. Murray and G. E. Dimock (trans.), *Homer*, vol. 4. (Cambridge, MA: Harvard University Press, 1995).

2 Herodotus, *Histories*, 8: 105 in A. D. Godley, ed. and trans. *Herodotus*, vol. 4 (Cambridge, MA: Harvard University Press, 1925).

3 Euripides, *Ion*, 554–56 in David Kovacs, ed. and trans., *Euripides*, vol. 4 (Cambridge, MA: Harvard University Press, 1999).

4 Aristophanes, *Frogs*, 693ff in J. Henderson, ed. and trans., *Aristophanes*, vol. 4 (Cambridge, MA: Harvard University Press, 2002).

5 *Ibid.*, 612–73.

6 Pseudo-Xenophon ("Old Oligarch"), *Constitution of the Athenians*, 1.10–11, in E. C. Marchant and Glen W. Bowersock, eds and trans, *Xenophon*, vol. 7 (Cambridge, MA: Harvard University Press, 1989).

7 Pseudo-Demosthenes, 53: 16 in A. T. Murray, ed. and trans., *Demosthenes*, vol. 6 (Cambridge, MA: Harvard University Press, 1939).

8 Euripides, *Suppliant Women*, 888–900 in David Kovacs, ed. and trans., *Euripides*, vol. 6 (Cambridge, MA: Harvard University Press, 1998).

9 Plato, *Republic*, in P. Shorey, ed. and trans., *Plato*, vol. 6 (Cambridge, MA: Harvard University Press, 1935), 578d–e.

10 Demosthenes 19.196–98, in C. A. Vince and J. H. Vince, eds and trans., *Demosthenes*, vol. 2 (Cambridge, MA: Harvard University Press, 1926).

11 Juvenal, *Satires*, in 6, 474ff S. M. Braund, ed. and trans., *Juvenal and Persius* (Cambridge, MA: Harvard University Press, 2004).

12 Seneca, *On Anger*, 3.40 in J. W. Basore, ed. and trans., *Seneca*, vol. 1 (Cambridge MA: Harvard University Press, 1989).

13 *The Digest of Justinian*, 48.8.11.2 in A. Watson, ed. and trans., *The Digest of Justinian*, vol. 2. (Philadelphia: University of Philadelphia Press, 1985), Justinian, *Institutes*, 1.8.2 in J. A. C. Thomas, ed. and trans., *The Institutes of Justinian: Text, Translation and Commentary* (Amsterdam: North Holland Publishing Co., 1975), 1.8.2.

14 *Digest, op. cit.*, 47.10.15.44; 47.10.15.35.

15 *Digest, op. cit.*, 48.8.3.4; 48.8.5–6.

16 Tacitus, *Annals*, 12.1–3, in J. Jackson, ed. and trans., *Tacitus*, vol. 4 (Cambridge, MA: Harvard University Press, 1937).

17 *Galatians* 3.28 in *The Good News Bible* (London: Collins, 1976).

Bibliography

Andreau, J., "The Freedman", in A. Giardina, ed., *The Romans* (Chicago: University of Chicago Press, 1993), 175–98.

Bradley, K. R., *Slaves and Masters in the Roman Empire: A Study in Social Control* (Oxford: Oxford University Press, 1987).

——, *Slavery and Society at Rome* (Cambridge: Cambridge University Press, 1994).

Cartledge, Paul A., *Sparta and Lakonia: A Regional History 1300–362 B.C.* (London: Routledge, 1979).

De Ligt, Luuk, "The Economy: Agrarian Change during the Second Century", in N. Rosenstein and R. Morstein-Marx, *A Companion to the Roman Republic* (Malden, MA: Blackwell Publishing, 2006), 590–606.

DuBois, Page, *Slaves and Other Objects* (Chicago: University of Chicago Press, 2003).

Finley, Moses I., *Ancient Slavery and Modern Ideology* (Princeton, NJ: Marcus Wiener, 1998).

Fisher, N. R. E., *Slavery in Classical Greece* (London: Bristol Classical, 2003).

Fitzgerald, William, *Slavery and the Roman Literary Imagination* (Cambridge: Cambridge University Press, 2000).

Foxhall, Lin, Cartledge, Paul and Cohen, Ed, *Money, Labour and Land: Approaches to the Economies of Ancient Greece* (London: Routledge, 2002).

Garlan, Yvon, *Slavery in Ancient Greece* (Ithaca: Cornell University Press, 1988).

Garnsey, Peter, *Ideas of Slavery from Aristotle to Augustine* (Cambridge: Cambridge University Press, 1996).

Glancy, Jennifer A., *Slavery in Early Christianity* (Oxford: Oxford University Press, 2002).

Hodkinson, S., "Spartiates, Helots and the Direction of the Agrarian Economy: Towards an Understanding of Helotage in a Comparative Perspective", in Enrico Dal Lago and Constantina Katsari, eds, *Slave Systems: Ancient and Modern* (Cambridge: Cambridge University Press, 2008), 285–320.

Hopkins, Keith R., *Conquerors and Slaves* (Cambridge: Cambridge University Press, 1978).

Hunt, Peter, *Slaves, Warfare, Ideology in the Greek Historians* (Cambridge: Cambridge University Press, 1998).

Jameson, M. H., "On Paul Cartledge, The Political Economy of Greek Slavery", in Lin Foxhall *et al.*, eds, *Money, Labour and Land, op. cit.* (2002), 167–74.

McKeown, Niall, *The Invention of Ancient Slavery?* (London: Duckworth, 2007).

Mirhady, David C., "The Athenian rationale for torture", in Virginia J. Hunter and Jonathan Edmondson, eds, *Law and Social Status in Classical Athens* (Oxford: Oxford University Press, 2000), 53–74.

Morris, I. M., "Hard surfaces", in Lin Foxhall *et al.*, eds, *Money, Labour and Land, op. cit.* (2002), 8–43.

Patterson, Orlando, *Slavery and Social Death. A Comparative Study* (Cambridge, MA: Harvard University Press, 1982).

Scheidel, Walter, "Human Mobility in Roman Italy II: The Slave Population", *Journal of Roman Studies*, 95 (2005), 64–79.

Urbainczyk, Theresa, *Slave Revolts in Antiquity* (Stocksfield: Acumen, 2008).

Vlassopoulos, K., "Slavery, Freedom and Citizenship in Classical Athens: Beyond a Legalistic Approach", *European Review of History/Revue europeenne d'histoire*, 16 (2009), 347–63.

Watson, Alan, *Roman Slave Law* (Baltimore: Johns Hopkins University Press, 1987).

Whitehead, David, *The Ideology of the Athenian Metic* (Cambridge: Cambridge Philological Society, 1977).

Whittaker, C. R., *Land, City and Trade in the Roman Empire* (Aldershot: Variorum, 1993), ch. 5.

2

SLAVERY IN AFRICA

Paul E. Lovejoy

Introduction

Slavery has been known in Africa for a long time – how long is not known because of a lack of documentation. However defined, slavery has been important in the history of Africa; indeed there have been major transformations in the political economy of Africa over the past millennium that can be attributed to slavery. The evidence suggests that slavery was indigenous, as was also the case elsewhere in the world. The trade in enslaved people, moreover, was multifaceted. Slavery affected social and political structures from early times to the present. This chapter examines the nature of slavery, from enslavement to trafficking, and the impact on Africa of the external trade in slaves across the Sahara, Indian Ocean and Atlantic. An examination of the uses and abuses of enslaved individuals demonstrates that the persistence of slavery is a factor in African history (Lovejoy, 2000a). In addition, this chapter examines how patterns of slavery in Africa changed over time.

Slavery, no matter how otherwise defined, involved the possibility that individuals could be bought and sold, with little and usually no consultation with the enslaved. Should we be concerned about whether or not we can use the term "slavery"? This philosophical question has challenged history and anthropology to define terms. The fact that people could be bought and sold affected the ideological context of society, which is important in understanding the relations of dependence and exploitation that are here defined as "slavery". Slavery was ubiquitous both in Africa and in the various parts of the world where Africans went, but the context varied and circumstances changed, often influenced by religious, sociological and political factors, and by opportunity. Slavery involved absolute power over another person, often resulting in psychological subordination, with intermittent expressions of resistance and attempts at escape. The relationships inevitably contained tensions that helped to define slavery in each situation. Language reflected the nature of this relationship, the word for "slave" being different in virtually every language, attesting to the ubiquity and antiquity of the practice of slavery. We can translate "slave" into any language in Africa, such as *nikla* (Tamasheq), *bawa* (Hausa), but also *bella* (Songhay), *maccuBe* and *rimaaybe* (Puular), *'abd* (Arabic), *jam* (Wolof), among others.

Sometimes, it has been argued, "slavery" did not exist in Africa, but whatever we are talking about is confused with other social relationships that are better described through the use of local terminology, which varies widely according to language and even dialect, as is argued by Joseph Inikori (1996). It could be argued equally convincingly, however, that the great variety of terms for "slavery" indicates the antiquity of the institution, evolving with each language and the people who spoke these languages, rather than being borrowed from other cultures or imposed from outside. Indeed, it is essential to distinguish slavery from other forms of servitude, such as human pawnship, some forms of marriage, and the status assigned to those freed from slavery. Usually these social relationships of dominance and subordination were specifically contrasted with, and referred to through the use of terms different from, slavery. Hence the descendants of slaves who were considered free were called *buzaye* in Tamachek, the language of the Tuareg, so that former slave status was remembered although the people in question could not be bought or sold legally.

Definitions of slavery in Africa

Slavery is a form of exploitation, whether in Africa or elsewhere, historically or in contemporary times. Its definition derives from the idea that slaves are property, and that slaves are outsiders who are alien by origin or who could be denied their heritage through judicial or other sanctions. With slaves, coercion could be used at will, and their labor power was at the complete disposal of the master. They did not have the right to their own sexuality or, by extension, to their own reproductive capacities and gender options. Enslaved women separated from their children and eunuchs are examples of this complete subordination. Slave status was inherited unless provision was made to ameliorate that status. Slavery was fundamentally a means of denying outsiders the rights and privileges of a particular society so that they could be exploited for economic, political, and/or social purposes.

The classic debate over the definition of slavery in the African context has revolved around efforts to find suitable terminology to allow comparisons with slavery in other places. On the one hand, Igor Kopytoff and Suzanne Miers (1977) have attempted to define the practice of slavery in terms of what they have called "institutions of marginality", in which individuals are perceived as more or less "belonging" to a society, and the extent to which acculturation and legal norms have allowed outsiders to be incorporated into the framework of society. On the other hand, Claude Meillassoux (1975, 1991), among others, has emphasized the alienation of individuals whose subordination has been reduced to the same status as livestock, who can be bought, sold, exchanged as gifts, bequeathed or otherwise disposed of without the consent of the person in question, and whose status was inherited. This emphasis on slaves as property is reflected in the western Sudan through the comparison of slaves with chickens. It is often said in Sudan that whoever owns the hen by right also owns the chickens: that is, the children of slaves are also the property of the master of the slaves, and as such have a monetary value (Klein, 1998). Whether the definition of "slavery" emphasizes the marginality of social and political status, or the property relationship, it is generally agreed that individuals who have been considered slaves could not be fully incorporated as fully equal members of society. Among the Akan, for example, matrilineal rules of identity defined individuals according to their kinship with the family of their mother, so that outsiders could never achieve legitimate and recognized status within society as free people, since their ties with the kin of their own mother, usually "outsiders" or alien to Akan society, had been severed (Lovejoy, 2000a: 123). Thus, what was very important in African slavery was that slaves were people who, in important ways, did not "belong" within existing social structures.

Historically, slavery has to be viewed as a common theme in the history of not only Africa, but virtually everywhere, always in historical context and never as a generalized and timeless concept applied to different historical situations. This approach is essential in examining the history of slavery in Africa and the dispersal of enslaved Africans within Africa, as well as to the Mediterranean via the Sahara, to Asia by caravans or across the Indian Ocean, and to the Americas and the "Middle Passage" of the Atlantic. The enslavement of people was intimately associated with the trade in slaves. Africa "produced" slaves, traded them and consumed its own people. The academic discussion of this theme in history has now become a major area of research, transcending older scholarship that ignored the issue, or treated slavery as an anachronism, or was dismissed by a colonial perspective that considered "African slavery" benign. Moreover, scholars have been encouraged to treat African slavery within wider contexts. It is now widely recognized, for example, that to study slavery in Africa is a way of showing that African history is not only the history of the continent, but also that of the regions where enslaved Africans were taken.

As the debate over the meaning of "slavery" demonstrates, usually outsiders have been perceived as ethnically different from insiders. A person who spoke the same language as his master, without an accent, who shared the same culture, believed in the same religion, and understood the political relationships that determined how power was exercised was far more difficult to control than an outsider and was unlikely to become enslaved. When differences in culture or dialect were relatively unimportant, the level of exploitation and the social isolation of slaves were usually limited; such situations suggest that slave holdings were small and that political and economic stratification was minimal. There are many such examples from societies that were decentralized and not part of a state, such as along parts of the upper Guinea coast in the fifteenth and sixteenth centuries, or in areas of central and eastern Africa that were relatively isolated from trading networks and international markets, even as late as the nineteenth century (Lovejoy, 2000a: 127–32). The most developed forms of slavery, nevertheless, were those where enslaved individuals were removed a considerable distance from their birthplace, thereby emphasizing their alien origin. This uprooting was as dramatic within Africa as was the transport of Africans across the Atlantic or the Sahara Desert, or as tragic as the seizure of people who lived only 100 kilometres or less from the home of the enslavers. Both situations helped to define the slave as an outsider, at least in the first instance. Over time, cultural distinctions tended to blur, so that the extent to which alien origin was a factor varied, which is why terminology also was different. Those who had been enslaved in their own lifetime were distinguished from those who were "born in the house", that is, had been born into slavery. Among the Hausa, for example, *cucanawa* referred to the children of slaves, who were nonetheless also *bawa* (slaves), and could be bought and sold just as their parents could be.

In Africa, the status of individuals under slavery influenced what was meant by ethnicity, which must be understood as a dynamic model of social and individual identity formation and not as an essentialist, timeless concept of belonging or not belonging to a group. Ethnicity involved ascription (by self and others), conscription (through immigration and slavery), and removal (through sale, kidnapping or slave raiding). A historical consideration of slavery in Africa helps to explain the emergence and persistence of ethnicity, the influence of religion in sustaining social relationships based on coercion, and the dichotomy between external influences of market demand for human labor and internal politics of controlling people and land. In most parts of West Africa, but to a much lesser extent elsewhere, practices of body and facial scarification were used as a means of identifying ethnicity, social status, and sometimes occupational specialization, which also had the effect of distinguishing between slave and free and protecting those with specific markings from enslavement. Facial and body markings among the Yoruba, for example, indicated which state or province a person was associated with, while among the Igbo of south-eastern Nigeria, the *ichi* scarification on a man's forehead indicated that he was a free person and part of the village or town council, and therefore was not legally subject to the possibility of enslavement (Afigbo, 1981).

Methods of enslavement in Africa

Historically, warfare, military raids and kidnapping were the most common means of enslavement in Africa. In each of these situations, enslavement involved violence, in which people were killed or wounded, and in which moveable property such as livestock, food and other goods were seized as well. The violence underlying enslavement needs to be emphasized. As Orlando Patterson has argued, enslavement in effect was a form of "social death" that severed individuals from their natal societies, eliminated ties with kin, and removed people against their will from their homelands, even resulting in the destruction of their villages and farms (Patterson, 1982). Whether as a form of punishment or as a means of acquiring captives for purposes of sale and exploitation, slavery was integrated into the political economy and social structures of African societies.

In a letter dating from 1391–92, for example, the government of Borno, an early kingdom located in present-day Nigeria and Chad, protested that Arab raiders were seizing its free subjects and taking them as slaves to North Africa. According to Uthman ibn Idris, the King of Borno, nomadic warriors were raiding across the Sahara for the purpose of enslaving people.

> These Arabs have pillaged our land, the land of Bornu, and continue doing so. They have taken as slaves free men and our fathers, the Muslims, and they are selling them to the slave-dealers of Egypt, Syria, and elsewhere, and keep some for themselves.
>
> (Palmer [1936], 1970: 218)

As this account demonstrates, there was no real division between Africa north and south of the Sahara, but rather there was continuity across the desert in terms of slavery and enslavement. In the specific context of this case, Borno was issuing complaints as a Muslim state against another Muslim state. The Muslim regions of sub-Saharan Africa were closely intertwined with the Muslim world of North Africa and the Middle East, which has remained the case until the present. This account chronicles raids across the Sahara, but slavery and raiding were well established south of Borno. The reference, rather, shows that sub-Saharan Africa was not isolated or distant. Moreover, lest it be thought that these trans-Saharan excursions for slaves were only an invasion, it should also be pointed out that documents from Borno also chronicle the enslavement of people by the Borno state for its own purposes, including the sale of slaves across the Sahara.

Even though forms of slavery existed in Africa before the maritime arrival of Europeans, and long before the emergence of the American slave systems, the European demand for African slaves had a transforming impact on African societies. The imposition of a racially defined slavery system changed Africans' understanding of slavery. According to William Snelgrave, a slave trader on the coast of the Bight of Benin in the 1720s, "It has been the Custom among the Negroes, time out of Mind, and it is so to this day, for them to make Slaves of all Captives they take in War ... [to] employ in their own Plantations." Now, Snelgrave noted, Africans "had an Opportunity of selling them to white People".[1] Snelgrave understood that the demand for slaves in the Americas transformed a local method of labor exploitation into an intercontinental system that was now based on racial categories. In addition, people were enslaved for judicial reasons, enslavement being considered a form of punishment, and many children were also born into slavery. In the sixteenth century, Jesuit priest Baltasar Barreira learned that not only were slaves taken in war, but people were enslaved for what were perceived to be criminal offenses.

> There are other ways of enslaving in a legal way, as when it is proved that one black is a witch, or if he confesses it himself; or that has killed another with poison; or that he is intimate with any of the king's wives; or that he is inciting war against the king; or that he asks for "chinas" – so they call their idols – to kill the king, in which case if the king happens to fall ill, not only do they kill the delinquent or sell him outside the kingdom, and confiscate all his possessions, but they also enslave and sell all his relatives, for fear that any of them, in revenge, also asks the "chinas" to kill him.
>
> (Hair, 1975: 67)

This report also refers to collective punishment for actions and suspicions that were considered illegal and threatening to the established political order. Enforcement inevitably required violence or the threat of violence. According to the report of Francis Moore, who was a slave trader in Senegambia in the 1730s,

> Since the Slave Trade has been us'd, all Punishments are changed into Slavery; there being an advantage on such condemnations, the strain for Crimes very hard, in order to get the Benefit of selling the Criminals. Not only Murder, Theft and Adultery are punished by selling the Criminal for Slave, but every trifling case is punished in the same manner.[2]

References to "trifling cases" indicates that European – that is, foreigner – observers were often not attuned to the reasons behind punishment and had little understanding about the nature of alleged crimes. Despite such reservations about the justification for enslavement, the fact remains that individuals were being enslaved, and this included delinquent members of society.

Slavery and labor

The central feature of slavery was the virtual lack of choice on the part of slaves. Their total subordination to the whims of their master meant that slaves could be assigned any task in the society or economy. Slavery was fundamentally tied to labor. It was not the only form of forced labor, but slaves could be made to perform any task in the economy. They had to do what they were told; hence they often performed the most menial and laborious tasks and sometimes undertook great risks. In the Kingdom of Kongo in the late sixteenth century, for example, it was reported that free people did not "cultivate the ground", but rather

> only slaves labour and serve. Men who are powerful have a great number of slaves whom they have captured in war or whom they have purchased. They [even] conduct business through these slaves by sending them to markets where they buy and sell according to the master's orders.
> (Cuvelier and Jadin, 1954: 135; also see Fage, 1980: 305)

As this account makes clear, slaves not only performed agricultural tasks but also traded on behalf of their owners, if individual slaves had been assimilated into local society and could be trusted. Similarly, in the hinterland of Sierra Leone, as observed in the 1560s, people were taken in war as slaves, "whome onely they kept to till the ground".[3] In the case of slaves, the concept of labor was not perceived as separate from the slave as a person. The slave was an instrument through which work could be accomplished, and coercion could be used to force compliance with particular orders. The slave was told what to do and, if he or she did not do it, he or she was punished, often severely.

Masters not only controlled the productive capacities of slaves, but also regulated their sexual and reproductive capabilities. When slaves constituted a significant proportion of the population, then sexual access and reproduction were strongly controlled. Women (and men too) were treated as sexual objects; the ability to marry was closely administered, and males could be castrated. The significance of sex is most strikingly revealed in the market price of slaves. Eunuchs were often the most costly, with pretty women and girls close behind, their price depending upon their sexual attractiveness. These two opposites of an engendered perspective – castrated males and attractive females – demonstrate most clearly the master's power over sexual and reproductive functions (Robertson and Klein, 1983). Slaves implicitly lacked the right to engage in sexual relationships without the consent of their masters. Their children, once slaves were given the opportunity to have children, were not legally their offspring but the property of their master. Biologically, they were the offspring of slave parents, but the right to raise the children could be denied. Instead, slave children could be taken away, and even when they were not sold, they could be redistributed as part of marriage arrangements, trained for the army or administration, or taken as concubines.

Moreover, the power of masters over slaves extended to the right of life and death. In many places, such as among the Igbo, slaves could be sacrificed at funerals of important individuals, as a sign of wealth and as one form of offering to gods. While in some cases, slaves of the house might be sacrificed, often individual slaves were bought specifically for the purpose of sacrifice. Where such practices were common, as among the Igbo, individual slaves might well fear being sold because the sale might lead to their death. Similarly, among the Yoruba, slaves could be sacrificed at religious ceremonies and annual festivals. The most well known public executions of slaves occurred in Dahomey, where hundreds of captives were killed at annual festivals (Lovejoy, 2000a: 165–86).

Those born into slavery found themselves in a different position from those who had been enslaved in their own lifetime, as the initial act of violence became an abstraction. Parents might tell their children of their enslavement, but this was not the children's experience. Children could also learn about enslavement from new captives. The threat of violence within African enslavement practices was also present. Legally, slaves could be separated from their parents and sold, even if in practice such separations were rare. Violence was still a crucial dimension of social control. People who had been enslaved could not necessarily expect that their children would be incorporated fully into local society, or otherwise expect emancipation, because the threat of re-enslavement in war and through raids on rural communities could result in their transfer to distant lands, if not their death along the way.

For various reasons, slaves tended not to sustain their numbers naturally, and slave populations usually had to be replenished. One reason for this situation was the relatively short life span for many slaves. Death could result from particularly harsh work, while funeral sacrifices and unsuccessful castration operations took their toll. Travel conditions for slaves destined for distant markets were also a factor, both because individuals were moved from one disease environment to another, thus increasing mortality rates, and because rations were often inadequate. Another reason was the demographic imbalance between the sexes in slave populations. Populations with an excess number of males led to a general decline in total population, not just slaves, unless more slaves were imported. When slave women were distributed unevenly, the general population did not necessarily decline, only the proportion of slaves in the population. Free men usually took the women as wives or concubines, so that they still bore children. Because the status of concubines and slave wives changed, often leading to assimilation or full emancipation, the size of the slave population decreased accordingly. The children of slave wives and concubines by free fathers were often granted a status that was completely or almost free. Under Islamic law, this was most pronounced. Concubines could not be sold once they gave birth, and they became free on the death of their master. The children of such unions were free on birth. These features of gradual assimilation or complete emancipation contradict the aspect of slavery that emphasized inherited status, but were compatible with the master's power to manipulate sexual and reproductive functions for his own purpose.

Slavery as but one form of labor

As indicated above, slavery in Africa should be distinguished from other forms of servile labor and from other patterns of organizing work. There were cases in which people were tied to the land, such as in Christian Ethiopia before the twentieth century, and hence were analogous to serfs in Europe, where obligations were fixed by custom. Elsewhere, however, such relationships were rare or non-existent. Patterns of raiding and warfare usually meant that people were enslaved and sometimes even re-enslaved so that "feudal" type arrangements could not develop. Moreover, there were forms of clientage, in which individuals voluntarily attached themselves to political and military elites that involved services without fixed remuneration. Such was often the case for people of slave descent, as in most Muslim areas and in regions plagued by warfare, as was true among the Yoruba in the nineteenth century. People did work for wages, such as porters who carried goods along trade routes or between the countryside and towns, but in many cases these people were in fact slaves who were being allowed to work on their own account, subject to payment of fixed fees to their masters.

Pawnship was also widely practiced, in which individuals were held as collateral for debts contracted by their relatives. Pawns were expected to reside with the creditors, and their labor was at the disposal of the creditor as a form of interest on the debt. In these cases, labor was redistributed within societies as a means of securing credit and therefore was closely tied to trade and marketing. Individuals could not be redeemed until the original debt was fully paid, which meant that pawning arrangements might be inherited or might become part of marriage contracts. In these contracts, pawned girls might marry within the household of the creditor as a means of liquidating debts, the whole process being conceived of as a substitute for marriage payments. Pawnship was found widely in West and Central Africa (Lovejoy and Falola, 2003). In some places, such as in Old Calabar and in the trade castles on the Gold Coast, European merchants accepted pawns as a way of guaranteeing that slaves and various commodities would be delivered when imported goods had been extended on credit to resident African merchants (Lovejoy and Richardson, 2001). In these cases, however, the terms of repayment usually involved a time limit on the contract that was based on the date of departure of ships. Local practices were not normally subject to specific time restrictions. It should be noted that not only people could be pawned, but also gold, other valuables, and fruit-bearing trees.

It is important to note that labor was organized on the basis of families, communal work parties, marriage contracts, and other arrangements. These forms of organization could involve coercion or more subtle forms of pressure. Financial and labor obligations associated with marriage contracts often involved arrangements in which future husbands worked for the family of the bride. Men or their kin might be required to make payments to the bride's family – often described as "bride price" – to reflect the financial dimensions of such contracts. These arrangements were usually intended to cement relations between kin groups and therefore help to secure the longevity of the marriage. However, whether slaves or not, pawns and clients were involved in these arrangements, which affected the nature of marriage and introduced other factors of labor mobilization and control into the equation. These various forms of social and economic structures demonstrate that slavery was widely recognized as one type of relationship among many that existed in West and Central Africa.

Islamic slavery

There was an important distinction in how slavery was established and how slaves were treated between Islamic areas and areas where Islam was not important or not present. In an Islamic context, slavery was governed by reference to legal and religious traditions, which were codified either by reference to the Qu'ran, or in *hadiths*, and legal schools, especially Maliki. It was also reflected in legal opinions and commentary, including those of al-Maghili and Ahmad Baba (Willis, 1985). Hence we need to look for similarities to, and differences from, other parts of the Muslim world. The influence on sub-Saharan politics of the Sharifian dynasty in Morocco and the Ottoman Porte should be stressed. Through pilgrimage and literacy, Muslim scholars were trained in Islamic law, which began from an early date in West Africa. Far from being isolated from the rest of the Islamic world, Muslims south of the Sahara were in close contact. Hence the literary and legal tradition was extended and expanded through the nineteenth century. Technical and legal problems were resolved through the issue of *fatwa*, or legal opinion.

Ahmad Baba (1556–1627), basing his interpretation on earlier scholarly opinions, wrote in 1614 in his *Mi'raj al Su'ud ila Nayl Hukm Majlub al-Sud* that:

> the reason for slavery is non-belief [in Islam] and the Sudanese non-believers are like other kafir whether they are Christians, Jews, Persians, Berbers, or any others who stick to non-belief and do not embrace Islam. … This means there is no difference between all the kafir in this respect. Whoever is captured in a condition of non-belief, it is legal to own him, whosoever he may be, but not if he was converted to Islam voluntarily.[4]

Specifically, as most notably argued in his famous treatise, a treatise widely cited as authoritative in subsequent Islamic texts in West Africa, the *jihad* leadership opposed the sale of enslaved people to non-Muslims as being illegal. Ahmad Baba argued that some people who were not Muslims – and he identified a number of ethnic groups, including the Yoruba, whom he called by that name – could be enslaved. It is instructive that the term Yoruba is a Muslim designation that was subsequently adopted as a common name only in the late nineteenth century. By contrast, he stated that people who had long been Muslim – specifically Hausa, Songhay, Mandingo, Soninke, Wolof and others – should never be enslaved. Later generations found it difficult to abide by the legal *fatwa* of Ahmad Baba, but even if ignored in practice these *fatwa* were well known in Muslim areas of Africa. According to Ahmad Baba, therefore, Muslims were morally and legally prohibited from selling people to non-Muslims, and especially to Christians.

The discourse surrounding slavery in Muslim regions indicates that the subject was widely discussed in Africa long before the abolition debate in Britain and elsewhere in the European world. It is instructive that the problem of "legal" and "illegal" enslavement pervaded many parts of Africa. In the Kingdom of Kongo, to the south of the Congo River, and in places along the Angola coast, some individuals claimed that they had been "wrongfully" enslaved, such as in the case of Nbena, a woman seized from Luanda in the eighteenth century (Curto, 2003). Similarly, two merchants at Old Calabar were seized and taken to Barbados in 1767, even though they were not slaves, encouraging them to use evidence about their previous status in order to prove that their enslavement was wrong (Sparks, 2004). By doing this, they subsequently secured their release and returned to Old Calabar. Other cases, too, demonstrate that slavery was a contentious issue whose legitimacy was contested in Africa, as well as elsewhere.

The trade in slaves

The trade in slaves within Africa was an aspect of commerce in general. When individuals were bought and sold in Africa, there were always many commodities also exchanged. Hence the slave trade was part of economic life, involving the use of money, the provision of credit, and the fixing of prices for exchange. In the context of African history, the interrelationship of internal forms of slavery and servility with the export trade in slaves is an important consideration, and a topic of debate among scholars. The trans-Atlantic and trans-Saharan slave trades removed millions of enslaved Africans from their homelands. This could not have happened unless slaves were being bought and sold. The relative impact of external trade in slaves on internal developments within Africa varied with proximity to the Sahara, the Indian Ocean, and, after the late fifteenth century, along the Atlantic coast. There were wide-ranging networks that were dominated by Muslim merchants, along the East African coast and from the Red Sea to the Atlantic shores of the upper Guinea coast, and from these areas far into the interior. While some of these merchants came from North Africa, the Middle East and India, there were also many merchants who were resident in sub-Saharan Africa and East Africa, and who dominated the trade in slaves well before the opening of trans-Atlantic commerce.[5] Moreover, trade in slaves was also found in areas beyond Muslim influence, precisely because enslaved individuals had to be moved some distance from areas and peoples whom they knew and to which they might attempt to escape. Slavery was based on control and the threat of repeated violence and coercion, which could best be effected through removal via commerce.

Most estimates of the numbers of enslaved Africans who were shipped to the Americas after the early sixteenth century through the nineteenth century range in the order of 12.5 million people. The numbers of people sent as slaves across the Sahara Desert, the Red Sea, and the Indian Ocean have been more difficult to establish, but the scale of this trade was historically very large as well. As reflected in Table 2.1, rough estimates of the scale of this slave trade suggest that about 17.5 million people were forcibly removed from Africa between 1500 and 1900, of which more than 70 per cent went to the Americas and the rest to the Muslim regions of North Africa, the Middle East and the Indian Ocean world. These estimates do not include the number of slaves sent into the Muslim world before 1500, which was considerable, or indeed after 1900. Nonetheless, one feature of slavery in Africa and the relationship of the export trade in slaves is clear. Until very recent times, Africa suffered from a demographic drain in population that was not matched by an inward migration of people to Africa. Slavery meant that economic, social and political development within Africa was constrained by a loss of population, which under other circumstances would have significantly altered the course of African history.

Because of the survival of extensive documentation on the movements of slaves to the Americas, it is possible to estimate the scale and direction of enforced migration of Africans under slavery and thereby provide as assessment of the impact of trans-Atlantic slavery on different parts of Africa (Table 2.2). Information on this traffic has been compiled into an accessible database, which demonstrates that about one out of every two Africans who went to the Americas came from non-Muslim areas centered in West and Central Africa, particularly Angola, Congo and the interior, and extending to Mozambique in south-east Africa. These are areas of Africa which were, and still are,

Table 2.1 Enslaved Africans destined for the Americas and the Islamic world, 1500–1900

	Americas	Percentage	Islamic world	Percentage	Total
1500–1700	2,150,000	55.4	1,650,000	44.6	3,700,000
1700–1800	6,500,000	83.3	1,300,000	16.7	7,800,000
1800–1900	3,870,000	77.4	1,130,000	22.6	5,000,000
Total	12,520,000	71.8	4,910,000	28.2	17,430,00

Sources: Lovejoy (2000a: 26, 47, 62, 142); Eltis *et al.*, www.slavevoyages.org/tast/index.faces

Table 2.2 Departures from Africa to the Americas by coastal origin, 1500–1867

Coastal origin	Number	Percentage
West Central Africa	5,694,600	45.5
Bight of Benin	1,999,100	16.0
Bight of Biafra	1,594,600	12.7
Gold Coast	1,209,300	9.7
Senegambia	755,500	6.0
South East Africa	542,600	4.3
Sierra Leone	388,700	3.1
Windward Coast	336,900	2.9
Total	12,521,300	100.2

Source: Eltis *et al.*, www.slavevoyages.org/tast/index.faces

inhabited by Bantu-speaking peoples. Moreover, a significant number of slaves in the trans-Atlantic slave trade, about 12 per cent, came from the Bight of Biafra, an area largely unaffected by the influence of Muslims. These areas were at the heart of the trans-Atlantic migration. Combined with the region from the Bight of Benin westward, which also accounted for substantial numbers of enslaved Africans, it can be seen that the Muslim regions of Africa accounted for only a small proportion of slaves destined for the Americas, probably fewer than 10 per cent of trans-Atlantic migrants. Africa was pulled in two directions, one focused on the Atlantic and the development of a diaspora of Africans in the Americas and the other orientated and largely restricted to the Muslim world. It seems clear that there was a relatively sharp separation between the Islamic world of sub-Saharan Africa and the trans-Atlantic system of commerce and interaction.

The emergence of new states along the Atlantic coast of Africa and in its immediate hinterland was closely associated with the development of the trans-Atlantic slave trade. The Bight of Benin and the Gold Coast were dominated by centralized states – the Yoruba states, particularly Oyo, after the middle of the seventeenth century, the Akan states, particularly Asante after 1700, Allada until 1724, and Dahomey after 1727 (Law, 1991, 2004). Dahomey emerged as a state whose structure required the enslavement of people. Slaves were either sold to Europeans to raise essential revenue for the state, killed in public ceremonies associated with the political power of the Dahomey monarchy, or, after the ending of the trans-Atlantic trade in slaves, settled on plantations to produce palm oil and to harvest palm kernels. The principal point of disembarkation from the Bight of Benin was Ouidah, from where about one million people left for the Americas. Lagos emerged as the dominant port in the nineteenth century. On the Gold Coast, slaves were embarked at Elmina, Cape Coast, Anamobu, and Koromantyn, whence the name Coromanti, used in the Americas is derived.

For the Bight of Biafra, almost all enslaved Africans left from one of two ports, either Old Calabar on the Cross River, or Bonny in the Niger River delta. Moreover, a majority, perhaps a large majority, of these people were ethnically Igbo, with a significant minority of Ibibio. Aro merchants dominated the trade of this region; their commercial network of slave traders was largely responsible for sending slaves to the coast (Brown and Lovejoy, 2010; Nwokeji, 2010). Whether or not the region was comprised of small-scale societies that lacked any centralized authority is a subject of controversy. The data suggest that the form of governance and politics in this region was under the umbrella of a network dominated by the Aro, who emerged only in the late seventeenth century, and who consolidated their grip on the interior in the eighteenth century in direct response to trans-Atlantic slavery, which is when the vast majority of Africans left this region.

The formation of Muslim governments in the savanna region of West Africa did not end slavery, even if the protection of Muslims from enslavement was official policy, but rather intensified enslavement. *Jihad* states instituted one significant policy, however. They attempted to close the trade to the coast.[6] As with most state policies, efforts to prevent deportation to the coast were not always successful. The amazing feature is that there was an attempt to do so at all. Moreover, it is recognizable in the statistics. At the same time as large numbers of people were being sent across the Sahara and even more were being kept enslaved within Muslim states, the number of people sent to the coast barely increased. The impact of *jihad* is reflected in the figures of the trans-Atlantic slave trade: the number of people who left West Africa surged with each *jihad*.

The question is, why were more people not sent out? Could they have been? Preliminary estimates of the size of the enslaved populations who were retained within Muslim states suggest that there were probably as many enslaved people in 1860 in the Sokoto Caliphate, in the interior of West Africa, as the number of enslaved African Americans who were in the United States at the outbreak of the American Civil War (Lovejoy and Hogendorn, [1993] 2000). Moreover, Futa Jallon, Futa Toro, and other Muslim states in the western Sudan appear to have had large numbers of enslaved people. Hence the reason why relatively few slaves came from these regions had little, if anything, to do with the ability of these regions to supply enslaved people into the intercontinental trade. Rather, factors other than market conditions limited the flow of enslaved Africans to the coast. While not all Muslim merchants respected religious pro-hibitions, the structure of trade and Muslim society placed severe limitations on the ability of merchants to circumscribe the rules. Indeed, because of religious restrictions, virtually no women or children entered the trans-Atlantic trade from these areas, so virtually the only Muslims to be found in the Americas were young adult males, who were capable of military service and hence often included enemies of Muslim states, whether they were Muslim or not. It has been estimated that as many as 80 per cent of the people from the far interior of the western Sudan were young adult males, while the proportion of males entering the Atlantic migration from the Central Sudan was perhaps as high as 95 per cent (Lovejoy, 2007). In understanding the history of slavery, it is important to distinguish areas that had substantial Muslim populations or that were under governments that were Muslim.

Slavery and colonialism

The abolition of the British slave trade in 1807 inaugurated a process of change that undermined the legality and viability of slavery, first in the Atlantic world and then globally. Inevitably, the resulting campaign affected those parts of Africa that were the source of enslaved peoples. Haltingly, yet slowly, slavery was restricted and then elimi-nated in many parts of the world. For Africa, anti-slavery became associated with European conquest and the establishment of colonial rule beginning in the nineteenth century. Sierra Leone was founded as a refuge for those freed from slavery by the

British navy. After 1834, slaves were emancipated in the British colony of South Africa, although not in the interior of Sierra Leone, which was considered a "protectorate" and not a colony. Similarly, the French conquest of Algeria undermined the legitimacy of slavery there. For all European powers after the Berlin Congress of 1884, fighting slavery became a justification for European partition and colonial occupation (Law, 1995). However, slavery did not end in Africa as European colonial empires expanded. Indeed, slavery continued under colonial rule well into the twentieth century. In most colonies, the enslaved population was not freed, but the legal status of slavery in the colonial courts was no longer recognized. Instead, enslavement and the trade in slaves were made criminal offenses punishable by imprisonment. The result was a gradual ending of slavery that took decades to achieve, as only children born under colonialism were recognized as being born free.

Meanwhile, those people who were already slaves had to fend for themselves as best they could. In the confusion of colonial occupation, many chose to run away. Hundreds of thousands of people fled their masters in the western Sudan in the first decade of the twentieth century (Klein and Roberts, 1980). A similar migration occurred in northern Nigeria (Lovejoy and Hogendorn, [1993] 2000: 1). Some fled to the invading colonial armies; others returned to their homelands; others tried to find employment in the new colonial economies. Without the support of the courts and no longer in control of political institutions, slave masters were forced to renegotiate their relationships with the enslaved population. Colonial policies of taxation and various types of vagrancy law were imposed to encourage a transformation in slave–master relations, and in some places, such as in the Protectorate of Northern Nigeria, slaves were now given the right to work on their own account and thereby earn money to purchase their emancipation. Previously, this provision had been a means by which masters had forced slaves to earn money, part of which had to be paid to the masters, and was at the discretion of the masters. Now this became a right that individuals could insist upon.

The questions now being asked attempt to understand why it is that in some parts of Africa, including South Africa, Angola, and scattered locations elsewhere, slavery continued as an institution. In South Africa, the East African coast, and Angola, slavery "looked" more like its counterpart in the Americas, with European and mulatto landowners attempting to develop plantation agriculture for export, and in the case of Zanzibar, Pemba, and the Swahili coast, with slave owners coming from Oman and India as well as from the local elite. In South Africa, British emancipation in 1834 transformed slaves into "apprentices", as was the case in other British colonies, but not within British protectorates. The imposition of this "gradual" emancipation prompted many Afrikaners (descendants of Dutch settlers) to undertake the Great Trek to escape British rule, found the breakaway states of the Transvaal and the Orange Free State, and thereby continue slavery under the name of apprenticeship. In Portuguese-controlled territories, slaves were declared to be *"liberatos"*, the only difference being in terminology.

In the twentieth century, colonial officials and anthropologists, often government-appointed, discovered that slavery was widespread almost everywhere in Africa. Despite efforts sometimes to describe "slavery" there as something different from slavery elsewhere in European colonies, especially the slavery in the Americas, it was clear to all that slavery continued, in modified and reshaped forms, in many places (Miers and Roberts, 1988). The revelation that, even after the termination of the trans-Atlantic slave trade and confinement of the trade in Islamic regions, slavery persisted and, indeed, its frequency even increased in some locations, indicates that colonial policy was far from effective in the emancipation of slaves unless individuals took action themselves. Despite political motivations underlying the reports of the League of Nations in the 1920s and 1930s, slavery was widespread, to such an extent that some colonial regimes tried to cover up its presence. British administrator Lord Frederick Lugard, who had previously served in Uganda and most notably in Nigeria, phrased the transition the "slow death" of slavery, which was expected to last the whole of the twentieth century. Despite the massive desertion of slaves at the time of the European colonial conquest, Lord Lugard has been proven to be right. Slavery has persisted, even if its legality has been ended.

Contemporary African slavery

More recently, since the independence of African countries in the 1960s and 1970s, slavery has become largely a subterranean force, no longer legal in most countries but continuing in various contexts, just as slavery has persisted almost everywhere in the world. Some Muslim countries that include territory in the Sahara, such as Mauretania, Niger, and elsewhere, have been particularly reticent in ending slavery, and when slavery has been suppressed, dependent relationships arising from former servitude have persisted, limiting the access of the descendants of slaves to land and other resources (Rossi, 2009). Moreover, in some cocoa-producing areas such as Côte d' Ivoire, children have been enslaved in order to harvest crops (Miers, 2003). In some Muslim areas such as Niger and northern Nigeria, the continuation of concubinage has also sustained the demand for enslaved women. These contemporary issues highlight the continuation of slavery in Africa well into the twentieth century, despite apparent colonial and post-colonial efforts to undermine and eliminate the institution. In these cases, the trade in enslaved children and women is illegal, but impossible to suppress.

Conclusion

Today, we know more than ever before about the origins of enslaved Africans who went to the Americas and to various parts of the Muslim world. Moreover, the relationship of slavery to the history of Africa, and the factors that made possible the establishment of identifiable communities of enslaved Africans in the Americas, and indeed in North Africa, the Sahara, and in West Africa itself, is much more clearly understood. As everywhere, slaves in Africa resisted their bondage as best they could. The methods of trade and marketing, either by Muslims or non-Muslims, and the impact of slavery on society and economy more generally, are major themes in the reconstruction of the African past. The trans-Atlantic slavery was indeed devastating for many parts of Africa, and the response of Muslims within West Africa, although buffering the region from trans-Atlantic forces to some extent, nonetheless resulted in the intensification of the institution within Africa.

The migration through slavery reveals a legacy of violence and insecurity that has punctuated the African past. Domestically, there were transformations as a result of population loss in specific places and at specific times through loss of life associated with wars and enslavement. There were adjustments in social, religious, and communal life that can be identified as responses to, and protection from, slavery. The formation of an

African diaspora in the Islamic world and in the Americas each represents the legacy of slavery, as is the continuing history in Africa of ethnic and religious strife, and indeed achievement, under colonialism and in the period of independence since then. Slavery has survived. Distinctions arising from an association with slavery continued through the colonial and post-colonial eras into contemporary times. A preoccupation with trans-Atlantic slavery or the African diaspora in the Americas risks losing perspective on the long trajectory of slavery in Africa. Historically, Africa has witnessed a steady, if varied, drain in population, an outward emigration that was forced and that was not matched by an influx of population of comparable numbers, except perhaps in South Africa. The impact of this demographic loss has to have been considerable, just as the arrival of Africans in the Islamic world and the Americas definitely affected economic and social development. This essay is intended to provide an introduction to the study of slavery in African history. From an African perspective, such a study includes the history of the victims of slavery and where they were taken, and how they were able to retain memories and sometimes direct connections with the homeland.

Contemporary slavery is different from the slavery of the past because of its illegality. We all understand how enslavement differed over time and depending upon location, but for anyone who is enslaved, such subtle scholarly distinctions hardly matter. The voices of those who are enslaved are often silenced. What we have to accept is that slavery has not been abolished in the world today, but it must be. The continuity in practices of servility in West Africa is a legacy, different from the legacy of the Americas, but no less real for the people who are affected. We have to increase the level of awareness among scholars, and indeed the public at large, about the differences and similarities in the experiences and conditions of the enslaved through history. We have to close the gap in knowledge dissemination in order to restore or establish the dignity of peoples who have suffered the experience and legacy of slavery.

Notes

1 William Snelgrave, *A New Account of Some Parts of Guinea and the Slave Trade* (London: Frank Cass, 1734 [repr. 1971]), 158; also see Law (1977: 573).
2 Francis Moore, *Travels into the Inland Parts of Africa* (London: E. Cave, 1738), 42. Also see Rodney (1966).
3 John Hawkins, as quoted by Elizabeth Donnan, ed., *Documents Illustrative of the Slave Trade to America* (Washington, DC, 1930–35), vol. 1, 48–49.
4 Ahmad Baba, *Miʿraj al-Suʿud: Ahmad Baba's Replies on Slavery* (Rabat: Institute of African Studies, Université Muhammad V, [1614/15], 2000, trans. John Hunwick and Fatima Harrak).
5 For trade on the East African coast and in the interior, see Campbell (1988); Zimba (2005); Alpers (2009).
6 On Muhammad Bello's attempt to prevent sales to Christians, see Lovejoy (2000b).

Bibliography

Afigbo, E. A. *Ropes of Sand. Studies in Igbo History and Culture* (Ibadan: University Press, 1981).
Alpers, Edward, *East Africa and the Indian Ocean* (Princeton, NJ: Markus Wiener, 2009).
Barry, Boubacar, *Senegambia and the Atlantic Slave Trade* (Cambridge: Cambridge University Press, 1998).
Brown, Carolyn and Lovejoy, Paul E., eds, *Repercussions of the Atlantic Slave Trade: The Interior of the Bight of Biafra and the African Diaspora* (Trenton, NJ: Africa World Press, 2010).

Campbell, Gwyn, "The Economics of the Indian Ocean and Red Sea Slave Trades in the 19th Century: An Overview", *Slavery and Abolition* 90 (1988), 1–20.

Curto, José C., "The Story of Nbena, 1817–20: Unlawful Enslavement and the Concept of 'Original Freedom' in Angola", in Paul E. Lovejoy and David V. Trotman, eds, *Trans-Atlantic Dimensions of Ethnicity in the African Diaspora* (London: Continuum, 2003).

Cuvelier, J. and Jadin, L., *L'Ancien Congo d'aprés les archives romaines (1518–1640)* (Brussels, 1954).

Eldredge, Elizabeth and Morton, Fred, *Slavery in South Africa: Captive Labor on the Dutch Frontier* (Boulder, CO: Westview Press, 1994).

Eltis, David, Behrendt, Stephen, Florentino, Manolo and Richardson, David, *The Trans-Atlantic Slave Trade Database.* www.slavevoyages.org/tast/index.faces

Fage, John D. "Slaves and Society in Western Africa, c. 1445–c. 1700", *Journal of African History* 21, 3 (1980), 289–310.

Hair, P. E. H., "Sources on Early Sierra Leone: (6) Barreira on Just Enslavement, 1606", *Africana Research Bulletin* 6 (1975), 52–74.

Inikori, J. E., "Slavery in Africa and the Transatlantic Slave Trade", in Alusine Jalloh and Stephen E. Maizlish, eds, *The African Diaspora* (Arlington: Texas A& M University Press, 1996), 39–72.

Klein, Martin A., *Slavery and Colonial Rule in French West Africa. Senegal, Guinea, and Mali* (Cambridge: Cambridge University Press, 1998).

Klein, Martin A. and Roberts, Richard, "The Banamba Slave Exodus of 1905 and the Decline of Slavery in the Western Sudan", *Journal of African History* 21, 3 (1980), 375–94.

Kopytoff, Igor and Miers, Suzanne, "African 'Slavery' as an Institution of Marginality", in Suzanne Miers and Igor Kopytoff, eds, *Slavery in Africa: Historical and Anthropological Perspectives* (Madison: University of Wisconsin Press, 1977), 3–81.

Law, Robin, "Royal Monopoly and Private Enterprise in the Atlantic Trade: The Case of Dahomey", *Journal of African History* 18, 4 (1977), 555–577.

——, *The Slave Coast of West Africa 1550–1750. The Impact of the Atlantic Slave Trade on an African Society* (Oxford: Clarendon Press, 1991).

——, ed., *From Slave Trade to "Legitimate" Commerce: The Commercial Transition in Nineteenth-Century West Africa* (Cambridge: Cambridge University Press, 1995).

——, *Ouidah. The Social History of a West African Slaving "Port" 1727–1892* (Athens: Ohio University Press, 2004).

Lovejoy, Paul E., *Transformations in Slavery. A History of Slavery in Africa* (Cambridge: Cambridge University Press, 2nd edn, 2000a).

——, "The Clapperton-Bello Exchange: the Sokoto *Jihad* and the Trans-Atlantic Slave Trade, 1804–37", in Christopher Wise (ed.), *The Desert Shore: Literatures of the African Sahel* (Boulder, CO: Lynne Rienner, 2000b), 201–28.

——, "Internal Markets or an Atlantic-Sahara Divide? How Women Fit into the Slave Trade of West Africa", in Gwyn Campbell, Suzanne Miers and Joseph C. Miller, eds, *Women and Slavery* (Athens: Ohio University Press, 2007).

Lovejoy, Paul E. and Falola, Toyin, eds, *Pawnship, Slavery and Colonialism in Africa* (Trenton, NJ: Africa World Press, 2003).

Lovejoy, Paul E. and Hogendorn, Jan, *Slow Death for Slavery. The Course of Abolition in Northern Nigeria, 1897–1936* (Cambridge: Cambridge University Press [1993], 2nd edn 2000).

Lovejoy, Paul E. and Richardson, David, "The Business of Slaving: Pawnship in Western Africa, c. 1600–1810", *Journal of African History* 42, 1 (2001), 67–89.

Meillassoux, Claude, ed., *L'Esclavage in Afrique précoloniale* (Paris: Maspero, 1975).

——, *The Anthropology of Slavery. The Womb of Iron and Gold* (Chicago: University of Chicago Press, 1991).

Miers, Suzanne, *Slavery in the Twentieth Century: The Evolution of a Global Pattern* (Oxford: Rowman & Littlefield, 2003).

Miers, Suzanne and Roberts, Richard, eds, *The End of Slavery in Africa* (Madison: University of Wisconsin Press, 1988).

Nwokeji, G. Ugo, *The Slave Trade and Culture: Atlantic Commerce and the Aro Trade Diaspora in the Bight of Biafra* (New York: Cambridge University Press, 2010).

Palmer, H. R., *The Bornu Sahara and Sudan* (New York: Negro University Press [1936], reprint 1970).

Patterson, Orlando, *Slavery and Social Death. A Comparative Study* (Cambridge, MA: Harvard University Press, 1982).

Robertson, Claire C. and Klein, Martin A., eds, *Women and Slavery in Africa* (Madison: University of Wisconsin Press, 1983).

Rodney, Walter, "Slavery and Other Forms of Social Oppression on the Upper Guinea Coast in the Context of the Atlantic Slave Trade", *Journal of African History* 7, 4 (1966), 431–43.

Rossi, Benedetta, ed., *Reconfiguring Slavery: West African Trajectories* (Liverpool: Liverpool University Press, 2009).

Shell, Robert, *Children of Bondage. A Social History of the Slave Society at the Cape of Good Hope 1652–1838* (London: James Currey, 1994).

Sheriff, Abdul, *Slaves, Spices and Ivory in Zanzibar* (London: James Currey, 1987).

Snelgrave, William, *A New Account of Some Parts of Guinea and the Slave Trade* (London: Frank Cass [1734], reprint 1971), 158.

Sparks, Randy, *The Two Princes of Calabar: An Eighteenth-Century Atlantic Odyssey* (Cambridge, MA: Harvard University Press, 2004).

Willis, John Ralph (ed.), *Slaves and Slavery in Muslim Africa* (London, 1985, two vols).

Wright, John, *The Trans-Saharan Slave Trade* (London: Routledge, 2007).

Wright, Marcia, "Women in Peril: A Commentary on the Life Stories of Captives in Nineteenth Century East Central Africa", *African Social Research* 20 (1975), 800–819.

Zimba, Benigna, *Slave Routes and Oral Tradition in Southeastern Africa* (Maputo, Mozambique: Filsom Entertainment, 2005).

3

SLAVERY IN THE INDIAN
OCEAN WORLD

Gwyn Campbell

Introduction

In the conventional view, Indian Ocean World (IOW) slavery shared the same essential features as the Atlantic slave system. Studies, inspired by the Atlantic model, have concentrated overwhelmingly on the export of East Africans by Arabs to Zanzibar and the Persian Gulf, and by Europeans to European enclaves in the IOW, notably the Mascarene Islands and the Cape. At these destinations, imported chattel labour underpinned "slave modes of production".

What is missing from the bulk of these studies is an authentic IOW dimension. This is generally true even of the few studies of other forms of slavery indigenous to the IOW.[1] This contribution is offered as a corrective to conventional views of IOW slavery. It first defines the term "Indian Ocean World" and discusses its historic significance as the location of the first "global economy". It then analyses the meaning and significance in IOW history of the slave trade and slavery.

In order to distinguish forms of servitude in the IOW from those in the Atlantic World, it is vital to establish the meaning and historical significance of the IOW – a concept fundamentally different from that of the "Atlantic" or "Pacific" World. It was introduced from the 1980s by Asia-centric historians in order to counter Eurocentric historiography that emphasised Europe as the centre of the first global economy and, from the "Age of Discoveries", European domination of the major commodities and sea lanes of the Indian Ocean arena (Wallerstein, 1974). Instead, Asia-centric historians posited Asia as the centre of the first global economy, one that developed by at least AD 1000 – possibly much earlier – and which remained dominant until at least the mid-eighteenth century. Some historians would argue it remained dominant until the early nineteenth century.[2]

These historians' argument is based on the adaptation of Braudelian concepts of "oceanic" space to the Asian region. Fernand Braudel, a major French historian in the post-1945 era, argued that conventional frameworks for historical analysis, notably territorial entities such as nation states, empires and continents, were inadequate because they largely ignored human–environment interaction. Thus, while Paris exercised political dominance over southern France, the material existence of people who lived in southern France had more in common with other inhabitants of the Mediterranean littoral, including northern Africa, being largely shaped by the

Mediterranean Sea and its climate, than with residents of northern France (Braudel, 1996).

Braudel's theories inspired not only the development of the *Annales* School of historians in Europe, but also the new Asia-centric school of historians, who highlighted the role of the Asian monsoons – a complex system of winds and currents governing the waters of the northern Indian Ocean, the Indonesian Sea, and the South and East China Seas. Unique to this macro-region, the monsoons both regulated agricultural production and facilitated the early development of trans-oceanic trade.

The monsoons were critical to the emergence of specialist crop zones in the northern sector of the IOW. The most basic division was between winter "dry" crop wheat cultures of the Middle East, North India, Central Asia and northern China, where some irrigation was required if winter rains proved insufficient, and the summer "wet" rice cultures of Southeast and South Asia (and later of Madagascar) (Chaudhuri, 1985: 23). The technology of water control and storage techniques associated with economies based on irrigation emerged during the "Neolithic Revolution", characterised by a concentration of population, the development of water conservation techniques and irrigation, and the domestication of wild food crops and animals.

This agricultural specialisation helped lay the basis for inter-regional trade. More fundamentally, the monsoons promoted the rise of trans-oceanic exchange. From April to September, as the Asian land mass heats up, hot air rises producing a vacuum that sucks in the air from the ocean, creating the southwest monsoon. During the other six "winter" months of the year, the opposite reaction occurs, creating the northeast monsoon. The monsoons thus comprise an alternating system of strong winds that blow from the northeast for six months of the year and from the southwest for the other six months, permitting the early development of trans-oceanic, intra-Asian sail. In addition, the monsoons, supplemented by a perennial system of equatorial winds and southern hemisphere southeast trade winds, offer a potential for regular trans-oceanic sail and commerce unparalleled in other oceans. As a result, purposeful two-way trans-oceanic trade emerged during the course of the first millennium AD, which by about the tenth century connected the major productive areas of Asia, China, India and Mesopotamia (present-day Iraq) in a sophisticated and durable network of long-distance maritime exchange of commodities, money, technology, ideas and people (Abu-Lughod, 1993: 78–79). It is this system that constituted the first "global" economy.

The IOW is thus a new conceptual framework. Whereas the Atlantic World is defined by oceans and land masses, the IOW is defined by the monsoons. Oceanic trade in the European global economy that developed from the fifteenth century was characterised by mercantilist precepts, reflected in an alliance between the state and the merchant class. By contrast, maritime exchange in the IOW global economy was, throughout the macro-region, dominated by littoral mercantile communities that retained a large degree of political and juridical independence from the centralised land-based polities in the hinterland. These polities, nevertheless, realised the advantages of having strong mercantile societies, and in many cases tried to protect such networks through the use of state power. These mercantile communities were externally oriented, developing trading networks and diaspora along the coastlines of neighbouring and overseas regions. They were also closely connected with riverine and overland trade arteries.

Enslavement in the Indian Ocean World

It is impossible to discuss bondage in the IOW without reference to forms of enslavement and trafficking in humans. Societies that developed economies based on irrigated agriculture required unprecedented labour inputs to create and maintain water channel and storage systems, and to harvest, store and transport the enhanced agricultural output of "wet" agricultural systems. It also required an extremely large and highly concentrated coerced labour force, notably in societies located alongside major rivers. Over time, the demographic growth stimulated by greater agricultural production generally allowed slave owners to easily acquire the labour they needed. The capture by the elite of surplus agricultural output, and their control of natural and human resources required to maintain the system, led to the emergence of highly stratified centralised hierarchical polities by around 2500 BC in Mesopotamia, Egypt and the Indus Valley (Ponting, 1993: 43–44, 55–56, 60), and separately in China by about 1750 BC (*ibid.*, 49, 61). The leaders of such polities placed major restrictions on the geographical mobility of subject populations in order to ensure vital labour input into agriculture.

From around 2000 BC, the wealth generated by the water storage and control technology, along with associated increases in agricultural output and demographic growth, enabled the major centralised states, such as the Middle Kingdom in Egypt and Babylonia in Mesopotamia, to form powerful armies and engage in military expansion. As they pushed forward the frontiers of the state through the conquest of less powerful neighbouring populations, these armies were faced with the problem of what to do with captives. This resulted in two broad systems of enslavement that were maintained throughout the IOW up to the end of the nineteenth century. In the first system, most adult male captives from pastoralists and hunter-gatherer societies were executed, while female and child captives were enslaved, taken back to the imperial centre, and sold. The killing of male captives was largely motivated by the expense of enslaving men, who were more likely to flee or rebel than women or children (Goody, 1980: 32–34; Campbell, 1991). This system was the reputed origin of slavery in Mesopotamia in the third millennia BC (Goody, 1980: 18), and was widely practised throughout the IOW down to the nineteenth century (Boomgaard, 2004).

In the second system, adult male captives from advanced and settled agricultural regions were commonly maintained *in situ* alongside captive women and children in a state of community bondage. Some scholars believe this to have been the origins of praedial servitude in India in the first millennia BC (Patnaik, 1985: 3). It also seems to have motivated the emergence of caste-like regulations that, as in India and Imerina (central highland Madagascar), served to curtail geographical mobility and thus ensured a permanent agricultural workforce in fertile, conquered regions (Campbell, 1985: 112–33). Such factors made viable the enslavement and surveillance of male captives (Goody, 1980: 21–22).

Nevertheless, over the long term, the majority of people entering slavery in the IOW probably did so through debt. Enslavement was legally enforced for defaulting debtors and their relatives in many IOW regions. In addition, the punishment for certain crimes was exacted in fines, which often led to indebtedness and subsequent enslavement (Reid, 1983: 10). Indebtedness was normally expressed in monetary terms, although it was often incurred in non-cash forms such as food or tools. As enslaved debtors were from the dominant slave-owning society, however, they generally enjoyed a higher status than imported slaves. Once they had paid off their debt, they could regain non-slave status.

Here, enslavement for indebtedness needs to be distinguished from debt bondage, even if both systems of enslavement could overlap. Enslavement for indebtedness was involuntary, whereas most people entered debt bondage voluntarily as a credit-securing strategy. Debt bondage embraced a vast range of people in the IOW, from farmers mortgaging future harvests and potential grooms borrowing a bride price, to small traders living off credit from larger merchants, to the ubiquitous rural gambler of Southeast and East Asia getting into short-term financial trouble, and including opium addicts in nineteenth-century China (Boomgaard, 2004; Delaye, 2004). Those subject to debt bondage often outnumbered those conventionally described as "slaves". For example, enslaved people in debt bondage were the most numerous of the social categories in Majapahit, in Java, while in central Thailand in the eighteenth and nineteenth centuries they formed up to 50 per cent of the total population. Their servitude was generally taken as paying off interest on the loan they had contracted, to which was added the cost of their accommodation, food and clothing. Consequently, their indebtedness invariably increased. Their servitude often became permanent, and sometimes became hereditary – at which point there was little to distinguish debt bondage from "slavery" (Rae, 2004).

Non-slave servile labour in the IOW was also sold or transferred involuntarily. People who were sold or transferred to others included "serfs" in Asia and Africa. In Africa, forms of pawnship were developed whereby children, especially girls, were "pawned" in return for money or an equivalent value in goods. They became "slaves" if they were not reclaimed within an established time period. Some were transferred as tribute or ransom. In open and private markets, people sold family members into temporary and permanent slavery. Other common forms of entry into bondage were through kidnapping by criminal gangs and through legally imposed enslavement for crime.

Some people entered slavery voluntarily, notably due to natural disasters. The Southern Oscillation or El Niño effect, produced every seven to ten years by changes in the pressure gradient across the Pacific Ocean, often provokes severe droughts throughout the IOW. Moreover, it tends to be followed in consecutive years by La Niña – a weather system that causes unusually heavy rain (Atwell, 2001: 39–40). Flooding that was destructive to property and harvests also frequently accompanied monsoons and cyclones. Moreover, Southeast and East Asia were centres of volcanic activity that could wreak both immediate local destruction and, through cloud veil-induced lower temperatures, years of depressed agricultural productivity across the macro-region and beyond. When El-Niño or La Niña coincided with sulphur rich volcanism, as in 1641, the effect could be catastrophic.

Natural disasters were frequently accompanied by famine and disease, which independently could have catastrophic consequences. For example, the bubonic plague that erupted in epidemic form in China in 1331 and spread along the main caravan routes of Asia to reach Crimea and Europe in 1346, killing an estimated 90 per cent of those infected, had a far greater impact in the IOW than in Europe. It killed some 50 per cent of China's population, and was probably as devastating in centres of population in India, the Middle East and Africa linked to trans-Asian commercial routes (Ponting, 1993: 228–29).

Natural disasters could so impoverish households that *in extremis* they sold family members into bondage in order to enhance the chances of survival of both the individual sold and the remaining family members. In Africa, in times of famine, a kinship group might transfer its rights in a kinship member to another lineage in return for goods or money, children and young adults being the most marketable. If not redeemed, these transferred "pawns" were retained by the creditor lineage (Kopytoff and Miers, 1977: 10–11). In China, in bad times, fathers often sold their daughters or secondary wives, though only non-elite households broke the taboo against selling sons. Throughout the IOW, parents also let their children out for adoption in exchange for money, while debt bondspeople could sometimes be exchanged, as could other servile people as part of a marriage dowry or a monastery donation. Even in relatively prosperous times poor low-status non-slaves occasionally offered themselves for sale to a member of the elite because of the promise of a higher standard of living and a higher status as the slave of a powerful or wealthy master. It was for these reasons, for example, that in the nineteenth century certain Filipino girls became concubines of high-status Sulu males (Warren, 2004; see also Watson, 1980: 227–36; Boomgaard, 2004).

Indian Ocean World slave trades over time

Indian Ocean World slave trades should thus be considered in the context both of the IOW global economy and of natural disasters. Demand for servile labour generally correlated directly with economic cycles and with high mortality associated with major natural disasters, famines and epidemic disease. Long-term economic cycles appear clear, with sustained peaks from c. 200 BC to AD 200 AD; c. AD 800–1300; and c. 1780–1910. Records clearly illustrate the disastrous impact of natural disasters in the mid-seventeenth century. However, much more research is required to flesh out medium- and short-term economic cycles, other periods of high mortality, and intra-IOW regional variations in both economic performance and natural disasters.

During sustained economic booms, high demand existed for servile labour for both directly productive work (agriculture, craft, commerce, transport) and non-productive work (military and guards, domestic labour, entertainment, sexual services). As periods of economic prosperity correlated directly with agricultural output and demographic growth, demand for productive labour was met chiefly by traditional forms of local servile labour. Consequently, many imported bondspeople, especially women and children, became items of conspicuous consumption. Women were deployed as domestics, wet-nurses, secondary wives, and providers of childcare, entertainment and sexual services. Girls were groomed for similar roles, while boys were employed as grooms, guards and soldiers. In royal circles, enslaved boys, if talented or particularly favoured, could become bureaucrats or advisers.

At times of economic slowdown, stagnation or regression, demand declined for both productive and non-productive forms of labour. The fall in demand for imported servile labour was initially more marked in non-elite circles, where masters might first enter joint-ownership schemes, and eventually divest themselves entirely of servile labour. Some elite owners engaged in conspicuous consumption went bankrupt because of their desire to maintain a vast retinue of unproductive bondspeople. On the supply side, the quantity and quality of servile labour varied chiefly according to the incidence of warfare, slave raiding and kidnapping, natural disasters, and indebtedness – factors that could often, but not necessarily, overlap.

No precise estimates exist of the number of slaves traded in the IOW, chiefly due to the limited nature of extant records, and the fact that, in contrast to the Atlantic system,

IOW slaves rarely constituted a specialist cargo. However, it is likely that the cumulative number of slaves traded in and across the IOW over the centuries far exceeded the 10 to 12 million landed in the Americas. In the nineteenth century, when the IOW slave trade peaked, possibly 1.5 million slaves were exported from East Africa. Slaves comprised between 20 and 30 per cent of the population of many IOW societies, rising to over 50 per cent in parts of Africa and in Indonesian ports (Campbell, 1988: 474–75). The greatest IOW slave traffic was probably overland, notably in Africa, Hindu India and the Confucian Far East. In India alone, there were an estimated eight million to nine million indigenous slaves in 1841, double the number of black slaves in the United States in 1865.

Throughout the IOW, markets were supplied with slaves chiefly from neighbouring regions, because local slaves were cheaper to capture and transport. Consequently, merchants shipping such slaves suffered fewer losses *en route* than they did when trying to transport slaves from more distant regions (Arasaratnam, 1995: 200). In the eastern IOW, China and other centralised states obtained many of their slaves from attacks against decentralised hill "tribes" and "maritime" communities. Nevertheless, slaves were also exported from the eastern to the western IOW and further afield. For example, Indonesians were shipped to Southeast Asia and Cape Town, while in the nineteenth century Chinese slaves were sent to Singapore and San Francisco.

The bulk of studies of slavery in South Asia focus on imported Africans, mainly due to an Atlantic bias in the literature (Harris, 1971; Alpers, 1997). Nevertheless, the majority of the servile population in South Asia were of local origin (Kidwai, 86–8; Miller[25]). Moreover, most slaves imported into India, at least in medieval times, were probably of Turk and Slavic origin. South Asia also exported bondspeople: Indians, for example, were exported as slaves to Macao, Japan, Indonesia, Mauritius and Cape Town.

In the Middle East, Circassians and Central Asians formed a clear majority of imported slaves until the tenth to thirteenth centuries, when their numbers may have been equalled by imported Africans, who possibly formed an absolute majority of slaves there in the nineteenth century (Lewis, 1990). In the early twentieth century, slaves were also imported into the Middle East from the Makran coast of Iran, Western India, Indonesia and China (Miers, 120–36).

The long nineteenth century witnessed enormous quantitative and qualitative difference in demand for servile labour in the IOW. The changes in IOW slavery were shaped primarily by the new forces of the international economy, by the attempts of indigenous states to modernise, by secondary imperialism, and by a growing commercialisation of labour. Much of the growing demand in the West for tropical produce from the mid-eighteenth century was supplied from the IOW. This demand, disrupted during the Napoleonic War, revived after 1815 and was sustained at ever higher levels by the industrial consumption of products such as copra, animal and vegetable oils, wax and rubber, and by an expanding Western taste; generalized for cash crops such as tea, coffee and sugar; and bourgeois tropical luxuries such as ivory, exotic feathers and animal trophies.

All these commodities needed to be produced or collected, sometimes treated, transported to docks, loaded onto vessels, and shipped to IOW and external markets, while the return flow of goods in exchange required shipping, offloading, and overland transport and distribution. Thus the growing commercial activity in the IOW associated with the international economy required a huge input of labour. Western scholars have focused attention initially on African slaves, and increasingly, as British anti-slave trade pressure increased in East African waters in the early nineteenth century, on the millions of Indian and Chinese indentured labourers recruited to work cash crop plantations across the IOW. By 1900, there were about one million Indians indentured on European-managed plantations in India. Between 1834 and 1920, two million Indians were shipped to overseas plantations (Chandra, 1993: 11). Often overlooked, however, is the fact that indigenous IOW elites also profited from the commercial opportunities afforded by an expanding international economy. In part, they profited from slavery designed to meet regional demand. For example, the luxury market in the Middle East, South Asia and the Far East, particularly for tropical animal products, was much more varied and dynamic than that of the West. However, another reason for an increase in slavery in the IOW in the nineteenth century was to cater for increased demand within the IOW. Thus indigenous IOW demand for Chinese indentured labour was greater than European-generated demand. Of the approximately 6.7 million people who emigrated from South China to Southeast Asia in the period 1851–1901, only about 4 per cent ended up as "indentured" labour on European estates.[3]

European warfare and imperialism also led to increased demands for labour in the IOW. High mortality and sickness in tropical zones among European troops and seamen inevitably resulted in growing demand for indigenous IOW replacements. Thus the British in India increasingly attempted to recruit from the Sikhs, Gurkhas, and other so-called "martial races" to secure and expand their interests not only in South Asia but also throughout the IOW and beyond.

Demand for female servile labour also increased dramatically in the nineteenth century so that in the IOW, in direct contrast to the Atlantic slave system, the proportion of females in servitude increased in the modern era. This was often due to the demand for sexual services established by men in sexually unbalanced situations, including indigenous and European long-distance traders, soldiers and ships' crews. Chinese emigration to Southeast Asia and the creation of Portuguese, French, Dutch and British outposts in the IOW had, from the early seventeenth century, created a considerable business in hired and purchased female slaves to serve Chinese and European traders as sexual partners, domestic servants and commercial agents. By the early nineteenth century, this aspect of IOW slavery constituted what Anthony Reid terms a large-scale "marriage market" (Reid, 1983: 26–27).

This demand for enslaved labourers increased dramatically during the nineteenth century. In part, this was due to the commercial boom associated with the expansion of the international economy and thus leading to increased numbers of single traders (European and indigenous) operating in the IOW. Second, there was a massive growth in the number of military, both indigenous and foreign. Academic research has concentrated on the impact of Europeans garrisoned in the IOW, which further stimulated the trade in females (Chatterjee, 150–68).

Increased demand for female prostitutes also emanated from the rise of mass migration of indentured labour. Although Indian indentured labour was generally sexually balanced, nineteenth-century labour migration in the IOW overall led to concentrations of predominantly male workers. This was particularly pronounced in the case of the millions of impoverished Chinese men who, between the 1840s and 1890s, emigrated to the new commercial centres in the Americas, Africa and Southeast Asia since Chinese women were officially forbidden to travel abroad. For instance, between the 1840s and 1890s, millions of impoverished Chinese males emigrated to the new commercial centres in the Americas, Africa and Southeast Asia. The result was large groups of poor Chinese men in Singapore and Hong Kong, both places falling under British rule in 1821 and 1842, respectively (Jaschok and Miers, 1994: 19–20). Chiefly due to male immigration from south-eastern China, Singapore's population quadrupled from the 1880s, resulting in a huge sexual imbalance of fourteen males for every female.

The demand for sexual services among enslaved people was in part met by "voluntary" prostitution. This trend was most marked as a response to "traditional" demand, from Muslim markets and from traders. Most "concubines" in the Middle East, free and servile, enjoyed a better lifestyle than the majority of female peasants (see e.g. Reid, 1983: 25–26). Above all, the greater assimilation of female slaves into the local slave-holding society meant that, although around three-quarters of slaves imported into the Gulf region were female, women comprised only one quarter of slaves seeking manumission from British consular officials.

Demand from traders, and occasionally from European visitors, was met in some regions voluntarily by indigenous "entrepreneurs" who hired out their services to traders, often on a seasonal basis. Thus in Madagascar, parents commonly hired out their daughters to serve as concubines and agents of foreign traders.

In the nineteenth century, however, there was a marked increase in the commercialisation of sexual services, which in turn led to increased involuntary prostitution and the exploitation of young females. Overlapping with debt bondage, the IOW trade in females has continued to this day. Wherever war or insecurity becomes endemic, as recently in the Sudan, it has expanded. Moreover, over the past few decades of rapid globalisation, it has also become more brutally commercial. An estimated 400,000 girls are trafficked each year in India alone. Precious little protection is offered to such females, while traditional possibilities of gaining economic independence have largely been closed as the trade has fallen increasingly into the hands of male-dominated, mafia-type structures. The very high risk of contracting HIV and dying young of AIDS has further stigmatised and sharply reduced the life expectancy and living standards of such women.[4]

Servitude in the Indian Ocean World

From the foregoing analysis, it is evident that there existed in the IOW complex and shifting slave trades that started well before the Common Era, remained vigorous into the twentieth century, and in some areas are still maintained. In all of these trades, sources, markets, routes and slave functions varied considerably. Thus, with the exception of a minority of European settlements such as Réunion and Mauritius, the characteristics of IOW slavery contrasted sharply with those of the Americas. In the American "model" of slavery, 10–12 million African slaves were put to work mostly on plantations and in mines; they formed large concentrated communities of visibly servile "foreigners" of African descent, deprived of civil rights, and whose status was hereditary. Moreover, violence against them was intrinsic to the system.

In the IOW, outside the few plantation economies such as Mauritius, slaves rarely lived in large communities. Moreover, slaves were employed in a vast range of functions, the range and responsibilities of which were much wider than those encompassed by the Atlantic model. Slaves may have performed most field labour in Africa and India, but there, as elsewhere in the IOW, peasant slave owners generally worked alongside their slaves in predominantly subsistence production. Slaves also laboured in mines, craft-work, porterage, fishing, commerce, and, if they were female, in textile production (Goody, 1980: 21, 32). Some slaves received shelter, food and clothing from their owners; others were given land, from which they were expected to obtain the resources to sustain themselves. Yet others were rented out or left free to seek livelihoods. However, in the IOW most slaves were probably acquired as symbols of conspicuous consumption, to reflect the power and wealth of their owners.

Outside European-managed plantations, violence was rarely used extensively against slaves. Slaves represented a substantial capital asset worth maintaining or even enhancing, while maximum slave productivity could be achieved only through acknowledging the essential humanity of slaves (Klein, 1993: 11–12; Meillassoux, 1991: 9–10). Indeed, slaves in the IOW generally enjoyed an array of traditional and prescribed rights unknown on the American plantations. Even in European settlements, outside the Mascarenes, their treatment was tempered by local economic and political forces. Even in Korea and China, where the most extreme systems of hereditary slavery were practised, slaves possessed a legal status and were immune from state corvées, and their marriages were generally respected.

It is at this point that the application of the simplistic, literally black-and-white dichotomies of the Atlantic model in IOW slavery studies become nonsensical. The terms used in languages indigenous to the IOW, and which are conventionally translated as "slave", do not derive from a common root, as in most European languages (*slav*), and rarely carry the conventional Atlantic connotations of the term. There exist, even within the same cultures, a variety of terms signifying different levels of servility, the meanings of which vary according to place and time (Eno, 83–93). Not only do servile statuses often overlap, they can move up and down in the hierarchy of statuses, and some of those conventionally described as "slaves" were sometimes also owners of "slaves". Most slaves possessed some rights, many that were upheld in law – as in the wide band of Islamic societies that ran in a wide arc across the IOW. For example, in late eighteenth- and early nineteenth-century Sulu, *banyaga* slaves married, owned property and performed wide-ranging functions on the same terms as non-slaves. Again, most female slaves probably enjoyed a lifestyle and a respect often superior to that of both male slaves and female peasants. There are instances of concubines in the Middle East sending for family members to join them – albeit as non-slaves. In some cases, as in nineteenth-century imperial Madagascar, some slaves even refused freedom to avoid being subject to a corvée system that reduced "free" subjects to comparatively worse living standards and a lower life expectancy than slaves.

This renders irrelevant the application to the IOW of the conventional dichotomy between slave and "free" that is central to any analysis of slavery based on the Atlantic model. The slave–free dichotomy that characterised New World slave societies was premised on the notion of the absence or possession of individual liberty. This concept was largely absent in IOW societies, where each person had an allotted status that carried with it a multiplicity of rights and obligations, but which could also overlap with other status and change position in the hierarchy of statuses, This fluidity makes it difficult to forge hard-and-fast distinctions between types of servitude, or to contrast "slave" with "free". As Anthony Reid underlines, the concept of personal freedom can be pitched against that of slavery only when all other forms of servitude are subsumed into a clearly defined category of "slaves" (Reid, 1983: 21).

The meaning of IOW systems of bondage becomes clearer if conceptualised within a hierarchy of dependency in which "slaves" constituted one of a number of servile groups. It was a reciprocal system in which obligation implied servitude to an individual with superior status, to a kin group or to the crown in return for protection. The highest status was enjoyed in acephelous societies by a group of elders, and in centralised societies by a sovereign who theoretically "owned" all those of inferior status: this was possibly most visible with corvée labour imposed on subjects who, in most IOW countries, were considered crown "property". In this sense, it could be argued, corvée fits the concept of "property" performing "compulsory labour" used by some authors as a defining characteristic of slavery (see Watson, 1980: 7).

Moreover, in the worldview of pre-industrial societies, there was no division between the temporal and the spiritual; the supernatural could bless or curse human activities and so required respect and appeasement from mortals. Thus in most communities the living and the dead were incorporated into a giant hierarchy of overlapping statuses, each with associated rights and obligations, in which the concept of bondage transcended temporal life. Kings were considered to be imbued with sacred power, but were in turn governed by the ancestors or gods. In Islam, for example, all Muslims were "slaves" of Allah.

Conclusion

To date, most studies of slavery in the IOW have been inspired and informed by the Atlantic model of slavery, in which there is a clearly distinct black "foreigner" community, of permanent and inheritable slave status, deprived of civil rights, and in which the violence exercised by the white slave-owner community on slaves is pervasive. Historians have concentrated overwhelmingly on the experience of East Africans shipped as slaves to European and Muslim settlements and plantations in the Western Indian Ocean.

However, slavery in the IOW cannot be understood outside the context of the IOW global economy, which arose during the first millennium AD and lasted into the nineteenth century, when the forces of the international economy increasingly embraced the macro-region. The IOW global economy was a sophisticated and durable system of long-distance exchange that linked China to Southeast and South Asia, the Middle East and Africa. It established a demand for different types of servile labour, primarily met by the military and political conquest of neighbouring peoples, but which also gave rise to complex slave trades involving enslaved peoples of many different origins, cultures and skin colours. During the history of the IOW slave trade, probably many more slaves were traded than in the Atlantic system and, overall, black Africans formed a minority of slaves traded. Moreover, most slaves were probably objects of conspicuous consumption by elites – whose wealth and power they were purchased to reflect. These slaves, who performed little economically productive labour, enjoyed a status and standard of living higher than most nominally "free", yet still servile, peasants.

Notes

1 A salutary exception is William Gervase Clarence-Smith, who, however, concentrates on an analysis of the Indian Ocean slave trade within the context of the burgeoning international economy of the nineteenth century, rather than within the pre-1800 global economy (Clarence-Smith, 1989).

2 Janet Abu-Lughod considers that a nascent global economy existed by the second century AD. However, she argues that its core was not Asian economies but the Roman Empire, and that it failed to survive the collapse of the latter in the third century (Abu-Lughod, 1993: 80).
3 My thanks to Jesse Sayles for this calculation based on information from Adam McKeown, "Global Chinese Migration, 1850–1940", paper presented at ISSCO V (5th Conference of the International Society for the Study of Chinese Overseas), Helsignor, Denmark, May 10–13, 2004.
4 Liz Stuart, "Journey's End for Trafficked Humans", *Guardian Weekly*, 13–19 February 2003, 21.

Bibliography

Abu-Lughod, Janet Lippman, "The World System in the Thirteenth Century: Dead-End or Precursor", in Michael Adas, ed., *Islamic and European Expansion. The Forging of a Global Order* (Philadelphia, PA: Temple University Press, 1993).

Allen, Richard B., *Slaves, Freedmen, and Indentured Laborers in Colonial Mauritius* (New York: Cambridge University Press, 1999).

Alpers, Edward A., *Ivory and Slavery in East Central Africa* (Berkeley: University of California Press, 1975).

Suzanne "The African Diaspora in the Northwestern Indian Ocean: Reconsideration of an Old Problem, New Directions for Research", *Comparative Studies of South Asia, Africa and the Middle East* 17 (1997), 62–81.

Arasaratnam, S., "Slave Trade in the Indian Ocean in the Seventeenth Century", in K. S. Mathew, ed., *Mariners, Merchants and Oceans. Studies in Maritime History* (New Delhi: Manohar, 1995).

Atwell, William S., "Volcanism and Short-tern Climatic Change in East Asian and World History, c. 1200–1699", *Journal of World History* 12 (2001), 29–98.

Braudel, Fernand, *The Mediterranean and the Mediterranean World in the Age of Philip II* (Berkeley: University of California Press, 1996).

Boomgaard, Peter, "Human Capital, Slavery and Low Rates of Economic and Population Growth in Indonesia, 1600–1910", in Gwyn Campbell, ed., *The Structure of Slavery in Indian Ocean Africa and Asia* (London: Frank Cass, 2004), 83–96.

Campbell, Gwyn, *An Economic History of Imperial Madagascar, 1750–1895. The Rise and Fall of an Island Empire* (Cambridge: Cambridge University Press, 1985).

——, "Slavery and Fanompoana: The Structure of Forced Labour in Imerina (Madagascar), 1790–1861" *Journal of African History* 29 (1988), 463–86.

——, "The State and Pre-colonial Demographic History: The Case of Nineteenth Century Madagascar", *Journal of African History* 31 (1991), 415–45.

——, ed., *The Structure of Slavery in Indian Ocean Africa and Asia* (London: Frank Cass, 2004).

Chandra, Bipan, "The Colonial Legacy", in Bimal Jalan, ed., *The Indian Economy. Problems and Perspectives* (New Delhi: Penguin, 1993).

Chatterjee, Indrani, "Abolition by Denial? Slavery in South Asia after 1843", in Gwyn, Campbell, ed., *Abolition and its Aftermath in Indian Ocean Africa and Asia* (London: Routledge, 2005), 150–68.

Chaudhuri, K. N., *Trade and Civilisation in the Indian Ocean, from the Rise of Islan to 1750* (Cambridge: Cambridge University Press, 1985).

Clarence-Smith, William Gervase, ed., *The Economics of the Indian Ocean Slave Trade in the Nineteenth Century* (London: Frank Cass, 1989).

Cooper, Frederick, *Plantation Slavery on the East Coast of Africa* (New Haven, CT: Yale University Press, 1977).

Delaye, Karine, "Slavery and Colonial Representations in Indochina from the Second half of the Nineteenth to the Early Twentieth Centuries", in Gwyn Campbell, ed., *The Structure of Slavery in Indian Ocean Africa and Asia* (London: Frank Cass, 2004), 129–42.

Goody, Jack, "Slavery in Time and Space", in James L. Watson, ed., *Asian and African Systems of Slavery* (Berkeley: University of California Press, 1980), 16–42.

Harris, Joseph E., *The African Presence in Asia: Consequences of the East African Slave Trade* (Evanston: Northwestern University Press, 1971).

Jaschok, Maria and Miers, Suzanne, "Women in the Chinese Patriarchal System: Submission, Servitude, Escape and Collusion" in Maria Jaschok and Suzanne Miers, eds, *Women and Chinese Patriarchy. Submission, Servitude and Escape* (London and New Jersey: Zed Books, 1994).

Klein, Martin A., ed., *Breaking the Chains: Slavery, Bondage, and Emancipation in Modern Africa and Asia* (Madison: University of Wisconsin Press, 1993).

Kopytoff, Igor and Miers, Suzanne, "African 'Slavery' as an Institution of Marginality", in Igor Kopytoff and Suzanne Miers, eds, *Slavery in Africa. Historical and Anthropological Perspectives* (Madison: University of Wisconsin Press, 1977).

Lewis, Bernard, *Race and Slavery in the Middle East: An Historical Enquiry* (New York: Oxford University Press, 1990).

Mason, John Edwin, *Social Death and Resurrection: Slavery and Emancipation in South Africa* (Charlottesville: University of Virginia Press, 2003).

Meillassoux, Claude, *The Anthropology of Slavery. The Womb of Iron and Gold* (Chicago: University of Chicago Press/London: Athlone Press, 1991).

Miers, Suzanne, "Slavery and the Slave Trade in Saudi Arabia and the Arab States on the Persian Gulf, 1921–63", in Gwyn, Campbell, ed., *Abolition and its Aftermath in Indian Ocean Africa and Asia* (London: Routledge, 2005), 120–36.

Eno, Omar A., "The Abolition of Slavery and the Aftermath Stigma: the Case of the Bantu/Jareer People on the Benadir Coast of Southern Somalia", in Gwyn, Campbell, ed., *Abolition and its Aftermath in Indian Ocean Africa and Asia* (London: Routledge, 2005), 83–93.

Patnaik, Utsa, "Introduction", in Utsa Patnaik and Manjari Dingwaney, eds, *Chains of Servitude, Bondage and Slavery in India* (Hyderabad: Sangam Books, 1985).

Patnaik, Utsa and Dingwaney, Manjari, eds, *Chains of Servitude, Bondage and Slavery in India* (Hyderabad: Sangam Books, 1985).

Ponting, Clive, *A Green History of the World* (London: Penguin, 1993).

Rae, Kim Bok, "Nobi: A Korean System of Slavery", in Gwyn Campbell, ed., *The Structure of Slavery in Indian Ocean Africa and Asia* (London: Frank Cass, 2004), 155–68.

Reid, Anthony, "Introduction: Slavery and Bondage in Southeast Asian History", in Anthony Reid, ed., *Slavery, Bondage and Dependency in Southeast Asia* (St Lucia: University of Queensland Press, 1983).

——, ed., *Slavery, Bondage and Dependence in Southeast Asia* (St Lucia: University of Queensland Press, 1983).

Sheriff, Abdul, *Slaves, Spices, and Ivory in Zanzibar* (London: James Currey, 1897).

Vaughan, Megan, *Creating the Creole Island: Slavery in Eighteenth Century Mauritius* (Durham, NC: Duke University Press, 2005).

Wallerstein, Immanuel, *The Modern World-System. Capitalist Agriculture and the Origins of the European World-Economy in the Sixteenth Century* (New York: Academic Press, 1974).

Warren, James Francis, "The Structure of Slavery in the Sulu Zone in the Late Eighteenth and Ninetenth Centuries", in Gwyn Campbell, ed., *The Structure of Slavery in Indian Ocean Africa and Asia* (London: Frank Cass, 2004), 111–28.

Watson, James L., ed., *Asian and African Systems of Slavery* (Berkeley: University of California Press, 1980).

Worden, Nigel, *Slavery in Dutch South Africa* (Cambridge: Cambridge University Press, 1985).

4

THE ORIGINS OF SLAVERY IN THE AMERICAS, 1500–1700

Betty Wood

Introduction

The wholesale enslavement by Europeans of West and West Central African peoples throughout the Americas was neither predetermined, nor was it the outcome of a series of "unthinking decisions".[1] Rather, beginning with the Iberian powers in the early fifteenth century, at different times in different places, it stemmed not so much from a backwards glance at the assumed benefits of the various slave systems of the ancient and medieval worlds of Western Europe as it did from quite self-conscious, pragmatic and forward-looking assumptions about the likely profits to be derived from the exploitation of this particular form of labour.[2] Those assumptions interacted, or more accurately were conveniently made to interact, with self-serving European assessments of the human worth – or lack of it – relative to their own of both Africans and the newly encountered indigenous inhabitants of the "New World". But these assumptions also interacted with something else that, until comparatively recently, has been largely ignored by many historians of slavery in the Americas: the continuing willingness, well into the nineteenth century in some cases, of many West and West Central African leaders to fuel the trans-Atlantic slave trade that evolved relatively rapidly during the course of the sixteenth century.

Over the years, partly because of "Old World" ideologies, and partly because of the realities posed by the indigenous peoples and the physical environments encountered by Europeans in the "New World", the slave systems they introduced came to differ in degree but not in essential kind. It was during the latter part of the fifteenth century, albeit in an "unthinking" fashion, that the ideological and pragmatic pieces of the Western European jigsaw that would culminate in a conscious decision to enslave West and West Central Africans in the Americas were beginning to slot into place in the Iberian Peninsula. By this time, the Iberian powers had a close familiarity with African peoples. Years of North African, or "Moorish", occupation of large parts of Spain had been brought to an end. Significantly for the future, the Spanish were willing to enslave some of those who remained within their midst. If any justification for this process was required, then it was to be found in the very traditional Western European concept that being captured in just wars – wars that were waged against non-Christians, usually Moslems – legitimated the captive's enslavement. Also relevant was the degree of unification that stemmed from the marriage of Ferdinand of Aragon and Isabella of Castile in 1469, something that helped encourage Spaniards to emulate their Portuguese neighbours. They began to look outwards, towards securing the wealth that might derive from establishing trading links with parts of the world that were hitherto unknown – at least to Europeans.[3]

Iberian precedents

The English and French were latecomers as colonisers compared with the Spanish and Portuguese, who, by the mid-sixteenth century, had firmly established themselves as the dominant European powers in South America, the Caribbean basin and the lands surrounding the Gulf of Mexico. This is not to say, though, that they were ignorant of the natural environments and indigenous peoples of the eastern Atlantic seaboard. Far from it. Beginning with John Cabot's trans-Atlantic voyage in 1497, West Country merchants developed important seasonal trading links, principally in fish and furs, with the peoples who inhabited the coasts of what the English came to call Newfoundland, Canada and New England. Those links were a crucial component of the ways in which metropolitan English people came to regard Native Americans as valuable trading partners.

Spanish power largely confined English trading ventures, and later colonising enterprises, to the more northerly reaches of the North American continent. However, the steady stream of precious metals being shipped back to Spain both reinforced the notion of the enormous wealth that could be obtained from the New World, and provided a target for English privateers.

The ways in which the Portuguese in Brazil and the Spanish in the Caribbean basin were acquiring immense wealth from the production of sugar, a commodity that became known in some quarters as "white gold", provided the English with another model for the exploitation of the Americas. Plantation agriculture relied upon enslaved African labour as early as the 1530s and 1540s. This dependence made the Atlantic slave trade important. Initially, the Dutch dominated the trade. They were displaced by the English in the latter part of the seventeenth century.

The planters who bought captive Africans literally could afford to work their slaves to death. They were able to replace dead workers with newly imported men and women. In fact, the average life expectancy of an enslaved worker on the sugar estates of Brazil and the Caribbean was only around seven years after arrival from Africa. As long as the trans-Atlantic trade continued, sugar planters showed little interest in exploiting the reproductive, as well as the productive, potential of African women by encouraging them to have children. Enslaved women and men struggled against horrendous odds to carve out for themselves something resembling familiar and secure relationships.

It was, then, an ever-growing European demand for sugar and tobacco that could be produced in many parts of the Americas that was the prime stimulus for the development of the trans-Atlantic slave trade. From the early sixteenth century onwards, that trade allowed for the continued expansion of racially based systems of bondage. Before the middle years of the eighteenth century, the main opposition to these processes would be offered by those being enslaved, whether on the slave ships or after their arrival in the Americas, rather than by Europeans.

By the middle years of the sixteenth century, when the English began to think in terms of establishing permanent colonies – as opposed to temporary trading posts – in the Americas, they were well aware of the different dimensions of the paths blazed by Spain and Portugal. Wealth, and what it might mean to individuals, as well as to the English nation and its standing in Europe, was the driving force of the schemes that got under way in the mid-1580s with what would quickly prove to be the ill-fated settlement at Roanoke.

True, Protestant churchmen were keen to spread their version of Christianity in the Americas, partly through the migration of English people and partly through missionary work among indigenous peoples. But it was the prospect of untold riches that fuelled the initial colonising efforts of the English. Despite their knowledge of one route to wealth – slave-based plantation economies – the founders of Virginia, which eventually proved to be England's first permanent colony in North America, rejected this in favour of what they anticipated would be an even quicker way of making money for themselves and their investors: exploiting the precious metals that they expected to find in the region of Chesapeake Bay. The Virginia Company also assumed that trade with Native Americans would provide another lucrative source of income. Looking more to the future, they also anticipated that expeditionary voyages along the waterways of Chesapeake Bay would reveal a secure and readily accessible passage to the untold riches of the Orient (Mancall, 2007).

Labour relations in the early seventeenth century

Within a very few years of the first settlement at Jamestown in 1607, each of these expectations had been dashed. The fledgling colony was on the point of collapse. Diseases of one kind or another ravaged the all-male settlement. Those who survived were either too weak or unwilling to undertake the agricultural tasks that would enable them to survive. A cluster of reforms introduced by the Virginia Company during the 1610s, together with its continuing ability to produce compelling propaganda that continued to attract migrants, ensured the settlement's survival, at least in the short term. However, it took something else, over and above the privatisation of land and the introduction of representative government, to ensure that, beginning in the 1620s, Virginia would begin to generate the wealth dreamed of by the Virginia Company and the colony's first settlers.

It was readily apparent that the environment around Chesapeake Bay precluded the production of sugar and the wealth known to stem from that commodity. Largely due to the experiments conducted by John Rolfe during the mid-1610s, however, it became evident that this region could produce another crop that was much in demand in Europe: tobacco. The land reforms introduced by the Virginia Company encouraged private initiative in the introduction and subsequent expansion of a crop that, unlike sugar, required a minimal investment in capital equipment. All that was needed to make handsome profits was enough land, occupied by indigenous peoples who greatly outnumbered the English settlers, and sufficient labour, which could not be supplied by a migrant population that was still decades away from growing significantly by natural reproduction.

Following a Native American assault on Jamestown in 1622, which almost wiped out the settlement, the English did not hesitate to take land from Native Americans by force. And so began hostilities that would continue for the remainder of the colonial period. Any notion that Native Americans might have any legal or moral right to the lands they occupied was simply swept aside by pragmatic, avaricious tobacco planters. But securing the lands they needed by force solved only part of the problem: labour, and large amounts of it, was required to maximise profits from those lands.

Beginning with the tobacco boom of the 1620s, the options available to planters were clear enough. First, they could have tried to emulate the early Iberian sugar planters in Brazil and the Caribbean basin by putting captive Native Americans to work in their tobacco fields. On the face of it, this would seem to have been the cheapest option available to them because no transportation costs were involved. Had they felt any need to justify the bondage of Native Americans, then they could have fallen back, as did the settlers of Massachusetts a few years later, on the longstanding Western European belief that capture in a just war could result in enslavement. Yet the planters of Virginia did not turn to Native American workers, and the reason for rejecting this solution to their labour shortages was pragmatic rather than ideological.

That there were positive English images of Native Americans, which might be said to have precluded their enslavement on any significant scale, is undeniable. Late sixteenth-century English portrayals of Native Americans, strikingly evident in the images produced by John White at the time of the Roanoke venture, depicted peoples who were organised into tribes or nations, with clear, almost Europeanised social hierarchies. These nations and hierarchies might fall somewhat short of the English ideal, but they showed that Native Americans were not wholly irredeemable. These were peoples with whom sixteenth- and early seventeenth-century English colonisers hoped to trade; these were peoples whom the Protestant English, like their Western European Roman Catholic contemporaries, thought capable of being converted to Christianity.

Significantly, and in marked contrast to contemporary English images of West and West Central African peoples, not for one moment did either the metropolitan promoters of colonisation or the early colonists deny the humanity of Native Americans. However, positive images of Native Americans were balanced, and in Virginia after the early 1620s became completely outweighed, by a far more negative stereotyping. In the aftermath of the attack on Jamestown, the English depicted Native Americans as treacherous, violent and dangerous enemies. Yet, simultaneously, another stereotype emerged: that of the lazy Native American, especially the Native American man. It seemed to the English that it was Native American women who did most of the work, particularly the agricultural work, in their societies. The introduction of alcohol to Native Americans as part of continuing trading relationships prompted yet another stereotype: that of the drunken "Indian". Finally, as elsewhere in the Americas, Native American health was severely damaged by the Old World diseases imported by European settlers. All in all, then, it seemed to the Virginia tobacco planters of the 1620s and 1630s that Native Americans were simply not worth employing as bound labourers. Even if they could be controlled, they remained dangerous, idle and dissolute. Moreover, the possibility of them escaping and returning to their tribe was high. All in all, then, Native Americans scarcely fitted the ideal or practical requirement of being docile, hardworking agricultural labourers, and so were rejected as a workforce.

Nevertheless, Indian slavery was not absent from the New World. It began with Columbus and led to one of the most famous set pieces in New World history, Bartolomé de Las Casas' fiery denunciation of the Spanish treatment of Indians. The English, too, fostered slavery, despite their protestations that they were different from the cruel Spaniards, in what became the Black Legend of Spanish depravity. In King Philip's War, New Englanders took at least 400 Indians captive and shipped them to the

West Indies. In 1708, Carolina contained 1400 Indian slaves as opposed to 4100 Africans, while in Louisiana there were 229 Indian slaves in a population that contained 1540 African slaves. Moreover, English involvement in Native American slavery, especially as slave traders, pre-dated any systematic English trade in African slaves. Indian enslavement may have been minor compared with the enslavement of Africans, but it had important consequences. The enslavement of Indians often had dramatic effects on Indian communities, especially communities suffering from other calamities, such as extensive population decline. It also encouraged Europeans to see Indians as people physically and culturally separate from themselves. English enslavement of Indians raised intriguing questions about the status of Indians in civil society. In the eighteenth century, Britons and Americans were concerned to try and reject the very idea of Indian bondage, but that rejection did not entail a rejection of the idea of Indian subordination. As Indians were released from bondage, they tended, especially in the new United States, to be denied the status of citizen. Those Indians who remained within areas of white settlement were redefined using categories of "blackness", which suggests a considerable overlap between how Indians and African-Americans were viewed by Europeans, and indicates how the manner in which Native Americans were freed established a way in which African Americans could be freed but not given civil equality (Chaplin, 2005; see also Brooks, 2002; Gallay, 2002; Rushforth, 2003).

On the face of it, the Virginia tobacco planters of the 1620s and 1630s needed to look no further than West and West Central Africans to provide a continuing supply of all the labour they required. They, as well as other English people, were very well aware of the fact that this had been the solution adopted by their Iberian rivals elsewhere in the Americas. Moreover, sixteenth-century English stereotyping of West and West Central Africans certainly provided an ideological framework – an ideological justification – for their enslavement. Although English thinking was deeply rooted in the Bible, especially in the Old Testament, as well as in mediaeval travel accounts, it took on new and potent dimensions as they first began to encounter these peoples during the first half of the sixteenth century.

The earliest of these encounters took place in what proved to be the somewhat contradictory motives behind English voyages to the West African coast. The English had no interest in establishing colonies there and, unlike their Portuguese and Dutch contemporaries, displayed no interest in attempting to convert to Christianity the indigenous peoples they came across. What the earliest English voyagers to West Africa were interested in was trade. It was for this reason that in 1555 a trader named John Lok returned to England with five West African men. He intended that these men should be trained in the intricacies of English commerce and then returned to Africa to assist subsequent English mercantile ventures. But, almost simultaneously, another side of English thinking was being revealed by the quite contrary activities of Englishmen such as John Hawkins.

Not content with trying to take the Spanish galleons carrying precious metals back to Europe, Hawkins and others saw another way to make money from the Iberian powers in the New World: satisfying what seemed to be Iberians' insatiable demand for enslaved workers. Anglo-Spanish rivalries led to the exclusion of the English from this trade for another century, leaving it open to the Dutch. However, what these early English attempts to penetrate the trans-Atlantic slave trade reveal is abundantly clear: not only willingness to be complicit in the enslavement of West Africans by other Europeans, but also the possibility that, should the need ever arise, they too would not demur from the brutal exploitation of West Africans in any colonies that they might establish at some future date.

These English voyagers, particularly those who ventured to the West African coast, returned home with West and West Central Africans. These people formed the nucleus of a black population, based principally in London and Bristol. What English lawyers in particular were unclear about was the legal status of this population. The issue was: could slavery exist under English Common Law? There was certainly no contemporary precedent for slavery in England. Even serfs had a limited degree of freedom and rights in terms of customary law and natural entitlements. This is not to suggest that the English had no understanding of the circumstances under which slavery might exist, or the grounds upon which it might be justified. They could find justifications in the Old Testament and cite examples from the ancient world, but there was little guidance in the writings of English jurists, save for the enslavement of captives taken in war. In fact, the English Common Law favoured personal liberty, if only because the Christian tradition could be interpreted to make personal freedom the norm. For the English, enslavement was akin to the complete loss of freedom, to what amounted to dehumanisation. Consequently, to treat a man like a slave was to treat him as a beast.

Although the legal status of Africans in sixteenth- and early seventeenth-century England was uncertain, to say the least, in the present context two points are particularly significant. First, and obviously, there was no unambiguous legal model for colonial proprietors and colonists, who everywhere enjoyed some degree of self-government, to follow. Moreover, and in no small measure because of the riches that stemmed from slavery and the trans-Atlantic slave trade, successive English monarchs and Parliaments were happy to leave colonial governments to determine the legal status of all members of their populations as they saw fit. Second, despite the confusion and uncertainty in England about the precise status of its growing African population, encounters in England were instrumental in shaping stereotypes that were firmly in place even before the first settlers set foot in Jamestown.

Arguably even more important than the first-hand contacts that took place in England itself were the second-hand reports that English seafarers brought back with them from their voyages to West Africa. Some of these reports were published as an integral part of more wide-ranging travel accounts; less accessible are those that became part of an oral tradition as returning sailors regaled their families, friends, and even strangers with no doubt heavily embellished tales of the exotic people and places they had experienced on their voyages. Metropolitan English people who crossed the Atlantic to establish colonies subscribed to deeply unfavourable stereotypes about West and West Central Africans that facilitated, but did not necessarily dictate, a move towards racially based systems of bondage in English America. By the late sixteenth century, the English thought negatively about West Africans. These thoughts were in marked contrast to the positive thread in their images of Native Americans.

As far as the English were concerned, three things in particular set Africans irrevocably apart from themselves and other Western Europeans. First, and arguably most important of all, was the "blackness" of their skins, a blackness that, for sixteenth-century English people, was loaded with negative connotations of evil, sin, dirtiness, danger and the Devil himself. It was a blackness that contrasted with the "whiteness", and perceived purity, of the English. Contemporary attempts to explain the blackness of

West Africans only compounded this negative image. If, as contemporary thinkers assumed, all humanity derived from a single source, Adam and Eve, held to be white-skinned, then how could the blackness of Africans be explained? The explanation that satisfied most acknowledged that Africans were part of the common creation, but were descendants of Ham, whose curse by his father Noah was not only that he should be "ugly and dark-skinned", but also that he would become the "servant of servants". That is to say, the blackness of West Africans had originated as a divine punishment for sinful behaviour.

Yet there was also a strand in sixteenth-century English writings about West Africa that actually doubted the very humanity of that region's indigenous peoples. To the English, Native American culture seemed sufficiently advanced for a mission of civilisation, grounded in Christianity, to seem at least a possibility. The reverse was true of their thinking about West Africans. Travel accounts accused them of cannibalism, female mutilation, and engaging in sexual relations with animals. What these same accounts singularly failed to acknowledge was the political sophistication and economic achievements of many West African societies. In effect, the English saw what they wanted to see: peoples who in every respect were different from, and distinctly inferior to, themselves.[4]

Given these highly negative assumptions, together with the fact that they had long been aware of the racially based plantation economies of Latin America and the Caribbean, the question naturally arises as to why the labour-hungry Virginia tobacco producers of the 1620s did not turn immediately to enslaved African workers. After all, John Rolfe, the same John Rolfe who had been principally responsible for the introduction of tobacco as a commercially viable crop to Virginia, reported the arrival in Port Comfort of "twenty Negars" who had been "sold" to the colonists by a Dutch man-of-war. One might have imagined that this would have opened the floodgates to a whole-sale dependence upon enslaved workers, but it did not. By the mid-1620s, at the height of Virginia's first tobacco boom, there were fewer than 100 Africans in the colony; 30 years later they still numbered fewer than 1000. Moreover, whatever their status might have been prior to their arrival in Virginia, once there, it was shrouded in ambiguity. It may well have been that, in terms of their conditions of employment, they were regarded in the same legal light as English servants. What is clear, however, is that they were not immediately consigned to perpetual servitude, a status that in a very traditional manner followed that of the mother, or denied all personal rights. In Virginia, these fundamental components of slavery would not begin to slot into place until the second half of the seventeenth century. There is no great mystery as to why this was the case. The answer lay not so much in the racial attitudes and assumptions of Virginia's burgeoning planter class as it did in the colony's northerly location and the economics of a trans-Atlantic slave trade dominated by the Dutch.

As far as Dutch slave traders were concerned, there were two obvious American markets for the human cargoes they shipped across the Atlantic: the sugar colonies of Brazil and the Caribbean. These long and well established markets enabled the Dutch to sell their human cargoes, which, depending upon mortality rates on the Middle Passage, could amount to 400 or 500 people, quickly and usually at a handsome profit. The relatively rapid turnaround time of slave ships optimised the number of voyages per annum. The Virginia of the 1620s and 1630s had none of these commercial advantages. Tobacco prices might have been high, and planters able to afford to purchase enslaved workers, but this is not how the Dutch saw things. What they saw was not only a population that numbered just over 1200, but also a population that was becoming ever more dispersed along the waterways of Chesapeake Bay. Jamestown could scarcely be described as a thriving commercial centre, one that had the necessary infrastructure to enable the rapid sale of enslaved people. Allied with this was the additional time and expense that it would take slave ships to sail north to Virginia, when it was still entirely possible that their prospective customers had been wiped out by Native Americans. The Dutch saw absolutely no point in trying to exploit the Virginia planters' demand for labour.

We know that in 1619 the Virginia colonists were willing to recruit "twenty Negars" into their workforce. What we can never know for certain is how they would have reacted during the 1620s and 1630s had West and West Central Africans been made available to them on a regular basis. Certainly, the prices they were receiving for their tobacco suggests that they could have afforded the prices being charged by the Dutch. There is no evidence to suggest that they found either the idea or the practice of a racially based system of slavery unpalatable. Indeed, evidence of English behaviour elsewhere in the Americas suggests that, had they been offered enslaved workers, they would have had no compunction in accepting them.

It was in the 1620s that the English acquired their first two possessions in the Caribbean: St Kitts (also known as St Christopher) and, at the most easterly edge of the Caribbean basin, Barbados. Both were ideally suited to the production of sub-tropical commodities, including sugar. In the short term, however, it was Virginian tobacco that provided the economic model for these settlements. That they would be willing to employ African workers, and that there were English merchants and shippers willing to compete with the Dutch and supply them, is suggested by the fact that, as early as 1626, a merchant named Maurice Thompson landed 60 Africans on St Kitts. By the mid-1630s, Barbados also was moving rapidly towards an ever-increasing reliance on African workers, workers whom they had no reluctance in enslaving.

In many respects, Englishmen in Virginia, St Kitts and Barbados before 1640 were willing to employ African workers as and when they could acquire them. But at this stage in their development, no English colony was dependent on African labourers. African labour was useful, but what sustained their emerging and highly profitable tobacco economies was a fortuitous coincidence of colonial labour needs and the state of the English labour market. Before its demise in the mid-1620s, the Virginia Company had been enormously successful in attracting settlers to its colony. The most important element of its propaganda had been the lure of the freedom that awaited in Virginia, a freedom that, in contemporary terms, meant a lack of dependence upon others; a freedom that meant that in due course the servant could become the master; a freedom that was rooted in the ownership of land, something that was virtually unattainable by the vast majority of English people.

For those who could not afford their trans-Atlantic passage, the price to be paid for this eventual freedom and elevated social status was their labour for a clearly defined number of years. There was nothing arbitrary about the terms and conditions of this labour. Either before they left England, or upon their arrival in America, servants and their masters signed a legally binding contract of indenture. This document clearly stipulated the length of service, what the employer was to provide by way of material support, and, in many cases, the promise of what were known as the freedom dues to be enjoyed by servants at the end of their indenture. During the late 1620s and 1630s, a similar system evolved in Barbados.

It may have been the attraction of the Americas, or the push of sheer economic desperation, that encouraged thousands of English people to cross the Atlantic as indentured servants during the course of the seventeenth century. The demographic, socio-economic and gender dimensions of this outflow were broadly similar, regardless of the intended destination. Most were young adults; men outnumbered women by as many as six or seven to one; and the majority came from agricultural backgrounds. English commentators may have depicted servants as unruly riff-raff, but this did not matter to the tobacco producers of Virginia and Barbados. These were youthful workers who could easily be trained up in the tasks associated with tobacco cultivation. They would provide the one thing that was absolutely essential to the continuing generation of profits.

As long as sufficient numbers of English people could be persuaded to cross the Atlantic as indentured servants, the unavailability of African workers was of no great economic consequence. All of this began to change in the middle years of the century. The English Civil War was the all-important catalyst that fuelled the transformation of the labour base of Barbados from a heavy dependence upon indentured servants to an even greater dependence upon enslaved African workers. Quite coincidentally, another transformation was also in the process of taking place in Barbados during the late 1630s: a shift from tobacco to sugar production.

Although tobacco could be produced in Barbados, it was of poorer quality than that grown in Virginia. In their search for an alternative cash crop, Barbadian planters looked to Brazil. The Brazilian model showed them not only how to cultivate and process cane, but also the cheapest and most productive workforce. The beginnings of what is often known as the "Sugar Revolution", and one that within a quarter of a century would make Barbados England's richest and most valuable colony, coincided with the political turmoil of the English Civil War. Trading patterns were disrupted and, just as seriously for Barbadian planters, the flow of indentured servants began to dry up. England's major commercial rivals, the Dutch, were on hand to offer these planters the two things they desperately needed: a means to get their sugar to market, and the labour necessary to produce it. Barbados was on the direct route between West Africa, Brazil and the Caribbean basin, and its demand for labour gave Dutch traders every incentive to shorten their voyages and exploit this new market for their human cargoes. Unlike early Virginia, mid-seventeenth-century Barbados was capable of absorbing an entire shipload of enslaved people. Barbadian planters displayed no reluctance in switching to this new type of labour.

In 1630, there were roughly 200 West Africans in a total Barbadian population of around 2000; by 1660, the West African component had increased more than a hundredfold to just over 27,000. In that same year they outnumbered the island's white residents by about 1000, forming the first black majority anywhere in Anglophone America. The legal status of these African workers had been clarified in what was the earliest pronouncement anywhere in English America legitimising slavery and linking it specifically to ethnicity. In 1636, Governor Henry Hawley decreed that any "Negroes that come here to be sold [would] serve for life". His decree went unchallenged not only in Barbados, but also in England. Neither politicians nor Anglican churchmen saw fit to intervene and seek to overturn this momentous declaration. On the contrary, in the decades that followed, influential Englishmen motivated by self-interest would both defend and promote a Barbadian policy soon to be emulated by English colonists everywhere on the North American mainland.[5]

Mid-century transitions

Beginning with the disruptions caused by the English Civil War, several circumstances would change, both in England and in the Americas, in ways that together hastened the development of clearly defined slave systems in England's mainland American colonies. The first of these systems emerged in South Carolina during the 1670s. It was a system that reflected the economic imperatives of Barbadian planters and a heightened emphasis on both commerce and colonisation in Restoration England.

By the mid-1660s, the relatively small size of Barbados was already severely limiting both the potential for leading sugar planters to expand their operations, and their scope to offer a declining number of indentured servants post-indenture opportunities in the shape of land ownership. They readily grasped a proposal that was being hatched in England between the King and some of his leading courtiers: to found a new colony on the American mainland in a region that seemed ideally suited to plantation agriculture.

The entire area to the south of Virginia was claimed by Spain, but that did not stop the English and their Barbadian allies from establishing a new colony, Carolina. Barbadian planters would have had no interest in moving to Carolina had it not been for one thing: a cast-iron guarantee from the English Crown that they would be allowed to take their slaves with them. Given the revenue it expected from Carolina, the Crown was only too keen to oblige. In 1669, the Earl of Shaftesbury and his secretary, the political thinker John Locke, drew up a document entitled the "Fundamental Constitutions" for Carolina in which, amongst other things, the right to hold property in the form of slaves was legitimated. Carolina would be the only Anglophone American colony in which a racially based system of slavery was present from the outset.

During the latter part of the seventeenth century, the population of Carolina grew rapidly, with many of the new settlers making their way there from the Caribbean. It would take several years, however, before Carolina realised its full economic potential, not in the shape of sugar, which could not be grown anywhere along the eastern Atlantic seaboard, but in the form of rice, a commodity that by the 1720s and 1730s was proving to be a lucrative export crop. Within a few years, rice would make South Carolina the wealthiest of England's mainland colonies, a wealth that derived from the often brutal and completely unapologetic exploitation of enslaved African workers.

Even though it took time to develop Carolina's rice economy, the colony's enslaved population grew rapidly during the late seventeenth and early eighteenth centuries. By 1708, for example, with an enslaved African population of around 4000, Carolina was already half black; during the next 20 years, as rice cultivation became increasingly important, that percentage soared to around 60 per cent. Out of all of England's mainland colonies, only Carolina would have a black majority. The rapid growth of Carolina's enslaved population stemmed from the trans-Atlantic slave trade, a trade that had fundamentally altered during the 1660s and 1670s with England's defeat of its major commercial rival, the Dutch.[6]

England's victory in the Anglo-Dutch wars not only ensured its dominance in Atlantic trade, but also secured for it the vast mainland territories of New Netherland, territories that during the late seventeenth century were carved up into the English colonies of

New York, Pennsylvania and the Jerseys. The jewel in this particular crown was the port of New Amsterdam, renamed New York, the best natural port on the eastern Atlantic seaboard and one that would facilitate all facets of English and colonial commercial activities throughout the Atlantic world, including the lucrative trans-Atlantic slave trade. What remained largely unremarked, and uncontroversial, in the aftermath of England's decisive victory over the Dutch was the fact that in claiming New Netherland they were also inheriting the slave system introduced by the Dutch earlier in the century. Unsurprisingly, perhaps, that system would go unchallenged and remain intact for the English to build upon.

A heightened emphasis on commerce and colonisation, together with the defeat of their Dutch rivals, enabled the English to enter the trans-Atlantic slave trade on a significant scale, especially from 1672 with the organisation in London of the Royal African Company. Although it may be argued that this monopoly restricted opportunities for private English and colonial slave traders, for the first time Caribbean and mainland American planters were being offered a steady and guaranteed supply of enslaved African workers. The question was: did they want them, and could they afford them? In Barbados and Carolina, the answer was clear enough: yes, slaves were wanted and yes, they could easily be afforded. As the seventeenth century drew to a close, Virginia tobacco producers, too, were beginning to answer in the affirmative. Circumstances had changed in ways that now meant the large-scale employment of enslaved workers was not only economically advantageous, but also socially and politically desirable.

During the 1660s and 1670s, Virginia's tobacco planters began to encounter a new cluster of difficulties. Partly due to overproduction, tobacco prices were poor. In large measure this overproduction stemmed from demographic changes. What is usually known as demographic normalisation was occurring in this part of the mainland, one crucial outcome of which was that more servants were surviving their term of indenture. If they could acquire land, which usually meant renting it from wealthier planters, there was no incentive for servants to return to the indentured labour market. After all, the prospect of land ownership was what had lured many of these ex-servants to Virginia in the first place. More tobacco was being produced, which lowered prices and simultaneously diminished the standard of living.

If this was not enough, elite planter–politicians squabbled over various issues, not least over the best policies to be pursued regarding Native Americans in the frontier regions of the colony. All these tensions exploded in 1676 in the shape of Bacon's Rebellion, a virtual civil war in Virginia. If a deeply divided planter elite could agree on anything, it was their horror of armed black workers fighting alongside white servants and ex-servants for Nathaniel Bacon's cause. Bacon was defeated and, within a quarter of a century, Virginia had been transformed into one of the most stable societies anywhere on the North American mainland. It was no coincidence that this coincided with another transformation: that from indentured European to involuntary African servitude.

Neither was it coincidental that, in the aftermath of Bacon's Rebellion, Virginia's planter elite paid careful attention to the intersection between social rank and race. They became ever more determined to drive a wedge between underclass whites and the Africans who they were in the process of enslaving. They were in no doubt that, not least because of what they knew of enslaved peoples' resistance elsewhere in the

Americans, the hegemony they sought depended upon enlisting the unquestioning support of underclass whites.

Regardless of anything else, the Virginia planters of the late seventeenth century continued to require workers. The demographic normalisation that was under way was still not generating enough of those workers through natural reproduction. Planters were still being forced, as they always had been, to look outside Virginia for the labour that was absolutely essential if they were to continue to make profits. Predictably, the cost and productivity of their workforce, especially at a time of relatively low tobacco prices, was a fundamental consideration. In many ways, this situation was the very reverse of that half a century earlier. Then, tobacco planters had been able to resolve their labour problems by exploiting the voluntary flow of indentured servants from England. By the 1680s and 1690s, this was becoming a more difficult solution. An economic upturn in the late-seventeenth-century English economy diminished the prospective pool of migrants willing to exchange their labour for a trans-Atlantic passage. At the same time, the colonies created by English interests during the second half of the century, beginning with Jamaica taken from Spain in the mid-1650s, and followed by Carolina and those carved from New Netherland during the 1670s and 1680s, heightened the competition for a diminishing pool of migrants.

Significantly, England's entry into the trans-Atlantic slave trade, together with declining rates of mortality in Virginia, began to make African peoples an economically more attractive type of labour for the colony's tobacco planters. As far as slave traders were concerned, Virginia was now attractive as a market in a way that had not been the case during the 1620s and 1630s. The colony was secure against any Native American assault that might threaten to overwhelm it, and appeared equally resilient to any attack that might be launched by England's European rivals. Crucially, Virginia's expanding tobacco economy also meant that now it was possible for slave traders to sell an entire human cargo at one location.

For their part, Virginia planters knew that in Barbados and South Carolina, as well as in the sugar economies of Brazil, Africans were being forced to work not for a legally limited term of years, but for their entire lives. Moreover, any children born to enslaved mothers were forced to inherit their status. Africans offered the prospect of a perpetual agricultural workforce in a way that indentured Europeans did not. Not only this but, if necessary through harsh physical coercion, Africans not only could be made to work longer hours than indentured Europeans, but also could be maintained much more cheaply.

The consequences of the transition to enslavement

During the last two decades of the seventeenth century, the African component of Virginia's population grew at a rate comparable with that of Barbados 40 years earlier. In 1680, there were roughly 4000 people of African descent in Virginia; by 1710 that number had grown to around 23,100. Africans accounted for just over 40 per cent of the colony's total population. Simultaneously, the planter-dominated Virginia government took steps to ensure there could be no doubts whatsoever about the legal status of this black element.

Although there might have been some ambiguity about the exact status of the Africans first taken to Virginia in the late 1610s and 1620s, it is clear that the colonists regarded them as being both different and also inferior to themselves. This can be seen, for example, in the use of the label "Negar", as well as in the separate categorisation of Africans in a census taken in the mid-1620s. Yet as long as the African component of the population remained relatively small, and could be controlled in a similar manner to indentured servants, there was no pressing need to place them in an entirely separate legal category, one that would define them as property rather than as persons, and thereby relegate them to a situation beyond the bounds of recognised civil society. But as the black population began to grow during the middle years of the seventeenth century, so a racial ideology developed that increasingly concerned itself with defining the ways in which those who for decades had been identified by the English as being irredeemable heathen savages could best be controlled. As in Barbados, which increasingly provided a model for the planter–politicians of Virginia, there were no countervailing forces, either locally or coming from England, to halt this process. Ironically, the more Africans resisted this hardening racial ideology, be it on the slave ships or once in the Americas, the more that confirmed in English and colonial minds the need for the imposition of the firmest of controls.

The last 40 years of the seventeenth century witnessed a flurry of legislation in Virginia that confirmed the legal status of slave upon its growing black population. The first hint that people of African descent might be legally dehumanised came in 1669, when the Virginia government decreed that Africans formed a part of their master's "estate", that is, a part of their property. Other laws sought, albeit unsuccessfully, to prohibit interracial sex and marriage, and equally unsuccessful restrictions were placed on black people's freedom of movement. In 1705 these laws were codified, leaving no doubt that Virginia's growing black population was a population that had been stripped of all its human rights.

During the second half of the seventeenth century, and in common with their counterparts in Barbados and Carolinas, Virginia's legislators had easily dismissed the one traditional argument that might have prevented the enslavement of Africans, or at least of those Africans who were willing to abandon their traditional belief systems in favour of Christianity: the argument that one Christian could not hold another Christian in perpetual bondage. Like the Anglican planters and churchmen of the other plantation colonies, those of Virginia took the self-serving position that, provided they attended to the spiritual needs of those in their service, it was perfectly legitimate for Christian masters to hold other Christians as slaves. The notion that any freedom implicit in Christianity was spiritual, not secular, and that the acceptance of Christianity made absolutely no difference to an individual's status, was endorsed by the Anglican authorities in England, and remained its official position through the era of the American Revolution.

Slavery in New England in the seventeenth century

That economic imperatives embedded in long-held English racial attitudes fuelled the enslavement of West and West Central African peoples in England's evolving plantation colonies seems evident enough. Yet a version of slavery, albeit a very different version of that institution, developed in parts of English America that were environmentally unsuited to plantation agriculture. The question is whether a similar explanation holds true for these more northerly regions and, more especially, in

New England. The answer is that, in the albeit very different context of New England and its labour requirements, economic factors also played a role in ensuring the enslavement of the smaller number of African peoples to be found in that region by the end of the seventeenth century.

The Puritans who began the settlement of New England in the early 1630s under the leadership of John Winthrop certainly did not eschew the idea of profit but, unlike their counterparts in Virginia and Barbados, their motivation for migration, and their blueprint for their colony of Massachusetts, was essentially religious in nature. They had a very clear idea of the "Godly Society" that they wished to establish. The guide that they adopted for that society, the Old Testament, provided them with every justification that they might have needed for the introduction of bondage into that society.

In 1641, in one of the earliest acknowledgements that slavery might exist in English America, the Puritans set out the circumstances under which an individual might be enslaved, circumstances that would have been entirely familiar to their contemporaries, and that would not have been unfamiliar to mediaeval English people. In the Puritan scheme of things, captives in a just war could be enslaved, as could those "strangers" who chose to sell themselves, or who were sold into, slavery. In an equally familiar fashion, the Puritans also decreed that Christian masters were obliged to attend to the spiritual wellbeing of their bond servants, their dependants. Drawing upon the Old Testament distinction between Jewish and non-Jewish bond servants, and the rights that attached to each, the Puritans accepted that bond servants should not be totally denied their humanity, but should continue to enjoy a cluster of rights. Thus it was that those who came to be enslaved in Massachusetts would enjoy, or endure, the ambiguous status of being considered both as property and as person in the eyes of the law.

Significantly, the definitions of bondage set out by the Puritans made no mention of ethnicity; instead, as their emphasis on just wars signified, they attached rather more importance to religion – to Christianity or to the lack of it. Yet these self-same Puritans shared the racial thinking of their English contemporaries and, together with the lack of Christianity of the handful of Africans brought to Massachusetts from the Caribbean in the late 1630s, bondage seemed the most appropriate and most convenient, category in which to place these dark-skinned "strangers".

True, the mixed family farms of Massachusetts never generated the same demand for large gangs of workers as did the sugar estates of Barbados and the tobacco fields of Virginia, something that is reflected in the relatively small numbers of African peoples to be found in New England during the seventeenth century. In 1660, for example, there were just over 500 Africans in a total New England population of roughly 33,000. Fifty years later, Massachusetts' population of around 61,000 included about 1300 Africans. As their number suggests, these Africans were never as economically significant as Africans in the plantation colonies, but even so, they filled important niches in New England's agricultural and urban economies. Insofar as New Englanders derived crucial economic benefit from slavery, then it was from the transportation of commodities produced by enslaved labour elsewhere in English America, supplying the sugar islands with the various goods they could not or did not produce for themselves, and, eventually, by their wholehearted participation in the trans-Atlantic slave trade.[7]

Everywhere in English America, including New England, the racially based slave systems that emerged during the course of the seventeenth century were rooted in pragmatism. The English did not begin their colonisation of the Americas with a view to enslaving West and West Central African peoples, but turned to these peoples – to those whom they could depict as the Sons of Ham – as irredeemable sub-humans, as and when they deemed it both possible and in their economic self-interest to do so.

Notes

1 This was the argument advanced by Winthrop D. Jordan, particularly for Virginia, in his influential *White over Black* (Jordan, 1968).
2 For this emphasis on pragmatism, see Morgan (1975) and Blackburn (1997).
3 For Western European voyages of "discovery", see Abulafia (2008).
4 For a lengthier discussion of these stereotypes, see Jordan (1968).
5 For Barbadian labour systems in the seventeenth century, see Beckles (1989).
6 For an excellent account of the development of South Carolina's slave system, see Wood (1974).
7 For slavery in seventeenth-century New England, see Twombly and Moore (1967).

Bibliography

Abulafia, David, *The Discovery of Mankind: Encounters in the Age of Columbus* (New Haven, CT: Yale University Press, 2008).

Beckles, Hilary McD., *White Servitude and Black Slavery in Barbados, 1627–1715* (Knoxville, TN: University of Tennessee Press, 1989).

Berlin, Ira, *Many Thousands Gone: The First Two Centuries of Slavery in North America* (Cambridge, MA: Harvard University Press, 1998).

Blackburn, Robin, *The Making of New World Slavery: From the Baroque to the Modern* (London: Verso, 1997).

Brooks, James F., *Captives and Cousins: Slavery, Kinship, and Community in the Southwest Borderlands* (Chapel Hill: University of North Carolina Press, 2002).

Chaplin, Joyce B., "Enslavement of Indians in Early America: Captivity Without the Narrative", in Elizabeth Mancke and Carole Shammas, eds, *The Creation of the British Atlantic World* (Baltimore, MD: Johns Hopkins University Press, 2005), 45–70.

Davis, David Brion, *The Problem of Slavery in Western Culture* (Ithaca, NY: Cornell University Press, 1969).

Eltis, David and Richardson, David, eds, *Routes to Slavery: Direction, Ethnicity and Mortality in the Transatlantic Slave Trade* (London: Frank Cass, 1997).

Gallay, Allan, *The Indian Slave Trade: The Rise of the English Empire in the American South, 1670–1717* (New Haven, CT: Yale University Press, 2002).

Jordan, Winthrop D., *White Over Black: Attitudes toward the Negro, 1550–1812* (Chapel Hill: University of North Carolina Press, 1968).

Mancall, Peter C., ed., *The Atlantic World and Virginia, 1550–1624* (Chapel Hill: University of North Carolina Press, 2007).

Morgan, Edmund S., *American Slavery, American Freedom: The Ordeal of Colonial Virginia* (New York: W.W. Norton, 1975).

Rushforth, Brett, "'A Little Flesh We Offer': The Origins of Slavery in New France", *William and Mary Quarterly* 3rd ser 60 (2003), 707–808.

Thornton, John, *Africa and Africans in the Making of the Atlantic World, 1400–1680* (New York: Cambridge University Press, 1992).

Twombly, R.C. and Moore, R. H., "Black Puritan: The Negro in Seventeenth Century New England", *William and Mary Quarterly* 3rd ser 24 (1967): 224–42.

Wood, Betty, *The Origins of American Slavery: Freedom and Bondage in the American Colonies* (New York: Hill and Wang, 1997).

Wood, Peter H., *Black Majority: Negroes in Colonial South Carolina from 1670 to the Stono Rebellion* (New York: W. W. Norton, 1974).

5

THE ATLANTIC SLAVE TRADE

Trevor Burnard

Introduction

The Atlantic slave trade, which lasted from the mid-fifteenth century until the last quarter of the nineteenth century, was a distinctive event in both global history and the history of slavery. There have been, of course, other large coerced migrations in history, notably in the mid-twentieth century when millions of people in Europe and Asia were moved from place to place in a very short period of time. Moreover, voluntary migration has often exceeded the levels of migration recorded in the Atlantic slave trade. Between 1815 and 1930, 51.7 million people left Europe for other destinations, mostly in the New World, of whom the British alone contributed 18.7 million, or 36 per cent (Richards, 2004: 4–6). As Gwyn Campbell notes in Chapter 3 of this volume, the total volume of the slave trade in the Indian Ocean World probably equalled and perhaps exceeded the volume of captives in the Atlantic slave trade.

Yet the Atlantic slave trade was distinctive in a number of important ways. As David Eltis and David Richardson argue, the Atlantic slave trade was "a new phenomenon in the human experience". It was "the largest transoceanic forced migration in history" whereby "relatively small improvements to the quality of life of a people on one continent [Europe] … were made possible by the removal of others from a second continent [Africa], and their draconian exploitation on yet a third [the Americas]" (Eltis and Richardson, 2008: 1, 2, 45). As other essays in this volume show, the Atlantic slave trade was the means whereby the Americas were repopulated by Africans, and made profitable to Europeans in the process. The repopulation process was demographically very significant. Before 1820, about four Africans arrived in the Americas for every single European. Between 1760 and 1820, this emigrating flow amounted to 5.6 Africans per one European. By the end of this period, nearly 8.7 million Africans had been taken against their will to the Americas, as opposed to just 2.6 million Europeans, only a small proportion of whom came to the Americas voluntarily (*ibid.*: 45).

Without the Atlantic slave trade, and the continual inflow of forced labour that went to the plantation societies of the American South, the Caribbean and Iberian America, the Americas would have been much less profitable, much less quickly than they were. As Barbara Solow (1991) notes, it was slavery that ensured colonial economic growth: those areas that had slaves prospered, those that were too poor to be able to exploit slaves languished. Through the Atlantic slave trade, African chattel slavery was made possible in the Americas and, in turn, the plantation system was able to succeed. The disease environment in tropical and sub-tropical regions of the Americas was malign, and the work that labourers were forced to do, especially when required to cultivate sugar cane, proved very injurious to health. Before the nineteenth century, no sugar-producing region and few plantation areas outside the American South were able to have a self-sustaining labouring population. In order to keep the plantation system going, a system that, as Richard Follett argues in Chapter 7 of this volume, devoured human lives, fresh inputs of labour were always required. These inputs were achieved through the increasingly more economically efficient transportation of captive Africans from West and Central Africa in what became known as the triangular trade (ships coming from Europe, picking up slaves in Africa, and depositing them in the Americas before returning to Europe). The consequences of this trade were profound for all four continents involved. It was a primary way in which an Atlantic world was created in "one of the most ambitious experiments in social engineering of the early modern era: the establishment of slave plantations" (*ibid.*; Osterhammel and Petersson, 2005: 47).

Nevertheless, the Atlantic slave trade was more than just an economic event. It was both a profound tragedy, one of the worst and most sustained crimes committed in history, and also an arena of dramatic social transformation. The Atlantic slave trade was the most visible indication in the Atlantic of how the Columbian encounter had opened up a virtually unconstrained form of capitalism, in which morality was placed below economic gain, and where slave traders devised new and ingenious ways in which to reduce everything, including people, to the status of commodities. The commodification of people was, as Stephanie Smallwood argues, an ultimate expression of the power of the market to alter social sensibility. The Atlantic slave trade, she suggests, was where "individual paths of misfortune merged into the commodifying Atlantic apparatus – the material, economic, and social mechanisms by which the market molded subjects into beings that more closely resembled objects – beings that existed solely for the use of those that claimed to hold them as possessions". At bottom, the slave trade became a battle for souls, to use the religious language favoured by abolitionists in late-eighteenth-century Britain, who saw in the slave trade a visible manifestation of original sin. Slavers tried to deny slaves' full personhood through the commodification of Africans into slaves. Africans, as Smallwood states, "tried to restore through her unassisted agency the pulse of social integration that saltwater slavery threatened to extinguish". The Atlantic slave trade, therefore, was crucial in helping to shape African diasporas in the New World (Smallwood, 2007a: 63, 182, 187).

Why not Europeans?

The Atlantic slave trade is not just distinctive. It is also curious. Certainly, European settlers in the Americas, especially in plantation regions, needed labour. As Betty Wood shows in Chapter 4 in this volume, those labour demands could not be met solely by the exploitation of Native Americans. Nevertheless, one has to ask why Europeans had to travel to Africa to get labourers when they might have met their labour needs from transporting and enslaving the lower social strata of European society, strata that caused European rulers no end of problem, and members of which, when criminals, they had little compunction in torturing and executing.

David Eltis and Robin Blackburn have raised the idea of a "white Atlantic" without a trade in slaves between Europe and Africa. Such a "white Atlantic" would have mirrored what happened after 1820 as European and Asian migration to the Americas picked up.

Blackburn (1997: 350–63) thinks that development may have been possible without any form of enslavement. Eltis's less cheery version makes a counterfactual argument for the enslavement of Europeans. Eltis (2000: 63–80) argues that not only would it have been cheaper for Europeans to stock the plantations with enslaved Europeans, but also that doing so would have been welcomed by racist planters, uneasy about having to deal with Africans whose social characteristics they despised and feared. Moreover, making Europeans slaves might have been beneficial for the rulers of European nations, solving an American labour problem while transferring to the New World the social problem of what to do with a rising tide of master-less and potentially criminal men. He suggests, however, that his counterfactual argument would never have happened because Europeans had a visceral distaste for enslaving their own people. He argues that Europeans did not enslave other Europeans because they thought doing so was taboo: Europeans believed that other Europeans, if not Africans, were members of their own moral community.

Eltis's counterfactual raises some powerful and disturbing questions about the reasoning behind the making of the Atlantic slave trade. As Seymour Drescher points out in an important critique, implicit in Eltis's argument is a claim that, even in the beginnings of the Atlantic slave trade, Europeans had sufficient doubts about the morality of slavery to reject it as a condition for themselves, just as Muslims thought it wrong to enslave fellow adherents of Islam. As Eltis suggests, twice in the history of the Atlantic slave trade, at its beginning and from around 1770, when the slave trade first came under concerted attack from British humanitarians, libertarian and psychological inhibitions carried the day against economic incentives. European squeamishness about enslaving fellow Europeans shows that European cultural constraints were always at odds against the rigorous logic of European commercial rationality (Drescher, 2004: 37–38).[1]

Nevertheless, there are some obvious problems with Eltis's counterfactual argument. First, as Blackburn notes, Europeans did not need to turn to slavery in order to work plantations. They could have continued to use indentured labour, as in the Chesapeake before the 1670s; or wage labour, as in plantation systems throughout the world after 1850. Second, Eltis probably overstates the supply of available people able to be enslaved in Europe. Strong, mentally sane and law-abiding young men were in continual demand throughout Europe and the Americas in the early modern period. More importantly, these poor people showed repeatedly, as in England during the English Civil War in the mid-seventeenth century, that they had a considerable capacity for resistance. Reintroducing slavery into England or France from the sixteenth century onwards would probably have led to mass popular revolt by poor people, who were as convinced as rich people that they were entitled to the rights and privileges of free people. European monarchs may have fantasised about ridding their realms of poor troublemakers and putting them to productive work in the Americas, but Drescher argues that to implement such fantasies would have been not just unthinkable but undoable, especially in smaller European nations such as Portugal. As he states, "any attempt to enslave European outsiders by one of Europe's smaller powers would most likely have been a formula for national disaster". In Portugal, "Europe's pluralistic state system guaranteed a step rise in the frequency, ubiquity and intensity of violence against any attempt to deliver 650,000 European slaves to Brazil in its vulnerable formative period." Moreover, Drescher asserts, the policing costs of keeping European slaves in check on ships and in the colonies would have been prohibitive (*ibid.*: 47, 52, 60).

Why Africans?

The obvious question we have to ask, then, is why it was not problematic to enslave and transport Africans across the ocean, when enslaving Europeans would have been close to impossible except in a permanently authoritarian state? What was true for Europeans should also be true for Africans. Recent research by historians has made clear that the key players in determining the shape of the Atlantic slave trade were African merchants and rulers. Europeans came to Africa upon sufferance and were dependent on local leaders for access to goods, including slaves. The whole Atlantic slave trade was founded on the willingness of Africans to sell other Africans to Europeans, and on the ability of African rulers to conduct such sales without facing local rebellion. The conduct of trade generally followed African dictates until European colonialism began in earnest from the late-nineteenth century, by which time the Atlantic slave trade had largely ended (Law, 1994).

One reason for African willingness to engage in the Atlantic slave trade was their long experience with slavery within northern and western Africa. Islamic societies were particularly keen on enslavement. Muslims were prepared to enslave anyone, regardless of colour, as long as they were people who were not Muslim. In the five centuries before the start of the Atlantic slave trade, about 5000 slaves per annum were sent across the Sahara from West Africa. In addition, the nature of political authority in much of West Africa encouraged slavery. Like other regions where slave trading was common, such as the Caucasus, the Balkans and pre-Norman England, West Africa was politically fragmented. The result of such fragmentation was frequent internecine warfare that often generated captives. Most slaves in West Africa were the unintended by-products of war. The prevalence of slavery in many West African societies made it easy for Africans to accept enslavement as natural and legitimate. Europeans were able to tap into existing slave supply networks, whereas such networks would have had to have been created afresh in Europe from the fifteenth century.

Moreover, as John Thornton argues, social relations in West and Central Africa were marked by the objective of controlling labour rather than land, as in Western Europe. Slaves were thus a source of wealth and a common form of currency. Moreover, and in distinction from Europe, African merchants seldom saw the victims of the Atlantic slave trade as their brothers or sisters. They saw them as aliens. Africans generally sold people they considered foreigners and enemies, although they would make some exception for countrymen guilty of serious offences (Thornton, 1998: 102).

Most importantly, of course, Africans sold slaves because they received valuable goods in return for them. It should be kept in mind that the trade in slaves did not become the dominant form of exchange between Europeans and Africans until the late seventeenth century. Before then, the African trade good most desired by Europeans was gold. This gold came mainly from the Akan gold-fields of the interior of modern-day Ghana. Palm oil was also important. Nevertheless, slaves became increasingly important in European–African trade. By the 1780s, when the Atlantic slave trade was at its apogee, slaves comprised over 90 per cent of the value of all African exports. The trade was significant enough to encourage African kingdoms, notably Dahomey, to start wars in order to take captives who could become slaves. In return for the people they sold to Europeans, Africans received a variety of goods, the most important of which were Indian cotton textiles. Africans were highly selective about the kinds of goods they received, and used their market power in Africa to extract favourable terms from slave traders, who were generally under appreciable time constraints, both in trying to load their ships with Africans so that their cargoes would not become ill, and also in leaving the African coast at the optimal time to get to the Americas so that profits from slave sales could be maximised. Over time, African merchants received better and better terms. By 1800, African traders were getting three or four times the value of goods that they were receiving in 1700, increasing considerably the price that planters on the other side of the Atlantic had to pay for their slaves. The Atlantic slave trade was, at all points, a sellers' market (Morgan, 2009: 225–29; Thornton, 1998: 72–97).

The organisation of the trade

Few early modern transatlantic trades were as complex as the Atlantic slave trade. It was inherently risky, as it involved myriad business decisions that had to be undertaken in combination with a variety of people in several places across the Atlantic world, and required a great degree of entrepreneurial skill as well as steely nerves. It is often described as the triangular trade, as ships involved in the slave trade followed a triangular route between Europe, Africa and the Americas. Goods produced in Europe were placed on ships that sailed to Africa, where these goods were exchanged for slaves. These slaves were transported to the Americas in the second leg of the voyage, usually termed the Middle Passage – a particularly risky leg of the voyage for merchants and ship captains, and a notoriously dreadful experience for traumatised African captives. On arrival in the Americas, these captives were sold in various forms of auction, with most captives becoming slaves on American plantations, producing tropical crops such as sugar, rice and similar goods. The final leg of the voyage saw ships returning to Europe, carrying either tropical produce or, more often over time, bills of exchange and specie that had been gained through the sale of slaves. If it all went well for the slave traders, which it often did not, then the profits that could be made were considerable. Evidence from Bristol and Liverpool in the 1770s and 1780s suggests that merchants could expect a rate of return between eight and ten per cent from slave-trading voyages. Such returns on invested capital were over twice what might be gained from less risky investments, such as government consols, and justified the risks and long-drawn-out nature of the voyages (Morgan, 2007: 81).

Europeans faced numerous difficulties in organising this complex trade, a trade, it should be emphasised, which involved trade cargoes that would be the equivalent of several millions of pounds sterling in today's money. Stephen Behrendt has shown how extraordinarily fine-tuned were the functionings of the transaction cycles of the Atlantic slave trade, cycles that slave traders had to get right if they were to make a profit from their merchandise. As Behrendt notes, seasonal transaction cycles shaped the direction, composition and geographical structure of the trade (Behrendt, 2001).

Even before merchants could enter into these cycles, they had to acquire finance – the slave trade was an expensive undertaking. Before 1700, slave trading was conducted mostly under the aegis of government companies that were given monopoly privileges over trade with Africa. The Dutch West India Company, founded in 1621, and the Royal African Company, founded in 1672, were two such companies. By the eighteenth century, the monopoly privileges of these companies were challenged by private traders, notably in Britain, where traders in London, Bristol and Liverpool eventually became market leaders, and in France, where similar market leadership was taken by merchants in Nantes. In good times, such as in many years of the eighteenth century, credit could easily be obtained. But in wartime, credit was squeezed. During the American Revolution, for example, the tightening of credit, and the extra military costs traders faced in defending their ships from privateering attacks, led to the volume of the British slave trade halving, and in 1778–79, when a liquidity crisis added to slave traders' problems, dropping by two-thirds.

Climatic concerns and agricultural cycles in both Africa and the Americas shaped when and how slaves were delivered to plantations. Traders wanted their ships to arrive in the most profitable markets, notably in the Caribbean and north-eastern Brazil, outside the hurricane season and during the dry-season harvest (usually between December and February in Jamaica and Rio de Janeiro), when planters had money to buy slaves and crops to send back to Europe in payment. There was a considerable increase in the number of slaves sold in this period in all the regions that specialised in growing sugar. In smaller, non-sugar-growing regions, planters were comparatively more likely to buy slaves during rainier months. Even more important, however, were African ecological patterns. In Old Calabar, for example, the ideal for African merchants and British slave traders was to buy slaves during the four-month yam harvest and sell them in the West Indies during the "in-crop" season at the start of the calendar year, when planters demanded more labourers to harvest sugar. At other places in Africa, with different ecologies and types of agricultural production, the buying of slaves might be less seasonal than year-round. Behrendt concludes: "The seasonal regularity of slave-supply lines from the African interior to coastal inlets to Atlantic ports depended upon optimal ecological conditions upon land and at sea. Non-optimal precipitation, temperature, or winds increased the likelihood that merchants and captains would not deliver slaves at predicted times, to predicted markets." The British were so successful as slave traders in the eighteenth century not only because they managed these seasonal factors very well, but also because they had more sources of supply throughout West Africa, where they could reduce the risks inherent in a time-dependent trade (Behrendt, 2009: 84–85).

Other factors were also important. Merchants were reliant upon African merchants to supply them with captives, and these African merchants in turn operated within the constraints of often volatile African political systems. European traders, in order to be successful, needed to understand how African political and economic systems operated, especially as the parts of West Africa most involved with supplying slaves to Europeans reoriented their social and political systems around the demands of the Atlantic slave trade. They needed, in particular, to establish close relationships with African merchants, which they did through paying duties and by giving preferential prices, as well as through extensive rounds of present-giving. It was only by doing this that they could evaluate levels of competition among slave buyers and sellers and thus assess the rates at which African merchants could sell slaves. Different parts of Africa required different marketing strategies. In general, merchants sent small ships to politi-cally decentralised coastal markets with intermittent slave supplies, in case it proved difficult to load captives quickly, and sent large ships to ports or lagoon sites which were politically centralised and which had the commercial infrastructures that could support large-scale slave shipments. The Windward Coast was an example of the former; Bonny and Ouidah were examples of the latter (Behrendt, 2001: 188; Law, 2004: 123–54).

The ultimate aim for slave traders was to minimise transaction costs and to maximise profits. Much of that was related to seasonality – when ships arrived in Africa, how quickly merchants could purchase and load captives, how easy slave voyages were and how little disease was experienced by slaves, and when and at what places slaves arrived in the Americas. The key part of the process was in Africa and, if they could, merchants tried to disperse their slaving voyages among as many African markets as they could in order to minimise both over-competition and delays in loading. Some European nations were better at this process than others. The Portuguese drew heavily on their contacts in Angola and were less likely than other European nations to try and diversify their sources of supply. In part, this reliance on Angola reflected the long-standing presence of a Portuguese colony there. It also reflected the ease of the linkages between Angola and Brazil – the transatlantic passage from Angola to southeast Brazil and Bahia was much shorter than transatlantic routes between Africa and the Caribbean. In addition, it reflected the unitary culture of Central Africa, allowing the Portuguese relatively easily to develop sophisticated delivery systems. One result of this close relationship between Angola and Brazil, the longest such relationship in the history of the Atlantic slave trade, was that the African cultures that developed in Brazil, especially in Bahia, were less hybrid than in other regions. Central African migration into Bahia provided Africans in this area with a common regional background. Conversely, the British had home manufacturing strengths that allowed them to trade competitively at more than 30 slaving markets north of Angola. The provenance of Africans purchased by the British was more diverse than for any other European trading nation, leading to African-American communities in British America being hybrid and ethnically mixed. What was most important to British traders was coordinating supply-and-demand cycles. They were not very concerned about meeting planters' preferences about what type of Africans they preferred to have as slaves. Planters were reluctant to be sold slaves from Old Calabar or from the Gabon River, but these were good markets where slaves could usually be bought. British merchants ignored planters' complaints about getting African captives from these places, knowing that planters' demand for slaves during the harvest season was so great that they would buy slaves regardless of the African provenance region (Miller, 1988; Behrendt, 2001: 199–201; Heywood and Thornton, 2007).

The above discussion suggests how the system was meant to work. But as the slave trade was an extraordinarily complicated system – what James Field Stanfield, in a long poem on the brutalities of the slave trade, called "the vast machine" – it was a system prone to faults. Things could go wrong at every point in the system. It might be difficult to raise capital in Europe; slaves might not be available at the right time and at the right price in Africa; the voyage across the Atlantic might be disrupted by slave rebellion or illness might break out on board; or slave ships might arrive into markets in the New World that were glutted with slaves. In such cases, the slave ship might become a living hell for crew and cargo, and the commercial environment might move from profit to financial disaster. Stanfield, a rare ordinary seaman who wrote about his experiences in front of the mast, experienced one such voyage when things went badly wrong. He left Liverpool for Benin on 7 September 1774 on the *Eagle*, under the command of David Wilson. The *Eagle* was old and leaky, and was abandoned at Benin. Stanfield lived in Africa for eight months waiting for another ship, *True Blue*, to arrive, which it did in June 1775. Wilson took command of this new ship and hired 15 sailors, including Stanfield, to take a cargo of captives to Jamaica. Stanfield portrayed Wilson as a monster. Depriving his crew and slave cargoes of food and water, he dined lavishly himself and flogged mercilessly anyone who offended him. The floggings were not done just to keep order; they were part of a campaign of terror in which there was a significant measure of sado-masochistic delight. Wilson was ill and took to his bed, but insisted that those flogged be tied to his bedpost so he could "enjoy their agonizing screams". If the sailor or slave was not flogged as hard as the captain commanded, the flogger would himself be flogged. The depravity of Wilson, Stanfield argued, had no end, even including what must have been a rape of a small girl eight or nine years old. Illness ravaged the ship, with half the crew dying, forcing Wilson to use enslaved men as sailors. Only four men who had embarked on the *Eagle*, including Stanfield, made it back to England on 15 April 1776. Earlier, in December 1775, 190 slaves had been offloaded in Kingston, Jamaica, out of 233 Africans who had been embarked in Benin. Stanfield noted how these Africans – "dumb and almost lifeless" – had been hauled onto the deck, cleaned up, and then subjected to the final indignity of sale, where the ship was rushed by "dread fiends" who "with impetuous sway, fasten rapacious on the shudd'ring prey". The scene was literally hellish, as "frantick mother calls her sever'd child" and as "one dreadful shriek assaults th' affrighted sky".[2]

The Middle Passage

The most notorious section of the triangular trade was the Middle Passage. It was one of the worst experiences in human history, where hundreds of traumatised men, women and children were sent in tightly packed, foul-smelling ships on a four-to-six-week journey across the Atlantic. Henry Smeathman, a botanist who wrote revealingly about his time in Africa, has left a vivid impression of its terrors:

> Alas! What a scene of misery and distress is a full slaved ship in the rains. The clanking of chains, the groans of the sick and the stench of the whole is scarce supportable ... two or three slaves thrown over board every day dying of fever, flux, measles, worms all together. All the day the chains rattling or the sound of the armourer riveting some poor devil just arrived in galling heavy irons.[3]

Few Africans, however, have left any evidence about their experiences of these stinking, frightful places. The most famous account is by Olaudah Equiano, who wrote a vivid account about his horror on being in a place where "the closeness of the place, and the heat of the climate added to the number in the ship, which was so crowded that each had scarcely room to turn himself". This led Equiano to reflect that "such were the horrors of my views and fears at the moment that, if ten thousand worlds had been my own, I would have freely parted with them to have exchanged my condition with that of the meanest slave in my own country". Some doubt, however, has been cast over whether Equiano was actually transported across the Atlantic. If true, then we would have virtually no direct testimony on a trade where Africans were stripped of much of their humanity and self-respect. As if to mirror that spiritual nakedness, most Africans travelled either naked or with minimal clothing or possessions. They were confined by chains, separated by gender, deprived of food and wilfully mistreated at every point of the passage.[4]

Not surprisingly, Africans were made to endure such torments only through the application of extreme force. The slave ship was a floating prison, full of weapons to keep Africans in check, and over-crewed by poorly paid seamen, a large proportion of whom succumbed to illness at some point of the triangular trade. About 15–20 per cent of British seaman undertaking service on a slaver in the eighteenth century died at some point on the several voyages in the Atlantic. This percentage was even higher than that experienced by Africans. Our best estimate of slave mortality on the Middle Passage is that 22.6 per cent of slaves died on slave ships before 1700, but that this reduced significantly over the eighteenth century, so that between 1801 and 1820 slave mortality rates were 9.6 per cent. Overall, 11.9 per cent of Africans embarking upon ships going across the Atlantic did not survive to face disembarkment. Such rates are historically high. Only 6.6 per cent of British convicts sailing on the much longer voyage from Britain to Australia perished *en route*, 1788–1814. Captives departing from ports in the Bight of Biafra died in disproportionate numbers to other Africans, with 18.3 per cent dying during the whole period, and a massive 36.8 per cent dying in voyages taken in the first half of the eighteenth century.[5]

Slave traders had good reason for over-crewing their ships. Africans did not accept their captivity aboard ships passively. Historians have discovered that there was much more resistance on slave ships than previously thought. David Richardson has counted at least 485 acts of violence done by Africans either on shore or at sea against the captains of slave ships and their crews, 90 per cent of which occurred between 1698 and 1807. These figures suggest that around one in ten voyages was affected by violence. Usually these revolts were unsuccessful and were put down with great force, but a number of revolts were successful. Africans occasionally forced slave ships to return to shore. Just as often, their acts of violence led to the total destruction of the slave ship when it was at sea. The greatest possibility of slave revolt occurred when the slave ship set sail from Africa. Captives were distraught at leaving African shores, often believing the fate that was in store for them was to be eaten by their European oppressors. The possibility of shipboard revolts made ship captains expend a great deal of money on securing their ships against attack. Richardson speculates that estimates of such costs suggest that if Africans had been more docile, then another 10 per cent, or one million slaves, might have been shipped across the Atlantic than actually were shipped. Moreover, higher levels of slave revolts in some African regions, notably Senegambia, helped to provoke political instability in these regions and made slaving activities more difficult, with the result that fewer Africans were shipped from these regions than might be expected. Thus, even if revolts failed, "they ultimately reduced the numbers of Africans forced into slavery and thus moderated the impact of the Atlantic slave trade on African societies" (McGowan, 1990: 21–22; Richardson, 2001: 72, 89).

The risk of revolts on slave ships had a major impact on how the ships were organised. In particular, it led to a dramatic increase in the number of seamen employed on ships. These seamen were employed less to sail ships than to keep order. Keeping order became easier as weaponry, especially small arms, improved substantially during the latter half of the seventeenth century, occurring alongside similar transformations in land-based armies. Guns made a great difference: sailors could aim them directly at humans with some degree of precision, and could also use them to deter potential rebels (Smallwood, 2007b: 706–8). Moreover, seamen learned on board ship the technologies of power that were used from the late seventeenth century to subdue plantation slaves on large estates. It is no accident that the rise of the very large West Indian plantation, with over 100 slaves, coincided temporally with the transformation of the English slave trade in the late seventeenth century and the evolution of more military relationships among seamen aboard slave ships. Seamen were customarily abandoned when ships reached their New World destination. A proportion of these abandoned seamen found positions as overseers on slave plantations, where what they had learnt about how to dominate slaves physically at sea stood them in good stead among slaves working on plantations.

The slave ship was a distinctive social place. It was, as Marcus Rediker argues, "a strange and potent combination of war machine, mobile prison and factory". All these functions depended upon the application of violence. The slave ship's extraordinary array of cannons and guns made it clear that the ship was able to both wage war on ships from other nations, and also defend itself from incursions from hostile European enemy ships or from pirates. Inside the ship, war also raged in a triangular fashion. Seamen were at war with captains. Rediker sees their conflict as a particularly ugly and brutal microcosm of the war between merchant capital (represented by captains) and wage labourers (seamen). The Atlantic slave trade was thus, he argues, part of a larger drama, the rise and movement of capital in the Atlantic world. Yet seamen were not just class warriors, trying and usually failing to assert themselves against highly skilled bosses, licensed to use extreme forms of power and instruments of terror to maintain proper subordination of both crew and captives. They were also complicit in the tyranny of life and death on the slave ship. The crew were the subalterns in the "vast machine". They were the prison guards who battled slaves with any weapon, physical or psychological, that they had at hand. But more than this, sailors were essential as "producers", keeping Africans alive and healthy if possible, so that they could be sold as labourers in the Americas. In producing workers for the plantations, sailors also played a crucial role in producing modern understandings of race. Africans went on board as Africans and emerged in the New World as "negroes". Sailors were hired as labourers in Europe, but became "white men" on the coast of Africa and on board the floating prison of the slave ship (Rediker, 2007, 9–10, 352; Smallwood, 2007a, 151).

Seamen occupy a curious position within the historiography of the slave trade. They were at once victims – poorly paid, proleterianised men who took up positions on slave vessels because they had few other alternatives, and oppressors – capable of horrific acts of cruelty against African captives. Contemporaries thought them, as Hugh Crow declared in 1800, "the very dregs of the community". Seamen themselves hated the trade. A satirical seaman's prayer of 1801 asked for good food and wine and "handsome doxies", but also that the penitent might be saved from the "Guinea-man and the tender". As Emma Christopher comments, "with very high mortality rates … mistreatment and slave revolt as well as all the dangers of the sea – only needy or imprudent men would enlist on a slave ship". The ill-treatment of seamen became so notorious that alleviating their plight became an early objective of campaigners against the slave trade in Britain (Christopher, 2006: 28–29).

Nevertheless, the real victims of the Middle Passage were African captives. It was a transformative event in their lives, and seldom one that signified improving life prospects. As Alexander X. Byrd writes, "the men and women who set off from one side of the Atlantic were not the same men and women who arrived at the other" (Byrd, 2008). They were people who were degraded by the process they had undergone, "socially dead" people who not only had lost their contacts in their native land, but whose experience aboard ship involved so much ritual dishonouring that it resulted in close to complete disempowerment. Male slaves, for example, were chained so tightly that they could hardly move and were forced to wallow in their own excrement, being unable to reach buckets provided to them as toilets. It made observers think them as beasts and their living environments as hellholes. A British seaman testified before parliament that "the floor of their rooms was so covered with blood and mucus which had proceeded from them having flux, that it resembled a slaughter-house ... I was so overcome by the heat, stench and foul air that I nearly fainted". The seaman could always go up on deck; the captives remained chained to fellow captives. It was extremely hard to preserve dignity in such an environment (Christopher, 2006: 167, 170).

The Middle Passage was a traumatic physical ordeal for Africans, not all of whom survived the process. It was also an emotional trauma, or ontological crisis of identity, in which Africans were disoriented by the hellish conditions in which they were placed. Olaudah Equiano described the slave ship as a "hollow place", suggesting, Smallwood argues, that at stake in the Middle Passage was African captives' "wholeness as fully embodied subjects". When Africans entered the ship, they moved from one phase, in which captives would become slaves in a system of slavery where slaves were conceived of as socially dead, to another phase, in which slaves had to work out means whereby they could preserve their humanity in an inhumane setting, where their individual worth was now assessed by how much money they might fetch at market. The slave ship, Smallwood insists, was indeed a "hollow place", distinguished by its many lacks – material and social misery, cognitive dissonance, and defencelessness in the face of the supernatural. All that was left was violence, terror, personal self-disintegration and death, physical and spiritual (Smallwood, 2007a, 125–26).

The Middle Passage was a forced migration, but one that was fundamentally different from other kinds of forced migration, because what slavers tried to do to captives was to deny their personhood. The Middle Passage was a kind of purgatory, in which people were temporarily suspended from being people. It was a limbo period that pre-dated their full commodification as slaves. We have little evidence as to what African captives thought about this process of dehumanisation, but we can see its manifestations in the dry accounting records of slavers, where deaths aboard ship were duly tabulated – "thin and dyed of a flux", "fell overboard in the night and was lost". Only occasionally do captives as individuals emerge in records, and usually then only *in extremis*. One rare example came in the trial of James D'Wolf, a New England slave captain, accused of murdering a woman suspected of having smallpox and thus likely to infect other slaves. One of D'Wolf's sailors testified that D'Wolf "lashed her in a Chair & ty'd a Mask round her Eyes and Mouth & there was a tackle hooked upon the Slings round the Chair when we lowered her down on the starboard side of the Vessel". Cranston was asked whether the woman made any noise as she was hoisted aloft (D'Wolf did want to touch her and thus get smallpox) and then thrown into the sea. He explained that the mask tied around was done so as to "prevent her making any Noise that the other Slaves might not hear, least they should rise". The answer was significant. Slave captains might not see captives as humans, but as commodities that could be disposed of without ceremony. Nevertheless, they were forced to recognise that captives were peculiar kinds of commodities because they always remained human enough that other humans might "rise" when a captive was callously murdered. Even here, however, the individual slave was silenced, literally in this case (Rediker, 2007: 343–44).

Volume and distribution

A vexed issue in the history of the Atlantic slave trade is the number of Africans involved as unwilling migrants. Until the mid-twentieth century, historians could only guess at the numbers involved, making the Atlantic slave trade similar to that other great Atlantic imponderable, the extent of demographic catastrophe among Native Americans following the Columbian encounter. A giant step forward was made in 1969 with the publication of Philip Curtin's painstaking reconstruction from primary sources of the volume of traffic across the Atlantic. Curtin suggested that just over 11 million slaves were transported to the Americas over four centuries. Brazil received about 4 million of these slaves, while similar numbers went to the Caribbean (Curtin, 1969). Since Curtin's pioneering contribution, historians have worked hard to refine the numbers that he presented. Foremost among these refinements has been the work of a group of scholars, headed by David Eltis, David Richardson, Herbert S. Klein and Stephen D. Behrendt. These scholars published a database on CD-Rom in 1999 that stands as a monument to the possibilities of collaborative work in the humanities. The database was revised again and published as a publicly accessible website in 2008. The database lists as much information as possible about 34,941 slave voyages between 1501 and 1866. It does not, and never will, list all voyages that set out to obtain slaves, as not all records survive. But the database does give us a wealth of information that allows for in-depth investigations of this singular historical event. It probably has some details of about 80 per cent of all slave voyages that took place in the Atlantic slave trade.[6]

According to their best estimates, the total number of people leaving Africa in the Atlantic slave trade between 1501 and 1866 was 12,521,336. Of this number, 10,702,656 are known to have disembarked from the ships they were carried on. The slave trade started slowly, with 44,909 people involved in the first half of the sixteenth century, and 154,376 placed on ships between 1551 and 1600. The trade increased in volume during the seventeenth and eighteenth centuries, reaching its peak in the latter half of the eighteenth century, when 3,440,981 Africans were transported out of Africa. The abolition of the slave trade by the British and the United States, and the destruction of Saint Domingue in a slave revolt, reduced the inexorable growth of the trade, but the development of a flourishing plantation system in Cuba and the continued vitality of slavery in Brazil meant that over 3 million Africans participated in the Atlantic slave trade between 1801 and 1850.

The largest European carriers were the Portuguese (and, in the nineteenth century, the Brazilians). The Portuguese started first in the trade and finished last. They carried 5,848,265 Africans, mostly to Brazil. They accounted for nearly 47 per cent of all slaves who embarked on slave voyages. Britain was the next biggest European carrier, taking 3,259,440 Africans to the British West Indies and British North America. The British were most important in the eighteenth century, carrying 964,634 Africans between 1701 and 1750 and 1,580,658 between 1751 and 1800. In that latter half century, the French joined them as major carriers, taking 758,978 to their flourishing West Indian colonies. Spain became an important European carrier in the nineteenth century, while the Netherlands and Denmark also transported slaves to their West Indian possessions. The United States was involved only for the last quarter century of the eighteenth century and the first decade of the nineteenth century, but managed to transport 305,326 Africans out of Africa, of whom 252,653 disembarked in the United States.

North America, however, was not a principal destination for slave traders. Only 472,381 Africans arrived in the region that became the United States before 1807. Brazil was easily the most important region of disembarkation, accounting for 5,532,118 or 52 per cent of Africans who survived the Middle Passage. Of these, 2,608,573 went to south-east Brazil, 1,736,308 arrived in Bahia, and 960,475 went to Pernambuco. Most of the remaining slaves went to the Caribbean. Jamaica had the most with 1,212,351; but Saint Domingue with 911,142, Cuba with 889,990, and Barbados with 608,958 were also substantial slave importers. The height of importations into the Caribbean came in the eighteenth century. Over 2 million Africans were landed in the British Caribbean in that century. Over 800,000 slaves went to the French Caribbean, mostly to Saint Domingue, in the last half of the eighteenth century, with imports in the 1780s particularly high. In the nineteenth century, Brazil once more became the major destination for Africans: 2,367,329 arrived there between 1801 and 1850.

The Africans transported to the Americas came from a wide range of African locations. Using the regional classifications employed in the Trans-Atlantic Slave Trade Database, the largest provenance region was West-Central Africa, from where 5,694,574 Africans left over four centuries.[7] A further 2 million left from the Bight of Benin, while Biafra and the Gold Coast both accounted for more than 1 million captives apiece. The importance of different regions changed over time. In the sixteenth century, Senegambia sent more slaves to the Americas than any other region. But by the seventeenth century, the most important provenance region was West-Central Africa. This region remained important into the mid-nineteenth century as a source of African slaves. In the early eighteenth century, the Gold Coast was an important source of slaves but it was eclipsed during that century by the Bights of Benin and Biafra. Sierra Leone was a smaller source of supply than the two Bights, but it peaked as a place for acquiring slaves in the late eighteenth and early nineteenth centuries.

Sale in America

The final, and least studied, part of the triangular trade was the sale of captives in the Americas. The arrival of a slave ship in an American port was hard to escape: slave vessels were notorious for their stench. Most ships disembarked captives at a pre-arranged port, but if the port seemed glutted with slaves, they might try to sail to another port within the same imperial jurisdiction. After duties were paid and sick slaves (or "refuse") were unloaded and sold at taverns for whatever slave factors could get for them, the factor in charge of selling sold slaves, probably by auction. The likely purchasers were either planters or merchants, with merchants becoming more prominent in the trade over time. By the mid-eighteenth century, at least in Jamaica, a retail trade in slaves, conducted in merchant pens in Kingston, existed alongside a wholesale trade in captives, usually conducted on ship or on rooms near the docks. Purchasers tended to pay by credit, meaning that wealthier purchasers, especially merchants with lines of credit, were favoured in the auctions through which slaves were sold. In the mid-eighteenth century, 65 per cent of the purchasers of slaves in Kingston were Kingston residents, buying 73 per cent of all slaves. The average number of slaves bought per purchaser was nine. Men received higher prices than women, and although planters expressed preferences for certain ethnicities rather than others, prices tended to be influenced by the quality of individual slaves and the time of arrival rather than by African place of origin (Burnard and Morgan, 2001).

An analysis of Royal African Company records of slave sales for the late seventeenth and early eighteenth centuries in Jamaica shows that, although merchants and planters may have wanted to purchase slaves who came from the Gold Coast and Slave Coast regions of West Africa, in practice they got slaves from wherever they could. Few planters stocked their plantations with slaves from just one region of Africa. Of 22 slave purchasers who bought sizeable parcels of slaves, all bought from more than one general area of West Africa, with 17 buying slaves from at least three regions. Sir Henry Morgan, the buccaneer governor, was typical. He bought 67 slaves in the early 1680s, 14 from the Gold Coast, 20 from the Bight of Benin, 28 from the Bight of Biafra and five from unspecified places in Africa. The end result was that in any plantation of any size in Jamaica, there would be slaves from a variety of African regions. Moreover, slave purchasers tended to buy small numbers of slaves from large numbers of slave shipments. It was therefore unlikely that more than four or six slaves on any plantation would have come from the same vessel arriving in Jamaica. The result was that slave gangs were ethnically diverse – a function of the dispersed way in which Africans were sold. We can track the ethnic origins of slaves owned by 11 substantial planters in one Jamaican parish, St John, in 1680. These men owned 299 slaves, with 128 coming from the Gold Coast, 81 from Biafra, 54 from Benin, 19 from Senegambia and 17 from Central Africa. The regional origins of the first African slaves bought by Jamaican sugar planters in the latter third of the seventeenth century were heterogeneous (Burnard, 2007: 145–51).

One implication of these findings is that the process of sale increased the degree of social alienation that Africans faced when arriving in the Americas. Commodification was a psychologically arduous process that left Africans, now slaves, disoriented. That disorientation was enhanced by how slaves were sold – as individuals or as a set of a few people, in a several-stage process that encompassed being treated like livestock on arrival; being conducted to a merchants' yard, where, Equiano tells us, "we were all pent up together like so many sheep in a fold, without regard to sex or age"; and then sold, possibly in a "scramble", more likely by individual negotiation between merchant and planter, and transferred to a plantation where a slave was "seasoned" or "broken" so that he or she could become a suitable slave. By the last stage in the process, the commodification and dehumanisation of the African was close to complete. It was not unusual for Africans to feel completely isolated and alone, probably because they were lost from their countrymen and countrywomen. Equiano speaks movingly about the pain of separation and the feelings of isolation and hopelessness he felt as he went through the several stages of sale and transformation into a chattel slave: "Not saleable among the rest, I now totally lost the small remains of comfort I had enjoyed in conversing with my countrymen; the women too, who used to wash and take care of me, were all gone different ways, and I never saw one of them again." Within a little time, "only myself was left … grieving and pining, and wishing for death".[8] What Equiano was feeling was extreme marginalisation, a kind of social death marked by an absence of kin, a reduction of personhood as a person became property, and the suffering of social abnegation. As Smallwood suggests, "If in the regime of the market, Africans' most socially relevant feature was their exchangeability, for Africans as immigrants the most socially relevant feature was their isolation, their desperate need to restore some measure of social life to counterbalance the alienation engendered by their social death." (Smallwood, 2007a: 189).

Legacies

As the largest forced migration in history, the Atlantic slave trade left an enduring impact on the Atlantic world. Its impact on Africa continues to be debated, although there is now a consensus that the larger claims for the slave trade being systematically responsible for African underdevelopment cannot be substantiated. The relationship between the slave trade and the development of capitalism continues to be debated 65 years after Eric Williams introduced the question by claiming that the profits of the transatlantic slave trade and colonial slavery played a crucial role in Britain's industrial revolution. The stronger version of Williams' thesis is no longer sustainable but, as Kenneth Morgan shows, there were significant links between Atlantic trade in general and the Atlantic slave trade in particular, and British (and by extension European) economic development. The linkages were not direct: private fortunes made in the slave trade, and in plantation produce resulting from the labour of people acquired in the slave trade, had limited effects on metropolitan capital accumulation. What the slave trade did do, however, especially in Britain, where business practices were most sophisticated, was accentuate demand for manufactures and help make more sophisticated and effective business institutions, such as long-term credit, banks and marine insurance. So too, as Joseph Inikori argues, was the role of West Africa as a market for European manufactures. The amount of the trade was significant. But what was more important was the crucial role the West African market played in instigating improvements to manufacturing technologies. In Britain, these developments contributed considerably to industrial development (Morgan, 2000: 94–98; Inikori, 2002).

The slave trade may also have contributed to cultural development. It played, as Matt Childs writes in Chapter 10 of this volume, an important role in disseminating African cultures into the New World. Scholars have been very concerned with correlating specific streams of African migrants to specific cultural forms in the Americas, such as slave culture in Bahia, which James Sweet (2003) sees very much as a derivation of Angolan culture; and the development of rice culture in South Carolina, which Judith Carney (2003) attributes to patterns of migration to the region that brought people from rice cultivating areas in Africa to low-country plantations. (For criticism of Carney's methodologies, see Eltis *et al.*, 2007.) Tracing such cultural survivals is important, in part because it suggests that creative elements of Atlantic culture could emerge even from the slave ship. Nevertheless, it is somewhat perverse to look at the slave ship as a place of cultural creation when it was overwhelmingly a place of terror and violence and, for many, a place of death. Joseph Miller has argued, in a magnificent overview of all aspects of the slave trade, that in the Angolan trade to Brazil so many Africans died in Africa, in the Middle Passage, and in Brazil that the survivors probably amounted to about one in three of those caught up in it (Miller, 1988).

Yet some did survive the slave trade and left descendants to wonder about what its legacies mean. In some ways, it is the musings of these descendants who give us the best understanding of a trade that, for all its importance, left few first-hand accounts of its true horrors – we know nothing, really, about life in the darkness below decks, what Stanfield call the "noisome cave" that from above seemed "rank maw, belched up in morbid stream/The hot mist thickens in a side-long beam". What happened there can only be reclaimed through imagination. That process of reclamation is difficult, as the novelist Caryl Phillips shows in two books, one a novel imagining the slave trade, the other a travelogue with novelistic elements that insists that there is not a historical disjuncture between the slave trade and contemporary black diasporas; and as Saidiya Hartman illustrates in her moving, poignant but problematic memoir of her personal experience as a modern African-American wanting modern Africans to acknowledge their role in facilitating the slave trade (Phillips, 1994, 2000; Hartman, 2007). Both writers caution us against seeing the Atlantic slave trade as past and as resolved. For them, and for historians trying to understand this trade, the ordeal of the Atlantic slave trade is part of a continuing history of exploitation and resistance in West Africa, Europe and the Americas that shows the willingness of the rich to victimise and dehumanise the poor and the lost.

Notes

1 Drescher also makes the point that European distaste for enslaving fellow Europeans was overcome in the mid-twentieth century as Nazi Germany created a short-lived but extensive slave society.
2 James Field Stanfield, *The Guinea Voyage, A Poem in Three Books* (London: James Phillips, 1789).
3 Cited in Miles Ogburn, *Global Lives: Britain and the World 1550–1800* (Cambridge: Cambridge University Press, 2008), 212–13.
4 Handler (2009); Olaudah Equiano, *The Interesting Narrative of the Life of Olaudah Equiano* (London, 1789), ed. Vincent Carretta, 2nd edn (New York: Penguin Putnam, 2003); Vincent Carretta, *Equiano, the African: Biography of a Self-Made Man* (London: Penguin, 2005), xiv–xv.
5 Klein *et al.* (2001). An especially vivid evocation of the Middle Passage is given in Rediker (2007).
6 The authors of the database estimate that the total number of voyages that set out to obtain slaves in the Atlantic slave trade was 43,600, on which 12.5 million captives embarked. Some problems remain that are an inevitable part of the process by which records were organised. For example, the database selects, rather arbitrarily, eight provenance regions in Africa from which captives were obtained, but these regions correspond only imperfectly to Africanists' understandings of African regions and linguistic groupings (www.slavevoyages.org).
7 These regional classifications are imperfect and reflect more European ideas of African cultures than African realities.
8 Equiano, *The Interesting Narrative of the Life of Olaudah Equiano, op. cit.*, 61–62.

Bibliography

Behrendt, Stephen D., "Markets, Transaction Cycles, and Profits: Merchant Decision Making in the British Slave Trade", *William and Mary Quarterly* 58 (2001), 171–204.

Behrendt, Stephen D., "Ecology, Seasonality, and the Transatlantic Slave Trade", in Bernard Bailyn, ed., *Soundings in Atlantic History: Latent Structures and Intellectual Currents, 1500–1830* (Cambridge, MA: Harvard University Press, 2009).

Blackburn, Robin, *The Making of New World Slavery: From the Baroque to the Modern, 1492–1800* (London: Verso, 1997).

Burnard, Trevor, "The Atlantic Slave Trade and African Ethnicities in Seventeenth-Century Jamaica", in David Richardson, Suzanne Schwarz and Anthony Tibbles, eds, *Liverpool and Transatlantic Slavery* (Liverpool: Liverpool University Press, 2007), 139–64.

Burnard, Trevor and Kenneth Morgan, "The Dynamics of the Slave Market and Slave Purchasing Patterns in Jamaica, 1655–1788", *William and Mary Quarterly* 58 (2001), 205–28.

Byrd, Alexander X., *Captives and Voyagers: Black Migrants across the Eighteenth-Century British Atlantic World* (Baton Rouge: Louisiana State University Press, 2008).

Carney, Judith, *Black Rice: The African Origins of Rice Cultivation in the Americas* (Cambridge, MA: Harvard University Press, 2003).

Christopher, Emma, *Slave Ship Sailors and their Captive Cargoes, 1730–1807* (Cambridge: Cambridge University Press, 2006).

Curtin, Philip D., *The Atlantic Slave Trade: A Census* (Madison: University of Wisconsin Press, 1969).

Drescher, Seymour, "White Atlantic? The Choice for African Slave Labor in the Plantation Americas", in David Eltis, Frank D. Lewis and Kenneth L. Sokoloff, eds, *Slavery in the Development of the Americas* (Cambridge: Cambridge University Press, 2004).

Eltis, David, *The Rise of African Slavery in the Americas* (Cambridge: Cambridge University Press, 2000).

Eltis, David and David Richardson, "A New Assessment of the Transatlantic Slave Trade", in David Eltis and David Richardson, eds, *Extending the Frontiers: Essays on the New Transatlantic Slave Trade Database* (New Haven: Yale University Press, 2008).

Eltis, David and David Richardson, eds, *Extending the Frontiers: Essays on the New Transatlantic Slave Trade Database* (New Haven: Yale University Press, 2008).

Eltis, David, Philip D. Morgan and David Richardson, "Agency and Diaspora in Atlantic History: Reassessing the African Contribution to Rice Cultivation in the Americas", *American Historical Review* 112 (2007), 1329–58.

Handler, Jerome S., "The Middle Passage and the Material Culture of Captive Africans", *Slavery & Abolition* 30 (2009), 1–26.

Harms, Robert, *The Diligent: A Voyage through the Worlds of the Slave Trade* (New York: Basic Books, 2002).

Hartman, Saidiya, *Lose Your Mother: A Journey along the Atlantic Slave Route* (New York: Farrar, Strauss and Giroux, 2007).

Heywood, Linda M. and John K. Thornton, *Central Africans, Atlantic Creoles, and the Foundations of the Americas, 1585–1660* (New York: Cambridge University Press, 2007).

Inikori, Joseph, *Africans and the Industrial Revolution in England: A Study in International Trade and Economic Development* (Cambridge: Cambridge University Press, 2002).

Klein, Herbert S., Stanley L. Engerman, Robin Haines and Ralph Shlomowitz, "Transoceanic Mortality: The Slave Trade in Comparative Perspective", *William and Mary Quarterly* 58 (2001), 93–118.

Law, Robin, "'Here is No Resisting the Country': The Realities of Power in Afro-European Relations on the West African 'Slave Coast'", *Itinerario* 18 (1994), 50–64.

Law, Robin, *Ouidah: The Social History of a West African Slaving "Port" 1727–1892* (Athens, OH and London: Ohio University Press and James Currey, 2004).

Miller, Joseph C., *Way of Death: Merchant Capitalism and the Angolan Slave Trade 1730–1830* (Madison: University of Wisconsin Press, 1988).

McGowan, Winston, "African Resistance to the Atlantic Slave Trade in West Africa", *Slavery and Abolition* 11 (1990), 5–29.

Morgan, Kenneth, *Slavery, Trade and the British Economy, 1660–1800* (Cambridge: Cambridge University Press, 2000).

Morgan, Kenneth, *Slavery and the British Empire: From Africa to America* (Oxford: Oxford University Press, 2007).

Morgan, Philip D., "Africa and the Atlantic, c. 1450–1820", in Jack P. Greene and Philip D. Morgan, eds, *Atlantic History: A Critical Appraisal* (New York: Oxford University Press, 2009).

Osterhammel, Jürgen and Niels P. Petersson, *Globalization* (Princeton: Princeton University Press, 2005).

Patterson, Orlando, *Slavery and Social Death: A Comparative Study* (Cambridge, MA: Harvard University Press, 1982).

Phillips, Caryll, *Crossing the River* (London: Bloomsbury, 1994).

Phillips, Caryll, *The Atlantic Sound* (London: Faber and Faber, 2000).

Postma, Menne, *The Dutch in the Atlantic Slave Trade, 1600–1815* (Cambridge: Cambridge University Press, 1991).

Rawley, James A., *The Transatlantic Slave Trade: A History*, revised edn (Lincoln: University of Nebraska Press, 2005).

Rediker, Marcus, *The Slave Ship: A Human History* (New York: Penguin, 2007).

Richards, Eric, *Britannia's Children: Emigration from England, Scotland, Wales and Ireland since 1600* (London: Hambledon & London, 2004).

Richardson, David, "Shipboard Revolts, African Authority, and the Atlantic Slave Trade", *William and Mary Quarterly* 58 (2001), 68–92.

Richardson, David, Suzanne Schwarz and Anthony Tibbles, eds, *Liverpool and Transatlantic Slavery* (Liverpool: Liverpool University Press, 2007).

Smallwood, Stephanie E., *Saltwater Slavery: A Middle Passage from Africa to American Diaspora* (Cambridge, MA: Harvard University Press, 2007a).

Smallwood, Stephanie, "African Guardians, European Slave Ships, and the Changing Dynamics of Power in the Early Modern Atlantic", *William and Mary Quarterly* 64 (2007b), 679–716.

Solow, Barbara, "Slavery and Colonization", in Barbara Solow, ed., *Slavery and the Rise of the Atlantic System* (Cambridge: Cambridge University Press, 1991), 21–42.

Sweet, James H., *Recreating Africa: Culture, Kinship, and Religion in the African-Portuguese World, 1441–1770* (Chapel Hill: University of North Carolina Press, 2003).

Thornton, John K., *Africa and Africans in the Making of the Atlantic World, 1400–1800*, 2nd edn (Cambridge: Cambridge University Press, 1998).

Voyages: The Trans-Atlantic Slave Trade Database, www.slavevoyages.org

Part 2

THE CHARACTER OF SLAVERY

6

WORK AND THE SLAVE ECONOMY

Lorena Walsh

Introduction

Acute labour shortages prevailed in almost all colonies that Europeans established in the New World. Given the high costs of transportation across the Atlantic and the reluctance of ordinary Europeans to risk their lives in strange lands, free migrants could not develop outposts and produce enough profits to sustain colonial enterprises. Europeans tried to remedy the shortfall by appropriating the labour of Native Americans outright, or by recruiting and shipping European indentured and convict servants. Portuguese trade and colonization in Africa opened up possibilities for exploiting a new source of labour: enslaved Africans. These labourers were captured from rival European ships or colonies, or purchased as commodities in Africa in a form of commerce in people unregulated by European law or precedent. They were subsequently treated as commodities, without recourse to the residual rights that European migrants were accorded, or to the occasional protections European intruders extended to native inhabitants.

Early staple regimes

The labour system that evolved in the first half of the seventeenth century involved intense and unremitting forced labour. In the frenetic years of first settlement, when immediate profits were the primary goal and immigrant life spans were often measured in months rather than years, the full benefits of hereditary slavery were seldom realized. Enslaved Indians were decimated by European diseases. Transported Europeans fared only marginally better in unaccustomed New World disease environments. Africans, too, suffered high death rates, but in the tropics a higher proportion survived than did Europeans, creating the stereotype that Africans were uniquely suited to working in hot climates. Where supplies of new Africans were readily available, however, labour owners were loath to forego immediate profits in order to encourage future natural increase.

Initially, Africans were set to work clearing land, raising livestock, and growing staple crops such as tobacco, cotton, and sugar. Labour forces often included a mix of enslaved Africans, Native American servants or slaves, and European servants. Mixed workforces proved inconvenient for the labour-owning elite, since the presence of bound workers who had some minimal legal protections made it harder fully to exploit the unprotected Africans, and harder to wring maximum profit from their costly investment in slaves. Consequently, as soon as elites could purchase enough Africans, they assigned them to

101

separate quarters where they could more readily cut rations, ratchet up work quotas, and impose harsher discipline.

Another reason for separating slaves from servants was that the one area in which slaves had privileges that servants did not was sexual relations and child bearing. A servant woman was severely punished for depriving the owner of her labour by giving birth to a child while in service. On the other hand, sex was tolerated among labourers bound for life, since transgressors could not be punished by adding extra time to their term. Owners recognized that however inconvenient children might be in the short term, they might profit in the long run from the sale or labour of surviving children. Separating slaves from servants thus furthered both profit and plantation discipline. The next step, which started among the richest tier of planters and later trickled down to less wealthy planters, was to make a full transition to a system in which all field workers were enslaved Africans, and in which only a few European servants, whose status was enhanced with special privileges to discourage their making common cause with slaves, were retained for craft and supervisory positions (Beckles, 1985, 21–45; Walsh, 2010).

Historians of slave work patterns initially devoted most attention to the technological requirements and cycles of planting, harvesting, and processing dictated by demanding staple crops such as sugar, cotton, rice, and tobacco, and to the organization and work patterns required in industrial enterprises such as gold mining, iron mining, and manufacturing. These studies have greatly expanded understanding of slaves' work routines in major staple-growing regions, where the seasonal rhythms of particular crops shaped the lives of all residents, enslaved and free. Studies have also looked at other cash crops and extractive industries – indigo, coffee, cacao, naval stores, cattle-penning, and lumbering, for example – the labour demands of which similarly shaped the lives of those compelled to produce them (Berlin and Morgan, 1993: 2–3).

The limitations of staple-centred studies have also become apparent. When lucrative staple crops were first adopted, most efforts were directed to producing them. Virtual monoculture was, however, a phase of early development that almost universally gave way to a more diverse array of cash crops and other income-generating activities. Whatever the requirements of the primary crop, diversification changed the work that slaves were forced to do, and was accompanied by increasing uniformity in the number of days slaves worked per year. Only comparative analyses across crops and regions can disentangle local innovations and shifts related to changes in the composition of the enslaved population from widely shared pan-Atlantic patterns (Berlin, 1998; Morgan, 1998).

Staple-centred accounts also describe generic and, by implication, unchanging work routines and management decisions. While slave-owners invariably sought to profit from their investment in, or inheritance of, bound labourers, their willingness to innovate, tolerance for risk, and levels of attention to business varied. Differing management styles adopted by planter families affected the nature and intensity of the work performed by enslaved men, women, and children attached to their estates. Similarly, Africans faced different challenges of adaptation and acculturation than did native-born workers. Recent studies of individual plantations or family estates reveal how diversification, the addition of complementary crops to the primary staple crop, and the adoption of more elements of labour-intensive Old World agriculture altered and increased the work required of the enslaved in a way generalized accounts cannot convey. Plantation histories, informed by evidence about the composition of enslaved workforces, and the varying skills, coping strategies, modes of resistance, and material conditions of Africans and creoles, provide concrete insights into the evolution of slave culture and communities. Finally, a focus on individual plantations illuminates the unique challenges posed by local environments, and the kinds of agricultural and self-provisioning expertise slaves developed in particular ecosystems (Walsh, 1997; Higman, 1998; Roberts, 2006; Nelson, 2007).

Gender was the most crucial determinant of slaves' occupations. Native American and African women had a more prominent role in agriculture than did women in European societies in both the Old and New Worlds. New World slave-owners appropriated the gender conventions of the enslaved to the detriment of women. The reasons are obscure, as the practice emerged in the sparsely documented first half of the seventeenth century. Colonists knew about Native American and West African work customs, but given their sense of ethnic superiority, the Europeans might be expected to have imposed their own gender conventions on the enslaved rather than to adopt those of other groups whom they considered culturally inferior. Indeed, in colonies where slavery remained peripheral, slave-owners followed European gender conventions defining men's and women's work. Enslaved Native American women were present in most colonies, but seldom in large numbers, and they were most often assigned domestic duties rather than field labour. Larger numbers of Native American women, however, were enslaved in the sugar-growing regions of Brazil, where in the late 1500s they were set to the same field labour as men. When African slavery replaced Indian slavery in the early 1600s, the sugar growers continued this practice (Schwartz, 1985; Beckles, 1999).

Slaveholders in all early European staple-growing colonies probably copied labour allocation practices developed by Brazilian sugar growers in the first decades of the 1600s, although evidentiary proof of such copying is absent. We do know that African women were commonly assigned to agricultural labour with work requirements equal to those of men in Virginia and Barbados in the 1640s, and on Martinique and Guadeloupe no later than the 1650s. Barbadian and Chesapeake planters also used indentured European servant women in tobacco, cotton, and sugar fields whenever merchants transported more women and girls than were needed for domestic service. In the case of the Europeans, qualms about this violation of gender conventions stemmed mainly from the adverse effect the practice had on servant recruitment in England. The high proportion of women in African cargoes, rather than planters' knowledge of women's active role in farming in their homelands, may have been sufficient reason for assigning most African women to the fields (Beckles, 1985; Brown, 1996; Moitt, 2001; Morgan, 2004). Enslaved males were also forced to perform activities, such as hoeing crops and winnowing and pounding grain, that the Africans would have considered traditional women's work. Imposition of unaccustomed kinds of labour was one method, albeit an unknowing one, that slave-owners employed to enforce racial supremacy on enslaved men (Beckles, 1999; Carney, 2001).

Slave-owners' abandonment of European conceptions about work appropriate for women helped reinforce stereotypes of African and African-American women as unfeminine, uniquely suited to hard unskilled labour, brutish in nature, and capable only of limited emotional and intellectual development. Such stereotypes led to a devaluation of maternity, with forced hard labour during pregnancy contributing to low fertility, high infant mortality, and low birth weights, coupled with a disregard for motherhood.

Over time, colonists revised their conceptions of enslaved men's capabilities, but not those of enslaved women (Beckles, 1999).

Agricultural intensification

As early-settled islands and coastal regions of mainland plantation colonies matured, the work assigned to slaves was no longer limited to clearing, farm building, and cultivation of a staple, along with food – and sometimes livestock – for on-plantation consumption. Having reaped the windfall benefits of farming virgin soils, diminishing returns set in. Planters averse to change had to be satisfied with smaller outputs of staple crops per worker or else to establish new quarters where slaves replicated extractive monocultures on lands further in the interior or on newly settled islands. Otherwise, planters needed to find technologies that could significantly expand output per worker (as in tidal rice culture) to counter the periodic gluts in supply and falling prices that inevitably followed increased output of a new staple (Eltis, 2000; Walsh, 2010). Alternatively, they compensated for smaller yields of the primary staple by making slaves work in other cash crops, or in fishing or lumbering.

The result was increased slaves' workload. Common solutions adopted in the first half of the eighteenth century were raising more livestock and further processing of staple crops. In Barbados, sugar planters changed from exporting raw muscadavo sugar to whiter, more refined, clayed sugar. They also began raising more cattle and routinely setting slaves to manuring cane fields, adding a further work requirement that became one of the most arduous tasks field workers had to perform. In Virginia, growers of sweet-scented tobacco had their workers stem tobacco leaves, which added value and allowed more tobacco to be pressed into a hogshead, thus saving on freight. Throughout much of the tidewater Chesapeake, planters also began raising surplus corn for market. Increased outputs were achieved by training slaves to use ploughs to prepare ground for planting and later for weeding. This technological change got around two bottlenecks. One was in the spring, when hoe technology alone imposed limits on the numbers of hills workers could prepare in time for planting tobacco and corn; the other in mid-summer, when both crops required extensive weeding. As a consequence, slaves had to spend more time in off-season ground preparation and in making fences to protect larger fields. In addition, night work began to be imposed for tasks such as stripping tobacco and husking and shelling corn that could be done by firelight.

South Carolina planters substituted diked tidal irrigation for freshwater swamp irrigation for rice, overcoming dual problems of flooding and drought. A steady supply of water drowned weeds, reducing the time slaves spent weeding. Decreased weeding, however, was more than offset by increased ploughing-under of rice stubble after harvest, and by the addition of hated "mud work" – constructing and maintaining embankments and ditches in winter. Hand processing of the increased volume of rice also taxed slaves to the limit in the post-harvest season. Until effective water-powered rice mills were developed in the 1770s, beating rice in a mortar and pestle to remove hulls was so arduous that stints of pounding at the mortar were imposed morning and evening, and extended late into the night during the winter (Chaplin, 1993; Edelson, 2006).

These mid-eighteenth century innovations in staple agriculture were colonial solutions to the problem of declining profits. They were effective because there were few restrictions on planters' ability to increase the slaves' workloads. In the early 1750s, however, a few elite planters in the Chesapeake and in the British West Indies turned agricultural "improvers," rejecting colonial land-extensive, labour-saving methods for modified versions of "English husbandry" that they considered economically and culturally superior. In the Chesapeake, improving planters replaced less labour-intensive rotation of fields for more labour-intensive rotation of crops. In the West Indies, early improvers also advocated using ploughs to minimize slaves' work in ground preparation and weeding. Initially, few of the crusaders' contemporaries embraced such radical changes (Sheridan, 1960; Edelson, 2006; Walsh, 2010).

At the end of the Seven Years' War, three developments propelled larger-scale planters throughout the British Empire into adopting Old World improvement schemes. First, grain shortages in Europe raised the price of wheat, encouraging planters in the Chesapeake and South Carolina either to increase acreage devoted to wheat, or to switch to it entirely. Second, the campaigns of the Seven Years' War revealed the strategic weaknesses of colonies with large black majorities, as well as exposing the naked violence that undergirded the empire's most valuable colonial possessions. This led to the first serious questioning of the morality and efficacy of British colonial slavery, both in the metropolis and in the colonies. Planters throughout the colonies responded to criticisms of their labour system by adopting more elements of English husbandry that they hoped would make colonial agriculture more profitable, and slavery less exploitative and perhaps eventually unnecessary. Third, beginning with the 1765 Stamp Act Crisis, the planter elite on the mainland generated a widespread resolve to diversify crops and to promote home manufactures so that colonists could better mount an effective campaign of commercial resistance to Britain and reduce the economic vulnerability inherent in single-staple colonies.

Although many elite planters contented themselves with reducing consumption of British manufactures and setting a few slaves to making coarse cloth, others concluded that a total reorganization of agriculture was imperative in order to counter British tyranny and to achieve economic independence. Chesapeake planters began devising plans for three- to six-course crop rotations (some including tobacco and some not) on continuously cultivated fields. By the early 1770s, a few planters had implemented these ambitious changes. The South Carolina elite turned older rice plantations in the vicinity of Charleston into grain-and-produce farms, directed more to provisioning and providing timber and firewood for Charleston than to generating profits from rice and indigo. Slaves in long-settled areas suddenly found themselves putting in more time on secondary than on staple crops. They spent more days ploughing ground for small grains, making fences to protect expanded corn and wheat acreage, raising fodder or creating water meadows, caring for livestock and dairying, hauling and digging-in manure, and growing or harvesting tertiary crops and firewood for sale in urban or regional markets. The work that enslaved men (and to a much lesser extent enslaved women) were required to do changed dramatically as planters diversified their crop mix and adopted more labour-saving technologies (Walsh, 1989; Edelson, 2006).

In British North America, the outbreak of war in 1775 brought an end to non-essential investments. Within two years nothing was being produced except subsistence crops. Throughout the American South, slaves were set to raising cotton, a step toward increased self-sufficiency that was retained well into the 1800s. In the West Indies, the closing of the provisioning trade after 1776 forced planters to put slaves to raising more food crops. On Barbados, slaves grew more food and livestock, and began raising cotton as a secondary crop. Still, in the 1790s Barbadian slaves spent only one-third of their time on sugar, dividing the rest of their time between cotton and provisions. Jamaica planters were less inclined to sacrifice maximum sugar production to grow more provisions, but some added coffee as a secondary crop to fill in slack periods in the sugar cycle, while at the same time requiring enslaved workers to raise more food in their own time (Walsh, 1995; Roberts, 2008).

After the American Revolution, the nature of slaves' work changed again. In the Chesapeake, the closing of continental tobacco markets at the onset of the French Revolution prompted most tidewater planters to abandon tobacco. Only in the Virginia Piedmont and Southside and on Maryland's lower western shore did slaves regularly tend tobacco after 1792. In the rest of the region, slaves were put to European-style mixed farming with wheat as the primary cash crop. The improving planter elite promoted wheat as a less arduous, less destructive, and morally superior crop. Moreover, planters who favoured gradual slave emancipation argued that the lesser toil associated with wheat would contribute to a decrease in the size of workforces and to increased manumissions. This might have been the case if wheat were the only crop slave-owners raised. A study of work logs at Mount Vernon in the 1790s reveals that George Washington's enslaved field hands spent only a fifth of their time working in wheat. Growing corn and caring for and raising food for livestock each required more hours per year than did the cash crop. When other chores and crops are added in, Mount Vernon and other grain-farm slaves worked almost as many hours a year as did sugar hands on Barbados. Wheat enthusiasts routinely glossed over the many hours slaves had to spend producing forage crops and ploughing in the volume of green and animal manure required just to maintain yields. The further work of marling or plastering to remedy overly acidic tidewater soils still lay in the future (Walsh, 1989; Roberts, 2008).

On the western frontier of the United States, in contrast, slaves were uprooted from homes in the east to clear land and to raise tobacco, cotton, and sugar with older colonial-style labour-saving methods on the more fertile soils of the interior. Production expenses were lower and profits higher in the newer region, leading to further export of slaves from older, declining areas. As these regions matured, however, the same changes in crop mix and work requirements that had been adopted earlier in the east were repeated. In the 1830s and 1840s, south-western planters began diversifying crops and instituted more concerted campaigns to expropriate as much daily and year-round labour as possible. In the mid-nineteenth-century US cotton south, slaves spent only about one-third of their time growing and processing the cash crop. The remaining two-thirds was allocated to raising food crops and livestock, pursuing crafts, and other miscellaneous farm and service activities (Smith, 1997; Follett, 2005).

The work assignments of enslaved Africans and African-Americans in regions where staple crops could not be grown, in urban areas, and in crafts and industries not unique to the New World, have received less attention than has been given to work patterns of slaves growing tropical crops. The work of slaves in places where slaves were a minority in the total workforce, for example, New Spain after 1640, Cuba until the last decades of the eighteenth century, and the North American northern farm colonies, often was not very different from the work pattern of non-enslaved labourers. Rather than being directly involved in producing for the export economy, slaves' ordinary work in fields and houses allowed other members of slave-owning households to pursue professions or to engage in inter-colonial trade. Nonetheless, slaves in these places were assigned work quotas that exceeded those later imposed on free wage, peonage, or convict workers, were forced to work on religious holidays, and were subjected to more violence than the government tolerated for other groups. Slaves were always worked harder than other groups of labourers (Hodges, 1999; Proctor, 2003; Bergad, 2007).

African contributions to colonial agriculture

The contribution enslaved and maroon Africans may have made to the development of New World staple crop regimes, especially in respect to rice cultivation, is a contentious topic. Judith Carney argues that Africans from rice-growing regions of West Africa transferred "an entire cultural system, from production to consumption" not only to rice-growing areas in South Carolina, but also to Surinam and Brazil. Types of seed, sowing skills, irrigation technologies, and processing techniques were among the expertise enslaved peoples contributed to wet-land rice farming in the New World. She contends it was Africans who "tutored planters in growing the crop," and that slave buyers' "pattern of selecting ethnic groups experienced in cattle herding was repeated with rice cultivation as planters in the early colonial period learned of the ethnic groups and geographical areas of West Africa specialized in growing rice on wetlands," and especially about the women who had gendered knowledge of sowing, milling, winnowing, and cooking the grain (Carney, 2001: 2, 81, 89).

On the whole, slave-owners valued Africans' agricultural expertise in inverse proportion to their numbers in the workforce. In Spanish America, Africans were valued for a variety of skills rather than simply for forced labour. In the 1610s, English settlers on Bermuda turned to Africans captured from Spanish colonies to teach them to grow and process tobacco. In the 1640s, Virginia Governor William Berkeley consulted Africans when experimenting with rice. French slavers were instructed in the 1710s to procure captives with rice-growing skills to help start an industry in Louisiana. Once European settlers developed the basics of the various staple crop and industrial regimes, however, slaveholders ceased to recognize African contributions (Hall, 1992; Bergad, 2007; Walsh, 2010).

Arguments for significant African agency based on planter preferences for Africans from rice-growing regions are problematic. Studies based on the recently assembled Trans-Atlantic Slave Trade Database (www.slavevoyages.org) demonstrate that the mix of labourers delivered to any New World locality "depended on a combination of African supply, winds and ocean currents, and strategies of competing European shippers," and that any preferences buyers had for particular ethnic groups "were subject to trends beyond their control." In the cases of South Carolina, Amazonia, and Surinam, the proportion of slaves brought from rice-growing areas of Upper Guinea did not differ significantly from the proportion of slaves from this region delivered to other colonies producing different staples. Half or more of new Africans entering South Carolina after 1750 came from rice-growing areas, but by then South Carolina planters had already developed a distinctive Carolina rice complex based mostly on European and colonial technologies. Moreover, the discount at which enslaved women sold in South Carolina does not support the hypothesis that rice planters were willing to pay a higher premium for female workers from Upper Guinea with expertise in rice-growing than were planters elsewhere (Eltis *et al.*, 2007).

Although the search for connections between the arrival of Africans with specific kinds of agricultural and technical expertise and the development of New World staple crop regimes appears increasingly unpromising, nonetheless the issue of specific African agricultural "survivals" – or more accurately adaptations – is far from settled. In the case of South Carolina, even the most severe critics of the "Black Rice" hypothesis acknowledge that African sowing, winnowing, and processing techniques were incorporated into tidal rice culture. It is also widely recognized that, in their own time, slaves raised African food crops that proved more suitable than European ones to tropical climates. Similar connections between African expertise and New World crops and industries have been posited for tobacco, indigo, gold mining, and cattle herding, while a generalized expertise is claimed for slash-and-burn clearing. On Saint Domingue, sugar and coffee planters purchased Africans from different ethnic groups to work the two crops, decisions that may have been influenced by their perceptions of differing expertise. Planters also assigned slaves from particular groups to privileged positions on the basis of perceived ethnic traits (Geggus, 1993).

Our understanding of the range of skills brought to New World agriculture by forced African migrants is rudimentary, given a lack of information about the multiple low-technology, labour-saving, gender-specific strategies prevailing among both West Africans and Native Americans in the early modern period. Slash-and-burn clearing, long fallowing, and hoe-and-hill culture were techniques that Europeans accustomed only to ploughing and the culture of small grains had to learn. How they learned these techniques, and from whom, is frustratingly vague.

The staple crop regimes that emerged in the sixteenth, seventeenth, and early eighteenth centuries derived from a combination of indigenous, African, and European technologies. These regimes were unambiguously structured by "the capital, entrepreneurship, organizational capacity, and drive for profit of European and European-American merchants and planters." The unintended or coerced contributions of both indigenous residents and transplanted Africans remains a topic open for further research. Studies of techniques used today in sub-Saharan Africa have potential for providing new insights into earlier practices. While present-day developing-country practices have likely changed from those used in past centuries, studies of low-technology, long-fallow agriculture remain especially valuable for understanding the kinds of gendered expertise that women may have introduced, skills that planters habitually overlooked or devalued (Eltis *et al.*, 2007, 1353).

Improving agriculture, diversification and gender

As colonial economies matured and diversified, the scope and scale of occupations assigned to enslaved men increased. More men and boys were trained in crafts previously reserved for indentured servants or free whites. Expanding commerce afforded more work for carters, watermen, pilots, and sailors. Slave men also more often worked in industries such as iron forges and furnaces and shipyards, some rising to posts involving considerable skill and responsibility. By the last quarter of the eighteenth century, the majority of craft work in the West Indies and in the Lower and Upper South was done by enslaved men and boys. In sugar, rice, and indigo, male sugar boilers, irrigation trunk minders, and indigo makers occupied positions of privilege. Diversified agriculture, especially work associated with various forms of "English" husbandry, also increased the number of skilled posts assigned to enslaved men, as men were trained in ploughing and ditching, and in sowing and cradling European grains (Carr and Walsh, 1988; Berry, 2007).

Although slave-owners in some regions favoured native-born and mixed-race males for skilled positions, widespread agricultural diversification and quickening commerce, rather than the emergence of a sizeable creole population, is the best explanation for changing work patterns for enslaved men. Everywhere after 1750, the most significant increase in occupational opportunities for enslaved men in rural areas was in agricultural management, transportation, and domestic service rather than in crafts, and was most pronounced on large plantations. By the last quarter of the eighteenth century, one in ten male slaves in the Chesapeake and in Georgia were tradesman or drivers, a higher percentage than on sugar plantations on Barbados, where about one in twelve were skilled. The proportion was even higher in South Carolina, where white craftsmen were seldom available and where Charleston offered more work for skilled slaves than did smaller West Indian and Chesapeake towns. By the end of the eighteenth century, one in four enslaved men in South Carolina had escaped field labour.

Although enslaved craftsmen were usually accorded a lower status than white artisans, regardless of the level of their skill, they began to do jobs recognizable in European labour systems such as carpentry, coopering, and masonry. Enslaved women, on the other hand, remained overwhelmingly as field workers. Females were regularly assigned arduous tasks such as carrying heavy loads of manure to cane fields and grubbing swamps in winter. Planters who adopted new technologies began to associate long-used farm hand implements – hoes and baskets – with women; and craft tools and newer, more efficient agricultural tools – ploughs, spades, and cradles – with men. Slave-owners trained men and boys in the use of the new implements on the newly formed assumption that African and African-American males, like European males, possessed greater manual dexterity and were better learners than women (Carr and Walsh, 1988; Ward, 1989; Morgan, 1998; Roberts, 2008).

In the United States in the 1790s, unprecedented urban growth further expanded the occupations of enslaved men. Rapidly growing cities such as Baltimore, Richmond, Norfolk, and New Orleans offered opportunities for slave-owners to hire, apprentice, or sell for a term skilled slaves. They also often agreed with enslaved people that slaves could hire themselves out in return for some proportion of enslaved people's earnings. City employers had to pay a premium over what slaves could earn for their owners in agriculture. Urban slaves could thus make considerable amounts of money when hired out. The money they earned was used to purchase freedom for themselves or other family members. In towns, as on the plantation, enslaved women did not have the advantages that men had. Opportunities for marketing provisions and for domestic service increased, but women seldom possessed skills that commanded wages high enough to negotiate self-hire arrangements (Whitman, 1997).

Intensity, duration and physical effects of work

How hard did slaves work? This question has been controversial ever since Robert Fogel and Stanley Engerman argued in the mid-1970s that slave labour was more efficient than free labour (Fogel and Engerman, 1974). Today, most scholars concede that the labour appropriated from the enslaved was generally more efficient and more profitable than free labour. Debate continues, however, over why this was so. The most widely accepted explanation is not that slaves worked longer hours, but rather than that, during the hours they worked, they worked more intensely. Throughout the British colonies, slaves worked approximately 280 days a year, with Sunday being a day of rest and with three-day holidays at Christmas, Easter and Whitsuntide. Few days anywhere were lost to bad weather; conditions had to be severe indeed to halt plantation work altogether. Nonetheless, economic historians estimate that many free northern farmers worked longer days than did southern slaves. Around 1860, for example, northern dairy farmers worked more than 3000 hours each year (Olsen, 1992).

Given the relatively abrupt transition between light and dark in regions close to the equator, the work day in West Indian fields was closely confined to the hours between sunrise and sunset. (During harvest, however, sugar mills ran around the clock six days a week, and workers were required to put in a three- to six-hour additional shift following a full day of field labour.) The assumption some economic historians have made, that on the mainland the slaves' work day similarly ran from sunrise to sunset, is debatable, especially in more northerly latitudes. Scattered evidence from the eighteenth-century Chesapeake suggests a customary dawn-to-dusk regimen of 13 to 15 hours from April through September. By the mid-nineteenth century, planters used clock time to extend the start of the working day into pre-dawn hours, forcing slaves to rise as early as 3:30 a.m. so that they were in the fields at first light. Work logs show that in the 1790s, slaves on sugar plantations worked longer hours (3288 hours per year on Jamaica, 2973 on Barbados) than did those on Chesapeake grain farms (2919). The hours worked on lower South cotton plantations (2800) in the mid-nineteenth century were even fewer. However, the figure for cotton farms may underestimate the length of the work day and overestimate the amount of time allowed for meals and rest during the day (Smith, 1997; Roberts, 2008).

Studies of skeletal remains are another source that contributes to understanding of the impact of heavy work on enslaved bodies, as well as health, nutrition, and the intensity of labour. "Skeletal changes associated with demanding physical labour were ubiquitous, as shown by arthritic changes at the major joints and by the early onset of vertebral degeneration," as can be seen in the remains of South Carolina and Maryland slaves (Rathbun and Steckel, 2002). Stiffened spines were stressed by years of wielding heavy hoes or axes. The upper arm bones and shoulder bones of men and women, both young and middle-aged, were robust and showed exceptional muscle development, evidence of upper body strength built by repeatedly doing tasks such as pounding grain in a mortar and pestle or hauling buckets of water and washing clothes by hand. The backbones of enslaved South Carolina and Maryland women also provide evidence for retention of the African work technique of carrying considerable weights on the head (*ibid.*; Walker, 2009).

A project comparing health indicators from over 12,000 skeletons from North and South America from before 1000 BC to the early twentieth century ranked slaves from South Carolina among the least healthy of the historical populations examined. These slaves were in the same range as "pre-Columbian populations facing extinction or demographic disaster." Childhood stress and anaemia caused by poor diets and heavy parasite loads appeared in over 60 per cent of the remains. Skeletal analysis confirms documentary evidence that slave children were exceptionally short (and, by inference, poorly nourished), but experienced catch-up growth in early adolescence when entry into the workforce was accompanied by an increase (typically a doubling) of meat rations. The skeletons also reveal that females of all ages, along with older males, ate less meat than did prime-age adult men (Rathbun and Steckel, 2002).

A newer form of analysis, that of stable carbon isotopes that are absorbed by bones when people consume green plants, not only supplies information about diet, but in some cases provides clues to a person's birthplace and to how long he or she had been in the New World. The bones of people who ate a corn-based diet have different carbon isotopes from those of people whose diet was based on small grains or other starches. It takes about 20 years for a bone's carbon content to be completely replaced by a pronounced dietary change. Since many migrants to tropical climates did not survive as long as 20 years, the length of time they spent in the New World can be estimated. To date, most carbon isotope analysis has involved European migrants. The carbon signatures of common historical West African diets require further research, but the technology offers significant potential for differentiating the remains of Africans and native-born individuals, and consequently for comparative analysis of health, nutrition, and work-related stresses between generations (Walker, 2009).

Comparative rates of sickness are also pertinent in assessing the work experience of the enslaved. The meaning of sick days recorded in plantation work logs is ambiguous, however, as identification and treatment of illness was always an area of tension and negotiation. On one hand, slaves feigned illness as a form of resistance to work demands. On the other, slave-owners so feared losing labour to malingering that those claiming to be sick were often incarcerated in the hospital (if there was one) or forced to stay indoors and to take a course of owner-prescribed "physic." Hence many slaves did not plead illness until they were so sick they could no longer work at all, since treatment often became a form of control, discipline, and punishment. Justin Roberts' analysis of work logs found that in the 1790s, slaves on Jamaica (who were primarily Africans) missed more than 40 (15 per cent) of possible work days. Adult field hands were even sicker, missing almost 20 per cent of work days, especially during the wetter months when the labour of holing, dunging, and planting cane was heaviest. Sick days declined in periods of lighter work such as weeding. Slaves on Barbados (who were mostly native-born) averaged about 20 days lost to illness, half the rate for Jamaica. Virginia slaves (also mostly native-born) were healthier, missing only 6 per cent (or a median of 12) possible work days per annum, primarily in winter (Roberts, 2008). Late-eighteenth-century Virginia planters were seldom chronically short-handed, as sugar planters often were, so owners were less willing to sacrifice slaves' health in order to make a crop. Cold weather that affected older slaves (who accounted for a high proportion of the sick days) most adversely was the primary cause of illness. Despite having low survival rates as infants and poor health as children, the greater immunity the native-born possessed to local diseases contributed to better health as adults.

The productivity debates

Overall, the number and length of work days and skeletal evidence suggest that slaves were more productive than free labourers because they worked more intensely. Although slaves toiled for long hours, their work days were about ten per cent shorter than those of free northern farmers. Initially, economic historians attributed the productivity difference to slaves doing synchronized work in organized gangs under a driver's whip.

The alternative task system protected the principle of slaves having time of their own. It did not preclude redefinition of tasks or expansion of work demands that reduced private time. When indigo was introduced as a new crop in the mainland low country, where tasking was the customary arrangement, for example, it was usually raised by gangs. By the mid-nineteenth century, the distinction between the two systems became increasingly blurred, as some steps previously undertaken by gangs were turned into tasks. In most cases, slaves preferred tasking because it allowed them more autonomy. Masters became more willing to make these tactical concessions because tasking usually reduced supervision costs. The skeletal evidence suggests that what affected productivity levels most was not whether slaves worked in gangs or in task work, but how much they had to operate in work speedups, where they needed to expend greater physical effort per hour (Morgan, 1988; Coclanis, 2000).

Better organization of work also contributed to productivity increases by meshing the complex seasonal requirements of two or three staple crops, and by utilising off-season labour in preparing and manuring fields, clearing land, and fencing. Slaves could cut timber in winter when field chores were few. Slaves were also engaged in short-term activities such as seine fishing. The labour of young, old, and partially disabled slaves was turned to spinning thread and weaving cloth; helping with processing crops such as coffee, corn, and tobacco; and picking cotton, all tasks that did not require strength. Planters found that they could minimize the cost of maintaining the workforce by incorporating more self-sufficient activities – for example, on Barbados raising more provisions to reduce expensive food imports, and on Chesapeake grain farms and lower-south cotton plantations raising and processing cotton, flax, and wool. These tasks could be fitted, in whole or in part, into slack periods in primary staple cultivation cycles, and much of the labour was assigned to slaves too young, old, or sick to perform efficiently in the fields (Metzer, 1992).

Nonetheless, where overall productivity per worker (as measured by outputs of major cash crops or gross agricultural revenue) rose, increased labour inputs accounted for most of the gains. With the exception of tidal rice culture (which involved elaborate systems of dikes, water-control devices, and pounding mills), of cotton ginning, and of the Cuban sugar industry in the later nineteenth century, where large, capital-intensive, mechanized mills were introduced, the contribution of increased capital investment in the form of better tools or machines, improved livestock, and specialized buildings was minimal in regions where slavery predominated.

Slave-owners in the seaboard southeast realized rising profits from diversified plantations into the 1810s, after which period production levels stagnated. Contemporaries and some modern-day historians have placed most of the blame on inefficient and unmotivated slaves. Some of the more pronounced failures – that of tidewater Chesapeake grain farms, for example – were nonetheless primarily due to environmental factors and the climate of the US south. Agricultural improvers looking to England and to the Northern United States did not fully appreciate that, because of environmental factors, systems of continuous cultivation were poorly suited to the region (Helms, 2000).

Slavery and improving agriculture could be compatible, as can be seen in an examination of farming practices in Maryland's Upper Eastern Shore, in the portions of the Shenandoah Valley and western Maryland settled by eastern slaveholders, and in the Bluegrass region of Kentucky. In these areas, planters cultivated a high percentage of their land, and enslaved workers implemented integrated grass, grain, and livestock husbandry.

The flat topography of the Eastern Shore and the fertile limestone soils of the western areas enabled slave-owners fully to adopt intensified farming. Moreover, employing slaves in southern industries was always profitable. Some historians, however, have argued that problems inherent in using either all-slave or mixed-race workforces curtailed industrial development and the adoption of new technologies. In the iron industry, which in the United States was manned almost entirely by slaves, bondspeople were sometimes able to turn initially established work quotas into customary tasks, thus impeding efforts to increase outputs and to change technologies. On the other hand, the high rates of absenteeism and worker turnover that hampered northern ironworks posed fewer problems for managers of enslaved labour forces. In industries such as chemicals, and in various crafts that employed enslaved people, free blacks, and free white labourers, the refusal of whites to accept equal or subordinate status to blacks, whatever their degree of skill, discouraged the advanced training of slaves and free blacks. The main reason for limited employment of slaves in southern industries, however, was that in urban industrial settings, free workers were readily available. In staple agriculture, on the other hand, slaves could be forced to be markedly more productive in work that free whites refused to do. Consequently, whenever staple prices rose, enslaved workers were shifted out of industries and back into the fields (Dew, 1994; Bezis-Selfa, 1999).

Internal slave economies

How slaves worked for themselves is an important topic. Whether land was abundant or scarce, whether labour was organized according to the task or gang system, whether essential food crops were raised as part of regular work requirements (and whether these were sufficient to meet at least basic caloric requirements) or whether the slaves had to produce or procure them in their "leisure" time, all affected the nature of the internal economy. During the phase of early settlement, when land clearing was crucial and the culture of staple crops was just getting under way, raising sufficient corn or other starches (and, on the mainland, livestock for minimal rations of meat) to feed plantation workers was normal. As staple production intensified, the time labour-owners allocated to cultivation of provisions was often minimized and was sometimes abandoned entirely (Berlin and Morgan, 1991; McDonald, 1993; Hudson, 1997).

The extreme case was sugar. Slaves working in sugar were allotted provision grounds on inferior parts of plantations, of small size on islands where land was scarce, and larger but often at a distance from dwellings on islands where land was more abundant. In the Chesapeake, as in societies where slaves were a small proportion of the population, small garden plots were the norm, since the slaves received at least minimally adequate corn and meat rations raised on the owners' land and time. Masters might impose other restrictions, such as prohibiting slaves from raising livestock other than poultry and from growing the region's staple crop. Some masters discouraged or proscribed selling of produce to anyone other than the owners' family through fear that trading in provisions might serve as cover for trading in stolen goods, or that slaves would procure too much alcohol (Walsh, 1995).

The greatest constraints on slaves' independent production, however, were time and energy. In regions where the gang system prevailed, slaves could work for themselves only on Sundays and occasionally on Saturday afternoons. The task system theoretically made more time available for enslaved people to work on their own account. Daily work quotas in tasking, however, were sometimes set so high that weaker workers were hard pressed to complete them by nightfall. Under both systems, those with the most surplus energy could make the most of the opportunities the internal economy afforded. Those who benefited most were slaves with a spouse living on the same plantation, extended families that included several members of productive age, and artisans exempted from gang labour. By the mid-nineteenth century, slaves in the lower mainland south and in Louisiana sometimes were able to accumulate stocks of hogs and cattle, and other property, that they passed on to heirs. On the other hand, those who were sick, weak, old, or not connected to an extended family were sometimes barely able to raise enough food to sustain themselves, much less to earn money with which to purchase a few non-essentials.

Occupations assigned in the master's economy also played a central role in slaves' standing within the internal plantation hierarchy. Those with privileged occupations often received better rations, housing, clothing, larger allocations of provision grounds, freedom from gang labour, and more chances for travel off the plantation. These privileges enhanced status and allowed them to maintain their family better. More access to the master's or manager's family offered better chances of having their children trained for similar positions, thus transmitting status across generations. Ordinary field hands were conversely disadvantaged in terms of time, energy, and chances for improving their own or their children's standing (McDonald, 1993; Hudson, 1997).

Garden plots and provision grounds offered slaves a chance to supplement meagre rations with additional calories, and with fresh vegetables and fruits. They could raise rice, yams, cowpeas, and okra that were not part of owner-provided rations. They also adopted unfamiliar crops such as Irish potatoes that provided additional calories with a minimum of labour. Archaeologists have demonstrated, through analysis of faunal remains, that slaves improved a diet low in meat by hunting and trapping small game animals, by catching fish in waterways near their quarters, and by harvesting shellfish. More infrequent analyses of botanical remains demonstrate a similar heavy reliance on wild fruits and vegetables used both for food and for medicine (Berlin and Morgan, 1991; Carney, 2001).

Slave-owners and slaves continually fought over how much time slaves could spend working in their own time, and over what enslaved people could do with the fruits of their own labour. When prices fell, slave-owners tried to cut out-of-pocket costs by shifting more responsibility for self-provisioning onto the slaves. When prices rose, they sought to increase profits by forcing slaves to work more hours to make bigger crops. Some Virginia slaves, for example, were required in the mid-eighteenth century to sell enough produce every year to buy cloth for a second shirt. In late-eighteenth-century Jamaica, if bondspeople did not voluntarily raise enough food to provision themselves, they were compelled to work provision grounds on Sundays in labour gangs supervised by a driver (Morgan, 1998).

Trade disruptions during the American Revolution changed the work routines of slaves throughout the British Empire. On the mainland, planters drastically cut back on production of staple crops or dropped them altogether. To compensate for the absence of imported manufactures, slaves in the Upper and Lower South raised cotton, produced cloth, and made shoes and salt. Some slaves in the West Indies were ordered to raise cotton, and, more critically, almost all were set to raising food crops, since the cut-off of the provisioning trade with the mainland could (and sometimes did) lead to starvation.

The average size of provision grounds was nearly doubled. Owners sought to compensate for inadequate clothing allotments or food rations by allowing slaves more time to work their gardens and to engage in hunting, gathering, and income-producing crafts such as basket- and broom-making. In a time when owners were most vulnerable, slaves were able to expand their rights to produce and to market independently. After the war, internal economies on the mainland grew dramatically, stimulated in part by unprecedented urban growth that raised demand for the vegetables, poultry, fish, shellfish, and wild fruits that slaves could most readily raise or gather. Trading quickly shifted from barter to a cash basis, which further facilitated exchanges and increased bondspeoples' ability to purchase small amenities in country stores (Walsh, 1995; Roberts, 2008).

In the nineteenth century, slave-owners increasingly endorsed the internal economy as a means of encouraging bondspeople to develop habits of "industry," and as means of reconciling them to slavery by urging them to buy into the system. Slaves were sometimes allowed to raise staples, such as cotton, that were marketed along with the owners' crops. They were more often paid for articles crafted in their leisure time or for working on Sundays or holidays, and given cash rewards for good performance. By mid-century, earnings in the informal economy in the American South were substantial. Increased use of tasking in at least some steps in cultivation and processing of cotton, coffee, and even sugar afforded more slaves time to participate in income-generating activities (McDonald, 1993; Hudson, 1997).

Determining how far self-produced subsistence and earnings from the internal economy improved slaves' health and material culture is difficult. Documentary sources tend to exaggerate the gains from independent production, and to gloss over those who refused to participate or who lacked time and energy to raise enough to survive. Demographic and anthropometric measures such as natural population increase and height reveal an inverse correlation between health and high levels of self-subsistence. The Digital Archaeological Archive of Comparative Slavery (www.daacs.org), a web-based, consistently classified and measured database of artifacts and of the contexts in which they were found on slave sites in the Chesapeake, the Carolinas, and the Caribbean, offers another measure for comparing kinds and amounts of consumer goods found in slave quarters, and of the various elements of slaves' diets. Early results comparing sites in Virginia and Jamaica find higher levels of material amenities on mainland sites, corroborating other types of evidence for inverse relationships between arduous work in staple monoculture accompanied by requirements for high self-subsistence, and comparatively better health and material comfort.

Conclusion

The work slaves did in the master's economy was profoundly shaped by the requirements of the tropical and semi-tropical staples they raised. Work routines were far from unchanging, however – as plantations matured, emphasis shifted from land-clearing and virtual monoculture to greater diversity in both cash and subsistence crops. The pan-Atlantic shift towards agricultural improvement initiated by large-scale planters, beginning in the latter half of the eighteenth century, resulted in longer work days, work speedups, and more encroachments on slaves' free time. Profit almost always won out over humanitarian impulses to ameliorate slavery. Modest technological innovations redefined the nature and status of enslaved men's work. Enslaved women experienced few benefits. Most enslaved women continued to be relegated to unremitting field labour. But at the same time as slaves were forced to work harder to maintain or increase their owners' profits, they also managed to work more intensively and effectively for themselves. Between 1750 and 1850, the internal economy expanded dramatically, evolving from barter to a cash basis, and increasingly responding and connected to changes in the formal economy.

Bibliography

Beckles, Hilary McD., "Plantation Production and White 'Proto-Slavery': White Indentured Servants and the Colonisation of the English West Indies, 1624–45", *The Americas* 41 (1985), 21–45.

Beckles, Hilary McD., *Centering Woman: Gender Discourses in Caribbean Slave Society* (Kingston, Jamaica: Ian Randle, 1999).

Bergad, Laird W., *The Comparative Histories of Slavery in Brazil, Cuba, and the United States* (Cambridge: Cambridge University Press, 2007).

Berlin, Ira, *Many Thousands Gone: The First Two Centuries of Slavery in North America* (Cambridge, MA: Harvard University Press, 1998).

Berlin, Ira and Philip D. Morgan, eds, *The Slaves' Economy: Independent Production by Slaves in the Americas* (London: Frank Cass, 1991).

Berlin, Ira and Philip D. Morgan, eds, *Cultivation and Culture: Labour and the Shaping of Slave Life in the Americas* (Charlottesville: University Press of Virginia, 1993).

Berry, Daina R., *"Swing the Sickle for the Harvest is Ripe": Gender and Slavery in Antebellum Georgia* (Champaign: University of Illinois Press, 2007).

Bezis-Selfa, John, "A Tale of Two Ironworks: Slavery, Free Labor, Work and Resistance in the Early Republic", *William and Mary Quarterly* 56 (1999), 677–700.

Brown, Kathleen M., *Good Wives, Nasty Wenches, and Anxious Patriarchs: Gender, Race, and Power in Colonial Virginia* (Chapel Hill: University of North Carolina Press, 1996).

Carney, Judith A., *Black Rice: The African Origins of Rice Cultivation in the Americas* (Cambridge, MA: Harvard University Press, 2001).

Carr, Lois Green and Walsh, Lorena S., "Economic Diversification and Labour Organization in the Chesapeake, 1650–1820", in Stephen Innes, ed., *Work and Labour in Early America* (Chapel Hill: University of North Carolina Press, 1988), 144–88.

Chaplin, Joyce E., *An Anxious Pursuit: Agricultural Innovation and Modernity in the Lower South, 1730–1815* (Chapel Hill: University of North Carolina Press, 1993).

Coclanis, Peter A., "How the Low Country was Taken to Task: Slave-Labor Organization in Coastal South Carolina and Georgia", in Robert L. Paquette and L. A. Ferlerger, eds, *Slavery, Secession, and Southern History* (Charlottesville: University Press of Virginia, 2000), 59–78.

Dew, Charles B., *Bond of Iron: Master and Slave at Buffalo Forge* (New York: W.W. Norton, 1994).

Edelson, S. Max, *Plantation Enterprise in Colonial South Carolina* (Cambridge, MA: Harvard University Press, 2006).

Eltis, David, *The Rise of African Slavery in the Americas* (Cambridge: Cambridge University Press, 2000).

Eltis, David, Philip D. Morgan and David Richardson, "Agency and Diaspora in Atlantic History: Reassessing the African Contribution to Rice Culture in the Americas", *American Historical Review*, 112 (2007), 1328–58.

Fogel, Robert W. and Stanley L. Engerman, *Time on the Cross: The Economics of American Negro Slavery* (Boston: Little, Brown, 1974).

Follett, Richard, *The Sugar Masters: Planters and Slaves in Louisiana's Cane World, 1820–1860* (Baton Rouge: Louisiana State University Press, 2005).

Geggus, David Patrick, "Sugar and Coffee Cultivation in Saint Domingue and the Shaping of the Slave Labor Force", in Ira Berlin and Philip D. Morgan, eds, *Cultivation and Culture: Labour and the Shaping of Slave Life in the Americas* (Charlottesville: University Press of Virginia, 1993), 73–98.

Hall, Gwendolyn M., *Africans in Colonial Louisiana: The Development of Afro-Creole Culture in the Eighteenth Century* (Baton Rouge: Louisiana State University Press, 1992).

Helms, Douglas, "Soil and Southern History", *Agricultural History* 74 (2000), 723–58.

Higman, Barry W., *Montpelier, Jamaica: A Plantation Community in Slavery and Freedom, 1739–1912* (Kingston: University Press of the West Indies, 1998).

Hodges, Graham R., *Root and Branch: African Americans in New York and East Jersey, 1613–1863* (Chapel Hill: University of North Carolina Press, 1999).

Hudson, Larry E., Jr, *To Have and to Hold: Slave Work and Family Life in Antebellum South Carolina* (Athens, GA: University of Georgia Press, 1997).

McDonald, Roderick A., *The Economy and Material Culture of Slaves: Goods and Chattels on the Sugar Plantations of Jamaica and Louisiana* (Baton Rouge: Louisiana State University Press, 1993).

Metzer, Jacob, "Rational Management, Modern Business Practices, and Economies of Scale in Antebellum Southern Plantations", in Robert W. Fogel and Stanley L. Engerman, eds, *Without Consent or Contract: Markets and Production: Technical Papers*, Vol. I (New York: W.W. Norton, 1992), 191–215.

Moitt, Bernard, *Women and Slavery in the French Antilles, 1635–1848* (Bloomington: Indiana University Press, 2001).

Morgan, Jennifer, *Labouring Women: Reproduction and Gender in New World Slavery* (Philadelphia: University of Pennsylvania Press, 2004).

Morgan, Philip D., *Slave Counterpoint: Black Culture in the Eighteenth-Century Chesapeake and Lowcountry* (Chapel Hill: University of North Carolina Press, 1998).

Morgan, Philip D., "Task and Gang Systems: The Organization of Labor on New World Plantations", in Stephen Innes, ed., *Work and Labour in Early America* (Chapel Hill: University of North Carolina Press, 1988), 189–220.

Nelson, Lynn A., *Pharsalia: An Environmental Biography of a Southern Plantation, 1780–1880* (Athens, GA: University of Georgia Press, 2007).

Olsen, John F. "Clock Time versus Real Time: A Comparison of the Lengths of the Northern and Southern Agricultural Work Years" in Robert W. Fogel and Stanley L. Engerman, eds, *Without Consent or Contract: Markets and Production: Technical Papers*, Vol. I (New York: W.W. Norton, 1992), 216–40.

Proctor, Frank I., III, "Afro-Mexican Labour in the Obrajes de Paños of New Spain, Seventeenth and Eighteenth Centuries", *The Americas* 60 (2003), 33–58.

Rathbun, Ted A. and Richard H. Steckel, "The Health of Slave and Free Blacks in the East", in R. H. Steckel and J. C. Rose, eds, *The Backbone of History: Health and Nutrition in the Western Hemisphere* (Cambridge: Cambridge University Press, 2002), 208–25.

Roberts, Justin, "Working between the Lines: Labor and Agriculture on Two Barbadian Sugar Plantations, 1796–97", *William and Mary Quarterly*, 63 (2006), 551–86.

Roberts, Justin, "Sunup to Sundown: Plantation Management Strategies and Slave Work Routines in Barbados, Jamaica and Virginia, c. 1780–1810" (PhD thesis, Johns Hopkins University, 2008).

Schwartz, Stuart, *Sugar Plantations in the Formation of Brazilian Society, Bahia, 1550–1835* (Cambridge: Cambridge University Press, 1985).

Shepherd, Verene A., ed., *Slavery Without Sugar: Diversity in Caribbean Economy and Society Since the Seventeenth Century* (Gainesville: University Press of Florida, 2002).

Sheridan, Richard B., "Samuel Martin, Innovating Sugar Planter of Antigua, 1750–76", *Agricultural History* 34 (1960), 126–39.

Smith, Mark M., *Mastered by the Clock: Time, Slavery, and Freedom in the American South* (Chapel Hill: University of North Carolina Press, 1997).

Walker, Sally M., *Written in Bone: Buried Lives of Jamestown and Colonial Maryland* (Minneapolis, MN: Carolrboda Books, 2009).

Walsh, Lorena S., "Plantation Management in the Chesapeake, 1620–1820", *Journal of Economic History* 49 (1989), 393–406.

Walsh, Lorena S., "Work and Resistance in the New Republic: The Case of the Chesapeake, 1770–1820", in Mary Turner, ed., *From Chattel to Wage Slaves: The Dynamics of Labour Bargaining in the Americas* (Bloomington: Indiana University Press, 1995), 97–122.

Walsh, Lorena S., *From Calabar to Carter's Grove: The History of a Virginia Slave Community* (Charlottesville: University Press of Virginia, 1997).

Walsh, Lorena S., *Motives of Honor, Pleasure, and Profit: Plantation Management in the Chesapeake, 1607–1763* (Chapel Hill: University of North Carolina Press, 2010).

Ward, J. R., "The Amelioration of British West Indian Slavery, 1750–1834: Technical Change and the Plow", *Nieuwe West-Indische Gids/New West Indian Guide* 63 (1989), 41–58.

Whitman, T. Stephen, *The Price of Freedom: Slavery and Manumission in Baltimore and Early National Maryland* (Lexington: University Press of Kentucky, 1997).

7

THE DEMOGRAPHY OF SLAVERY

Richard Follett[1]

Introduction

The winding road to Codrington College climbs the steep cane-covered hills to the oldest Anglican seminary in the New World. Within earshot of the eighteenth-century college buildings, Atlantic waves crash into Conset Bay on Barbados' rugged eastern coastline. Christopher Codrington bequeathed his Barbadian estates in 1710 to the Society for the Propagation of the Gospel. At his death, he empowered the Society to establish a missionary seminary on the Codrington estates, and to manage his large sugar plantations and the 300 enslaved people upon them. Codrington's wishes, however, were only partly fulfilled. While the buildings rose, the slave population of the Codrington plantations underwent massive decline. Low birth rates, infant and adult death, and widespread disease so debilitated the slave population that, despite purchasing 450 additional slaves from 1712 to 1761, the total number of slaves on the Codrington plantations numbered 190 in 1760. Every year, the Society bought dozens of Africans from slave traders in Bridgetown, but the number of births and new acquisitions failed to keep pace with death on the plantation. Young and old, African and creole succumbed to tropical disease and to the physical rigors of New World slavery (Bennett, 1958: 1–3, 52, 61).

The experience of the enslaved population on the Codrington plantations was replicated on thousands of estates throughout the Caribbean from the seventeenth to nineteenth centuries. Death defined plantation America, and its omnipresence encouraged slaveholders to be callous about life. Planters and slaves lived on the "threshold of death" and, as Vincent Brown observes, "in one of history's greatest episodes of creative destruction", the vibrant, profitable economies of New World slavery ultimately "consumed its inhabitants". On the Codrington estates, as elsewhere in tropical America, frequent death winnowed the slave population, particularly among the newly arrived, but the slaveholders' predilection for males also ensured an unnaturally small population of women. There were accordingly fewer babies, and those infants faced a range of infections that killed regularly. Children who survived their infant years embarked on a life where the slaveholder's lash drove them to toil long hours in desolate conditions. That labor was undertaken with a diet inadequate in nutrients, minerals, and calories to ward off infection or to fuel the basic energy requirements of cane work. Death, disease, and destruction dictated life, and only frequent acquisitions from the Atlantic slave trade sustained the population. With mortality ranging between 5 and 7.5 per cent on mid-eighteenth-century sugar estates, Barbadian planter Henry Drax calculated that to maintain an estate of 200 slaves required the acquisition of between 10 and 15 new hands annually. In no small measure, it was the persistent annual and daily fatalities within the slave populations that spurred the volume and longevity of the Atlantic slave trade (Brown, 2008: 57–58; Amussen, 2007: 96).

By 1761, the Society recognized the crippling financial cost of replacing the slave population with new acquisitions. Having purchased hundreds of enslaved Africans, the slave population was more than a third smaller than that bequeathed by Codrington. As Archbishop Thomas Secker observed, "I have long wondered and lamented that the Negroes in our plantations decrease, & new Supplies become necessary continually. Surely this proceeds, from some Defect, both of Humanity, & even of good policy." Secker's point was well made; the Society's policy of acquiring two males for every female was culpable for the slave population's incapacity to grow by natural means, and the reliance on "unseasoned" African imports ensured that, on average, one in every two new recruits died within the first three years of Caribbean slavery. Slaveholders recognized the expense of child-rearing (the reduction in physical labor when relatively more women were acquired, the loss of field-labor by mothers, and the cost of raising children to maturity, many of whom would die in childhood), though once the price of slaves began to rise sharply in the 1760s, planters saw a potential cost advantage in encouraging child birth among the enslaved rather than buying new African slaves. From 1780 to 1807, the cost of purchasing a male slave within the British West Indies rose by 141 per cent, almost three times the relative increase in the price of the primary export, raw sugar. Planters responded in kind, ameliorating conditions and encouraging population growth. As the Surveyor General William Senhouse observed of the planters' new-found enlightened self-interest, "the owner's humanity will in a few years be amply rewarded by a valuable increase in his property". Senhouse proved prescient in his commentary. Slightly improved food, medical treatment, and care of the new-born on the Codrington estates soon paid dividends as the number of infant mortalities decreased and the gender balance of slave population gradually stabilized. By 1792 women were in the majority, and by the turn of the century births surpassed deaths. After 70 years of Society management, the slave population on the Codrington estates was finally growing by natural means (Bennett, 1958: 89, 96; Eltis *et al.*, 2005: 680; Handler and Lange, 1978: 84).

The demographic transition experienced on the Codrington plantations was early within the context of West Indian slavery. It was not, however, exceptional. Across the Caribbean, though at different times and rates, population dynamics shifted from low fertility and high mortality toward relative demographic stability from the late eighteenth to mid-nineteenth centuries. At the same time, the slave populations became increasingly creolized or American-born. This in turn had a positive long-term effect on birth rates, as the creole born gradually equalized the imbalanced sex ratios of the eighteenth century. Since American-born slaves tended to have a relatively stronger immunological response to New World tropical diseases than newly arrived Africans, mortality rates also began to fall. In Barbados, this demographic transition was well advanced by 1800, but the abolition of British slave trading from 1808 forced West Indian planters to pay greater attention to child-births and natural increase. Progress, however, advanced unevenly and sporadically. In fact, between 1807 and 1834, the slave population of the British West Indies declined from 770,000 to 665,000. The expansion of cane sugar plantation agriculture through the first three decades of the nineteenth century in Jamaica, and particularly in the newly acquired cane colonies of Trinidad,

Tobago, and Demerara-Essequibo, hampered the prospects of demographic growth in the British Caribbean. No other crop was produced under such physically exhausting conditions as sugar. Long shifts, gang labor, and night work characterized life on a sugar plantation and distinguished it from the relatively less demanding regimes associated with coffee, cotton, pimento, cocoa, or food provisioning. Although the rate of natural increase rose on those estates where material or laboring conditions improved, the erosive effect of high adult and infant mortality on the cane estates (particularly in the "new" sugar colonies) undermined the positive effect of amelioration long into the nineteenth century. Thus, despite the introduction of pro-natalist policies and the increased number of women within the slave population, it was not until the 1840s (a full decade following emancipation) that the black population of Jamaica finally began to show positive growth. The demographic histories of Jamaica and Barbados differed, but the gradual rise in the number of women and creole born within the slave labor forces created a pattern of marginal (though positive) natural growth for the nineteenth-century slave populations (Higman, 1984: 72–78, 307–78; 1995: 134–35).

If gradual demographic stability characterized the last decades of British West Indian slavery, the most striking aspect of the eighteenth-century slave systems was their failure to create self-sustaining populations. The combination of low natality and high mortality bequeathed a devastating demographic legacy throughout tropical America. Almost one in four Africans sold into slavery, nearly four million people, were destined for Brazil from 1700–1850, yet Brazilian planters counted just 1.5 million slaves in the 1872 census. Cuba, an island economy that converted to cane sugar and coffee monoculture in the 1790s, imported some 780,000 slaves between 1790 and 1867, but in 1862 just 370,000 slaves resided on the island. Neighboring Jamaica and Saint Domingue fared no better. Jamaica imported over one million slaves, mostly between 1700 and 1807, but by 1832 just 312,876 were registered on the colonial returns. In Saint Domingue, almost 800,000 slaves were imported from 1680 to 1777, though the slave population numbered no more than 290,000 by the end of that period (Bergad, 2007: 96–97; Bergad *et al.*, 1995: 38; Higman, 1995: 54; Hall, 1971: 14).

The United States, however, stood apart. Before Congress prohibited American involvement in the Atlantic slave trade in 1808, some 360,000 slaves were imported to the United States and its colonial antecedents. Less than 4 per cent of the entire volume of the Atlantic slave trade entered the United States, but by 1860, 3.95 million slaves lived in the American South. The rate of population growth was exceptional. In 1810, some 1.1 million slaves resided on American soil, but by 1825, the US was the largest slaveholding nation on Earth. Slavery in the American South was exceptional on several levels: the nineteenth-century slave population grew swiftly (without reliance on the international slave trade), practically every slave in 1860 was creole born, and the growth of US slavery underpinned the rapid emergence of American cotton, cultivated by native-born African-American slaves from the Carolinas to Texas. It was, in turn, the value of their cotton and slaves that made American slaveholders stalwart defenders of chattel bondage. The American slave population boomed because of even sex ratios, comparatively low infant and adult mortality, a substantially higher birth rate than death rate, and high levels of per capita food consumption (a scenario shared with the British Bahamas, where the slave population also expanded naturally). Conditions elsewhere in the tropics nonetheless remained dismal, irrespective of the pro-natalist policies exhibited in the British West Indies and in Cuba (Eltis, 2001: 45; Fogel, 1989: 123–32).

As Charles Pennell, the British Consul in Salvador, Bahia noted in 1827, "the annual mortality on many sugar plantations is so great that unless their numbers are augmented from abroad the whole slave population would become extinct in the course of about twenty years". The proprietors, Pennell concluded, "act on the calculation that it is cheaper to buy male slaves than to raise Negro children". By 1832, the rate of decline within the Brazilian slave population stood at 5 per cent per year, ensuring that if no additional purchases were made, the slave force would be reduced to half its size in seven years. The factors eroding the slave population's capacity to expand were not dissimilar to those on the Codrington estates a century earlier. There was a high proportion of males to females, exacerbated by male-orientated gender ratios within the international and inter-regional slave trade. In addition, crude birth rates hovered at about 34 per 1000, while death rates of between 47 and 65 per 1000 were not uncommon in the plantation belts of Bahia, a prime location for newly arrived Africans for the first half of the nineteenth century. Infant mortality and the death of recently imported Africans, furthermore, contributed to the demographic phenomenon Pennell described. Indeed, so high were the prospects of morbidity among Brazilian slaves that life expectancy at birth was 18.3 years for males, almost half of that of US slaves (35.5) in 1850 (Schwartz, 1985: 365–71; Eltis and Engerman, 1993: 310–12; Graham, 2004: 299).

Sugar and slavery

Of the New World plantation crops (sugar, coffee, tobacco, rice, and cotton), the cultivation and manufacture of cane sugar was the most extensive and demographically destructive. From its northerly outcrop in Louisiana to its southern extremes in Brazil, sugar, suffering, and death were synonymous terms. As Clement Caines of St Kitts observed, "the excess of toil, which our field slaves are obliged to ensure, brings on premature infirmity and decay". One former slave in Louisiana's sugar belt put it more bluntly, "it like a heathen part o' de country". Physical labor was common to all slave systems, but it was the intensity of labor required to harvest cane that made the sugar colonies so dreaded. Throughout the Caribbean, harvest lasted for five to six months, commencing in December and culminating in May. During that period, enslaved workers toiled from early morning to evening, cutting the cane and transporting it to the sugar mill, where operators (mostly male slaves) ground the canes, expressing the juice from within the sucrose-rich shoots and collecting the syrup. This was then reduced in a series of open kettles and finally transferred to coolers, where the molten sugar granulated and drained. The production process was sequential and relied on speed, discipline, and team work. Since practically every sugar estate possessed both milling and manufacturing facilities on one self-contained site, the intense pattern of harvest work was replicated both island-wide and regionally. Crop over, the enslaved conducted plantation maintenance, cultivated the growing canes, and dug cane holes for planting new sugar canes in October and November (Goveia, 1980: 234; Follett, 2005: 46).

The intensity of sugar work reached its nadir in the nineteenth-century sugar colonies, where high labor:land ratios were employed to maximize output, and where steam-powered sugar mills introduced a semi-mechanized cadence to plantation life. In Cuba and Louisiana, planters rationalized the practice of night work, introducing labor shifts that ensured the mills never stopped turning and the evaporation kettles kept simmering. As John Wurdemann observed on his tour of the nineteenth-century Cuban sugar fields, the slaves were permitted but five hours sleep daily, their bodies appearing as "mere skeletons" from overwork. They were quite simply "worn out", one commentator recalled. On the Mesopotamia Estate in western Jamaica, hard labor in sugar increased mortality appreciably. Between 1736 and 1762, absentee planter Joseph Foster Barham purchased 168 new people, mainly Africans, to labor on his large sugar estate. But by 1762, most of these men and women were dead. In fact, almost 290 slaves had died during that period, or more than 11 per year. Others survived, but only just. One quarter of the adults inventoried in 1762 were described as non-working invalids; there were not even enough prime-aged slaves (in their twenties to thirties) for effective sugar production. Although some of the Africans died from tropical diseases contracted during the first two years in Jamaica, the frequency of early fatalities and broken health suggests that the managers of Mesopotamia were driving their slaves to death. Women probably fared the worst. As one recent study of fecundity (the biological capacity for reproduction) among slave women in Louisiana's cane belt indicates, the sugar regime exacted a serious toll on the capacity of slave women to conceive and carry births to term. Extreme physical labor and inadequate nutrition prompted delayed menarche, irregular menstrual cycles, amenorrhea, and weight loss. This in turn depressed the number of live births, as even modest weight loss contributes to ovarian dysfunction. In all probability, slave women also suffered from luteal phase progesterone deficiency, itself triggered by heavy labor. Progesterone deficiency ensures that the womb is unsupportive for the successful implantation and sustained growth of the fertilized egg. At Mesopotamia, progesterone deficiency may have been partly culpable for the high number of miscarriages recorded. From 1762 to 1831, almost the half the recorded pregnancies ended in miscarriage, stillbirth, or the death of infants within a few days of birth. Facing a lethal combination of overwork, physical punishment, and dietary deficiencies, and quite possibly wishing to save their unborn children from the horrors of bondage, some women committed abortion. However culturally significant self-induced abortion was for slave parents, it is improbable that it made a substantial impact on slave population growth. Far more significant was the material nature of sugar work and the epidemiological conditions that contributed to the low natality recorded among Caribbean slave women (Hall, 1971: 18; Fraginals, 2001: 287; Dunn, 2007: 46–47; Follett, 2008: 54–78; Morgan, 2006: 248–51).

If the sugar regime impaired the reproductive capacity of women, it was the persistently high death rates among sugar-working slaves that stopped populations from increasing naturally. In nineteenth-century Cuba, for instance, death rates remained high, with more than 5 per cent of active workers dying annually. Although fertility rates improved (once slaveholders began to import substantial numbers of slave women), the gross death rate was, Manuel Moreno Fraginals observes, "the logical end-product of the work system on the plantations". It was, moreover, high enough to erase the pronatalist policy in Cuba. In neighboring Jamaica, on the eve of emancipation, the sugar regime continued to be deadly. There were 22.7 births per 1000, yet 35.1 deaths per 1000 on the island's sugar estates, a natural decrease of −12.4. Elsewhere, there were 25.1 births to 23.3 deaths, giving a modest increase of 1.8 on Jamaican coffee farms and 25.9 births to 23.8 deaths (an increase of 2.1) on pimento estates. Sugar, however, was so dominant in the island's economy that, irrespective of positive population growth in other crop-combinations, the Jamaican slave population shrank by −8.6 from 1829 to 1832. The odds of survival for slaves laboring on sugar estates were also lower than for slaves of any other type of plantation. In nineteenth-century Trinidad, the odds of survival for an adult male slave on a cotton plantation were twice those for a sugar estate and 1.7 times greater than on a cocoa farm (Fraginals, 1977: 193–97; Higman, 1995, 123; John, 1988: 116).

Even when compared with European cities, where chronic ill health plagued the poorest residents, the demographic experience of the Caribbean sugar islands is striking. Mortality rates in industrial Europe were high, but much lower than those on Jamaican cane estates. By the 1870s, death rates in Manchester and Liverpool reached 28.4 and 26.1 per 1000 and surpassed 30 per 1000 in the first decade of the twentieth century. Elsewhere in Europe, birth rates (35–40 per 1000) outstripped death rates (23–28 per 1000) by a considerable margin. Death rates in industrializing Bremen were thus no worse than a West Indian coffee plantation, but were compensated by buoyant birth rates. On Caribbean sugar estates, by contrast, death rates were dreadful, as were the feeble birth rates. Indeed, had the slave population of the United States ultimately mirrored the devastating losses of the West Indian sugar regime, it is probable that of the one million slaves in 1800, no more than 180,000 would have been alive at the start of the nineteenth century. In Europe (and among American slaves too), relatively buoyant birth rates sustained population growth, but in the Caribbean, low birth rates and high death rates combined to produce demographic decline (Vögele, 1999: 86, 89; Livi-Bacci, 1986: 435; Lee and Marschalk, 2000: 379–86; Fogel and Engerman, 1974: 29).

Sex ratios and demography

Although the demands of labor placed a heavy burden on slaves, the imbalanced sex ratios associated with the Atlantic slave trade and New World sugar production imposed a further demographic restraint on population growth. From the late seventeenth to nineteenth centuries, the demand for male African labor by Euro-American planters created a slave population characterized by sexual imbalance, a relatively small number of women, and low fertility rates. At the outset of the plantation revolution in the late seventeenth century, slave traders dispatched relatively gender-balanced cargoes of Africans to the Americas, but as staple-crop production intensified in the early eighteenth century, so too did the planters' reliance on male labor. From 1715 to 1792, males outstripped females by 179:100 in the French slave trade, and this pattern was replicated elsewhere. Between 1764 and 1788, for instance, British slave traders to Jamaica shipped 165 males per 100 females, while Portuguese officials in north-eastern Brazil recorded sex ratios of 166:100 between 1756 and 1788. By the close of the century, Spanish vessels *en route* for Havana trafficked sex ratios of 2.2 enslaved males for every female. The number of children sold into Atlantic slavery oscillated by African region, the slave trader's nationality, and chronology, but throughout the eighteenth century, children represented between 20 and 30 per cent of all slave crews. A typical French slave ship in the eighteenth century, sailing from the Bight of Benin or Loango on the coast of Congo to the sugar plantations of Martinique and Saint Domingue, carried beneath its decks a frightened, alienated, and diverse cargo. Almost half (47.4 per cent) of the enslaved on that vessel were men, 26 per cent were women, and 26.6 per cent were children (Geggus, 1989: 23–29; Eltis and Engerman, 1992: 237–57; Nwokeji and Eltis, 2002: 202).

Planters demonstrated their broad preference for men by paying a 10 to 20 per cent premium for male slaves. That price differential closed once planters began to emphasize the reproductive possibilities of acquiring females, but even in New Orleans in 1859, the average price of a male aged 16–20 was US$1596, compared with $1395 for a similarly aged woman. Driven by sugar planters' preference for male slaves, the price of male and female labor in the lower Mississippi valley reflected the continuing effect of age and gender selectivity on population dynamics even as late as the mid-nineteenth century. Throughout the Louisiana sugar belt, planters privileged youth, brawn, and reproductive potential, with young men constituting approximately 60 per cent of all adult sugar workers in the cane fields. By 1860, adult males outnumbered females (age 15–49) in the leading sugar-producing parishes by 28,205 to 19,946. To supply this highly gendered and age-distorted demand, traders transported thousands of slaves from the upper to the lower South, selling males aged 25 and women aged 22 at a premium. The impact of such gender-selective purchasing in Louisiana led to slave populations with relatively few women and children. High levels of mortality associated with the rigors of the sugar regime thinned the ranks of slave population still further, ensuring that the region's plantations suffered natural decrease of about 13 per cent per decade. Thus, in contrast to the rest of the USA, where in 1860 there were 1320 enslaved children (aged 0–9 years) per 1000 women (aged 15–49), there were 922 children per 1000 females in the sugar region. The impact was demographically disastrous. In fact, had Louisiana's slave population broadly mirrored that of the rest of the American South (with its equitable sex ratios and high fertility rate), there would have been 13,500 more children living in the sugar parishes in 1860. By contrast, there was a relative dearth of children. In the sugar-growing parishes that follow the snaking course of the Mississippi River, males outnumbered females by 13,565 to 10,677 in 1860. There were 7792 children aged 0–14, or 32 per cent of the entire slave population. In Dallas County, Alabama, by contrast (located within the cotton belt), the slave population numbered 12,907 males and 12,853 females. In this population there were 10,752 children, or approximately 42 per cent of the county's enslaved population. The imbalanced sex ratios associated with sugar work in Louisiana and elsewhere thus compromised fertility rates and lowered the total number of children born, while overwork-induced miscarriage and high levels of infant death additionally cut into the slave population's capacity to increase[2] (Higman, 1995: 192; Bergad et al., 1995: 71–73; Tansey, 1982: 167; Kotlikoff, 1992: 34, 42–45; Tadman, 2000: 1549–50).

Louisiana's demographic record mirrored that of the eighteenth-century Caribbean, where imbalanced sex ratios closely reflected the gender-specific nature of the international slave trade and the planters' desire for male labor. These factors were structural impediments to population growth. First, the importation of men exacerbated the problem of low fertility. Second, mortality (particularly among African imports) remained so high that populations declined, irrespective of slave acquisitions. And third, it was the continual restocking of plantation communities with newly enslaved African males that slowed the emergence of a creole-born population. At Mesopotamia, Jamaica, only the acquisition of some 423 African- and Jamaican-born slaves between 1762 and 1831 sustained the population. Between those years, estate officials recorded 410 live births (from 504 females), but 749 fatalities forced Joseph Foster Barham II, the absentee proprietor, to buy slaves in Kingston. The owners of Worthy Park, another Jamaican sugar plantation, similarly watched their slave population wither from the now familiar combination of low birth rates and stubbornly high mortality. When Rose Price assumed management of the estate in 1791, the population of Worthy Park numbered 357. The preceding decade, however, had seen deaths surpass births by almost 2:1. Only the acquisition of 225 slaves from 1792–93, at the cost of £13,472, enabled the slave force to expand. Yet despite massive investment, death rates soared to 5.7 per cent. The newly acquired Africans, especially the Congolese, succumbed to dysentery and a range of newly acquired infections that flourished among the enslaved. By 1795, after three years of "seasoning", Price calculated that almost one-quarter of the new African slaves had died. All told, 115 slaves had perished on the estate during his residency. Had Price looked to the 174 slave women who had reached or passed their child-bearing years by May 1795, the slaveholder would have found little cause for comfort. Only 89 of the women had given birth in recent years, but of these, 70 had lost one or more children to miscarriage or early death. Of the 352 pregnancies recorded on Worthy Park, live births totaled 275, indicating a miscarriage rate of 1:4.6 births. In addition to the 77 miscarriages, 116 of the offspring were dead by 1795, leaving just 159 children alive on Rose Price's register. The low birth rates at Worthy Park thus derived from the relatively small number of women engaged in childbearing, persistent miscarriage (and there are probably many more unrecorded incidences of early fetal loss), infant death, and possibly lower levels of fertility among newly acquired African women. Relatively widespread syphilis might account for the high numbers of stillbirths, but above all, it was the combination of low fertility and high mortality that suppressed growth at Worthy Park (Dunn, 1987: 797; Craton and Walvin, 1970: 130–34; Craton, 1978: 87; Jacobi et al., 1992: 145–58).

Skewed sex ratios and low fertility compromised the capacity for population growth, but in areas where women equaled the number of men, and where a creole population of native-born slaves emerged, the conditions for natural increase improved. In the North American colonies, sex ratios in the Chesapeake and South Carolina reached parity by 1700 and with that, the number of children also began to increase. In Maryland, child:woman ratios rose from 106 (children per 100 women) in the 1680s to 140 in 1700. Further south in Virginia, the slave population began to grow naturally by the 1720s. Sex ratios among newborns were roughly equal, ensuring a stable demographic base for the next generation. Equally significant, many of these children survived into adulthood. Even in South Carolina, where a large number of African males were imported in the 1730s and in the 1750s and 1760s, the rate of natural increase reached 1.5 per cent by the 1770s. Such demographic growth ultimately enabled American planters to be less reliant on the international slave trade than their compatriots in the Caribbean sugar islands. In colonial North American slave societies, the role of native-born bondswomen proved central to demographic growth. These bondswomen lived longer, were healthier, and were more likely to have children at a younger age than their African parents. Creole women usually conceived their first child in their late teens, had relatively short birth intervals, and could expect to bear eight or nine children. Recently enslaved West Africans, by contrast, began child-rearing later than the creole-born, they breastfed for longer (availing of the contraceptive effect of breastfeeding), and thus experienced birth intervals of between 36 and 48 months. African-born women accordingly had smaller families than their creole-born counterparts (Morgan, 1998: 80–95; Klein and Engerman, 1978: 368–71).

Creolization and greater gender equity, however, did not guarantee population increase. On the Mesopotamia Estate, plantation managers addressed the skewed gender imbalance by acquiring Jamaican-born family units. By 1809, over 80 per cent of Mesopotamia slaves were creole-born. Despite Barham's attention to pro-natalism (women were in the majority in every age group above 14 and especially in the prime childbearing age, 20–29), birth rates were feeble (18.9 per 1000) while death rates averaged 34.5 per 1000. Once again, low fertility was a result of working in sugar. As elsewhere in the late eighteenth-century Caribbean, bondswomen at Mesopotamia were relegated to unskilled manual labor. Women conducted two-thirds of the field work on Barham's estate, toiling through the four-month harvest, and conducting the burdensome task of cane holing (whereby slaves prepared the soil for cane planting) by hand. Slave women did the heaviest manual labor conceivable and this, in turn, compromised their fecundity. Of the 200 women who lived on this estate from 1799–1818, about 55 per cent had children, and those who did so had relatively small families. The reasons for this were many. Women on Mesopotamia lived relatively short lives (at age 17 a female could expect to live until 31), they may have practiced African child-rearing habits (longer birth intervals), and they suffered from chronic malnutrition (with associated fetal, neonatal, and infant death). On Mount Airy, a Virginia plantation raising wheat and corn, the picture was almost entirely reversed. There the birth rate was 39.8 per 1000, while the death rate of 20.6 per 1000 was considerably smaller than that of Mesopotamia. Slave women at Mount Airy could expect to live to 39, two-thirds of all women had children, and those mothers had an average of 6.4 births. Mesopotamia mothers, by contrast, had on average 3.1 live births. The actual percentage of women on Mesopotamia was in fact slightly higher than on Mount Airy, but what fundamentally distinguished the two plantations was the nature of labor. At Mesopotamia, it was sugar work, conducted mainly by women, that physically debilitated slaves; while at Mount Airy, the less onerous duties associated with mixed farming fell mainly on males. Elsewhere in the Caribbean, where women were the majority or near majority of the population by the 1780s, populations did not grow naturally. On the La Barre plantation in Saint Domingue, for instance, where women became a majority of the population between 1790 and 1796, improvements in birth rates were negligible. At Galbaud du Fort, a sugar plantation on the Léogane plain in western Saint Domingue, where the slave population rose from 120 to 190 over the course of the eighteenth century, the number of births remained depressingly low: just two to three per annum. The contrasting experience of Virginia and Caribbean slave women forcefully underscores the impact of crop type on slave demography. Even in the sugar islands, the age–sex profile of the increasingly creolized population should have created robust positive increase. But it did not. The slave population at Mesopotamia ultimately declined from 364 in 1799 to 309 in 1818; the reasons were multi-causal, but the hard labor associated with the cultivation of sugar lay at the axis of demographic decline (Dunn, 1977: 41–46, 54, 57; Moitt, 2001: 32, 91).

Significantly, in locations where cane sugar was not the primary crop, slave populations increased, particularly when balanced sex ratios and creole majorities existed. Such were the conditions in the Minas Gerais region of Brazil, where the economy shifted from gold mining (performed by males) to a diversified economy based on mixed farming, ranching, coffee, and domestic textiles (conducted by men and women) in the nineteenth century. In this location, sex ratios narrowed from 201 males per 100 females in 1786 to 135:100 in 1855. The number of African-born within the slave population similarly declined to 7.6 per cent in 1872, despite the maintenance of international slave trading until mid-century. Creolization and improved sex ratios created the basis for population growth, but relatively high fertility rates ensured lots of children. Even by 1820, the number of enslaved children (aged 0–9 years) per 1000 women (aged 15–45) was 1230, slightly fewer than the 1482 in the American South, but significantly higher than the 560 children (aged under 10) to women (aged 15–49) in three São Paulo slave-holding districts where coffee cultivation expanded and the importation of male slaves continued apace in the 1820s. The relatively high slave fertility rates documented in the Minas Gerais sharply distinguished the region from the specialized mono-crop export economies of the Caribbean or Bahia, where sugar held sway and where laboring and living conditions were very harsh. By contrast, in the Minas Gerais, the slave population grew by natural means and without reliance on the African slave trade. The demographic history of the Minas Gerais was among the only cases in Latin America and the Caribbean where the slave population expanded in ways not dissimilar to that of the United States (Bergad, 1999: 105–7, 142–44, 219; Barickman, 1998: 155–61).

Sugar cultivation reaped a grim harvest, but the epidemiological conditions on Caribbean plantations made life short, miserable, and deadly. Sickness was not confined to the "hott-houses" or plantation hospitals. As estate manager Thomas Thistlewood discovered, semi-permanent ill-health defined life among the living, too. On Egypt Plantation in western Jamaica, where Thistlewood worked in the 1750s and 1760s, one-third of the slaves were either ill or disabled. At Galbaud du Fort in Saint Domingue, between 20 and 25 slaves in a workforce of between 160 and 180 were similarly hospitalized through ill-health. In much of tropical America, the general health of the slaves was abysmally low. At least one in ten were sick, though these figures rose particularly after the exertions of the harvest season. Even in the climatically and epidemiologically mild American South, slaves complained of tooth decay, rickets, skin lesions, syphilis, tuberculosis, and pneumonia. Bio-archeological investigation of the osteological remains of slaves in Jamaica, Barbados, and Maryland confirm the physical stresses of slavery. Chronic periodontal disease associated with severe vitamin D, C and calcium deficiency plagued slaves. Males and females showed evidence of anemia and osteomyelitis (bacterial infection of bones), while tibial bowing (due to poor childhood nutrition) and arthritis affected many. Diarrhea (exacerbated by vitamin A and thiamine deficiency) weakened the enslaved still further, as did geo-helminths such as the intestinal round-worms and threadworms (*Ascaris* and *Trichuris*), which instigated the coughing and bronchial complaints (caused by worm larvae passing through the lungs) and the stomach pains and bouts of diarrhea that slaves so frequently complained of. Lymphatic filariasis (or elephantiasis, a disorder of the lymphatic system with associated swelling) was known as "Barbados leg" and was transmitted to humans by mosquitoes carrying the larvae of parasitic worms. Leprosy and yaws similarly afflicted slaves, as did congenital syphilis, which may have affected one in ten enslaved people. Chigoe fleas made working barefoot a dangerous occupation. The fleas burrowed into feet, causing ulcers and the loss of toes that made the slaves, James Grainger MD clinically observed, "less useful upon a plantation". Many of these illnesses were not fatal in themselves, but they so debilitated enslaved Africans that they frequently fell prey to more lethal infection. Grainger labeled the Caribbean "the Torrid Zone", and for those incapacitated by the rigors of slavery, life was both torrid and distressingly painful (Burnard, 2004: 182; Debien, 1974: 319; Wood and Clayton, 1985: 100–102; Savitt, 1978: 49–80; Corruccini *et al.*, 1987: 183; Armstrong and Fleischman, 2003: 55–61; Kiple, 1984: 71–74, 95–102; 136–43; Hutson, 2005: 16, 19).

Diseases and diets

The misery slaves endured was made more taxing by the plethora of infectious diseases they faced. On practically every New World plantation, three separate disease environments (tropical Africa, temperate Europe, and the American tropics) collided, facilitating a rapid exchange of infection. Native Americans suffered in the first instance, their population being decimated by Euro-Asian smallpox and measles, but the Europeans and Africans who settled on the tropical and semi-tropical American lowlands had little immunity to the epidemiological infections they now encountered. Chronic illnesses that Africans brought with them, such as malaria and yellow fever, proved deadly to colonial settlers and Amerindians alike. The stock British émigré to the colonies, "Johnny New-Come", quickly succumbed to tropical infection, dying at rates that occasionally surpassed those of the enslaved. By the mid-eighteenth century, recent arrivals in Jamaica could not expect to survive more than 13 years in the tropics. Their lives were short, fragile, and punctuated by high infant mortality. Death and dislocation so ravaged the white population that more than 50,000 European migrants were needed to increase the white population of Jamaica by 5000. Those migrants also transported bacterial pneumonia to the New World. Africans lacked immunity to these unfamiliar infections, and in the crowded plantation huts respiratory illnesses and whooping cough proliferated among the enslaved. Since immunity is, in most cases, acquired (through repeated exposure) and not inherited, newly arrived Africans and Europeans faced especially acute risks of mortal infection upon their arrival. Dysentery or the "bloody flux" (characterized by bloody diarrhea) particularly afflicted those who had recently endured the Middle Passage or who died soon after their arrival in the colonies. Both bacillary and amebic dysentery were present in tropical Africa, the former killing many on the slave ships, while the latter reached epidemic proportions on Caribbean estates, leading to intestinal hemorrhage, peritonitis, and death. Between 25 and 50 per cent of newly imported Africans died during the initial two to four years on the tropical American plantations, euphemistically called the "seasoning" period. As many as half of these deaths occurred during the first year, approximately 30 per cent of which were deaths from amebic dysentery. Slaveholders replaced those who perished with new African imports who, in turn, possessed little immunological resistance to the fevers that raged on a New World plantation. The acquisition of creole-born slaves helped break the cycle of seasoning deaths, but the low birth rates exhibited by slaves throughout the sugar islands ensured that most planters relied on African imports (and not creoles) to sustain their losses. Africans who boarded the slave ships were generally malnourished, and within their bodies they transported a high degree of latent amebiasis to the Americas. The low protein–high carbohydrate diet consumed by the enslaved, and the unsanitary conditions aboard slave ships, exacerbated the spread of amebic dysentery, which, after 25–90 days' incubation, surfaced on the plantations with devastating losses. The slave and migrant trades accordingly functioned as disease vectors, transporting immunologically unprotected Africans and Europeans to the New World along with the infectious parasitic diseases they carried with them. The scale and longevity of the slave trade enhanced the communication of disease across the Atlantic, ensuring that for several centuries, gastrointestinal and bronchial infections afflicted Afro-Caribbean slave communities (Brown, 2008: 17; Burnard, 1994: 63–82; Sheridan, 1985: 1–11, 209–10; Kiple, 1984: 59, 65, 71–73; Kiple and Higgins, 1992: 323–27).

At Worthy Park, the principal killers were dysentery, flux (diarrheal diseases), yaws, and dropsy. Eighteenth-century medics commonly misdiagnosed the cause of death and illness on many estates, but the overcrowding, poor sanitation, and proximity of drinking water and earth closets (let alone the animal pens) enhanced the risks of parasitical infection. Dropsy, or fluid retention within the body, was also a significant cause of reported death. One in ten slaves on Worthy Park died of the dropsy, a poorly understood term that described hypertension but also wet or cardiac beriberi, a disease that thrives among thiamine-deficient peoples. Yaws was similarly blamed for nine deaths at Worthy Park, but these were possibly misdiagnosed cases of advanced, life-threatening pellagra (including delirium and extreme physical wasting) or were mistaken as leprosy (where bone or joint lesions occur). Africans were particularly susceptible to pleurisy, tuberculosis (consumption), and various pulmonary infections to which they had little immunological resistance. On Worthy Park alone, 15 slaves succumbed to consumption, while on Newton Plantation in Barbados, one in eight deaths were tuberculosis-related. Smallpox proved a major killer until inoculation suppressed the disease, but typhoid fever raged throughout tropical America and, along with pneumonia, it was responsible for many of the slave "fever" deaths. During the nineteenth century, cholera ravaged the Caribbean, killing 19,000 blacks and 4000 whites in the Havana district in 1836. In 1855, cholera similarly struck Puerto Rico, killing 12 per cent of the island's slave population. Africans possessed some, though by no means complete, immunity to falciparum malaria, yellow fever, and hookworm disease (the principal afflictions of whites), but what made the Caribbean such a morbid location for the enslaved was the combination of infectious and parasitic disease, heavy workloads, and associated fatigue. These factors combined perniciously on sugar estates, where tuberculosis, dropsy, and diarrheal disease contributed to unsanitary living conditions. Overcrowded plantation villages similarly brought the slave population and their highly contagious infections into physical proximity, but it was the poor and unvaried quality of the slave diet and the epidemiological consequence of malnutrition that proved lethal to generations of slaves (Craton, 1978: 19, 123–33; Kiple, 1984: 96–100, 138–46; Figueroa, 2005: 74).

Slave diets were monotonous and unhealthy. On most estates, slaves received half a pound of animal protein daily (salted fish, jerked beef, and pork) and a pint of cereal (cornmeal or rice). Slaves supplemented this diet with plantains, yams, and vegetables cultivated in their own provision grounds. This tedious diet sufficed for raw caloric intake (approximately 3000 calories) but lacked nutritional balance. The beef–cornmeal or fish–rice diets provided scarcely enough protein to maintain good health (83 or 88 per cent of the recommended daily allowance), the high salt content in the fish or meat contributed to hypertension, and the fat content of the diet was chronically low (especially for fish eaters), ensuring low intake of fat-soluble vitamin A. Despite cooking in iron pots, slaves were also iron-deficient, and although vitamin C-rich fruits were readily available, the slow cooking of meals destroyed most vitamin C.

These inadequate nutritional intakes prompted poor health: diarrhea and night blindness are symptomatic of vitamin A deficiency, anemia is related to low iron intake, while bruising, slow wound recovery, loss of appetite, and scurvy indicate vitamin C deficiency. Slaves also consumed inadequate levels of thiamine (particularly those consuming rice), niacin and riboflavin (notably those eating corn), and calcium. The common dental complaints among slaves derived from low calcium intake. Pellagra thrives among niacin-deficient peoples, while beriberi is caused by thiamine deficiency. Most of the vitamin and mineral deficiencies were not fatal, but in the case of pellagra and beriberi, which were commonly misdiagnosed as yaws, leprosy, or dropsy, nutritional deficiencies unleashed major killers. Even at non-life-threatening levels, pellagra would have led to diarrhea, dermatitis, and dementia, while beriberi can either strike quickly (cardiac failure) or slowly rob an individual of the energy required to conduct even the most basic of tasks. At the very least, thiamine and niacin deficiency prompted fatigue, irritability, weight loss, depression, insomnia, and bowel complaints. They also made slaves highly susceptible to typhoid fever (Kiple, 1984: 62, 76–103, 125–33, 145; Sheridan, 1985: 162–78).

Diets improved in the nineteenth century (leading to increases in the height of slaves, notably in the USA and Cuba), but food supply in the eighteenth-century Caribbean was intermittent and was marked by periods of scarcity and hunger followed by abundance. Indeed the period from July to November was known as "the hungry season", when semi-starvation led to fatigue, body wasting, irritability, apathy, and introversion. Whatever scant nutritional reserves the body could draw on were also shared by intestinal worms that grew restless without sufficient food, prompting abdominal pain, swelling, and diarrhea among their hosts. For slave women, malnutrition additionally led to amenorrhea, irregular menstrual cycles, and higher rates of miscarriage. When combined with hard physical labor, maternal undernutrition slows fetal growth, harms the development of the child's immune system, and augments fetal, neonatal, and infant mortality. Even in the nineteenth-century USA, where slaves were comparatively well fed (4200 calories daily but lacking in key vitamins and nutrients), bondswomen delivered children weighing 5.10 pounds at birth. American slave newborns were small compared with the poorest populations of the developing world in the mid-twentieth century, and it is probable that slave women on Caribbean sugar estates gave birth to still smaller infants. Undernourished slave women, moreover, produced nutritionally inferior (calcium- and thiamine-deficient) milk, and inadequate quantities of it (Fraginals, 2001: 310–14; Fogel, 1989: 132–38; Steckel, 1986: 182; Follett, 2003: 527–28).

The nutritional debt was thus transferred from mother to child, even before birth. During their first year, infants were exposed not only to the nutritional deficiencies of their mother's milk, but to lethal infections that killed between one-third and half of those born. In some cases, infant mortality increased to 65 per cent, wiping out any gains accrued from an already negligible birth rate. At Codrington College, 10 of the 23 children born from 1743–48 had died by 1748, most perishing in their first year. Infantile beriberi (prompted by maternal thiamine deficiency) and neonatal tetany (triggered by depleted calcium reserves among nursing mothers) killed many newborns, but it was lockjaw or neonatal tetanus (stemming from infection of the umbilical cord stump) that was the primary cause of infant death during the first weeks of life. Whooping cough, croup, and diphtheria similarly spread among the very young. Congenital syphilis among children kills between 25 and 50 per cent of those infected; given the high level of infection in adults, it is probable that the broad medical terms used by planters to describe childhood illnesses (consumption, dropsy, yaws, convulsions) actually masked syphilis. Malaria, too, represented a major danger to infants, for immunity is acquired only by repeated exposure to the disease. Africans, of course, possessed some inherited immunity via the genetic modification of red blood cells and the production of sickle-shaped corpuscles, which are less readily parasitized by the malarial plasmodium. Only one in four or five Africans possessed the sickle-cell trait (the same proportion gaining malarial protection from G6PD deficiency), but when both parents of a child possess the sickle-cell trait, then the odds are one in four that the child will develop sickle-cell anemia, a life-threatening disease whose symptoms (fever, acute chest pain, swelling, fatigue, jaundice) usually appear at about four months. Approximately one-third of children who face an acute sickle-cell crisis die from stroke, others from hypovolemic shock. Sickle-cell anemia victims are also highly susceptible to meningitis and pneumonia (Moitt, 2001: 92; Bennett, 1958: 55; Jacobi *et al.*, 1992: 154–55; Kiple, 1984: 14–17, 120–32, 148).

Slave infants who survived their first months faced still greater risks in weaning. The cessation of breast milk and the lactose intolerance to bovine milk deprived slave children of calcium, inducing tetany-related convulsions, shortened breath, and larynx and joint spasms which afflicted babies during teething. Calcium- and vitamin D-deficient children also suffered from rickets, while post-weaning stress arrested teeth development. The high-carbohydrate and low-protein diet consumed by children triggered protein-energy malnutrition and relatively mild cases of kwashiorkor, characterized by distended or "pot" bellies, muscle wastage, and diarrhea. At this point in their lives, slave children would also have acquired worms, which proliferate quickly among young children, particularly vitamin A-deficient individuals. Worms afflicted adults and infants with abdominal pains, lethargy, and diarrhea, but malnourished children infested by worms suffered from anemia, stunted growth, and lowered immunity to infection. High levels of infant mortality were not uncommon throughout the nineteenth century, of course. In the poorest neighborhoods of industrial Sheffield, 27.9 infants died per 100 births in 1905, but even these indices were half that of the Caribbean sugar islands. As previously indicated, the number of slave births was problematically small for most of tropical America, but what compounded the problem of demographic decline was the erosive effect of high infant mortality and the grim reality that fewer than half of those born would reach adulthood (Kiple and King, 1981: 17–20, 96–118; Vögele, 1999: 89).

For those who survived, bodily and nutritional harm was matched by the psychological stress of enslavement. The prospect of sale from family and friends haunted slave communities, but it was the frequent use of corporal punishment and the prospect of forced sex with their owners that terrorized the enslaved. The Jamaican slave owner Thomas Thistlewood, for example, wielded the whip forcefully against those who challenged his authority. Slaveholders like Thistlewood well understood that they were surrounded by hundreds of people who would kill them if given the opportunity. Eighteenth-century slaveholders employed every weapon in their arsenal to intimidate slaves, especially in areas such as Westmoreland Parish, Jamaica, where blacks (mostly male and recently enslaved) outnumbered whites by 12:1. Some of the methods used were sadistic. Thistlewood whipped slaves, rubbing salt, lime juice, or pepper into their wounds; he made one slave defecate in another's mouth and then gagged him; he forced slaves to urinate in each other's eyes; he cropped the ears and slit the nostrils of those who ran away; he chained others in "bilboes" or stocks (occasionally coating the prisoner in molasses to attract flies); he branded slaves with his initials; and he decapitated fugitives only to display the head on a pole for all to see. He forced slave women to have sex with him and, although he possessed a black mistress, Thistlewood's sexual exploits extended to 138 bondswomen over almost 40 years. In this violent and volatile world, slaves responded accordingly, launching revolts, escaping to maroon communities, hampering operations by acts of sabotage, or just unhappily getting along as well as they could. Others killed themselves (87 per cent of reported suicides in Cuba 1839–46 were committed by slaves). As with other episodes of suicide and infanticide among slaves, those who took their own lives possibly hoped that their soul would journey back to Africa. The majority of nineteenth-century slave masters did not employ the brutalizing tactics adopted by Thistlewood, but the psychological harm and clinical depression associated with plantation slavery should not be underestimated. Slaves were physically, emotionally, and psychologically abused. Under such circumstances, it is hardly surprising that slaves fell ill so regularly and perhaps, once afflicted, they lacked the physical and emotional resources to recover (Burnard, 2004, 149–51, 156, 178; Hall, 1989: 72–73, 124, Hall, 1971: 21–22; Barcia, 2008: 71–83).

Conclusion

Slave populations declined for many inter-related reasons. The multi-causal factors included low natality and high mortality, uneven sex ratios among adults and a correspondingly small number of children, the slow process of creolization, chronic ill-health among adults and children alike, and severe malnutrition. Added to these endogenous factors was the fundamental role of the slave-plantation regime. The brutal working conditions associated with sugar dictated the lives of the bondspeople; it led to physical exhaustion, it severely impinged on the slave woman's biological capacity to bear children, and it was central to the high mortality rates recorded on the Codrington estates and elsewhere in the Caribbean. The frequency of death on the sugar estates cheapened the lives of the living and bequeathed a precarious and frenetic tenor to West Indian life. In short, the sugar islands were a "demographic disaster area". Where slave populations increased, however, sugar was conspicuous by its absence. Most notably in the American South, balanced sex ratios, early creolization, and relatively high fertility rates ensured population increase. But even there, adult and infant mortality ravaged the slave quarters. And nowhere more so than on Silver Bluff Plantation (Dunn, 1973: 334).

Located on the banks of the Savannah River, a dozen miles from Augusta, Georgia, Silver Bluff was the home to 147 slaves and James Henry Hammond, Governor, US Senator, and leading proponent of the pro-slavery cause. Hammond believed slavery to be a positive good, a gift of Providence, in fact. But for slaves on Silver Bluff, the picture was not quite so rosy. Adults and children alike perished in staggering numbers from "fevers", pneumonia, and intestinal parasites. Even Hammond was shocked by the frequency and regularity of death. "One would think", he disdainfully observed, "that I was a monster of inhumanity". After ten years of plantation management, Hammond noted shamefacedly in September 1841, "it is most melancholy to record that my negroes have in that period actually decreased in the course of nature. There have been 73 births and 82 deaths". Of the children, 72 per cent died before their fifth birthday. Hammond nevertheless attempted to stem the population decline. He followed mid-nineteenth-century medical advice, he introduced sanitary regulations, and he believed stable family life was essential for the smooth running of a plantation. Such sentiments, however, did not preclude Hammond's own sexual exploits within the slave community. As he confided in 1856, Hammond had fathered several of the children on the estate. Putting aside Hammond's personal contribution to the slave population, his interventions in sanitary and medical care steadily reduced child mortality on Silver Bluff to 26 per cent in the 1850s. More significantly, the crude death rate of Hammond's slaves more than halved. By purchasing young men and women, and encouraging family formation, the ratio of births to deaths on Silver Bluff improved from 0.7 (1832–36) to 2.09 (1857–61). This in turn contributed to a 40 per cent increase in the number of children (aged under 10) to women (aged 15 to 49). Hammond grumbled that slaves were "demoralized" by the high levels of morbidity, but the growth of the slave population at Silver Bluff stood in signal contrast to the demographic history of enslaved peoples throughout the Americas. For those in "miserable slavery" as Thomas Thistlewood accurately rejoined, death was omnipresent, an exhausting labor regime taxed the reserves of the very strongest, the distortions of age- and gender-selective purchasing led to low natality, while chronic malnutrition contributed to systemic population decline (Faust, 1982: 75–87; Hall, 1989: 80).

Notes

1 The author expresses his gratitude to Trevor Burnard, Robert Cook, and Rhiannon Stephens for their comments and editorial suggestions on this paper.
2 US Census data for Ascension, St James, St John the Baptist, and St Charles Parishes, LA; Dallas country, AL. http://fisher.lib.virginia.edu/collections/stats/histcensus

Bibliography

Amussen, Susan Dwyer, *Caribbean Exchanges: Slavery and the Transformation of English Society, 1640–1700* (Chapel Hill: University of North Carolina Press, 2007).

Armstrong, Douglas V. and Fleischman, Mark L., "House-Yard Burials of Enslaved Laborers in Eighteenth-Century Jamaica", *International Journal of Historical Archaeology* 7 (2003), 55–61.

Barcia, Manuel, *Seeds of Insurrection: Domination and Resistance on Western Cuban Plantations, 1808–1848* (Baton Rouge: Louisiana State University Press, 2008).

Barickman, Barick J., *A Bahian Counterpoint: Sugar, Tobacco, Cassava, and Slavery in the Recôncavo, 1780–1860* (Stanford: Stanford University Press, 1998).

Bennett, J. H. Jr, *Bondsmen and Bishops: Slavery and Apprenticeship on the Codrington Plantations of Barbados, 1710–1838* (Berkeley: University of California Press, 1958).

Bergad, Laird W., *Slavery and the Demographic and the Economic History of Minas Gerais, Brazil, 1720–1888* (Cambridge: Cambridge University Press, 1999).

Bergad, Laird W., *The Comparative Histories of Slavery in Brazil, Cuba, and the United States* (Cambridge: Cambridge University Press, 2007).

Bergad, Laird W., Iglesias García, Fe and del Carmen Barcia, Maria, *The Cuban Slave Market, 1790–1880* (Cambridge: Cambridge University Press, 1995).

Brown, Vincent, *The Reaper's Garden: Death and Power in the World of Atlantic Slavery* (Cambridge: Harvard University Press, 2008).

Burnard, Trevor, "A Failed Settler Society: Marriage and Demographic Failure in Early Jamaica", *Journal of Social History* 28 (1994), 63–82.

Burnard, Trevor, *Mastery, Tyranny, and Desire: Thomas Thistlewood and his Slaves in the Anglo-Jamaican World* (Chapel Hill: University of North Carolina Press, 2004).

Campbell, Gwyn, Miers, Suzanne and Miller, Joseph C., eds., *Women in Slavery: The Modern Atlantic* (Athens: Ohio University Press, 2008).

Corruccini, Robert S., Jacobi, Keith P., Handler, Jerome S. and Aufderheide, Arthur C., "Implications of Tooth Root Hypercementosis in a Barbados Slave Skeletal Collection", *American Journal of Physical Anthropology* 74 (1987), 179–84.

Craton, Michael, *Searching for the Invisible Man: Slaves and Plantation Life in Jamaica* (Cambridge: Harvard University Press, 1978).

Craton, Michael and Walvin, James, *A Jamaican Plantation: The History of Worthy Park, 1670–1970* (London: W.H. Allen, 1970).

Debien, Gabriel, *Les Esclaves aux Antilles Françaises* (Basse Terre: Société d'Histoire de la Guadeloupe, 1974).

Dunn, Richard S., *Sugar and Slaves: The Rise of the Planter Class in the English West Indies, 1624–1713* (New York: W.W. Norton, 1973).

Dunn, Richard S. "A Tale of Two Plantations: Slave Life at Mesopotamia in Jamaica and Mount Airy in Virginia, 1799–1828", *William and Mary Quarterly* 3rd ser 24 (1977), 32–65.

Dunn, Richard S., "'Dreadful Idlers' in the Cane Fields: The Slave Labor Pattern on a Jamaican Sugar Estate, 1762–1831", *Journal of Interdisciplinary History* 17 (1987), 795–822.

Dunn, Richard S., "The Demographic Contrast between Slave Life in Jamaica and Virginia, 1760–1865", *Proceedings of the American Philosophical Society* 151 (2007), 43–60.

Eltis, David, "The Volume and Structure of the Transatlantic Slave Trade: A Reassessment", *William and Mary Quarterly* 3rd ser 58 (2001), 17–46.

Eltis, David and Engerman, Stanley L., "Was the Slave Trade Dominated by Men?" *Journal of Interdisciplinary History* 23 (1992), 237–57.

Eltis, David and Engerman, Stanley L., "Fluctuations in Sex and Age Ratios in the Transatlantic Slave Trade, 1663–1864", *Economic History Review* 46 (1993), 308–23.

Eltis, David, Lewis, Frank and Richardson, David, "Slave Prices, the African slave trade, and productivity in the Caribbean, 1674–1807", *Economic History Review* 58 (2005), 673–700.

Faust, Drew Gilpin, *James Henry Hammond and the Old South: A Design for Mastery* (Baton Rouge: Louisiana State University, 1982).

Figueroa, Luis A., *Sugar, Slavery, and Freedom in Nineteenth-Century Puerto Rico* (Chapel Hill: University of North Carolina Press, 2005).

Fogel, Robert W., *Without Consent or Contract: The Rise and Fall of American Slavery* (New York: W.W. Norton, 1989).

Fogel, Robert W. and Engerman, Stanley L., *Time on the Cross: The Economics of American Negro Slavery* (New York: W.W. Norton, 1974).

Follett, Richard, "Heat, Sex, and Sugar: Pregnancy and Childbearing in the Slave Quarters", *Journal of Family History* 28 (2003), 510–39.

Follett, Richard, *The Sugar Masters: Planters and Slaves in Louisiana's Cane World 1820–1860* (Baton Rouge: Louisiana State University Press, 2005).

Follett, Richard, "Gloomy Melancholy: Sexual Reproduction among Louisiana Slave Women, 1840–60" in Gwyn Campbell, Suzanne Miers and Joseph C. Miller, eds, *Women in Slavery: The Modern Atlantic* (Athens: Ohio University Press, 2008), 54–78.

Fraginals, Manuel Moreno, "Africa in Cuba: A Quantitative Analysis of the African Population in the Island of Cuba", in Vera Rubin and A. Tuden, eds, *Comparative Perspectives on Slavery in New World Plantation Societies* (New York: New York Academy of Sciences, 1977) 187–201.

Fraginals, Manuel Moreno, *El Ingenio: Complejo Económico Social Cubano del Azúcar* (repr. Barcelona: Crítica, 2001).

Geggus, David, "Sex Ratio, Age and Ethnicity in the Atlantic Slave Trade: Data from French Shipping and Plantation Records", *Journal of African History* 30 (1989), 23–44.

Goveia, Elsa V., *Slave Society in the British Leeward Islands at the End of the Eighteenth Century* (repr, Westport: Greenwood Press, 1980).

Graham, Richard, "Another Middle Passage: The Internal Slave Trade in Brazil", in Walter Johnson, ed., *The Chattel Principle: Internal Slave Trades in the Americas* (New Haven: Yale University Press, 2004), 291–324.

Hall, Douglas, *In Miserable Slavery: Thomas Thistlewood in Jamaica, 1750–86* (London: Macmillan, 1989).

Hall, Gwendolyn Midlo, *Social Control in Slave Plantation Societies: A Comparison of St. Domingue and Cuba* (Baltimore: Johns Hopkins University Press, 1971).

Handler, Jerome S. and Lange, F. W., *Plantation Slavery in Barbados: an Archaeological and Historical Investigation* (Cambridge: Harvard University Press, 1978).

Higman, B. W., *Slave Populations of the British Caribbean, 1807–1834* (Baltimore: Johns Hopkins University Press, 1984).

Higman, B. W., *Slave Population and Economy in Jamaica, 1807–1834* (repr, Kingston: University of West Indies Press, 1995).

Hutson, J. Edward, ed., *On The Treatment and Management of the More Common West-India Diseases* (Kingston: University of West Indies Press, 2005), 16, 19.

Jacobi, Keith P., Cook, Della Collins, Corruccini, Robert. S. and Handler, Jerome S., "Congenital Syphilis in the Past: Slaves at Newton Plantation, Barbados, West Indies", *American Journal of Physical Anthropology* 89 (1992), 145–58.

John, A. Meredith, *The Plantation Slaves of Trinidad: A Mathematical and Demographic Enquiry* (Cambridge: Cambridge University Press, 1988).

Kiple, Kenneth F., *The Caribbean Slave: A Biological History* (Cambridge: Cambridge University Press, 1984).

Kiple, Kenneth F. and Higgins, Brian T., "Mortality caused by Dehydration during the Middle Passage", in J. E. Inikori and Stanley L. Engerman, eds, *The Atlantic Slave Trade: Effects on Economies, Societies, and Peoples in Africa, the Americas, and Europe* (Durham: Duke University Press, 1992), 323–27.

Kiple, Kenneth F. and King, Virginia Himmelsteib, *Another Dimension to the Black Diaspora: Diet, Disease, and Racism* (Cambridge: Cambridge University Press, 1981).

Klein, Herbert and Engerman, Stanley L., "Fertility Differentials between Slaves in the United States and the British West Indies: A Note on Lactation Practices and their Possible Implications", *William and Mary Quarterly*, 3d ser. 35 (1978), 357–74.

Kotlikoff, Lawrence J., "Quantitative Description of the New Orleans Slave Trade, 1804–62", in Robert W. Fogel, ed., *Without Consent or Contract: Conditions of Slave Life and the Transition to Freedom, Technical Papers*, Vol. I (New York: W.W. Norton, 1992), 31–53.

Lee, William Robert and Marschalk, Peter, "Demographic Change and Industrialization in Germany, 1815–1914: Bremen in Comparative Perspective", *History of the Family* 5 (2000), 379–86.

Livi-Bacci, Massimo, "Fertility, Nutrition, and Pellagra: Italy during the Vital Revolution", *Journal of Interdisciplinary History* 16 (1986), 435.

Moitt, Bernard, *Women and Slavery in the French Antilles, 1635–1848* (Bloomington: Indiana University Press, 2001).

Morgan, Kenneth, "Slave Women and Reproduction in Jamaica, c. 1776–1834", *History* 91 (2006).

Morgan, Philip D., *Slave Counterpoint: Black Culture in the Eighteenth-Century Chesapeake and Lowcountry* (Chapel Hill: University of North Carolina, 1998), 80–95.

Nwokeji, G. Ugo and Eltis, David, "Characteristics of Captives Leaving the Cameroons for the Americas, 1822–37", *Journal of African History* 43 (2002), 191–210.

Savitt, Todd L., *Medicine and Slavery: The Diseases and Health Care of Blacks in Antebellum Virginia* (Urbana: University of Illinois Press, 1978).

Schwartz, Stuart B., *Sugar Plantations in the Formation of Brazilian Society: Bahia, 1550–1835* (Cambridge: Cambridge University Press, 1985).

Sheridan, Richard B., *Doctors and Slaves: A Medical and Demographic History of Slavery in the British West Indies, 1680–1834* (Cambridge: University of Cambridge Press, 1985).

Steckel, Richard H., "Birth Weights and Infant Mortality among American Slaves", *Explorations in Economic History* 23 (1986), 173–98.

Tadman, Michael, "The Demographic Cost of Sugar: Debates on Save Societies and Natural Increase in the Americas", *American Historical Review* 105 (2000), 1534–75.

Tansey, Richard, "Bernard Kendig and the New Orleans Slave Trade", *Louisiana History* 23 (1982), 159–78.

Vögele, Jörg, *Urban Mortality Change in England and Germany, 1870–1913* (Liverpool: Liverpool University Press, 1999).

Wood, Betty and Clayton, T. R., "Slave Birth, Death, and Disease on Golden Grove Plantation, Jamaica, 1765–1810", *Slavery and Abolition* 6 (1985), 99–121.

8

GENDER AND FAMILY LIFE

Jennifer L. Morgan

Introduction

African women were more important to the project of constructing the Americas – both literally and symbolically – than historians have been willing to acknowledge. Four-fifths of all women who migrated to the Americas before 1800 were African. During the same period, the numbers of enslaved forced migrants outnumbered European migrants by almost three to one (Eltis, 2000: 97; Morgan, 2007: 122). We know, of course, how this came to pass. The trans-Atlantic slave trade set in motion a massive transformation of the Atlantic world – arguably, the trade itself created the Atlantic world – setting in motion structural, material, cultural, and demographic changes with which historians continue to grapple. Recently, historians and scholars of the Atlantic have exhibited a new appreciation for the multiple ways in which the trans-Atlantic slave trade produced and mobilized gendered articulations of power. In the context of this circulation of commodified bodies, African women emerge and disappear from the historical record in ways both predictable and also startling. Racial slavery produces them as both brute and sexualized labour. Contemporaries relied upon Old World ideologies of gender and difference in order to articulate a natural order in which black women's bodies were especially degraded. By giving birth to children, women were the natural reproducers of hereditary racial slavery. Thus women's involvement in family life was always imbricated with the racial logic on which their enslavement rested. For women caught in the circuits of trade and exchange that characterized slavery in the Americas, family life was always problematic. As European traders put the trans-Atlantic slave trade into motion, they simultaneously constructed images of African people as enslavable in ways that situated women's bodies and reproductive possibility as a fulcrum upon which racial difference depended.

Gender and racial difference

In a collection of essays published in English in 1587, Richard Hakluyt showed how England was ready to engage in the trans-oceanic trade that Iberia had dominated for almost a century. Deeply concerned by both the economic and the religious implications of Spanish ascendancy in exploration and colonization, Hakluyt deployed his editorial skills to construct an England that must engage in overseas trade or else lose its Protestant legitimacy (Bartels, 1992: 517–38; Griffin, 2002). Many of the narratives collected by Hakluyt were concerned with exploration and trade. He was especially interested, for example, in discussions of navigable rivers, and was full of advice about which local peoples were in possession of valuable mineral wealth. For Hakluyt, what was at stake was imposing an "English" system of human geography upon Africa. In the aftermath of Queen Elizabeth's defeat of the Spanish Armada in 1588, the relationship between England and Spain would be increasingly marked (on the English side) by an ethnically or racially coded notion of Spanish immorality. But in this relationship, accusations of racialized impurity became enmeshed in sexuality. In 1590, for example, Edward Daunce reminded English readers that "the *Mores* in eight monthes conquered *Spaine* ... and ... the Spaniards were eight hundred years before they recovered that losse: during which time, we must not thinke that the Negroes sent for women out of *Aphrick*."[1] Such a characterization shows us that careful attention to racial and sexually coded difference is crucial to understanding the gendered experience of enslavement.

In the early modern European imagination, it was in Africa and Asia that oddities and monsters, such as anthropophagi, troglodytes, and pygmies, had their home (Burke, 2004: 27). It was a relatively short step for European commentators to equate the Africans they saw in Africa with the monsters that they imagined lived there. In the process, naked human savages were transformed into commodities. Literal monsters became figurative ones. This kind of short-hand indication of savagery shifted as the planting of the Americas intensified. Europeans increasingly justified enslavement by reference to the strangeness of African bodies, paying particular attention to female bodies (Morgan, 2004: 12–49). As Kim Hall has written, "blackness begins to represent the destructive potential of strangeness, disorder, and variety, particularly when intertwined with the familiar, and familiarly threatening, unruliness of gender" (Hall, 1995: 28).

Hall's assertions notwithstanding, there was not a singular trajectory from the strange to the racist. Europeans' shifting interests in African souls and bodies mean that their responses to Africans were different depending on the various stages of their involvement with Africa. For example, French missionaries in the Antilles heaped more vitriol upon Africans in the 1630s, when Africans were scarce in the French West Indies, than they did 20 years later, as increased sugar cultivation meant that priests had the possibility of making thousands of African converts to Catholicism (Peabody, 2004). Nevertheless, as the degree to which enslaved Africans were degraded changed in response to how useful various European nations found them, their enslavement was made increasingly natural. Moreover, gender assumptions were an important part of this process of naturalization. Europeans expressed increasingly derogatory views about the bodies of female Africans in order to justify African enslavement.

These derogatory views became more prevalent as the plantation system took hold in Barbados and Virginia. English propagandists, for example, argued that an African woman's work was interrupted neither by childbirth nor childcare – her distended breasts allowed for an imaginary perfection at hard labour. English thinkers hardly gendered African women as female, for their descriptions of African female bodies severed the connection between childrearing and the domestic sphere. What was crucial in the English imagining of African women was that African women, unlike European women, could leave the home to work even while nursing children. Such descriptions and images were crucial components of early racial ideology. Long before scientific racism emerged in the mid-nineteenth century, Europeans had begun to conceive of the African body as inherently both distinct and also diminished. An absence of pain in childbirth meant that African women, having sidestepped the curse of Eve, were not of the same genus as Europeans. African women who were enslaved in the Americas had to try and fashion social and familial identities for themselves in the face of these wide-spread corporeal images, mobilized in conjunction with a commercial imperative to exploit African labour.

These visual and literary images were necessary because, before the legitimacy of the slave trade and Atlantic slavery became established, some Africans had to be marked both as significantly different from English people and also as people in need of trans-formation. Thomas Herbert's 1637 description of a Hottentot woman suckling over her shoulder is a striking example of how racialist logic was made visible in the strange bodies of African women.

For the claim ultimately was not that enslaved Africans were not human, but rather that their humanity was so strange and deformed that it was Europeans' duty to help lead African into useful, or civilized, patterns of social interaction. Images and descrip-tions of African women giving birth without pain, suckling newborn children over their shoulder with distended breasts, and needing no recovery time after public and indiffer-ent births, all situated African women well outside European gender conventions. Africans' principal purpose as humans was to work, and to work hard. It is important to note also that had European observers been able to see these women outside the lens of commodification, they might have understood something about the centrality of West African women to local economies. The imperative to extract value from the American colonies, however, displaced other ways of seeing. These images of African women then, even those not immediately identifiable as derogatory, produced a body marked for slavery.

Gender and the slave trade

From its inception, European observers embedded their descriptive language of the slave trade in their gendered notions of humanity and of the family. Gomes Eannes de Zurara described the first large shipment of Africans to Lisbon in 1444 as follows:

> ... though we could not understand the words of their language, the sound of it right well accorded with the measure of their sadness. But to increase their sufferings still more, there now arrived those who had charge of the division of the captives, and who began to separate one from another, in order to make an equal partition ... and then was it needful to part fathers from sons, husbands from wives, brothers from brothers. No respect was shewn either to friends or relations, but each fell where his lot took him ... And who could finish that partition without very great toil? For as often as they placed them in one part the sons, seeing their fathers in another, rose with great energy and rushed over to them; the mothers clasped their other children in their arms, and threw themselves flat on the ground with them, receiving blows with little pity for their own flesh, if only they might not be torn from them.[2]

For de Zurara, the pathos of enslavement was best evoked by the thwarted ties of family, the wrenching of parent–child bonds, and ultimately by a mother's willingness to sacrifice herself in an effort to protect her child. In 1444 he could articulate the violation of parental bonds without grappling with its importance. As opposed to slavery in the classical world, slavery in the Americas, rooted as it was in a commodified biological inheritance, made the family life of the enslaved problematic. The enslaved mother was simultaneously rendered impossible (as the child was wrenched from her grasp) and crucial (as her womb marked the child as a product legitimately offered onto the Atlantic market). The institution was founded on the constantly recurring process of subverting the parental bond in favour of the commercial link. Regardless of sex ratios and disease environments that would, far more often than not, leave enslaved women incapable of conceiving children, as noted by Richard Follett in Chapter 7 of this volume, an African woman whose maternity was either potential or actualized was crucial to the enterprise of perpetual racial slavery. Whether she appears in the archives as an effort to dismiss or to proclaim the humanity of the African slave, a figure of black maternity is central to the claim that blackness actually exists.

We need to stress that there were significant numbers of women caught in the trans-Atlantic slave trade and put to work in the fields and industries of the American colonies. While there has been promising growth in scholarship on women and slavery, gender continues to be an acknowledged but largely under-theorized area in slavery studies or in studies of early modern racial formation; as a result, women still tend to disappear from broad assertions of what slavery was and whom it affected.

Significantly more males than females were exported from the various regions of Africa. Over the entire 400-year history of the trans-Atlantic slave trade, the ratio was approximately 179 males to 100 females (Eltis and Engerman, 1993: 256). Nevertheless, women and girls were always present in the slave trade, even when they were fewer in number than men and boys. Moreover, male majorities were not uniform. The imperative to pay close attention to differences in slavery over time and space is, perhaps, nowhere more fully rendered then around questions of sex ratio, family formation, and labour in slave economies throughout the Americas. Over the course of the entire period of the Atlantic slave trade, adult men – although they were the largest group of persons transported – constituted less than half of the total number of adults and children brought to the Americas. Women, boys, and girls combined outnumbered them in the trade. In the last four decades of the seventeenth century, overall, women constituted almost 40 per cent of those who crossed the Atlantic, men constituted 50 per cent, and children made up the remainder. During the eighteenth century, the proportion of children (those thought by slave traders to be under the age of 15) was 20 per cent, women were 30 per cent of all captives, and men were half of all those transported across the Atlantic. North American import patterns were different in that the sex ratios tended to be lower: 158 males to 100 females. By the end of the eighteenth century, import patterns to North America mirrored those to the Caribbean in the seventeenth century, when traders brought relatively even numbers of males and females to the regions. Elsewhere in the Americas, it was not until the nineteenth century that the proportion of women would fall to almost 15 per cent.

These sex ratios become part of the process of ethnogenesis that was initiated throughout the Atlantic as dispersed peoples worked to craft both new and also rooted identities. In the seventeenth century, for example, ships leaving the Bight of Biafra carried 20–25 per cent fewer men than those leaving the Upper Guinea Coast or West Central Africa. Indeed, during the entire period of the slave trade, the Bight of Biafra was the port of origin for more enslaved women than any other. Ugo Nwokeji argues that the distance from the Saharan slave market (where slaveowners paid high prices for women) and the relative marginality of local female slavery helped to explain the high rate of female captives sold for transport to the Americas from the Bight of Biafra (Nwokeji, 2001: 47–68). Despite the broad truth that the Bight of Biafra sold the highest proportion of women into the trade, here too, particularities matter. The slave trade shaped life across the Atlantic in many ways, linking identity with ethnicity in ways interdependent with the power and dislocation of the trade in human beings. Women designated "Ibo" by New World slave traders may have experienced some discomforting resonance. The term signified "Stranger" prior to the eighteenth century in the areas from which they were captured (Byrd, 2006). Once in the Americas, first generations of enslaved Africans tended to organize themselves around their ethnic identity – choosing marriage partners and kin from among those who shared a common original location, if not a shipboard confinement (Mintz and Price, 1976 [1992]: 42–51; Bennett, 2003: 79–126). For women who may have understood their enslavement as the result of categories of exclusion that were mobilized by people to whom they were now linked by language and place of origin, the experience of endogamy – marrying within a social group – must have been rife with contradiction. It couldn't have been otherwise.

The trans-Atlantic trade was ultimately an attempt to create an entirely new category of people. The women and men who supplanted those categories of social despoilment and commercial value with meaningful relationships and powerful assertions of their complex humanity in turn crafted new categories of social and cultural meaning in the Americas (Smallwood, 2007). For women and men on board slave ships, the process of rejecting the categories that legitimated their capture and transport sometimes happened even before the ships left the African coast. Female captives were often granted more mobility on board slave ships than were men. This mobility facilitated crewmen's ability to sexually assault captive women, but it also meant that women were frequently at the heart of plotting and executing shipboard revolts. In 1721 on board the *Robert*, anchored offshore of Sierra Leone, a woman was hung by her thumbs and whipped to death for leading a plot that ended in the death of three crew members. Women on board the *Thomas* in 1797 stole weapons from the ship's armoury and passed them to the men below. When faced with the unthinkable – that a starving crew would feed off the body of a dead African child – women on board the *Thomas* rebelled and killed three crew members (Taylor, 2006: 85–103). For most female captives, of course, their efforts at resistance on slave ships were thwarted, but what is important is seeing how from the very start of the enslavement process women were prepared to use collective action to change their situation.

Once in the Americas, the common experience for slave women was that work and reproduction were central to their lives. Work is dealt with in detail by Lorena Walsh and Richard Follett in Chapters 6 and 7 of this volume. There is a singular experience of demography among those enslaved in North America – entwined with birth and infant mortality rates – which meant that, for better or worse, children born to enslaved parents tended to survive their infancy and grow to adulthood. It was only in North America that slave populations increased naturally (they began to do so in the Chesapeake from the 1740s and in the Lowcountry from the 1760s). In North America, by the mid-eighteenth century, women found themselves parenting children whose survival enriched the holdings of slave owners: on the sugar islands, pregnancies were thwarted by the death toll meted out by sugar cultivation. But it is here, in the work that slave owners made these women perform, that one finds the alchemy of race and gender most powerfully illuminated.

Gender before the plantation

Early in the development of slave societies in the Americas, sex ratios in the slave trade were relatively equal. Enslaved women tended to do the same types of work as men. European and African gender conventions of appropriate work clashed as African men found themselves performing the women's work of agricultural labour, and as slave owners put women to work building colonial roadways, which was men's work in Africa. The social logic of labour was transformed for both the enslaved and the free. In an effort to fully comprehend what the parameters of this change might have meant, some scholars have suggested that this transformation was akin to "de-gendering". They have argued that the violation under way was so profound that to express the extent of the violation, we need to evoke the unthinkable, an un-gendered body.[3] It is perhaps evidence of the limits of our own imagination that we turn to gender as a metaphor for this kind of violent disembodiment. Much of the scholarly work on the history of slavery is, indeed, a search for metaphor. But, given the extent to which early modern formulations of the racial difference that enables such violence draw on and deploy gender as means of conveying difference, it seems inadequate to suggest that the ultimate manifestation of racialized violence could be felt in an imaginary vacuum created by the absence of gender. It is difficult to speculate as to how this shift in notions of work was experienced – in the context of the brutality and disorientation of forced transport to the Americas, perhaps the old cultural meanings assigned to the work one was now performing in such a new context would seem a relatively meaningless violation. On the side of the slave-owning class, these newly inscribed parameters of work became part of the fabric of racial logic; for the enslaved, forced labour became the lived environment through which efforts to form families and establish kin ties were made.

English law articulated settlers' understanding that work had a strong gender dimension, modified by race. The essential difference between black and white women lay, according to a 1643 Virginia statute, in the different kinds of work each did. In this first act in the English context to legislate racial difference, black women's work was defined as permanently taxable – tithable regardless of any change in their status from slave to free – while white women's could be free of tax (Brown, 1996: 116–20). This legislation happened well before the colony of Virginia moved firmly over to slavery on a large scale. In the 1640s, the enslaved population in Virginia was negligible. The turn to full reliance on enslaved labour in the Chesapeake was almost 50 years away. Nevertheless, the spectre of black freedom was alarming enough to encourage lawmakers to craft legislative boundaries where what blacks could or could not do was spelled out. Such clarity around the criteria of women's work helps to illuminate the process by which racial differences become naturalized in the interplay between notions of work and shifting hierarchies of gender difference. Difference that had formerly been tautological was redeployed along newly intensified lines of race and work. These redeployments happened throughout the Atlantic littoral at different times and places but, collectively, they signalled a process that had been well under way by the time the Virginian legislators penned their distinction about black women's fieldwork.

Legislative efforts to regulate racial purity on the North American mainland similarly testify to the centrality of gender as a tool for crafting racial logic in early American life. Slave-owning assemblies in Maryland and Virginia initiated drawn-out statutory processes of regulating contact between slave and free over the course of the seventeenth century, interventions that would ultimately be borrowed by planters in other New World slave societies. By the eighteenth century, the laws of slavery, especially those relating to gender differences, were similar in every Anglo-American slave society. But just because the final outcome turned out to be the same, we still need to look at the process by which slave owners came to regulate slave women and came to control their behaviour, because these processes show how anxieties about connections between black, brown, and white bodies were a central concern of those in positions of power.

The 1662 Virginia Act that defined that all children born of the bodies of black women were slaves, even if their fathers were free and white, made gender a central component of an emerging discourse of race. Faced with children born from women whose humanity could not be questioned, economic concerns trumped those of paternity. A similar kind of process occurred in French American slave societies. Although the 1685 *Code Noir* allowed for interracial marriage, in fact seventeenth century Martinique planters passed legislation convicting white men of crimes for fathering mulatto children. Those children could be purchased but were ordered to be freed at the age of 21. In Guadeloupe, in 1680, the island's legislators passed a law that echoed the 1662 position of Virginian slave owners in which the condition of a child followed that of its mother, at least if that mother was black. The association between blackness and forced labour was now legally complete. In 1664, Maryland passed a law that decreed that "whatsoever free-born woman shall intermarry with any slave. ... shall serve the Master of such slave during the life of her husband; and that all the issue of such free-born women, so married shall be slaves as their fathers were."[4] Punishing white women for giving birth to black babies rendered the apprehensions of the colony's slave owners transparent; for even as racial categories came into focus for white settlers, interracial sexual and social contact were a constant reminder that claims of immutable racial difference had to be constantly bolstered by the law. But if the spectre of white women engaged in sexual acts with African men was one area of concern for legislators, it was white men's sexual access to black women that was a more significant problem. Ultimately, the logic of paternity would have to be entirely set aside in the context of the chimera of racially distinct bodies. Statutes passed by both French and English colonial assemblies suggest that colonial slave owners saw questions of racial constancy as critical. They highlight the intensity of efforts to establish legal boundaries between white men and the people they enslaved. These laws also remind us that the dividing line between the realms of labour and family were essentially rendered non-existent by the ideologies of racial dominance. Slaves who tried to have families stumbled into a quagmire of racial meaning, the outcomes of which indelibly marked one's future and that of one's child. The concerns about sexual liaisons made explicit by the Chesapeake legislators were the implicit foundations for laws that conflated racial identity and forced labour, and which imposed significant barriers for slaves in trying to create viable family life.

The Virginian statutes, moreover, occurred in the absence of a fully developed slave society. These legislators were not, in other words, looking out the windows of the Assembly over fields filled with black labourers. Indeed, through much of the seventeenth century, settlers in British North America only aspired to the level of slave ownership that planters in the West Indies had achieved by mid-century and that the Latin American colonies had experienced since the early sixteenth century. But throughout the Atlantic, as Europeans devised strategies to rationalize the alchemy of race, work, and intimacy that was at the heart of slave societies in the Americas, gender and family life remained crucial. In mid-seventeenth-century Martinique and Guadeloupe, a significant proportion of slave owners had invested in female-only or in female-majority holdings (Moitt, 2001: 13). They probably did so intentionally in order to breed a labour force rather than build a slave force through purchase from the slave trade.

Regardless of the desires of slave owners, however, enslaved women and men in these early moments in the history of American slave societies established families for their own reasons. On the first sugar island in the Americas, Hispaniola, Spanish settlers began to enslave African labourers in small numbers beginning in 1504, turning more intensely to African labourers by 1529 – the date of the first African slave revolt that Christmas. The Spanish Crown suggested that each African slave be accompanied to the West Indies by "his wife" in order to stop slave rebellion (Guitar, 2006: 51). In 1626, Dutch settlers imported the first 11 Africans to serve as slaves to the Dutch West India Colony. They were all male. The company imported three women two years later for "the comfort of the company's Negro men". Outnumbered almost four to one, these first women enslaved to the Dutch West India Company in New Amsterdam experienced an isolation that later dissipated when slave imports became more sex-balanced. By the final year of Dutch settlement, Peter Stuyvesant dispatched a "lot of Negroes and Negresses" to the highest bidders. Of those who purchased more than a single labourer, only one did not buy enslaved women. A few months later, the *St Jacob* arrived in the colony with 160 men and 140 women – an imbalance, to be sure, but one that supplied slave owners with labouring women and men. Here, as elsewhere in the colonies, enslaved women were seen as a natural part of the work force. They were neither relegated to the last chosen and least desirable part of the cargo, nor were they put to work only in domestic spaces. Indeed, for women of African descent, the connection between femaleness and domesticity was effectively severed by the beginning of the seventeenth century by the racialist ideology circulating in the Atlantic.

In the hands of slave owners and others benefiting from the new structures of labour in the colonies, domesticity became part of the technologies of slave ownership. Domesticity is an important lens through which we can view both the violence and the strategic resistance of the enslaved. It is not only in the wrenching depiction of families torn asunder in an Iberian slave market that marriage existed as part of the fabric of racial slavery. In the 1660s, Peter Stuyvesant sold an enslaved man whom he recognized as married and then "urged" the purchaser to buy the man's wife as well. He wielded the marriage as a moral imperative for the buyer – though this was an imperative he failed to recognize as the seller.

Stuyvesant and the enslaved men and women labouring in New Amsterdam thought quite differently about marriage. In February 1644, a group of enslaved Africans petitioned for a change in their status. Pleading that they had faithfully served the Dutch West India Company for the past 18 years, the petitioners argued for their freedom. In doing so, they argued that "they are burthened with many children so that it is impossible for them to support their wives and children, as they have been accustomed to do, if they must continue in the Company's service". In response, the Council of

New Netherlands conferred what historians have called "half-freedom" upon the named petitioners "and their wives".[5] These women were appendages to the petition and, presumably, were the same to the petitioners. It is hard for a historian to know what to make of them. However, they were absolutely central both to the logic of the petition and to the Dutch West India Company's efforts to maintain control of petitioners. In exchange for freedom, the petitioners were required to make an annual payment to the Dutch West India Company in the form of wheat and a hog valued at 20 guilders, and to accept that "their children at present born or yet to be born, shall be bound and obligated to serve the Honorable West India Company as Slaves". The mothers of these children understood what this meant. Children born to freed parents would produce profit by their work; but their real importance to the colony lay not in what they could carry or grow or build or clean, but rather in their ability to fix their parents as docile and willing workers. Dorothe Angola, the adoptive parent of an orphaned Anthony (child of half-free parents), and Maria Portogys, who apprenticed her daughter as a household servant to a Dutch family, for example, both became historical actors by leaving records in which they tried to protect their children by getting them formalized apprenticeships (Harris, 2003: 26).

Both Dutch and English colonial slave owners in New York paid careful attention to the reproductive lives of enslaved women in order to try and maximize their investment in slave property. Crowded urban conditions meant that in most slave owning households there was only one enslaved person. Natural reproductive increase proved difficult to achieve. One slave owner advertised a woman for sale, noting that "she had been married for several years without having a child". Another wrote "to be sold, a likely barren Negro Wench" (Foote, 2004: 75). It seems that colonial slave owners looked upon the children or potential children of the women they enslaved as burdensome and potentially dangerous. Natural increase among the enslaved in New York did not commence until the 1740s and 1750s, despite the early achievement of balanced sex ratios in the slave population.

Despite the hostility of slave owners to women having children, enslaved women did bear children in colonial New York City. Recent work on African burial grounds in lower Manhattan indicates that 30 per cent of the examined remains belonged to infants under the age of 2, while 10 per cent were children between the ages of 2 and 12. The children buried were likely to have suffered from malnutrition, and the mortality rate of young persons of African descent was considerably higher than that in the slave-owning class (Blakey, 2001: 412). Children were, clearly, being born but they were dying young after much mistreatment. It is difficult, of course, to know or to speculate about the cost of their suffering, both that borne by themselves and by their parents.

Slave owners did acknowledge an enslaved person's right to a family life and associated freedom with family circumstances. In a petition submitted to Holland, Protestant settlers in New Amsterdam protested the enslavement of free black children, saying that the West India Company enslaved these children "though it is contrary to the laws of every Christian people that anyone born of a free Christian mother should be a slave and compelled to remain in servitude". In response, the Dutch West India Company argued that they had not separated children from parents. Children were ideologically essential in another arena addressed in the Protestant petition. Between 1639 and 1655, some 57 African converts were baptized in the Dutch Reformed Church – of those, 49 were children. Accused of neglecting the spiritual life of adults, church officials responded that adults come to the church out of "worldly and perverse aims ... they want nothing else than to deliver their children from bodily slavery without striving for piety and Christian virtue" (Foote, 2004: 49). In other words, slave owners and their critics alike mobilized conventional notions of family ties to mitigate the denial of those same family ties under slavery. Thus reproduction, family, and racial slavery come together under a rubric of demography and religion, and in the process crafted a kind of painful intimacy that augured no kind of respite from racial violence.

As slave societies came into full fruition, the alchemy of race, hereditary slavery, and intimacy became increasingly complicated. As Trevor Burnard has shown in the case of eighteenth-century Jamaica, a slave owner such as Thomas Thistlewood could live in extremely close proximity to the women and men he enslaved without conceding that they shared anything approaching civil space. For the enslaved women under Thistlewood's control on the Egypt plantation in Westmoreland Parish, Jamaica, this translated into incessant danger of rape at the hands of a man who carefully recorded most, if not all, of his close to 4000 sexual acts meted out on the bodies of enslaved women. Their work in the fields, their pregnancies and miscarriages, and their efforts to protect themselves from Thistlewood all speak to the ways in which sexual vulnerability – intimate violence – defined female lives under slavery (Burnard, 2004: 133).

Southern frontiers of plantation: postscript

My interest thus far in charting a set of ideologies crucial to, yet distinct from, plantation-based economies is to place both women and gendered ideologies of intimacy within the ground of racial slavery. It is in the example of plantation work that the idea that women were ungendered by labour holds the most powerful sway. The notion that brute labour is fundamentally male leads to the presumption either that women did not perform such labour or that, if they did so, they lost their gendered identity in the process. Instead, I argue that as an analytic category as well as an experiential one, gender retained its definitional power for women and men under slavery. Well before South Carolina turned to rice, or before the West Indies became a sugar-producing region, slave owners made women work in agricultural labour. In the Americas, women performed plantation work alongside men. Indeed, the entire system of hereditary racial slavery depended upon slave owners' willingness to ignore cultural meanings of work that had been established in England and to make Africans work in ways that the English or the Spanish or the French could not conceive of working themselves. Once slave owners received almost equal numbers of African men and women from slave traders, they inverted the gender ideology that they applied to white women and work. As more and more enslaved persons were brought to the Americas, African women and girls increasingly found themselves in the fields. Such practices were solidified by the mid-eighteenth century on plantations like *Roaring River* in Jamaica, where, for example, 76 per cent of enslaved women were field workers compared with only 33 per cent of enslaved men. These women, it should be noted, were also the parents of 43 boys and 36 girls; most of whom were too young to work at the time of the plantation's inventory in 1756 (Sheridan, 1974: 257). In the sugar plantations of the French Antilles, as early as the seventeenth century, women were the majority of the field gangs: both in the so-called 'first gangs' of strongest workers and in the 'second gangs' – the latter mistakenly associated with women's work, as they were the site for weaker, sick, young workers and women who were pregnant or nursing. Moreover, once cane was harvested, the business of feeding the stalks into the mills – a job whose obvious dangers were mitigated by the ready presence of a sharp bill to sever the hand or arm of the unfortunate sleepy worker found caught in the grindstones – was women's work (Moitt, 2001: 40, 49).

The importance of women's labour to the cultivation of rice in the South Carolina Lowcountry has attracted much historical interest. Given the centrality of the field to the lives of the enslaved, work would acquire a pressing influence much larger than its bounded confines. Slave work was about more than work; it was also a form of cultural expression. African women, for example, played a particular role in the harvesting and processing of rice. In order to make rice edible, the indigestible outer husk must be removed while keeping the inner kernel whole. This involves a delicate balance of strength and finesse. Harvesting rice was undertaken completely by hand until the advent of mechanized threshing in the 1760s and 1770s. Rice was among the most onerous and labour-intensive food crops cultivated by slave labour in North America, and the duration of the growing season and the dangerous and repellent nature of the work placed it at the extreme end of any continuum of forced agricultural labour in the early Atlantic world.

The demands of rice cultivation ultimately increased the risks associated with childbirth for enslaved women. Women tended to conceived children during periods when they had relatively less onerous work and more abundant caloric intake. The result was that children were most often born in the late summer and early fall, months when work demands were at their highest and when the disease environment was at its most debilitating (Cody, 1996: 69). Cultivating the crop over the duration of its 14-month growing season involved clearing the land of trees, bushes, and shrubs in January and February; planting acres of seeds by hand and foot; weeding constantly with hoe and hand; spending weeks in knee- and waist-deep water scaring birds away from the ripening crop; harvesting and stacking the rice over the course of three to four weeks; and finally threshing, winnowing, and pounding the rice to remove the kernel from the husk. Runaway numbers peaked during the hoeing and weeding seasons of June through early August, as enslaved men and women stole away in search of respite from the "laborious and tedious" task of hand-picking grass from around the rice shoots that had taken root.

The pounding of the harvested rice was especially arduous and dangerous work. The constant work of lifting a 10-pound pestle over one's head for hours a day was exhausting, so much so that the task was often divided into two separate sessions in the mornings and evenings. The act of pounding the rice required not only physical strength but acumen as well. If the rice was pounded too strenuously, it resulted in less valuable broken rice that displeased planters interested in maximizing profits. The information necessary to cultivate and harvest rice drew heavily on the experience of women from places such as Senegambia, where rice cultivation had long been practiced. These women found they had to teach men in Carolina how to perform this task efficiently and carefully. The skills needed to cultivate rice successfully were then transferred from Africans to Englishmen, and from women to men to women again (Carney, 2001).

Rice culture in South Carolina differed from staple crop cultivation elsewhere in the New World not only because of the gruelling demands of the crop, but because of the relationship between indigenous African female knowledge and rice cultivation.

Women's expertise was important at every stage of the crop's cultivation in the West African rice region – from seed selection, to the use of the long- and short-handled hoe, to the use of the mortar and pestle, to the construction and design of the fanner baskets for winnowing and, finally, to cooking. Enslaved women and their families might even have relished the familiarity wrought by the steady rhythmic cadences of the mortar and pestle at the start of the day. But as South Carolina slave owners wrested the crop from household use and applied it to plantation agriculture, the cadence of the mortar and pestle resonated differently.

Work, then, was attached to ethnicity and to the emotional lives of the enslaved in ways that are not always immediately visible. For some Senegambian women who found themselves enslaved in South Carolina rather than elsewhere in the Americas, the crop that debilitated them, that was the source of malaria in the summer and killingly brutal labor in the fall, also evoked home. Fundamentally, of course, crops meant wealth for slave owners and exploitation for the enslaved but, in the interstices, something else altogether could emerge.

In the antebellum period, Frances Kemble argued that fieldwork destroyed women's habits as "mother, nurse, and even housewife" by reducing them to "hoeing machines".[6] Leslie Schwalm has suggested that the hoe itself might be considered the "universal implement of slavery", one with particular significance for women across the Americas (Schwalm, 1997: 21). If the hoe is the universal implement of slavery, it is an implement that women wielded constantly. We must remember that, even in places where males were in the demographic majority, female majorities in the fields were normal. On the St Domingue *Breda* Plantation in 1789, 40 per cent of enslaved men were field workers compared with 88 per cent of enslaved women. Moreover, while mortality rates foreclosed parenting to many, Bernard Moitt has shown that for mothers of surviving daughters, fieldwork was an unchanging, generationally carried burden that left mothers like Felice on Guadeloupe watching, perhaps with a numbed sense of horror, as each of her seven daughters trailed behind her in the cane fields (Moitt, 2001: 43–44).

An over-determined connection between women and domestic work still dominates the ways in which we think about women's work. The very phrase "women's work" conjures the domestic – cleaning, childcare, food preparation – and inevitably leans in the direction of the family. Images of enslaved female house servants tend to populate the collective imaginary with as much tenacity as do gentle-hearted mammies. But as slave owners perused the bodies of their newly purchased human property, they quickly made decisions about the kind of work each was capable of performing. In almost all cases, they put women to work cultivating land. The rhythm of fieldwork was punctuated by family life, but slave owners understood motherhood to conform to the specific contours of the field. Failure to cede family to the field resulted in severe punishments, such as whipping a nursing mother if she exceeded the allotted time during a break to feed her child (Camp, 2004: 22). To be exempted from the field in favour of the house happened to very few enslaved women, particularly in the colonial period, when the luxury of large houses and the niceties of china, silver, and fine furniture were purely part of the slave owners' imaginary future rather than their tangible present. And for those who did labour in houses, their work lives were always dictated by the interpretive frame of slave owners. Fieldwork in a plantation-based society defined even the lives of those who escaped its demands: Mary Ann, a house servant in Charleston, found herself exiled from town and put to "as hard lauber and coarse food as is on the plantation" until she relinquished her affection for a "rascally fellow" of whom her owner disapproved (Chaplin, 1993: 125).

Mary Ann's presumption that she could autonomously consort with any "rascally fellow" she chose was explicitly interrupted by fieldwork. For many others, the interruption was simply part of daily life, as identities as spouses, as mothers and as labourers overlapped. To build affinity between parents and children was a dangerous gesture in a slave society. In North America, the growth of the plantation south fuelled an internal slave trade that wreaked havoc on family life – separating parents from children and spouses from one another, and introducing the threat of that separation throughout the enslaved population (Tadman, 2004: 131). Elsewhere in the Americas, the toll taken on family life was meted out in the epidemiology of sugar production. Alone in North America, women and men enslaved in the sugar fields of Louisiana found their potential for family formation violently thwarted by the "distorting intensity" of the sweet crop (Follett, 2005). Mortality rates were so high that the birth and survival of infant children was anomalous. The intimate lives of the enslaved were expanded primarily through the constant arrival of newly enslaved African men and women, either from Africa or, in the nineteenth century, from the Chesapeake, who were themselves extremely vulnerable to the mortality associated with sugar. The result was extremely high infant and child mortality. In Jamaica, when Abba's son died at the age of six in 1771, she was "quite frantic and could hear no reason" (Hall, 200: 184–85). In the context of these death rates, family ties became even more valuable as death and rites around death increasingly came to signify the ties that wove black communities together. As Vincent Brown has recently argued, in the midst of the constancy of death, "the living regularly reached over the threshold to draw potency from the afterlife" (Brown, 2008: 56).

Conclusion

The economic expansion of territories throughout the Caribbean and the Americas depended upon planters' willingness to devastate black families. It is no surprise then, that in the face of this wrenching of private life into the service of public gains, we should understand that family was no private matter under enslavement. Rather, family, like labour, was transformed by the terms of enslavement. In the context of a slave society based on claims of heritable racial difference, the ties of affinity between kin functioned on myriad levels. Those ties were the source of subjection and suffering. But family could also be a place from which to refute the slave owners' claim that ties among Africans and their descendents were either facile or easily thrown down. Likewise, slavery saturated those places where ties of kin and community were affirmed. Strategies of self-protection were also about pleasure: about love, and music, and faith, and a commitment to the notion of a future. Crafting family life and maintaining it in the face of economies of loss became part of the arsenal in the fight against slavery; intimacy and private life were forced into a new and radically public sphere. Maintaining affection and fighting separation become strategies for the preservation of individual families, but they also disrupted the racial logic of the slavery system. As women and men responded to their enslavement, their family life was indelibly marked by the terms of racial slavery. What emerged was saturated by the violence of a system that transformed reproduction into a commercial act, but also imbued family and its constancy with profound meaning.

Notes

1 Edward Daunce, *A Brief Discourse of the Spanish States* (London, 1590), 31.
2 Gomes Eannes de Azurara, Crónica dos Feitos da Guiné, trans. in Robert Edgar Conrad, ed., *Children of God's Fire: a Documentary History of Black Slavery in Brazil* (Princeton: Princeton University Press, 1983), 5–11, 10.
3 I am drawing here on Spillars (1987); see also Moitt (2001: xiv, 34).
4 "An Act Concerning Negroes and other Slaves," in Willie Lee Rose, ed., *A Documentary History of Slavery in North America*, (reprint edn, University of Georgia Press, 1999), 24.
5 For a discussion of "half-freedom" see Higginbotham (1978: 105–9).
6 Fanny Kemble, *Journal of a Residence on a Georgian Plantation in 1838–1839* (New York: Harper & Brothers, 1864), 121.

Bibliography

Bartels, Emily, "Imperialist Beginnings: Richard Hakluyt and the Construction of Africa", *Criticism* 34 (1992), 517–38.

Bennett, Herman L., *Africans in Colonial Mexico: Absolutism, Christianity, and Afro-Creole Consciousness, 1570–1640* (Bloomington, IN: Indiana University Press, 2003).

Blakey, Michael L., "Bioarchaeology of the African Diaspora in the Americas: Its Origins and Scope", *Annual Review of Anthropology* 30 (2001), 387–422.

Brown, Kathleen M., *Good Wives, Nasty Wenches, Anxious Patriarchs: Gender, Race, and Power in Colonial Virginia* (Chapel Hill: University of North Carolina Press, 1996).

Brown, Vincent, *The Reaper's Garden: Death and Power in the World of Atlantic Slavery* (Cambridge, MA: Harvard University Press, 2008).

Burke, Peter, "Frontiers of the Monstrous: Perceiving National Characters in Early Modern Europe", in Laura Lunger Knoppers and Joan B. Landes, eds, *Monstrous Bodies/Political Monstrosities in Early Modern Europe* (Ithaca, NY: Cornell University Press, 2004).

Burnard, Trevor, *Mastery, Tyranny, and Desire: Thomas Thistlewood and his Slaves in the Anglo-Jamaican World* (Chapel Hill: University of North Carolina Press, 2004).

Byrd, Alexander, "Eboe, Country, Nation, and Gustavus Vassa's Interesting Narrative", *William and Mary Quarterly* 3d ser. 63 (2006), 123–48.

Camp, Stephanie, *Closer to Freedom: Enslaved Women and Everyday Resistance in the Plantation South* (Chapel Hill: University of North Carolina Press, 2004).

Carney, Judith A., *Black Rice: The African Origins of Rice Cultivation in the Americas* (Cambridge, MA: Harvard University Press, 2001).

Chaplin, Joyce, *An Anxious Pursuit: Agricultural Innovation and Modernity in the Lower South* (Chapel Hill: University of North Carolina Press, 1993).

Cody, Cheryll Ann, "Cycles of Work and of Childbearing: Seasonality in Women's Lives on Low Country Plantations", in David Barry Gaspar and Darlene Clark Hine, eds, *More Than Chattel: Black Women and Slavery in the Americas* (Bloomington, IN: Indiana University Press, 1996).

Eltis, David, *The Rise of African Slavery in the Americas* (Cambridge: Cambridge University Press, 2000).

Eltis, David and Engerman, Stanley L., "Was the Slave Trade Dominated by Men?" *Journal of Interdisciplinary History* 23 (1993), 237–57.

Follett, Richard, "'Lives of Living Death': The Reproductive Lives of Slave Women in the Cane World of Louisiana", *Slavery and Abolition* 26 (2005), 289–304.

Foote, Thelma Wills, *Black and White Manhattan: The History of Racial Formation in Colonial New York City* (New York: Oxford University Press, 2004).

Gaspar, David Barry and Hine, Darlene Clark, eds, *More Than Chattel: Black Women and Slavery in the Americas* (Bloomington, IN: Indiana University Press, 1996).

Griffin, Eric, "From Ethos to Ethnos: Hispanising the 'Spaniard' in the Old World and the New", *CR: The New Centennial Review* 2 (2002), 69–116.

Guitar, Lynne, "Boiling it Down: Slavery on the First Commercial Sugarcane Ingenios in the Americas (Hispaniola, 1530–46)", in Jane Landers and Barry Robinson, eds, *Slaves, Subjects, and Subversives: Blacks in Colonial Latin America* (Alberqueque: University of New Mexico Press, 2006).

Hall, Douglas, *In Miserable Slavery: Thomas Thistlewood in Jamaica, 1750–86* (revised edn, University of West Indies Press, 200).

Hall, Kim, *Things of Darkness: Economies of Race and Gender in Early Modern England* (Ithaca, NY: Cornell University Press, 1995).

Harris, Leslie M., *In the Shadow of Slavery: African Americans in New York City, 1626–1863* (Chicago: University of Chicago Press, 2003).

Higginbotham, A. Leon Jr, *In the Matter of Color: Race and the American Legal Process, The Colonial Period* (Oxford: Oxford University Press, 1978).

Mintz, Sydney and Price, Richard, *The Birth of African American Culture: An Anthropological Perspective* (1976; repr. edn Uckfield, UK: Beacon Press, 1992).

Moitt, Bernard, *Women and Slavery in the French Antilles, 1635–1848* (Bloomington, IN: Indiana University Press, 2001).

Morgan, Jennifer L., *Laboring Women: Reproduction and gender in New World Slavery* (Philadelphia: University of Pennsylvania Press, 2004).

Morgan, Philip D., "The Cultural Implications of the Atlantic Slave Trade: African Regional Origins, American Destinations and New World Developments", *Slavery and Abolition* 18 (2007), 122–45.

Nwokeji, Ugo, "African Conceptions of Gender and the Slave Traffic", *William and Mary Quarterly* 3d ser. 58 (2001), 47–68.

Peabody, Sue, "A Nation Born to Slavery: Missionaries and Racial Discourse in Seventeenth Century French Antilles", *Journal of Social History* 38 (2004), 113–26.

Schwalm, Leslie, *A Hard Fight for We: Women's Transition from Slavery to Freedom in South Carolina* (Urbana: University of Illinois Press, 1997).

Sheridan, Richard B., *Sugar and Slavery: An Economic History of the British West Indies* (Bridgetown, Barbados: University Press of the West Indies, 1974).

Smallwood, Stephanie E., *Saltwater Slavery: A Middle Passage from Africa to American Diaspora* (Cambridge, MA: Harvard University Press, 2007).

Spillars, Hortense, "Mama's Baby, Papa's Maybe: An American Grammar Book", *Diacritics* 17 (1987), 65–81.

Tadman, Michael "The Interregional Slave Trade in the History and Myth-Making of the U.S. South", in Walter Johnson, ed., *The Chattel Principle: Internal Slave Trades in the Americas* (New Haven, CT: Yale University Press, 2004), 117–42.

Taylor, Eric Robert, *If We Must Die: Shipboard Insurrections in the Era of the Atlantic Slave Trade* (Baton Rouge: Louisiana State University Press, 2006).

9

REMEMBERED PASTS
African Atlantic religions

Sylvia R. Frey

Religious patterns: 1400–1551

The history of African Atlantic religions is an epic story of continuous creation. It cannot be simply told because it is multilayered and moves through multiple transformations. In order to understand the bewildering complexity of African Atlantic religions, it is best to consider them in successive stages. Stage one begins in Africa, whose rich and multiple religious traditions animate African Atlantic religions to this day. The second stage begins in the Americas, with the establishment of the Luso-Hispanic Catholic world from roughly 1500 to 1700. Although there is no neat dividing line, the third stage begins with the period of massive African imports and extends well into the nineteenth century. Within each stage there are marked variations in the historical trajectory of different groups as local circumstances shaped religious expressions in distinctive ways. There are also deep patterns that bear the unmistakable signature of Africa.

Geographically and historically African Atlantic religions begin on the continent of Africa, with its mix of traditional religions, Islam, and Christianity. The overwhelming majority of Africans adhered to traditional religious forms, although by the time Islam and Christianity arrived indigenous religions had already experienced substantial change in response to massive transformations in communication and commerce. Despite great variations among different societies, certain unifying elements defined traditional cosmologies: a developing concept of a supreme being or ultimate power who controlled the universe; and a pantheon of subordinate deities, many of whom had a dual nature that recognized female participation in the divine, and each of whom had a cult with its own priests and priestesses, societies, and religious activities. Ancestral spirits occupied a special place in the spiritual hierarchy. Endowed with power to do good or harm, ancestral anger was appeased and their mercy implored through ritual objects and ceremonies, which were universally condemned by missionaries as *fetich* or *grisgris*.

The great majority of Africans adhered to traditional religions, but communities of black Jews, Muslims and Christians had existed in antiquity. Islam had made deep inroads on the continent, arriving in Africa through two gateways. Commercial networks established as early as 780 by Muslim merchants from the Arabian Peninsula formed the basis for the spread of Islam from the coastal towns of modern Somalia and Mozambique. Although Islam became a majority faith between 1200 and 1500, until the nineteenth century it remained largely confined to the coast. In North Africa, Berber Muslims were the first practitioners of Islam. Camel caravans engaged in the gold trade crossed the vast Saharan desert with the riches of Africa into the states of Ghana, Mali, Songhay, and Kamen, introducing Islamic influences into West Africa.

In West Africa, the long process of Islamization developed in stages, and was closely linked to urbanization and to the work of Muslim scholars who travelled with the caravans. An early account of the conversion of the king of Mali points to the importance of rulers as early recipients of Islam, and to its nominal acceptance by common people. Assailed by droughts and a series of calamities, the king asked a Muslim guest of his kingdom for help. Throughout the night the Muslim led the king through a series of Muslim rituals and prayers. When dawn broke and rain fell, the king converted and "ordered the idols to be broken and expelled the sorcerers from his country. He and his descendants as well as his nobles were sincerely attached to Islam, while the common people of his kingdom remained polytheists" (quoted by Levtzion, 2007: 65). The development over centuries of Muslim religious and communal institutions such as Mosques and Qurani'c schools, the institution of public prayer and Islamic festivals, and the introduction of Islamic commercial law encouraged the conversion of the literate and commercial classes of West African towns such as Timbuktu, by the fourteenth century one of the great centers of Islamic learning. Nevertheless, the expansion of Islam into the countryside among the peasants was a slow process. Mystic poems written in vernacular languages were the medium through which the largely illiterate rural populations learned about Islam, but pre-Islamic beliefs and customs persisted among the rural populations of West Africa until the *jihads* of the eighteenth and nineteenth centuries achieved conformity and orthodoxy.

Islam had been established in West Africa for perhaps 500 years before Portuguese caravels brought Christianity to the African Atlantic coast. Flourishing Christian churches existed in Egypt, Ethiopia, and Nubia from the sixth century, but the modern phase of Christian activity in West and Central Africa began after the "reconquest" of the Iberian Peninsula by Christian armies. Expeditions to "cause injury to the Moors" established small Portuguese enclaves on the Atlantic islands of São Tomé and Cape Verde and in a few coastal towns in Senegal and on the Gambia River. In the 1570s, the Portuguese established a toehold in the Niger Delta kingdom of Warri. Christianity's greatest impact, however, was in the West-Central African kingdom of Kongo, where Catholicism was embraced by King Nzinga a Nkuwu, baptized João da Silva. João's son, baptized Afonso, established what John Thornton and Linda Heywood describe as "one of the most ambitious bilateral cultural programs in the period of European expansion" without resort to conquest or forced coercion (Heywood and Thornton, 2007: 62–63).

The engagement of Africans with Christianity is inextricably linked to the history of African Atlantic religions, and more broadly to Atlantic cultures and the roles played by Africans in shaping those cultures. Ira Berlin's argument that West Africans who lived in close proximity to Europeans had already incorporated European cultures and religious ideas before they were enslaved, and further that the cultural predisposition of these "Atlantic Creoles" was a critical influence in shaping African American cultures and religions in the formative period of North American slavery, has been broadly influential (Berlin, 1996; Law and Mann, 1999). While not denying the importance of cultural connections between Africa and the Americas, recent studies challenge Berlin's thesis on the grounds that he exaggerated the extent of cultural creolization in West Africa and the numerical significance of Atlantic Creoles among exported slaves. Recent work by African scholars has produced a more nuanced concept of Atlantic Creole cultures that emerged along the coasts of West and West Central Africa during the seventeenth century.

What they suggest is that different African Creole cultures – defined by language, religion, clothing, foodways, and music – developed in relation to their principal orientation: the Gold Coast (present-day Ghana) had links to Protestant Britain, Denmark, and the Netherlands; the Bight of Benin was overwhelmingly oriented toward Britain. Despite Dutch Calvinist penetration, Central Africa had continuous contacts with Portugal and with Catholic Christianity throughout the seventeenth century. The flood of new religious ideas created endless chances for complexity as some ideas were absorbed into and through traditional religions. The early history of African Creolization in Central Africa is the best documented, and can serve as a model of the process. A recent study by Linda Heywood and John Thornton (2007) defines two core areas of Atlantic Creole culture, Kongo and Portuguese Angola, where Catholic Christianity was voluntarily embraced. Anchored at one end by traditional religion beliefs and practices and on the other end by Catholic beliefs and rituals, the Kongolese variant of Catholic Christianity that emerged in Central Africa was rooted both inside and outside of European Christianity.

As ruler of the most highly centralized state in Central Africa, King Afonso established Catholicism as a royal cult under his direct control. In a pattern repeated elsewhere in Africa and later in the Americas, missionary culture and ritual were imported into the kingdom, and selective elements of Christian faith were incorporated into local beliefs and practices in such a way as to mutually enrich and inform both religious traditions. For example, to accommodate Kongolese belief that salt warded off evil, priests consented to "salt" baptism, which involved placing a small amount of salt on the tongue of the baptizand. Well versed in Catholic theology, Afonso and his advisors translated Christian terminology into Kikongo so that, for example, the "house of idols" became a church, a priest a *nganga a ukisi*.

If originally Kongolese Catholicism was state-sponsored, its expansion into rural areas was primarily an indigenous activity. Missionaries, hampered by language barriers, relied heavily upon native teachers, interpreters, and translators to prepare people in remote villages for baptism, a model successfully adapted by Moravians in the Dutch Caribbean and by evangelical Baptists and Methodists in the British Caribbean and North America. By 1516, Afonso had established a network of schools taught by Kongolese priests and teachers. Kongolese missionaries established a second center of Christianity in Angola in the early 1500s and in Loango in the 1580s. By the end of the sixteenth century, Kongo was a Christian country, Angola was a center of Christianity, and Ndongo and Matamba were influenced by Christianity but essentially adhered to traditional religions.[1]

The crucial question is, of course, how thorough was African conversion? Skeptics do not deny the existence of an Africanized Catholic Christianity, but they maintain that it existed in parallel fashion and in separate spheres with traditional religions so that Kongolese are more accurately described as "bi-religious". They point out that only a limited number of Africans were Christian, and the majority of them were converted in mass baptisms without benefit of religious instruction, one example being the 5000–6000

Mbundus baptized in Angola in 1582. Rural villagers shared in the new African religious culture even while retaining many of their older traditional beliefs, including reverence for local deities and local *nganzas* and the power of amulets to ward off evil, and they continued to resist Christian marriage (Sweet, 2003: 112–150).

Central African Christianity was not orthodox, as Heywood and Thornton emphasize, but an Africanized version of Catholic Christianity. In the early modern world the practice of dual religious participation was a widespread phenomenon. A classic African example was Doña Beatriz Kempa Vita, who was both part of the process of change and a catalyst of change. Born of noble parentage in 1684, Beatriz was, like many of her social rank, baptized Catholic, probably by a mulatto, Father Luis de Mendoça. She was taught the basic elements of Catholicism from a catechism, first published in Portuguese, later translated into Kikongo. Growing up in a period of tumultuous civil war, Beatriz established a Christian religious movement dedicated to bringing peace between contenders for the Kongolese throne and to reuniting the Kingdom of Kongo under one king. Her leadership was based on her claim that she was possessed by St Anthony, a simultaneous borrowing from traditional religion and a continuing identification with Catholicism. She preached a radical version of Catholic history, claiming, for example, that Jesus and Mary were Kongolese and that in Heaven "no one has any color". She conducted Mass, distributed statues of St Anthony to replace the Cross and other symbols of Christianity, attempted to create an order of nuns, and commissioned "Little Anthonys" to spread her message. Ironically, although she tried to eradicate witchcraft, she was convicted of witchcraft and was burned to death in 1706.

Beatriz's followers and thousands of others were caught up in the civil war of 1708–09 and the wars of 1714 and 1715. All told, perhaps as many as 12,000 of them ended up enslaved in the Caribbean, the Spanish Indies, and North America (Thornton, 1998b: 17, 28, 110, 120, 124–25, 148). The military skills of veterans of the wars and memories of Catholicism, particularly Kongolese veneration of the Virgin Mary, appear to have influenced the timing, shape, tactics, and form of the Stono Rebellion of 1739 in South Carolina (Thornton, 1991; Smith, 2001). Directly or indirectly, Beatriz's followers and millions of other Africans caught in the dark undertow of slavery bequeathed to succeeding generations in the Americas an ability to imagine and generate new religious ideas and practices. Along the way, as they embraced what was useful and abandoned what was not, they remade rich and multiple variations of religious practices, all of which were connected by an attachment to an ancient cosmology.

Transmission to the Americas: 1519–1700

The slave vessels that transported no fewer than 11 million men, women, and children into the abyss of slavery in the Americas were carriers of spiritual matter as well as people. What scholars do question is the impact of African traditional religions and Africanized versions of Islam and Christianity on slave societies in the diaspora. What was transmitted? What survived and in what form; to what extent, if any, did African religious forms influence the shaping of African American religions? The first waves of enslaved men, women, and children to arrive in the Americas were relatively few in number, and many of the early arrivals were "creolized". Whether people were adherents of traditional religions, Africanized Islam or Africanized Christianity, most clung to the religious beliefs and practices of their African past. They carried with them certain cosmological constants and a cultural memory that allowed disparate religious elements to co-exist.

Traditional religions are a case in point. There is convincing evidence that core beliefs and ritual practices persisted in relatively pure forms that are clearly visible in divination, healing rituals, and conjure. Statistical quantification of the slave trade makes it possible to link specific ritual practices to particular regions and in some cases to specific African ethnic groups. Torn away from their roots and thrown into the buffeting winds of history, Africa's sacred specialists had neither the time nor the opportunity to gather the regalia and implements of their practices as they were herded aboard slave ships, but they carried the knowledge of the rituals with them into Atlantic slave societies. Take divination, for example. A form of spiritual intervention, divination was widely practiced not only in Africa but throughout early modern Europe to explain disasters, disease, death, and social conflict. The first generations of Africans to arrive in Atlantic slave societies would have encountered the strong presence of magic and divination among European populations. Until occult practices began to fade under the combined influence of Enlightenment philosophy and English Protestant opposition, African religious specialists were probably able to perform their religious ceremonies in public, sometimes in the presence of and with the approval of whites, especially when white judicial systems proved inadequate instruments to control restive enslaved populations.

In Central Africa, divination operated as a form of trial to determine the guilt or innocence of suspected criminals. Descriptions of the ordeal of a hand in boiling water ceremony in Bahia and a needle ceremony on a small coastal island link the Brazilian rituals to a Central African trial of *jaji*, both in form and function. The benne seed ritual among South Carolina's Gullah people is reminiscent of Poro-Sande culture. Reading objects or cosmograms to establish the cause of illness are also of clear Kongolese origins. Mina slaves, who began arriving in Brazil near the end of the seventeenth century, discovered divinatory messages in a pan of water, or used snakes, idolized among the Ewe, Fon and Yoruba as deities, to help them interpret omens. Spirit possession, in which a diviner or medium was taken over by ancestral spirits, was a religious form used to determine the cause of illness or death, to resolve social conflicts, or punish the possessed. Although the settings and contexts were different, the broad contours of spirit mediumship functioned in a similar fashion in all slave societies in the Americas. Forms derived from Central Africa were common in Brazil, where it was known as *calundu* (Sweet, 2003: 120–26, 129–30, 139–52). A seventeenth-century depiction of a *calundu* in which Africans possessed by ancestral spirits danced to the beat of drums contains some of the core elements of the possession-inducing *Myal* dance reported in early nineteenth-century Jamaica, where it later became the *Cumina* cult, and in the possession of female dancers in Dutch Surinam (Frey and Wood, 1998: 58–59; Sweet, 2003: 150). The invocation of ancestral and supernatural powers persists in almost all former slave societies in modified form later known as voodoo and hoodoo.

Instead of using possession rituals to determine the cause of illness, Mina religious specialists in colonial Brazil relied on ancient remedies and herbal cures. Sacks or baskets filled with herbs, roots, powders, and various objects imbued with spiritual powers were their preferred instruments of divination (*ibid.*: 156–57). North American slave societies lack the Inquisition records that provide detail about African religious practices in Brazil and Mexico, but archaeologists are unearthing finds that connect religious practices with West African roots. What appears to be a divination bundle discovered recently in

Annapolis, Maryland is believed to have arrived directly from Africa around 1700, presumably carried by a recent African immigrant. X-rays reveal that the bundle contains about 300 pieces of metal compacted in clay and a stone ax. Because divination was common among many different African cultures, it is difficult to link it to a particular ethnic group. But its most striking component, the stone ax, suggests an association with Yoruba practices related to Shango, god of thunder and lightning, or with Angolan spirit mediums, for whom the ax sometimes functioned as a visual representation of the spirit of a powerful warrior.[2]

Africanized Islam and Africanized Catholicism also arrived intact in the Americas, where their histories are so closely intertwined it is impossible to separate them. In the Luso-Hispanic Catholic world, religious transmission unfolded against a background of centuries of conflict between Christianity and Islam reaching back to the Crusades and culminating in the expulsion of the "moors" from Spain in 1492. It is difficult to gauge the number of African Muslims in the Americas and the Caribbean. One estimate suggests that 2.25–3 million Muslims from Islamized West Africa were enslaved in Mexico, Jamaica, Brazil, Trinidad, Cuba, and Central and North America (Diouf, 1998: 46–48). Until the trade shifted to Angolans between 1615 and 1640, the majority of enslaved people in Spanish America came from the Senegambia, Sierra Leone, and the Bight of Benin, which means that few of them were familiar with Catholic Christianity. Many, however, were potential Muslims. The first wave of 156,000 enslaved Africans to arrive in the Americas during the second half of the fifteenth century came from the Senegambia and Upper Guinea, areas heavily influenced by Islam. But the faith did not develop uniformly. There was a Senegambian and potentially Muslim presence in Costa Rica and Panama in Central America, in New Spain (Mexico), and in Spanish Puerto Rico and Cuba from the sixteenth century. By the end of the sixteenth century, the number of Moorish slaves in Mexico was negligible, while Muslims in Brazil and Trinidad had influence out of all proportion to their actual numbers. The explanation lies in the demographic distinctiveness of Mexico and in the institutional strength of the Spanish church.

Mexico and Peru were the two largest importers of slaves in the sixteenth and seventeenth centuries. Between 1521 and 1639, Mexico imported over 110,000 Africans. For a brief period between 1545 and 1556, the enslaved population was predominantly Senegambian, which means that numbers of them were possibly Muslim. Clustered in urban centers along the coast, their distinctive dress and dietary habits and their corporate expressions of faith made them highly visible and led to efforts to ban or exile Muslims from Spanish America in 1501, 1530, 1532, 1543, and 1577. As a minority in a sea of Catholics and non-Muslim Africans, Muslims in New Spain (Mexico) had to create new ways to observe the Five Pillars of Islam, for example, by resorting to private worship instead of common prayer, by inventing new ways to observe *zakah* or alms-giving, by the quiet observance of dietary rules and Islamic feasts, and ultimately, perhaps, by abandoning all hope of the pilgrimage to Mecca, where the Prophet Muhammad is said to have received the first words of the Koran.[3] The shift in the trade from the Senegambia to Angola in the seventeenth century led to a steady decline in the number of Muslims in Mexico, and by the end of the century they had effectively disappeared.

The growth of sugar and the opening of silver mines led to a spectacular rise in slave imports after 1650, the vast majority of them from Central Africa, principally Angola, an important center of Africanized Catholicism for 200 years. The Church had no distinct conversion policy for Africans, but after his election as emperor in 1519, Charles V granted permission to transport *bozales*, Africans imported directly from West Africa, to Spanish territories on condition that "they be Christians" or that they "become Christians on reaching each island". Although canon law forbade forced conversion and some Spanish theologians like the Dominican priest Francisco de Vitoria insisted that "faith must be received voluntarily" or it would be "empty and ineffective", a precedent for the conversion of "unbelievers" by "violence and the sword" existed in the forced baptism of Muslims in Spain and the expulsion of those who refused to accept Christian baptism. Moreover, the legitimacy of the monarch's power seemed to find affirmation in Papal bulls (proclamations) granting dominion (*dominium*) over New World lands, and by implication over peoples, to Spanish and Portuguese monarchs.[4]

Historians of Latin America have not been especially concerned with how the clergy introduced Christianity to *bozales*, but anecdotal evidence hints at mass conversion as hundreds were baptized even as they were herded aboard slave vessels in Luanda or upon landing at the debarkation ports of Cartagena and Vera Cruz (Bennett, 2003: 11, 41–42, 47–48; Sweet, 2003: 196–7). A royal order of 1697 required slaves to be baptized at African ports and provided with religious instruction on the slave ships, but slaves continued to arrive in Bahia unbaptized (Gudeman and Schwartz, 1984: 51). Beginning in 1524, a more systematic approach was put into place in response to perceived challenges to Catholic sovereignty following the Protestant Reformation. The process began in Hispaniola as part of the effort to convert indigenous populations. Known as *congregacion*, it separated the population into two parts, indigenous people on one side, and all others, including *bozales* and *ladinos*, or creoles, on the other. In Mexico, for purposes of administration people were assigned to residential neighborhoods and placed under the supervision of regular clergy and staff attached to a cathedral and its bishop. Technically, at least, this meant that Africans received the same instruction in matters of faith as Spaniards. Standing apart from the enslaved population, but interacting with it, was a large and partially creolized *ladino* population. Clustered together in distinct *barrios*, descendant Africans began to create an elaborate social network based on ethnic affinity and ties forged during the transoceanic voyage. By the early seventeenth century, an urban free black population began to outnumber the enslaved population; by mid-century, Mexico had the largest freed and free creole population in the Western Hemisphere. Although they represented only 2 per cent of the vice-regal population, African descendants made up a majority of Catholics in Mexico (Bennett, 2003: 26).

It was through the Mexican Inquisition that the Catholic Church insinuated itself into the lives of Mexico's African descendant population. The advent of the Protestant Reformation and the flight of European Jews and Muslims to the New World to escape the Spanish and Portuguese inquisitions created new anxieties over threats to Catholic orthodoxy, and led to the establishment of an arm of the Inquisition in the New World to reassert religious orthodoxy. The operation of the inquisitions in the New World offers an important perspective on differences in the structure and the character of Spanish and Portuguese orthodoxy and, more importantly for this chapter, on the vast differences in the curve of conversion in the religious landscapes of African Atlantic communities.

In Spanish America, branches of the Inquisition were set up in 1569 in Mexico, Cartagena, and Lima. Technically established to suppress heresy, most of the time the tribunal in Mexico was occupied with the enforcement of a distinctive form of Spanish Christianity anchored in the patriarchal family. The Inquisition tribunals and ecclesiastical courts imposed orthodoxy through various mechanisms of control, the preferred form being the spectacle of the *auto-de-fé*. The first *auto-de-fé* in Mexico in 1574 signaled the opening of the Catholic offensive against Protestant "enemies of God". It consisted of the public humiliation of persons charged with heresy. After being tortured, the hapless victims were dressed in yellow "fooles coats" and, with nooses tied around their necks, were paraded to the central plaza to be garroted and burned to death. Although the initial targets were Protestants and *conversos*, descendants of baptized Jews, nearly 50 per cent of the proceedings of the Mexican Inquisition involved persons of African descent, who in 1571 outnumbered Spaniards by 11,645 to 9495.[5]

The intended purpose of the Inquisition in Mexico was to control the behavior of the expanding African population by imposing conjugality on *bozales*. But the Creole and enslaved populations transformed it into a weapon to subvert the authority of the master by appropriating the instruments originally meant to control them. As Christians, Africans were entitled to the same right to marriage as Spaniards, but subject to the same obligation of monogamy. The embrace of the Christian moral code represented a departure for descendant Africans, but the large *ladino* population, which was the first target of the Inquisition, quickly acquired the cultural dexterity to appreciate the advantages of formal marriage ties. Thousands of petitions for marriage licenses contained in tribunal records reveal the ease and frequency with which they navigated the judicial system to secure the right to marry without the owners' consent, win regular conjugal visits, and protect their families against forced separation. The conscious choice to marry within the same ethnicity calls attention to the existence of a cohesive, self-conscious people. Based initially on the trauma of the transoceanic voyage and reinforced by residence in distinct *barrios*, the redefinition of social identity was facilitated by the shared experience of religion (Bennett, 2003: 72, 78, 89–91, 94, 98, 101, 109, 129, 150–51). As the demographic balance began to shift in favor of a Creole as opposed to an African-born enslaved population, Afro-Mexican Catholic culture ceased to be recognizably "African", although it retained certain African elements.

The "Africanness" of Brazil's bewildering diversity of religions stands in marked contrast to Mexico. How this process occurred is complex, but it is clear that demographics and the Inquisition played key roles. It is not by accident that Catholic Brazil had the most complex and diverse religious universe and the largest African Muslim presence in all of the Americas. The slave trade to Brazil did not begin until the 1560s, decades after the first slaves arrived in Spanish America, and Africans were not imported into the Amazon in significant numbers until the mid-eighteenth century. There was, however, a constant influx of Africans, the great majority from Central Africa. Although they shared a common ethnic origin with enslaved Afro-Mexicans, they were dispersed through different regions of Brazil to provide labor for the expanding sugar and mining industries in Northeast and Southeast Brazil and in Bahia, instead of being clustered in coastal towns where they could organize their lives as a community.

Brazil had no tribunal or resident officials and instead relied on occasional tribunals called *visitas* and the local religious establishment. Until the early seventeenth century, the temporary courts depended on *familiares*, local informers who reported on such mundane transgressions as smoking tobacco or wearing clean clothes on Saturday. Persons charged with more serious "crimes", including blasphemy, practicing Islam or

Judaism, Lutheranism or Calvinism, witchcraft, superstition, or pacts with the devil, had to be sent to the Lisbon tribunal. Up until the middle of the eighteenth century, the targets were overwhelmingly Judaism, bigamy, witchcraft, and heresy. In contrast to Mexico, where Africans were involved in almost 50 per cent of cases, very few cases involving Africans or Indians were brought to full trial by the Bahian tribunal.[6] The absence of intense supervision by church authorities made it possible for the small Islamic community to survive and for African-based religions not merely to endure, but to live.

Religious transformation: 1700–1800

As the seventeenth century drew to a close, the vast majority of Atlantic Africans remained outside institutional Christianity. A century later, the religious landscape had changed more radically than at any time since the Protestant Reformation. A complex combination of forces distinct from, and sometimes opposed to, one another coalesced to radically transform the religious landscape of the African Atlantic. As the century advanced, African religions entered a new phase, characterized in some cases by a fusion of different religious traditions, in others by entirely new inventions, and by the gradual disappearance of others. The dynamics of change were not the same everywhere. They depended on a number of factors: the shift in the demographic balance in favor of creoles as opposed to those of African origin in some places and alternatively the rapid growth of African imports in others; the entry of creolized Africans into mainstream churches and the simultaneous reinvigoration of traditional religious beliefs and practices; a movement toward the creation of socio-religious organizations within institutional churches and the incorporation of both re-Christianization and re-Africanization tendencies.

The immediate triggers were the international slave trade and international revivalism. The ramifications of these two globally connected developments do not form a single narrative, but rather split and change in time and in space. Over the course of the eighteenth century, the Americas experienced a massive demographic transition as the international slave trade reached its peak. Over 100,000 Africans, most of them captured in raiding expeditions, were carried into slavery before international bans on the trade by Britain and the United States limited its growth. Supplied to British, Dutch, and French traders principally by the West African kingdoms of Oyo (Yoruba), Dahomey (Benin) and Asante (Gold Coast), the shift in the locus of trade brought in over 45 ethnic groups, the majority to Brazil and the Caribbean, giving new life to traditional beliefs and practices. Warfare and slave raids that transformed human beings into commodities changed the meaning of some traditional religious practices in the diaspora. Belief in witchcraft was common throughout the early modern Atlantic world although its meaning and purpose varied. To early modern Europeans, witchcraft was inextricably associated with the devil, which triggered some of the most notorious episodes in Virginia in 1626 and in Salem's 1692 witch trials. Most Africans, on the other hand, conceived of witchcraft as a religious power used to balance the forces of good and evil. Some scholars believe that the African association of witchcraft with malevolent human agency developed under the impetus of the slave trade and that the coincident rise of witch-finding divinations such as the poison ordeal was a means to resist slavery (Shaw, 1997: 856–76; Sweet, 2003: 161–71).

161

The growing presence of African "witches" in the diaspora and their tendency to use their powers to take revenge on white masters coincided with the decline in the occult among Europeans, and contributed to the linkage of the most pernicious images of witchcraft with Africans. In traditional society, the Mandingo viewed sorcery as a neutral force, but under slavery they used their occult powers against slave-owners. In Cuba and the Spanish Caribbean, it gave birth to a new word in the slave-holders' lexicon, *mandinga*, to denote sorcery for evil purposes (Diouf, 2003: 145). After the abolition of the British slave trade in 1807, the British Royal Navy "liberated" Africans on ships bound for Spanish and Portuguese plantations. Thousands were resettled in British colonies such as Trinidad and the Bahamas. The fresh infusion of African religious traditions revived or reinforced traditional religions. Rada, for example, was carried to Trinidad by 8000 Africans from Dahomey in the 1860s. Settled in Belmont Valley Road, they practiced their ancestral religion in spite of persecution as Obeahmen (Brereton, 1981: 134).

The increase in the traffic in slaves paralleled the rise of evangelical Protestantism, an international movement that successfully implanted itself in the British Caribbean and North America. Ultimately the shift in the trade and the spread of international revivalism generated a crucial transition in the socio-religious landscape of the African Atlantic. The religious metamorphosis can be refracted through the lives of two black evangelical leaders.

Rebecca Freundlich, a young ex-slave woman, was a member of the Moravian mission that launched international revivalism. As the earliest known black Protestant missionary, Rebecca's itinerant mission from Germany to the Danish island of St Thomas and from there to the Gold Coast of Africa broke the rules of female travel and established an enduring pattern of female agency in religious conversion. Unable to communicate with the Creole spoken by most Africans on the Dutch islands, Moravian missionaries turned to black "helpers" whose genealogy can be traced to the Capuchins in Central Africa. From St Thomas, the movement established infant missions in Jamaica in 1754, Antigua in 1756, Barbados in 1765, and Salem, North Carolina in 1772.[7]

The missionary techniques pioneered by the Moravians were adopted by other evangelical groups and applied with notable success in the British Caribbean and North America, where the subjects of proselytization became themselves proselytizers. The spiritual passage of George Liele, one of the first converts, is an extension of the arc of religious change represented by Rebecca Freundlich. Enslaved in Virginia, Liele was taken by his master to Georgia. After a lengthy conversion experience he was ordained a New Light Baptist. Liele's success in preaching to enslaved people up and down the Savannah River puts him in the vanguard of continental revivalism. The First African Baptist Church of Savannah, established by Andrew Bryant, was also the model for dozens of independent black churches that sprang up across the country. Before it was interrupted by the American Revolution, bi-racial, ecumenical revivalism stretched across the young republic, challenging racial and gender conventions and implanting distinctive expressions of black evangelical Protestantism. Although women had no formal leadership roles, they discovered unprecedented opportunities to speak and to exhort. As charismatic leaders, they played a leading role in exuberant revivalism.

The emergence of popular Protestantism in the Caribbean and its spread to the United States unleashed a powerful wave of black evangelism that resonated around the

North Atlantic. The ending of the American Revolution precipitated a sizable exodus of African Americans and the circulation of black forms of Protestantism to the Caribbean, where Liele laid the foundation of the Baptist mission in Jamaica; to Nova Scotia and West Africa, where David George, one of Liele's converts, formed the first permanent black Baptist Church; to the Canadian Maritimes, where Moses Wilkinson, a black Methodist preacher and a Huntingdonian, John Marrant stamped their own versions of radical evangelicalism on the landscape. In Jamaica, the revivalistic, egalitarian tradition of black evangelical Protestantism metamorphosed into the Native Baptist movement, a more Africanized form of Christianity. In North America, the connection with black radical theology found concrete expression in the nineteenth-century rebellions led by Gabriel Prosser in Virginia and Denmark Vesey in South Carolina (Frey, 2004).

If African descendants were attracted to the radical promise of evangelical Protestantism and the opportunity to play leadership roles, the adaptability of the pantheon of saints, the elaborate visual and aural rituals, and the tendency to extend rights and protections to all baptizands, made Catholicism amenable to growing numbers in the French and Iberian worlds. Outside of Mexico, until the eighteenth century few Atlantic Africans were affected by Catholicism. Over the course of the eighteenth and early nineteenth centuries, growing numbers adopted and translated Catholicism to suit their own religious and social needs. The way they organized their religious and social worlds bears several of the hallmarks of Afro-Mexican Catholicism, specifically the ability to maximize the advantages of the hard hand they had been dealt in life, which passed virtually intact from Mexico as an ethnic and cultural legacy of Africa.

The power of cultural patterns is strikingly clear in baptism, the ritual occasion for entry into the spiritual community, and the rights and protections it afforded. In keeping with the Catholic practice of infant baptism, the Code of Canon Law mandated that infants must be sponsored by an adult or adults in consideration of their inability to speak for themselves. Much as their Kongolese ancestors had used the spiritual power of salt baptism to protect the converted, or as Afro-Mexicans used the sacrament of marriage to preserve family integrity, enslaved and free people of color co-opted the ritual practice to achieve a deeply personal and political end – freedom for their children.

Enslaved parents almost always chose as godparents someone with the potential to purchase the child's freedom. In some cases the godparent was a free person of color, in other cases another enslaved person. The ritual co-partnership between the sponsors or godparents and the infants' biological parents, and between the child and his or her godparents, was a major building block of social organization in emerging black Catholic communities everywhere in the Atlantic world. In places as disparate as the free black town of Gracia Real de Santa Teresa de Mose in Spanish Florida, in the French frontier community of New Orleans, in the plantation zone of Bahian Reconçavo, in the Brazilian city of Rio de Janeiro, creolized Africans manipulated the religious practice of god-parenthood to forge intricate social networks by marrying within the group, serving as witnesses at each others' weddings, and god-parenting each others' children, and they used it as a mechanism to incorporate new Africans into the socio-religious community.[8]

Both Protestantism and Catholicism welcomed enslaved Africans into ecclesiastical organizations but limited their participation. African men had served as lay priests in Kongo-Angola and played a prominent role as lay teachers everywhere in the Americas, but they could not enter the priesthood until well into the nineteenth century. Ursula de

Jesus, the Afro-Peruvian mystic, spent her days as a servant to a white nun of the black veil in the large and wealthy convent of Santa Clara in Lima, the religious capital of the Vice-Royalty of Peru. Ursula's experience echoes in the circumstance of Henriette DeLille, 28 times a godmother to new Africans and creole infants in New Orleans, and Marie Elizabeth Lange, part of the Haitian diasporic stream to Baltimore. Protestant churches did ordain some black preachers, but the great majority were self-appointed and unlicensed. Church authorities initially accepted the charismatic leadership of black women but denied them formal religious authority on biblical grounds (van Deusen, 2002).

Yet within these systems of institutionalized restrictions, Atlantic Africans turned a means of survival into unique vehicles of spiritual expression both within and without the institutional framework of Protestantism and Catholicism. In Protestant North America, where the legal slave trade ended in 1808, creolized men and women began laying the cornerstones of the black church as early as 1787, when black congregations first began seceding from bi-racial churches to protest discrimination. Dozens of autonomous black churches, Masonic lodges, and social clubs sprung up in Boston, New York, Philadelphia, and Charleston. In the absence of ordained black priests, a remarkable new breed of female leaders emerged out of the nineteenth-century diasporic stream that carried thousands of French-speaking Catholics from the Caribbean to the mainland. Bound together by French language and culture and religious faith, they built the religious, social, and educational framework of Afro-Catholicism in Baltimore and New Orleans. A Haitian émigré, Marie Elizabeth Lange, founded the Oblate Sisters of Providence, the oldest black religious sisterhood in the world. In New Orleans, the black Creole Henriette Delille and the Cuban-born Josephine Charles formed the Sisters of the Holy Family in 1842 to serve the French-speaking population of the city.

Societies that continued to receive direct African imports followed a quite different arc. Nowhere are the links between African ethnic groups and Europeans more evident than in Brazil, Haiti, and Cuba, the great creative cauldrons of the African Atlantic. Although the slave trade ended in Brazil in 1851 and in Cuba in 1862, the final abolition of slavery did not happen until 1886 in Cuba and 1888 in Brazil. In the meantime, Central Africans continued to be funneled into both places, but near the end of the century growing numbers of Yoruba from the Mina Coast were carried into Cuba, St Domingue (Haiti), and Bahia, Brazil. Bahia, a major supplier of sugar and diamonds to Europe and a sponge for all things African, absorbed approximately one-quarter of Yoruba-speaking peoples, Cuba about one-sixth, and St Domingue nearly a third (Roberts, 2004: 178). The convergence of different ethnicities and their intersection with Catholic Christianity created what historians have called neo-African religions: *Santeria* in Cuba, *Candomblé* in Brazil, and *Vodun* in St Domingue.

The rapidly growing enslaved populations led church authorities in the Iberian colonies to import European institutions to convert, instruct, and control the African populations. The *irmandades* or brotherhoods of Brazil originated in Portugal in the late fifteenth century, but African religious brotherhoods existed in São Tomé, the Kingdom of Kongo, and Angola. This raises the possibility that they were brought to Brazil by African creoles who had first experienced them in Portugal, or by Africans who had been converted in Africa and were sold into slavery in Bahia (Kiddy, 2007: 158). A similar institution, the *cofradía*, based on models developed in Spain, emerged in Cuba, Lima, New Grenada, and Santo Domingo. Both institutions were intended to enforce conversion on Africans. More often they functioned as "veiled African societies" reminiscent of the Kimpasi in Kongo, or the Poro and Sande initiation societies of Sierra Leone. Dedicated to Our Lady of the Rosary or to black saints such as St Anthony, many of the brotherhoods admitted only members of the same ethnicity or occupational group. Although they publicly called themselves Catholics, the *irmandades* and *cofradías* incorporated African elements almost invisibly. Members privately practiced African rituals, incorporated African-derived music and dance, and transformed the cult of the saints into African-styled spirits. Under the guise of Christianity, the *cofradías* created a popular religion known as *Santeria* or *La Regla de Ocha*, the law of Orisha. Under the guise of Catholic saints (*Santeria*), they developed a range of rituals to worship the *orishas* of Africa and staged their own versions of Catholic festivals such as the *Dia de los Reyes* on Epiphany[9] (Sweet, 2003: 202–6, 209; Reid, 2004: 119–21; Ocasio, 2005: 92, 94–96, 98).

Like *Santeria*, *Candomblé* appears to have developed in the interstitial spaces of the *irmandades*. An African-derived religion that originated in Salvador, the capital of Bahia, its early beginnings are associated with Angolans and other ethnic groups, but the Yoruba, or Nagô as they were known in Bahia, had the decisive influence. The principal components of worship involve multiple deities called *orixas* and the practice of divination and spirit possession, which is generally viewed as feminine, not surprising considering the commanding female deities in the African pantheon. Dancing was a central element in the performance of *Candomblé*. Often described by Europeans as "disorganized" or "wild and wanton", in fact *Candomblé* is a highly choreographed ritual through which the dancers, driven by drum beat, call the *orixa*, or spirit, to occupy the body, at which point the dancer enters the trance state.

Vodou had already emerged in Haiti before the Yoruba began arriving in large numbers. An amalgam of several African religious traditions with Catholic elements, *vodou* began to crystallize as an identifiable religion beginning around 1760. In contrast to urban-based *Candomblé* and *Santeria*, *vodou* was created by African plantation workers and was controlled by rural Haitian elites. Until recently, most scholarship emphasized Dahomean and Yoruban influences, the most salient expressions of which are the Yoruban deities Ogun, the lord of fire and Ezilie, the water goddess of love, and the Dahomean deity Rada. Current scholarship stresses the importance of Kongolese Catholicism in the creation of *Vodun*. Conditioned to Catholicism by almost 300 years of Portuguese and Italian missionary activity prior to enslavement, the baKonga brought with them to Haiti Catholic imagery, prayers, objects such as the crucifix, and devotion to the cult of the Virgin Mary and St James the Great. The familiar figure of the Kongolese lay priest reappeared in Haiti in the person of the *prêt savanne* or "bush priest". Far from being introduced by Catholic missionaries in Haiti, *vodou* appropriated Catholicism and merged it with various West African cults to create a neo-African religion (Vanhee, 2002; Rey, 2002). The syncretic culture created by an amalgam of ethnic groups was dispersed throughout the circum-Caribbean, where it found its most articulate expression in Louisiana.

Catholic-based neo-African religions such as *Vodun*, *Santeria*, and *Candomblé* and the Trinidadian *Shango* share integral features with distant but related Protestant-based religions such as Myalism of Jamaica or the Trinidadian spiritual Baptist Church. They had in common a complex of African religious beliefs and a common focus on the presence of *orishas* or *loas*. Although men were almost always titular leaders, possession performances were usually led by women, who often made up the majority of adherents. Sometimes the connections between the different religious expressions are visual and sometimes musical. Dancing, singing, and drumming played a crucial part of the experience of trance. What all neo-African religions shared in common was the ability to fuse disparate influences into something useful and completely original (Burton, 1997: 99–100, 235).

In contrast to the growth of Protestantism and Catholicism and the infinite variations on both is the story of one faith coming undone. Muslim communities still survived in Trinidad and Rio de Janeiro, and in some locations actually increased in the early nineteenth century. Neither England nor France had a history or traditions of hostility toward Muslims, and the British slave trade carried thousands of Muslims from islamized West Africa to Jamaica and Trinidad, to coastal Georgia and South Carolina and New Orleans. The majority of them were Mande-speakers from the Senegambia, Sierra Leone, and the Gold Coast. There are no reliable estimates of the number of Muslims in North America, but estimates are in the tens of thousands. Much of what we know about Islam in mainland America is distilled in the figures of literate, educated African Muslims such as Muhammad Kaba (a.k.a. Robert Tuffit), Abd Rahman, enslaved in New Orleans, and Salih Bilali, a driver on the Georgia island of St Simons. Each continued to practice Islam and led a relatively privileged life (Diouf, 1998: 55–56, 58–59).

Islam has rightly been termed a "supranational" religion for its ability to transcend ethnic and even linguistic differences. Muslim leaders in Trinidad created one of the most vibrant and influential religious communities in the Americas by doing just that. Led by Jonas Mohammed Bath, who arrived as a slave in Port of Spain in 1804 or 1805, they formed a mutual aid society of about 140 members, including some who were not of Manding ethnicity. They retained their African identity and religion, along with their Muslim and new Creole names. Using the profits from trade, moneylending and cocoa planting, they manumitted fellow believers from slavery. A company of demobilized soldiers from West Indian regiments who had served with the British in the War of 1812 resettled in a company village in Quare on the east coast of Trinidad. They converted many villagers to Islam, and by 1840 Quare was predominantly Muslim (Brereton, 1981: 67–68).

Although they belonged to different religious traditions, Yoruba Muslims shared a common language with the Nagô of Brazil, and as part of the urban labor force they found common ground with other street workers and African healers in *cantos*, organizations composed of the same ethnic groups. Like Brazilian and Cuban brotherhoods, these ethnic networks promoted solidarity and encouraged collective resistance. The strong bonds of cohesion sometimes led to violent rebellions, such as the one led by François Makandal in 1757 Haiti, and the well known Mâle War of 1835, which united Muslim Nagô, Hausa, Tapa, and Borno (Reis and Mamigonian, 2004: 86–87, 89, 94–96). Over the long term, however, orthodox Islam did not survive. In many cases, the Muslim presence was not numerically sufficient to support communal institutions such as Qurani'c schools, mosques or brotherhoods that are essential to a corporate religion such as Islam. A highly skewed sex ratio made it difficult to develop families through which the basic tenets of the faith could be passed down. Unlike Catholicism, Islam was not a syncretist faith, although Islamic traits were incorporated into other faiths (Diouf, 1998: 179–84).

Conclusion

As this general survey suggests, African religions have not merely endured – they have lived. Rich, endlessly refreshed, ever-changing, African Atlantic religions reveal constant themes, boundless variations, and deep patterns. Each variation occurred in a specific context, yet each carries historical resonances that flow from ancient and intimate connections to Africa, preserved through unconscious bonds shared by people linked by blood or memory. The linkages seem to be rudimentary until seen in a sustained sequence, when the connections become seamless and multiple. Viewed across porous imperial and national boundaries, the first faint hints of an incipient global culture begin to appear: in a worldview that was inclusive instead of exclusive; in the yoking of Christian religious traditions with African spirituality; in the persistence of community loyalty and collective values; in the deployment of magic and medicine and rituals of justice for protection and healing; in the commanding influence of spiritual leaders and diviners, male and female; in the structural configuration of popular religion. At the very center of change are the remnants of memory passed on to succeeding generations of witnesses.

Notes

1 The preceding paragraphs follow the interpretation of Heywood and Thornton (2007: esp. 57, 62–65, 170, 177, 186, 196–98).
2 "Under Maryland Street, Ties to African Past", *The New York Times*, 21 October 2008, D1, D3.
3 For the demography of the trade in the early period, see Elbe (1997); for Mexico, see Bennett (2003: 22–27, 91, 99, 101), also Gomez (2005: 13, 16–20, 24–25, 28, 31–33, 59); for Muslims in Brazil, see Sweet (2003: ch. 4).
4 "Francisco de Vitoria, 'On the Evangelization of Unbelievers', Salamanca, Spain [1534–35]", reprinted in Kenneth Mills, William B. Taylor and Sandra Lauderdale Graham, eds, *Colonial Latin America: A Documentary History* (Wilmington, DE: Scholarly Resources Inc. Imprint, 2002), 65–77.
5 Bennett (2003: 9); the Inquisition was abolished in 1834.
6 "Confessing to the Holy Office of the Inquisition, Bahia, Brazil [1592–1618]", in Mills *et al.*, *Colonial Latin America, op. cit.*, 234–36; Wadsworth (2007: 21–24, 42–43, 45–47).
7 Frey and Wood (1998); for the Moravians in North Carolina see Sensbach (1998).
8 For Bahia, see Gudeman and Schwartz (1984: 35–56); for Rio de Janeiro, see Karasch (1987: 256–57), also Landers (1990: 23–25); for New Orleans, see Clark (2007: 177–81, 184–87).
9 Mills *et al.*, *Colonial Latin America, op. cit.*, 281.

Bibliography

Barnet, Miguel, *Afro-Cuban Religions*, trans. Christine Renata Ayorinde (Princeton, NJ: Marcus Wiener, 2001).

Bennett, Herman L., *Africans in Colonial Mexico. Absolutism, Christianity and Afro-Creole Consciousness, 1879–1640* (Bloomington and Indianapolis: Indiana University Press, 2003).

Berlin, Ira, "From Creole to African: Atlantic Creoles and the Origins of African-American Societies in Mainland North America", *William and Mary Quarterly* 3rd ser 53 (1996), 251–88.

Brereton, Bridget, *A History of Modern Trinidad* (Kingston: Heinemann, 1981).

Burton, Richard D. E., *Afro-Creole Power, Opposition, and Play in the Caribbean* (Ithaca, NY: Cornell University Press, 1997).

Chireau, Yvonne P., *Black Magic: Religion and the African America Conjuring Tradition* (Berkeley: University of California Press, 2003).

Clark, Emily, *Masterless Mistresses. The New Orleans Ursulines and the Development of a New World Society, 1727–1834* (Chapel Hill: University of North Carolina Press, 2007).

Creel, Margaret Washington, *"A Peculiar People": Slave Religion and Community Culture among the Gullahs* (New York: New York University Press, 1988).

van Deusen, Nancy E., "Ursula de Jesus: A Seventeenth-Century Afro-Peruvian Mystic", in Kenneth J. Andrien, ed., *The Human Tradition in Colonial Latin America* (New York: Rowan & Littlefield, 2002), 88–103.

Diouf, Sylviane A., *Servants of Allah. African Muslims Enslaved in the Americas* (New York and London: New York University Press, 1998).

——, "Devils or Sorcerers. Muslims or Studs", in Paul E. Lovejoy and David V. Trotman, eds, *Trans-Atlantic Dimension of Ethnicity in the African Diaspora* (London: Continuum, 2003).

Egerton, Douglas R., *Gabriel's Rebellion: The Virginia Slave Conspiracies of 1800 and 1802* (Chapel Hill: University of North Carolina Press, 1993).

——, *He Shall Go Out Free: The Lives of Denmark Vesey* (Madison, WI: Madison House, 1999).

Elbe, Ivana, "The Volume of the Early Atlantic Slave Trade, 1450–1521", *Journal of African History* 38 (1997), 31–75.

Frey, Sylvia R., "Cultural Migrations: A Time and Space Outline of Black Evangelical Protestantism", in Genevieve Fabre and Benedicte Alliote, eds, *Diasporas: Consciousness and Imagination* (Amsterdam and New York: Rodopi, 2004), 83–99.

Frey, Sylvia R. and Wood, Betty, *Come Shouting to Zion. African American Protestantism in the American South and the British Caribbean to 1830* (Chapel Hill: University of North Carolina Press, 1998).

Gomez, Michael A., *Exchanging Our Country Marks: The Transformation of African Identities in the Colonial and Antebellum South* (Chapel Hill: University of North Carolina Press, 1998).

——, *Black Crescent: The Experience and Legacy of African Muslims in the Americas* (New York: Cambridge University Press, 2005).

Gudeman, Stephen and Schwartz, Stuart B., "'Cleansing Original Sin:' Godparenthood and the Baptism of Slaves in Eighteenth-Century Bahia", in Raymond T. Smith, ed., *Kinship Ideology and Practice in Latin America* (Chapel Hill: University of North Carolina Press, 1984).

Heywood, Linda M. and Thornton, John K., *Central Africans, Atlantic Creoles, and the Foundation of the Americas, 1585–1660* (Cambridge: Cambridge University Press, 2007).

Horton, Robin, *Patterns of Thought in Africa and the West: Essays on Magic, Religion and Science* (Cambridge: Cambridge University Press, 1993).

Law, Robin and Mann, Kristin, "West Africa and the Atlantic Community: The Case of the Slave Coast", *William and Mary Quarterly* 3rd ser 56 (1999), 307–34.

Levtzion, Nehemia, "Islam in the Bilad al-Sudan to 1800", in Michel Abitbol and Amos Nadan, eds, *Islam in Africa and the Middle East* (Aldershot, UK: Ashgate, 2007).

Karasch, Mary C., *Slave Life in Rio de Janeiro, 1805–1850* (Princeton, NJ: Princeton University Press, 1987).

Kiddy, Elizabeth W., "Who Is the King of Congo? A New Look at African and Afro-Brazilian Kings in Brazil", in Linda M. Heywood and John K. Thornton, eds, *Central Africans, Atlantic Creoles, and the Foundation of the Americas, 1585–1660* (Cambridge: Cambridge University Press, 2007).

Landers, Jane, "Gracia Real de Santa Teresa de Mose: A Free Black Town in Spanish Colonial Florida", *American Historical Review* 95 (1990), 9–30.

MacGaffey, Wyatt, *Religion and Society in Central Africa: The BaKongo of Lower Zaire* (Chicago: Chicago University Press, 1986).

Ocasio, Rafael "Dancing to the Beat of Babalu Aye: Santeria and Cuban Popular Culture", in Patrick Bellegarde-Smith, ed., *Fragments of Bone Neo-African Religions in a New World* (Urbana: University of Illinois Press, 2005).

Raboteau, Albert, *Slave Religion: The "Invisible Institution" in the Antebellum South* (New York: Oxford University Press, 1978).

Reid, Michele, "The Yoruba in Cuba: Origins, Identities, and Transformations", in Toyin Falola and Matt D. Childs, eds, *Yoruba Diaspora in the Atlantic World* (Bloomington and Indianapolis: Indiana University Press, 2004).

Reis, João Jose and Mamigonian, Beatriz Gallotti, "Nagô and Mina: The Yoruba Diaspora in Brazil", in Toyin Falola and Matt D. Childs, eds, *The Yoruba Diaspora in the Atlantic World* (Bloomington and Indianapolis: Indiana University Press, 2004).

Rey, Terry, "Kongolese Catholic Influence on Haitian Popular Catholicism: A Sociohistorical Exploration", in Linda M. Heywood, *Central Africans and Cultural Transformations in the American Diaspora* (Cambridge: Cambridge University Press, 2002), 265–85.

Roberts, Kevin, "The Influential Yoruba Past in Haiti", in Toyin Falola and Matt D. Childs, eds, *The Yoruba Diaspora in the Atlantic World* (Bloomington and Indianapolis: Indiana University Press, 2004).

Robinson, David, *Muslim Societies in African History: New Approaches to African History* (Cambridge: Cambridge University Press, 2004).

Sanneh, Lamin and Joel A. Carpenter, eds, *The Changing Face of Christianity: Africa, the West and the World* (New York: Oxford University Press, 2005).

Sensbach, Jon K., *A Separate Canaan. The Making of an Afro-Moravian World in North Carolina, 1763–1840* (Chapel Hill: University of North Carolina Press, 1998).

——, *Rebecca's Revival: Creating Black Christianity in the Atlantic World* (Cambridge, MA and London: Harvard University Press, 2005).

Shaw, Rosalind, "The Production of Witchcraft/Witchcraft as Production: Memory, Modernity, and the Slave Trade in Sierra Leone", *American Ethnologist* 24 (1997), 856–76.

Smith, Mark M., "Remembering Mary, Shaping Revolt: Reconsidering the Stono Rebellion", *Journal of Southern History* 67 (2001), 513–34.

Sweet, James H., *Recreating African Culture, Kinship, and Religion in the African-Portuguese World, 1441–1770* (Chapel Hill: University of North Carolina Press, 2003).

Thornton, John K., *Africa and Africans in the Making of the Atlantic World, 1400–1800* (Cambridge: Cambridge University Press, 1998a).

——, *The Kongolese St. Anthony. Dona Beatriz Kempa Vita and the Antonian Movement, 1684–1706* (Cambridge: Cambridge University Press, 1998b).

——, "African Dimension of the Stono Rebellion", *American Historical Review* 96 (1991), 1101–13.

Vanhee, Hein, "Central African Popular Christianity and the Making of Haitian Vodou Religion", in Linda M. Heywood, ed., *Central Africans and Cultural Transformations in the American Diaspora* (Cambridge: Cambridge University Press, 2002), 243–264.

Wadsworth, James E., *Agents of Orthodoxy Honor, Status, and the Inquisition in Colonial Pernambuco, Brazil* (Plymouth: Rowman & Littlefield, 2007).

10

SLAVE CULTURE

Matt D. Childs

Introduction

African slaves and their masters and mistresses created new cultures in the Americas out of the ordeal of Atlantic slavery. The cumulative effects of the slave labor system served to radically change people's perceptions of their own culture, and their own self. Prior to 1450, few people in Europe, the Americas, or Africa would have defined themselves as white or black. Yet, after the development of slavery in the Americas, racial categories became the primary method of self-identifying and identifying others. This cultural phenomenon became common even in areas that did not experience large-scale plantation slavery. The greatest cultural legacy of slavery in the Americas, and its most unique feature, was not brutalizing labor conditions, but how slavery shaped notions of blackness and whiteness and shaped understandings of racial identity in the New World.

Analyzing "slave culture" is difficult. Cultures are dynamic and constantly changing. Defining a specific culture often freezes cultural forms at a specific and static moment. In order to avoid this problem, I place considerable emphasis on how Africans struggled to survive slavery while creatively drawing from their own African-derived cultural resources and stressing how diverse cultures were recreated and reformulated on the other side of the Atlantic.

Let me be clear about what I mean by "culture". In 1983, Raymond Williams famously wrote, "culture is one of the two or three most complicated words in the English language" (Williams, 1983: 87). More than 25 years later, the latest historical literature about slave culture only confirms Williams's statement. William Sewell offers a methodological overview of how historians have used the concept of culture, stressing that it is most frequently used as an abstracted part of social existence:

> In one meaning, culture is a theoretically defined category or aspect of social life that must be abstracted out from the complex realities of human existence. Culture in this sense is always contrasted to some other equally abstract aspect or category of social life that is not culture, such as economy, politics, or biology.

Yet, as Sewell emphasises, culture also includes economic practices, politics and biology. Sewell suggests that culture can be analyzed and assessed in five ways: (1) as a learned social behavior; (2) as an institutional place of meaning; (3) as a product of social agency; (4) as a system of symbols and meanings; and (5) as practice and expression.

In analyzing the transformation, recreation, and reformulation of African cultures as a product of enslavement and slavery, this chapter addresses these five aspects of slave culture (Sewell, 1999: 35–61).

The first section examines the process of enslavement in Africa to understand the learned social behaviors and meanings Africans brought from their places of origin. The second section focuses on the Middle Passage itself to study how the trans-Atlantic voyage served as a transformative experience in forging new cultural meanings and practices for Africans. The third and final section examines how Africans recreated and reformulated their culture through institutional spaces, family and ethnic relations, religious beliefs, and labor practices in the Americas.

As historians continue to study and flesh out the historical, cultural, and social consequences of slavery, several modes of inquiry can be broadly identified. The pioneers in the field of slave cultural studies were anthropologist Melville Herskovits, who created a typology of cultures identifying those that were more or less African depending on cultural practices; Brazilian sociologist Nina Rodrigues, who studied enslaved Muslims; and Cuban anthropologist Fernando Ortiz, who coined the term "transculturation" to convey the new culture that emerged between Spanish and African interactions. All three scholars charted important empirical and conceptual territory, but they tended to read current religious practices observed through fieldwork among people of African descent back onto the past. For example, one common feature in their analyses was a tendency to regard African cultures as being "transplanted" in their entirety and thus being a clear "continuation" of African beliefs and practices (Herskovits, 1941; Rodrigues, 1935; Ortiz, 1940).

By contrast, in a widely influential essay Sidney Mintz and Richard Price argued that as result of what they concluded was the random nature of the slave trade, Africans imported into the Americas "did not compose at the outset, groups" that could be identified with a single specific and unifying culture traced to an Old World homeland. Rather, they argued that African slaves brought to the New World represented "crowds" of disparate groups and cultures "and very heterogeneous crowds at that". Mintz and Price did not ignore the cultural traditions Africans brought with them, and even analyzed some of their practices, but they forcefully suggested that scholarship should examine the creation of Creole cultures and innovations in the New World in response to "[w]hat they [slaves] undeniably shared at the outset was their enslavement". Mintz and Price cautioned scholars against looking for similarities between Old World and New World African traditions. Instead, they focused on how diverse African cultures came together and began to form and invent new bonds of association and identity born out of slavery through the process of Creolization. In brief, Mintz and Price argued that scholars should concentrate on the "organizational task of enslaved Africans in the New World and that of creating institutions—institutions that would prove responsive to the needs of everyday life under the limiting conditions that slavery imposed upon them" (Mintz and Price, 1992: 18–19). Mintz and Price provided the greatest challenge to the view of slave culture advanced by Herskovits, Rodrigues and Ortiz. These two points of view about African survivals in the New World continue to shape most scholarship on slave culture.

Since the 1970s, the literature on slavery in the Americas, especially on United States slavery, has generally followed the Mintz and Price Creolization model with its emphasis on New World innovations in the formation of African-American cultures. Ira Berlin, for example, built upon the "creolization model" by connecting the paradigm to early African/European interactions when he developed the term "Atlantic Creole". According to Berlin, "Atlantic Creoles" emerged during the encounter between Africans and Europeans in West Africa during the sixteenth century. These trans-Atlantic cultural brokers served as cultural and political intermediaries between nascent slave communities and European settler communities, were often fluent in multiple languages, and were able to deftly bridge cultural divides. Ten years after Berlin first coined the term, "Atlantic Creole" has now become a regular title in books and articles on slave culture in the Americas with special attention drawn to the remarkable skills and fascinating lives of these individuals Berlin (1998: 17–46).[1]

Nevertheless, at the same time as Berlin was developing the concept of the "Atlantic Creole", African Diaspora studies began to challenge the Mintz and Price Creolization model. Scholars such as John Thornton and Paul Gilroy argued that the African Diaspora was a process shaped by events and experiences on both sides of the Atlantic (Thornton, 1998; Gilroy, 1993). At the same time, historians of Africa such as Joseph Miller, Paul Lovejoy, Michael Gomez, Robin Law, John Thornton, James Sweet, and David Eltis took an increasing interest in slavery in the Americas (see, for example, Miller, 1988; Lovejoy, 2000; Gomez, 1998; Sweet, 2003). In particular, the study of the trans-Atlantic slave trade has been revolutionized by collaborative scholarly efforts, computer assistance, and the construction of long-term data sets spanning centuries. As a result, it has become easier for scholars to eschew the generic non-descriptive terms "Africa" and "African", and identify more precisely the cultural origins of slaves and their New World destinations. The statistical databases on the trans-Atlantic slave trade assembled by an international team of researchers, headed by David Eltis, and work on trans-Atlantic cultural links between Africa and the Americas by the scholars brought together by Paul Lovejoy's Nigerian Hinterland Slave Trade Project at York University, have gathered a massive amount of demographic and biographic source material on the lives and experiences of slaves in the Diaspora.[2] The quantitative and qualitative data in these works fundamentally challenge the conclusions made by Mintz and Price about the random nature of the slave trade that supposedly resulted in a "crowd" of different cultures. Historians have begun to identify specific migration patterns from statistical and cultural sources that link slave-exporting regions in Africa with specific destinations in the Americas. Increasingly, scholars are focusing on a single exporting region in Africa and upon a single destination in the Americas to trace out in detail how both sides were intimately connected through the slave trade (see, for example, the chapters in Heywood, 2002; Falola and Childs, 2005; Curto and Lovejoy, 2004; Hall, 2005).

An additional paradigm for understanding slavery in the Americas extends back to work on Ancient Slavery by Moses Finley. Finley (1980: 79–80) made a distinction between "slave societies" and "societies with slaves". In the "slave societies" of the Americas, the enslaved often made up the demographic majority of a colony or nation's population. In these societies, the master–slave relationship served as the dominant social, political and economic relation. Brazil, Jamaica, and Saint Domingue are examples of "slave societies". In "societies with slaves", by contrast, African slaves were only one among many laboring populations. In these societies, the master–slave relationship was not the determinative social, political, and cultural influence. Moreover, economic activities tended to be diversified rather than concentrated around slave-produced tropical goods. New Spain, Peru, Pennsylvania, and New York are examples of "societies with slaves". These typologies are particularly useful for understanding the emergence and transformations in slave systems. The great slave societies of the Americas in Brazil, the Caribbean, and the southern part of the United States all started as "societies with slaves" before they became "slave societies". The distinctions between the two different slave systems provide useful analytical tools for studying the specific roles of demographics and labor in shaping such topics as family relations, possibilities for manumission, and more broadly cultural accommodation and resistance.[3]

These interpretive paradigms have strengths and weaknesses. The "Creolization" model gets at the heart of the creative adaptive process all slaves had to go through, but does not distinguish this process very clearly from the creative adaptations to new environments that all migrants, slave or free, had to go through. The Atlantic approach, in the words of Paul Lovejoy (2000: 2), "is important because it places the 'middle passage' in the middle of the slaves' experiences". Nevertheless, this approach underplays the ways in which African-American cultural forms were developed within and during enslavement. The "Atlantic Creole" model conceptually bridges the "Creolization" model and the Atlantic approach, but here some problems can also be discerned. Most of the literature on "Atlantic Creoles" focuses on those Africans who were conversant and even comfortable operating in European worlds, and who used certain markers of western civilization, such as European languages and the mastery of writing, as well as being people who practiced European religion. In addition, there were many generations of Atlantic Creoles in the Americas, not just an initial generation. For Berlin, Atlantic Creoles are a generational phenomenon produced through initial African–European interactions. Yet every time European traders created new zones and *entrepôts* for the trans-Atlantic slave trade to thrive, a new group of "Atlantic Creoles" came into existence. The "slave society" versus "society with slaves" typology also has certain limitations for studying slave culture because ultimately it is the structural factors of the slave systems that distinguish the two, not cultural factors. Collectively, the insights of these various models and approaches help historians to understand the dynamics influencing the transformation, recreation, and reformulation of slave culture in the Americas. The limitations of these models, however, do not invalidate them as explanatory tools, but powerfully underscore that ultimately there was not one slave culture, but many slave cultures that require many perspectives to understand Atlantic slavery across time and place.

The enslavement process in Africa

African American slave cultures had their origin in Africa, a culturally diverse continent. As early as the sixteenth century, large populations of Africans practicing Catholicism could be found in the Kingdom of Kongo and in the Portuguese colony of Angola. In addition, Islam had extended its influence from East Africa to the West African Atlantic coast, beginning in the eighth century. In the process, Islam created many Muslim converts and centers of political power organized by caliphates. Beyond monotheistic religions familiar to Western civilization, complex indigenous African religions could be found throughout West and Central Africa. African religious diversity alone during the era of the slave trade, not to mention other markers of culture, such as language, were far more numerous and more complex than anything in Europe.

For the purposes of understanding the transformation, recreation, and reformulation of Africans' culture, and their ancestral origins on the other side of the Atlantic, three large provenance zones can be identified as the homelands for Africans with shared linguistic and cultural understandings: Upper Guinea, Lower Guinea, and Central Africa. The region of Upper Guinea extends from the Senegal River down to present-day Sierra Leone. The dominant ethnic groups of Africans in this region are the Wolof, Fula, Mandinga, and Cabo Verdeans. Many Muslims could be found among this group, and the initial population of slaves brought to Europe in the fifteenth century came from this region. The second region, Lower Guinea, geographically extends from Sierra Leone south into the Bight of Biafra, with slaves particularly drawn from the Ivory Coast, the Gold Coast, and the Slave Coast between 1600 and 1850. The region was composed of Akan and Yoruba speakers and included such ethnicities as the Mina, Lucumi, Nago, Igbo, and Coromante. The third region, Central Africa, extends from Loango in the north to Benguela in the south, with the major sources for enslaved Africans from this region being the Kongo and Angolan regions. This region exhibited more cultural and linguistic similarities than the other two cultural regions. Within the Central African cultural zone, Kikongo and Kimbundu represented the two dominant spoken languages, which themselves were mutually intelligible. It would have been common for Africans to draw somewhat narrow circles of political and cultural inclusion, reflecting kinship (family) and kingship (political) associations. Africans drew upon these broad shared cultural and linguistic similarities as they forged new cultures in the Diaspora.[4]

Historians have recently emphasized the political, military, and cultural forces contemporary to West and Central Africa during the era of the trans-Atlantic slave trade in order to understand the transferences and transformations in culture that occurred among the enslaved in the New World. Beginning in the fifteenth century and continuing long into the nineteenth century, the enslavement process in Africa transformed African politics, society, economics, and culture. Broadly speaking from 1450 to 1900, the military and political leaders of West and Central Africa attempted to consolidate large areas into centralized states through the forceful incorporation of small polities. Kingship networks in service of state building began to assert authority over kinship associations. Warfare and enslavement in the service of political centralization and empire building drastically reduced the number of stateless societies all along the Atlantic basin, but no large single empire emerged to exert political influence over the region as a whole. The simultaneous process of political inclusion of small states and the rise and subsequent political fragmentation of larger states in Africa, combined with the rapid expansion of slavery on the other side of the Atlantic in such places as Brazil, the Caribbean, the mainlands of Spanish America, and the United States provided a deadly scenario for the Atlantic slave trade to flourish (Thornton, 1983; 1998: 304–17). The political and military conflicts in Africa served to infuse slave cultures in the Americas with a certain degree of cultural multilingualism and cosmopolitanism because it made Africans familiar with various processes of spatial and cultural dislocation.

Assessing the process of how Africans become transformed into Atlantic slaves requires an exploration of how Africans understood the enslavement of Africans on the continent. First, they did not regard slavery as "Africans" enslaving "Africans" or "Blacks" enslaving "Blacks", just as Europeans would not regard the Nazi Holocaust as simply "White" Europeans indiscriminately committing genocide against other "White" Europeans. Africans had developed their own concepts of who could and could not be enslaved. None of these criteria emphasized racial characteristics. Enslavement could often be justified for religious purposes, as slavery served to tutor unbelievers in the belief system of the enslavers. At least theoretically under Islamic law, a fellow Muslim could not be enslaved and those who shared belief systems also could not be enslaved. If a slave showed mastery of the religion of the master, he or she might be able to justify emancipation. Other concepts that served to justify enslavement included not being part of an ethnic community, being the subject of an existing rival polity, or people who found themselves outside kinship relations. Similarly to other groups throughout history, religious, ethnic, and political differences among West and Central Africans often manifested themselves through warfare. Captives captured in war often became enslaved. It should be stressed, however, that slavery within West and Central African societies was often a transitory state, and it was not uncommon for slaves to move in and out of enslaved status several times during their lifetime.[5]

There are two features of slavery in Africa that distinguish it from racial slavery in the Americas. The first distinguishing feature was that Africans had a very narrow and restricted concept of who belonged to a community and a polity. Polities were often constructed around extended kin lines or ancestry traced to a particular founding member of their society. Africans "outside" that cultural network could be subject to enslavement. Europeans, by contrast, were extremely hesitant to enslave other Europeans, even when Europeans were constantly at war with each other for political, religious, and military reasons. In fact, it was far more common for Europeans to sentence fellow Europeans to death for crimes rather than punish them to enslavement for life. Indentured servants often labored as part of a criminal or debt sentences, but these punishments were usually for less than ten years and, except in rare cases, this was not a status that passed to heirs. By contrast, Europeans had no such reservations about enslaving Africans, indicating to a certain degree that they regarded people from Africa as beyond the fold of humanity. These two cultural concepts – how Africans drew narrow circles of inclusion, while Europeans drew very broad circles of exclusion – created the conditions for the trans-Atlantic slave trade to thrive (see Eltis, 2000).

A second distinguishing feature of slavery in Africa compared with slavery in the Americas was that enslaved status often was not permanent. While the goal of providing "civilization" to the enslaved was most certainly a self-serving justification, to a certain degree Africans were less hypocritical than their European counterparts. Once an enslaved African could demonstrate some mastery of the dominant culture and had the economic resources to have their freedom purchased, they often could leave enslavement and become part of mainstream society. In the Americas, such transitions between slavery and freedom were exceptional rather than normal, as John Garrigus discusses in Chapter 14 of this volume. Moreover, even where a freed population did emerge in the Americas, most notably in cities and towns, masters never regarded free people of colour as their equals. As slavery in Africa was not associated with race, but was concerned with many other factors such as debt, kin networks, ethnicity, political conquest, warfare, and dependency, African enslavement was a more flexible and transitional status than the relatively rigid nature of American enslavement. The important point to emphasize is that while African slavery was distinct from its New World counterpart, the institution did exist in Africa itself. That most of the enslaved had experiences with slavery in Africa prior to shipment to the New World allowed for some continuities in

African cultures, even while the enslaved had to adapt and survive in a new environment on the other side of the Atlantic.

Three examples illustrate the relationship between state building and enslavement in Africa. In West Central Africa, the Portuguese established their presence at the colony of Angola in 1575 and worked within the existing Kingdom of Kongo networks to obtain slaves for the trans-Atlantic trade. The Kingdom of Kongo acquired slaves through waging war on neighbours. As the Kingdom of Kongo extended its political boundaries in Central Africa during the sixteenth and seventeenth centuries, slaves were acquired by military conquest and then used in economic activities, especially urban labor in the major cities of the Kongo. For example, beginning in the 1520s, the Kongo and the Portuguese battled against the Ndongo. Captured Ndongo slaves were taken to the Kongo and put to work, thereby somewhat depopulating and weakening the Ndongo. Similarly, in order to gain a foothold at the colony of Angola, the Portuguese had to fight political and territorial wars to establish their presence on the African continent. In the process of doing so, war captives became enslaved in Africa and many ended up being funneled to the trans-Atlantic slave trade. The slaves who came from Kongo and Angolan regions brought with them varying degrees of knowledge about Christianity. Consequently, the imposition of Christianity on slaves in the New World most likely was not the first encounters Central Africans had with that religion. Linda Heywood and John Thornton (2007: esp. chs 2–3) argue that Catholicism represents continuity rather than a rupture in African culture.

In the Bight of Benin, two powerful empires extended their political influence, mainly through slave raiding activities. For several centuries, the political kingdoms on the Slave Coast, such as Allada and Whydah, had engaged in slave trading activities with the immediate hinterland and European traders on the coast. The Dahomey Empire, by contrast, became the dominant military and political force in the region through slave raiding. The "success" of Dahomey in acquiring and producing slaves extended its political and military influence both towards the interior and on the coast. As enslavement in Africa became entangled with the escalating demand of the trans-Atlantic slave trade, the social, cultural, political, economic, and military traditions particular to Africa were exported along with slaves to the other side of Atlantic (Law, 1991).

The Oyo Empire, also in the Bight of Benin, followed a similar rise to that of the Dahomey Empire as a result of slave raiding activities. The Oyo Empire benefited materially and militarily from its participation in the trans-Atlantic slave trade as the slaves were provided by its neighbors. The enslavement of neighboring groups weakened their rivals and contributed to the centralization of kingly power. Over time, however, the growth of royal authority and centralization produced opposition by non-Oyo leaders, who saw their power and prestige decline rapidly. Ultimately, the never-ending European demand for slaves resulted in tensions within the Oyo polity itself, reaching the point where civil wars erupted, and the Oyo themselves became for the first time the principal slaves leaving the region. European demand for slaves proved to be one of the key factors in explaining the rapid rise of the Oyo Empire and its downfall by civil war (Law, 1977). Historians have recently begun to link these military conflicts on the African continent to creating cultures of resistance in the Americas. Knowingly or not, slave traders and masters often imported slaves from militarized cultures. Historians have argued that the military and cultural background of African slaves shipped to the Americas represented a central, if not decisive, feature of the 1739 Stono revolt in

South Carolina, the Haitian Revolution, and the 1835 Malê revolt in Brazil, rather than simply representing a response to New World enslavement (Thornton, 1991a: 1108–13; 1991b: 50–80; Lovejoy, 1994).

In summary, the enslavement process in Africa developed out of slavery practices indigenous to West and Central Africa itself. Over time, however, and as the trans-Atlantic slave trade developed and intensified, enslavement in Africa increasingly became linked with slavery in the Americas. Among the major exporting regions in Africa, enslavement often resulted from the process of military warfare in the service of political empire building.

The Middle Passage

The Middle Passage refers to the trans-Atlantic shipments of slaves from the African continent to the Americas. The experience of the Middle Passage, however, did not just begin and end at ports of embarkation on the African coast and disembarkation in the New World. Historians of slavery in Africa and the Americas over the past 20 years have emphasized that slavery in the New World began with the long trek from the African interior to the coast. The "middle" in the "middle passage", consequently, does not refer exclusively to the period between enslavement in Africa and toiling in the Americas. Rather, the horrific trans-Atlantic voyage experienced by the estimated 11 million Africans who crossed the Atlantic represents one common feature of a "middle" experience. That experience included enslavement, transportation, and waiting for shipment to the New World while penned at slave forts on the African coast, and arrival in American port cities, waiting to be sold to new masters, and then being funneled to rural plantations. Collectively, this Middle Passage experience served as an important foundational moment that transformed Africans into Atlantic slaves. Further (and as this volume attests), it should be emphasized that the diversity of slavery in the Americas makes it difficult cogently to synthesize the slave experience. That stated, one of the commonalities shared by all slaves who came to the Americas was that they left from African slave ports, experienced a trans-Atlantic voyage, and arrived at American ports. Given that most slave societies in the Americas did not produce a Creolized slave population by natural increase, the trans-Atlantic slave trade was the one historical experience most commonly shared by all slaves spread across time and place throughout the history of New World slavery (see, for example, Smallwood, 2007; Byrd, 2008).

Although European slave traders called at ports all along the Atlantic coast of Africa and at some ports in the Indian Ocean, several dominant streams in the movement of enslaved Africans from the interior to the coast can be identified. One way to conceive of the capturing, enslaving, and movement of Africans from the interior to be sold to European traders along the Atlantic littoral is to see Africa and its hinterland geographically as several funnels. The wide mouth of the funnel extends into the interior, with the narrow tip emptying its content at African port cities. From the fifteenth to the nineteenth centuries, the length and width of the enslavement funnels became more extensive. While there were many and overlapping funnels, several stand out: the Angolan/Kongo funnel from West Central Africa to the Portuguese controlled port of Luanda; the Biafran funnel from the Cross River region of Calabar to the Bight of Biafra; the Yoruba funnel of the Nigerian hinterland to the Bight of Benin; and the Akan funnel from the region of present-day Ghana to the Gold Coast. Alex Byrd (2008: 21–22) stresses that from a comparative perspective "the overseas voyage from the African littoral to the Americas represented perhaps the shortest leg of captives' whole disparaging odyssey ... even before reaching the ships, slaves from the interior could be many months moving from their former homes to the coast". One of the major cultural consequences of being uprooted from natal kin-based communities and forced into new social roles as moveable commodities of labor was the creation of new cultural identities.

Historians of slavery in the Americas have long recognized that the enslavement funneling process often resulted in ethnic communities emerging in the Americas, such as Kongos, Igbo, Minas, Lucumis, and Nagos.[6] Ethnonyms (ethnic names) commonly found in the Diaspora were widespread among the enslaved population in the Americas. Nevertheless, these ethnonyms are not found with the same regularity and frequency in west and central Africa. For example, while "Mina" slaves took on a collective identity in the Americas, locating "Mina" communities in Africa is more difficult. Similarly, the unified Yoruba identity such as Lucumi or Nago that developed in the Diaspora is difficult to locate in Yorubaland beyond very restricted locations prior to 1850. Further, such terms as Kongo, Igbo, Carabali, and Coromante, while frequently used to designate Africans' place of origin and a common identity, may tell scholars only the ports and regions from which the enslaved left (Law, 1997; 2005).

The wide-scale employment of ethnic designators in the African Diaspora, and their relative absence on the African mainland, serve as indices about the transformations in African culture produced by Atlantic slavery. In Yorubaland, for example, the multiple ethnicities, languages, and kin-based communities became enveloped into an overarching Yoruba identity in the Diaspora. As João Reis argues, the "Yoruba of the Oyo, Ehba, Ijebu, Ilesha and Ketu kingdoms became Nagôs in Bahia through complex exchanges and convergences of cultural signs with the help of a common language, similar divinities (Orishas), the unification of many under Islam, long experience as subjects of the Oyo *alafins* (kings), Yoruba urban traditions and, obviously a life of slavery in Bahia" (Reis, 1997). In other words, the Yoruba wove an identity based upon commonalities of culture in the Diaspora, and did not draw rigid lines of cultural distinctions by kinship and kingship, as would have been done in Africa. In the case of Biafrans, scholars are now suggesting that the term "Igbo" was at first used to refer to outsiders who arrived at the exporting Atlantic ports of Bonny, Old Calabar, and Elem Kalabarri. Over time, Biafrans from the interior adopted and embraced an Igbo identity as part of a transformation from their natal/kin communities of the interior to create ties of solidarity with fellow captives during the trek to port cities, imprisonment at the coastal slave forts while awaiting shipment across the Atlantic, and then most forcefully as a result of the intimate bonds that emerged during the horrific trans-Atlantic crossing. That these ethnic identities were to a certain degree created by the slave trade and were forged from Diaspora experiences does not make them any less African or authentic.

We can see how African culture became reshaped through Atlantic slavery by looking firstly at cosmological beliefs, and secondly at the terms the enslaved used to describe their experience. Slaves exported from the Kongo/Angolan region by the Portuguese often referred to each other as "*malungo*", a Kimbundu-derived word that could mean either brother, relative, or comrade, and, in Brazil, shipmate. But *malungo* was more than just a tie of solidarity born out of the slave trade. It also referred to a Central African deity that had the authority to re-establish broken kin relations and create new hierarchies of lineage (Slenes, 1991).

In the Americas, among slaves exported from the Bight of Benin, several deities associated with cholera and smallpox became more prominent than they had been in Africa. In the Kingdom of Dahomey, Sakpata, the god of smallpox, became more important as the interior slave trade increased incidences of disease (Law, 2004: 90, 93). As enslaved Africans called upon the supernatural to seek out assistance and guidance in dealing with their liminality, these transformations in belief systems serve as a cultural index at the level of consciousness of being converted from Africans to Atlantic slaves.

As Africans arrived at the coast, European slave traders, African merchants, and the slaves themselves began to draw clear distinctions between indigenous African slavery and trans-Atlantic slavery. In the eighteenth-century Angolan slave trade, Africans morbidly referred to slave traders, slave ships, and slave merchants all by the term *tumbeiros*, meaning "undertakers", "tombs", and "bearers of tombs" (Miller, 1988: 314). Upon arrival at Atlantic slave forts, local merchants and traders separated the enslaved Africans brought from the interior from the local slave population who worked at the slave forts owned by African and European merchants. These "castle" or "factory" slaves, as they became known, had different customary rights from the Atlantic slaves, usually maintained some ties with their local kin and ethnic communities, and some family members even redeemed them from slavery. European traders stationed at slave forts frequently ran into trouble with African rulers when they violated local customs about the treatment of castle slaves. In ports in the Bight of Biafra and the Bight of Benin, an "Igbo" or a "Lucumi" from the interior was treated more harshly, as they did not have any of the limited security that kinship and kingship communities could offer. In a cultural and legal sense, Africans on the coast drew distinctions between those slaves still connected to kinship and kingship communities in Africa and those separated from such associations (see Byrd, 2008: ch. 1; Smallwood, 2007: 52–53).

The cultural process whereby Africans were changed into enslaved Atlantic laborers was not unlike sand passing slowly through the narrow neck of an hourglass. It became crystallized during the Middle Passage. Thousands of Africans violently resisted the trans-Atlantic slave trade, and some did indeed succeed in freeing themselves, but their actions did not abolish the trans-Atlantic slave trade dominated by European political imperatives and merchant capital (for examples, see Diouf, 2003). Ties of ethnic solidarity intensified during the trans-Atlantic voyage. Sidney Mintz and Richard Price (1992: 43–44) insightfully drew attention to this intimate bonding encounter on the slave ship, yet they erred in assuming that the Africans would have been complete strangers and that they only met for the first time on the slave ship. The trans-Atlantic crossing represented the third phase in the formation of ties of enslaved solidarity.

For those Africans who survived the cramped, unhealthy, disease-infested, and deadly Middle Passage, arrival in the Americas resulted in slaves being held in yards, stockades, and baracoons until prospective buyers came calling for purchase. As a result, the funneling process that transformed Africans into Atlantic slaves continued in the New World at American port cities. Penned up once again until sold or auctioned off, Africans continued to forge associational ties among those who shared a common cultural background and a historical experience of the Middle Passage. The first year for Africans in the Americas resulted in exceptionally high mortality rates that only compounded the demand for more slaves. Slave trade transactions in the Americas are littered with the word "refuse", which traders applied to slaves as a result of their sex, age, or health upon arrival. Africans who survived the Middle Passage now had to adjust and reformulate their culture to their New World environment (Smallwood, 2007: 176–94; Byrd, 2008: 61–71).

Recreating Africa in the Americas

The cultural priorities and strategies employed by the enslaved upon arrival in the New World were similar to those of voluntary migrants, even if their available choices and opportunities were far more constrained. Enslaved Africans attempted to recreate cultural familiarity in their strange new land by congregating with fellow countrymen, by speaking African languages, by practicing African religions, by performing songs and dances similar to those from Africa, by cooking sacred and everyday food items to provide a taste of Africa under slavery, and most importantly by struggling to establish kin and family relations to provide some personal stability. In this sense, Africans were not unlike the Irish of Boston or the Italians of New York in the nineteenth century, for example, who established ethnic communities like those they had left behind. Nevertheless, enslaved Africans were involuntary migrants whose ability to recreate their past lives was restricted. That Africans ultimately could not recreate African culture as it existed in Africa should come as no surprise, given their enslaved status. What should come as a surprise, however, and serves as a testament to Africans' cultural ingenuity under severe duress, is that they did create a Diasporic culture which spoke to both their African origins and their New World experiences.

Masters throughout the New World recognized that Africans did not represent an undifferentiated mass of laborers, but brought with them forms of social organization and cultural differences that they perpetuated and refashioned in the Americas as survival strategies. Robert Jameson, a British observer in Cuba, recognized how both masters and slaves identified Africans by "nations" in the early nineteenth century: "The different nations to which the negroes belonged in Africa are marked out in the colonies both by the master[s] and the slaves; the former considering them variously characterized in the desired qualities, and the latter joining together with a true national spirit in such union as their lords allow."[7] David Eltis's detailed study of trans-Atlantic slave trade documents led him to conclude that "[w]hile the planters' basic requirement was slave labor from anywhere in Africa, no one can read the trans-Atlantic correspondence of the early modern slave systems without recognizing the importance of African nationhood in the shaping of the plantation regimes"(Eltis, 2000: 244). Africans asserted their humanity by adopting cultural practices and an identity that reflected their place of origin, whereas masters imposed their dominion over slaves by defining them as racialized instruments of labor.

In Iberia and Latin America, the practice of recognizing ethnic cultural differences among Africans occurred through religious lay brotherhoods. Slavery had been firmly established in Seville a century before the Conquest of the New World in 1492. Municipal authorities appointed a steward to settle disputes between slaves and masters, and allowed the African population the right to gather on feast days and perform their own dances and songs. In addition, black congregationalists established religious brotherhoods (Pike, 1967: 344–46). These practices were then carried to the Americas. From the very beginning of Atlantic slavery and New World colonization, the Catholic Church played a fundamental role in justifying slavery and in creating spaces for an African collective identity.

Spain and Portugal organized enslaved and free Africans into religious brotherhoods in the New World by grouping them together by place of origin. Mariza de Carvalho Soares' detailed examination of religious brotherhoods in Rio de Janeiro documents how Africans who shared a similar ethnicity often formed their own sodalities (Soares, 2000). These brotherhoods gave an institutional framework to a Catholic ethnic identity. The same phenomenon occurred in various locations of the Spanish empire. By the end of the sixteenth century, the names of sodalities in Lima often reflected African ethnicity, such as the Dominican brotherhood for the "negros Congos", and the brotherhood of Nuestra Señora del Socorro for Angolans (Bowser, 1974: 249–50, 339). In Mexico City, Africans outnumbered Spaniards two to one by the end of the sixteenth century. Unsurprisingly, religious brotherhoods populated by and catering to the population of African descent proliferated, as Nicole von Germeten (2006) has shown. From the northern borderlands of Saint Augustine to the far southern extreme of Buenos Aires, Catholic brotherhoods made up of Africans could be found throughout the Spanish empire (Landers, 1999: ch. 5; Andrews, 1980).

For the Spanish Caribbean island of Cuba, the presence of Catholic brotherhoods that included the population of African ancestry can be traced to the sixteenth century. In 1573 the Havana Town Council reported that Africans took part in the procession of Corpus Christi, and several wills indicate they regularly made donations to sodalities. Jane Landers found that many African ethnic groups proliferated in Havana and organized important brotherhoods. Most of the brotherhoods selected a patron saint who they honored on his or her feast day with elaborate festivals and ceremonies (Landers, 1999: ch. 5). As an eighteenth-century Havana bishop lamented, these brotherhoods often disregarded their religious duties and sacraments and created "scandalous and grave disorders … when they congregate on festival days" (cited in Marrero, 1980: VIII, 159). By carving out an institutional space for themselves within the Catholic Church, Africans refashioned their New World institutions to speak, in part, to their places of origin on the other side of the Atlantic.

Colonial authorities reluctantly allowed Africans to form ethnically organized mutual-aid and religious societies that displayed a great deal of independence from the Catholic Church. Over time, these somewhat more independent organizations became known as *cabildos de nación*. These societies thrived in port cities throughout Latin America. They were largely an urban phenomenon. The key to the success of the *cabildos* and the lay brotherhoods was the ownership of a house where Africans could collectively meet. The shared house could be a boarding-house that rented rooms; a conference center for holding meetings and reunions; a school for education and training in the artisan trades; a bank collecting membership dues, offering loans, and even purchasing freedom for slaves; a theater for dances; or even a funeral parlor. The *cabildo* houses provided a sacred space for ethnic solidarity in a society increasingly divided along racial lines between slavery and freedom (Howard, 1998; Childs, 2006: 209–45).

The origins of the New World African lay brotherhoods and *cabildos* can be traced to Catholic brotherhoods of Spanish origin, but analogous societies were common to West and Central Africa. At the port of Old Calabar and surrounding regions in the Bight of Biafra, an all-male secret society known as Ekpe formed as early as the second half of the seventeenth century. According to Paul Lovejoy and David Richardson (1999: 347–49), Ekpe society created an "interlocking grid of secret associations [that] served to regulate the behavior of members". The secret organization crossed the Atlantic and resurfaced in nineteenth-century Cuba through an altered form in the Abakuá society. In the Yoruba Kingdom of Oyo a semi-secret organization known as the Ogboni society advised the King on religious and political matters. When Yorubaland funneled thousands of Africans to Cuba and Brazil in the nineteenth century, detailed knowledge of the organization crossed the Atlantic and influenced the *cabildos* (Law, 1977: 61).

Various other societies existed in West and Central Africa that performed charitable, recreational, political, and economic functions for members sharing the same language, ethnicity, and nationality. The collective and communal organizing principles of these organizations often translated into mutual-aid societies in the Americas. The African-born and Creole population of African descent regularly met with their fellow nationals in various formal or informal organizations. These cultural associations often linked the more fortunate and well placed members of an ethnic group with their poorer and severely exploited co-nationals through patron–client networks. The Yoruba in West Africa, for example, operated mutual-aid societies as early as the eighteenth century through the Ajo and Esusu saving institutions. Each member paid dues into a collective fund that would then be available for individual loans. When Yoruba slaves began to be exported across the Atlantic, the Esusu savings association emerged in the Caribbean and Brazil (Falola and Akanmu, 2000). Latin American colonial administrators and Catholic priests regarded African brotherhoods and *cabildos* as an extension of European religious sodalities. The organizations for Africans, however, surely did not represent something entirely of Iberian origin, but an Old World African institution modified to a New World setting.

Syncretic African religions grew out of the institutional space accorded Africans within the Catholic Church. As indigenous African religions were not tied exclusively to a specific text or scripture, they regularly evolved by incorporating other deities and beliefs. This tendency towards syncretism, coupled with the familiarity Africans already had with Islam and Christianity prior to arrival in the Americas, culturally prepared Africans to adapt their religions to Christian practices. Africans from Yorubaland, for example, channeled deities called *orisas* into Roman Catholic saints. This syncretism between Yoruba *orisas* and Roman Catholic saints gave birth to some of the central religious beliefs and practices of *Candomblé* in Brazil, *Santeria* in Cuba, and *Vodun* in Haiti. For example, in Brazil, Ogun, the *orisa* of iron and war, is matched with St George, who carries a sword, whereas in Cuba, Ogun is commonly linked with Saint Peter, who holds an iron key. In Haiti, iconography depicting Saint Jerome in battle carrying a metal sword linked him to Ogun as the deity of blacksmiths. Changó, the *orisa* god of thunder and lightening, is linked to Santa Bárbara because her father was struck dead by lightning as a punishment for killing her when she refused to give up her Christian faith. The high volume of the slave trade to Cuba, Brazil, and Saint Domingue during the eighteenth and nineteenth centuries resulted in a constant influx of belief systems, which created the demographic conditions for syncretic religions to thrive. It should be stressed, however, that religious continuities required a transformation of African religious imagery and symbols into imagery and symbol that contained significant Christian elements (see for example Matory, 2005).

Protestant slave societies of the Americas also produced their own variants of African-influenced Christianity. From the seventeenth to the nineteenth centuries, masters and missionaries in the British Caribbean and United States went from showing very little interest in the spiritual wellbeing of slaves to demonstrating a religious zeal that helped produce a distinct Afro-American Christianity. The emergence of evangelical Christianity, with its emphasis on a personal relationship with God, rather than access to God being through exclusive instruction by theologically trained scholars, braided with creolized slave populations in North America during the eighteenth century. In particular, Baptists and Methodists took an active evangelizing role. Some groups even spoke out against slavery and allowed slaves and free people of colour to form their own independent churches, such as First African Baptist Church in Augusta, Georgia and the African Methodist Episcopal Church, formed by Richard Allen. Employing biblical scripture, slaves created a distinct Afro-American Christianity that linked their religious experiences to stories of the biblical exodus of the Jews from Egypt. Slaves in the USA and the British Caribbean refashioned their religious worldview to claim that they were God's chosen people, who would be redeemed from slavery and racial oppression through conversion. Slaves forged the beliefs of Evangelical Christianity that swept through the Anglo-Protestant world into a weapon to attack master dominion. By comparison, there are few equivalents from the Catholic French, Spanish, or Portuguese slave societies of the Americas where biblical inspiration from the Old Testament and mastery of the written word of the Bible served as powerful tools in shaping the slaves' religious experience.[8]

Slave culture varied dramatically between urban and rural areas. Catholic brotherhoods and *cabildos* were almost exclusively an urban phenomenon. Further, while slave religion thrived in both urban and also rural locations, religion took on a particular organized and institutionalized form in American port cities tied to Atlantic networks, such as Philadelphia, Savannah, Charleston, New Orleans, Le Cap François, Havana, Bahia, and Rio de Janeiro. The vitality and strength of these organizations and their accompanying religious practices reflected the opportunities that urban slaves had to move outside the close supervision of their masters in order to make associations with other slaves and with free people of colour.

This relative freedom of movement and slaves' dynamic and diverse associational and religious experience also carried over in the marketplace. João Reis has found, in his detailed studies of slave markets in Bahia, Brazil (Reis, 1997), that the customs governing the selling of goods and the organization of the markets reflected practices and traditions in West Africa. In one dramatic case in the 1850s, slaves organized a strike after municipal authorities attempted to impose a new set of regulations that disrupted the African marketing system organized by "*cantos*" in Bahia, Brazil. This marketing system was similar to those common in the Bight of Benin. Slaves and free people of color were often both buyers and sellers in New World Atlantic port cities. More than 50 years ago, Sidney Mintz (1955) drew attention to the central role slaves played in marketing goods in Jamaica. Most of the foodstuffs sold at markets were produced by Africans. Moreover, slaves were trusted by their masters to make purchases on their behalf – masters only rarely interfered with how slaves conducted their business in slave markets.[9]

Conclusion

The cultural transformations that began with slavery in Africa, transportation to the New World via the Middle Passage, and recreating Africa in the Americas provided a wealth of historical experiences for the population of African descent as they made the cultural, legal, and social transition from slave to freed person. In the years, decades, and centuries since abolition, the descendents of slaves throughout the Americas had drawn upon the experiences they suffered during enslavement in Africa, trans-shipment to the Americas, and slavery in the New World to create vibrant cultures that mixed Old-World and New-World elements. The legacy of slavery still weighs heavily among the living as the descendants of slaves continue to emphasize their black racial identity, born out of the cultural processes of slavery, to campaign for cultural inclusion in the nation state, political equality, and an end to racial discrimination, all of which had it origins in converting Africans into Atlantic slaves.

Notes

1 For authors who build upon and employ Berlin's model, see Sparks (2004); Heywood and Thornton (2007); Landers (2010).
2 Eltis *et al.* (1999); for the activities and publications of Paul Lovejoy's Nigerian Hinterland Slave Trade Project, see www.yorku.ca/nhp/areas/nhp.htm
3 Various other scholars have employed the typology, see for example Morgan (1991).
4 The division of West and Central Africa into three cultural areas is derived from Thornton (1998: xii–xxxviii).
5 For a concise overview of African slavery, see Manning (1990).
6 For an overview linking ethnic homelands in Africa to ethnic slave communities in the Americas, see Hall (2005).
7 Robert Francis Jameson, *Letters from the Havana during the Year 1820; Containing an Account of the Present State of the Island of Cuba and Observations on the Slave Trade* (London: John Miller, 1821), 21.
8 Among the numerous works on this topic, see Genovese (1974); Sidbury (2007).
9 For the importance of African ethnicity and marketing practices in the Americas see Reis (1997); see also Mintz (1955).

Bibliography

Andrews, George Reid, *The Afro-Argentines of Buenos Aires, 1800–1900* (Madison: University of Wisconsin Press, 1980).

Berlin, Ira, *Many Thousands Gone: The First Two Centuries of Slavery in North America* (Cambridge, MA: Harvard University Press, 1998).

Bowser, Frederick P., *The African Slave in Colonial Peru, 1524–1650* (Stanford: Stanford University Press, 1974).

Byrd, Alexander X., *Captives and Voyagers: Black Migrants across the Eighteenth-century British Atlantic World* (Baton Rouge: Louisiana State University Press, 2008).

Childs, Matt D., "'The Defects of Being a Black Creole': The Degrees of African Ethnicity in the Cuban Cabildos de Nación" in Jane A. Landers and Barry Robinson, eds, *Slaves and Subjects: Blacks in Colonial Latin America* (Albuquerque: University of New Mexico Press, 2006), 209–45.

Curto, José C. and Lovejoy, Paul E., eds, *Enslaving Connections: Changing Cultures of Africa and Brazil during the Era of Slavery* (Amherst, NY: Humanity Books, 2004).

Díaz, María Elena, *The Virgin, The King, and the Royal Slaves of El Cobre: Negotiating Freedom in Colonial Cuba, 1670–1780* (Stanford: Stanford University Press, 2000).

Diouf, Sylviane A., ed., *Fighting the Slave Trade: West African Strategies* (Athens: Ohio University Press, 2003).

Eltis, David, *The Rise of African Slavery in the Americas* (Cambridge: Cambridge University Press, 2000).

Eltis, David, Richardson, David, Behrendt, Stephen D. and Klein, Herbert S., eds, *The Trans-Atlantic Slave Trade: A Database on CD-ROM* (Cambridge: Cambridge University Press, 1999).

Falola, Toyin and Akanmu, Adebayo, *Culture, Politics, & Money Among the Yoruba* (New Brunswick: Transaction Publishers, 2000).

Falola, Toyin and Childs, Matt D., eds, *The Yoruba Diaspora in the Atlantic World* (Bloomington: Indiana University Press, 2005).

Finley, Moses I., *Ancient Slavery, Modern Ideology* (New York: Penguin, 1980), 79–80.

Genovese, Eugene D., *Roll, Jordan, Roll: The World the Slaves Made* (New York: Pantheon Books, 1974).

Gilroy, Paul, *The Black Atlantic: Modernity and Double Consciousness* (Cambridge, MA: Harvard University Press, 1993).

von Germeten, Nicole, *Black Blood Brothers: Confraternities and Social Mobility for Afro-Mexicans* (Gainesville: University of Florida Press, 2006).

Gomez, Michael A., *Exchanging Our Country Marks: The Transformation of African Identities in the Colonial and Antebellum South* (Chapel Hill: University of North Carolina Press, 1998).

Hall, Gwendolyn Midlo, *Slavery and African Ethnicities in the Americas: Restoring the Links* (Chapel Hill: University of North Carolina Press, 2005).

Herskovits, Melville J., *The Myth of the Negro Past* (New York: Harper, 1941).

Heywood, Linda M., ed., *Central Africans and Cultural Transformations in the American Diaspora* (Cambridge: Cambridge University Press, 2002).

Heywood, Linda M. and Thornton, John K., *Central Africans, Atlantic Creoles and the Foundation of the Americas, 1585–1660* (Cambridge: Cambridge University Press, 2007).

Howard, Philip A., *Changing History: Afro-Cuban Cabildos and Societies of Color in the Nineteenth Century* (Baton Rouge: Louisiana State University Press, 1998).

Joyner, Charles W., *Down by the Riverside: S South Carolina Slave Community* (Urbana: University of Illinois Press, 1984).

Karasch, Mary C., *Slave Life in Rio de Janeiro, 1808–1850* (Princeton, NJ: Princeton University Press, 1987).

Landers, Jane G., *Atlantic Creoles in the Age of Revolutions* (Cambridge, MA: Harvard University Press, 2010).

——, *Black Society in Spanish Florida* (Urbana: University of Illinois Press, 1999).

Law, Robin, *The Slave Coast of West Africa, 1550–1750* (Oxford: Clarendon Press, 1991).

——, *The Oyo Empire, c. 1600–c. 1836: A West African Imperialism in the Era of the Slave Trade* (Oxford: Clarendon Press, 1977).

——, "Ethnicity and the Slave Trade: 'Lucumi' and 'Nago' as Ethnonyms in West Africa", *History in Africa* 24 (1997), 205–19.

——, *Ouidah: The Social History of a West African "Port", 1727–1891* (Athens: Ohio University Press, 2004).

——, "Ethnicities of Enslaved Africans in the Diaspora: On the Meanings of 'Mina' (Again)", *History in Africa* 32 (2005), 247–67.

Lovejoy, Paul E., "Background to Rebellion: The Origins of Muslim Slaves in Bahia", *Slavery & Abolition* 15 (1994), 151–80.

——, *Transformations in Slavery: A History of Slavery in Africa*, 2nd edn (Cambridge: Cambridge University Press, 2000a).

——, "Identifying Enslaved Africans in the African Diaspora", in Paul E. Lovejoy, ed., *Identity in the Shadow of Slavery* (London: Continuum, 2000b).

Lovejoy, Paul E. and Richardson, David, "Trust, Pawnship, and Atlantic History: The Institutional Foundations of the Old Calabar Slave Trade", *American Historical Review* 104 (1999), 333–55.

Mann, Kristin, and Bay, Edna G., eds, *Rethinking the African Diaspora: The Making of a Black Atlantic World in the Bight of Benin and Brazil* (London: Routledge, 2001).

Manning, Patrick, *Slavery and African Life: Occidental, Oriental, and African Slave Trades* (Cambridge: Cambridge University Press, 1990).

185

Marrero, Levi, *Cuba: Economía y sociedad, del monopolio hacia la libertad comercial (1701–1763)* (Madrid: Editorial Playor, 1980).

Matory, J. Lorand, *Black Atlantic Religion: Tradition, Transnationalism, and Matriarchy in the Afro-Brazilian Candomblé* (Princeton, NJ: Princeton University Press, 2005).

Miller, Joseph C., *Way of Death: Merchant Capitalism and the Angolan Slave Trade, 1730–1830* (Madison: University of Wisconsin Press, 1988).

Mintz, Sidney W., "The Jamaica Internal Marketing Pattern", *Social and Economic Studies* (1955), 95–103.

Mintz, Sidney W. and Price, Richard, *The Birth of African-American Culture: An Anthropological Perspective* (Boston: Beacon Press, 1992).

Morgan, Philip D., "British Encounters with Africans and African-Americans, circa 1600–1780", in Bernard Bailyn and Philip D. Morgan, eds, *Strangers within the Realm: Cultural Margins of the First British Empire* (Chapel Hill: University of North Carolina Press, 1991), 157–219.

——, *Slave Counterpoint: Black Culture in the Eighteenth-century Chesapeake and Lowcountry* (Chapel Hill: University of North Carolina Press, 1998).

Ortiz, Fernando, *Contrapunteo cubano del tabaco y el azúcar* (Havana: J. Montero, 1940).

Pike, Ruth "Sevillan Society in the Sixteenth Century: Slaves and Freedmen", *Hispanic American Historical Review* 47 (1967), 344–46.

Reis, João José, "'The Revolution of the *Ganhadores*': Urban Labour, Ethnicity and the African Strike of 1857 in Bahia, Brazil", *Journal of Latin American Studies* 29 (1997), 355–94.

Rodrigues, Nina, *Os Africanos no Brazil* (São Paulo: Companhia Editora Nacional, 1935).

Schwartz, Stuart B., *Sugar Plantations in the Formation of Brazilian Society: Bahia, 1550–1835* (Cambridge: Cambridge University Press, 1985).

Sewell, William H., Jr, "The Concept(s) of Culture", in Victoria E. Bonell and Lynn Hunt, eds, *Beyond the Cultural Turn: New Directions in the Study of Society and Culture* (Berkeley: University of California Press, 1999).

Sidbury, James, *Becoming African in America: Race and Nation in the Early Black Atlantic* (Oxford: Oxford University Press, 2007).

Slenes, Robert W., "'Malungu, ngamos vem!': África coberta e descoberta do Brasil", *Revista da Universidade de São Paulo* 12 (1991), 48–67.

Smallwood, Stephanie E., *Saltwater Slavery: A Middle Passage from Africa to American Diaspora* (Cambridge, MA: Harvard University Press, 2007).

Soares, Mariza de Carvalho, *Devotos da cor. Identidade étnica, religiosidade e escravidão no Rio de Janeiro, século XVIII* (Rio de Janeiro: Civilização Brasileira, 2000).

Sparks, Randy J., *The Two Princes of Calabar: An Eighteenth-Century Atlantic Odyssey* (Cambridge, MA: Harvard University Press, 2004).

Sweet, James H., *Recreating Africa: Culture, Kinship, and Religion in the African-Portuguese World, 1441–1770* (Chapel Hill: University of North Carolina Press, 2003).

Thornton, John K., *The Kingdom of Congo: Civil War and Transition, 1641–1718* (Madison: University of Wisconsin Press, 1983).

——, "African Dimensions of the Stono Rebellion", *American Historical Review* 96 (1991a), 1108–13.

——, "African Soldiers in the Haitian Revolution", *Journal of Caribbean History* 25 (1991b), 50–80.

——, *Africa and Africans in the Making of the Atlantic World, 1400–1800*, 2nd edn (Cambridge: Cambridge University Press, 1998).

Williams, Raymond, *Keywords: A Vocabulary of Culture and Society* (New York: Oxford University Press, 1983).

11

THE PLANTER CLASS

Trevor Burnard

Introduction

Slaves generally had masters, and those masters were generally wealthy men of high status, even if the ranks of slave owners sometimes included women, free coloureds, and the state. Masters' authority in the family, community, and polity was enhanced by owning slaves. If one is to understand the world of slaves, then one needs to look at the world of their masters, not only because the purpose of enslavement was to make masters' lives easier, but also because slavery tended to be an intensely personal institution. One particular set of masters and mistresses deserves close study if we are to understand the distinctive features of slavery in the Americas. This group was planters, the owners of large-scale agricultural establishments, populated by enslaved people through whose labours tropical produce was made that was transported throughout the world, especially to Europe. The planter class of the Americas was a New World invention. Their lives, ideas, and interactions with slaves were of paramount importance in shaping slave life in the Americas. Although planters existed wherever there were plantations – in places such as the tea plantations of Assam, the sugar plantations of Fiji, the rubber plantations of Malaya, and the tobacco plantations of Zimbabwe, the plantations and the planter class who ran them took a special form in the Americas. This chapter examines who planters were, what they did, how they interacted with their slaves, and how their power in the Americas came to be reduced by the mid-nineteenth century.

Initially, "plantation" was synonymous in English with "colony", making all colonists planters and *vice versa*.[1] By the end of the seventeenth century, however, the word "plantation" had taken on a specific and narrow definition: an overseas settlement producing a cash crop for export through the labour of enslaved people of African heritage. The owners of these plantations form the subject matter of this essay. The planter was a discernible social type, the progenitor of a powerful yet usually colonial class that exercised enormous power within society, and especially over slaves. It was backward looking in many of its social assumptions, but forward thinking in its racial and economic ideas, and was the closest group of people in the New World to the aristocracy of early modern Europe. Sustained through slavery, the planter class in its most important locations – Brazil, the Caribbean, and the American South – left an indelible imprint on political and social development in large swathes of tropical and semi-tropical America.

Origins and changes over time

The planter class developed in conjunction with the growth of cash crops for export, especially sugar, the most important New World plantation crop. The planter as a social, economic, and political type first emerged in the eastern Mediterranean in the late medieval period, and became fully formed in the Atlantic islands of São Tomé and Madeira by the mid-fifteenth century. By the time the potential of large-scale plantation agriculture had been realised in north-east Brazil in the mid-sixteenth century, long-lasting features of the planter class and the plantation complex had been established (Blackburn, 1997: 31–94).

Philip Curtin (1990) has usefully summarised the principal features of this emerging plantation complex. The plantation was an agricultural enterprise organised around capitalist principles, in which the great majority of the workers were enslaved people (after the mid-sixteenth century, invariably from Africa rather than from the Americas). These slaves lived on estates containing from 50 to several hundred labourers. The size of the plantation labour force differentiated it from almost all European business enterprises prior to the advent of the industrial factory in the nineteenth century. Indeed, plantations were novel enough in size, and in the regimented labour that enslaved people were forced to do, to be described as factories in the field. Nevertheless, while plantations were capitalist entities, the plantation retained several feudal features, notably that the owners of enslaved workers controlled those workers, and tried to control them at other times of their lives, not only during their working day. Moreover, the power that planters had over slaves was immense, including *de facto* legal jurisdiction of their slaves' bodies.

The planter was the chief architect of the plantation complex and the major beneficiary of the often substantial wealth that his workers produced (although women were planters, most were male, and male assumptions, notably paternalism, operated as important ideologies). The planter owned land, labour, and capital equipment, and managed all steps of the production process, whether directly or, more commonly, through agents. The power that planters had in their plantation "kingdoms", their close to absolute power over their slaves, and the political clout they exercised as a result of their wealth and control over labour made planters feel that they were a class akin to European nobles. They adopted manners of living that accorded well with established European norms of aristocratic practice. Nevertheless, planter power was always constrained by outside forces. The plantation generally retained many of its colonial features. The fact that political control over plantation societies usually resided elsewhere than in the hands of planters (either in the imperial metropolis or, in the case of the antebellum South and nineteenth-century Brazil, in centres of mercantile capital in the American North and in Europe), and the fact that plantations were designed to supply distant markets with specialised tropical or sub-tropical products (sugar, tobacco, rice, cotton, and coffee, to name the most important commodities), meant that the close to total power that planters exercised over slaves was not replicated in their relations with the outside world.

Changes over time

These features of the plantation complex were constant. The first planters of the Azores in the mid-fifteenth century, and the planters of mid-nineteenth century South Carolina and Louisiana, were fundamentally similar. Nevertheless, the plantation complex and the planters who controlled that complex did change over time. One pattern was established in mid-sixteenth-century north-east Brazil. In Bahia, the sugar economy comprised two classes, *senhores de engenhos* and *lavradores de cana*. The former owned the sugar mills necessary to produce sugar and the land upon which cane was grown. Many of the slaves necessary to make sugar, however, were owned by the latter group, tenanted farmers who rented land and access to sugar mills from *senhores de engenhos*. Although *lavradores* were clearly inferior in wealth and social standing to mill owners, and were treated by *senhores de engenhos* as servants rather than as equals, the two groups together formed a powerful planter class. The feudal nature of their relationship, however, precluded Brazilian planters from making the best utilisation of resources (Schwartz, 1985).

A major advance was made in Barbados in the mid-seventeenth century when sugar planters developed the integrated plantation in which both the growing and the processing of sugar was done on one plantation. In addition, planters perfected the gang-labour system of production, and developed, through the commission system, an effective way to market their crop in Europe. The perfection of the plantation system made Barbados a very rich place and Barbadian planters the envy of the Americas. Richard Ligon explained in his encomomium to Barbados in 1657 that through "the sweet negotiations of sugar", Barbadians had "in a short time ... [grown] very considerable", both in "Reputation and Wealth". The most "Industrious" settlers, men who had the most "percing sights and profound judgements", had established "very great and vast estates". Their wealth was so great that "they economise on nothing" as one French visitor explained. They paid outrageous sums for clothes, furnished their houses "sumptuously", went "well-mounted on very handsome horses ... covered with rich saddle-cloths", they ate very well and drank "the best wines from more than six areas in Europe". The system that Barbadian planters invented was attractive and thus often emulated, especially as the slave trade became sufficiently efficient to allow relatively easy replacement of an enslaved labour force which could not, except in the American South, maintain natural population growth. By the mid-eighteenth century, the large-scale integrated plantation containing hundreds of enslaved people of African descent, forced to work during the day for planters and then grow their own food in their limited free time, was a dominant form throughout the British and French West Indies and in the more southerly regions of the American South (Menard, 2006).[2]

British abolition of the slave trade in 1807, the destruction through revolution of the Saint Domingue planter class, and the advent of industrialisation initiated further changes in plantation culture. These events helped to spell the decline of planter power in the British and French West Indies, especially from the second quarter of the nineteenth century. Planters, however, became notably more important in other places. In what Dale Tomich has called "second stage slavery", planters in Brazil, Puerto Rico, Cuba, and especially in an expanding US South, embarked on an aggressive period of agricultural expansion in which slavery was successfully integrated into industrial systems (Tomich, 2004: 56–74). Planters were more powerful in these new nineteenth-century slave systems than they had been in any previous era. Industrialisation was crucial, but so too was slave reproduction. Alone of the major slave-owning regions, planters in the antebellum American South did not require an external slave trade to support their moneymaking endeavours. In Cuba and Brazil, planters wavered in the mid-nineteenth century between wanting to maintain slavery as the principal system of labour exploitation, and wishing to avoid racial war through transforming plantation labour into waged labour by white immigrants and the descendants of black slaves. In the American South, however, the continuing economic vitality of slavery, and the demographic success not only of an increasingly native-born black population but also of a numerically dominant white population, encouraged southern white intellectuals to devise a pro-slavery defence of the privileges of the planter class and the moral superiority of coerced labour over wage labour. American pro-slavery ideology had no counterpart in any other slave society.

Composition and wealth

The planter class, like the European aristocracies it mimicked, was always tiny in number. It was a sub-set of the larger group of slave owners, most of whom owned only a few slaves and who were either small farmers or involved in other occupations. Planters, on the other hand, were masters of many slaves, whom they worked hard, and over whom they exerted significant physical and psychological control. Planters varied in respect of their wealth and slave ownership, but the quintessential planters of legend and fact were very rich and owned hundreds of slaves. In a mature slave society such as eighteenth-century Jamaica, the average sugar planter owned between 150 and 250 enslaved persons. The richest sugar planters, men such as John Tharp and Sir Simon Taylor, wealthy planters in early nineteenth-century Jamaica, possessed over 2000 slaves each (Petley, 2009). Slave ownership on this scale meant that only a few people could legitimately call themselves planters. In Jamaica in 1804, a map of the island suggested that there were no more than 830 sugar planters. B.W. Higman's careful analysis of slave registration returns indicates that of 12,453 slave holders in Jamaica in 1832, perhaps not many more than 2000 could call themselves planters. Similarly, there were not many more than 300 *senhores de engenho* in mid-seventeenth century and perhaps 500 in mid-nineteenth century Bahia. In Cuba, a slave population of over 350,000 in 1860 lived mostly on 1365 *ingenios*. Only in the antebellum American south were the numbers of planters substantial. Even there, the proportion of the white population who could call themselves planters and be recognised as such was extremely small. Only one in eight southern white families owned more than 20 slaves, but this group owned over half of America's 3 million enslaved persons (Higman, 1976; Schwartz, 1985: 167–68; Barickman, 1998; Oakes, 1982).

The planter class was very rich. In North America, the southern planter class by 1850 was disproportionately numerous among the wealthiest Americans. The 338 planters who owned more than 250 slaves in America in 1860 owned 104,327 slaves, or 2.6 per cent of all American slaves (Scarborough, 2003). By that date, northern merchants and industrialists rivalled the wealth of the richest planters, although as a group, planters probably had more wealth. In previous centuries, however, no group of people in the New World group were as rich as planters. Plantation wealth made Jamaica, with not many more than 12,000 white inhabitants, worth as much in gross domestic product in 1774 as British American farm colonies such as Massachusetts and Pennsylvania (Burnard, 2001). It had wealth per white capita of a quite different order than was achieved in places with few slaves. Thomas Thistlewood, for example, a man of modest origins who was far from the top ranks of the planter class, and whose diaries are an excellent guide to the mores and way of life of ordinary white Jamaicans, died in 1786 with £2408 sterling in personal property, including 34 slaves and land worth perhaps £1000. This amount of wealth made him ten times as wealthy as the average wealth holder in England and Wales. The wealthiest Jamaicans were colossally rich. Sir Simon Clarke died a decade before Thistlewood, with a fortune estimated at half a million pounds. John Tharp died in 1805 with a ducal income of £362,000 in personal estate, including 2900 slaves and another £300,000 in landed property. The wealthiest antebellum southern planters were just as rich. Nathaniel Heyward of South Carolina died in 1851 owning 1834 slaves. Edward Lloyd VI, of an old Maryland family, owned plantations in Maryland, Louisiana, and Mississippi where 658 enslaved people worked. Stephen Duncan of Natchez had property conservatively valued at over $2 million in 1855.[3]

The authority of wealth tended to sanctify the social origins of these very rich people. Nevertheless, the origins of most members of the planter class were not as distinguished as filiopietist ancestors liked to imagine. Certainly, planters were not a literal extension of European nobility in the New World. Occasionally, planters came from humble stock. Daniel Defoe described how his hero, Robinson Crusoe, became a Bahian sugar planter. He first raised tobacco and food crops, subsequently sending to Africa for a few slaves. After a couple of years, he had enough capital to apply to a local merchant for credit to become a sugar planter. Another fictional planter, Thomas Sutpen, the protagonist of William Faulkner's *Absalom, Absalom*, came from similarly murky origins. Born of poor white stock in West Virginia, he worked as a plantation overseer in Haiti, where his sturdiness in putting down a slave rebellion encouraged his boss to allow him to marry his mulatresse heiress and thus acquire the money needed to establish a cotton plantation in the Mississippi wilderness.

Such ascents from poverty and obscurity to planter wealth occurred more often in fiction than in fact. Most often, planters came from merchant stock. The brothers Pacoal and Dinis Bravo were New Christian merchants who came to Bahia from Oporto, Portugal in the early seventeenth century. Their commercial prowess allowed them to acquire some land belonging to the Engenho Sergipe, and they began to grow cane and supply the mill as *lavradores de cana*. Dinis expanded his operations until he set up his own *engenho* on Cajaíba Island. The first planters in the Matanzas sugar region near Havana that developed in the 1790s came from similar origins. The founders of *ingenios* were powerful and well connected Havana merchants, such as the Junco family and the Lamar and O'Farrell brothers. These were men already familiar with methods of production and the vagaries of international markets. Crucially, they had access through their commercial contacts to substantial sources of capital from within Havana, from Spanish commercial interests, and from linkages with North American merchants, slave traders, and planters (Bergad, 1990).

The merchant origins of planter wealth are important, given that planters often liked to distance themselves from merchant competitors, and given debates in the historiography that see planters as opposed to the representatives of merchant and industrial capital. Although planters tended to reduce their involvement in commercial activities once they became planters, it was not uncommon from the sixteenth century through to the mid-nineteenth century for planters to have at least short-term investments in commercial ventures. For some planters, such as Zachary Bayly, uncle of the historian Bryan Edwards, in mid-eighteenth century Jamaica, and Stephen Duncan, mid-nineteenth century Natchez planter and the principal banker in the antebellum Lower South, planting was just part of a range of profit-making activities that were as likely to involve commerce as planting.

Whatever their social origins, planters everywhere cemented their power through intermarriage into other planter families. Planter genealogies in long-established planter societies such as Cuba, Brazil, and the American South resemble what Bertram Wyatt-Brown calls, in respect of the landed families of the Old South, a "tangle of fishhooks" (Wyatt-Brown, 1982: 219). Planter elites were often a great cousinhood, connected in multiple ways through marriage, political connections, and economic interactions. These multiple interactions gave planters solid class cohesiveness. Nevertheless, the conditions of plantation life meant that there was always a degree of social mobility into and out of the planter class. In the Caribbean, ferocious mortality rates made it very difficult to sustain planter dynasties over more than one or two generations. The constant presence of early death gave societies like seventeenth-century Barbados and Virginia, and eighteenth-century Jamaica and Saint Domingue, a particular character. Planters were as "careless of futurity" as were their slaves, living for the moment rather than for a future in which neither they nor any descendants were likely to be present. Planting was also an uncertain business, and planters were often undone by unanticipated changes in market conditions. A bad crop, unwise guesses about the future, and sudden downturns in international commodity markets led many planters into ruin. The chances of disaster were compounded by indebtedness, brought on mostly by the large capital demands for labour and equipment that planters daily faced and sometimes by the strong tendency of planters to lapse into unsustainable extravagance.

Planters enjoyed the wealth and social prestige that owning a plantation conferred. They did not always enjoy living in rural backwaters among hundreds of slaves, away from urban excitement, and always fearful of what their resentful slaves might do to them. Almost as soon as planter classes began developing, complaints began to be heard that planters were abandoning their social duty to keep their slaves in order through constant personal supervision, and instead were "absentees" (the word itself implies a degree of moral opprobrium) from their estates. Absenteeism is often put forward as the curse of the planter class, leading to economic in efficiency and political dysfunction. That wealthy planters were delinquent absentees was a charge most often hurled at eighteenth-century West Indian planters resident in Paris and London, who derived their income as rentiers rather than active managers. In truth, planters were more often resident than they were absent (fewer planters were able to remove to Europe than is usually suggested in the literature) and, even when they were not resident on estates, devolved power to plantation operatives who were as likely to be as effective managers of slaves as planters. B.W. Higman's careful study of attorneys in Jamaica suggests that management practices on plantations actually improved when management was passed over to a cadre of professional managers. Moreover, even when planters appeared to be resident on their estates, as in north-eastern Brazil and the antebellum American South, they were likely to spend much of their time off their properties (Higman, 2005). Bahian planters congregated in Salvador just as South Carolinian rice planters spent much of their time in Charleston. In addition, the richest planters had multiple estates, meaning that few slaves on large estates would have much experience of their owner's personal attention.

The overwhelming majority of planters were white men of European descent. Whiteness could, however, be a relative term. Planters in early nineteenth-century

Martinique, for example, sniffed that all of their counterparts in Guadeloupe were, to a lesser or greater degree, descendants of Africans. But these planters were men whose racial origins, however murky, did not stop them from being accepted as European. Money and power whitened families, which was important, as whiteness was highly valued in societies where blackness was denigrated. In some places, however, free coloured planters were an integral component of the slave-owning class. Free coloured planters were most numerous in eighteenth-century Saint Domingue, where they owned probably a majority of coffee estates in the south and west of the island. Julien Raimond, a free coloured indigo planter who played a prominent role in the early 1790s in raising colonial racism as an issue for French revolutionaries to consider, was, along with the failed revolutionary Vincent Ogé, the most famous member of this wealthy subset of the planter class in Saint Domingue. Raimond famously declared that his class controlled one-third of the wealth in the richest plantation colony of its time. That was an overstatement, but free coloured planters in Saint Domingue were indeed a rich and politically unified group. Raimond's tale, however, is one of tragedy. Despite owning hundreds of slaves and an impressive plantation house, Raimond faced increasing discrimination from a nakedly racist planter regime that from the 1770s tried to ensure that only white people were treated as full members of the political polity. Saint Domingue's free people of colour responded to such deliberate humiliation by attacking colonial oppression with liberal ideals. In the French Revolution, free coloured planters' campaign for civil rights led them to turn against white planters and helped to provoke the conflagration that led to Haitian independence. The effect of earlier discrimination, however, was that Raimond was forced to abandon the life he most wanted, that of a colonial planter equal to his white counterparts (Garrigus, 2007).

Character of the planter

As a distinctive social type, the planter everywhere shared similar social and cultural characteristics. To their supporters, the planter was a model of a New World gentleman. Andre Joaô Antonil wrote an important guide for Brazilian planters in the early eighteenth century in which he declared that "To be a *senhor de engenho* is a title which many aspire to because it means to be served, obeyed, and respected by many ... [it] is considered like having a title among the nobles of Portugal." Antonil emphasised how Bahian planters ought to cultivate affability and hospitality, but his main emphasis was on his role as the central person upholding rural social and economic relations. He needed to treat his subordinates fairly. Most importantly, as Father Luís Vellozo affirmed in 1720, the *senhor de engenho* "keeps the slaves of the said engenho well controlled and instructed, so that they do not bother anyone". Planters ought to treat slaves humanely, but most importantly they needed to make sure that enslaved people knew their place (Schwartz, 1985, 273, 284–85).

For Virginia planter William Byrd II, writing in the early eighteenth century, the plantation was an idyll and the planter was God's representative on Earth. He described himself as living "like one of the patriarchs, I have my flocks and my herds, my bond-men and bond-women, and every soart [sic] of trade amongst my own servants, so that I live in a kind of independence on every one, but Providence." In Byrd's vision, the planter was at the top of a harmonious social hierarchy, where he assumed individual, personal authority over all people below him, especially servants and slaves. He was responsible for the welfare of all those below him. In return, people below him in the social order owed him respect and, above all, obedience. The planter historian Edward Long elaborated on planters' virtues and responsibilities in his virulently pro-planter history of Jamaica. The Jamaican planter, he declared, was a paragon of an English gentleman. He was "tall and well-shaped" with "penetrating sight". More importantly, he was "sensible, of quick apprehension, brave, good-natured, affable, generous, temperate and sober; unsuspicious, lovers of freedom, fond of social enjoyments, tender fathers, humane and indulgent masters; firm and sincere friends" and always hospitable, gay and fond of entertainments and music. Indeed, he concluded that "there are no people in this world that exceed the gentlemen of this island in a noble and disinterested munificence" (Lockridge, 1987; Craton, 1991).

Of course, this self-image of an agreeable, public-spirited, and aristocratic master class seldom lived up to the facts. Like all ruling classes, the planters of the New World worried about whether their subordinates held them in the same high esteem as they held themselves. As the diaries of eighteenth-century Virginia planter Landon Carter reveal, it was not unusual that a conservative patriarch would feel himself beset from all sides by disobedient dependents – a frustrated spouse, resentful children, disrespectful tenants, and recalcitrant servants and slaves. To be a planter even when planters formed a cohesive and effective ruling class, as in eighteenth-century Virginia, was to be a man beset by anxieties. As Kathleen Brown argues, "authority was a delicate project ... require[ing] constant vigilance against even small usurpations of power". As she states, "tiny fissures" in the ability of planters to command obedience from others "not only indicated larger weaknesses in the construction but constituted a nagging reminder of contradictions inherent in colonial masculinity" (Brown, 1996: 318).

But we should not overemphasise planters' anxiety about losing control over themselves and over others. Landon Carter was a weak, unimpressive man who inspired a risible lack of respect among his planter peers. He fretted about challenges to his authority because he was an undistinguished and disappointed man who failed to replicate the political success that his forebears had achieved. He wanted more than anything else to exercise a patriarchal role within his family and household, but found at every turn that his dependants resented his overbearing manner and his insistence on getting his own way. In truth, Carter was less a patriarch than a despot, a tyrant similar in his dealings with dependents to the Pashas of the Ottoman Empire he affected to despise. What is important, nevertheless, is that – despite his manifold failings – his possession of a large slave force, his ownership of plentiful acres, his descent from distinguished planter ancestors, and his position as the patriarch in a society predicated on patriarchal leadership meant that he was able to insist that, in public, at least, he received the grudging respect of inferiors. Even when Carter acted most outrageously, as when he disowned his daughter and, even more egregiously, usurped the authority of his grown son – a powerful patriarch in his own right – by whipping a saucy grandson in the presence of the boy's mother, he was able to survive "this domestic gust" by threatening disinheritance. Carter won this battle of wills because he had the power to enforce his will on others. One learns more about the power and authority of a class from its weakest members, such as Landon Carter, than from its greatest successes (Isaac, 2004).

To their detractors, planters were arrivistes who had pretensions to aristocratic gentility but were, in fact, *nouveau riche* pretenders. Their irreligiosity and unrelenting materialism offended some observers. The Jesuit priest Father Nóbrega lamented in the mid-sixteenth century that planters in Brazil cared little for religion and instead "give consideration to nothing but sugar mills and property even though it might be with the perdition of all the world's souls" (Schwartz, 1985, 272). Their indifference to intellectual pursuits also exposed them to ridicule. A few planters, such as Francisco Arango y Parreño in early nineteenth-century Cuba and Thomas Jefferson in late eighteenth-century Virginia were significant intellectuals, but it is hard not to agree with the judgement of Gordon Lewis for the Caribbean that "the plantocracy constituted the most crudely philistine of all dominant classes in the history of Western slavery" (Lewis, 1983: 109). Their arrogance and self-importance also met with derisive comment. One of the principal reasons why the English clergyman James Ramsay became an abolitionist in the 1780s was his distaste during a residence in Nevis for the excessive individualism, rampant consumerism, and narcissistic indulgence of the planters he derisively lampooned as belonging to "the Kingdom of I" (Brown, 2006: 227–53). Samuel Johnson was similarly unimpressed with the gap between what planters expected for themselves and what they were prepared to impose on others when he made his famous quip during the American Revolution about "how it is we hear the loudest yelps for liberty from the drivers of negroes".

Planters argued that such attitudes were evidence of their excessive attachment to precepts of liberty. Other observers were inclined to attribute planter self-centredness to the malign influence of slavery. "Bred for the most Part at the Breast of a Negro Slave, surrounded from their Infancy with a numerous retinue of these dark Attendants", planters, John Fothergill asserted, "were habituated by Precept and Example, to Sensuality, and Despotism". Their power over slaves allowed them to "play the Mogul and *lord* it" over their slaves "without Controul". Even planters admitted that the immense power they were able to exercise over enslaved men could make men born to command domestic tyrants. Thomas Jefferson thought one of the evils of slavery was that it led to corruption, as slave ownership "nursed, educated and daily exercised" habits of tyranny so that "the man must be a prodigy who can retain his manners and morals undepraved by such circumstances". Moreover, commentators were convinced that planters were hypocrites, especially in sexual matters. Planters proclaimed the purity of the white race at any opportunity, especially as attitudes to race hardened after the mid-eighteenth century, but they seldom thought their qualms about the physical and mental attributes of people of African heritage were much impediment to engaging in sexual relations with coloured women. Even defenders of the planter character had to admit that planters were obsessed with the sexual charms of black women. Edward Long fulminated that Jamaican planters preferred to "riot in the goatish embraces" of "some black or yellow *quasheba*" rather than "share the pure and lawful bliss derived from matrimonial, mutual love". Concubinage with coloured women was so common, he asserted, that "He who should presume to shew any displeasure against such a thing as simple fornication, would for his pains be accounted a simple blockhead".[4]

The vivid descriptions by planters of the black women they coveted make it clear that one of the attractions of being a planter was that it offered easy sexual opportunities. John Stedman, a traveller in late eighteenth-century Surinam, provided lurid descriptions of "Surinam marriages", in which nubile young slave women were provided to white men of all ranks to serve as domestics and concubines. He eulogised his coloured mistress in glowing terms, waxing lyrical about how Joanna's "face was full of native modesty, and the most distinguished sweetness. Her eyes, as black as ebony, were large, and full of expression, bespeaking the goodness of her heart. A beautiful tinge of vermillion glowed through her dark cheeks, when she was gazed upon." Stedman tried to suggest that his purchase of and cohabitation with this beauty was a mutually satisfactory passionate romance, but his description of how he came to acquire his mistress suggests a less equal exchange. His text shows that a perquisite of mastery was the ability to take sexual pleasure whenever one wanted. Stedman glamorised what were in fact tawdry encounters. Thistlewood's copious diaries detail a wealth of exploitative sexual relationships between white men and black women. Thistlewood himself used sex as a weapon of mastery, recording in laconic fashion his sexual encounters with over 100 slave women. He was at best a sexual predator; at worst a serial rapist. His comments on other white men's sexual behaviour in Jamaica suggest that such depredations were typical rather than unusual (Stedman, 1988: 20–21; Burnard, 2004, 156–64).

In more established slave societies, such as the antebellum South, open relationships between planters and slave concubines were frowned upon. Southern planters rarely acted like Thistlewood and lived openly with a slave mistress. Nevertheless, interracial liaisons were frequent. The astute diarist and planter's wife Mary Chesnut exploded against the willed ignorance of southern women to the mixed-race slave children, who were evidence of what southerners called miscegenation. "Wives and daughters, she declared, affect "purity and innocence" and thus pretend "never to see what is as plain before their eyes as sunlight. And they play their part of unsuspecting angels to the letter". As recent advances in medical technology have made evident in the confirmation that Thomas Jefferson had a long-standing liaison with a light-skinned slave (his deceased wife's half-sister, making his relationship quasi-incestuous as well as interracial, according to the standards of the time), connections between planters and black and coloured women occurred even at the most elevated social levels (Woodward, 1993; Gordon-Reed, 2009).

Interracial liaisons were almost always between white men and black or brown women. A feature of planter society, especially in mature slave societies, was how determined planters were to restrict the opportunities white wives and daughters had for social fraternisation, especially with black men. White women were usually as complicit in maintaining slavery as were white men. The more prescient among them, however, recognised that in societies predicated on planter dominance and the subordination of dependents to the will of masters, women's status was akin to that of slaves. It is no accident, first, that women played a prominent role in abolitionism and, second, that the position of women was considerably less advanced in slave societies than in Western Europe and the American North. Planters' relations with women were complex, and planters did not usually equate white women with slaves. White women's role as the reproductive legitimators of whiteness led to them being idolised by their menfolk, even if they were diminished by being desexualised and ideologically erased from a role in productive relations. But the social relations of planter society, with its emphasis on hierarchy and obedience to authority, meant that women were placed on the same conceptual order as other dependents.

Relations with slaves

Where planters offended European sensibilities most, however, was in how they treated their slaves, especially their indulgence in brutal methods of slave management. Slavery was maintained by force. Planters achieved mastery over slaves through keeping a monopoly over all forms of coercion, both private and public. Plantation societies were especially violent places, with Africans unfortunate enough to encounter planters in the first phase of building plantation societies particularly likely to be recipients of planter brutality. Ira Berlin describes how the arrival of the fully fledged plantation economy in the Chesapeake in the early eighteenth century was accompanied by a notable ratcheting upward of violence directed towards slaves. Chesapeake slaves faced the pillory, the whipping post, and the gallows far more frequently and in far larger numbers as the plantation regime kicked in. Moreover, Africans faced punishments designed not to only correct but also to degrade and humiliate. William Byrd, Virginia planter and a sophisticated colonial gentleman, noted, without embarrassment, in his diary how he forced a slave bed-wetter to drink a "pint of piss". These types of punishment were common on large plantations. The overseer Thomas Thistlewood, for example, devised an appalling punishment he called "Derby's dose", which involved one slave defecating into another slave's mouth, which was then wired shut. Through such punishments, slave men in particular were reminded both of how little their masters considered their feelings and also to what lengths masters were prepared to go to enforce obedience (Berlin, 1998: 115–16; Burnard, 2004, 104).

Punishments inflicted on slaves went well beyond humiliation. Planters had the power to do anything short of murder to their enslaved property. They showed little reluctance to use extreme force. To murder a slave was supposedly a crime in most jurisdictions, but planters could usually get away even with murder if they wanted. In 1788 Nicholas Lejeune, a psychopathic Saint Domingue planter, arrested, convicted, but then pardoned for torturing and killing slave women so viciously that even the authorities in Saint Domingue could not let his atrocities pass unnoticed, confirmed in a defiant declaration outside the court-room how wide he thought planters' powers were in slave societies. Lejeune celebrated terror as the best way of dealing with slaves. Since slaves "detest us", "if we do not make his chains as proportionate to the dangers we run with him, if we let loose his hatred from the present state in which it is stifled, what can prevent him from attempting to break the chains? ... It is not the fear and equity of the law that forbids the slave from stabbing his master, it is the consciousness of absolute power that he has over his person. Remove this bit, he will dare everything." (cited in Burnard, 2004, 149; for Lejeune, see Thibau, 1989: 17–93).

Severe punishments of slaves were less common in second-stage slavery than when plantations were first established, in part because planters became increasingly sensitive to outside criticism of them as brutes. But brutality remained at the centre of planters' relations with slaves until the very end of slavery. Planters used force because they feared their slaves. They knew, as Lejeune insisted, that the pretty words slaves might use to curry favour with masters masked a deep hatred of the men who forced them into degradation. They always expected slave rebellion. That slave rebellion was inevitable was clear to observers such as Abbé Raynal, who in his mid-eighteenth-century indictment of French colonial slavery in *Histoire des deux Indies* saw events such as Tacky's Rebellion in Jamaica in 1760 as "indicators of the impending storm". Echoing Lejeune, Raynal argued that slaves "only want a chief", a Spartacus or Crassus "sufficiently courageous to lead them to vengeance and slaughter". When Spartacus did emerge in the form of Toussaint Louverture, the shadow he and his fellow rebels in Haiti cast over planters' comfortable assumptions that their slaves actually loved them was never erased from planters' memories.[5]

When slaves did rebel, planters' responses were quick, overwhelming, and savage well beyond standards usually employed in Western Europe. The aftermath of Tacky's revolt saw Jamaican planters execute over 100 slaves, usually through exquisite tortures, such as leaving slaves to rot, without food and water, in gibbets until they died, or burning them slowly to death over a fire. A large-scale revolt in Demerara in 1823 saw planters resort to a similar wave of tortures and executions, creating martyrs out of slave rebels and abolitionist missionaries alike (da Costa, 1997). Planters, however, could be cruel without being bloodthirsty. João José Reis notes how in an 1835 Malê slave rebellion by African Muslims in Bahia, rebel slaves were seldom killed, but planters embarked upon a deliberate strategy of restricting the lives of slaves suspected of disaffection so that "treacherous" Africans would find so unbearable that they would leave Brazil, if free, or give up wanting to seek freedom, if slaves (Reis, 1993: 229).

Of course, planters realised both that their propensity to violence gave their opponents ammunition to denounce them as uncivilised and barbaric tyrants, and also that torture and killing were ineffective ways of making slaves obedient labourers. Slaves may have been property, but they were also people, and planters recognised the humanity of their charges as much when they treated slaves harshly as when they exercised other methods of control over them. It was only humans who were responsible for their own actions and who could be punished as slaves were punished. More importantly, planters recognised that their insistence on their own social and political independence masked their dependence on the enslaved people who worked for them, served them, and were often present at their birth and helped to prepare the coffins they were buried in. Planters were a parasitic class, whose lives would have been impossible without slave help.

A few planters, overwhelmingly in the antebellum South, fooled themselves that their enslaved people liked them and were happy in a system – what Elizabeth Fox-Genovese and Eugene Genovese have described as "slavery in the abstract" – where racially inferior people had found their natural place at the bottom of the social order. Charles Cotesworth Pinckney II of South Carolina declared in the early nineteenth century that "Beyond mere animal suffering the slave has nothing to dread. His family is provided in food, shelter, and raiment, whether he live or die." For white southerners, slavery was a pleasant condition, much to be preferred (with the proviso that one must have a good master) to the uncertainty, drudgery, and exposure to dearth that they believed was the inevitable consequence for poor people living in the industrial north. Antebellum planters' belief that their slaves were better off under slavery than under other systems of labour exploitation can be easily dismissed. What is important, however, as Eugene Genovese has outlined repeatedly, is that the ideology of the planter class was a serious alternative to the tenets of industrial capitalism and especially to the ideas of political economists like Adam Smith and John Stuart Mill. The American Civil War was a clash between two systems of thought as much as between two political polities (Fox-Genovese and Genovese, 2008: 84).

Planters did, of course, establish ties with slaves that involved a degree of personal intimacy. It may be, as Orlando Patterson comments, that "no authentic human relationship was possible where violence was the ultimate sanction" and that "intimacy was usually calculating and sadomasochistic". But the evidence of slaves themselves shows that, amidst the brutality slaves experienced, some kind feelings emerged between masters and slaves. Charles Ball, an antebellum southern slave who wrote a narrative of his life, inveighed against the cruelties of slavery. But Ball also noted "instances of the greatest tenderness of feeling" between masters and slaves, describing one mistress "as a true friend to me" (cited in Morgan, 1998: 269). Even a rapacious master such as Thomas Thistlewood developed close and loving relations with several of his slaves. He whipped them when they displeased him but he also healed them when they were sick, went fishing and shooting with them, and protected them from the attacks of whites and slaves from other estates. He had an especially close intimate relationship with Phibbah, his slave mistress of over 30 years.

The nature of the relationship between masters and slaves varied greatly. The two most important variables were the size of the white population in a slave society and the demographic characteristics of the slave population. Planters in societies like eighteenth-century Saint Domingue and Jamaica, where blacks outnumbered whites by ten to one and where nearly 80 per cent of slaves were traumatised, dehumanised, recently arrived migrants from Africa, had few illusions about their capacity to mould slaves' minds so that they worked willingly and without coercion. Slave management in these societies was predicated on cultivating white support for planter power and upon keeping enslaved people under firm discipline. Conversely, planters in such societies did not try to bend the minds of slaves to their will, as was common in the antebellum American South. They seldom tried to re-order the social and cultural world of Africans, leaving them to worship as they liked and form families in the African manner. White despotism in the period of the Atlantic slave trade did not extend to rooting out all traces of Africa in America. The major exception was in respect to cultural practices such as *obeah* and *vodou* that planters believed, with reason, to be influences on slaves contemplating rebellion.

Nevertheless, although planters outside the American South did not attempt to destroy the autonomy of the slave community as a means of reinforcing the authority of the master, the psychological pressure to obey that planters placed on slaves was not negligible, especially in the early modern period, where belief in immutable social hierarchies was strong. The most convincing exposition of such strategies of psychological control came in the American South, where planters fashioned an ideological strategy that combined paternalism and an explicitly racist assertion of white supremacy so as to implant in blacks an assuredness of their racial inferiority. Such strategies did not work as well as masters imagined, as slaves always had means whereby they could establish meaningful relationships and gain self-worth outside their connections to masters. Moreover, the messages that planters tried to implant about their own superiority were constantly undermined by abundant evidence of their ethical failings. But in societies such as the nineteenth-century American South, the antebellum notion of stewardship as a rule governing how superiors related to inferiors was sufficiently ingrained to enable planters to cow slaves psychologically as well as physically. Drew Faust, for example, has detailed the management strategies of South Carolina planter James Henry Hammond, in which he was able to present himself, with some degree of success, through elaborate ceremonies where he played the generous master from whom all blessings flowed, as "a beneficent master whose guidance and control represented the best of all possible worlds for the uncivilised and backward people entrusted to him by God" (Faust, 1982: 72–73).

Opposition to planters

Planters were probably the single most powerful class of wealth-holders in the Americas. Their possession of slaves gave them the economic means to solidify their economic, social, and political dominance in slave societies. They were the dominant ruling class in these societies for a very long time, from the fifteenth century through to the last years of the nineteenth century. Even after slavery was ended, planters remained an important, if diminished, class. It was not until after World War II, with the advent of widespread mechanisation and the end of colonialism, that planter power finally began to disappear. Their cultural power remained important, with the ideal of the plantation and the planter playing a role in popular culture in such classic works as the film *Gone with the Wind*, produced in 1939. The descendants of the planter class still occupy many of the upper social and economic positions in the societies that their ancestors controlled.

Nevertheless, planters were never as powerful as they imagined, even in their eighteenth-century heyday. A potent source of opposition always came from the slaves they owned, who did not accept that slavery was an inescapable condition and who, as other chapters in this volume attest, frequently rebelled against planter authority. Except in Haiti, however, such challenges to planter rule were always overcome by planters. They found it harder, however, to combat opposition from abolitionists. A previous historiography assumed that some of the conflict between planters and capitalists suggested that there was an ideological dichotomy between the two groups, with planters being fundamentally uncomfortable with the tenets of modern capitalism. Few historians would take such a position nowadays. Planters were capitalists, operating within the context of a capitalist colonial economy, always on the lookout for ways to increase private profit. A capitalist mindset did not preclude a paternalist outlook. As Richard Follett notes in describing antebellum Louisiana planters, "Shrewdly capitalist in their business affairs, the sugar masters defended slavery as an organic institution ... As aggressive promoters of the most industrialized sector of southern agriculture, the sugar masters found few discrepancies between their personae as slaveholders and as thoroughly modern businessmen." (Follett, 2006: 4).

Nevertheless, the capitalist mindset of planters did not mean that they accepted the social values of industrial societies. Increasingly, planters devoted to slavery, white supremacy, and an organic social order with themselves at the apex became objects of disdain to believers in a free-market economy and the economic efficiency of wage labour over slavery. From the late eighteenth century, these believers became increasingly opposed to slavery both on moral and economic grounds. What they perceived to be the wasteful inefficiencies of planter culture and of the slave economy led to abolitionist attacks on planters and the plantation system. Eventually, as detailed elsewhere in this volume, planters found these challenges impossible to ignore and difficult to resist. In the French and British Caribbean, planters were too few in number to prevail against determined metropolitan insistence that slavery had to be ended and the plantation system had to be reformed. After the abolition of slavery, these plantation societies became but shadows of their former selves. In the Spanish Caribbean and in Brazil, the challenges to the plantation system came from within, with an important subsection of planters deciding that if white supremacy was to be preserved, then slavery had to be ended by planters themselves. The only planter class powerful enough and stubborn enough to try and resist the powerful forces of anti-slavery percolating through the western world in the mid-nineteenth century was the only group of planters who developed a sophisticated defence of slavery – slaveholders in the American South. They chose self-immolation through the Civil War. Their defeat in 1865 marks the last gasp of authentic planter power and the end of the planter voice. Nevertheless, the plantation structures that sustained planters and the often pernicious ideologies that they developed to justify their social, racial, and political dominance in New World societies continue to have many modern echoes.

Notes

1 Other European nations had no precise equivalent for "plantation". In the Portuguese world, the closest equivalent is *engenho*, meaning a mill to crush sugarcane.
2 Richard Ligon, *A True and Exact History of the Island of Barbados*, 2nd edn (London, 1673; reprinted 1970).
3 Converting wealth from a different period into modern values is difficult. Tharp and Duncan would probably be ranked as centi-millionaires today (Burnard, 2001; Petley, 2009; Brazy, 2006).
4 John Fothergill, *Considerations Relative to the North American Continent* (London: Henry Kent, 1765), 41–42; Thomas Jefferson, *Notes on the State of Virginia* (1787; reprinted New York: W.W. Norton, 1972), 162; Edward Long, *History of Jamaica* … , 3 vols (1774; reprinted London: Frank Cass, 1970), II, 322.
5 Abbe Guillame Raynal, *A Philosophical and Political History of the Settlements and Trade of the Europeans in the East and West Indies*, 5 vols, trans. J. Justamond (Dublin: 1779), 5, 48.

Bibliography

Barickman, B.J., *A Bahian Counterpoint: Sugar, Tobacco, Cassava, and Slavery in the Recôncavo, 1780–1860* (Stanford, CT: Stanford University Press, 1998).

Berlin, Ira, *Many Thousands Gone: The First Two Centuries of Slavery in North America* (Cambridge, MA: Harvard University Press, 1998).

Bergad, Laird W., *Cuban Rural Society in the Nineteenth Century: The Social and Economic History of Monoculture in Matanzas* (Princeton, NJ: Princeton University Press, 1990).

Blackburn, Robin, *The Making of New World Slavery: From the Baroque to the Modern, 1492–1800* (London: Verso, 1997).

Brazy, Martha Jane, *An American Planter: Stephen Duncan of Antebellum Natchez and New York* (Baton Rouge: Louisiana State University Press, 2006).

Brown, Christopher Leslie, *Moral Capital: Foundations of British Abolitionism* (Chapel Hill: University of North Carolina Press, 2006).

Brown, Kathleen, *Good Wives, Nasty Wenches, and Anxious Patriarchs: Gender, Race, and Power in Colonial Virginia* (Chapel Hill: University of North Carolina Press, 1996).

Burnard, Trevor, "'Prodigious Riches': The Wealth of Jamaica Before the American Revolution", *Economic History Review* 54 (2001), 506–24.

——, *Mastery, Tyranny, and Desire: Thomas Thistlewood and His Slaves in the Anglo-Jamaican World* (Chapel Hill: University of North Carolina Press, 2004).

Chaplin, Joyce B., *An Anxious Pursuit: Agricultural Innovation and Modernity in the Lower South, 1730–1815* (Chapel Hill: University of North Carolina Press, 1993).

da Costa, Emilia Viotti, *Crowns of Glory, Tears of Blood: The Demerara Slave Rebellion of 1823* (New York: Oxford University Press, 1997).

Craton, Michael, "Reluctant Creoles: The Planters' World in the British West Indies", in Bernard Bailyn and Philip D. Morgan, eds, *Strangers within the Realm: Cultural Margins of the First British Empire* (Chapel Hill: University of North Carolina Press, 1991), 315–62.

Curtin, Philip D., *The Rise and Fall of the Plantation Complex: Essays in Atlantic History* (Cambridge: Cambridge University Press, 1990).

Dunn, Richard S., *Sugar and Slaves: The Rise of the Planter Class in the English West Indies, 1624–1713* (Chapel Hill: University of North Carolina Press, 1972).

Edelson, Max, *Plantation Enterprise in Colonial South Carolina* (Cambridge, MA: Harvard University Press, 2006).

Evans, Emory, *A "Topping" People: The Rise and Decline of Virginia's Old Political Elite, 1680–1790* (Charlottesville: University of Virginia Press, 2009).

Faust, Drew Gilpin, *James Henry Hammond and the Old South: A Design for Mastery* (Baton Rouge: Louisiana State University Press, 1982).

Figueroa, Luis A., *Sugar, Slavery, and Freedom in Nineteenth-Century Puerto Rico* (Chapel Hill: University of North Carolina Press, 2005).

Follett, Richard, *The Sugarmasters: Planters and Slaves in Louisiana's Cane World, 1820–1860* (Baton Rouge: Louisiana State University Press, 2006).

Fox-Genovese, Elizabeth and Genovese, Eugene D., *Slavery in White and Black: Class and Race in the Southern Slaveholders' New World Order* (Cambridge: Cambridge University Press, 2008).

Garrigus, John D., *Before Haiti: Race and Citizenship in French Saint-Domingue* (New York: Palgrave Macmillan, 2006).

——, "Opportunist or Patriot? Julien Raimond (1744–1811) and the Haitian Revolution", *Slavery & Abolition* 29 (2007), 1–21.

Gordon-Reed, Annette, *The Hemings of Monticello: An American Family* (New York: W.W. Norton, 2009, repr. edn).

Higman, B.W., *Slave Population and Economy in Jamaica, 1807–1834* (Cambridge: Cambridge University Press, 1976).

——, *Plantation Jamaica 1750–1850: Capital and Control in a Colonial Economy* (Kingston: University of the West Indies Press, 2005).

Isaac, Rhys, *Landon Carter's Uneasy Kingdom: Revolution and Rebellion on a Virginia Plantation* (Oxford: Oxford University Press, 2004).

Lewis, Gordon K., *Main Currents in Caribbean Thought: The historical evolution of Caribbean Society in its Ideological Aspects, 1492–1900* (Baltimore: Johns Hopkins University Press, 1983).

Lockridge, Kenneth, *The Diary, and Life, of William Byrd II of Virginia, 1674–1744* (Chapel Hill: University of North Carolina Press, 1987).

Menard, Russell R., *Sweet Negotiations: Sugar, Slavery, and Plantation Agriculture in Early Barbados* (Charlottesville: University of Virginia Press, 2006).

Morgan, Philip D., *Slave Counterpoint: Black Culture in the Eighteenth-century Chesapeake and Lowcountry* (Chapel Hill: University of North Carolina Press, 1998).

Oakes, James, *The Ruling Race: A History of American Slaveholders* (New York: Alfred A Knopf, 1982).

O'Brien, Michael, *Conjunctures of Order: Intellectual Life and the American South, 1810–1860* (Chapel Hill: University of North Carolina Press, 2003).

Petley, Christer, *Slaveholders in Jamaica: Colonial Society and Culture during the Era of Abolition* (London: Pickering and Chatto, 2009).

Reis, João José, *Slave Rebellion in Brazil: The Muslim Uprising of 1835 in Brazil*, trans. Arthur Brakel (Baltimore: Johns Hopkins University Press, 1993).

Scarborough, William Kauffman, *Masters of the Big House: Elite Slaveholders of the Mid-Nineteenth-Century South* (Baton Rouge: Louisiana State University Press, 2003).

Schwarz, Stuart B., *Sugar Plantations in the Formation of Brazilian Society: Bahia, 1550–1835* (Cambridge: Cambridge University Press, 1985).

Stedman, John Gabriel, *Stedman's Surinam: Life in an Eighteenth-Century Slave Society*, edited by Richard and Sally Price (Baltimore: Johns Hopkins University Press, 1988).

Thibau, Jacques, *Le Temps de Saint-Domingue: L'Esclavage et la revolution française* (Paris: Editions Jean-Claude Lattès, 1989).

Tomich, Dale, *Through the Prism of Slavery: Labor, Capital, and the World Economy* (Lanham, MD: Rowman and Littlefield, 2004).

Woodward, C. Vann, *Mary Chesnut's Civil War* (New Haven, CT: Yale University Press, 1993, repr. edn).

Wyatt-Brown, Bertram, *Southern Honor: Ethics and Behavior in the Old South* (New York: Oxford University Press, 1982).

Young, Jeffrey Robert, *Domesticating Slavery: The Master Class in Georgia and South Carolina, 1670–1837* (Chapel Hill: University of North Carolina Press, 1999).

12

RESISTANCE TO SLAVERY

James Sidbury

Introduction

Prior to 1780, slavery existed in all European settler societies in the Americas. For many years the historiography of American slavery was dominated by the study of those portions of Anglophone America that became the United States and by the study of Brazil, but during recent decades an explosion of scholarship has both broadened and deepened knowledge of slavery throughout the hemisphere. It has become clear that slavery was a remarkably flexible institution, taking different forms and playing different economic, social, and cultural roles in the gold and silver mines in South and Central America, the cities of Spanish and Luso America, the logging frontiers of Central America, the sugar plantations of the Caribbean, the ships plying the Atlantic, and the farms, towns, and plantations of North America. The wealth of local and regional studies that has revealed this variety has also uncovered a wide range of labor relations, living arrangements, family structures, and cultural responses. In all of these settings, however, historians have found evidence that the enslaved resisted their oppression.

The omnipresence of resistance in the historiography of slavery raises questions. In the hands of some historians, it can seem that any act committed by any slave that did not obviously reinforce slavery should be considered an example of resistance. When should attending a dance or a barbecue be considered an act of resistance, and when should it not? Limiting the definition of resistance is more difficult, however, than it might appear, because the wide array of contexts within which slavery developed means that broad, synthetic, and theoretical approaches to resistance threaten to homogenize the different meanings that similar acts carried in different settings. It is true, for instance, that slaves throughout the Americas ran away from those who claimed them as property. Under any theoretical umbrella, such behavior counts as resistance. But even in this seemingly clear-cut case, the similarity is deceiving. Were those African, African American, and Native American people who ran away to build and then defend the federated villages that comprised the famous seventeenth-century Brazilian *quilombo* of Palmares engaged in the same activity as an eighteenth-century African American slave who ran away from Landon Carter's Virginia plantation, but who remained hiding in the immediate vicinity until he was recaptured? How does either of those acts relate to Frederick Douglass' famous flight to freedom from Maryland to New York in 1838, or the attempt of Gabriel, the leader of an 1800 slave conspiracy in Richmond, Virginia, to stow away on board a boat sailing away from the state in an effort to escape those trying to capture him? (Schwartz, 1992: ch. 4; Isaac, 1982: 328–50; Sidbury, 1997: ch. 2, 3). No one doubts that all of these runaways were resisting the slave regimes in which they lived, but grouping them together threatens to obscure more than it illuminates about what they did and what they believed themselves to be doing.

To be sure, too much can be made of this problem. On one level, it is simply a specific instance of the tension inherent in all historical synthesis – that between respecting what is specific and idiosyncratic about an individual or event while drawing out broader patterns. On a more important level, it can sound a useful cautionary note about the complications involved in tracing patterns linking the efforts and perceptions of millions of men and women caught up in an institution that lasted from the beginning of the sixteenth century until the end of the nineteenth century, spanned North and South America as well as the islands of the Caribbean, and supplied labor for enterprises that ranged from small family farms and artisanal workshops to large mines, huge planta-tions, and major industrial concerns. Resistance could not help but take different forms and have different meanings at different times and places. In surveying the strug-gles of many of the enslaved peoples throughout the Americas, this chapter discusses three broad aspects of slave resistance: the search for cultural autonomy, the efforts of the enslaved to run away from their owners, and the physically violent responses of some enslaved people to their condition. In moving from a survey of the cultures of the enslaved to an examination of slave violence, the discussion moves from the most ambiguous forms of resistance to those acts whose status as resistance historians have been least inclined to question. It closes with a discussion of the relationships among these different kinds of resistance.

Cultures and resistance

The first peoples enslaved by the Europeans who came to the New World were Native Americans. Many Native Americans continued to suffer slavery long after 1492. However, the epidemiological disaster that hit native peoples in the wake of contact created ideological concerns and economic problems that helped fuel objections to enslaving Indians. As early as the sixteenth century, Europeans turned to Africa and the Atlantic slave trade to supply many of their most pressing needs for labor in the New World. With important local exceptions, Africans and their descendants came to dominate the slave populations of the Americas.

Victims of the Atlantic trade were sold out of ports dotting the western coast of Africa from Senegambia in the North to the greater Congo River basin in the South. Each port of embarkation serviced a hinterland that stretched toward the interior of the continent, meaning that the slave trade engulfed victims from an enormous geographical expanse that included a rich and diverse collection of societies and peoples. Without leaving Africa, most captives were sold to people who spoke different languages, who often worshipped different deities, and who expected them to work without compensa-tion. Those sold into the Americas had to make sense of the new and threatening world into which they were thrust. Understanding the cultures that emerged from these pro-cesses involves thinking through the relationships among the cultures of sixteenth- to nineteenth-century West and Central Africa and the cultures of enslaved peoples in the Americas.

The initial discussion of these questions took shape in the first half of the twentieth century, when E. Franklin Frazier and Melville J. Herskovits offered diametrically opposed interpretations of the effects of the slave trade on its victims. Frazier, focusing primarily on the United States, argued that being kidnapped and sold into slavery in Africa, followed by the traumas of the Middle Passage and the disorienting and dehumanizing experiences of being purchased and put to work in the New World, effectively stripped African captives of their cultures, forcing them to face American slavery without cultural resources drawn from their home societies. The cultures of African-descended people in the Americas were, for Frazier, American cultures without meaningful connection to Africa. Herskovits, an anthropologist who did a great deal of field work in the Caribbean basin, argued to the contrary that, notwithstanding the horrors of enslavement and the Middle Passage, Africans who arrived in the Americas sought to organize their spiritual and material lives according to the cultural heritages they brought from their African homes, and, in doing so, reconstituted recognizably African cultures in the Americas. For Herskovits, the cultures of the enslaved were best seen as extensions of African cultures (Frazier, 1939; Herskovits and Herskovits, 1936; Herskovits, 1958).

The debate took a major turn toward its modern form in 1976, when anthropologists Sidney W. Mintz and Richard Price formulated a theory of creolization designed to extend and revise Herskovits' work (Mintz and Price, 1976). Mintz and Price claimed that Africans arriving in America found themselves enmeshed in too ethnically diverse a population of enslaved people to recreate the local cultures of their homelands, but that they brought a common underlying set of cultural norms – Mintz and Price conceived of it as a cultural grammar – upon which they could draw to create African American institutions. Understanding the link between Africa and America had less to do with discovering cultural "survivals" or surviving cultures than with understanding the Old World foundations that lay beneath the creole cultures that enslaved African Americans developed in their new homes. For Mintz and Price, then, the slaves' struggles against the oppression they faced in plantation America led them to develop cultures which, while not directly traceable back to African predecessors, were recognizably African in their cognitive orientation and distinct from the cultures of their European owners. Mintz and Price's theory of creolization appeared on the scholarly scene at the same time as a rich body of scholarship which argued that slaves in the antebellum United States built sustaining communities that remained beyond the control or even the understanding of their masters.[1] The autonomous creole cultures of the enslaved, often explicitly linked to the musical, literary, and artistic achievements of twentieth-century African American cultures, came to be seen as a privileged site of slave resistance.

By the 1980s, however, some scholars grew increasingly uneasy with creolization as a framework, even as they continued to see slaves' defense of autonomous cultures as a key achievement of their resistance. They believed that the theory of creolization effectively blocked an appreciation of substantive continuities between the cultures of Africa and of African-descended people in the Americas, or that the creolizationists portrayed slave culture too much as a response to masters and oppression, rather than as the independent achievement of the enslaved. Some saw the scholarly triumph of creolization as the reflection of a poisonous, if often unconscious, tendency in Western history that denigrated black people and their culture (Asante, 1987). Others portrayed it more as the unintended effect of the slaves' success in shielding their culture from their masters, insisting that an essentially African culture nurtured slave resistance throughout the period of bondage, but did so only by remaining invisible to whites and thus concealed in the record (Stuckey, 1987). A third group looked to institutional causes. They argued that the failure of creolizationists to appreciate the persistence of West and Central African cultures in the Americas was rooted in their lack of grounding in West and Central African history, a lack of grounding caused by provincial traditions of graduate training, especially among those studying US history. Because historians of slavery in the United States knew little about Africa, they missed connections to the Old World, while too easily assuming that the story of those they studied began on the western side of the Atlantic (Thornton, 1992; Gomez, 1998, 2005).

The increasing breadth of slavery scholarship contributed to this critique of creolization. The growing literatures on Brazil and Spanish American slavery revealed that slaves and free people of African descent organized fraternal organizations among African ethnic groups (for example, Nago, Lucumi, Congo). This process was a clear example of the direct, one-to-one relationship between the identities and cultures of African and African American peoples that Herskovits had posited. Studies of Cuban *Santería*, Brazilian *Condomblé*, and Haitian *Vodun* underscored the presence of complex cultural institutions in the Americas with relatively clear African cultural genealogies. The publication of the *Trans-Atlantic Slave Trade Database* in 1999 and of David Eltis' important analysis of its data helped reinforce the peripheral role of North America in the Atlantic trade (Eltis, 2000). It opened the possibility that scholars might soon be able to map the transfer of specific African cultures to specific American places, uncovering in the process the ways that victims of American slavery resisted the hegemony of their putative masters' cultures.

This possibility rested, however, on an understanding of the "ethnic" cultures of West and Central Africa during the era of the slave trade that recent scholarship has called into question. From Ira Berlin's claims that the African littoral was peopled by cosmopolitan "Atlantic creoles," to J. Lorand Matory's demonstration that "Yoruban" identity is better understood as a product of the Diaspora than as something "indigenous" to West Africa, to Stephanie Smallwood, David Northrup, and Alexander Byrd's portrayals of intensely local, fluid, and changing identities among victims of the slave trade *within* West Africa, it has become problematic to assert that the ethnicities claimed by members of Cuban *cabildos* or Brazilian *irmandades* existed as stable identities in West and Central Africa during the era of the slave trade (Berlin, 1998; Matory, 1999; Smallwood, 2007a; Northrup, 2006; Byrd, 2008). The processes of cultural change that scholars following Mintz and Price label as creolization increasingly seem less a product of Africans' engagement with American cultural, social, and natural environments, than a continuation of patterns of cultural adaptation that were central to the conflicts and resulting internal migrations happening in seventeenth- to nineteenth-century Africa (Miller, 2004). The autonomous slave cultures that historians have seen as central to slave resistance throughout the hemisphere have less to do with either the transfer and defense of cohesive old world cultures or the cultural inventiveness stimulated by American conditions, than with the cultural hybridity and adaptability that characterized West and Central Africa in the era of the Atlantic trade. This fluidity is as true of the slave cultures scholars have seen as most "American" – such as those found in the antebellum United States – as of those in Brazil or Cuba that have conventionally been thought more "African".

If questions about the roots of slave cultures have produced heated scholarly debates, a growing consensus can be discerned in the ways that scholars analyze the patterns of daily resistance supported by and integral to these cultures. It's not that local studies of slaves in different American societies have portrayed slaves engaging in identical activities throughout the Americas. Instead, the careful and locally specific reconstructions of the ways that slaves responded to the conditions in which they found themselves, whether on sugar plantations, in gold mines, in urban settings, or in tobacco fields, fit a general framework. Throughout the Americas, masters or their proxies held enormous power over slaves, but it has become increasingly clear that even when laws gave masters almost complete power, the reality on the ground was more complicated. Slaves could and did develop strategies that created informal power, so that employers of slave labor who wanted to make a profit, which means virtually all employers of slave labor, had to reach understandings with their bondsmen. Historians increasingly believe that slaves and their masters, overseers, or employers negotiated the norms that governed the pace of work, the size of the realm of relative privacy that slaves could expect to see respected, the amount of time that slaves could consider their own, and the kinds of independent economic activities that slaves could pursue.[2]

The key to understanding these negotiations is to remember that they took place between parties who brought very different resources to the process. Slave owners and employers enjoyed a monopoly on the legal authority to use force, at least when they were supported by governmental power (as they were until the mid-nineteenth century in almost all slave societies), and a near monopoly on the control of the most efficient weapons with which force could be exerted. They also employed an array of other cultural and material advantages rooted in their control of the state and the economy. The enslaved brought what scholars, following theorist James C. Scott, have come to call the "weapons of the weak" – gossip, the willingness to cooperate in slowing the pace of work, tool-breaking and associated types of property destruction, and other forms of day-to-day resistance. Obviously, masters had the upper hand in these negotiations. Had that not been the case, the enslaved would have become free and their weapons would not have been those of the weak. But an enormous body of scholarship makes it equally clear that the weapons of the weak could be potent in the hands of slaves who understood how to use them, and masters had little choice but to compromise on issues they thought unessential. As Robin Blackburn puts it, "colonies with large slave majorities could not have survived" for long "if they had not reproduced the subjection of the forced laborers effectively" (Blackburn, 1988: 20). This observation is equally applicable to the plantation regimes in societies such as the United States and Brazil, in which most people were free, and may be even more applicable to urban settings in which slavery was important but more economically marginal (Whitman, 1997; White, 1991). In all of these settings, subjection could be more efficiently reproduced through negotiation than brute force, though the negotiation always took place under the shadow of masters' potential recourse to brute force.

Because the textures, terms, dangers, and triumphs of resistance through negotiation were locally specific, it is impractical to provide more than a few illustrative examples. One of the clearest arose in South Carolina during the early eighteenth century, where slaves were put to work growing rice in the swamps of the Lowcountry. The nature of the work and the scarcity of whites who were willing to work as overseers made gang labor impractical. A task system quickly evolved in which each full hand was given a task to complete each day, after which her time would be her own. In remarkably short order, the tasks became standardized across plantations, suggesting that slaves and masters effectively negotiated what constituted a legitimate day's work. The size of a task in the Lowcountry remained stable for more than a century – surely an indication of the ability of Lowcountry slaves to protect their customary rights by resisting their masters' efforts to intensify the pace of work. Working in the rice swamps was brutal, killing labor and should not be romanticized, but there is evidence that slaves preferred tasked labor to gang labor, for during the nineteenth century many sought to win the right to work tasks in regions beyond the Lowcountry (Morgan, 1982: 563–99, 1988: 189–220, 1998: 179–87).[3] Though the task system never prevailed in most of plantation America, the struggles over customary allocations of time that are best illustrated in the literature on tasking took place everywhere, with the enslaved using the tools at their disposal to maximize their own time (Blackburn, 1997: 347). In Spanish American societies, which provided greater legal recourse for the enslaved than did other American places, slaves turned to the courts to arrange a change of masters or to "force concessions from abusive or recalcitrant masters", a powerful weapon with which to establish and defend customary understandings (Andrews, 2004: 33–35). All of these acts of resistance share an orientation toward ameliorating slavery by using the best resources at hand to negotiate with enslavers, rather than toward overthrowing or escaping slavery, and that is a quality shared by a vast array of the efforts of enslaved people throughout the hemisphere.

The slaves' economy became one of the most important arenas for these ameliorative struggles. Though the primary staple economies of the Americas remained in the hands of Europeans and their descendants, the enslaved developed parallel economies in North and South America. Presumably in an effort to ease the economic burden of feeding their enslaved labor forces, masters throughout the hemisphere began early on to assign small plots of land to their bondspeople for the cultivation of subsistence crops. There was a degree of exploitation in this practice, especially when first instituted, since the grounds had to be tilled during slaves' free time on Sundays or after returning from the master's fields, but it quickly evolved into something else. The enslaved grew crops, and they acquired chickens, and sometimes livestock, all of which they used to enrich their diets. They also began to produce surpluses that they could market to their masters, to neighboring whites, and, in many cases, through sophisticated slave-controlled marketing systems into urban centers. Slaves came to understand that the garden or provision grounds were their own, and they passed them onto their children. While masters had no legal obligation to recognize the slaves' ownership of these plots of land, most came to recognize that violating their slaves' sense of customary right in that land was simply not worth the cost. In this way, slaves throughout plantation America won greater, if limited, economic autonomy from their masters, undercutting potential support for more radical forms of resistance.[4]

Historians' ambivalence about the long-term effects of slaves' engagement with the market parallel their uncertainties about the role of cultural autonomy and the day-to-day resistance that it both embodied and fostered. Through music, kinship, religion, economic participation, labor slowdowns, and a host of other activities or cultural achievements, the enslaved carved out arenas of life that remained relatively insulated from their masters. Doing so did not always entail risking the displeasure of those who controlled guns, whips, and gallows, but it often did. All of these efforts helped create cultural worlds in which the enslaved could find much more meaning to their lives than might seem to have been possible, given the stark realities of New World slavery.

It is less clear, however, how useful it is to think about these accomplishments under the rubric of resistance. Did the slaves' very success in building meaningful lives under slavery lessen the number committed to risking everything in an effort to bring slavery to an end? If so, should we follow William Dusinberre in speaking of "dissidence" rather than "day-to-day" resistance? Or is the privileging of those seeking "revolutionary" change an artifact of a period when scholars had much more faith in the promise of transformative change? (but cf. Dusinberre, 1996). Questions of this sort stimulated enormous debate among historians of slavery during the 1970s and 1980s, before receding into the background for a decade or two. They are currently re-emerging in ways that highlight arguments about the links between constant low-level resistance (dissidence?) and other ways that the enslaved resisted their oppressors.

Runaways and resistance

Slaves throughout the Americas ran away from their masters, and running away constituted an ongoing and ever-present problem for those who ruled slave societies. Running away was not, however, the same problem in all places or times, in part because slaves ran away for a variety of reasons and with different goals. Some absented themselves from the plantation, house or workshop for a few days, effectively registering a protest about bad treatment by denying masters their labor, or risking punishment to go off to visit friends or family. Others sought to escape slavery by seeking a berth as a mariner on an ocean-going ship, by fleeing to town and trying to blend into an urban free black community, or, especially in the antebellum United States, by trying to run to a polity where slavery had been abolished. Still others ran away to form or join maroon communities where they could live with other escaped slaves as free people. In virtually every slave society, and in many societies with slaves, there were individual slaves who pursued each of these strategies, but different patterns emerged among runaways in different places and times.

Comparing runaways across slave societies is difficult because the scholarship on runaways asks different questions of different places. Scholars studying societies that had numerous and powerful maroon communities – such as Jamaica, Brazil, or Suriname – see running away through the lens of *grand marronage*. They certainly do not deny that slaves ran away without seeking to join maroon communities, but maroons dominate the literature, as they may have dominated the ways the enslaved thought about running away. Scholars studying the United States, on the other hand, which had very weak traditions of *grand marronage*, but an abundance of local newspapers in which masters could advertise for the return of runaway slaves, have produced a large and sophisticated literature on individual runaways. In each case, it is difficult to tell the degree to which the differences in scholarly emphasis reflect differences in the behavior of slaves in the societies being analyzed, and the degree to which they reflect differences in what masters in those societies found most troubling.

When North American slaves ran away, their masters often advertised for their return in provincial newspapers. Analyses of the resulting advertisements suggest remarkable consistency across time and space. From the early eighteenth century until the Civil War, young males, ranging from late adolescence into the mid-twenties, were most likely to appear in the advertisements. Most are listed as having run away alone. Many masters listed some kind of precipitating event as an explanation for the escape. In the nineteenth century, those runaway slaves living in the border South – Maryland, Delaware, Kentucky, and Missouri – sometimes attempted to cross into freedom by running to a free state or to Canada. Those runaways living in the Mississippi River Valley were more like to run south or west, hoping to reach New Orleans and passage on a sea-going ship, or Mexico. Slaves from throughout the southern United States often ran to towns or cities, hoping to pass as free. Only a small percentage of those who fled slavery reached freedom; there was too much hostile terrain to cross, and even those who escaped the South faced danger from slave catchers in the free states.[5] Nonetheless, as James Oakes has shown, individual runaway slaves played an important role in bringing slavery to an end in the United States, for it was southern masters' desire to protect the Border South by stemming the perceived tide of runaways that inspired passage of the Fugitive Slave Act of 1850 and the Kansas–Nebraska Act of 1854. Those laws were instrumental in mobilizing opposition to the "Slave Power Conspiracy", and thus contributed to the rise of the Republican Party, the coming of the Civil War, and the abolition of slavery in the United States (Oakes, 1986).

Individual slaves in Latin America and the Caribbean also fled their masters using strategies that were specific to their locales. Runaways in nineteenth-century Barbados, with its heavily creole slave population, resembled those from the antebellum United States. They were overwhelmingly male and American-born, and a disproportionate number had artisanal skills. Like their North American counterparts, many ran to towns – Bridgetown or Speightstown – to pass as free, while others sought to hide among their kin in the countryside. Enslaved men in southern Brazil later in the nine-teenth century ran away and sought freedom by joining the Brazilian Army during the war against Paraguay. Runaways in pre-revolutionary Saint Domingue were over-whelmingly African, like the slave population of Saint Domingue, while runaways in Bermuda tended to be creole males who used their seafaring skills to steal a boat and try to sail to freedom (Heuman, 1985; Kraay, 1996; Geggus, 1985; Bernhard, 1999). The varying and problematic nature of surviving evidence regarding the number and identity of runaways makes it difficult to compare in meaningful ways the actions and effects of runaways in different slave societies, but that evidence leaves no doubt that slaves throughout the Americas ran away from their masters.

Individual runaways troubled slave regimes by costing their masters valuable labor. They also created political challenges when they ran across state, national or imperial borders. Slaves who escaped and remained at large while forming autonomous communities – maroons – created much greater headaches for those ruling slave societies. Communities of escaped slaves existed throughout the Americas, but *marronage* did not take deep root everywhere (Thompson, 2006). Maroons found it much easier to establish themselves where relatively forbidding terrain – usually mountains or jungles – sat adja-cent to large slave-worked plantations or mines. This allowed slaves to slip away from bondage and to organize relatively defensible communities without breaking entirely from their slave communities. Most, though not all, of those who founded maroon commu-nities were young, single men, and they tended to coalesce as bands of warriors willing and able to fight to maintain their independence. While maroons rejected life on the plantation, they frequently returned to the plantation zones to steal food, weapons, and livestock, and to entice or abduct others, especially women, to join them in the bush.[6]

It is surely true that most maroon settlements were small and temporary, and left little if any trace in the written record. Many were larger and survived for a number of years, fighting off intermittent military expeditions sent to re-enslave them (see, for example, Carroll, 1977; Corzo, 2003). A much smaller number of maroon settlements fought off sustained and well funded efforts by the slave regime to re-conquer them and became famous, both at the time and in subsequent scholarship, as emblems of successful slave resistance. Some of the most famous of these – the Windward and Leeward Maroons of Jamaica, and the Saramaka of Suriname – so successfully resisted their attackers that the British in Jamaica and the Dutch in Suriname gave up trying to defeat them and signed formal treaties recognizing their freedom and autonomy.

Treaty maroons existed in an ambiguous relationship to the slave regime. They agreed to help capture runaway slaves and to return any slaves who ran to them. They promised their military loyalty to the regime, both against hostile European powers, and against slave uprisings. Without looking beyond their legal standing, then, they simultaneously represented the promise of successful slave resistance and served as bulwarks against continuing slave resistance.

When one moves a bit closer to the ground, their roles become even less clear. As Trevor Burnard has shown, Jamaican maroons often preyed upon enslaved Jamaicans by stealing from their provision grounds (Burnard, 2004). On the other hand, when called upon by white Jamaicans to help repress Tacky's Revolt in 1760, the maroons took their time, leaving authorities unsure whom they planned to fight for. They did finally help put down the rebellion, but their uncertain allegiances came to the fore again during the Haitian Revolution, when the Leeward Maroons fought the beleaguered British to a draw in the Second Maroon War. By that time, white Jamaicans had grown so distrustful of the Maroons' allegiance that they ignored their own supposed commitment to the rule of law and betrayed the terms of the Treaty immediately after signing it by deporting the Maroons. The deported Maroons underscored their uncertain standing in the racialized Atlantic world when, after an unpleasant detour in Nova Scotia, they arrived at Great Britain's colony for freed slaves in Sierra Leone. Upon getting off the ship in Freetown, they helped repress an uprising by formerly enslaved black settlers against the white Sierra Leone Company's government (Sidbury, 2007: 127). There is probably no way to reconcile the contradictory roles that Jamaican Maroons played: sometimes emblems of freedom and resistance for slaves, at others they were a source of terror and division; sometimes a refuge for those running from plantations, at others, they were slave-catchers.

The history of Brazilian maroon communities – *mocambos* or *quilombos* – is as rich, complicated, and prominent as that of the Jamaican maroons. The spectacular history of the seventeenth-century Kingdom of Palmares looms over many discussions, but as Stuart Schwartz began to argue as early as 1970, and as others have also shown, however remarkable the size and longevity of Palmares, the biggest story of *marronage* in Brazil lies in the number of settlements that existed in close proximity to plantation regions, major urban centers, and mining regions (Schwartz, 1970; Nishida, 2003; Dantas, 2008; Andrews, 2004: 38–39). What seems most striking in hemispheric perspective is the degree to which Brazilian authorities appear to have tolerated the *quilombos*. They did not sign treaties with them, nor did they legitimize them in other ways, but their efforts at repression were intermittent and appear designed more to control than to eliminate communities of fugitive slaves. The *quilombos* co-existed with Brazil's slave regime, providing a haven for some escaped slaves, trading with people on the plantations and in town, and attracting periodic attempts at repression.

Slaves chronically ran from their masters. Doing so could be a part of the kind of day-to-day resistance through which the enslaved negotiated the terms under which they lived and worked, or it could be an attempt to achieve individual freedom while living within the boundaries of the slave regime, or it could be an escape from the regime into an autonomous community that existed in an uneasy relationship to that regime. In each case the slaves fleeing their masters were resisting slavery, but the nature of that resistance varied, as did its results. One must distinguish between the sense that the escaping slaves made of their actions and the effect of those actions. It is probably true that those slaves who fled to maroon communities issued the most fundamental challenge to slavery, because they sought to escape into an autonomous community and to defend that community against their former masters. Individual runaways, on the other hand, appear to have been most concerned with achieving their own freedom, and much less concerned to challenge the system of slavery. The runaways' intent is, however, only a part of the story, given the roles of individual runaways in stimulating the political conflicts that produced the American Civil War, and the roles of some maroons as slave catchers and soldiers fighting rebel slaves.

Violence and resistance

Slavery was brutal and violent. Paradoxically, that fact helps explain both the presence and the relative rarity – when it was rare – of violent resistance. Masters had regular recourse to the lash, and the records of slave societies abound in stories of stomach-turning physical and emotional violence that masters, overseers, and other whites visited on the enslaved when "mere" whipping did not accomplish all that they hoped. Slaves were decapitated for running away, they were tortured for disobedience, they were raped for their oppressors' pleasure, and they were publicly and symbolically dishonored in ways that offer disturbing testimony to mankind's capacity for senseless cruelty. Planters in the antebellum United States went to great pains to argue that abuses, by which they meant horrific punishments beyond whipping, were exceptional rather than the norm, and they may have been correct – horrific punishment would presumably have lost much of its effect if it were used routinely. But whether understood to have been exceptional, the norm, or something in between, the enslaved lived with ever-present threats of emotional and physical brutality. It is little surprise that slaves sometimes responded with violence. Nor is it surprising upon reflection that, faced with the prospect of being raped, decapitated, or having someone defecate in one's mouth, many enslaved people controlled their desire to lash back at their masters, and opted to run away or engage in safer forms of day-to-day resistance.

There may be little else to say about individual acts of violence by the enslaved than that, throughout the Americas, in response to specific abusive acts or to cumulative patterns of cruelty, slaves sometimes attacked whites. While most slaves lacked easy access to guns or swords, they worked every day with machetes, axes, hoes, shovels, scythes, hammers, and other agricultural tools that could easily be turned against their oppressors in a fight. Perhaps the most powerful account of such an incident comes at a climactic moment in the first autobiography of the antebellum abolitionist activist and post-bellum statesman Frederick Douglass.[7] While a slave in Maryland, he was hired out to a farmer who specialized in "breaking" recalcitrant slaves for their masters. Douglass suffered Edward Covey's abuses for the first six months of his year-long hire, but when finally pushed beyond his fear of white retribution, Douglass decided to stand up and fight. He describes getting the best of a long and brutal fistfight, and credits his victory with his transformation from slave into man. He never accepted another whipping, and soon sought to organize a group escape to the North. Douglass' rhetorical flourish and changed behavior serve as reminders of the stakes of such violent resistance, but he is also careful to inform readers that his resistance was successful not only because he won the fight, but also because Covey's economic wellbeing rested on his reputation as a slave breaker. As a result, Covey chose to cover up his defeat rather than to use the law to make an example of Douglass. Individual violent resistance more often brought swift and brutal exemplary punishment, regardless of the slave's initial success.

Collective violent resistance – slave rebellion – receives full treatment elsewhere in this volume, but no discussion of slave resistance can ignore it completely. Slave rebellions, like all rebellions, were exceptional events. Their history in the New World began on Hispaniola within the first decades of its settlement and continued through the era of slavery. Roughly 10 per cent of trans-Atlantic slave voyages experienced uprisings, and conspiracies or rebellions occurred in all American slave societies. A distinction must be made, of course, between conspiracies, in which slaves planned to rise against their masters but were betrayed before the battle began, and realized rebellions. Distinctions should also be made among the different kinds of uprising, from community actions designed to defend customary rights on a plantation; to efforts by men enslaved as prisoners of war in Africa to reconstitute themselves as a military force and strike out for freedom (Stono in South Carolina and the Malê Revolt in Salvador, Bahia); to efforts to overthrow a given slave regime (Gabriel in Virginia and Saint Domingue/Haiti); to reformist, ameliorative uprisings such as those that occurred in Barbados, Demerara, and Jamaica during the final decades of British slavery. Whether conspiracy or rebellion, and whether reformist or transformative in intent, slave uprisings required a confluence of forces and events that created the conditions in which the enslaved could secretly organize around ever-present grievances. Only one uprising – the Haitian Revolution – was "successful" in the sense that it permanently replaced the slaveholding regime with a polity organized by those who had been enslaved, and arguments about the long-term effects of slave rebellions continue. After all, the nineteenth-century efforts of enslaved Barbadians, Demerarans, and Jamaicans, though explicitly ameliorative in intent, strengthened metropolitan abolitionists and accelerated British emancipation.

Conclusion

Dividing a survey of patterns of slave resistance into day-to-day resistance, running away, and violent resistance provides a useful organizing framework, but it risks ignoring the stickiest questions facing historians writing about resistance. Were there causal connections among these different styles of resistance? Should we conceive of this tripartite division hierarchically – with daily resistance at the bottom and collective violent resistance at the top? If so, according to what criteria?

These questions have informed analysis of slave resistance since at least the 1930s, and between the 1960s and the 1980s or 1990s, a scholarly consensus reigned. Most historians shared a whiggish outlook. If they studied the United States, they saw slave resistance as a historical precursor to the Civil Rights Movement or, for a smaller group, the Black Power Movement. Historians from other American regions saw slave resistance through the lens of anti-colonialism, but the teleological implications of their work were similar. Slave resistance was important because it transformed the societies in which slaves lived or laid the groundwork for later transformative projects. The most important slave resistance was, in the language of the time, properly political.[8]

At first glance, approaching slave resistance, or most other forms of activism, in this way might seem self-evident. Upon reflection, however, many scholars who have been influenced by post-modern theoretical developments during the 1980s and 1990s worry that the political/pre-political distinction on which it is based rests on an unconvincing assumption that historians understand the continuing direction of historical change and thus can discern what contributed to that direction – to "progress" – and what did (and does) not. The loss of faith in progress, whether understood as the promise of revolutionary change or of reliably beneficent ameliorative change, has not, as it might have, led historians to lose interest in slaves' efforts to resist their oppression. Slave dress, slaves' celebrations, and a whole host of other activities, which may or may not have contributed to challenges to the slave system, attracted the attention and the careful and sensitive scholarship of historians. They came to see any act through which slaves asserted their humanity as an act of resistance.

Recent reactions to the tendency to see resistance everywhere in the history of slavery have run along two parallel tracks: one that foregrounds the empirical, the other the theoretical. Some historians moved away from broad interpretations of slaves' assertions of their humanity by asking narrower questions about what slaves had resisted, and what they had accomplished. These scholars do not necessarily see rebellion as the end point of resistance, but they do seek a clear and pragmatic endpoint for the different forms of resistance that they discuss. Liese M. Perrin noted that when slave women exercised forms of birth control, they not only gained greater control over their own lives, they effectively went on strike by refusing to perform the reproductive labor on which masters counted. Stephanie Camp ended a creative analysis of the ways that slaves, especially enslaved women, constructed alternative geographies in the antebellum South, by trying to tie these alternative geographies to the physical mobility of so-called "Contrabands" and of freed people, that proved so important during the Civil War and Reconstruction. Walter Rucker built on Sterling Stuckey's emphasis on cultural continuities between Africa and the Americas, but did so with a clear focus on the ways that Old World beliefs inspired violent attempts to overthrow slavery. David Richardson set the gold standard for empirically rigorous analysis of slave resistance with his analysis of its effects on the Atlantic slave trade, showing that slavers' fear of slave resistance steered the trade away from certain ports of embarkation and increased the cost of the trade, thus measurably decreasing the number of its victims, and sparing roughly one million potential African victims over the course of the trade (Perrin, 2001; Camp, 2004; Rucker, 2006; Richardson, 2001). While these studies do not share a single theoretical take on resistance, all move away from amorphous claims that slaves resisted simply by asserting their humanity. Resistance in each case involved the enslaved having acted in ways that either sought to prevent slaveowners from achieving some pragmatic and measurable goal, or had the effect of doing so.

Another response to increasingly expansive definitions of slave resistance that see asserting humanity as rejecting slavery has been to question whether the individualist assumptions behind these claims offer meaningful grounds for understanding the intentions of the enslaved. Stephanie Smallwood's creative reconstruction of the experiences of victims transported to the Americas by the Royal Africa Company, and her analysis of the role of enslaved guardians in the Atlantic slave trade, both show the problems of understanding slaves' behavior through a black–white binary in which slaves (blacks) resist owners (whites), for the slaves she studies came from societies in which local and kinship identities and rivalries governed their senses of self and shaped processes of enslavement and sale (Smallwood, 2007a, 2007b). Similarly, Trevor Burnard's portrayal of Jamaica as a society divided by multiple tribal identities, in which the white tribe played its trump cards in an attempt to keep the different black tribes divided, is built upon the assumption that enslaved people struggled constantly against their oppression (Burnard, 2004). His is not, however, a simple story of slaves resisting masters, because the brutalizing world of Thomas Thistlewood that he recovers is a world in which the cultures, friendships, alliances, and enmities that informed people's senses of identity did not match, despite always existing within the framework of, the straightforward distinctions in legal status between slave and free. Anthony Kaye studied a very different place – antebellum Natchez, Mississippi – but his questioning of the "anachronistic liberal" individualist framework of the literature on slave community and resistance led him to a remarkably similar story (Kaye, 2007: 9). Kaye's Natchez was not divided into ethnic "tribes", but it was tribal, with neighborhood lines determining who counted as an insider or outsider. Like Burnard, he sees the enslaved engaging in constant struggles within a complex matrix of collective identities that undercuts the simple binary story of slave resistance.

Walter Johnson has offered the most influential and sophisticated revision of the resistance paradigm within the historiography of North American slavery. He began that process somewhat by indirection in a reinterpretation of American slavery as seen through the lens of the New Orleans slave market (Johnson, 1999). Several years later, Johnson formulated an explicit critique of the resistance paradigm that pointed in a new direction by returning to an old question. In a meditation on the work that the concept of agency does in contemporary social history, Johnson focused much of his attention on the theoretical incoherence of the literature on slave resistance (Johnson, 2003: 113–24). He addressed this problem at a number of levels, but his main prescriptive move was prefigured by an invocation of Marx at the beginning of the essay. He noted the increasingly expansive definitions of resistance that have come to dominate scholarship on slavery, and offered a bracing normative critique of the progressive political work those broad definitions purport, but fail, to do in the broader culture.

Sandwiched between these moves, he called for a return to a more rigorous approach, one that foregrounds rather than sidesteps the links between individual and collective action. Johnson challenged historians interested in slave resistance to make specific and empirical links between the daily acts through which the enslaved learned how to trust one another in struggles with their masters, and broader collective movements: "if it is to be successful, collective resistance also depends upon the remapping of everyday life – of longing and hope and sadness and anger – in historical terms" (ibid.: 118). Historians seeking to understand slaves' resistance must reconstruct the ways slaves engaged in these processes of remapping; they must reconstruct, he argued, slaves' sense of their own history.

Johnson's prescription requires that scholars move away from timeless categories of the folk that too easily insinuate their way into analyses of the enslaved. Rather than seeking to prove that all American slave cultures were predominantly African or predominantly creole, scholars should ask how specific enslaved people forged the cultures they used to navigate the lives they found themselves living. Which parts of their heritages proved useful? When and how? Addressing these questions entails giving up the comforting assumption that by identifying with the enslaved and finding all that they did progressive – one of the effects of labeling their every act "resistance" – modern scholars ensure that they themselves are on the right side of history. It requires instead that one take seriously and think deeply about the ways that those victimized by American slavery drew upon their pasts to make sense of their lives, and that one recognize that to have been an ongoing process filled with contingency and uncertainty. It makes no more sense to see slaves as perpetual resistance machines than as docile victims. To return to the invocation of Marx with which Johnson begins "On Agency", slaves, like everyone else, made "their own history", but not "under circumstances chosen by themselves, but under circumstances directly encountered, given and transmitted from the past" (quoted by *ibid.*: 113).

Notes

1 For the best example of this body of scholarship, much of which was written in response to Elkins (1959), see Blassingame (1972). Genovese (1976) shares much with the "culture and community" historiography, though it moves well beyond it.
2 For synthetic works that show "negotiation" being used to explain day-to-day resistance throughout the Americas, see Berlin (2003: 116–17, 128, 149–50, 185, and throughout for North America); Andrews (2004: 12).
3 See Dusinberre (1996) for the brutality of Lowcountry slavery.
4 Berlin and Morgan (1993) offer a very useful discussion (Introduction) and four case studies. See Burnard (2004) for provision grounds undercutting the potential for radical resistance.
5 Franklin and Schweninger (2007: 21–39), which is a distillation of their *Runaway Slaves* (Franklin and Schweninger, 1999).
6 The best explanation of maroons' relationship to the plantations remains the Introduction to Price (1979).
7 See Chapter 10 of Douglass, *Narratve of the Life of Frederick Douglass, an American Slave, Written by Himself* (1845) at http://docsouth.unc.edu/neh/douglass/douglass.html
8 Genovese (1976) provides the most important, sophisticated and explicit explication of the distinction between political and pre-political resistance.

Bibliography

Andrews, George Reid, *Afro-Latin America, 1800–2000* (New York: Oxford University Press, 2004).
Asante, Molefi K., *The Afrocentric Idea* (Philadelphia, PA: Temple University Press, 1987).
Berlin, Ira, *Many Thousands Gone: The First Two Centuries of Slavery in North America* (Cambridge, MA: Harvard University Press, 1998).
——, *Generations of Captivity: A History of African American Slaves* (Cambridge, MA: Harvard University Press, 2003).
Berlin, Ira and Morgan, Philip D., eds, *Cultivation and Culture: Labor and the Shaping of Slave Life in the Americas* (Charlottesville: University Press of Virginia, 1993).
Bernhard, Virginia, *Slaves and Slaveholders in Bermuda, 1616–1782* (Columbia: University of Missouri Press, 1999).
Blackburn, Robin, *The Making of New World Slavery: From the Baroque to the Modern, 1492–1800* (London: Verso, 1997).
——, *The Overthrow of Colonial Slavery, 1776–1848* (London: Verso, 1988).

Blassingame, John W., *The Slave Community: Plantation Life in the Antebellum South* (New York: Oxford University Press, 1972).

Burnard, Trevor, *Mastery, Tyranny, and Desire: Thomas Thistlewood and his Slaves in the Anglo-Jamaican World* (Chapel Hill: University of North Carolina Press, 2004).

Byrd, Alexander X., *Captives and Voyagers: Black Migrants Across the Eighteenth-Century British Atlantic World* (Baton Rouge: Louisiana University Press, 2008).

Camp, Stephanie, *Closer to Freedom: Enslaved Women and Everyday Resistance in the Plantation South* (Chapel Hill: University of North Carolina Press, 2004).

Carroll, Patrick J., "The Evolution of a Mexican Runaway Slave Community, 1735–1827", *Comparative Studies in Society and History* 19 (1977), 488–505.

Corzo, Gabino la Rosa, *Runaway Slave Settlements in Cuba: Resistance and Repression*, transl. Mary Todd (Chapel Hill: University of North Carolina Press, 1988 [2003]).

Dantas, Mariana L. R., *Black Townsmen: Urban Slavery and Freedom in the Eighteenth-Century Americas* (New York: Palgrave Macmillan, 2008).

Dusinberre, William, *Them Dark Days: Slavery in the American Rice Swamps* (New York: Oxford University Press, 1996).

Elkins, Stanley M., *Slavery: A Problem in American Institutional and Intellectual Life* (Chicago: University of Chicago Press, 1959).

Eltis, David, *The Rise of African Slavery in the Americas* (Cambridge: Cambridge University Press, 2000).

Franklin, John Hope and Schweninger, Loren, *Runaway Slaves: Rebels on the Plantation* (New York: Oxford University Press, 1999).

——, "The Quest for Freedom: Runaway Slaves and the Plantation South", in Gabor Boritt and Scott Hancock, eds, *Slavery, Resistance, Freedom* (New York: Oxford University Press, 2007), 21–39).

Frazier, E. Franklin, *The Negro Family in the United States* (Chicago: University of Chicago Press, 1939).

Geggus, David, "On the Eve of the Haitian Revolution: Slave Runaways in Saint Domingue in the Year 1790", *Slavery and Abolition* 6 (1985), 112–28.

Genovese, Eugene D., *Roll, Jordan, Roll: The World the Slaves Made* (New York: Vintage, 1976).

Gomez, Michael Angelo, *Exchanging Our Country Marks: The Transformation of African Identities in the Colonial and Antebellum South* (Chapel Hill: University of North Carolina Press, 1998).

——, *Reversing the Sail A History of the African Diaspora* (Cambridge: Cambridge University Press, 2005).

Herskovits, Melville J., *The Myth of the Negro Past* (Boston: Beacon Press, 1958).

Herskovits, Melville J. and Herskovits, Frances S., *Suriname Folklore* (New York: Columbia University Press, 1936).

Heuman, Gad, "Runaway Slaves in Nineteenth-Century Barbados", *Slavery and Abolition* 6 (1985), 95–111.

Isaac, Rhys, *The Transformation of Virginia, 1740–1790* (Chapel Hill: University of North Carolina Press, 1982).

Johnson, Walter, *Soul by Soul: Life Inside the Antebellum Slave Market* (Cambridge: Harvard University Press, 1999).

——, "On Agency", *Journal of Social History* 37 (2003), 113–24.

Kaye, Anthony E., *Joining Places: Slave Neighborhoods in the Old South* (Chapel Hill: University of North Carolina Press, 2007).

Kraay, Hendrik, "'The Shelter of the Uniform': The Brazilian Army and Runaway Slaves, 1800–888", *Journal of Social History* 29 (1996), 637–57.

Matory, J. Lorand, "The English Professors of Brazil: On the Diasporic Roots of the Yoruba Nation", *Comparative Studies in Society and History* 41 (1999), 72–103.

Miller, Joseph C., "Retention, Reinvention, and Remembering: Restoring Identities through Enslavement in Africa and Under Slavery in Brazil", in José C. Curto and Paul E. Lovejoy, eds, *Enslaving Connections: Changing Cultures of Africa and Brazil During the Era of Slavery* (New York: Humanity Books, 2004), 81–121.

Mintz, Sidney and Price, Richard, "An Anthropological Approach to the Afro-American Past: A Caribbean Perspective", ISHI Occasional Papers in Social Change No. 2 (Philadelphia, PA: Institute for the Study of Human Issues, 1976).

Morgan, Philip D., "Work and Culture: The Task System and the World of Lowcountry Blacks, 1700 to 1880", *William and Mary Quarterly* 3rd Ser 39 (1982), 563–99.

——, "Task and Gang Systems: The Organization of Labor on New World Plantations", in Stephen Innes, ed., *Work and Labor in Early America* (Chapel Hill: University of North Carolina Press, 1988), 189–220.

——, *Slave Counterpoint: Black Culture in the Eighteenth-Century Chesapeake and Lowcountry* (Chapel Hill: University of North Carolina Press, 1998).

Nishida, Mieko, *Slavery and Identity: Ethnicity, Gender, and Race in Salvador, Brazil, 1808–1888* (Bloomington: University of Illinois Press, 2003).

Northrup, David, "Becoming African: Identity Formation among Liberated Slaves in Nineteenth-Century Sierra Leone", *Slavery and Abolition* 27 (2006), 1–21.

Oakes, James, "The Political Significance of Slave Resistance", *History Workshop* 22 (1986), 89–107.

Perrin, Liese M., "Resisting Reproduction: Reconsidering Slave Contraception in the Old South", *Journal of American Studies* 35 (2001), 255–74.

Price, Richard, ed., *Maroon Societies: Rebel Slave Communities in the Americas* (Baltimore: Johns Hopkins University Press, 1979).

Richardson, David, "Shipboard Revolts: African Authority, and the Atlantic Slave Trade", *William and Mary Quarterly* 3rd ser 58 (2001), 69–92.

Rucker, Walter C., *The River Flows On: Black Resistance, Culture and Identity Formation in Early America* (Baton Rouge: Louisiana State University Press, 2006).

Schwartz, Stuart B., "The Mocambo: Slave Resistance in Colonial Bahia", *Journal of Social History* 3 (1970), 313–33.

——, *Slaves, Peasants, and Rebels: Reconsidering Brazilian Slavery* (Urbana: University of Illinois Press, 1992).

Sidbury, James, *Ploughshares into Swords: Race, Rebellion, and Identity in Gabriel's Virginia, 1730–1810* (Cambridge: Cambridge University Press, 1997).

——, *Becoming African in America: Race and Nation in the Early Black Atlantic* (New York: Oxford University Press, 2007).

Smallwood, Stephanie E., *Saltwater Slavery: A Middle Passage from Africa to American Diaspora* (Cambridge, MA: Harvard University Press, 2007a).

——, "African Guardians, European Slave Ships, and the Changing Dynamics of Power in the Early Modern Atlantic", *William and Mary Quarterly* 3rd ser. 64 (2007b), 679–716.

Stuckey, Sterling, *Slave Culture: Nationalist Theory and the Foundations of Black America* (New York: Oxford University Press, 1987).

Thompson, Alvin O., *Flight to Freedom: African Runaways and Maroons in the Americas* (Mona, Jamaica: University of West Indies Press, 2006).

Thornton, John, *Africa and Africans in the Making of the Atlantic World, 1400–1680* (Cambridge: Cambridge University Press, 1992).

White, Shane, *Somewhat More Independent: The End of Slavery in New York City, 1770–1810* (Athens: University of Georgia Press, 1991).

Whitman, T. Stephen, *The Price of Freedom: Slavery and Manumission in Baltimore and Early National Maryland* (Lexington: University Press of Kentucky, 1997).

13

SLAVE REBELLIONS

Gad Heuman

Introduction

Slave rebellions have been a feature of slavery from its beginnings. This was the case for slavery in Greece and Rome as well for subsequent systems of slavery elsewhere. In the case of the Americas, slave rebellions have characterised slavery from the onset of European settlement in the sixteenth century to the end of slavery nearly four centuries later. While rebellions differed substantially in scale and in scope across the Americas, they often terrified slave owners. In the face of rebellions, many slave masters fled to the safety of towns, where they could be protected by the military authorities. In the most massive of all rebellions, the Haitian Revolution, there was no sanctuary for slave owners even in the island's towns; thousands of planters therefore fled to other parts of the Caribbean and to the United States. Yet it was not just planters who felt the consequences of the slave rebellion in Haiti. The enslaved across the Americas were aware of the outcome of the slave revolt in Haiti and saw it as an inspiration to rebel against slavery.

Rebellions had another effect: they forced slave owners to construct powerful mechanisms of control. In the first instance, this meant organising militias and having military forces available to put down rebellions. It also involved drafting slave codes to police the institution of slavery; in addition, masters devised severe punishments for those who rebelled. The drastic nature of those punishments was evidence of the planters' fears of the enslaved. In the end, abolitionists pointed to these brutally repressive measures to highlight the barbaric nature of slavery itself.

Planters' attempts to control the enslaved population and to put down rebellions did not rest solely on force. One of the intriguing aspects of slave rebellions involved the attitudes of those of the enslaved who did not rebel. In the midst of rebellions, some of the enslaved carried on working as usual. Others were armed by the authorities to help them defeat the rebels. In many outbreaks, members of the slave community themselves provided advance warnings of the plots to overthrow the system. Slave rebellions provide further evidence, then, of the complexity of a system that lasted for hundreds of years in the Americas.

This chapter provides an overview of slave rebellions, including conspiracies that were discovered before they could develop. The chapter first examines the conditions that were more likely to lead to rebellions, then discusses African- and creole-led rebellions. It also focuses on the role of religion in the outbreak of rebellions.

Conditions for rebellions

One of the early scholars of slavery, Herbert Aptheker, noted that the cause of rebellions was slavery itself (Aptheker, 1943 [1963]). Beyond that fundamental point, however, how is it possible to explain the significantly larger number of rebellions that occurred in Latin America and the Caribbean than in the United States? The United States experienced a handful of major rebellions and conspiracies, the largest of which resulted in the death of between 60 and 70 whites. By comparison, rebellions were more frequent in the Caribbean and Latin America. Jamaica alone had more rebellions than the United States, and these often involved thousands of slaves instead of less than 100 who took part in the most violent outbreak in the United States. The one revolt that succeeded in ending slavery occurred in St Domingue, and revolts elsewhere in the Caribbean in the nineteenth century played a significant role in the British government's decision to abolish slavery.

In *From Rebellion to Revolution*, Eugene Genovese explored some of the conditions that were conducive to rebellions across the Americas. One of the most important of these was the size of the units in which enslaved people worked. In the Caribbean and Latin America, plantations often had hundreds of slaves. For example, Worthy Park estate in Jamaica had between 300 and 500 enslaved men and women during the late eighteenth and early nineteenth centuries, and only a small white population to manage the plantation. At the same time, the average slaveholding in the American South was roughly 20 slaves.

For Genovese, large plantations such as Worthy Park "provided a favorable setting within which insurrectionary movements could mature" (Genovese, 1979 [1981], 13). Rebel leadership could develop more easily where there were significant numbers of enslaved people. Moreover, the culture of those communities was inevitably different, and more independent of white culture than in farms or units that were so much smaller on average, as in the United States.

It was not just the different size of plantations or farms across the Americas that influenced the incidence of slave revolts; it was also the ratio of blacks to whites in these communities that was significant. In eighteenth-century Jamaica, for example, blacks outnumbered whites by a ratio of roughly 10:1, while in neighbouring St Domingue the figure was even higher, 15:1. Although there were very significant black majorities in the Caribbean, blacks in the United States were a minority, except in South Carolina and Mississippi. The demography of the slave populations was therefore significant; as Genovese suggests, blacks in the Caribbean "could feel their strength, [while] the slaves in the United States could not but help feel their weakness" (*ibid.*: 15).

There were also other significant factors that could lead to rebellions. One of these was economic difficulties and distress. For example, on the island of St John in the Danish Virgin Islands, there was pronounced hunger among the enslaved before the outbreak of 1733. This was due to a drought and a hurricane that affected the provision grounds of the slaves. In 1760, the rebellion in Jamaica that year was partly a response to the problems caused by the Seven Years' War; because of the war, the cost of imported goods had doubled. Just before the slave rebellion in Jamaica of 1831–32, there was a severe drought and problems in the provisions grounds. Food was scarce and expensive; in addition, there was an epidemic of smallpox and dysentery in the period leading up to the rebellion.

Abolitionist politics and rumours of emancipation could also be important in the outbreak of rebellions. In the Aponte conspiracy of 1812 in Cuba, the enslaved on the island heard that the Spanish parliament, the *Cortes*, was debating the issue of slavery. It was not difficult for the enslaved to believe that the Spanish had actually ended slavery. There was also a rumour circulating in Cuba that the King of England had said that the slaves in Cuba were free. Even more curious was the belief among some of the enslaved in Cuba that the King of Kongo had declared that they were free, and that he was sending troops to aid in their rebellion. It was not just in Cuba that this was the case: at the time of the Denmark Vesey conspiracy in 1822 in Charleston, South Carolina, there was a Congressional debate about the admission of the Missouri territory as a slave state. The leader of the conspiracy, Denmark Vesey, used this debate to claim that Congress had freed the slaves; for Vesey, it was white people in South Carolina who were denying their freedom. Similarly, the Nat Turner Rebellion in Virginia in 1831 was preceded by a meeting of Virginia's politicians in 1829 to draft a new state constitution. From the slaves' point of view, there were rumours arising from this meeting that they might be liberated.

There was an additional element that was conducive to the outbreak of slave rebellions: splits in the ruling class. This helps to explain the slave rebellion in St Domingue. Prior to the slave revolt there of 1791, the *grands blancs* and the *petits blancs* (the wealthy and poorer whites) were split, as were the free people of colour. The ruling class was therefore divided. There were also instances in which the ruling class was poorly defended, since the military authorities were dealing with other problems. For example, in the rebellion in 1760 in Jamaica, the forces of control were occupied elsewhere because of the Seven Years' War, a factor that the slave leadership clearly took into account in deciding when to attack white authority.

The conditions that led to the outbreak of rebellions in the Americas were therefore varied. Nonetheless, they do help to explain the greater number of rebellions and conspiracies in the Caribbean and Latin America. In seeking to account for rebellions generally, it is also important to consider the role of Africans and African-led rebellions, since such outbreaks often differed significantly from those involving primarily creoles.[1]

African-led rebellions

African slaves strongly resisted slavery. Most of them had been free before their enslavement in Africa and their experience of the Middle Passage. Once in the Americas, some of them established maroon communities and sought to recreate aspects of their African societies. Others became involved in rebellions and conspiracies, hoping to end their own enslavement. Nevertheless, Africans were not always intent on ending slavery in the New World. Accustomed to slavery in Africa, Africans were sometimes prepared to enslave creole slaves and people from other African ethnic groups.

Whatever their intent, Africans led rebellions across the Americas. For example, an African-led uprising occurred on the island of St John in the Danish West Indies in 1733–34. Prior to the rebellion, St John had only recently begun sugar production; consequently, a significant number of African slaves had been brought to the island in the previous decade. The majority of the enslaved were from the Akan kingdoms of the Gold Coast, and they heavily outnumbered the whites on St John. Moreover, in 1733, the Danish authorities also passed draconian legislation against the enslaved.

In response, African slaves rebelled in November, 1733, first taking over the small fort on the island and then setting off the cannons to announce the general uprising. The rest of the enslaved responded, killed the whites who were unable to escape, and burned the canes and many of the plantation buildings. Short of troops, the authorities appealed for help, especially for armed forces from Martinique. Yet it was only after a month-long campaign against the enslaved that the whites were able to end the rebellion. They did so in a particularly horrific fashion, much like the colonists of nearby St Croix, who responded brutally when faced with a possible conspiracy several years later. As the historian of the Danish Virgin Islands put it, "gibbet, stake, wheel, noose, glowing tong – all were employed to impress upon the community the sinfulness of rebellion" (Westergaard, 1917: 246).

Six years later, in 1739, a rebellion broke out at the Stono River in South Carolina. A group of slaves led by an Angolan, Jemmy, stole guns from a local store and travelled south, killing whites and burning houses as they went. One of the historians of this rebellion, Mark Smith, described it as "both a mass act of escape and a genuine insurrection", because the slaves were heading south to Spanish-controlled Florida where they expected to be freed (Introduction to Smith, 2005: xii–xiii). In the rebellion, 20 whites and 40 blacks were killed; like other uprisings in the Americas, it involved ruthless killing and total surprise. Twenty of the rebels were described as "Angolan slaves": for John Thornton, they were Kongolese soldiers who had become prisoners of war and had been sent to South Carolina. Moreover, Thornton has described their military dancing during the outbreak as part of the African culture of war (Thornton, 2005).

There is an additional perspective on the Stono Rebellion that also reflects the importance of an African past. The Low Country of South Carolina was transformed in this period from a frontier society based on cattle herding to a plantation society producing rice. According to Edward Pearson, this fundamentally changed gender relations among the African slaves. Rice cultivation for the males violated their notions of the sexual division of labour: this was women's work in western and west-central Africa. It was therefore an additional insult for the enslaved males to be forced to do this work, especially in light of their relatively autonomous existence as cattle herders. Additionally, as in the case of other rebellions, there were problems of disease in South Carolina: there had been a smallpox epidemic and then yellow fever, and there were also food shortages at the time of the outbreak (Pearson, 1996).

Less than 30 years later, in 1760, African slaves in Jamaica led one of the largest revolts in the eighteenth-century Caribbean. The enslaved took advantage of the colonial forces having to fight elsewhere, as Britain was heavily involved in the Seven Years' War against France and Spain. Apart from weakening the imperial forces, the war resulted in a significant reduction in the export of Jamaican sugar and in a doubling of the cost of imported provisions. As in the case of St John, it was Akan slaves who were involved in the rebellion. According to Edward Long, the eighteenth-century historian of Jamaica, the leader of the revolt was an Akan slave named Tacky, who was intent on "the entire extirpation of the white inhabitants; the enslaving of all such Negroes as might refuse to join them; and the partition of the island into small principalities in the African mode; to be distributed among their leaders and head men".[2]

The revolt broke out in St Mary's parish, possibly because of the high concentration of Akan slaves in the district. On the night of Easter 1760, between 50 and 100 of the enslaved from several estates attacked the fort in the capital of the parish, Port Maria, killed the official in charge of munitions, and seized the muskets and gunpowder stored there. The rebellion spread across much of the country and may have involved as many as 30,000 slaves. In Kingston, Jamaica's chief town, there were reports that a female slave had been made Queen of Kingston; she was described as wearing a crown and sitting under a canopy. This may well have been an example of a West African custom, with the enslaved woman assuming the title of Queen Mother of the Ashanti. Although the Jamaican government eventually suppressed the rebellion, it took well over a year to do so. The cost was enormous: it exceeded £100,000. In the process, 60 whites died as well as an equal number of free coloureds and free blacks. Between 300 and 400 slaves were killed, another 100 executed, and at least 500 transported off the island (Craton, 1982: ch. 11).

Three years later, in 1763, a major rebellion broke out in Berbice, then a Dutch colony but later to be taken over by the British as part of British Guiana. There had been several slave revolts in the previous 30 years as well as more than a dozen slave conspiracies that had been stymied. In the 1763 rebellion, Cuffee, an enslaved Akan who was a cooper and had been a domestic, successfully led the enslaved from seven plantations bordering the Berbice River and forced the Dutch to evacuate the capital of the colony, Fort Nassau. The revolt nearly resulted in the expulsion of the Dutch from the colony.

One of the most significant aspects of this revolt was Cuffee's plan initially to take over the whole colony, but subsequently to divide Berbice into two sections. Cuffee would control upper Berbice, which would become an independent black federation of different African ethnic groups, while the other half of the colony would remain a plantation economy controlled by whites and retaining slavery. Although Cuffee was able to negotiate with the Dutch Governor as an equal, his plan for Berbice failed, largely because of divisions among the African leadership. Cuffee's rival, Atta, also an enslaved Akan, envisioned an Akan kingdom, in which other African groups would be enslaved. The rebellion ended when Cuffee committed suicide and two of his lieutenants brought Atta in to the Dutch (*ibid.*: 271–72).

Not all African-led rebellions broke out in the eighteenth century. In light of the very significant slave trade to Brazil in the nineteenth century, it is not surprising that a major rebellion involving Africans occurred there in 1835. Led by Malês, the term used to describe African Muslims, the rebels planned a great explosion in the centre of Bahia: the idea was to take over the government by attacking the military bases in the city. The revolt would then spread to the countryside. It was set to occur on 25 January, a Feast Day and a holiday which meant that many of the free inhabitants of the city would be away for the celebration.

However, rumours circulated in Bahia the day before the planned outbreak and the conspiracy was betrayed before the rebellion could be set in motion. As a result, the authorities made military preparations to quell the revolt, and the rebels lost the element of surprise. For the historian of the uprising, João Reis, this was "the most effective urban slave rebellion ... on the American continent" (Reis, 1993: xiii). Reis estimated that there were roughly 600 rebels involved in the outbreak, of whom 70 were killed and many more wounded. On the other hand, the rebels killed nine people. As was often the case, white loss of life in rebellions was less than whites expected, and far less than was exacted in retribution against captured rebels after a rebellion was quashed.

Although African Muslims – the Malês – played a central role in the rebellion, they were a minority among the Africans in Bahia and needed to recruit other Africans.

Reis maintains that the rebellion was therefore a Malê plot but an African uprising (*ibid.*: 123). As in the rebellion in Jamaica in 1760 more than 80 years earlier, the Africans were not intent on ending slavery or freeing all the slaves. There is little doubt that they sought to end white domination, but mulattoes and creole blacks may also have been targets of the rebels. From the Africans' perspective, mulattoes and creole blacks were part of the problem: they were not victims but aided the whites in dominating African-born slaves. Yet this was not always the case in Bahia. In an abortive Hausa-led conspiracy in 1814, the African rebels planned to incorporate creoles as well as free coloureds in their plans. As Stuart Schwartz has pointed out, this potential collaboration worried the slave owners (Schwartz, 2006: 256–57).

There were also a series of African-led rebellions in early nineteenth-century Cuba. Like Brazil, Cuba imported large numbers of African enslaved people in this period to work on the sugar and coffee estates on the island. According to Manuel Barcia, many of them had military experience before their arrival in the Americas. Some of the enslaved participated in rebellions, partly because of their loyalty to their captains in Africa who were also brought to Cuba. There were also African rituals that were often significant in these rebellions: in the Stono rebellion, for example, dancing and drumming in an African mode were common. Barcia also discusses the role of African sorcerers and the wearing of protective amulets in Cuban revolts. Again, the utilisation of African cultural symbols was an important feature of African-led rebellions across the Americas (Barcia, 2008: 41–46).

These examples of Bahia, Cuba, Jamaica, Berbice and St John all concern African-led rebellions. But Africans sometimes worked in concert with creoles, with aims similar to those employed in the creole rebellions of the late eighteenth and nineteenth centuries. One such conspiracy developed in 1736 on the island of Antigua. In the year leading up to the planned outbreak, a group of "Coromantee" slaves hatched a plan to kill all the whites and establish an African kingdom with an enslaved man named Court (alias Tackey) as the King. A "Coromantee" himself, Tackey was owned by Antigua's Speaker of the Assembly. He had been brought to the island when he was about ten years old and by the time of the conspiracy was around 35. According to one description of Tackey, "it was fully proved that he had for many Years covertly assumed among his Countrymen, the title of King, and had been by them address'd and treated as such" (Craton, 1982: 120–21). However, Tackey and the other leaders of the conspiracy realised that they needed the help of creoles. They therefore enlisted the aid of Tomboy, a creole master-carpenter, and several other elite creole slaves.

The rebels' plan was to blow up the governor and other whites who would be attending a ball in the capital of Antigua, St John's, on the night of 11 October 1736. Tomboy would be responsible for constructing the seating for the ball and, in the process, would place the gunpowder among the seats. The explosion at the ball would also provide the signal for the enslaved all over the island to revolt on their individual estates and then converge on the capital. However, the ball was delayed, and the planters learned about the plot. Their investigations uncovered the ringleaders almost immediately, and also gradually the names of conspirators across the island. As in the case of the other revolts across the Americas, the authorities acted with enormous ferocity. Of 88 slaves executed, five were broken on the wheel, six were starved to death, and 77 were burned alive. Many others were banished off the island. A significant proportion of those involved in the conspiracy were elite slaves: drivers, skilled slaves and domestics, not the type of the enslaved the planters expected to lead a conspiracy. Worryingly for the planters, the overwhelming majority of rebel slaves in Antigua were creoles (Gaspar, 1985).

There seem to have been differences in the aims of the creoles and the Africans in Antigua. The Africans were seemingly intent on killing the whites and setting up an autocracy on African lines. On the other hand, creoles were less committed to a war against the whites and may have considered the continued enslavement of the Africans as a viable strategy. At the same time, there were African overtones to the conspiracy, including an African ritual dance held a week before the planned outbreak. Although whites and creole slaves seem to have regarded the dance as little more than entertainment, for many African slaves, "it held a binding significance, for it was the authentic *Ikem* dance performed by the Ashanti king in front of his captains once had he had decided on war" (Craton, 1982: 123). In addition, as in the Jamaican rebellion of 1760, it was likely that a woman named Queen was to be a traditional Akan Queen-Mother. Her role would have been to advise Tackey and act as his principal confidant. Moreover, in advance of the conspiracy, there had been an African ceremony to crown the King of the "Coromantees" and to prepare the rebels for the intended war against the whites. African patterns were therefore significant in this conspiracy, but the role of elite creoles was also crucial.

Creole-led rebellions

Many creole-led rebellions shared the goal of the rebels in Antigua: they were seeking an end to slavery. Ultimately, that was the aim of the leaders of the one successful slave revolt in the Americas, the Haitian Revolution. Toussaint L'Ouverture, who emerged as the leader of St Domingue, was a French-speaking creole who occupied an elite position on the plantation where he worked. Freed before the Revolution, Toussaint had become a free person of colour; moreover, he owned slaves himself. But creoles did not act alone in the Haitian Revolution; more than 100,000 enslaved Africans were brought to St Domingue in the decade before the outbreak of the revolution. A significant number of these Africans had been soldiers in West Africa who had become prisoners of war and had been sent to St Domingue. Toussaint clearly made use of their experience in fighting the English and the Spanish in the course of the revolution (Dubois, 2004; Thornton, 1991; see also Laurent Dubois, Chapter 16 in this volume).

The Haitian Revolution clearly had an impact on slave rebellions across the Americas. The enslaved in the Caribbean and elsewhere in the Americas knew about the events in Haiti and often were aware of them relatively quickly. At least three rebellions and conspiracies, one in Virginia, one in South Carolina and one in Cuba, were inspired by the revolution in Haiti.

The first of these, Gabriel's Rebellion, was a conspiracy planned for 30 August 1800 in Richmond, Virginia, the capital of the state. Gabriel was a blacksmith who was hired out by his master and therefore had an element of quasi-freedom since he retained a share of his wages. The events in St Domingue and the end of slavery there clearly had an impact on Gabriel. According to Douglas Egerton, the lesson that enslaved people such as Gabriel learned from St Domingue was that slaves in Virginia not only "had a right to govern themselves but that victory was possible" (Egerton, 1993: 48).

Gabriel's plan was to organize a rebel army, seize the arms in the Capitol building of Richmond and take control of Richmond. This would have meant the end of slavery in Virginia and perhaps beyond; moreover, Gabriel expected that poor whites would join him. Most of the conspirators were skilled slaves, like Gabriel, or were enslaved people who hired out their time. This was an urban plot, also involving free blacks. But Gabriel neglected "to cast his appeals in messianic terms or to imply that he was the man chosen to bring on the day of jubilee" (*ibid.*: 51). By the middle of August, there were rumours of a possible plot circulating in Richmond, and on the appointed day of the rebellion there was a violent storm. As a result, the rebellion was postponed. The conspiracy was then betrayed, the arms stored in the Capitol building were moved, and blacks arrested. Twenty-seven blacks were hanged, including Gabriel.

Twelve years later, in 1812, there were a series of rebellions in Cuba that were linked to Aponte, a carpenter, a free person of colour and a captain in Havana's free black militia. When Aponte was subsequently arrested, he had drawings of maps and military garrisons in Cuba as well as his own book containing drawings of Toussaint L'Ouverture and Jean François, both leaders of the Haitian Revolution.

The rebellions themselves consisted of a series of attacks on plantations in the east-central region of Cuba during the first few months of 1812. For example, in January, over the course of two days, slaves and free people of colour attacked five plantations and killed several whites. Before that rebellion was suppressed, the rebels had killed eight whites, injured several others and burned several plantations. Fourteen slaves were executed as a result of this rebellion and over 100 slaves and free coloureds were transported out of the colony to serve prison sentences. There was also a short-lived rebellion in March in the same region and, subsequently, a plan to attack the Havana military forts and distribute weapons to slaves and free coloureds. The goal was to end slavery. But this was suppressed and Aponte and his fellow conspirators were hanged.

The link between the free coloureds and slaves frightened slaveholders, who had been worried about arming and training the free people of colour. In addition, while there was no proof of Aponte's involvement in the rebellions, his book of drawings clearly concerned the authorities. As Matt Childs has written, "the Haitian Revolution provided powerful images of a black king and military generals that inspired Aponte and others" (Childs, 2006: 169).

Free coloureds were also significant in a conspiracy known as La Escalera in Cuba. Discovered in 1844, the conspiracy was organised by free coloureds and free blacks, and designed to end slavery on the island. The alleged ringleader of the conspiracy, Gabriel de la Concepción-Valdés (Plácido), was a well known poet, and Plácido's fellow conspirators were also literate and included other artists. According to Manuel Barcia, La Escalera was a well coordinated movement, with cells in Havana and across the island. The British consul, David Turnbull, has long been implicated in the conspiracy; under interrogation, many of the rebels discussed British assistance in their planning. Moreover, the leaders of the conspiracy were well aware of the Haitian Revolution, even though it had broken out more than 50 years previously (Barcia, 2008: 27–29; see also Paquette, 1987).

Haiti was also the backdrop for the conspiracy led by Denmark Vesey in Charleston in 1822. It was not just that Vesey had spent some time as an enslaved boy working on a plantation in Saint Domingue. More importantly, the objective of his conspiracy was to escape to Haiti with as many slaves as he could. Vesey was aware that he could not end slavery in South Carolina, but he could flee to Haiti and take a large number of the enslaved with him.

Vesey had been born a slave and brought to Charleston, where he worked as an urban slave as in the city. But he won the lottery and was able to buy his freedom at the end of 1799. Although he was free, Vesey was not admitted into the society of the free people of colour in Charleston and continued to associate with the enslaved, especially skilled slaves like himself. Vesey's conspiracy therefore involved mostly artisans, and he organised the revolt with the help of a small number of elite slaves.

The plan was that the leaders would kill their masters and secure the arms stored in Charleston's Arsenal. They would burn the city in various key places, steal money from the banks and goods from the stores, and gather at the docks prior to their escape to Haiti. The revolt was scheduled to take place on Sunday 14 July: it was Bastille Day as well as the day that ex-slaves in Massachusetts celebrated their emancipation. Vesey expected other slaves to join the conspiracy; instead, one of the enslaved gave away details of the revolt and was then forced to confess. This led to the confessions of several others involved in the plot, the arrival of Federal troops, and the arrest of over 130 slaves and free blacks. Thirty-five of them were hanged, including Vesey (Egerton, 2004).[3]

The slave revolt in Haiti may also have inspired several very significant outbreaks in the Anglophone Caribbean in the first few decades of the nineteenth century. Led by creoles, these rebellions in Barbados, Demerara and Jamaica were intended to end slavery. Like other outbreaks in the Americas, they were affected by rumours of emancipation and by the politics of abolitionism.

In the case of Barbados in 1816, Barbadian slaves had become agitated about the Assembly's resistance to Imperial legislation seeking the registration of slaves. Since reports at the time equated the Registration Act with a plan for the emancipation of the enslaved, some of the enslaved believed that freedom was being withheld from them. One literate domestic slave, Nanny Grigg, claimed that the enslaved were to be freed on Easter Monday 1816, but "the only way to get it was to fight for it, otherwise they would not get it; and the way they were to do, was to set fire, as that was the way they did in Saint Domingo" (Craton, 1982: 261). When the slave rebellion broke out on Easter Sunday, it spread to a third of the island. The leaders of the rebellion timed it to coincide with the peak of the harvest season, and the enslaved made use of arson in an attempt to obtain their freedom. The damage to property on the island was estimated at £175,000, with a quarter of the year's sugar crop destroyed. However, the rebellion – subsequently known as "Bussa's Rebellion" after the name of one of its alleged leaders – proved short-lived. Like other rebellions in the Americas, the repression was savage (Beckles, 1990: 78–85).

As in Aponte in Cuba and Denmark Vesey in Charleston, free coloureds were involved in the Barbados rebellion. One of them, Washington Franklin, was reportedly to be made Governor of the island after the rebellion. While the evidence for this view was unreliable, there was no doubt about the importance of several other free coloured men in the rebellion. One of them, Cain Davis, held meetings with slaves on several plantations and reinforced the belief among many slaves that their masters were opposing abolitionist efforts to free them. The Barbadian House of Assembly was particularly concerned about the influence of William Wilberforce on the enslaved, and believed that Wilberforce had agents and spies working among the slaves in the island (*ibid.*: 82–83).

There was a similar backdrop to the Demerara slave rebellion in 1823. Again, the enslaved believed that local whites were withholding their freedom; in this case, the Imperial context of the rebellion was the formation of the Anti-Slavery Society and the beginning of the abolitionists' campaign in Britain. The rebellion broke out in August, involving thousands of the enslaved. One of the plans for the rebellion involved the enslaved along the East Coast of the Demerara River marching to the capital of the colony, Georgetown, and burning it down. This would provide a signal for the enslaved elsewhere in the colony to join the rebellion.

Like the Barbados uprising, the Demerara revolt was repressed severely, with the death of about 250 slaves. Many of the rebels were executed gruesomely; others who were spared execution were flogged with up to as many as 1000 lashes. The planters linked the rebellion to the work of the humanitarians and, more specifically, to the chapel in Demerara of Rev. John Smith, a missionary for the London Missionary Society. Smith was found guilty of complicity in the rebellion and died in prison while awaiting a reprieve from the Crown (da Costa, 1994).

As in Barbados and in Demerara, the enslaved in Jamaica in 1831 concluded that they had also been freed. The rebellion that the enslaved organised was the most serious in Jamaica's history: it broke out two days after Christmas 1831. Although the rebellion lasted less than two weeks, it did massive damage to property and involved thousands of slaves. One estimate suggests that 20,000 slaves may have been involved in the rebellion, more than 200 of whom were killed during the rebellion and a further 300 executed. Property valued at over £1,000,000 was destroyed. The Christmas Rebellion, or the "Baptist War" as it came to be known, was a crucial event in the abolition of slavery (Holt, 1992: 14; Brathwaite, 1981: 80–81; see also Brathwaite, 1982: 11–30).

In the period leading up to this rebellion, there was a heightened degree of political consciousness among the enslaved, stimulated by the resistance of local whites to the British government. In 1831, and under pressure from the Anti-Slavery Society, the British government took steps to ameliorate the condition of the slaves. It sent out legislation outlining improvements to be enacted locally on behalf of the slaves. The response in Jamaica was predictable: the whites organised a series of island-wide meetings to denounce the interference of the Home government in its internal affairs. Whites even began to reconsider their allegiance to the Crown: if Britain would not protect the institution of slavery, perhaps the United States could be encouraged to do so (Heuman, 1981: 84).

The whites discussed these developments openly, and apparently with little concern about the possible effects on the enslaved. The slaves were consequently made aware of the growing anti-slavery agitation in England. As the whites continued to denounce the British government, many of the enslaved concluded that the Crown had already freed them. Since they also believed that the whites were withholding their freedom, the enslaved surmised that they would not meet any resistance from the King's troops in the event of a rebellion; indeed, the soldiers might even come to their aid (Turner, 1982: 150–54).

Religion and resistance

In addition to the belief that they had been freed, the rebels in Jamaica used religion to help organise the rebellion. Religion in its various forms was therefore an important element in the outbreak of rebellions across the Americas. In the case of Jamaica in 1831–32, the leader of the rebellion, Sam Sharpe, was an urban slave, educated and well thought of by his master. He was highly articulate and became a leader in the Baptist Church as well as a "Daddy" or "Ruler" in the Native Baptist Church. Moreover, Sharpe used the organisation of the church to organise the rebellion. As Mary Turner has suggested, "the Baptist war … was essentially the Native Baptist war; its leaders shaped mission teaching to their own ends" (*ibid.*: 153).

Sharpe planned a campaign of passive resistance for the period just after Christmas, 1831: the slaves would simply cease work until their owners paid their wages and thereby conceded that the slaves were free. However, Sharpe also developed an alternative strategy of armed rebellion in case passive resistance failed. In addition, Sharpe made use of oaths to exact loyalty from his confederates. At a meeting before the 1831 rebellion, Sharpe asserted that "if 'Buckra' would pay them, they would work as before; but if any attempt was made to force them to work as slaves, then they would fight for their freedom".[4] The oath was taken on a Bible:

> Sharpe said we must sit down. We are free. Must not work again unless we got half pay. He took a Bible out of his pocket. [He] made me swear that I would not work again until we got half pay.

One version of the oath included promising "not [to] trouble anybody or raise any rebellion".[5] However, another oath taken just before the outbreak of the rebellion was more threatening: those accepting it vowed "not to flinch till they had succeeded in getting their freedom".[6]

The oaths taken by the slaves in 1831 represent a fusion of religion and politics, but one in which political goals were dominant. Although the Baptist War was a political movement, it was based around religious meetings, and partly inspired by Baptist and Native Baptist traditions. As Mary Turner has commented on the 1831 rebellion, it demonstrated "some degree of political maturity among the slaves. They had created a protest movement … in which religion had been subordinated to political aims" (Reckord, 1968: 123).

Earlier in the same year, 1831, there was a rebellion in Southampton, Virginia led by the slave Nat Turner. Turner was inspired by a series of heavenly visions to lead his people to destroy slavery. In a violent rebellion that only lasted a day, Turner and other rebels killed nearly sixty whites, including his master and his family. During their short-lived rebellion, the rebels killed every white man, woman and child they encountered.

Turner was motivated by an apocalyptic Christianity; like Sam Sharpe, he made use of the New Testament to provide a message of freedom. For Denmark Vesey, it was the Old Testament that provided a similar lesson: slavery was against the teachings of the Bible. Vesey became a class leader in the African Methodist Episcopal Church that was established in Charleston; moreover, many of his co-conspirators were also members of the Church. But other rebels used different religions to buttress their resistance. As Douglas Egerton has suggested, "whether the creed was Baptist or Catholic, Muslim or a pre-Islamic West African derivation, a devout sense of faith inspired numerous leaders from Southampton to Bahia to believe that the heavens were on the side of the oppressed" (Egerton, 2003: 137).

Conclusion

Only one slave rebellion was ultimately successful: the rebellion in St Domingue. That rebellion not only liberated the slaves, but also led to the independence of Haiti. Yet slave rebellions had other effects as well. Arguably, the United States ended its involvement in the slave trade just over 200 years ago, in 1808, because of the fear of another St Domingue. It is also clear that the Jamaican rebellion of 1831 had a significant impact on the abolition of slavery itself. The public in Britain became aware of the problem of trying to retain slavery in the face of that massive rebellion. The violence associated with the repression of the rebellion made the British question the system and, ultimately, its longevity.

Slave rebellions also demonstrate that the enslaved were often prepared to resist their enslavement violently, in spite of the odds against their success. Whether it was Africans or creoles who led the rebellions, slaves sought to bring an end to their own enslavement and often to slavery itself. This could mean attempting to flee the system, as in the case of the Stono rebels and Denmark Vesey. It could also be part of a sophisticated plan to overthrow slave holders: this was the objective of the Muslim rebels in Bahia in 1835. Alternatively, the slave rebellion could begin as a passive protest, an attempt to end slavery by refusing to work as slaves. Sam Sharpe in Jamaica had this vision of attaining freedom.

Whatever their plans, enslaved people planning revolts made use of their churches, their chapels and their mosques to help organise rebellions. They also had their own interpretation of political events around them: many of the enslaved seemed to have believed rumours of emancipation, even when these appeared to be implausible. One example of this was the belief that the King of Kongo would come to the aid of the Aponte conspirators in Cuba. Rebel leaders also made use of rumours of emancipation to inspire their followers. It is likely that the leaders of the Barbadian rebellion of 1816 would have known that the Act to register slaves did not free the enslaved.

But, ultimately, freedom was worth the fight for those who resisted the system violently or made plans to overthrow it. Sam Sharpe embodied their views when, just before he was hanged, he said: "I would rather die on yonder gallows than live in slavery".

Notes

1 The term "creole" is used here to mean men and women of whatever colour born in the Americas.
2 Edward Long, *The History of Jamaica*, 3 vols (London: T. Lowndes, 1774: vol. 2, 447–48.
3 For an alternative view that Vesey and the other rebels were victims of an imagined conspiracy, see Johnson (2001: 915–76). See also the subsequent "Forum: The Making of a Slave Conspiracy, part 2", *William and Mary Quarterly* 3d ser, 59 (2002: 135–202.
4 Henry Bleby, *Death Struggles of Slavery: Being a Narrative of Facts and Incidents which Occurred in a British Colony during the Two Years Immediately Preceding Negro Emancipation* (London: Hamilton, Adams and Co., 1853), 112.
5 National Archives, Colonial Office 137/185, Trial of Samuel Sharpe, 19 April 1832, ff. 308, 309.
6 *British Parliamentary Papers*, 1831/32, (561) XLVII, 35.

Bibliography

Aptheker, Herbert, *American Negro Slave Revolts* (1943 [repr. New York: International Publishers, 1963]).

Barcia, Manuel, *Seeds of Insurrection: Domination and Resistance on Western Cuban Plantations, 1808–1848* (Baton Rouge: Louisiana State University Press, 2008).

Beckles, Hilary, *A History of Barbados: From Amerindian Settlement to Nation-State* (Cambridge, Cambridge University Press, 1990).

Brathwaite, Edward Kamau, "Rebellion: Anatomy of the Slave Revolt of 1831/32 in Jamaica", *Jamaican Historical Society Bulletin* 8 (1981), 80–81.

——, "The Slave Rebellion in the Great River Valley of St. James – 1831/32", *Jamaican Historical Review* 13 (1982), 11–30.

Childs, Matt D., *The 1812 Aponte Rebellion in Cuba and the Struggle against Atlantic Slavery* (Chapel Hill: University of North Carolina Press, 2006).

Craton, Michael, *Testing the Chains: Resistance to Slavery in the British West Indies* (Ithaca: Cornell University Press, 1982).

da Costa, Emilia Viotti, *Crowns of Glory, Tears of Blood: The Demerara Slave Rebellion of 1823* (New York, Oxford University Press, 1994).

Dubois, Laurent, *Avengers of the New World: The Story of the Haitian Revolution* (Cambridge, MA: Harvard University Press, 2004).

Egerton, Douglas R., *Gabriel's Rebellion: The Virginia Slave Conspiracies of 1800 & 1802* (Chapel Hill: University of North Carolina Press, 1993).

——, "Nat Turner in a Hemispheric Context" in Kenneth S. Greenberg, ed., *Nat Turner: A Slave Rebellion in History and Memory* (New York: Oxford University Press, 2003).

——, *He Shall Go Out Free: The Lives of Denmark Vesey* (1999 [revised edn Lanham, MD: Rowman & Littlefield, 2004]).

Gaspar, David Barry, *Bondmen & Rebels: A Study of Master-Slave Relations in Antigua* (Baltimore: Johns Hopkins University Press, 1985).

Genovese, Eugene D., *From Rebellion to Revolution: Afro-American Slave Revolts in the Making of the New World* (1979 [repr. New York: Vintage Books, 1981]).

Greenberg, Kenneth S., ed., *Nat Turner: A Slave Rebellion in History and Memory* (New York: Oxford University Press, 2003).

Heuman, Gad J., *Between Black and White: Race, Politics and the Free Coloreds in Jamaica, 1792–1865* (Westport, CT: Greenwood Press, 1981).

Holt, Thomas C., *The Problem of Freedom: Race, Labor, and Politics in Jamaica and Britain, 1832–1938* (Baltimore: Johns Hopkins University Press, 1992).

Johnson, Michael P., "Denmark Vesey and His Co-Conspirators", *William and Mary Quarterly* 3rd ser. 58 (2001), 915–76.

Mullin, Michael, *Africa in America: Slave Acculturation and Resistance in the American South and the British Caribbean, 1736–1831* (Urbana: University of Illinois Press, 1992).

Paquette, Robert L., *Sugar is Made with Blood: The Conspiracy of La Escalera and the Conflict between Empires over Slavery in Cuba* (Middletown, CT: Wesleyan University Press, 1987).

Pearson, Edward A., "'A Countryside Full of Flames:' A Reconsideration of the Stono Rebellion and Slave Rebelliousness in the Early Eighteenth-Century South Carolina Lowcountry", *Slavery & Abolition* 17 (1996), 22–50.

Reckord, Mary (née Turner), "The Jamaica Slave Rebellion of 1831", *Past and Present* 40 (1968), 108–25.

Reis, João José, *Slave Rebellion in Brazil: The Muslim Uprising of 1835 in Bahia* (Baltimore: Johns Hopkins University Press, 1993).

Schwartz, Stuart B., "*Cantos* and *Quilombos*: A Hausa Rebellion in Bahia, 1814" in Jane G. Landers and Barry M. Robinson, eds, *Slaves, Subjects, and Subversives: Blacks in Colonial Latin America* (Albuquerque: University of New Mexico Press, 2006), 247–71.

Smith, Mark, ed., *Stono: Documenting and Interpreting a Southern Slave Revolt* (Columbia: University of South Carolina Press, 2005).

Thornton, John K., "African Soldiers in the Haitian Revolution", *Journal of Caribbean History* 25 (1991), 58–80.

——, "African Dimensions" in Mark Smith, ed., *Stono: Documenting and Interpreting a Southern Slave Revolt* (Columbia: University of South Carolina Press, 2005), 73–86.

Turner, Mary, *Slaves and Missionaries: The Disintegration of Jamaican Slave Society, 1787–1834* (Urbana: University of Illinois Press, 1982).

Westergaard, Waldemar, *The Danish West Indies under Company Rule, 1671–1754* (New York: Macmillan, 1917).

14

FREE COLOUREDS

John Garrigus

Introduction

Every slave society has had ex-slaves. In societies that enslaved many different ethnic groups, former slaves and their descendants could not be easily identified. In ancient Rome, for example, the descendants of freedmen were eligible to become citizens. But from the 1400s, when Europeans began to enslave large numbers of Africans in the Iberian Peninsula and then in the New World, ex-slaves and their descendants were often visually identifiable. US slave society tended to describe all such people as "free blacks", although most Caribbean and Latin American cultures developed more specific labels to designate mixtures of European, African and native American ancestry. With the rise of a self-consciously "scientific" racial ideology in the eighteenth century, racial ideologues claimed they could precisely determine a person's degree of African descent from his or her physical appearance. In practice, however, whether an observer described a free person as "black", "mulatto", "quadroon" or "white" depended heavily on clues such as gender, language or social class. In other words, racial labels, including the phrase "free person of colour", were social constructions, based on the observer's perceptions and stereotypes. For this reason, their use varied widely from one society to another.[1]

In the 1940s, scholars began to focus on these variations to better understand the nature of racism. Why was it that in many Spanish and Portuguese colonies during the height of slavery, anywhere from 30 to 80 per cent of African-descended people lived free, while in British and French territories, nearly all such people lived in bondage? In the late 1700s, there were approximately 1.3 million free people of colour in the western hemisphere. Slightly over 1.2 million of them lived in Spanish or Portuguese colonies (Klein and Vinson, 2007: 274). Moreover, in Latin America, free people made up a larger portion of the population of African descent than in any other part of the Americas. The intendancy of New Grenada, containing roughly the territory of modern day Panama, Colombia, Venezuela and Ecuador, had 80,000 slaves in 1789 but 420,000 free people of colour. In 1792 Cuba, which was only starting its great sugar expansion, had 85,000 slaves and 54,000 free people of colour. Mexico in 1810 had 10,000 slaves and approximately 300,000 free people of African descent. Brazil did not take a full national census until 1872, about a decade before slavery was abolished there. At that date, officials found that free people of colour outnumbered slaves 4.2 million to 1.5 million. They also outnumbered Brazil's whites 4.2 million to 3.8 million (*ibid.*: 197–98).

Despite such large numbers in Iberian America, much of what has been written about free coloureds since the 1950s comes from research on British and French colonies and their successor states. Here, masters perceived the freedom of even a few people of colour as a challenge to slavery. In the United States in 1790, for example, free people of colour were most numerous in the Upper South states of Maryland, Virginia and North Carolina. Yet even there, free coloureds made up only 1.8 per cent of the total population and only 5.5 per cent of the total population of African descent. Most free people in the Upper South were whites; free coloureds were only 2.7 per cent of the free population in this region.

Free coloured numbers were larger in the British Caribbean, but not by much. In Barbados in 1786, free people of colour were only 1.3 per cent of the African-descended population and 4.9 per cent of the free population ("Appendix: Population Tables", in Cohen and Greene, 1972: 335–39). In Jamaica in 1800, they made up only 2.2 per cent of the total population of African descent, but about 19 per cent of the free population. In France's Caribbean colonies, proportions were slightly higher but fundamentally similar. In Martinique in 1789, free people of colour amounted to 6 per cent of the non-white population and 26 per cent of the free population. Free people of colour in French Saint-Domingue (modern Haiti) came closest to the population levels seen in Latin America, making up 44 per cent of the free population in 1788. When seen as a fraction of Saint-Domingue's massive slave population, however, they accounted for only 5 per cent, much like the US Upper South or Barbados (Régent, 2007: 183, 336–37).

Scholars have turned to two competing sets of theories, one cultural and the other material, to explain these differences between Spanish and Portuguese America on the one hand, and British and French America on the other. The first of these explanations sees attitudes towards free people of colour as a product of the colonizing metropolitan culture. Enslaved and free Africans and their descendants had been living in Spain and Portugal for at least a century before Columbus reached the Caribbean. In the sixteenth century, an estimated 10 per cent of the population of Portugal and of southern Spain was enslaved. Not all of these people were Africans. Many Iberian slaves originated from the Black Sea, the Ottoman Empire, or North Africa. Others were Iberian Moslems enslaved during the long wars of the *Reconquista*. A long familiarity with slavery gave the Spanish and Portuguese a cultural framework for the slavery of Africans, including European-born Christian blacks. Iberian Christians inherited from their Moslem neighbours a particular disdain for Africans compared with other enslaved people. These negative physical and cultural stereotypes were already in place in the fifteenth century, when Gomes Eanes de Zurara chronicled Portugal's early expeditions into West Africa. Iberian Christians also had their own notion of *limpieza de sangre* or "purity of blood", which emphasized the otherness of people whose ancestors had not been Christian. They suspected that captured Moslems, Jews and Africans became Christians for political, not religious reasons.

The cultural explanation of New World racism points out that many of these Iberian prejudices were rooted in ideas about the souls, not the bodies, of black people. For this reason, Spanish laws allowed individuals who demonstrated their virtue or piety to win official recognition of their cultural purity, or *limpieza de sangre* (Martinez, 2004). In Spanish America, this legal custom continued into the late eighteenth century with the documents known as *cédulas de gracias al sacar*. These documents accorded a measure of civil status to people of African descent who had demonstrated their worth. In 1795, the Spanish Crown institutionalized the fees and procedures for these dispensations.

The long history of Iberian warfare and slavery also gave Portuguese and Spanish colonists in the New World a deep familiarity with manumission. The Arabic word *horro*, meaning "to free", explained what happened after Christian and Muslim soldiers captured and held each other for ransom. Many prisoners spent years in slavery before their relatives could deliver payment. *Horro* came to mean both freeing a slave and setting aside money, reflecting a notion of emancipation as something that could be purchased. These meanings persisted as slavery became a major system of labour in both kingdoms' American colonies.[2] In contrast, the French word *affranchissement* came out of a medieval tradition where bondsmen could acquire immunity [*franchise*] from certain feudal obligations in exchange for a payment or military service (Stella, 2000: 156).

The English word "manumission" was taken from the Latin, but English legal culture did not follow the Roman law procedures like the Spanish and Portuguese did. These legal systems required that an official notary draft all documents and witness their signing. This system, which had no widely practised equivalent in the English legal tradition, allowed disadvantaged persons, such as free people of colour, to prove that they had made agreements with members of the master class, including contracts to free a slave.

Another part of the cultural argument is that in Spanish and Portuguese territories, the Catholic Church gave free and enslaved people of African ancestry social identities that the master class had to recognize. In Europe and the New World, officials allowed free and enslaved Christian blacks to marry and to form their own religious confraternities and *cabildos* [councils] under white supervision. They believed these institutions would help people of colour accept the social hierarchy and their low status within it. With no experience of these black institutions in their home countries, masters in British and French America feared that allowing such freedoms would weaken slavery. Because these colonies were more egalitarian for whites than their Iberian counterparts, poorer members of the enslaving class felt threatened by free coloured prosperity. For these reasons, proponents of the cultural argument contend, British and French colonies restricted the numbers and freedom of free coloureds.

In contrast, the second explanation argues that it was material conditions that shaped free coloured numbers and treatment in the Americas. Regardless of the culture, masters in every slave society had extra-legal power over their workers. Economic and environmental facts led masters to insist on keeping nearly all African-descended peoples and their descendants in slavery, or, alternatively, to allow slaves to amass savings, join a religious confraternity, or buy their own freedom. In Brazil, Spanish America and the Caribbean, profits from sugar, coffee and mining allowed many masters to pay easily for new slaves to replace manumitted workers, especially when a thriving slave trade provided ready access to captives. In North America, however, few planters were able to buy large crews of new Africans, making them then less likely to free their slaves.

This materialist explanation includes an environmental dimension. Where farm- or ranch-land was readily available, free people of African descent were more able to support large families, or to buy enslaved family members out of bondage, than their counterparts in areas where land was scarce. In the eighteenth century, this was the case in Brazil's Minas Gerais mining region, for example, or in the largest Caribbean islands such as Jamaica, Cuba or Saint-Domingue, all of which developed relatively large free populations of colour over time. On the other hand, when restricted to cities, free people of colour found it more difficult to build large families. This constraint helps explain why free coloured populations in the islands of Barbados or Martinique were pro-portionately smaller than in Jamaica or Saint-Domingue. In cities, prosperity was limited to those with a valuable skill or capital for large-scale trading.

The materialist explanation explains Latin America's large free populations of colour by pointing to the region's long history of slaveholding. Faced with the death of millions of Native Americans in the 1500s, Spanish and Portuguese colonies imported large numbers of Africans to work in sugar fields, silver mines and urban workshops. But by the end of the 1600s, these enterprises were less profitable, while the gradual rebound of Indian populations provided cheaper labour. As African slave labour became less valu-able within Iberian economies in the New World, masters appear to have manumitted more workers: free coloured populations began to increase in New Spain, Cuba, Santo Domingo and Brazil in the late 1600s. In the 1800s, therefore, when the profitability of Cuban sugar and Brazilian coffee led to renewed slave imports, these societies already had large free coloured populations. Therefore the co-existence of large numbers of slaves and free people of colour does not show that slavery was "more humane" in these countries, materialists contend. Rather, over a long time period, enslaved people in Latin America took advantage of slavery's declining profitability.

Historians and free people of colour

Looking beyond the stark contrasts among various slave regimes, historians have been drawn to a number of common elements in the lives of free people of colour. Six themes in particular stand out. The first of these is manumission, the legal process by which an enslaved person became free. Only a small percentage of slaves were ever freed, though historians have had difficulty coming up with even approximate "rates of manumission" for a given society. In most countries, there are neither comprehensive manumission records nor detailed slave censuses, especially in the rural areas where most slaves lived. Even for Brazil, with its large free population of colour, manumission rates in eighteenth century Bahia were close to 1 per cent annually.

A deed of manumission by an owner was often the result of a slave's long years of service in close proximity to the master. Most historians conclude that such freedom was less an act of generosity by the enslaver than a way of motivating enslaved workers to be loyal and diligent. Men and women in domestic service were most likely to be able to negotiate this kind of arrangement. Creoles were more likely to find freedom than Africans. In Latin American societies, self-purchase was the most common method of manumission. In some Spanish and Portuguese territories, bondspeople benefited from a customary arrangement known as *coartación* in which their enslaver agreed to gradually sell them their liberty at a pre-arranged price. The slave gradually paid sums to the master for his or her liberty. Even so, one scholar estimates that it took a Brazilian slave 37 years of work to accumulate the price of his or her freedom in eighteenth-century Bahia, Brazil, a period much longer than the life expectancy of most captives arriving from Africa (Schwartz, 1974: 630; on *coartación*, see de la Fuente, 2007).

Final testaments were another kind of document in which masters relinquished their property rights over a worker. Such freedoms were full of difficulties for the slave, however. Heirs often resisted losing property. And testators often granted only condi-tional freedom, obligating the enslaved person to continue to serve for a certain amount of time. Moreover, many societies required that owners and slaves obtain official permission for a freedom document, which might involve paying an expensive tax. A dying master might provide funds to pay these freedom taxes, but often the bondsman would have to solve this problem himself.

As this suggests, governments tried actively to shape manumission policies. The first version of France's *Code Noir*, promulgated in 1685, allowed masters to free their slaves at will. Drafted by European jurists who worried about master/slave concubinage, the *Code* encouraged masters to marry their slave mistresses, ordering that local officials confiscate a man's concubines and his slave children. If he married his slave, the *Code Noir* specified that she and any children born to the couple would automatically be free. In practice, few French slave owners took this step, and local authorities turned a blind eye to slave mistresses. In fact, in the 1720s and 1730s, administrators increasingly limited a master's right to free slaves, requiring official permission and then a tax. Nevertheless, in the 1780s, dozens of free people of colour in Saint-Domingue used the marriage loophole in the *Code* to free their sexual partners while avoiding the expensive manumission tax. Like whites, free people of colour regularly owned slaves to exploit their labour, but they also bought friends and family. Throughout the hemisphere, slaves found freedom thanks to the efforts of family members or friends. Even if they could not pay the costs of a formal manumission, such purchases constituted a major step towards freedom. In Brazil and various parts of Latin America, there were also confraternities and other societies that raised money to buy the freedom of members and their kin.

Manumission taxes allowed governments both to raise revenue and discourage masters from "abusing" their ability to free slaves. Recognizing that sexual relationships motivated many masters, some governments made manumission taxes more expensive for enslaved women than any other category of person. Yet governments also encouraged manumission when it suited their interests. A number of colonial states, including Brazil and Cuba, granted freedom to individual slaves in exchange for extraordinary military service, particularly in emergencies such as coastal attacks or slave rebellions. In some societies, men who lived in freedom but did not have liberty papers could earn these documents through service in the slave police. This measure was aimed at the many people who lived in a kind of grey area between slavery and freedom, risking re-enslavement because they lacked official papers.

The most striking fact about manumission is that in nearly all societies, roughly two-thirds of all freedom deeds went to women and children. Yet the role of sexuality in acquiring liberty is unclear. In most cases sexual contact between masters and slaves did not produce lasting bonds. Thomas Thistlewood, an eighteenth-century Jamaican colonist who carefully recorded his daily activities, used sexual violence as a tool to control his slaves. He had sex with 138 women over 37 years, nearly all of them his slaves or the property of other colonists. He freed only one of those women, Phibba, his common-law wife, and she had to wait six years after he died for liberty. Thistlewood's former employers owned Phibba, but he had managed to convince the same family to free the couple's son John when the child was only two.

Masters did not free all the children they fathered, although contemporaries described this as a social obligation in some slave societies. The evidence that we can obtain from plantation inventories in French Saint-Domingue shows that 2 to 5 per cent of the enslaved population had some white ancestry. This suggests that there were between 15,000 and 25,000 children of white men living in slavery in Saint-Domingue, a figure equivalent to the size of the colony's free people of colour. In other words, white men freed fewer than half of the slave children they fathered in Saint-Domingue. Similarly, a recent study of manumissions in Mexico City reveals that the women and children manumitted there were not as frequently freed by white men who may have been the child's father, as they were by elite white women, who came into contact with the slave mothers and children in domestic service (Proctor, 2006).

A second theme of free coloured experience that historians have explored is what might be called "the colour line", the set of laws and practices whites used to bar free people of colour from full citizenship. Spanish American societies discriminated against all people of African ancestry. In the late sixteenth and early seventeenth centuries, Mexico City's 8000 white residents were heavily outnumbered by the 60,000 Indians living just outside the city. But they were also outnumbered inside the city walls by approximately 9000 free and enslaved people of colour (Martinez, 2004). These free people of colour were required to pay special taxes; moreover, there were restrictions on how they could dress in public. They were shut out from university enrolment, and they could not have careers in the military or other respected occupations, although they did come to serve disproportionately in the colony's coastal militia (Vinson, 2001: 2–4).

Other colonies passed similar laws, but in the sixteenth and seventeenth centuries colonists and officials in many societies routinely violated or disregarded them. In the ethnically complicated societies of mainland Spanish America, the few prosperous families of mixed African, European or Indian ancestry were able to change the racial labels that officials used to describe them, gradually "promoting" themselves into categories where they faced less discrimination. *Gracias al sacar* dispensations institutionalized this unofficial process by allowing wealthy individuals to attend university, serve in military units or join elite church societies. British Jamaica had a similar procedure in its so-called "special bills". Over the course of the eighteenth century, the Jamaican House of Assembly approved dispensations for 128 free people of colour. These men and women, mostly the children of powerful planters, were exempted from specific racial disabilities, and might be granted the right to serve in "white" militia units, vote in local elections, or hold local office.

In the second half of the eighteenth century, however, a pseudo-scientific ideology of race began to replace this earlier, more flexible social system, in the French and British worlds especially. Reinforced by Enlightenment science and a new rhetoric of national identity after the Seven Years' War, the emphasis on biological definitions of race was also caused by events in the Caribbean. White unease after the great 1760 slave uprising known as Tacky's Revolt led Jamaica to impose to new restrictions on free people of colour. In Saint-Domingue, after whites and free coloureds joined forces in a 1769 revolt, new laws segregated public spaces and compelled all free coloureds, even those born free, to carry papers proving that they were not slaves. A 1773 law required that those with "white" family names adopt new names of "African origin".

A third historiographical theme has been the question of free coloured wealth. The vast majority of free people of colour across the hemisphere were poor, often desperately so. Slaves worked for decades to buy their own freedom, or that of family members, and citizens or officials often complained about ex-slaves who had no honest way to support themselves. Yet many slave societies feared free coloured wealth and restricted these people's ability to inherit property. A few descendants of slaves did become wealthy, however, and historical scholarship points to three sources for that wealth: social networks, entrepreneurship, and use of the law. Saint-Domingue had the eighteenth century's wealthiest free population of colour, including several hundred free coloured planters. The most notable figures of that class acquired at least some of their property through social connections, most notably inheritance. Other French colonies restricted free coloured inheritances, but Saint-Domingue never applied these laws. By the 1780s, some free families of colour were descended from two or even three generations of French ancestors, often immigrants who had married or partnered with landowning free women. Marriage alliances between propertied families and, for ex-slaves, patron–client relationships with wealthy whites, were critical for many free people of colour. Brazil's most famous and wealthy free woman of colour, Chica da Silva, was a former slave who became the mistress of an administrator and merchant in the diamond district of Minas Gerais. In New Spain, free coloured militia officers in the 1790s ranked among the local elite in towns such as Puebla, and over 27 per cent of those marrying in this decade married white women (Klein and Vinson, 2007: 207; Vinson, 2001: 60).

Most wealthy free coloureds were also entrepreneurs. Julien Raimond of Saint-Domingue inherited land and slaves from his French father in the 1760s. But he had to share the estate with seven siblings and with his mother, whose dowry had been the nucleus of the family plantation. After partnering with his brothers, Raimond doubled his property by marrying his first cousin; after she died, he married a wealthy free coloured widow. Yet he also bought up abandoned plantations and planted indigo, using the latest information and technology to produce a high-quality dye. Raimond, who may have been the wealthiest man of colour in the New World to be completely excluded from civil rights, controlled over 200 slaves in the mid 1780s. By 1782, the value of his colonial property, combined with that of his wife, was equivalent to 254,000 *livres tournois*, making him richer than 60 per cent of nobles in the French city of Toulouse (Mousnier, 1979: 189). The truth of his much-cited claim that free coloureds owned one-third of Saint-Domingue's slaves is debatable. But in Jamaica in 1832, free coloureds owned 70,000 out of the 310,000 enslaved people in the island (Allen, 1994: 235). In Brazil, Chica da Silva owned 104 slaves, manumitting only one of them (Furtado, 2009: 154).

The Caribbean also had a handful of wealthy free coloured merchants. Some, like Vincent Ogé of Saint-Domingue, benefited from family connections and a European education to become part-owner of a ship, to serve as a broker for expensive real estate, and to buy and sell French goods at a wholesale level. Yet entrepreneurs existed at a lower level, too. In 1837, Joseph Thorne of Barbados, an ex-slave who had become a shoemaker and merchant, was wealthy enough to afford a study with finely bound books, natural history specimens and elegant furniture (Newton, 2008: 62). Zabeau Bellanton, a free black woman in Cap Français, found a lucrative niche in the local slave trade by acquiring sick or extremely young slaves, strengthening them, and then reselling them at a considerable profit. The United States benefited from the entrepreneurial traditions of Caribbean free people of colour. Many of Saint-Domingue's free coloureds moved to the mainland during the Haitian Revolution. In the period 1830–65, 14 of the 21 wealthiest free black entrepreneurs in the USA had French names or were from New Orleans. The first millionaire of African ancestry in the United States, William Leidesdorf (1810–48), was the son of a sea captain from the Danish West Indies (Walker, 1986: 354–55).

A final ingredient of free coloured economic success was access to the law. Both Raimond and Ogé initiated lawsuits against whites or filed legal declarations to protect themselves from potential legal attacks. Hundreds of poorer free coloured plaintiffs in Saint-Domingue initiated lawsuits on the local level in the 1780s. Many of them won (Rogers, 1999: 352–63). Some appealed their cases as far as Versailles. In Brazil, there were perhaps hundreds of cases in which slaves and free people of colour successfully appealed to the Portuguese monarch for redress of abuses. On the other hand, some applicants specified that they had tried the law and, because of their low status, they were not heard. Others didn't have the money to use legal channels. In many of these cases they had legal documents, but masters disregarded their freedom papers or refused to let slaves buy their freedom as legally pre-arranged (Russell-Wood, 2000: 329).

A fourth interest of historians has been the political stance of free coloureds on the issue of slavery. Some free people of colour defended slavery, politically and militarily. Yet free coloureds were also among the most prominent anti-slavery voices. Most striking, thousands of free coloureds joined enslaved people in taking up arms against the institution. But in Cuba, Brazil, Saint-Domingue, Jamaica and Suriname, free men of colour served in militias and other units that tracked escaped slaves and policed the enslaved population. During slave rebellions, wealthy free men of colour who wanted to join the white elite defended slavery. In Saint-Domingue, the pro-slavery free coloured mayor of the city of Saint-Marc joined white planters in supporting a British invasion during the Haitian Revolution. In the aftermath of Barbados' 1816 slave rebellion, the island's wealthiest free men of colour described themselves as pro-slavery when given the right to testify in court (Newton, 2008, 77). Brazil's Francisco de Soles Tôrres Homem, a free man of colour who was Brazil's Minister of the Treasury in 1858–59, argued for the maintenance of slavery, though as a senator in 1870 he voted for the free womb law, which specified that all children born to slave mothers would be free.

Far more numerous were the intellectuals and propertied men and women of colour who worked against slavery on a local, national and even transatlantic context. Sometimes that abolitionism expressed itself in literary terms, as in the cases of Mary Prince, a former slave in the Bahamas and Caribbean; the Cuban poets Juan Francisco Manzano and Placido; or the Brazilian poet João da Cruz e Sousa. Some free coloured abolitionists, such as Frederick Douglass and Manzano, were former slaves; others were born free, but to families only recently emerged from slavery, such as Martin Delaney and David Walker, prominent US opponents of slavery. Julien Raimond of Saint-Domingue was a rare case, a freeborn planter who allied with French abolitionists in Paris to work for free coloured citizenship. In early 1793, one and a half years after the beginning of the slave revolt in the colony, Raimond came to the conclusion that the French Revolution in Saint-Domingue could survive only if it offered the enslaved population a path towards freedom. Antônio Pereira Rebouças of Bahia, Brazil was a similar figure. A freeborn man of colour who married the daughter of a wealthy merchant, he became a slave owner in the 1830s, though he would be a prominent abolitionist later (Spitzer, 1990: 115–16).

In addition, there were free coloured revolutionaries. Perhaps the most important of these was François Dominique Toussaint, who was born into slavery in Saint-Domingue, but achieved legal freedom by 1776. Probably the most influential man of African descent in the history of the Americas, Toussaint closely guarded the fact that he was a free man who had adopted the cause of rebel slaves. Toussaint was committed to the end of slavery, but as Saint-Domingue's governor in the late 1790s, he insisted that the ex-slaves continue to work on the plantations that had made the French colony so wealthy before 1791. This policy led to numerous revolts and made it easier for a French expeditionary force to defeat him in 1802. Especially in the wake of Toussaint's victories, free men of colour were implicated in the leadership of other rebellions or conspiracies against slavery in Venezuela (1795), Bahia [Brazil] (1798), Cuba (1812) and South Carolina (1822).

A fifth theme in the experience of free people of colour was their importance as cultural innovators. A few achieved fame for their contributions to European or Euro-Creole colonial cultures. Joseph de Boulogne of Guadeloupe and Saint-Domingue was renowned as a composer, violinist and swordsman in late eighteenth-century Paris. Much of what survives of Brazilian sacred music from the colonial period was written by free Brazilians of colour, most notably the priest and composer José Maurício Nunes Garcia (1769–1830) of Minas Gerais, sometimes described as "the most important composer living in the Americas during the colonial period".[3]

Because of the size of its free population of colour, the possibilities for social advancement available to light-skinned Brazilians of colour, and the long duration of slavery there, Brazil produced more outstanding cultural figures of African descent than any other American society. Joaquim Maria Machado de Assis (1839–1908), the son of a mulatto housepainter and a Portuguese washerwoman, is often described as the greatest of all Brazilian writers. Other celebrated Brazilian artists of colour were the sculptors Antônio Francisco Lisboa, known as Aleijadinho (1730–1814); Valentim da Fonseca e Silva (active 1773–97); and the painter Leandro Joaquim (c. 1738–98). All three men were also architects, known for their fountains and churches. Outside Brazil, other well known free coloured innovators include the Cuban poet Gabriel de la Concepcion Valdes, known as Placido (1809–44); the Mexican painters Juan Correa (1646–1716) and José de Ibarra (1688–1756); Boston's African-born poet Phyllis Wheatley (1754–84); and the Louisianan inventor Norbert Rillieux (1806–94).

Free people of colour were also culturally significant because they ranked among the most creolized people in any New World society. Their cultural worlds probably reflected traditions and skills of different African and European societies as well as distinctive local achievements in religion, music, language, plastic arts, cooking and medicine. But colonial societies, or even independent New World nations, ascribed little value to such forms of creole culture until long after the end of slavery. A few such figures are known, but their names are mostly preserved for their role within European-style institutions, like the religious leaders Richard Allen (Pennsylvania) and Rebecca Protten (Danish Virgin Islands).

Finally, historians have recently begun to investigate a sixth set of issues at the heart of free coloured identity: definitions of gender and sexuality. Brazil's Chica da Silva, a mulatto ex-slave who became the mistress of a wealthy white man in the 1750s, became famous after a 1975 film presented her as the embodiment of mulatta sexuality, neglecting to depict the fact that the couple had 13 children in 16 years of cohabitation (Furtado, 2009: 104, 122). In the Caribbean, white creoles and European visitors alike marvelled at the beautiful free women of colour whose white lovers, some implied, were powerless to resist them.

Women's ability to use their sexuality to escape slavery was the exception, not the rule. Nevertheless, free women were manumitted far more frequently than enslaved men, and paradoxically in some societies, such as Brazil, they may have experienced more legal and economic autonomy than white women. A number of women of colour became owners of land, businesses and slaves. In the town of Diamantina in the mining district of Minas Gerais, women of colour made up 86 per cent of the 511 household heads in the 1770s, while free black men made up only 31.5 per cent. While most of the men of colour practised a trade, most of Diamantina's women instead lived by leasing out their slaves (*ibid.*: 111, 131). While free from the marriage laws that subjected a wife to her husband's legal guardianship, unmarried free women of colour also had no legal claim on the property of the men they lived with. New social arrangements arose to address this situation, such as the *plaçage* agreements of nineteenth century New Orleans, in which wealthy white men agreed in advance to compensate their free coloured mistresses with property.

In many societies, the economic, cultural and demographic prominence of women within the free coloured population became part of the negative stereotypes attached to all members of this class. Whites associated free people of colour with sexual and social immorality of all kinds, setting aside their own part in these activities. Authorities used this supposed lack of virtue, which some writers by the late 1700s described as biologically predetermined by the mixture of African and European "blood", to explain why even freeborn wealthy people of colour deserved to be excluded from white society. The military provided one stereotypically male institution where whites depended on free coloured participation. Their military role gave men of colour a symbolic as well as practical tool to assert their masculine virtues, through bravery, loyalty and discipline.

Changes over time

Three sets of events transformed the social position and aspirations of free people of colour throughout the New World. The most important was the Haitian Revolution (1791–1804), which in succession admitted free people of colour to citizenship, eliminated slavery, and finally became a successful war of independence. Such independence wars, taken as a group, constitute a second set of events with profound consequences for free people of colour, beginning with the struggle against Britain in North America (1775–83) and ending with Cuba's unsuccessful 10 Years' War against Spain (1868–78). The British anti-slavery movement constituted a third set of events that encouraged free coloured abolitionists, but put new pressures on free people of colour in Cuba and Brazil.

The decade-long struggle over racism and slavery in French Saint-Domingue was the single most important event in the history of the hemisphere for free people of colour. In Paris, Julien Raimond brought France's fledgling anti-slavery movement into his struggle against colonial racism. In 1791, Raimond and the *Amis des noirs* convinced French Revolutionary legislators that wealthy freeborn men of colour were worthy of citizenship. Saint-Domingue's colonists refused to accept this, and, as whites and free coloureds fought, slaves rose in a massive and well coordinated rebellion. Contemporaries accused free coloureds of prompting this uprising, and some biographers suggest that the freedman Toussaint of Breda may have been involved, though there is no hard evidence of this. He and other free men were part of the rebellion's leadership at the end of 1791, though most free coloureds continued to fight for their class alone, against the whites.

In 1792, France extended citizenship to all free men of colour. In 1793, the commissioners sent to Saint-Domingue to integrate free coloureds into the Revolution acknowledged the end of slavery by proclaiming emancipation, as they struggled against near-simultaneous British and Spanish invasions and against colonial counter-revolution. In February 1794, the French Revolutionary government ratified this act and extended emancipation to all French territories. Within six months, Toussaint, now calling himself Louverture or "the opening", brought his black soldiers into the French army, taking a place alongside lighter-skinned free coloured officers who had been co-opted earlier.

Once slavery was over, the former free coloured and ex-slave populations took new names, *anciens libres* and *nouvaux libres*, respectively. In 1802, Napoleon sent a massive French invasion to remove Toussaint, who in eight years had made himself governor. Yet Bonaparte's generals were suspicious of the *anciens libres* and their attempts to disarm the population alienated the *nouvaux libres*. Both populations united against the French, and on 1 January 1804 Jean-Jacques Dessalines, an ex-slave, declared national independence.

The changes in Saint-Domingue/Haiti affected free people of colour throughout the Atlantic world in four ways. Many of the revolts and conspiracies involving free and enslaved people of colour in the early 1800s had multiple causes, including declining troop levels as the Spanish and British pulled regiments from the colonies to fight Napoleon. But the example of Haiti inspired several conspiracies, notably a conspiracy in Curaçao (1795); a 1799 revolt in Cartagena; in modern-day Venezuela the Coro (1795) and Maracaibo (1799) uprisings; the Denmark Vesey conspiracy in South Carolina (1808); and the Aponte Rebellion in Cuba (1812). In Brazil, Cuba, Jamaica, Brazil, Gran Colombia and the United States, new free coloured political activism appears to be linked to news of Haiti.

Second, Haiti proclaimed itself as a refuge for "blacks", a term its government defined to include not only Africans, but Native Americans. By far the largest group who went to Haiti were between 6000 and 13,000 free people of colour from the USA in the 1820s, followed by another wave in the 1840s. They came with a certain amount of support from US whites, including the American Colonization Society, which was also attempting to send free blacks to Africa. While American free blacks established a colony in West Africa, which eventually became the nation of Liberia, British whites and free coloured abolitionists mounted two similar projects in the neighbouring territory, which is today the nation of Sierra Leone. There they resettled free blacks from London and Nova Scotia in the 1780s and 1790s.

As these examples suggest, the Haitian Revolution may also have made life more difficult for free people of colour. One scholar concludes that its impact remains "deeply ambiguous". There is no consensus on whether free coloureds in Jamaica and elsewhere saw Haiti as an example to follow or avoid (Geggus, 2001: 249). Many whites saw Haiti as proof that a multiracial society could not survive after slavery. Manumission rates in the new United States had surged after independence, and they now fell back dramatically. New laws in the US South, the British Caribbean, northern Brazil and the Spanish Caribbean restricted free coloured movements and gatherings.

Fourth, the end of enslaved labour in the Caribbean's largest sugar producer revived the sugar industry in many regions, especially Brazil and Cuba, where renewed sugar planting helped sustain the slave trade into the middle of the 1800s. In the United States, cotton plantation slavery expanded west, thanks in part to Napoleon's sale of the Louisiana territory to the USA, a direct consequence of the Haitian Revolution.

Wars of national independence were a second set of events that transformed the lives of free people of colour. Beginning with the American Revolution and continuing into the nineteenth centuries for most Latin American countries, these wars created a demand for soldiers. Revolutionaries also waged an ideological battle to win local people to their side, and this included explicit and implicit promises to correct the racial inequalities of colonial society. Many free men of colour became soldiers and even officers, paving the way for them to acquire citizenship and even non-military leadership roles after independence. One of the best known is Vicente Guerrero, who became Mexico's third president in 1829, abolishing slavery in that country.

Cuba is the best example of a struggling independence movement that found a potent source of strength in free coloured soldiers. The inconclusive 10 Years' War (1868–78) began on a plantation, when the white planter Carlos Manuel de Céspedes freed his slaves as a symbolic gesture. The identification of the independence movement with anti-slavery and anti-racism attracted men of colour, so that by 1872 they made up at least one-half of the rebel army. One of them, Antonio Maceo, became a leading general, and even his mother, a free Afro-Cuban woman, joined the rebel army. Like her son, Mariana Grajales became a powerful symbol of free coloured patriotism. Pro-Spanish forces used the diverse composition of the rebel forces as a powerful propaganda tool, playing on white fears that without Spain the island would become "another Haiti". Although this racial tension was a key factor in the failure of the war, the conflict nevertheless established the patriotism of Cuban free coloureds. When the struggle began again in 1895, after the 1886 abolition of slavery, Afro-Cubans were again at the fore-front. In a similar way, the actions of free coloured soldiers in the US Civil War (1861–65) and in the Brazilian army during the equally bloody War of the Triple Alliance (1864–70) won them new respect in some quarters.

A third set of events was the rise of anti-slavery activity in Great Britain. In 1772 a High Court decision ended slavery in the British Isles, freeing more than 10,000 enslaved workers. From this date, British abolitionism was an inspiration and source of assistance to free coloured activists. As the British movement moved from opposition to the slave trade to anti-slavery, pressure from British abolitionists helped free coloureds in the British West Indies get civil rights in the 1820s. In 1811 and 1813, free coloureds in Barbados and Jamaica, respectively, began petitioning for the right to give evidence in court. But it was only in the early 1820s, as abolitionists in London pushed for laws to improve slave conditions, that colonial whites began to respond. Finally, in 1832 all qualified free coloured and black men were allowed to vote.

After the Napoleonic wars, Britain's efforts to force an end to all transatlantic slave trading had a powerful effect on the lives of free coloureds, especially in Brazil. With the country's coffee sector in a period of rapid growth, neither planters nor the Brazilian government wanted to stop the slave trade. So from the 1830s to the 1850s, Brazilians purchased 700,000 captive Africans, despite the fact that the Brazilian government had passed a law emancipating all Africans smuggled into the country after 1831. Authorities simply did not enforce the 1831 law, but its existence made it impossible to produce legal records of slave sales. Because there was no way to prove, legally, that a given African in Brazil was being enslaved, there was also no way of proving, legally, that he or she was free. The 1831 anti-slavery law, ironically, made freedom far more precarious than it would otherwise have been for thousands of people. It may have led to the re-enslavement of free coloureds whose neighbours, friends or patrons could not convince the police that they were free.

The label "free people of colour" was a social and legal invention designed to ensure that ex-slaves and their descendants did not join the master class. Some societies did allow "free coloureds", especially wealthy, light-skinned people with powerful relatives, to enjoy some of the privileges of elite status. But in the later 1700s and 1800s, a new "scientific" idea of race justified Europe's colonial slave systems, teaching that Africans and their descendants possessed a kind of biological inferiority that could never be overcome. In nearly all Atlantic societies, this idea survived for more than a century after the end of slavery itself.

Although free people of colour were a far smaller and more privileged group than slaves, the story of their lives and of the institutions that tried to define them is a critical part of the history of slavery. For while slavery itself can be explained as a labour system, the history of the label "free coloured" shows how masters and the governments that supported them developed concepts of racial difference and tools of discrimination that far outlasted bondage.

Notes

1 This essay uses the term "free people of colour" to describe all people who were reputed to have some degree of African ancestry but who lived in freedom. It reserves the term "freedmen" for men and women who were ex-slaves.
2 These terms are *ahorrimiento*, a Spanish word meaning manumission; the Spanish *carta de ahorro* or Portuguese *carta de alforria*, referring to liberty papers; and *horro*, or ex-slave in Spanish.
3 Moehn (2005: 466) cites Henry L. Crowl's liner notes to a 1998 recording of Garcia's *Officium 1816*, Graham Griffiths, Camerato Novo Horizonte de Sao Paulo (Paulus 00068–2).

Bibliography

Allen, Theodore, *The Invention of the White Race* (London, New York: Verso, 1994).
Bergad, Laird W., *The Comparative Histories of Slavery in Brazil, Cuba, and the United States* (New York: Cambridge University Press, 2007).
Berlin, Ira, *Slaves Without Masters: The Free Negro in the Antebellum South* (New York: Pantheon Books, 1974).
Childs, Matt D., *The 1812 Aponte Rebellion in Cuba and the Struggle against Atlantic Slavery* (Chapel Hill: University of North Carolina Press, 2006).
Cohen, David W. and Greene, Jack P., *Neither Slave Nor Free: The Freedman of African Descent in the Slave Societies of the New World* (Baltimore: Johns Hopkins University Press, 1972).
Cox, Edward, *Free Coloureds in the Slave Societies of Grenada and St. Kitts and Grenada, 1763–1833* (Knoxville: University of Tennessee Press, 1984).
Ferrer, Ada, *Insurgent Cuba: Race, Nation, and Revolution, 1868–1898* (Chapel Hill: University of North Carolina Press, 1999).
de la Fuente, Alejandro, "Slave Law and Claims-making in Cuba: The Tannenbaum Debate Revisited", *Law and History Review* 22 (2004), 339–69.
——, "Slaves and the Creation of Legal Rights in Cuba: Coartación and Papel", *Hispanic American Historical Review* 87 (2007), 659–92.
Furtado, Júnia Ferreira, *Chica da Silva: A Brazilian Slave of the Eighteenth Century* (Cambridge, New York: Cambridge University Press, 2009).
Garrigus, John D., *Before Haiti: Race and Citizenship in Saint-Domingue* (New York: Palgrave Macmillan, 2006).
Geggus, David P., "Epilogue", in Geggus, David Patrick, ed., *The Impact of the Haitian Revolution in the Atlantic World* (Columbia: University of South Carolina Press, 2001).
Handler, Jerome S., *The Unappropriated People: Freedmen in the Slave Society of Barbados* (Baltimore: Johns Hopkins University Press, 1974).

Heuman, Gad J., *Between Black and White: Race, Politics, and the Free Coloreds in Jamaica, 1792–1865* (Westport, CT: Greenwood Press, 1981).

Katzew, Ilona, *Casta Painting: Images of Race in Eighteenth-Century Mexico* (New Haven, CT: Yale University Press, 2005).

Klein, Herbert S., "American Slavery in Recent Brazilian Scholarship, with Emphasis on Quantitative Socio-economic Studies", *Slavery & Abolition* 30 (2009), 111–33.

Klein, Herbert S. and Vinson, Ben, *African Slavery in Latin America and the Caribbean*, 2nd edn (New York: Oxford University Press, 2007).

Martinez, Maria Elena, "The Black Blood of New Spain: Limpieza de Sangre, Racial Violence, and Gendered Power in Early Colonial Mexico", *William and Mary Quarterly* 61 (2004), 479–520.

Moehn, Frederick, "Colonial-era Brazilian Music: A Review Essay of Recent Recordings", *Notes: Quarterly Journal of the Music Library Association* 62 (2005).

Mousnier, Roland, *The Institutions of France Under the Absolute Monarchy, 1598–1789*, trans. Brian Pearce (Chicago: University Of Chicago Press, 1979).

Newton, Melanie J., *The Children of Africa in the Colonies: Free People of Color in Barbados in the Age of Emancipation* (Baton Rouge: Louisiana State University Press, 2008).

Proctor, Frank Trey, III, "Gender and the Manumission of Slaves in New Spain", *Hispanic American Historical Review* 86 (2006), 309–36.

Régent, Frédéric, *La France et ses esclaves: De la colonisation aux abolitions (1620–1848)* (Paris: Grasset & Fasquelle, 2007).

Rogers, Dominique, "Les libres de couleur dans les capitales de Saint-Domingue: Fortune, mentalités et intégration à la fin de l'Ancien Régime (1776–89)" (Doctorat, Université de Bordeaux III, 1999).

Russell-Wood, A. J. R., "'Acts of Grace': Portuguese Monarchs and Their Subjects of African Descent in Eighteenth-Century Brazil", *Journal of Latin American Studies* 32 (2000), 307–32.

Schwartz, Stuart B., "The Manumission of Slaves in Colonial Brazil, Bahia, 1684–1745", *Hispanic American Historical Review* 54 (1974), 603–35.

Spitzer, Leo, *Lives in Between: Assimilation and Marginality in Austria, Brazil, and West Africa, 1780–1945* (Cambridge: Cambridge University Press, 1990).

Stella, Alessandro, *Histoires d'esclaves dans la péninsule ibérique*, Recherches d'histoire et de sciences sociales, 92 (Paris: Ed. de l'Ecole des Hautes Etudes en Sciences Sociales, 2000).

Tannenbaum, Frank, *Slave and Citizen: The Classic Comparative Study of Race Relations in the Americas* (Boston: Beacon Press, 1992).

Vinson, Ben, *Bearing Arms for His Majesty: The Free-Colored Militia in Colonial Mexico* (Palo Alto, CA: Stanford University, 2001).

Walker, Juliet E. K., "Racism, Slavery, and Free Enterprise: Black Entrepreneurship in the United States Before the Civil War", *Business History Review* 60 (1986), 343–82.

15

RACE RELATIONS IN
SLAVE SOCIETIES

Timothy James Lockley

The roughly 10 million Africans transported forcibly to the Americas between 1500 and 1850 were thrust headlong into a bewildering variety of different environments. Some cleared the jungles of South America, others grew sugar on small Caribbean islands, while a smaller number laboured in rice fields and tobacco farms, or on the wharves of ports on the North American mainland. In all these locations, enslaved Africans added to a pre-existing mix of Native Americans, immigrant Europeans and their descendants. Enslaved Africans were never completely isolated from these other populations, although in several Caribbean islands and in the coastal regions of South Carolina and Georgia nine out of ten individuals were enslaved (Goveia, 1965: 203). Historians writing on slavery have scrutinised the lives of the enslaved in detail, carefully documenting, amongst other things, religious experiences, family formation, cultural expression and resistance. Where historians have studied how slaves interacted with other people, they have concentrated on the master/mistress–slave relationship, exploring themes such as paternalism, hegemony and capitalism. The importance of the interaction between owners and the enslaved cannot be underestimated, since the master determined the amount of work required from slaves, the amounts of food and clothing dispensed, and how punishment would be determined and delivered. Trevor Burnard, in Chapter 11 of this volume, explores this relationship in depth.

Yet such approaches make it easy to overlook the encounters that enslaved people throughout the Americas had with people who were neither fellow slaves nor owners. The number of non-slaveholding whites was particularly large in North America, and even in the southern states they outnumbered slaveholders by three to one. Elsewhere in the Americas, Kingston, Havana, Bridgetown and Rio de Janeiro all had an artisanal class that encountered slaves on a daily basis. The 1834 census of Rio de Janeiro, for instance, documented *c.* 8000 white men of "lower status", including *c.* 4000 artisans, 900 street sellers and 1000 servants. A further 500 white women with low-status occupations were recorded in the Rio census. In Savannah, Georgia, more than 1500 white women were recorded as working in the 1860 census, including nearly 300 servants and 45 washerwomen, occupations they shared with free black and enslaved women (Karasch, 1987, 69–73; Lockley, 2002: 102–120). Poorer whites were often concentrated in urban environments since port cities were not only the point of arrival for new European immigrants. Ports also had the critical mass of population required for artisans to find sufficient work, as well as being favoured locations for factories and shipyards that offered employment.

Outside towns, a small number of whites continued to work their own farms on a subsistence basis. George Pinkard, visiting Barbados in the early nineteenth century, documented the existence of white farmers "who obtain a scanty livelihood by cultivating a small patch of earth, and breeding up poultry, or what they term stock for the markets".[1] These white Barbadians were also known as "Redlegs" and were descendants of the original indentured settlers of the island in the seventeenth century. By the time of the abolition of slavery in 1834 an estimated 8000 "Redlegs" lived in Barbados, working as servants or artisans or on small subsistence farms. In Antigua, by contrast, one visitor in 1774 noted that "everybody in town is on a level as to station", while in Jamaica the number of poor white farmers was very small since the strong demand for white overseers resulted in high wages that enabled most overseers to purchase their own slaves fairly quickly. Not without reason was it known as the "best poor man's country" (Goveia, 1965: 213; Burnard, 2004: 247–48). In Brazil, non-slaveholders constituted more than half of the white rural population, and on the North American mainland non-slaveholding farmers dominated certain parts of the southern United States, especially in the mountainous regions of western North Carolina and Virginia and eastern Tennessee and Kentucky. In these parts, only about 10 per cent of whites owned slaves. Yet even in the coastal lowcountry of the American South, where some wealthy planters counted their enslaved property in the hundreds, poor whites continued to subsist "on other men's land, or government districts – always the swamp or the pine barren", eking out a miserable subsistence on poor-quality lands (Klein and Luna, 2000: 937; Inscoe, 1989; Lockley, 2001: 26–27). In areas with large slave populations, such as coastal areas of North and South America, and the larger Caribbean islands, these poorer whites had numerous opportunities to interact with enslaved people. This chapter examines the significance and importance of these unofficial, and often clandestine, interactions.

Overseers

For the vast majority of plantation slaves, the non-slaveholding white they most frequently encountered was the overseer. The job of the overseer in the seventeenth and eighteenth centuries had been relatively respectable, and sometimes was taken by young men in order to learn the planting business. Those such as Thomas Thistlewood in Jamaica, or Roswell King in Georgia, perhaps started overseeing as men with modest means, but were able to earn sufficient money to buy their own land and slaves. By the nineteenth century, however, it was more common for overseers to be men of relatively low social status, willing to work on short-term contracts for comparatively little money in the heat of the plantations, while owners retreated to more comfortable coastal or mountain homes. John Luffmann, visiting Antigua in the 1780s, noted that the overseers were "generally poor Scotch lads" who had originally come over as indentured servants. Some slaves accurately described their overseers as "poor white trash" (Lockley, 2001: 32).[2]

Overseers had an awkward role: their position depended on their ability to deliver a crop that could be sold. So long as they did that, few owners concerned themselves with how it was done. In pursuit of this end, overseers would use the whip to get the most work out of the slaves, and the accounts of former slaves are replete with stories of the abuse regularly meted out by brutal overseers. Yet enslaved people were not completely powerless in the face of a brutal overseer. Excessive violence by an overseer, particularly when it led to the death of a slave, could land the overseer in court and even in jail, at least in the antebellum United States, and on occasion courts were prepared to support slaves who defended themselves from unprovoked attacks by overseers. In 1847 an Alabama slave was sentenced to death following a fight with his overseer that ended with both bloodied and bruised. The case went to the Alabama supreme court, where the death sentence was overturned on the grounds that a "defenceless" slave could offer a "self-defence" plea despite the law clearly stating that he was "forbidden to resist". The court ordered that the slave be re-tried on a lesser charge of "mayhem" that would not have merited a death sentence.[3]

There were other, less violent, methods used by slaves to undermine the overseer's position. Plantation tools could be "accidentally broken", rice fields could be drained or flooded at the wrong time, and the sugar harvest could proceed slowly with a portion of the crop lost to the first frost. All of this damaged the profitability of the plantation and endangered the position of the overseer. Some slaves would even risk a personal appeal to the benevolence of the owner over the head of the overseer. Since slaves represented an economic asset, it was not unknown for owners to protect those "assets" at the expense of the overseer's job. If an overseer wished to keep his position, he had to tread a fine line between using sufficient coercion to produce a crop, but not enough to lead to a complete breakdown of plantation discipline. Where overseers were permitted to use a portion of the plantation for their own crops, paying the slaves to work the land on Sundays, there was an even greater incentive for them to treat the slaves relatively well. In Antigua, John Luffmann saw overseers using "the ground of their employers" to raise "stock of every kind. ... they also grow exotics as well as vegetables natural to the climate" and crucially "they employ the slaves belonging to the plantation to vend such produce". Similarly, in South Carolina, Charles Ball's overseer hired 20 slaves on Sundays to work on his own land, "for which he gave them fifty cents each".[4] This economic dependency would have acted as a further check on the behaviour of overseers.

Economic relations

Away from the plantation, slaves working on hire regularly found themselves labouring alongside whites. One particularly experienced slave in Tennessee was hired out as a farm-manager by his master, and to his surprise found himself in charge of white labourers, recalling that "'Bossing' white hands and working with them, so as to make their labors profitable for my employer, was no easy task".[5] Cotton mills, iron forges and construction projects normally employed white labour in managerial or supervisory positions, though Irish immigrants in North America often did exactly the same work as the slaves, especially when it involved digging canals and laying railroads. Industrial work like this did not occur in every part of the Americas, and the scope for bi-racial interaction was limited by the managerial roles often taken by whites, that effectively recreated the racial divisions on the plantation. More widespread were the shops and other service industries in towns and cities that employed black and white workers on the same terms. Far from all chambermaids, shop assistants or artisans were black, and despite a widespread belief among elite whites that menial work would not be done by white people, there is sufficient evidence that poorer whites did a considerable amount of labouring work.

Poorer white residents often complained loudly about the competition they experienced from enslaved labourers, carpenters and blacksmiths. Slaves who were permitted to hire their own time by their owners in return for a weekly fee could afford to undercut white workers, since they did not have to support their enslaved family from their wages. In 1760, the South Carolina Grand Jury presented "as a grievance, negroes being allowed to make and sell bread, cakes, and many other articles, which prevents poor white people from getting a livelihood by such employment".[6] In 1793, the Master Coopers of Charleston complained to the South Carolina legislature "that at present as well as considerable time past the slaves of Charleston have been priviledged (although illegally) to sell, traffick, and barter, as well as to carry on different trades and occupations (free from direction or superintendence of any white person whatever) to their own emolument, and the great and manifest injury of the mechanical part of the community, selling their commodities and working at their trades much lower, and at much cheaper rates, than those persons who are priviledged by their citizenship and qualified from their former apprenticeship to exercise the different mechanical branches can possibly afford". The subsequent bill that would have protected the rights of white workers was ultimately voted down in the legislature.[7] The shoemaker's guild in Rio de Janeiro protested about exactly the same competition in 1813, but also to no avail (Karasch, 1987: 201). Since masters earned an easy income from the hire of surplus slaves, and since other whites benefited from the downward pressure on prices this competition engendered, the concerns of white artisans were rarely heeded. Laws that granted monopolies to white workers, for instance a 1770 Barbados law granting whites exclusive rights to sell goods on the street, and a 1758 Georgia law excluding slaves from all artisan trades, only ever operated for a set period and invariably were not renewed (Jones, 2007: 17; Lockley, 2001: 68–69). The competition between white and black artisans was a chronic problem, and it was only after the abolition of slavery removed the self-interest of slaveholders that white workers found their position receiving legislative support.

Only some of the economic interaction between slaves and non-slaveholding whites involved competition. As numerous scholars of the "informal" slave economy have established, slaves had some time to themselves in the evenings and on Sundays, time that was often spent growing crops, making items for sale, or hiring themselves out for wages. These activities created many opportunities to meet non-slaveholding whites. Slaves with items to sell often found that poor whites were willing trading partners, bartering alcohol, tobacco or other small luxury items in return for milk, eggs, chickens and fresh vegetables. The Rev. Richard Bickell described those selling at the marketplace in Kingston, Jamaica as "Jews with shops and standings as at a fair, selling old and new clothes, trinkets and small wares at a cent, per cent, to adorn the Negro person, there were some low Frenchmen and Spaniards and people of colour, in petty shops and with stalls; some selling their bad rum, gin, tobacco, etc.; others salt provision and small articles of dress, and many bartering with the slave or purchasing his surplus provision to retail again."[8]

Slaves living on plantations near towns such as Kingston, Savannah and Charleston established Sunday markets where they almost monopolised the sale of fresh foodstuffs. Some white urban residents complained about the high prices charged by enslaved vendors in these markets. In Savannah in 1818, the Grand Jury cited "as an evil of great magnitude the ordinance granting badges to colored and black women, for the purpose of hawking about articles for sale. These women monopolise in divers ways, many of the necessaries of life, which are brought to our market, by which the price is greatly enhanced, and the poor inhabitants of our city, proportionately distressed". Since masters themselves, however, rarely went to the market, preferring to send their domestic slaves instead, little was done to regulate prices.[9]

Criminal relations

The economic freedom afforded to slaves provided them with the opportunity to undermine the system that enslaved them. Slaves resisted their enslavement in numerous ways, some subtle and almost unnoticed, others overt and violent. Theft, for example, was a frequent form of slave resistance. Several scholars have described the moral economy whereby slaves rationalised these acts as a "redistribution" of goods among the master's property, or by claiming that since masters were guilty of stealing slaves from Africa, they could hardly complain when their own property was purloined. Stolen consumable items were most likely eaten quickly by the culprits, or shared among friends, thus disposing of the evidence. Other items, such as plantation tools or cotton, rice or sugar, that were obviously part of the main cash crop, had to be sold or bartered, and this proved to be a crucial nexus of interaction between slaves and poor whites.

The customary trading activities of slaves in the Sunday markets of town and cities throughout the Americas provided a suitable cover for a trade in stolen goods. Typically, slaves would receive either small amounts of cash, or goods such as alcohol or tobacco, in return for the goods they had stolen. The shopkeepers and traders who purchased these items would almost certainly have known they were stolen, but they were willing to collude with the slaves for two reasons. First, they paid a fraction of the true value for the stolen items, and thus would be able to sell them on at a significant profit. Edward Long said Jewish shopkeepers in Jamaica profited from slaves "by giving but a trifling value of their goods".[10] Second, the chances of shopkeepers getting caught were negligible. Since slave laws in the Americas rarely afforded slaves the right to testify in court against a white man, masters had great difficulties in proving any offence had taken place, unless they had witnessed it themselves. The *Charleston Standard* bemoaned the fact that "the negroes will steal and trade, as long as white persons hold out to them temptations to steal and bring to them. Three-fourths of the persons who are guilty, you can get no fine from; and, if they have some property, all they have to do is to confess a judgment to a friend, go to jail, and swear out".[11] Since slaves often traded such items at night, and via "secret" back doors, the chance of being observed by a white man was small. The economic incentives for shopkeepers, who rarely owned slaves themselves, easily outweighed any sense of racial duty to keep slaves in subjection. If a slave went home drunk and incapable of work, it was the master's problem, not the shopkeeper's.

The illicit trade between poor whites and slaves was not only confined to the urban markets. French officials in Saint Domingue complained in 1697 about various "bad-intentioned individuals" who purchased items from slaves "without troubling to find out where the slaves could have obtained these goods". This trading most often took place at night and in secret, and was so commonplace "that the public markets were poorly attended" (Hall, 1971: 67). Henry Bibb recalled that in rural Kentucky, local poor whites encouraged "slaves to steal from their owners, and sell to them corn, wheat, sheep, chickens, or anything of the kind which they can well conceal".[12] In Louisiana and coastal South Carolina and Georgia, white boatmen would use the network of rivers and creeks to land on a remote part of an estate in order to trade with slaves. The Georgetown, South Carolina Grand Jury singled out "the traffic carried on by negroes in boats upon our rivers, under the protection of white men of no character" as a matter of public concern in 1818. There was little chance of such traders being caught by the plantation owner and, if challenged, any incriminating evidence could swiftly be disposed over the side of the boat (McDonald, 1993: 71).[13] Where slaves traded key parts of plantation machinery used in the processing of cotton, sugar or rice, they disrupted production and ultimately hurt the master where it most mattered – in his pocket.

Masters made various attempts to control the illicit trade between white shopkeepers and slaves. Some attempted to limit the trading activities of their slaves, but soon found that dissent increased markedly on the plantation. Attempts were made to close Sunday markets, often cloaked in Sabbatarianism, though this just shifted trading activities to Saturday afternoons. Some local authorities even altered the law to permit the testimony of a slave against a white shopkeeper, declaring "it shall be taken for granted, (such probability appearing) that such persons are guilty". One shopkeeper in Charleston, South Carolina appealed his conviction for illegal trading to the state supreme court. After hearing evidence that "one Sunday morning there was a concourse of negroes about defendant's shop; that they continued in and about it during nearly two hours ... Defendant kept his gate closed and, from time to time, opened it to let negroes in or out", the court upheld his conviction stating "a presumption against the defendant, as imposed on him the necessity of proving that the negroes ... were not there unlawfully". Laws presuming the guilt of white defendants went against the very ethic of a slave society: consequently, few juries of their peers were willing to convict shopkeepers on slave testimony alone.[14]

Despairing of legal and official channels, some masters turned to extra-legal methods, banding together to destroy the homes and businesses of those "known" to be trading illegally with their slaves. One poor white man, living near Charles Ball's plantation in South Carolina, was suspected of purchasing stolen cotton from the slaves since "the overseer regarded the circumstance, that black people often called at his house, as conclusive evidence that he held criminal intercourse with them". When a search of the man's cabin revealed nothing, "the few articles of miserable furniture that the cabin contained, including a bed, made of flags, were thrown into a heap in the corner, and fire was set to the dwelling by the overseer". Ball's master proclaimed that "he had routed one receiver of stolen goods out of the country, and that all others of his character ought to be dealt with in the same manner".[15] In 1836, Mississippi newspapers reported that "there has lately been some *lynching* of some shop keepers ... for selling whiskey to and harbouring negroes. Each of the lynched received about one hundred lashes".[16]

Some poor whites went from being passive recipients of stolen goods to become more active participants in criminal activity with slaves. One young white sailor in colonial New York was quick to tell "some Negroes of very suspicious characters" with whom he had a "familiar acquaintance ... where they might have a fine booty, if they could manage cleverly to come at it" (Zabin, 2004: 47–48). In Savannah eighteenth-year-old Henry Forsythe and a slave, George, conspired together to steal more than a $100 from their employer, Savannah cabinet-maker Isaac Morell. Apprehended 135 miles away in

Augusta, Forsythe spent three years in jail for his part in this particular inter-racial conspiracy (Lockley, 1997: 57–72). Once caught and imprisoned, black and white prisoners were not above plotting joint escapes. One fugitive slave lodged in Georgetown jail escaped with a white prisoner "through a hole in the roof". The fact that the pair "had the range of the jail and were not locked up a night" certainly made their escape easier.[17] These marginalised whites evidently had few qualms about joining forces with slaves.

Much of the criminal interaction between slaves and poor whites was opportunistic and motivated by personal financial gain, but some might be classed as altruistic. Some whites wrote passes for slaves, that were subsequently used in an attempt to escape slavery. Others offered food and shelter to runaways out of sympathy for their plight, though if caught such individuals were often charged with "slave stealing", as it seemed incomprehensible to courts that someone would voluntarily help slaves escape. Those convicted of "harboring" a slave faced fines and possible jail sentences: a study of such individuals in North Carolina concludes that the only common factor they shared was their poverty (Forret, 2006: 137). For these poor whites, we can speculate that friend-ships, perhaps built up over a long period of time via a trading relationship or by working alongside each other, acted to break down racial barriers and stereotypes. Such individuals understood that their respective situations were not dissimilar and that they were both exploited by the white elite. It should be stressed that only a minority of poor whites came to this conclusion. Few, however personally sympathetic, genuinely desired to see all slaves freed.

At the most extreme end of the spectrum of bi-racial resistance were whites who joined together with slaves in violent opposition to the established regime. In 1663, slaves and white indentured servants in Virginia planned a joint revolt, and after Bacon's Rebellion in 1676 a mixed force of slaves and white servants held out longest against royal troops sent to restore order (Phillips, 1918: 472; Morgan, 1975: 269). While it was perhaps predictable that servants and slaves experiencing similar conditions would make common cause, less understandable were instances when free white people plotted with, or were suspected of plotting with, slaves to murder owners and destroy property. A white publican, John Hughson, and his wife were executed in New York in 1741 for supplying arms to slaves for an aborted rebellion. The plotters had used Hughson's pub, where whites and blacks freely intermingled, as the place to plan their rebellion. It was for this disregard for racial boundaries, as much as for the plot itself, that Hughson lost his life. The judge remarked that Hughson and his wife were "guilty not only of making Negroes their equals, but even their superiors, by waiting upon, keeping with, and entertaining them with meat, drink and lodging" (Hoffer, 2003: 62–64, 113). In 1821, a Virginia woman reported an "elderly white man ... who she understood was a gardener" to the state authorities after overhearing him telling a slave "that you all ought to be free, that a little time after three o'clock was the time" (cited in Johnston, 1932: 162). In the decades leading up to the American Civil War, nervous slave owners saw abolitionist agitators behind every corner and lashed out against suspicious characters. Whites who were recent immigrants, who had weak ties to the community, and who may have been involved in clandestine trading activities with slaves were lynched with increasing reg-ularity. Several white men were lynched in Mississippi in 1835, accused of plotting a large slave rebellion, while in 1860 "local farmers and artisans" in Texas had to endure a bout of lynching directed at covert abolitionists.[18]

Planned inter-racial violence did not always need to be writ large, striking against the system of slavery; it could also be personal, aimed at a particular slaveholder. In Georgia, a 31-year-old white carpenter, William Howell, attempted to persuade his enslaved "paramour", Sarah, to poison her master, and provided her with strychnine and arsenic to accomplish the task. After Sarah refused to do it, William took it upon himself to add the poison to the water used to make morning coffee for the master and his family. The dosage was not fatal, and suspicion quickly fell upon Sarah. In order to save his lover, William confessed to the crime, but the court determined that even her small part in "the most diabolical crime known" merited execution. As for Howell, he was jailed for seven years for "attempting to induce a slave to crime", and died in prison the following year (McNair, 2009: 142–43).[19]

Sexual relations

The relationship between William Howell and Sarah is just one example of a much larger issue of inter-racial sexual relationships in the Americas. Attitudes towards inter-racial relationships differed noticeably between North and South America. In Latin America and the Caribbean, it became accepted that white men would take black or Native American women as wives or concubines. Thomas Thistlewood lived in Jamaica for more than 30 years in the second half of the eighteenth century, yet never married a white woman despite his wealth, preferring instead a long-standing, though not exclusive, relationship with a slave woman, Phibbah (Burnard, 2004: 228–40). In North America such inter-racial unions faced public opposition and official sanction as early as the seventeenth century (Degler, 1959: 56). Of course, it was an open secret that white planters on the North American mainland, especially in South Carolina and Virginia, took sexual advantage of their female slaves and fathered mulatto children, thereby adding to their own wealth, but such relationships (if they can be so termed) were often coerced and almost never publicly acknowledged. As Mary Boykin Chesnut commented acidly in 1861, "Like the patriarchs of old, our men live all in one house with their wives and their concubines; and the mulattoes one sees in every family partly resemble the white children. Any lady is ready to tell you who is the father of all the mulatto children in everybody's household but her own. Those, she seems to think, drop from the clouds" (Chesnut, 1949: 21).

On rare occasions, white women took enslaved or free black men as lovers or partners, thereby posing a far more serious challenge to the social order, since the mixed-race children who resulted from such unions were free. In Barbados, authorities responded to such matters by removing the children from their mothers and binding them out as indentured servants (Jones, 2007: 34). In the early seventeenth century inter-racial marriage was still technically possible in many places, but during the late seventeenth and early eighteenth centuries laws were passed banning such unions, for instance in Maryland in 1692, in North Carolina in 1715, and in French Louisiana in 1724.

Despite the increasing level of official disapproval of inter-racial relationships, whether formal or informal, and the shame associated with illegitimacy, some individuals defied social conventions to continue such relationships regardless of the consequences. In 1809, a white man in Barbados was fined for living with a "woman of colour" and fathering six children with her. His defence, that he was only trying to "do a fatherly and Husband's part", was a bold statement against the prevailing social ethic, but ultimately did not mean he avoided a fine (Jones, 2007: 61). In Charlottesville, Virginia, David Isaacs and his free coloured wife-in-all-but-name, Nancy West, were together for 40 years in the early nineteenth century and had seven children together. The local Grand Jury indicted them for this arrangement, but only after they had abandoned the fiction of living apart after nearly 20 years together and made their relationship more public (Rothman, 2003: 57–87).

Another form of consensual bi-racial sexual relationship common in the Americas was prostitution. Brothels in port cities throughout the New World catered to the needs of visiting sailors, many of whom were black (Bolster, 1997: 186–87). In Antigua, James Adair reported that the "trulls who ply for the accommodation of the sailors" were often white. Thus it was not unknown for white prostitutes in the British West Indies to have mulatto babies by enslaved clients (Hoffer, 2003: 64).[20] White prostitutes were often poor immigrants from Europe, who realised only after arrival that life in the New World was harsher than they expected. Job opportunities for women were often limited to seamstressing or servile positions, neither of which paid enough money for rent and food. The Ladies' Benevolent Society in New Orleans lamented that "the stinted pittance, granted as the reward of woman's labor, is soon exhausted by the unceasing demand for food and shelter" and therefore it is not surprising that some white women turned to prostitution just to survive.[21] Black prostitutes were more likely to be free than enslaved, but not universally so, since some owners saw profit in pimping their female slaves in this manner. One slave trader in New Orleans observed that two young girls he was due to sell would "soon pay for themselves by keeping a whore house" (Baptist 2001: 1619). Local authorities were often highly critical of the "houses of ill-fame" that existed in their cities, especially when they were believed to be facilitating inter-racial sex, but it was difficult to entirely stamp them out. In truth, many people cared little that poor white women had sexual relations with black men, and rape accusations against black men were far less likely to result in a conviction or execution in the era of slavery than they were after abolition. As several scholars have now established, rape accusations against black men were relatively rare in themselves, and even when these cases came to court, it was by no means certain that a conviction would result. Slave owners had a financial vested interest in the lives of their slaves, meaning that they often opposed the execution of slaves except when absolutely necessary. Moreover, rape cases have always had low conviction rates due to lack of witness evidence and the issue of consent. When slave owners weighed the value of a slave against the word of a poor, perhaps "loose", white woman, it became possible to believe that consent had been willingly given and to acquit black men of what otherwise would have been a capital crime (Lockley, 2000: 230–53; Sommerville, 1995: 481–518).

Inter-racial sexual relationships most often occurred in the poorer parts of town, where black and white lived in close residential proximity. Cheap rents and poor-quality housing inevitably attracted those with least to spend, regardless of skin colour. The shops and other businesses in these neighbourhoods usually attracted a racially diverse clientele. In addition, most towns throughout the Americas had bars and gambling dens, often near the docks, where polite society would not venture. These places were frequented by working men, sailors, loose women and slaves, all attracted by the cheap alcohol and the prospect of easy money. Racial boundaries were blurred in such establishments, and we know that they were not racially exclusive, as tavern owners were often cited by grand juries for permitting slaves to enter their premises and to gamble.

The South Carolina Grand Jury, for example, complained in 1760 about "the evil practice of sailors, soldiers, and other disorderly persons and negroes, assembling, gaming, rioting and committing other disorders on the Sabbath-day".[22] Henry Bibb recalled that poor whites in Kentucky "associate much with the slaves; [and] are often found gambling together on the Sabbath".[23] Perhaps some element of segregation existed inside the bar itself, with blacks limited to certain areas and denied a chance to play certain games, but more likely whites and blacks drank side by side or gambled at the same table. When authorities in Chatham County, North Carolina jailed poor white farmer Archibald Campbell in 1840 for playing cards with slaves, his friends petitioned the Governor, stating that Campbell "lives in a section of the country where the same thing is often done [and] he knew no difference between playing with a white man or sporting with a coloured one" (cited in Bolton, 1994: 45). Such socialising might be understood to weaken the basis of racial slavery, since whites were interacting with slaves and free blacks as people rather than as chattel, but in reality the servile status of blacks was not threatened by such encounters. Of course, mixing alcohol and money often incited violence between players over accusations of cheating or inability to pay debts, and some poorer whites ended in court accused by an owner of harming a slave and thereby reducing both his value and his usefulness.

Religious interaction

A completely different kind of social environment where slaves and poorer whites were able to mix was church. The religious lives of the enslaved varied markedly throughout the Americas. In Latin America, Catholicism was universal and imposed on newly arrived Africans without their consent or any understanding of what it meant. Slaves were encouraged to attend mass, be married by a priest, have their children baptised, and be buried according to custom. The Catholic church in Brazil "insisted on the slave's right to equal access to the Church, its sacraments, and its code of morality", and masters were unable to prevent the Catholicisation of their slaves (Ramos, 1986: 439). While the universality of religion meant that no special status was afforded to black Catholics, the power and influence of priests could occasionally act as a check on the unbridled power of masters. In some parts of Latin America, it was even possible for blacks to be ordained as Catholic priests, and in the poorer parts of cities such as Rio de Janeiro they worked alongside white priests, ministering to both white and black Catholics. The higher clerical ranks were not open to black priests, but it was possible for a few slaves to achieve a relatively high social status because of their religious beliefs (Karasch, 1987: 87).

In the Caribbean, and in scattered locations elsewhere in the Americas, magic, *obeah*, *voodoo* and *hoodoo* were popular among slaves. These were belief systems with little or no cross-over to the white population. Even when Christianity began to make inroads among slaves, for example the Moravians in Antigua or the Baptists in Jamaica, the small number of white Christians normally worshipped separately in Anglican churches. In North America, by contrast, a multitude of different Protestant denominations flourished, and several were interested in converting or evangelising slaves, particularly after the American Revolution. The rapid growth of southern Baptist and Methodist congregations in the late eighteenth and early nineteenth centuries was in part due to the efforts made to convert slaves. In some regions, enslaved members constituted the vast majority of Baptist and Methodist congregations. Since the message of spiritual equality espoused by these denominations also attracted poorer whites, evangelical churches became a significant point of contact between the enslaved and non-slaveholding whites. Ex-slave Peter Randolph recalled that "I did not know of any other denomination where I lived in Virginia, than the Baptists and Presbyterians. Most of the colored people, and many of the poorer class of whites, are Baptists." One report of an early nineteenth-century outdoor camp meeting near Sparta, Georgia observed "about 3000 persons, white and black together, that lodged on the ground that night".[24] All members of evangelical churches, regardless of status, were according the title of "brother" or "sister" and were held, ostensibly, to the same code of morality that forbade drunkenness, adultery, gambling and bastardy. Enslaved members were able to make complaints about their owners to the quarterly discipline meetings that regulated the behaviour of members, but only if their owners were co-religionists. In this manner, some owners were occasionally held to account for their treatment of slaves, and slaves were afforded rights that no court would have recognised. Church discipline also served to undermine theories of racial superiority by demonstrating that whites were just as likely as slaves to commit immoral acts. In 1846, the Jones Creek Baptist Church, whose membership was split evenly between whites and slaves, heard a charge against Brother Daniel F. Sullivan "for an attempt to commit adultery with sister Anna Parker", ultimately determining to excommunicate him. Three years later they heard "a charge against Brother W J Gordon for drinking too much ardent spirits, Brother Gordon after some debat said he was sorry for drinking too mutch and for the future that he will not drink any at all".[25] For these white men, membership of the church meant that they were held to account for their personal behaviour in ways that were unusual in the Americas. As the nineteenth century wore on, however, religious organisations became more adept at discriminating between their members. Black members, and especially black women, were held to a higher standard of morality than whites, and were punished more harshly when found to have violated standards of behaviour. An enslaved member might be excommunicated and expelled from the church for drunkenness, whereas a white member, guilty of the same offence, might only receive an admonishment (Lockley, 2001: 153–54; Frey and Wood, 1998: 187–88).

Marronage

Just occasionally, church discipline meetings intervened in the place of the master, punishing slaves for lying, stealing, and even running away. Every society in the Americas had to deal with the chronic problem of slaves who fled from their bondage, and in some regions runaway slaves were so numerous that they eventually formed their own distinct societies in the Amazonian jungle, the mountains of Jamaica and the swamps of South Carolina. More often, however, slaves fled in very small groups, or alone, and lurked in the woods close to their family and friends before being captured and returned to slavery. In the seventeenth and eighteenth centuries, when white indentured servants in plantation colonies laboured under similar conditions to slaves, runaway groups could often be bi-racial, finding enough common cause to overcome any nascent racial antipathy. In the mid 1650s, Barbadian authorities sent troops into the sparsely populated centre of the island in search of "several Irish servants and Negroes" who had fled there. A century later, a Virginia planter advertised for "two English convict servant men, both blacksmiths by trade" who had fled taking with them "a Negro lad, about 18 years of age". All three took horses from their master's stable to speed their escape. Once in the woods, these bi-racial groups of "white persons and blacks" often continued to work together, committing "many outrages and robberys". Even when servants and slaves chose not to flee together, they sometimes aided and abetted each other's escape. In 1693, a white Barbadian servant "counterfeited and set Mr Walker Colleton's hand to a ticket for a negro woman" allowing her to travel freely about the island, while in the same year a slave was charged with "enticing and contriving the sending off of some white servants"[26] (Beckles, 1986: 81, 91; Lockley, 2009: 10). By the nineteenth century, some whites in the antebellum United States were actively helping slaves to escape, either out of personal sympathy or from abolitionist motivations. A ship's cook concealed one slave in his schooner just before it sailed from Alabama to "a northern port, with a view ... to secure her freedom". Wrongly charged with slave stealing "there being no intention to convert the slave to his own use", the cook was re-tried on a charge of "harboring".[27]

Running away was the activity most likely to bring enslaved Africans into contact with Native Americans. The degree of slave interaction with Native American people varied considerably over time and among regions. In the sixteenth century, when the number of Africans in the Americas was small, and the numbers of Native Americans very high, little contact occurred between the two groups, except in locations in Spanish American possessions where both Africans and Native Americans were enslaved. In such places, slaves had to work in whatever position their master ordered, regardless of ethnic origin. The infections brought by Europeans to the Americas, in particular smallpox and influenza, devastated Native American populations by as much as 90 per cent and hastened the import of slaves from Africa, who shared European immunity to old world diseases and who were often more resistant to tropical diseases such as yellow fever and malaria. Native Americans all but disappeared from the Caribbean islands, and were driven from the profitable coastal plantations of Brazil, Surinam and South Carolina into the interior jungles and mountains. However, the persistence of Native American tribal areas in relative proximity to white-controlled regions offered hope to fugitive slaves. Runaways could reasonably expect to find a safe haven among peoples who had also suffered terribly from European colonisation: some of the largest maroon communities in the seventeenth and eighteenth centuries were a fusion of Native American tribes and fugitive African slaves. For a period in the seventeenth century, Saint Vincent was divided between native Carib inhabitants and escaped slaves from Barbados, while some of the largest *quilombos*, or maroon settlements, in Brazil were populated by escaped African and Native American slaves (Beckles, 1986: 89–90; Lockley, 2009: xiv–xv).

Yet it was not unknown for colonial governments to use Native Americans against slaves, as they possessed the local knowledge that regular troops usually lacked. In North America, a deliberate English strategy of seeking alliances with powerful southern tribes meant that runaway slaves rarely found a welcome among the Cherokee or the Creek. Indeed, some colonial governments employed Native American tribes to hunt escaped slaves, rewarding them with blankets, weapons and food. In 1766, the South Carolina government employed the Catawba to hunt out fugitive slaves in coastal swamps, "and partly by the terror of their name their diligence and singular sagacity in pursuing enemies thro' such thickets soon dispersed the runaway Negroes apprehended several and most of the rest of them chose to surrender themselves to their masters and return to their duty rather than expose themselves to the attack of an Enemy so dreaded and so difficult to be resisted or evaded for which good service the Indians were amply rewarded" (Lockley, 2009: 32–33). Only in post-Revolutionary Florida did fugitive slaves and Native Americans make common cause against the new American government. In the Seminole wars, fought in the early nineteenth century, US military commanders noted the courage and tenacity of the "black Seminoles", who were often the military leaders.

Creating racial solidarity

The strategy of using Native Americans against runaway slaves successfully avoided the prospect of the two groups joining forces against white authority. In order to prevent a possible alliance between poorer whites and slaves, elites pursued a variety of tactics. Those who traded with slaves illegally or helped them escape bondage were harshly punished, while at the same time efforts were made to make poorer whites part of the policing system of slavery. Poorer whites disproportionately served on patrols that were supposed to be on the lookout for runaway slaves or those who had left their plantations without permission. While theoretically all white males were supposed to take turns at patrolling, in reality wealthy men either paid a fine, or paid a substitute to take their place, leaving men who could not afford the fine as the mainstay of patrols. About a third of patrollers were non-slaveholders, and only a small number among the rest owned more than five slaves (Hadden, 2001: 97). These patrols existed in every slave society as a means of keeping the enslaved population in check, since every slave taken up by a patrol would be beaten before being returned to their owner. The interviews conducted with former slaves in the United States during the 1930s are full of complaints about the actions of the "paddyrollers". Former Arkansas slave Frank Larkin recalled "But I tell you, you'd better not leave the plantation without a pass or them paddyollers would made you shout. If they kotch you and you didn't have a pass, a whippin' took place right there" (Rawick, 1972: II, pt 4: 240). The violent reputation of patrols was entirely justified. Occasionally, elite whites grumbled about patrollers who "maltreat[ed] the slaves", especially those who returned a slave in a condition that resulted in time away from work. Nevertheless, even here not all patrollers acted in such a manner towards slaves on every occasion. In Charleston, the Grand Jury cited "William Garres, one of the officers of the Watch, for entertaining Seamen and Negroes at unseasonable Hours" and in urban environments, where individuals were in regular contact, the normal patterns of interaction between the patrol and the enslaved could be subverted (Lockley, 2001: 41–43).[28] In 1772, Grand Jurors in South Carolina complained about "the licences which are annually granted to watchmen, or their wives, to keep dram-shops, whereby it becomes their interest to encourage Negroes, and others, to frequent their houses, and consequently to protect such disorderly persons in their male-practices".[29]

Perhaps aware that allowing poorer whites to act as patrollers did not create sufficient social distance between the races, elite whites also stressed the privileges of race. These included the right to vote, the right to testify in court, the right to carry weapons, and the right to travel freely, rights that were routinely denied to non-whites even in parts of the Caribbean and Latin America where free black populations were larger than in North America. If these privileges had been extended to free blacks in the seventeenth and eighteenth centuries, those rights were often removed by the early nineteenth century. Being white earned a disproportionate share of public poor relief and a monopoly on private benevolence, demonstrating clearly that both the state and elite whites were prepared to help indigent whites with food, clothing, shelter and even employment. For example, the School for Female Industry, founded in St John's Parish, Barbados in 1799, was for whites only, excluding not only the large slave population but also free blacks. Moreover, when universal systems of education started to become popular during the nineteenth century, they too were deliberately reserved for whites. South Carolinian William Henry Trescott made the association between race and access to education explicit: "the white race must preserve its superiority by making its work mental as well as bodily ... and the only way to preserve this distinction, it to give to every workman in the state the education of a responsible citizen [and] to afford that degree of education to every one of its white citizens which will enable him intelligently and actively to control and direct the slave labor of the state"[30] (Jones, 2007: 13–14). Pro-slavery writers used the latest scientific studies to argue that "the brain of the Negro ... is, according to the positive measurements, smaller than the Caucasian by a full tenth; and this deficiency exists particularly in the anterior portion of the brain, which is known to be the seat of the higher faculties", and hence "his want of capability to receive a complicated education renders it improper and impolitic, that he should be allowed the privileges of citizenship in an enlightened country".[31]

Being white thus brought sufficient privileges to put a brake on any genuine threat of inter-racial co-operation to overthrow slave regimes in the Americas. White people of whatever social and economic status benefited from numerous forms of positive discrimination: above all, they were part of the so-called "master race", something that could never be taken away from them, however miserable their own individual circumstances were. When a South Carolina judge stated "a slave cannot be a white man", he was articulating a truth held dear by many impoverished whites (cited in Williamson, 1995: 18). The psychological security that skin colour offered meant that poorer whites could trade with slaves, sleep with slaves, and even plot with slaves, safe in the knowledge that their whiteness, and hence their innate superiority, was inalienable and as permanent as the slavery to which their trading partners, lovers and co-conspirators were condemned.

Notes

1 G. Pinckard, *Notes on the West Indies written during the expeditions under the command of the late General Sir Ralph Abercromby* (London: Longman, Hurst, Rees, and Orme 1806), II, 132.
2 J. Luffman, *A Brief Account of the Island of Antigua* (London: J. Luffman 1789), letter 23.
3 See, for instance, the ten-year jail term given to an Alabama overseer in 1843 for beating a slave to death. H. T. Catterall, *Judicial Cases Concerning Slavery* (Shannon: Irish University Press, 1968), III: 151, 162 (1847 case).
4 Luffman, *op. cit.*, letter 11; C. Ball, *Slavery in the United States* (New York: John S. Taylor, 1837), 166.
5 C. Thompson, *Biography of a Slave* (Dayton, OH: United Brethren Publishing House, 1875), 63.
6 *South Carolina Gazette*, 25 October 1760.
7 South Carolina Assembly Records: Petition 0010 003 1793 0063 and Report 0010 004 ND 02591 South Carolina Archives.
8 R. Bickell, *The West Indies As They Are* (London: J. Hatchard 1825), 66.

9 *Savannah Republican*, 17 January 1818.

10 E. Long, *The History of Jamaica* (London, 1774), I: 578.

11 *Charleston Standard*, 23 November 1854, cited in F. L. Olmsted, *Journey in the Seaboard Slave States* (New York: Miller & Holman, 1856), 441.

12 H. Bibb, *Narrative of the Life and Adventures of Henry Bibb, an American Slave*, (New York, 1849), 24.

13 Presentment of Georgetown District Grand Jury, 3 November 1818, General Assembly Papers 0010 015 1818 00007 South Carolina Archives.

14 An Act For Ordering And Governing Slaves, 10 May 1770, Sec. 33. R. & G. Watkins, eds., *A Digest of the Laws of the State of Georgia to 1798* (Philadelphia, R. Aitkin, 1800), 175. Catterall, *Judicial Cases, op. cit.*, II: 376.

15 Ball, *Slavery in the United States, op. cit.*: 308, 312.

16 *Haverhill Gazette*, 13 August 1836. Lynching in the antebellum era might involve whipping or tar and feathering, and did not always result in the death of the victim.

17 Catterall, *Judicial Cases, op. cit.*, II, 406.

18 *Richmond Enquirer*, 28 July 1835; *Austin State Gazette,* 27 September 1856, cited in Addington 1950: 416, 433

19 Catterall, *Judicial Cases, op. cit.*, III, 71; State of Georgia, Board of Corrections Records, Georgia Archives, Morrow. North Carolina-born Howell was jailed on 29 April 1859 and died on 12 December 1860.

20 J. M. Adair, *Unanswerable arguments against the abolition of the slave trade* (London: J. P Bateman, 1790), 85.

21 *Annual Report of the Managers of the Ladies' Benevolent Society* (New Orleans: Sherman & Wharton, 1855), 5.

22 *South Carolina Gazette*, 25 October 1760.

23 Bibb, *Narrative of the Life and Adventures of Henry Bibb, op. cit.*, 24.

24 P. Randolph, *Sketches of Slave Life: Or, Illustrations of the "Peculiar Institution"* (Boston: 1855), 33; *Farmer's Gazette*, 8 August 1807.

25 Minutes of Jones's Creek Baptist Church, Mercer University, Macon, Georgia, 25 April, 25 May 1846; 24 February 1849.

26 *Virginia Gazette*, (Rind) 12 May 1768.

27 Catterall, *Judicial Cases, op. cit.*, III, 146.

28 *South Carolina Gazette*, 15 April 1745.

29 *South Carolina Gazette*, 29 October 1772.

30 W. H. Trescott, "The States' Duties in regard to Popular Education", *Debow's Review* 20 (1856), 148.

31 J. C. Nott, *Two Lectures on the Natural History of the Caucasian and Negro Races*, (Mobile: Dade and Thompson, 1844), 35; R. H. Colfax, *Evidence Against the Views of the Abolitionists, Consisting of Physical and Moral Proofs, of the Natural Inferiority of the Negroes* (New York: James T. M. Bleakley Publishers, 1833), 25.

Bibliography

Baptist, E., "'Cuffy,' 'Fancy Maids,' and 'One-Eyed Men': Rape, Commodification, and the Domestic Slave Trade in the United States", *American Historical Review* 106 (2001), 1619.

Beckles, H., "From Land to Sea: Runaway Barbados Slaves and Servants, 1630–1700" in Gad Heuman (ed.), *Out of the House of Bondage: Runaways and Resistance and Marronage in Africa and the New World* (London: Frank Cass, 1986).

Berlin, I. and Morgan, P., eds, *The Slaves' Economy: Independent Production by Slaves in the Americas* (London: Frank Cass, 1991).

Boles, J. B., *Masters and Slaves in the House of the Lord: Race and Religion in the American South, 1740–1780* (Lexington: Kentucky University Press, 1988).

Bolster, J., *Black Jacks: African American Seamen in the Age of Sail* (Cambridge, MA: Harvard University Press, 1997).

Bolton C. C., *Poor Whites of the Antebellum South: Tenants and Laborers in Central North Carolina and Northeast Mississippi* (Durham, NC: Duke University Press, 1994).

Burnard, T., *Mastery, Tyranny and Desire: Thomas Thistlewood and his Slaves in the Anglo–Jamaican World* (Chapel Hill, London and Kingston: University of North Carolina Press and University of the West Indies Press, 2004).

Bynum, V. E., *Unruly Women: The Politics of Social and Sexual Control* (Chapel Hill: University of North Carolina Press, 1992).

Chesnut, M., *A Diary from Dixie*, edited by Ben Ames Williams (Boston: Houghton Mifflin, 1949).

Degler, C. N., "Slavery and the Genesis of American Race Prejudice", *Comparative Studies in Society and History* 2 (1959), 49–66.

Flynt, J. W., *Dixie's Forgotten People: The South's Poor Whites* (Bloomington: Indiana University Press, 1979).

Forret, J., *Race Relations at the Margins Slaves and Poor Whites in the Antebellum Southern Countryside* (Baton Rouge: Louisiana University Press, 2006).

Frey, S. R. and Wood, B., *Come Shouting to Zion: African American Protestantism in the American South and the British Caribbean to 1830* (Chapel Hill: University of North Carolina Press, 1998).

Fronsman, B. C., *Common Whites: Class and Culture in Antebellum North Carolina* (Lexington: University of Kentucky Press, 1992).

Goveia, E. V., *Slave Society in the British Leeward Islands at the End of the Eighteenth Century* (Westport, CT: Greenwood Press, 1965).

Hadden, S., *Slave Patrols: Law and Violence in Virginia and the Carolinas* (Cambridge, MA: Harvard University Press, 2001).

Hall, G. M., *Social Control in Slave Plantation Societies: A Comparison of St Domingue and Cuba* (Baton Rouge: Louisiana State University Press, 1971).

Harris, J. W., *Plain Folk and Gentry in a Slave Society: White Liberty and Black Slavery in Augusta's Hinterlands* (Middletown, CT: Wesleyan University Press, 1985).

Heuman, Gad J., *Between Black and White: Race, Politics, and the Free Coloreds in Jamaica, 1792–1865* (Oxford: Clio, 1981).

Hodes, M., *White Women, Black Men: Illicit Sex in the Nineteenth Century South* (New Haven, CT: Yale University Press, 1997).

Hoetink, H., *Slavery and Race Relations in the Americas* (London: Harper and Row, 1973).

Hoffer, P. C., *The Great New York conspiracy of 1741: Slavery, Crime and Colonial Law* (Lawrence: University Press of Kansas, 2003).

Inscoe, J. C., *Mountain Masters, Slavery, and the Sectional Crisis in Western North Carolina* (Knoxville: University of Tennessee Press, 1989).

Johnston, J. H., "The participation of white men in Virginia negro insurrections", *Journal of Negro History* 16 (1932), 158–67.

Jones, C., *Engendering Whiteness: White Women and Colonialism in Barbados and North Carolina, 1627–1865* (Manchester: Manchester University Press, 2007).

Karasch, M. C., *Slave Life in Rio de Janeiro, 1808–1850* (Princeton, NJ: Princeton University Press, 1987).

Klein, Herbert S. and Luna, Francisco Vidal, "Free Colored in a Slave Society: São Paulo and Minas Gerais in the Early Nineteenth Century", *Hispanic American Historical Review* 80 (2000), 913–41.

Lockley, T. J., "Partners in Crime: African–Americans and Non–slaveholding Whites in Antebellum Georgia", in M. Wray and A. Newitz, eds, *White Trash: Race and Class in America* (New York and London: Routledge, 1997), 57–72.

——, "Gender and Justice in Antebellum Savannah: The Case of George Flyming", *Georgia Historical Quarterly* 84 (2000), 230–253.

——, *Lines in the Sand: Race and Class in Lowcountry Georgia, 1750–1860* (Athens: University of Georgia Press, 2001).

——, "Spheres of Influence: Working Black and White Women in Antebellum Savannah", in S. Delfino and M. Gillespie, eds, *Neither Lady, Nor Slave: Working Women of the Old South* (Chapel Hill: University of North Carolina Press, 2002), 102–120.

——, *Welfare and Charity in the Antebellum South* (Gainesville: University Press of Florida, 2007).

——, *Maroon Communities in South Carolina: A Documentary Record* (Columbia: University of South Carolina Press, 2009).

McDonald, R. A., *The Economy and Material Culture of Slaves: Goods and Chattels on the Sugar Plantations of Jamaica and Louisiana* (Baton Rouge and London: Louisiana State University Press, 1993).

McNair, G., "Slave Women, Capital Crime, and Criminal Justice in Georgia", *Georgia Historical Quarterly* 93 (2009), 135–58.

Mintz, S. W. and Hall, D., *The Origins of the Jamaican Internal Marketing System* (New Haven, CT: Yale University Press, 1970).

Morgan, Edmund S., *American Slavery, American Freedom: The Ordeal of Colonial Virginia* (New York: Norton, 1975).

Morgan, P. D., *Slave Counterpoint: Black Culture in the Eighteenth Century Chesapeake and Lowcountry* (Chapel Hill: University of North Carolina Press, 1998).

Oakes, J., *The Ruling Race: A History of American Slaveholders* (New York: Knopf, 1982).

Phillips, U. B., *American Negro Slavery* (New York: D. Appleton and Co., 1918).

Ramos, D., "Community, Control and Acculturation: A Case Study of Slavery in Eighteenth Century Brazil", *The Americas* 42 (1986), 419–53.

Rawick, G., *The American Slave: An Autobiography*, Arkansas Narratives (Westport, CT: Greenwood Press, 1972).

Roediger, D. R., *The Wages of Whiteness: Race and the Making of the American Working Class* (London: Verso, 1991).

Rothman, J. D., *Notorious in the Neighborhood: Sex and Families across the Color Line in Virginia, 1787–1861* (Chapel Hill and London: University of North Carolina Press, 2003).

Scarborough, W. K., *The Overseer: Plantation Management in the Old South* (Baton Rouge: Louisiana State University Press, 1966).

Schwartz, S. B., *Sugar Plantations in the Formation of Brazilian society: Bahia, 1550–1835* (Cambridge: Cambridge University Press, 1985).

Sommerville, D. M., "The Rape Myth in the Old South Reconsidered", *Journal of Southern History* 61 (1995), 481–518.

Thompson, E. T., *Plantation Societies, Race Relations and the South: The Regimentation of Societies* (Durham, NC: Duke University Press, 1975).

Williamson, J., *New People: Miscegenation and Mulattoes in the United States* (Baton Rouge: Louisiana State University Press, 1995).

Wood, B., *"Women's Work, Men's Work": The Informal Slave Economies of Lowcountry Georgia, 1750–1830* (Athens: University of Georgia Press, 1995).

Zabin, S. R., *The New York Conspiracy Trials of 1741* (Boston: Bedford, 2004).

Part 3

CHANGES AND CONTINUITIES

16

SLAVERY IN THE AGE OF REVOLUTION

Laurent Dubois

Introduction

During the period that stretched from 1770 to 1830, European empires in the Americas suffered a series of remarkable powerful blows. During this period, enslaved people consistently played pivotal roles in the shape and definition of political change. Of course, resistance to slavery was a permanent feature of slave societies in the Atlantic world and, despite the frequent claims of pro-slavery advocates, they needed neither outside instigators nor radical revolutionary ideas to inspire them to revolt and resistance. But to be successful, slave resistance had to be extremely careful and very strategic. Before the Age of Revolution, some of the most successful forms of resistance involved taking advantage of conflicts between empires, as in the case of slaves who escaped Georgia for Spanish Florida, where they often gained freedom. Starting with the American Revolution, however, the enslaved found a bounty of new opportunities through which they could confront and contest their situation. Abolitionists, meanwhile, also found the changing institutional and political situation propitious for the pursuit of attacks on slavery. For many of those who came to embrace the radical and egalitarian ideas that circulated during this period, slavery increasingly came to seem indefensible and untenable.

The paradox of the Age of Revolution is that it both weakened and strengthened slavery. In North America, for instance, as Ira Berlin writes, the age marked a major transformation in African American life, but with strikingly varied results, "propelling some slaves to freedom and dooming others to nearly another century of captivity". "At the end of the revolutionary era, there were many more black people enslaved than at the beginning", he notes, because of the expansion of slavery in much of the southern USA. At the same time, however, the "shock of revolution profoundly altered slavery", reconfiguring relations between masters and slaves in important ways (Berlin, 2003: 99–100). While slavery was decisively weakened north of Virginia, it emerged shaken but still strong in much of the southern plantation colonies, and indeed entered into a period of expansion and consolidation in the early nineteenth century. In the Caribbean, the period saw the demolition of an extremely powerful and profitable institution through the Haitian Revolution, and its weakening in the British Caribbean. But it also, precisely because of the decline of slavery in Haiti in particular, spurred the expansion of slavery in Cuba. In Spanish Latin America, the wars of independence sapped and often decisively weakened slavery, though the process of abolition was extremely slow in many cases, while in Brazil the system of slavery remained strong through the period, and would last through much of the nineteenth century.

In this chapter, I narrate the ways in which the events of the Age of Revolution changed the geography of slavery in the Americas, and seek to explain some of the differences between events in different empires and different regions. Throughout, I focus as much as possible on the ways in which the enslaved viewed, responded to, and transformed the meaning and impact of revolution. I concentrate here on two main issues that shaped enslaved responses to, and participation in, the Age of Revolution. The first was the circulation of revolutionary language and ideology, which created new opportunities for voicing protest and for being heard. Enslaved rebels as well as free abolitionists could, and did, point out the hypocrisy of those who embraced and touted ideas of equality and natural rights while defending the brutal practice of slavery. At the same time, when the enslaved demanded freedom they expanded the terrain of political ideas – and this is the second issue I focus on here – concretizing abstract ideas of universal rights, and making freedom mean something extremely real, and often extremely threatening to the social order in the plantation Americas.

The Age of Revolution was also an age of near-constant war. While war created a great deal of suffering, notably for the enslaved, it also opened up opportunities. The enslaved participated actively in revolutionary wars throughout the Americas, and in the case of Saint-Domingue, started such a war and ultimately won it. The recruitment of the enslaved into the army was enticing for commanders in wartime, but in a moment of intense political uncertainty and possibility, it also carried with it important dangers. This was particularly true because the figure of the citizen-soldier became one of the most potent symbols for a new political order based on equality and political rights. As soldiers, men of African descent became defenders and representatives of emerging nations, and they used this position to gain political power and lay claim on government institutions.

At the beginning of the Age of Revolution, slavery was relatively secure throughout the Americas. Indeed, in many places slavery was expanding rapidly. The system had seen its share of challenges, notably during the 1730s, when a wave of plots, uprisings and maroon wars shook many slave societies. The most serious threat to the planter order was probably presented by the strong maroon societies in Jamaica and Suriname. But these were attenuated in Jamaica at the end of the 1730s, when colonial governments signed treaties with the most powerful groups of maroons, exchanging an acknowledgement of their freedom for a promise that the maroons would not accept new runaways from the plantations, and would return those who showed up in their territory.[1]

But while some abolitionists and intellectuals warned that the slave system, because of its violence, was also inherently unstable, it was difficult to imagine the extent to which it would be challenged and, in several cases, undone within the next decades. By the early nineteenth century, however, the world of slavery had shifted decisively. During the American Revolution, slavery was abolished outright in a few states in the North, while gradual abolition was put in place in many others. The Revolution set off mass escape from plantations of the South when the British promised freedom to those slaves who would serve them against the rebels, though ultimately many found their hopes for a dignified freedom dashed. A decade later, enslaved insurgents in Saint-Domingue turned themselves into an army that was embraced first by the Spanish, and ultimately by the French, winning emancipation for themselves and the abolition of slavery throughout the French empire in the process. In the next decades, during the wars for Latin American independence, the abolition of slavery was set in motion in most of the New Republics, though in some places the total destruction of slavery took many decades. By 1830, both because of the dramatic events of the Age of Revolution and because of a shifting economic context, slavery occupied a very different place in the political and social order of the Americas than it had in the late eighteenth century.

The American Revolution

Robin Blackburn has argued that the Revolutions of this period, "American, French, Haitian, and Spanish-American" should "be seen as interconnected, with each helping to radicalize the next." "The American Revolution", he writes, "launched an idea of popular sovereignty that, together with the cost of the war, helped to provoke the downfall of the French monarchy. The French Revolution, dramatic as was its influence on the Old World, also became a fundamental event in the New World because it was eventually to challenge slavery as well as royal power" (Blackburn, 2006). Slavery was an important issue during the American Revolution, of course, and debates about slavery took place early on during the French Revolution as well. But it was, as Blackburn insists, the actions of the enslaved in Saint-Domingue that opened up the most powerful attack on slavery in the Age of Revolution. As he argues, "The first major breach in the hugely important systems of slavery in the Americas was opened not by English or American abolitionists but by Jacobin revolutionaries and the black peasantry of Saint Domingue (later Haiti)" (*ibid.*).

The movement for independence in North America opened up a new stage in the battle over slavery. The British decision to hold out the promise of freedom to those enslaved by their enemies, originally put into practice locally by a threatened British official, was expanded into a large-scale wartime policy as a result of the insistent response of slaves themselves to the promise of freedom. In this case, as in others, the fears of slave owners, the hopes of slaves, and the exigencies of war created a context ripe for the mobilization of slave communities. A pamphlet published in London in 1774 argued for suppressing patriot revolt by granting freedom to the slaves of the North American colonies. Echoes of this arrived in Virginia through personal correspondence. Some white Virginians magnified the strength of anti-slavery forces in the empire. After Edmund Burke noted in the British parliament in March 1775 that many members favoured slave emancipation in the colonies, James Madison heard in Virginia that a bill for slave emancipation had actually been introduced. A report of the House of Burgess in Virginia declared that the British had a "diabolical" plan "to offer Freedom to our Slaves, and turn them against their Masters". In a process that mirrored and helped drive what was happening among slaves in Virginia, whites heard rumours of an impending British intervention on behalf of the slaves. Some Virginia slaves, meanwhile, planned rebellions. A slave named Antonio, who had once sought to gain his freedom by unsuccessfully arguing in court in 1771 that he was "a free born subject" of the King of Spain, was one of those who plotted a revolt (Holton, 2000: 140–42).

In April 1775, Virginia's Governor, Lord Dunmore, threatened patriots with the spectre of emancipation. He declared that if any high-ranking British officials were harmed by American revolutionaries, he would "declare freedom to the slaves and reduce the city of Wmsburg [sic] to ashes", repeating the threat again a week later, after a group of "Negroes" presented themselves at the Governor's palace and offered their services to him. In July, a slave plot was uncovered in which the plan was apparently for slaves to rise up and travel to the West, where "they were to be received with open arms by a number of Persons there appointed and armed by [the] Government for their Protection". The rumoured greeting by the British took place soon enough, not in the West but on the coast, where Dunmore began accepting offers by slaves to serve with the British. One slave, Joseph Harris, who had worked as a pilot on the Chesapeake, distinguished himself by twice saving British ship captains from American rebels. British officers refused the demand of enraged Patriots to hand him over. In November, a troop serving under Dunmore, made up of a majority of former slaves, routed a Patriot militia unit. Two of Dunmore's soldiers captured the militia's commander, their former master. An elated Dunmore issued a declaration inviting all slaves and indentured labourers who could serve in the army to join the British. If they joined up, they would receive freedom. A thousand answered the call, and were organized into an "Ethiopian regiment" whose uniforms proclaimed "Liberty to Slaves". "The slaves' insurgency", writes Woody Holton, "played an important role in persuading Dunmore to ally with them and thus in prodding white Virginians further along the road to independence". The possibility of an alliance – circulated by fearful white Virginians and hinted at by slave conspirators – had become a reality (*ibid.*: 133–35, 143–61).

The slave-owners of South Carolina, too, were pushed towards independence through fear of slave insurrection. Their fears were compounded by paranoia and by Lord Dunmore's actions in Virginia, but they were also tied to the actions of slaves themselves. In 1775, before the war began, a slave named Jeremiah told another that "the war was come to help the poor negroes". When it began, he continued, they should join the British. In July of that year, a slave preacher named George was arrested as a leader of a conspiracy after he explicitly invoked an impending freedom decreed by the King of Britain. Drawing on Biblical symbolism, he declared that "the old King had reced [sic] a Book from our Lord by which he was to Alter the World ... but for his not doing so, was now gone to Hell, and punishment – That the Young King, meaning our Present One, came up with the Book, & was about to alter the World, & set the Negroes Free". Woody Holton writes about this that: "The rumor that freeing the slaves was one of Great Britain's principal aims – perhaps even the primary one – might have been fabricated by black leaders in the hope that it would serve as a self-fulfilling prophesy. If a real slave revolt crystallized around the apocryphal story of a British army of liberation, British statesmen might indeed be drawn into an alliance with the slave rebels" (Olwell, 1989: 21–48, 33–34; Frey, 1991: esp. 62; Schama, 2006; Nash, 2006: ch. 1; Holton, 2000, 154).

Slaves were inspired to run away by information about the possibility of finding refuge with their masters' enemies, and their flight propelled the creation of an alliance between the British and such slaves. Although, in the end, the promise of freedom that slaves saw in the British army remained unfulfilled, the vision of liberation they projected did shape British policy during the war in ways that allowed many slaves to find a tenuous freedom and an escape from their masters. For many enslaved men and women who successfully joined the British, this action was the beginning of a series of what Cassandra Pybus has dubbed "epic journeys of freedom". For officials in the British

Empire, deeply invested in plantation slavery in the Caribbean and heavily involved in the slave trade, the question of what to do with enslaved people who had escaped their masters and often served in the military was a delicate one. Many were resettled, often in extremely difficult circumstances, in places such as Nova Scotia and Sierra Leone, and some ended up as far away as Australia. They struggled against major odds to fulfil their hopes for a dignified and autonomous existence (Pybus, 2006).

The Revolutionary period in North America posed difficult challenges for slave insurgents. While the ideology of rights promulgated by the revolutionaries lent itself well to a challenge against slavery, the British government held out a concrete promise of liberty, albeit for strategic rather than for ideological reasons. In several Northern states, however, revolutionary ideas were used to challenge slavery and ultimately bring about abolition. "Emancipation came quickly in northern New England", writes Ira Berlin, "particularly in areas where slaves were numerically few and economically marginal". Vermont, New Hampshire and Massachusetts rapidly ended slavery. But the process was much more complicated in New York, New Jersey, Rhode Island and Pennsylvania. A gradual emancipation decree was put into effect in Philadelphia in 1780, and "by the first years of the nineteenth century every state north of the Chesapeake enacted some plan for emancipation". All of these plans, however, involved a very gradual access to freedom on the part of slaves, and "assured that the demise of slavery in the North would be a slow, tortuous process". It took at least a generation for most slaves to actually gain their freedom, and in New York and New Jersey there were still some people enslaved "until the mid-nineteenth century and beyond" (Berlin, 2003, 103–4).

Slavery, however, ultimately emerged shaken but still entrenched in the Southern United States. The rights to "life, liberty and the pursuit of happiness" famously proclaimed in the Declaration of Independence, writes Robin Blackburn, turned out to be "easier to reconcile with the enslavement of blacks than might be thought, since the rights it asserted could only be claimed by members of a people with their own properly organized government". He continues: "Natural-rights doctrines had traditionally declared that all men were born free but qualified this notion immediately by insisting that liberty could only be realized in specific communities organized by the law of peoples (*jus gentium*). Slaves lacked a community that would recognize their freedom." "Even Thomas Paine in *Common Sense* saw the New World", he writes, "as a haven for persecuted Europeans, not Native Americans or African Americans"; while "The chief author of the American Declaration later concluded that neither the slaves nor their descendants could ever become part of the American people and that they would need to find their own liberty somewhere else, perhaps in Africa." The three-fifths clause of the United States Constitution, which allowed slaveholding states to claim representation based on their white population plus three-fifths of their slave population, effectively embedded the right to slavery in the Constitution itself (Blackburn, 2006: 649).[2]

The struggle against slavery in the United States would henceforth solidify along regional lines, with the Northern states increasingly playing the role of sanctuary that the British briefly played during the revolutionary years, but within a system of government that made the kind of claims the federal government could make on states – and the kinds of claims slaves could make on the federal government – quite different from what had been the case during the Revolution. Furthermore, rising demand for cotton, as well as the Louisiana Purchase of 1804 and the development of sugar plantations in Louisiana, propelled an expansion of slavery after the end of the War of 1812. Indeed, as

Ira Berlin notes, on the cusp of the nineteenth century "slavery in the Lower south was primed for a half century of explosive growth". For free people of African descent in the North, conditions of life deteriorated in many ways, propelling some to pursue plans for repatriation to Africa through the creation of Liberia (Berlin, 2003, 124; Tyler-McGraw, 2007).

The American Revolution, however, did in one sense play a powerful role in propelling abolition. But it did so outside the new United States. During the Revolution, some in Britain, writes Blackburn, "used antislavery themes to discredit the rebellion. Both reactions helped antislavery in Britain." As a result, "British abolitionism was born of defeat in America. The Society for the Abolition of the Slave Trade was founded in Britain in 1787 and was soon able to demonstrate impressive popular and parliamentary support" (Blackburn, 2006: 650). As Christopher Brown has shown, the political and intellectual crisis incited in Britain as a result of loss of the American colonies made it possible for abolitionist ideas, which had been circulated for some time, to become a major vehicle for the claiming of "moral capital" and the assertion that Britain was the true home of ideas of freedom that the American Revolutionaries had mobilized in their war against Britain (Brown, 2006).

The French and Haitian Revolutions

In August of 1791, thousands of slaves on the sugar plantations of the Northern plain of Saint-Domingue began killing their masters. They burned and looted the great houses on their plantations, set alight the fields of sugar cane in which they had worked, and smashed the machinery that made the cane into sugar. They swept across the plain and attempted to capture the thriving port town of Le Cap, where representatives were gathered together for a meeting of the Colonial Assembly. Their original plan had been to take the town and wipe out the assembly, made up of the most prominent planters in the colony, in one stroke. They were unable to take the town, but ultimately they succeeded in their broader aims. The enslaved insurgents quickly transformed themselves into a revolutionary army, turning shattered plantations into rebel camps and retreating to the mountains when confronted by the large French missions sent against them. The rebels, many of them veterans of the wars then tearing apart societies in Africa, notably in the Kongo region of Central Africa, used sophisticated guerrilla tactics and ambushes to keep their enemies at bay for two years (Dubois, 2004; Fick, 1990; Geggus, 2002).

Those who organized this uprising saw an opportunity in 1791 that they had not seen before. That opportunity had a name, or at least a cause: the French Revolution. The question of how to understand the relationship between the French and Haitian Revolutions has intrigued and befuddled generations of historians. In fact, the 1790s saw a French Atlantic Revolution that played out on both sides of the Atlantic, and the currents of impact and effect were complex and varied, but never unidirectional. In the Caribbean, meanwhile, there were multiple revolutions, since the French colonies of Martinique and Guadeloupe also saw upheaval and transformation during this period. And the revolution that took place in Saint-Domingue really became a "Haitian Revolution", in the sense that it aimed to create an independent nation, only in 1802 and 1803. Before that, enslaved insurgents actually won their freedom by arguing for, and winning, a closer legal and political connection between France and the colony of Saint-Domingue.

The Revolution of 1789 in France shaped what happened in the Caribbean in many ways. First, most importantly, it shook up the system of colonial governance and weakened its power, inviting resistance and protest as a result. All social groups in Saint-Domingue saw an opportunity in the French Revolution. For many planters, who had long chafed at regulations that required most trade in their plantation products to be with France, as opposed to with the highest bidder, it was an opportunity to argue for greater economic freedom. For poorer whites in the colony, it was an opportunity to protest and fight against the social hierarchy within the colony that kept them marginalized and often landless. For free people of African descent, also called free people of colour and often described in the literature as "mulattoes" – though many were in fact not of mixed European and African ancestry – it was an opportunity to protest against decades of humiliating local legislation that constrained them from practising certain professions as well as controlling other aspects of their life, some as minute as the kind of clothes they could wear and the kind of transportation they could use.

But if the French Revolution created an opening by attacking the central authority, it also produced an outpouring of language and symbolism which could be powerfully mobilized in colonial society. With the 1789 Declaration of the Rights of Man, it produced a charter that was both immensely powerful and immensely vague in its articulation. Indeed, the discourse and ideals of the French Revolution were used in very different ways in different parts of the French empire. In the slave-trading port of Saint-Louis, Senegal, for instance, local merchants, many of them of mixed European and African ancestry, took advantage of the moment to demand an end to the monopoly still held by the Compagnie des Indes, insisting on *their* right to participate in the slave trade. Planters in Saint-Domingue similarly used the language of liberty to demand freedom from trade monopolies (Coquery-Vidrovitch, 2001). Free people of colour were particularly astute in how they harnessed the new language of rights to long-standing grievances about racial discrimination. Presenting themselves as wealthy, educated patriots, elite free people of colour – with leaders such as Julien Raimond and Vincent Ogé, both wealthy slave owners – they argued that they should have access to political rights alongside whites in the colonies. They allied themselves with the nascent abolitionist movement in France to take on the privilege of white planters, which they dubbed the "aristocracy of the skin". They found many were sympathetic to their arguments, which both drew on and buttressed the idea that a new era of equality was dawning in France. These debates over the rights of free people of colour, though they ultimately failed to bring about major change, at the time did help set the stage for what happened in Saint-Domingue in 1793. Nevertheless, it took the slave insurrection of 1791 to win political rights for all free people of colour, granted by a National Assembly that hoped such measures would help stop the advance of slave rebellion. One important fact was that two of the commissioners sent to the colony in 1792, Léger Félicité Sonthonax and Etienne Polverel, were familiar with and sympathetic to the arguments for racial equality and abolition that circulated in France during the 1780s and early 1790s.

In mid-1793, the French administrators in the colony, besieged by counter-revolutionary whites and attacked by both the Spanish and British, reached out to the insurgents, offering them freedom and citizenship if they fought for France. Many responded, and within a few months the French were pushed to abolish slavery outright in the colony. It was an unprecedented and thoroughly unexpected event: the most profitable slave colony in the Atlantic world was now populated by hundreds of thousands of free men and women of African descent. There was no period of transition between slavery and freedom, as there was in most of the Northern states of the USA, and no compensation for masters. Indeed, many masters were on the run. A group of representatives elected in the colony, including one African-born man who had survived the Middle Passage, Jean-Baptiste Belley, carried the news of events in Saint-Domingue to Paris. The National Convention ratified the local decision in February 1794, and extended it to the entire French empire. The decree was never applied in the Indian Ocean, where planters successfully resisted the application of the decree, or in Martinique, which fell to the English early in 1794 and which remained in their hands until 1802. But in Guadeloupe and its dependencies, in French Guiana, and for a brief time in St Lucia (which was successfully conquered by the French), slavery was abolished as a result of the National Assembly's decree.

The enslaved revolutionaries of Saint-Domingue had won a stunning victory, over-turning the system of slavery, the foundation for the entire Atlantic economy, in what had been its most profitable site. Saint-Domingue was the most productive and richest colony in the hemisphere, cherished by the French and sought after by the British and Spanish. The colony's profitability was directly linked to its brutality: from the expansion of its plantation economy in the early eighteenth century to the revolution of 1791, at least 700,000 slaves, and probably many more, had stepped off slave ships into Saint-Domingue to be sent to work in harsh conditions, producing sugar and other commodities for export. By the time the revolution began, however, there were only half a million slaves in the colony. The plantation experience had scarred these slaves, often quite literally: many were branded by their owners and bore the scars of whipping and other tortures inflicted on them to ensure discipline.

For those who oversaw the transition from slavery to freedom in the colony, the problems were immense. The economy was based entirely on the production of coffee and sugar for export. This production required gruelling field labour. The post-emancipation colony's leaders, both those sent from metropolitan France and those who were home-grown, were committed to maintaining the plantation economy, certain that it was the only way for Saint-Domingue to maintain a role in the broader Atlantic economy. Most former slaves, however, saw something very different in freedom: not a continuation of old forms of labour, now with wages, but rather autonomy, dignity and independence based on independent land-ownership and cultivation. Freedom was under assault from the moment it arrived in Saint-Domingue, for the British successfully invaded parts of the colony, maintaining slavery in the regions they controlled. But in the midst of a war between slavery and freedom, another, lower-grade conflict took shape on and around the plantations, between different visions of human work and human dignity, between a vision of export-oriented, highly regimented and industrialized production and one of production for and by families and communities. It was a conflict that would continue even after the French were expelled from the colony. It shapes Haiti's history into the present day.

The towering figure of the revolutionary period was Toussaint Louverture, who guided, defined and contained the transformations in his homeland. Born a slave, with an Arada father who had been brought to the colony from West Africa, he was freed over a decade before the revolution, and briefly owned his own slave as well as managing a rented coffee plantation. He navigated skilfully between the different worlds in the colony, maintaining ties with planters, various other men of African descent who were free before emancipation, and also with both Creole (that is, American-born) as well as African-born former slaves. Louverture was deeply committed to preserving emancipation, but because of this he also acted to constrain its meaning, insisting that the former slaves continue to work on plantations and that the colony continue to export its valuable plantation products. He was a skilful diplomat, showing a bold autonomy by negotiating independently of the French government with the British and the US, securing trade and even military assistance from the administration of John Adams. He worked closely with former slave-owners and succeeded in rebuilding the coffee economy and a part of the sugar economy on the war-torn island, doing his best to satisfy the French government and those who were clamouring for a return to the profits of the previous years. He was caught in a difficult paradox: in order to protect and sustain emancipation, he limited its content and sought to keep the economy of the old order alive.

Despite Louverture's efforts, the French regime of Napoleon Bonaparte ultimately turned against emancipation, seeing in the armies of ex-slaves a dangerous and perhaps uncontainable force. It dreamt of rebuilding the old plantation economy and its profits. Bonaparte briefly considered another alternative, one that might have led to a very different future for the Americas: working with Louverture and his army of ex-slaves, and continuing to use the promise of emancipation as a weapon of war against the slave colonies of France's enemies. But, in the end, he chose a much less imaginative and more brutal path that led to war and the loss not only of Saint-Domingue but also of his plans for Louisiana. The Republicans of the Caribbean, many deeply committed to the emancipatory and egalitarian dimensions of the French Revolution, were forced to make a choice between remaining free and equal and remaining French. Though it took some time, in the end the vast majority chose independence.

When Bonaparte's repressive representative to the colony, his brother-in-law Victor-Emmanuel Leclerc, arrived in the colony, he found and took advantage of the deep fissures in the colony. There were serious differences between those who had been enslaved before the Revolution, and those who had been free and often wealthy long before emancipation was decreed though of African descent. There were also some differences in attitude and political vision between those blacks who were African-born and those who were creoles. Moreover, important struggles went on between new elites, particularly military leaders, who had profited in the wake of emancipation and those whose experience of liberty had been circumscribed by poverty and coercion. The French succeeded in gaining support for their aims from many black officers and soldiers. After a series of battles, Louverture surrendered and then was tricked and bundled off to France, where he died in prison.

But as Haitians came to realize what French intentions really were, and as French tactics became more and more vicious, a group of black generals managed to unite various constituencies, all of whom could agree that they were not willing to go back to an era of slavery and racial subordination. The army flew as its flag the French tri-colour with the white ripped out of it, symbolizing a rejection of white power as well as the unity of the other groups in the colony. By late 1803, the French had been defeated, and the debris of their army, along with many white planters, fled the island. On 1 January 1804, a new nation was formed by the victorious army. They called it Haiti. The word, once used by the indigenous inhabitants of the island to name their homeland, was meant to signify that the new nation represented the rejection not only of slavery, but also of the broader brutalities carried out by Europeans in the Americas. Indeed, in 1805, defending a series of massacres of remaining white inhabitants that he had ordered, the nation's founder and first emperor, Jean-Jacques Dessalines, declared: "I have avenged America".

Dessalines, like the other leaders who soon followed him, faced a daunting task. Haiti had been deeply scarred not only by nearly a century of slavery, but also by a decade of brutal war that had left up to 100,000 dead. The economy was in shambles. Furthermore, most slaves found it unacceptable to return to the plantation system as it had previously been configured. Externally, Haiti was ostracized politically by most governments. France refused to recognize the new nation until 1825, when the Haitian government agreed to pay a large and ultimately debilitating indemnity that would go to reimbursing the lost property of the former planters of Saint-Domingue. The USA refused Haiti political recognition until 1862. Although Haiti's coffee economy grew and prospered during the nineteenth century, and although there were periods of relative political stability and progress, the mixture of deep social conflicts and external ostracism proved to be a toxic combination, hobbling the efforts of many Haitian leaders to secure peace and prosperity for their people.

The Haitian Revolution, meanwhile, reshaped the Atlantic world. Starting in 1791, but especially in waves in 1793 and again in 1803, thousands of refugees left, many of them ending up in the USA, notably in Charleston and Philadelphia. Others settled in Cuba, but were expelled in 1809. Most of them settled in the Louisiana Territory, which Napoleon had been forced to sell to the USA when his plans for a rejuvenated French empire in the Americas were decimated, along with his troops, in Saint-Domingue. These migrants, many of them free people of colour, were to have an important impact on New Orleans. They shaped the cultural life of the city, infusing it with French language and theatre, and many free people of colour continued the struggle for racial equality that had begun in Saint-Domingue in the United States, establishing a tradition of activism that stretched through the nineteenth century.

Haiti came to symbolize many things to peoples in the Americas. It was a symbol of black dignity and resistance, a vision that inspired slaves from Virginia to Brazil. The figure of Toussaint Louverture was widely celebrated and eulogized. The young Haitian state assisted in, and influenced the course of, the Latin American wars of independence, hosting Simon Bolivar and other revolutionary leaders and urging them to abolish slavery when they won independence. At the same time, proponents of slavery pointed to the violence of the Haitian Revolution and to the political and economic difficulties of post-independence Haiti to argue that black people were better off enslaved than free. While the Revolution had ended slavery in the most profitable colony in the Americas, it also opened the way for its expansion elsewhere, particularly in Cuba. That island dramatically expanded its sugar production; this was also the case in the Louisiana territory whose sale by France to the United States was triggered by the defeat of French troops in Saint-Domingue.

Spanish American Revolutions

In Cuba in 1812, the aspiration for emancipation and independence came together in a particularly striking way through the revolt led by the free man of colour José Antonio Aponte. A carpenter and militiaman, Aponte was very interested in the history of the

Haitian Revolution, and kept a book in his house that included images of revolutionary leaders such as Toussaint Louverture, which he used to recount what had happened in the neighbouring island. The Cuban planter class was enthusiastically trying to fill the void in sugar production left by the loss of Haiti, and slave imports into Cuba were skyrocketing as the society became increasingly dominated by sugar plantations. Using his militia connections, as well as those developed in the religious brotherhoods called *cabildos*, Aponte and his co-conspirators organized a widespread rebellion, issuing demands for emancipation and independence from Spain. The rebellion was quickly crushed and its leaders executed, and it would take many years before the twin aspirations of emancipation and independence were fulfilled in Cuba. Indeed, even as much of Latin America broke away from Spain, the Cuban elite, notably its planter class, remained loyal to Spain partly because of a concern that a war for independence would lead to a struggle for freedom on the part of the enslaved in the colony (Childs, 2006; see also Gad Heuman's Chapter 13 in this volume).

The Latin American wars of independence began with the French invasion of the Iberian peninsula, which created a political opening, as well as "a series of questions" for leaders in Spanish America. "Would they accept the French conquest of the mother country? Would they reject French rule and remain loyal to the deposed Bourbon monarchy? Or would they follow the example of the United States and strike for independence?" The choices they faced were complex, and the answers they came up with were shaped predominantly by the events in the Caribbean during the preceding decades, according to George Reid Andrews, who notes that "as Spanish Americans grappled with these questions, they paid greatest attention of all to the Haitian Revolution" (Andrews, 2004: 53).

But what, precisely, was the lesson of the Haitian Revolution? On the one hand, the events there highlighted the "enormous risks of trying to overthrow central authority" in societies based on slavery, as Andrews has argued. "For dominant classes throughout the hemisphere," he states, "the lessons to be drawn from Haiti were obvious: wherever large populations of nonwhites lived under conditions of forced labour, political revolution could all too easily become social revolution." So elites in mining and plantations regions of Latin America, notably Peru, Cuba and Puerto Rico, remained cautious and loyal to Spain after 1808. Where movements for independence did emerge, however, was "on the peripheries, where mestizos outnumbered Indians and where whites and free blacks and mulattoes outnumbered slaves". Nevertheless, the bids for independence launched in 1809 and 1810 set off a series of complex and widespread civil wars that would last over a decade. These wars, like the American Revolution, created an opportunity for enslaved men because each side increasingly needed recruits. As a result, throughout the region "the independence wars broke the back of colonial slavery, dealing the institution a fatal blow". In no place were slaves the "overwhelming majority of the population" that they had been in Haiti. Throughout Latin America, it was slaves themselves who "took up arms to fight for their freedom", and it was slaves who played a crucial role in propelling emancipation (*ibid*.: 54–55).

The involvement of free people of African descent as well as the enslaved in many ways helped to crystallize and set the terms of the conflict between Latin American creoles and Spanish governors and their allies. "During the struggle for independence," writes Marixa Lasso, "full citizenship for people of African descent thus shifted from being the goal of a few American and Spanish radicals to becoming one of the main issues dividing Spaniards from American patriots." The debate about whether people of African descent would gain citizenship began in 1810, when a gathering of representatives from Spain and the Americas came together to draft a new Spanish constitution. For representatives from the Americas, granting citizenship to free people of African descent, or *pardos*, would provide political advantages, since representation in the Cortes was proportional to population, and they would therefore gain more seats. But some Spanish representatives counter-attacked by questioning the capacity of *pardos* to exercise their citizenship rights. Through a series of debates, representatives from the Americas came to insist in increasingly radical terms on the equality of *pardos*. Debates over the question also took place in Latin America itself, notably in 1811 at a Constitutional congress created by republican rebels in Venezuela. These debates, of course, were also propelled by the shape of the military conflicts breaking out throughout the region, in which *pardos* were insistent and important participants. Importantly, once arguments for racial equality and larger claims that the American republics should be spaces defined by racial harmony had been articulated and put on paper, they provided a foundation for demands by *pardos* for equal treatment in all domains of life (Lasso, 2007: 35).

There were also, however, demands for a more radical application of ideas of equality: the abolition of slavery itself. The 1810 Hidalgo rebellion in Mexico called for the abolition of slavery and, after its initial defeat, rebel leaders mobilized plantation slaves in guerrilla campaign that lasted until 1817. Though the Spanish offered an amnesty to rebels in that year, they did not free the enslaved, many of whom continued a guerrilla campaign for another decade until 1829, when slavery was ultimately abolished in Mexico. In Venezuela, meanwhile, many slaves joined the ranks of both sides of the conflict pitting pro-independence forces against those loyal to the Spanish crown. Even for those who did not join armies, the chaos of warfare often opened up opportunities when masters fled and the enslaved in some areas took over plantations and began working on their own terms, for their own profit (Andrews, 2004, 58–60).

Abolition came much more slowly than it had in Saint-Domingue in the early 1790s, however. Still, as Andrews argues, "by 1825 almost every Spanish American country had banned further imports of slaves from Africa and enacted programs of either gradual or immediate emancipation". The first country to abolish both slavery and the slave trade was the Dominican Republic, though that was as a result of an invasion by Haiti in 1822. In 1811 Chile, with a very small slave population, had led the way by abolishing slavery and putting in place a "free womb law", which meant that all children born after that date were born free, though they had to stay on their plantation until the age of maturity. Such laws were originally put in place by elites eager to recruit enslaved men into military service: they represented a compromise between the aspirations of the enslaved and the interests of masters, since they represented a very slow and highly contained demand for emancipation. Legislators found many ways to limit their impact, notably by increasing the age of maturity at which those who were technically born free would actually be able to enjoy their freedom. In 1839, the government of Peru went so far as to declare that, for people of African descent, they would not reach the age of majority until they were 50 (*ibid.*: 56, 64; Klein and Vinson 2007: 231–33).

By the end of the 1820s, most of the new Latin American Republics had abolished slavery, though final abolition would come to most only in the 1850s, and Bolivia and Paraguay lagged behind. Puerto Rico and Cuba, meanwhile, remained under Spanish rule, in large part because the planter classes in these islands did not want to start a war for independence that they felt could easily become a re-run of the Haitian Revolution. The situation in Brazil varied again. The Portuguese crown took refuge in Brazil in 1808 after the French invasion of Portugal, and so the colony became, for a time, the political centre of the empire. The period led to important changes in the social and economic order in Brazil, notably in terms of trade. But slavery remained in place, and would be undermined only gradually over the course of the nineteenth century, until the final abolition in 1888. Moreover, unlike Britain and France, Portugal continued its heavy involvement in the slave trade through the 1860s (Andrews, 2004: 57; Adelman, 2006; Marques, 2006).

Conclusion

The Age of Revolution left behind an imperial Atlantic that had been profoundly shaken and deeply reconfigured. Within a few decades in the late eighteenth and early nineteenth centuries, most of the American hemisphere had gone from being controlled by competing imperial governments to being governed by independent states. In many areas, most strikingly Haiti, but also in the Spanish Latin American Republics and the Northern states of the USA, slavery had been either completely eliminated or set on a steady path to disappearance. In other areas, however, slavery still flourished, and indeed was on the rise. Slavery would remain a pillar of Atlantic economy and society throughout much of the nineteenth century. Everywhere, however, the Age of Revolution opened up important possibilities, anchoring and institutionalizing ideas of rights and sovereignty that provided a foundation for ongoing struggles against slavery and racial inequality.

Notes

1 The classic study on the maroons of Suriname is Price (1983, reprinted 2002). On the maroons of Jamaica, see the excellent study of Bilby (2005).
2 For a careful analysis of the reasons why slavery was not abolished, see Nash (2006: ch. 2).

Bibliography

Adelman, Jeremy, *Sovereignty and Revolution in the Iberian Atlantic* (Princeton, NJ: Princeton University Press, 2006).

Andrews, George Reid, *Afro-Latin America, 1800–2000* (Oxford: Oxford University Press, 2004).

Berlin, Ira, *Generations of Captivity: A History of African-American Slaves* (Cambridge, MA: Harvard University Press, 2003).

Bilby, Kenneth, *True-Born Maroons*, (Gainesville: University of Florida Press, 2005).

Blackburn, Robin, "Haiti, Slavery and the Age of Democratic Revolution", *William and Mary Quarterly* 63 (2006), 643–74.

Brown, Christopher, *Moral Capital: Foundations of British Abolitionism* (Chapel Hill: University of North Carolina Press, 2006).

Childs, Matthew, *The 1812 Aponte Rebellion in Cuba and the Struggle Against Atlantic Slavery* (Chapel Hill: University of North Carolina Press, 2006).

Coquery-Vidrovitch, Catherine, "Nationalité et citoyenneté et Afrique occidentale français: Originaires et Citoyens dans le Sénégale Colonial", *Journal of African History* 42 (2001), 285–305.

Dubois, Laurent, *Avengers of the New World: The Story of the Haitian Revolution* (Cambridge, MA: Harvard University Press, 2004).

Fick, Carolyn, *The Making of Haiti: The Saint Domingue Revolution from Below* (Knoxville: University of Tennessee Press, 1990).

Frey, Sylvia, *Water from the Rock: Black Resistance in a Revolutionary Age* (Princeton, NJ: Princeton University Press, 1991).

Geggus, David, *Haitian Revolutionary Studies* (Bloomington: Indiana University Press, 2002).

Holton, Woody, *Forced Founders: Indians, Debtors, Slaves and the Making of the American Revolution in Virginia* (Chapel Hill: University of North Carolina Press, 2000).

Klein, Herbert and Vinson, Ben, III, *African Slavery in Latin America and the Caribbean*, 2nd edn (Oxford: Oxford University Press, 2007).

Landers, Jane, "Gracia Real de Santa Teresa de Mose: A Free Black Town in Spanish Colonial Florida", *American Historical Review* 95 (1990), 9–30.

——, *Black Society in Spanish Florida* (Bloomington: Indiana University Press, 1999).

Lasso, Marixa, *Myths of Harmony: Race and Republicanism during the Age of Revolution, Colombia 1795–1831* (Pittsburgh: University of Pittsburgh Press, 2007).

Marques, João Pedro, *The Sounds of Silence: Nineteenth-Century Portugal and the Abolition of the Slave Trade* (New York: Berghahn Books, 2006).

Nash, Gary B., *The Forgotten Fifth: African-Americans in the Age of Revolution* (Cambridge, MA: Harvard University Press, 2006).

Olwell, Robert A., "'Domestick Enemies': Slavery and Political Independence in South Carolina, May 1775-March 1776", *Journal of Southern History* 55 (1989), 21–48.

Price, Richard, *First Time: The Historical Vision of an Afro-American People* (Chicago: University of Chicago Press, 2002).

Pybus, Cassandra, *Epic Journeys of Freedom: Runaway Slaves of the American Revolution and Their Global Quest for Liberty* (Boston: Beacon Press, 2006).

Schama, Simon, *Rough Crossings: Britain, the Slaves and the American Revolution* (New York: Ecco, 2006).

Tyler-McGraw, Marie, *An African Republic: Black & White Virginians in the Making of Liberia* (Chapel Hill: University of North Carolina Press, 2007).

17

ABOLITION OF THE ATLANTIC SLAVE TRADE

Christopher Leslie Brown

Introduction

There was nothing quite like the Atlantic slave trade in the long and varied history of the trafficking in enslaved men, women, and children. Although the trans-Saharan slave trade conveyed captives to North Africa and the Middle East over a longer span of time, no previous system approximated the more than 12.5 million embarked from Africa for the Americas from 1492 to 1867.[1] In many eras before and after, slave traders transported their victims across vast distances, far from their place of birth. Yet the thousands of miles covered by the typical slave voyage, from Europe to Africa to the Americas, had few if any institutional precedents. The Atlantic slave trade, too, was exceptional in the way that it came to an end. Within the span of four decades, each of the nations responsible for its organization and conduct came to renounce it. In little more than a half century, the slave trade would be effectively suppressed. In other places and in other times, the long-distance trafficking of enslaved peoples sometimes experienced rapid fluctuations too, rising and falling with the onset of war, economic change, or shifts in the political fortunes of the authorities that made the trade possible. Never before, though, had a trade in slaves been denounced and then abolished by the governments of the same peoples who had created it. It is the singularity of this history that accounts in part for the volume and complexity of the scholarly literature about it.

The importance of the subject derives also from the many and varied consequences that slave trade abolition entailed. Because the traffic connected and entangled the histories of Europe with the history of Africa and the Americas, the effects of abolition would be felt on each continent, upon the content, direction, and regulation of overseas trade from Europe, upon the recruitment and management of labour in the Americas, and upon patterns of economic change across West Africa. For these reasons, the subject holds an important place in the international history of the first half of the nineteenth century. Slave trade abolition reveals, as well as any subject, the ways that individual nations, individual colonies, particular peoples could and did have their fates decided by those who lived at a distance. At the same time, the relatively sudden and relatively quick success of the campaign to abolish the slave trade raises fundamental questions regarding morals, politics, and economics as engines of historical change. Explaining the abolition of the slave trade has seemed to many historians like a useful way to approach much broader problems concerning the possibility of humanitarian action and the power of the profit motive. For all of these reasons, the scholarly literature on slave trade abolition not only bears upon the specifics of its own history, but also carries implications for a wide variety of subjects pertinent to the making of the modern world.

This chapter considers in turn the five principal problems around which that scholarly literature has coalesced: the origins of abolitionist ideas and opinion; the emergence and evolution of antislavery movements; the enactment of abolitionist legislation or the declaration of abolitionist ordnances; the suppression of the Atlantic slave trade; and the effects and legacies of that suppression.

Origins of abolitionist opinion

For more than two centuries, the occasional complaint about the horrors and injustice of the Atlantic slave trade had no discernible effect on opinion in Europe or in the Americas.[2] There was no more reason to think that the slave trade could be brought to an end in 1750 than there had been in 1550. Indeed, closing the trade had become more unthinkable by the mid-eighteenth century since, by then, it had become entwined with every aspect of American colonial development, overseas commerce, and the demands of international competition. Until the late eighteenth century, the political history of the slave trade consisted of contests over who would conduct it and on what terms, rather than whether the trade should continue. Expressions of shock and disgust with the traffic, which litter the history of the trade, always fell before the more commanding imperatives of economic necessity and political calculation. Over time, there had developed, too, a series of assumptions and understandings that helped legitimate the traffic on moral grounds. Apologists explained that the captives had been taken in just wars in Africa, and that removal to the Americas rescued the victims from heathen lands and introduced them to Christianity.

Such justifications of the Atlantic slave trade attracted some sceptics among Portuguese and Spanish theologians both in Europe and the Americas, particularly in the sixteenth and seventeenth centuries. They doubted that the enslavement of Africans in Africa could be described as the result of just wars, or that the labour regimes that prevailed in the Americas could be described as a rescue from barbarism or as providing a sanctuary in Christ (Russell-Wood, 1978: 35–37; Boxer, 1978: 34–34; Gray, 1987: 52–68). Most of the arguments against the Atlantic slave trade had been articulated long before the development of the abolitionist campaigns of the late eighteenth century. But, in most instances, they were articulated by isolated commentators who found themselves ruminating upon a system so pervasive that they could scarcely imagine the most modest of reforms, and certainly not abolition. By the early eighteenth century, moreover, critics concentrated less on the horrors and injustice of the Atlantic slave trade, and rather more on the abuses attending colonial slavery. It was the latter that entered the personal experience of a large number of European observers in the Americas.

Before 1750, the most consistent opposition to the Atlantic slave trade occurred in West Africa, as a small but growing scholarship on African resistance to the traffic has begun to show. For some time, scholars have understood that the Atlantic slave trade thrived because of active participation by West African political and military elites, who seized and sold vulnerable men, women, and children to European traders in exchange for commercial goods. But that emphasis on African agency has tended to obscure the countless attempts by Africans in Africa to stop the traffic or limit its growth. For many ordinary people throughout Atlantic Africa and its hinterlands who were vulnerable to capture, the insatiable demand for new captives seemed like a form of witchcraft, like the work of evil spirits who had corrupted all forms of earthly and divine power for the sake of nefarious ends. In response, where slaving became endemic, the endangered sometimes constructed elaborate defences to protect themselves from slavers, by consolidating their residences, by constructing fortified villages, or taking refuge in swamps. The unlucky, who could not escape captivity, fled when they could, either during the march to the ocean or from the palisades and warehouses that held them on the coast. Resistance did not end there. Perhaps one in ten slave-ship voyages experienced a shipboard insurrection either on the West African coast or during the Atlantic crossing. These attacks on the Atlantic slave trade in Africa by Africans did not and could not cause its abolition. But they did discourage slave trading in some parts of Africa and raise costs for shippers everywhere and, as a consequence, perhaps they saved some lives as well. If every people and every state in Africa had cooperated, the volume of the Atlantic slave trade would have been larger still. Some, however, refused: they would not sell slaves; they would not allow slave traders to pass through their territory; and they attacked European shippers who tried to conduct business there. Often that initial opposition to the Atlantic slave trade eroded over time because of the persistence of European demand for captives, and because of an increasing desire across Atlantic Africa for the goods that slave traders supplied. This was the case in the Kongo in the early sixteenth century, Dahomey and Benin in the seventeenth century, and the Galinhas Country along the Ivory Coast in the eighteenth century. In each of these places, a European demand for more captives overcame the reservations of those African elites who at first had been hesitant to supply them (McGowan, 1990; Inikori, 1996; Thornton, 2003; Diouf, 2003; Taylor, 2006; Thornton, 2010).

Unhappiness with what the Atlantic slave trade wrought developed in the Americas as well. There, those unlikely to benefit from the use of slaves sometimes denounced the importation of African captives. Some resented the ways that large-scale slaveholding enabled the emergence of planter aristocracies. Some expressed concern about the inability of free white labour to compete with enslaved African labour. Others worried that a too-rapid growth of the slave population would lead to social unrest and insurrection. Where the imbalance between black and white workers was too great, unsuccessful efforts to recruit white migrants in greater numbers tended to be initiated by planter authorities. These anxieties about the impact of the slave trade on colonial societies has been documented most extensively in the historiography on colonial North America, which witnessed an unusually high degree of European migration across the colonial period. But such resentments surfaced at other times and in other places too, as in Cuba and Brazil, for example, in the middle decades of the nineteenth century, when the quickening pace of sugar and coffee production led to a rapid influx of African captives. In British North America, these concerns sometimes moved individual colonies to regulate and, in some instances, temporarily to close the slave trade. The middle Atlantic and northern colonies pursued such ends most avidly in the first half of the eighteenth century by, now and again, instituting prohibitive tariffs on slave imports – tariffs that the British government frequently disallowed. Even in the southern colonies, officials sometimes attempted to curtail slave-ship arrivals. The founders of Georgia banned slave imports to the infant colony for two decades in order to encourage white migration, to discourage the formation of a plantation economy, and to render the new settlement defensible. The colony of South Carolina decided also, for almost a decade after the Stono Rebellion of 1741, that the importation of slaves presented too many dangers to public safety to tolerate. Fears of insurrection raised doubts even in Jamaica, where some residents proposed a halt to the traffic in the era of the Seven Years' War. Doubts about the Atlantic slave trade spread across most of the North American colonies on the eve of the American War for Independence. Then, desires to curtail the traffic became entangled with a broader push in the colonies for political and economic autonomy. Closing the Atlantic slave trade to North American shores numbered among the first acts of the newly established Continental Congress in 1774 (Brown, 2006: 75–91, 134–43; Paquette, 1988: 81–103; Bethell, 1970: 70–72, 290–91, 311–12; Marques, 2006: 54–61; Wood, 1984: 1–89; Wax, 1982).[3]

This growing opposition to the Atlantic slave trade in North America owed much to the work of an emerging circle of antislavery activists. The intelligentsia in Europe and the Americas occasionally had derided and condemned the Atlantic slave trade before 1760, but no-one had tried to suggest that the immorality of the practice required those in power to pursue its abolition. That point of view first crystallized in Revolutionary America, particularly among Quakers in the Delaware valley and the allies they recruited across British North America. Within the Society of Friends, there had been critics of the Atlantic slave system from the beginning. Dissident Quakers long had insisted that slavery and the slave trade demeaned Africans and dehumanized those who traded slaves or owned them. Successive years of warfare and political division from 1756 to 1783 prompted the Society of Friends as a whole to seek greater fidelity to professed values and to find new ways to exert moral leadership. It would be difficult to exaggerate the importance of Anthony Benezet to the transformation of abolitionist sentiments to abolitionist politics. Benezet, more than any other Quaker, turned Friends from a focus on self-purification to a broader campaign to reshape how the wider society looked at the institution of the slave trade. With respect to abolitionist ideas, he was an innovator: he distilled and simplified the case against man-stealing that had gained some purchase among Spanish and Portuguese theologians more than a century before, but then added new emphases upon the devastation that the Atlantic slave trade brought to African society and upon the barbarities that attended the Middle Passage. Benezet, a pioneer in these matters, decided that governments both in the colonies and in Europe should be persuaded to abolish the traffic in total. Because he circulated his writings widely in North America, Britain, and France between 1762 and 1784, the moral case against the Atlantic slave trade received wider circulation and much greater visibility than before. This circulation of Quaker ideas, arguments, and politics in the era of the American Revolution led historian David Brion Davis to label their campaign "The Antislavery International" (Jackson, 2009; Davis, 1975: 213–32).

Abolitionist publics

Anthony Benezet's propaganda campaign had its most pronounced impact in Great Britain. Nowhere else among the major slave-trading powers did a popular, public campaign against the traders emerge. That this campaign crystallized in Britain at the close of the eighteenth century might seem odd at first glance. In the second half of the eighteenth century, British merchants were the leading slave traders in the Atlantic world. There were good commercial and political reasons to favour a continuation of the trade. Antislavery sentiments, moreover, did not always lead to antislavery commitments. That seems to be one lesson that arises from the history of antislavery thought in France, where there was a critique of the trade's inhumanity but only the most minimal attempt to address it (Seeber, 1937; Miller, 2008). It would be a mistake also to attribute the new antislavery campaigns to the cultural consequences of merchant capitalism, as the historian Thomas Haskell once proposed, given the complete absence of abolitionist organizing in the Netherlands, where merchant capitalism was strong (Bender, 1992). A number of historians have detailed how the first British abolition campaign came to fruition in the 1780s – the Quaker petition to the House of Commons calling for abolition, the alliance between Quakers and Evangelicals that culminated in the formation of the London Committee for Effecting the Abolition of the Slave Trade in 1787, and the series of investigations and debates in parliament that raised and then thwarted hopes before the somewhat sudden achievement of abolition in 1807 (Anstey, 1975; Oldfield, 1995; Jennings, 1997). Only recently, however, has the prior transition from antislavery thought to antislavery action received close scrutiny. The formation of antislavery commitments in the British Isles during the 1780s depended in part upon the changing politics of empire that attended the expansion of British dominions after the Seven Years' War and the loss of 13 North American colonies in the American Revolution. A new concern developed in this period that imperial practices needed to be assessed against the standards of virtue and liberty. Among Quakers in England, and among aspiring young reformers within the Church of England, Thomas Clarkson and William Wilberforce most notably, turning the nation against the Atlantic slave trade looked to be one way to improve the moral character of overseas enterprise and to foster a greater commitment to religion at home (Brown, 2006: pt III, IV).

The British campaign against the Atlantic slave trade enjoyed unusual public success. The London Abolition Committee and the numerous allies it attracted proved skilful in devising persuasive and memorable propaganda. Iconography conceived in the first years of the campaign – the kneeling bondsman asking "Am I Not a Man and a Brother", and the woodcut of the fully loaded slave-ship Brookes – became recurring images for nineteenth-century antislavery movements. From the start, the campaign's organizers behaved as if the nation had a right to decide policy. In 1787 and 1788, they recruited abolition petitions from every major town in England. At the height of public agitation for British abolition in 1791 and 1792, more than 500 petitions reached the House of Commons, bearing more than 400,000 signatures. As these numbers indicate, the movement drew in those typically excluded from British politics. The abolitionists put sailors before members of Parliament to testify about the workings of the trade. Former slaves, Olaudah Equiano most prominently, published accounts and presented lectures on their experience of the slave trade and work on the plantations. For the first time, women figured prominently in public political discourse, as subscribers to the London Abolition society, as petitioners for abolition, as authors of antislavery tracts, and as, themselves, political organizers. Defenders of the British slave trade used this popularity to hurt the antislavery movement after 1792, as the Haitian Revolution and the war with France stigmatized antislavery and radical politics of all kinds. Yet, as Seymour Drescher has shown, the abolitionist consensus that took shape at the end of the 1780s would persist in British culture up to the abolition of the British slave trade in 1807 and after. Perhaps 750,000 individuals signed the 1370 petitions sent to the House of Commons in 1814, which asked the British government to seek an international agreement on slave trade abolition that would prevent Britain's rivals from re-entering the Atlantic slave trade at the close of the Napoleonic Wars (Drescher, 1986, 1994; Wood, 1997: 14–77; Rediker, 2007: 319–26; Sandiford, 1988; Midgley, 1992).

In the United States, by contrast, there was an abolitionist consensus without a national abolitionist movement. Between 1783 and 1787, the great majority of the newly independent American states refused entry to slave-ships. At the time of the Constitutional Convention in 1787, only the state of Georgia was importing slaves. In the ensuing two decades, before the abolition of the US slave trade on 1 January 1808, only Georgia and South Carolina took in sizable shipments of captives from Africa, although, throughout this period and for many years after, American merchants, ships, sailors, and capital would continue to carry slaves to the Caribbean. This apparent tension between a general reluctance to receive slaves in the new nation and the toleration of their shipment and landing elsewhere indicates a characteristic tendency in attitudes towards the Atlantic slave trade in the United States after the American War for Independence. Americans wanted to profit from slavery while, at the same time, they wanted to reduce the risks, costs, and stigma associated with it. During and after the American Revolution, many Americans had come to regard the traffic as barbaric and a stain on national honour. Some in the Chesapeake thought the further import of Africans was unnecessary, since the US slave population was increasing without new captives; dangerous, because new captives seemed more difficult to assimilate; and potentially ruinous, since abundant slave imports threatened to throw incautious slave owners into irretrievable debt. Yet that broad consensus on the problems of the slave trade, unlike in Britain, had no outlet in national politics. The new constitution ratified by 1788 explicitly removed the subject from national debate by forbidding a ban on the traffic for two decades.[4]

Elsewhere, too, in the other polities engaged in the slave trade, abolitionist publics were slow to emerge, if they emerged at all. In France, as Seymour Drescher puts it, abolitionism was "ideologically robust and institutionally weak". Several French political economists toyed with various schemes for ameliorating colonial slavery, with gradual emancipation as a distant hope in some instances. But these schemes almost never became more than thought exercises, and rarely emphasized the problems of the slave trade. The impetus for French organizing would instead come from the British Isles, when, beginning in 1789, Thomas Clarkson and other London activists tried to encourage antislavery enthusiasms. Slave trade abolition, though, never ranked highly among the various grievances that stimulated political reform, and then revolution, in France. That was true even for those intellectuals who founded the Amis de Noirs in 1789, a society that pledged to promote both slave trade abolition and emancipation. If the Haitian Revolution led to an end to slavery in Saint Domingue, and for two decades, an end to the French slave trade, it also for two generations produced in France an association between antislavery, revolutionary violence, and the loss of wealth and power.[5] In Spain and Portugal, slave trade abolition never became a political cause and rarely generated political debate, at least before British lobbying forced these governments to address the question after 1807. Before then, though, the Spanish and Portuguese crowns, Brazil and the Spanish American colonies deepened their investment in the Atlantic slave trade to capitalize on the economic opportunities opened up by the Haitian Revolution (Murray, 1980; Marques, 2006: 2–15).

This sustained resistance to abolitionist pressure and the abolitionist example indicates that the Atlantic slave trade enjoyed extensive political support in the late eighteenth century and after. At present, though, historians have written far more on the defence of slavery than on the defence of the slave trade in the Age of Revolutions. In many instances, of course, the interests and arguments overlapped, since those dependent upon slave labour often needed the Atlantic trade in slaves to continue. Nonetheless, the case for slavery and the case for the slave trade often had to be argued differently, since, in some ways, the Atlantic slave trade was the more vulnerable of the two. Slave trade abolition, unlike slave emancipation, fell well within the ambit of commercial regulation and thus seemed susceptible to government intervention. The Atlantic slave trade proved more difficult to defend on moral grounds. Very few, by the late eighteenth century or thereafter, insisted that the Atlantic slave trade was a positive good that served the interests of the captives too. Instead, in both Europe and the Americas, the defence of the slave trade turned upon its apparent economic and strategic necessity. Few people could imagine how the valuable plantation colonies of the Americas could get on without it. Those arguments, in most instances, proved far more influential to the stewards of wealth and power than the moral and political arguments for its abolition. Moreover, no nation could abolish the slave trade, some observed, unless all agreed to do so. Some in the halls of power both in Britain and elsewhere feared that abolition would simply allow competitors to claim a larger share of Atlantic trade. To the defenders of the traffic in France, Spain, Portugal, and Brazil, the British campaign to abolish all Atlantic trades after 1807 looked less like a moral crusade and more like an attempt to suppress the commerce of Britain's competitors. In those places, particularly in France and Brazil, the defence of the slave trade would become entwined with a defence of the nation (Rawley, 1993; Ryden 2003, 2009; Kielstra, 2000; Marques, 2006: 20–28, 48–54, 78–83, 127–49; Bethell, 1970: 5–6, 63–66, 218–19, 232–33, 249–50; Murray, 1980: 147–48).

Explaining abolition

Still, notwithstanding the economic and strategic importance of the Atlantic slave trade, the participating nations agreed to the formal abolition of the traffic with striking rapidity. In 1790, the slave trade was legal and encouraged by every maritime power in the Atlantic world. By 1830, within four decades, they each had outlawed the trade, although an extensive illicit traffic would take another 30 years to be fully suppressed. The British antislavery movement played a decisive role in this process, and not only in the British Isles. Immediately after the cessation of the British slave trade in 1807, the British government sought a prohibition of the traffic of its allies and rivals. That aim was greatly aided by British victories at the close of the Napoleonic Wars, which left Britain in a position to dictate terms. British diplomats imposed upon their more vulnerable and more dependent allies and rivals treaties that led to the formal abolition of the Dutch slave trade in 1814, the French slave trade in 1818, the Spanish slave trade in 1820, and the Portuguese and Brazilian slave trades in 1830. Only Denmark in 1803, the United States in 1807, and newly independent republics in mainland South America from 1810 to 1813 enacted abolition on their own, without prodding from the British Isles. Even in these instances, though, the British campaign sometimes mattered. The Danish decision to act in 1792 – legislation that allowed the Danish slave trade to continue for another ten years – took shape in part because the Danes believed that the British trade would soon be abolished. The new Latin American Republics prohibited slave imports after 1810, in part to win British recognition of their independence. The crucial importance of the British government in the enactment of abolitionist measures everywhere, therefore, gives the history of British abolition, and explanations of it, international importance. For, without an end to the British trade, and the subsequent British commitment to prohibiting the traffic as a whole, it is certain that the Atlantic slave trade would have continued to expand deep into the nineteenth century, and perhaps beyond (Eltis, 1987: 81–101; Mason, 2000; Green-Pedersen, 1979; King, 1944).

Few subjects in the study of comparative slavery and slavery have received more extensive or searching scrutiny than the problem of British abolition.[6] The question of motivation, which, in one way or another, has dominated subsequent scholarly investigations of the subject, was a matter of controversy immediately after 1807. This is in part because British abolitionists, the British government, and the British nation more generally often described the measure as a triumph of good over evil, as a renunciation of a public sin, and as an emblem of national virtue. That interpretation received its first and most detailed articulation in Thomas Clarkson's *The History Of The Rise, Progress, and Accomplishment of the Abolition of the African Slave-Trade by the British Parliament*, which appeared less than a year after the enactment of the formal ban. Its emphasis on the triumph of humanitarianism informed how most British men and women thought about abolition and their nation's abolitionist commitments across the nineteenth and into the early twentieth century, even as the moral character of colonial rule drew increasing criticism both in the empire and at home. That way of thinking about British abolition, with its stress on humane and principled selflessness, drew pronounced and sustained criticism, however, outside the British Isles, particularly among the European and American nations that Britain dragged, reluctantly, into abolitionist commitments. For critics in France, Spain, Portugal, Brazil, Cuba, the United States, and elsewhere, British slave trade abolition and British abolitionism represented a combination of fanaticism, hypocrisy, and self-interest. These critics devoted particular attention to the ways that a ban on all the Atlantic slave trades stood to benefit Britain's economic interests by legitimating the surveillance of all merchant shipping and suppressing the economic development of Britain's competitors. Yet the sceptics noted, too, that British manufacturers and British capital continued to profit from slavery and the slave trade outside the empire, even as the nation and its government made a show of their collective renunciation of in humanity. Suspicions about British motives and distrust of British self-righteousness became a lasting legacy of this era, even as the initially hesitant and unwilling in Europe and the Americas came themselves to embrace the abolitionist ethos with more ardour and more purpose from 1850.[7]

These nineteenth-century controversies about the character of British motives informed twentieth-century controversies over their historical interpretation. The 1933 centennial of emancipation in the British Empire occasioned a slate of works that consolidated and popularized the humanitarian narrative, perhaps most influentially in *The British Anti-Slavery Movement* by Reginald Coupland, Beit Professor of Colonial History at Oxford University. Those works, in turn, inspired a revival of nineteenth-century critiques in the landmark book *Capitalism and Slavery* by Eric Williams (1944). The final chapters offered a sustained reorientation in the way that slave trade abolition had been understood. Williams drew attention anew to the "fanaticism" of the abolitionists, and lingered upon evidence of their hypocrisy. But he gave even more attention to the way that material interests, more than morals, explained the history of slave trade abolition, and not only in the British suppression of the European and American trades, but in the prohibition of the British traffic as well.

Two changes in the economic climate during the Age of Revolutions were crucial to Williams. There was, first, the separation of the North American colonies from the Caribbean plantations and a consequent decline in the British commitment to the West Indian monopoly on the home market. In addition to the rise of free-trade ideology there was, secondly, Williams argued, a crisis of overproduction in the West Indian colonies in 1806 and 1807 that made the abolition of the British slave trade feasible. Williams acknowledged the determination and skill of the abolitionist leadership, but insisted that they prevailed only because the economic interests of the nation had shifted dramatically by the early nineteenth century.

For more than 30 years after the publication of *Capitalism and Slavery*, the economic interpretation of British abolition became what one chronicler of these debates called "the new orthodoxy".[8] Accounts of British antislavery, abolition, and emancipation continued to narrate the rise and progress of the abolitionist movement, but in most instances took care to stress also that changing economic conditions and ideologies assisted their efforts and contributed to their success. Only in the 1970s did the "new orthodoxy" begin to receive detailed critique. Roger Anstey (1975) published, in a highly detailed account of the origins and course of the campaign against the British slave trade, an account that credited the energy and skill of the abolitionists and revealed, through their apparent absence, the relative unimportance of economic interests in the success of 1807. Seymour Drescher (1977) published *Econocide: British Slavery in the Age of Abolition*, which painstakingly investigated and dismantled the key aspects of *Capitalism and Slavery*'s explanation of British abolition. Using the same economic data upon which Williams relied, Drescher demonstrated that the British West Indian economy was expanding economically, and would have continued to expand if the abolitionists had not intervened. The turn to free-trade principles, which supposedly had led to British contempt for the West Indian monopoly on the home market, occurred much later, Drescher demonstrated. It occurred after the achievement of abolition in 1807, not before.

Since the publication of *Econocide*, few historians have continued to adhere to the economic interpretation of British abolition. The continuation or expansion of the British slave trade after 1807 stood to aid economic growth in the British West Indies as a whole, according to the new scholarly consensus, even if abolition, in some instances, promised to ease a crisis of sugar overproduction in the short run.[9] If the economic interpretation no longer holds court, however, the humanitarian narrative, with its emphasis on principled politicking and savvy parliamentary manoeuvring, wields less influence too. Since 1980, historians of British abolition have extended the range of actors pertinent to understanding the movement's achievement, and have emphasized in particular the impact of broad-based popular pressure. At the same time, they have brought to the fore the wider range of concerns that figured in the success of 1807, concerns that do not fall neatly on either side of the conventional divide between economics and morals. Most importantly, the Haitian Revolution, and the military and political history of the Caribbean more generally, begins to claim a larger place in histories of British, as well as French, abolition. For some time, historians have understood that the 1805 ban on slave shipments to colonies acquired during the war with France, colonies that might be returned after the peace, cleared the way for the complete prohibition of the entire British trade in 1807. More recently, though, several scholars have shown that concerns for the security of the British plantation colonies in time of war led some in parliament to question the wisdom of importing tens of thousands of Africans into the British settlements each year. Creole slaves, slaves born in the West Indies, increasingly were viewed as more pliable than those born in Africa. That view, when combined with a growing confidence in the economic benefits of less coercive strategies of slave management, helped abolitionists portray abolition as a path to amelioration, as a way of reconciling humanity and interest without compromising plantation production. This expectation, that the slave trade could be abolished without undermining plantation production in the British West Indies, became an article of faith among British abolitionists and their supporters by 1807 (Hochschild, 2005; Richardson, 2007; Ryden, 2009; Fergus, 2009; Morgan, 2010).[10] It informed British abolitionist diplomacy thereafter, and bewildered governing elites elsewhere, who doubted that a comprehensive abolition could yield economic benefits.

Suppression of the slave trade

It was one thing to outlaw the Atlantic slave trade. It was something else to stop it. Slave traders transported more than two million captives Africans to the Americas illegally in the nineteenth century, after the formal abolition of the individual slave trades (Eltis, 1981: 155). Most of these captives went to Brazil and Cuba, where they were both the cause and the effect of a rapid increase in the production of coffee and sugar in these two regions during the nineteenth century. They arrived on ships flying the flags of those states – Portugal, Brazil, Spain, and the United States – that proved most reluctant to enforce the terms of the prohibitions to which they had agreed. That conflict, between the formal obligations of national and international law, and the actual practices of the individual states, occupies an important place in the diplomatic history of the half-century after 1815, after the close of the Napoleonic Wars. It provided the central theme for W. E. B. Dubois' *Suppression of the African Slave Trade to the United States of America*, one of the first scholarly histories of the Atlantic slave trade. Since then, slave trade suppression has been the subject of several detailed national histories, and has been placed in broad international context by David Eltis.[11] The impact of slave trade abolition, like the aftermath of emancipation, remains a vibrant area of scholarly research, even though the origins of abolition have tended to attract more controversy than its consequences.

At the Congress of Vienna in 1814, Britain sought an international accord that would not only make the Atlantic slave trade illegal for all European powers, but also would establish a joint agreement to enforce it. British diplomats came away from that and subsequent meetings with little more than a collective acknowledgment that the trade was an "odious commerce" that ought to be suppressed. As an alternative, thereafter, the British government worked to forge bilateral agreements on the slave trade with each of the individual nations. Britain could not win the right to search and condemn French or American ships suspected of illegal trafficking. Both governments refused to surrender this marker of sovereignty. Instead, the United States and France agreed to police their own merchants by establishing naval squadrons in West Africa, a commitment that the French government would honour in practice, but the United States would not. By contrast, Portugal, Spain, the Netherlands, and, after 1822, Brazil, proved less able to resist British diplomatic pressure, in part because they depended upon British economic support. As a consequence, they each acceded to the establishment of courts of mixed commission, in which a British judge would join with a Portuguese, Spanish, Dutch, or Brazilian jurist in deciding when a ship suspected of trading illegally should be condemned. (For detailed assessments of each case, see Fehrenbacher, 2001: 150–204; Kielstra, 2000; Murray, 1980; Bethell, 1970; Marques, 2006; Emmer, 1981.)

These courts of mixed commission have been described recently as the first international human rights courts. In truth, though, these courts often were international only in the most limited sense. The British navy captured more than 90 per cent of the ships brought into these courts. A disproportionate number of the cases were heard at Sierra Leone, a British colony, where the British Commissioner often acted unilaterally because the other justice was absent. These courts liberated perhaps 80,000 enslaved men, women, and children before the final end of the slave trade. Yet, at the same time, they were unable to bring the slave trade itself to an end. Many slave traffickers flew an American flag; the United States, until the election of Abraham Lincoln, refused to join the system of mixed commissions and would not enforce its own laws. Slave-ships that skirted the British royal navy in African waters in most instances could disembark their cargo in Brazil and Cuba unmolested, where government officials and a wider public supported slave imports long after they had been formally declared illegal (Bethell, 1966; Martinez, 2008).

The sociologists Robert Pape and Chaim Kaufman have described the six-decade campaign to suppress the Atlantic slave trade as "the most expensive international moral effort in modern history". From 1807 to 1867, Britain expended on average, they estimate, nearly 2 per cent of its national income on the enforcement of slave trade abolition. Over time, the size of the West African squadron grew incrementally across the 1820s and 1830s, and then dramatically in the 1840s. Eltis estimates that the royal navy captured one out of every eight ships employed in the slave trade. This was sufficient to increase the purchase price of slaves in the Americas and, in turn, increase the profits for those traders whose ships made a successful crossing, but not enough to stop the traffic entirely. In 1838, there were as many slaves shipped to the Americas as there had been in 1788, the year when the formal campaign against the Atlantic slave trade began. That uncertain record would lead some both in and outside of Parliament, from the late 1830s to the late 1840s, to question if the investment, in terms of money and lives, had been and was still worth the effort (Kaufmann and Pape, 1999; Lloyd, 1949).

The evident limits of diplomacy moved the British government to contemplate other strategies. Some abolitionists began to think that the use of force was immoral, even when the Atlantic slave trade was the target; or that discouraging the slave trade in Africa, rather than attempting to intercept it on the high seas, might achieve abolition more quickly. That point of view inspired the disastrous Niger expedition of 1840 orchestrated by Thomas Fowell Buxton, who had hoped that the promotion of Christianity, commerce, and civilization in the West African hinterland would bring to an end traditions of captive-taking and slave trading. Others thought that more emphasis might be placed on policing Africa's Atlantic coast. Veterans of the West African squadron, such as Joseph Denman, argued that a blockade of the principal slaving ports would make it impossible for illicit traffickers to operate. That strategy, which received support from the Foreign Office, led to a series of treaties with West African states that authorized the policing of certain ports, and, to prevent slave exports from Dahomey, would culminate with the annexation of Lagos in 1851. Britain took unilateral action with growing frequency, even when this meant skirting or violating international law (Temperley, 1991; Law, 2010). The Palmerston Act of 1839 and the Aberdeen Act of 1845 empowered the Royal Navy to condemn Brazilian and Spanish ships suspected of trading illegally in British Vice-Admiralty Courts, effectively abandoning the system of mixed commission in the process.

The Atlantic slave trade could only come to an end, David Eltis has concluded, when the individual nations each decided to enforce their own laws. For most of this period, Britain had too few active partners in the campaign to achieve its goals. France put a stop to the illicit use of the French flag in the slave trade in 1831, in part because of strengthening abolitionist commitments there. Elsewhere, though, ambivalence about abolition was revealed by the lack of resources devoted to it. The United States government under-funded its West African squadrons for four decades, thereby allowing US ships, or ships flying the US flag, to import tens of thousands of African captives to Cuba. Brazil, too, made no attempt to police its own waters until 1850, when the British navy began to do so on Brazil's behalf. The suppression of the slave trade to Cuba, the last surviving branch of the traffic after 1850, depended in part upon declining demand for slaves in Cuba after 1860, but it owed something also to the firm turn against the illegal slave trade in the United States after the election of Abraham Lincoln (Daget, 1981; Bethell, 1970: 351–63; Murray, 1980: 298–323). Britain initiated, organized, and conducted the suppression of the Atlantic slave trade but, in the end, could succeed only with the assistance, however grudging, of others.

Legacies

The campaign to suppress the Atlantic slave trade led to the liberation of more than 200,000 captives from more than 2000 slave-ships. Those set free by British officials found themselves scattered to the peripheries of the British Atlantic Empire – to the Bahamas, to Trinidad, to the Cape Colony and, most frequently, to Sierra Leone. In many instances, they were apprenticed or indentured to British colonists, or British officials, seeking to rectify labour shortages in new settlements or within the British army or navy. The *"emancipados"* liberated by the Iberian powers in the Americas usually experienced a similar fate – re-enslavement in practice if not in name (Asiegbu, 1969; Thompson, 1990; Adderley, 2006; Murray, 1980: 271–97; Conrad, 1973: 50–70; Mamigonian, 2009). Their vulnerability to further exploitation indicates the persistent demand across the Atlantic world for coercible labour, even as the Atlantic slave trade fell out of favour. In the United States and in Brazil, those demands would lead to the rapid extension of internal slave trades, which would funnel labour to the most prosperous plantation economies, the cotton South in the antebellum United States and the coffee plantations of southern Brazil. If abolition ended the continued import of new African labour, and thus further facilitated the creation of Creole societies on the plantations, it also encouraged the separation of kin. Where the inter-colonial slave trade was forbidden, the end of the Atlantic slave trade would lead, after emancipation, to the formation of new labour migration schemes from India and China (Johnson, 2004; Walton, 1993). The economic consequences of slave trade abolition in the Americas were mixed. In some places, such as the United States, where the slave population grew extensively without new imports, the impact was modest. In other places, in the French and Danish Caribbean and, later, in Brazil and Cuba, the ban on the Atlantic slave trade brought about a significant reduction in the export of staple crops (Eltis, 1987: 232–40).

In Africa, by contrast, the suppression of the Atlantic slave trade was attended by a rapid growth in the export of what the abolitionists liked to refer to as "legitimate commerce". Starting in the late eighteenth century, the opponents of the Atlantic slave trade had argued that the commerce in captive Africans had discouraged the export of tropical goods that might have found extensive markets in Europe and elsewhere. They justified abolition, in part, as a way of opening up access to these under-valued and under-utilized trades. Such ambitions figured explicitly in the Danish abolition decree of 1793, and would inspire experiments in plantation agriculture throughout West Africa by both the British and the French in the first half of the eighteenth century. Portugal feared that British suppression of the Atlantic slave trade aimed, in part, to seize Portuguese dominions in West-Central Africa for British exploitation and colonization. These ambitions outraced European capacities until the very end of the nineteenth century (Brown, 2006: 262–82, 314–30; Curtin, 1964; Roge, 2008; Klein, 2009; Hopkins, 2001, 2009; Marques, 2006: 193–248). But the export of tropical commodities did grow quickly during and after the years of suppression. The transition to legitimate commerce was most apparent in the Bights of Benin and Biafra, where the palm oil trade by the third quarter of the nineteenth century came to exceed the value of the Atlantic slave trade in the years before. That shift to a commodities trade, in turn, intensified the employment of slave labour, the prices for whom declined within Africa with the end of the Atlantic slave trade. Abolition, then, had the ironic consequence of reducing the number of captives taken in West Africa, but increasing the number of slaves engaged in economic production there (Eltis, 1987: 223–32; Law, 1995; Lovejoy, 2000).

In time, by the end of the nineteenth century, every nation in Europe and the Americas would come to see antislavery as the British did, as an emblem of moral progress and an instrument for the improvement of those peoples benighted by archaic, savage traditions. Just as antislavery in the early nineteenth century helped the British define what it meant to be British, in the late nineteenth century it helped European nations bring further clarity to the idea of the "West". Indeed, antislavery seemed to mark off Christian Europe from the Muslim and pagan states of the Middle East, Africa, and Asia. As with the late medieval crusades against infidels in Palestine, this marker of moral superiority made it easier to conceive of European expansion as a war against barbarism. To sanctify the scramble for African colonies, the European delegates meeting in Berlin in 1885 pledged themselves to the protection and advancement of the "native tribes". Even as decolonization movements gathered force during the twentieth century, and even as the moral authority of the West came under critical scrutiny, the League of Nations and, after, the United Nations reasserted the commitment of the "civilized world" to bringing an end to slavery around the globe. The campaign that started in the late eighteenth century as an attempt to stop the British slave trade had extended by the twentieth century into a worldwide campaign against human bondage, which, in its peculiar mixture of philanthropy and imperialism, would mark, and continues to mark, relations between the world and the West (Davis, 1984: 279–315).

Notes

1 *Voyages: The Trans-Atlantic Slave Trade Database*, www.slavevoyages.org
2 This paragraph and the next draw upon Davis (1988).
3 W. E. B. Dubois, *The Suppression of the African Slave Trade to the United States of America, 1638–1870* (New York: Longman, Green and Co., 1896), 7–37.
4 For the United States slave trade after 1783, see McMillan (2004); Eltis (2008). For the Atlantic slave trade in US politics and Chesapeake opposition to the traffic in the latter half of the eighteenth century, see Fehrenbacher (2001); Deyle (2009).
5 The large literature on antislavery thought and action in France during, before, and immediately after the Haitian Revolution is well summarized in Drescher (2009: 146–80, 173). See also the scholarship cited therein.
6 This paragraph and the four that follow draw from Brown (2006: 3–22).
7 On tensions between hostility to British high-handedness and respect for the British example, see Mason (2009).
8 Temperley (1987). The essays in this volume provide a useful overview of scholarly responses to *Capitalism and Slavery* (Williams, 1944) as of the mid-1980s.
9 For the persistence of dissenting views, see especially Carrington (2002). Ryden (2009) also has argued for the importance of decline, but in a way that stresses politics as well as economics.
10 For a dissenting view, which questions the impact of events in the Caribbean on abolition in 1807 and thereafter, see Drescher (2009, 169–74, 182–86, 223–28). Recent assessments of the parliamentary context include Farrell (2007); Hilton (2010).
11 Eltis (1987). The five paragraphs that follow draw primarily on this book, except where indicated.

Bibliography

Adderley, Roseanne Marion, *"New Negroes from Africa:" Slave Trade Abolition and Free African Settlement in the Nineteenth-Century Caribbean* (Bloomington: Indiana University Press, 2006).
Anstey, Roger A., *The Atlantic Slave Trade and British Abolition, 1760–1810* (Atlantic Highlands, NJ: Humanities Press, 1975).
Asiegbu, Johnson U. J., *Slavery and the Politics of Liberation, 1787–1861: A Study of African Emigration and British Anti-Slavery Policy* (New York: Longmans, Green, and Co., 1969).
Bender, Thomas, ed., *The Antislavery Debate: Capitalism and Abolitionism as a Problem in Historical Interpretation* (Berkeley and Los Angeles: University of California Press, 1992).
Bethell, Leslie, "The Mixed Commissions for the Suppression of the Transatlantic Slave Trade in the Nineteenth Century", *Journal of African History* 7 (1966), 79–93.
——, *Abolition of the Brazilian Slave Trade: Britain, Brazil, and the Slave Trade Question, 1807–1869* (Cambridge: Cambridge University Press, 1970).
Boxer, C. R., *The Church Militant and Iberian Expansion, 1440–1770* (Baltimore: Johns Hopkins University Press, 1978).
Brown, Christopher Leslie, *Moral Capital: Foundations of British Abolitionism* (Chapel Hill: University of North Carolina Press, 2006).
Carrington, Selwyn H. H., *The Sugar Industry and the Abolition of the Slave Trade, 1775–1810* (Gainesville: University Press of Florida, 2002).
Conrad, Robert, "Neither Slave nor Free: the Emancipados of Brazil, 1818–68", *Hispanic American Historical Review* 53 (1973), 50–70.
Curtin, Philip, *The Image of Africa: British Ideas and Action, 1780–1850* (Madison: University of Wisconsin Press, 1964).
Daget, Serge, "France, Suppression of the Illegal Slave Trade, and England, 1817–50", in Eltis, David and Walvin, James, eds, *The Abolition of the Atlantic Slave Trade: Origins and Effects in Europe, Africa, and the Americas* (Madison: University of Wisconsin Press, 1981), 155–76.
Davis, David Brion, *The Problem of Slavery in the Age of Revolution, 1770–1823* (Ithaca, NY: Cornell University Press, 1975).

——, *Slavery and Human Progress* (New York: Oxford University Press, 1984).

——, *The Problem of Slavery in Western Culture*, Second Edition (New York: Oxford University Press, 1988).

Deyle, Steven M., "An 'Abominable' New Trade: The Closing of the African Slave Trade and the Changing Patterns of U.S. Political Power, 1808–60", *William and Mary Quarterly* 3rd ser. 66 (2009), 833–52.

Diouf, Sylviane, *Fighting the Slave Trade: West African Strategies* (Athens: Ohio University Press, 2003).

Drescher, Seymour, *Econocide: British Slavery in the Age of Abolition* (Pittsburgh: University of Pittsburgh Press, 1977).

——, *Capitalism and Antislavery: British Mobilization in Comparative Perspective* (Basingstoke, UK: Macmillan, 1986).

——, "Whose Abolition? Popular Pressure and the Ending of the British Slave Trade", *Past and Present* 143, (1994), 135–66.

——, *From Slavery to Freedom: Comparative Studies in the Rise and Fall of Atlantic Slavery* (Basingstoke, UK: Macmillan, 1999).

——, *Abolition: A History of Slavery and Antislavery* (Cambridge: Cambridge University Press, 2009).

Eltis, David, "The Impact of Abolition on the Atlantic Slave Trade", in Eltis, David and Walvin, James, eds, *The Abolition of the Atlantic Slave Trade: Origins and Effects in Europe, Africa, and the Americas* (Madison: University of Wisconsin Press, 1981).

——, *Economic Growth and the Ending of the Transatlantic Slave Trade* (New York: Oxford University Press, 1987).

——, "The U.S. Transatlantic Slave Trade, 1644–1867", *Civil War History* 54 (2008), 347–78.

Eltis, David and Walvin, James, eds, *The Abolition of the Atlantic Slave Trade: Origins and Effects in Europe, Africa, and the Americas* (Madison: University of Wisconsin Press, 1981).

Emmer, Pieter C., "Abolition of the Abolished: The Illegal Dutch Slave Trade and the Mixed Courts", in Eltis, David and Walvin, James, eds, *The Abolition of the Atlantic Slave Trade: Origins and Effects in Europe, Africa, and the Americas* (Madison: University of Wisconsin Press, 1981), 177–92.

Farrell, Stephen, "'Contrary to the Principles of Justice, Humanity and Sound Policy:' The Slave Trade, Parliamentary Politics and the Abolition Act, 1807", in Farrell, Stephen, Unwin, Melanie and Walvin, James, eds, *The British Slave Trade* (Edinburgh: Edinburgh University Press, 2007) 141–71.

Fehrenbacher, Don E., *The Slaveholding Republic: An Account of the United States Government's Relations to Slavery*, completed and edited by Ward M. McAfee (Oxford: Oxford University Press, 2001).

Fergus, Claudius, "'Dread of insurrection': Abolitionism, Security, and Labor in Britain's West Indian Colonies, 1760–1823", *William and Mary Quarterly* 3rd ser. 66 (2009), 757–80.

Gray, Richard "The Papacy and the Atlantic Slave Trade: Lourenco da Silva, the Capuchins, and the Decisions of the Holy Office", *Past and Present* 115 (1987), 52–68.

Green-Pedersen, Svend E., "The Economic Considerations Behind the Danish Abolition of the Negro Slave Trade", in Gemery, Henry A. and Hogendorn, Jan S., eds, *The Uncommon Market: Essays in the Economic History of the Atlantic Slave Trade* (New York: Academic Press, 1979), 239–60.

Hilton, Boyd, "1807 and All That: Why Britain Outlawed Her Slave Trade", in Peterson, Derek, ed., *Abolitionism and Imperialism in Britain, Africa, and the Atlantic* (Athens: Ohio University Press, 2010), 63–83.

Hochschild, Adam, *Bury the Chains: Prophets and Rebels in the Fight to Free an Empire's Slaves* (Boston: Houghton Mifflin, 2005).

Hopkins, Daniel P., "The Danish Ban on the Atlantic Slave Trade and Denmark's African Colonial Ambitions, 1787–1807", *Itinerario* 25 (2001), 154–84.

——, "Peter Thonning, The Guinea Commission and Denmark's Post-abolition African Colonial Policy, 1803–50", *William and Mary Quarterly* 3rd ser. 66 (2009) 781–808.

Howard, Warren S., *American Slavers and the Federal Law, 1837–1862* (Berkeley: University of California Press, 1963).

Inikori, Joseph E., "Measuring the Unmeasured Hazards of the Atlantic Slave Trade: Documents Relating to the British Slave Trade", *Revue Francaise d'histoire d'outre-mer* 83 (1996), 53–92.

Jackson, Maurice, *Let This Voice Be Heard: Anthony Benezet, Father of Atlantic Abolitionism* (Philadelphia: University of Pennsylvania Press, 2009).

Jennings, Judith T., *The Business of Abolishing the British Slave Trade, 1783–1807* (London: Frank Cass & Co., 1997).

Johnson, Walter ed., *The Chattel Principle: Internal Slave Trades in the Americas* (New Haven: Yale University Press, 2004).

Kaufmann, Chaim and Pape, Robert A., "Explaining Costly International Moral Action: Britain's Sixty-Year Campaign against the Atlantic Slave Trade", *International Organization* 53 (1999), 631–68.

Kielstra, Paul, *The Politics of Slave Trade Suppression in Britain and France, 1814–1848: Diplomacy, Morality, and Economics* (New York: St Martin's Press, 2000).

King, James Ferguson, "The Latin American Republics and the Suppression of the Slave Trade", *Hispanic American Historical Review* 24 (1944), 387–411.

Klein, Martin A., "Slaves, Gum, and Peanuts: Adaptation to the End of the Slave Trade in Senegal, 1817–48", *William and Mary Quarterly* 3rd ser. 66 (2009), 895–914.

Law, Robin, *From Slave Trade to "Legitimate Commerce:" The Commercial Transition in Nineteenth-Century West Africa*, papers from a conference of the Centre of Commonwealth Studies, University of Stirling (Cambridge: Cambridge University Press, 1995).

——, "International Law and the Suppression of the Atlantic Slave Trade", in Peterson, Derek, ed., *Abolitionism and Imperialism in Britain, Africa, and the Atlantic* (Athens: Ohio University Press, 2010), 150–74.

Lloyd, Christopher, *The Navy and the Slave Trade: The Suppression of the African Slave Trade in the Nineteenth Century* (London: Longmans Green, 1949).

Lovejoy, Paul, *Transformations in African Slavery: A History of Slavery in Africa*, 2nd edn (Cambridge: Cambridge University Press, 2000).

Mamigonian, Beatriz G., "In the Name of Freedom: Slave Trade Abolition, the Law and the Brazilian Branch of the African Emigration Scheme (Brazil–British West Indies, 1830s–1850s)", *Slavery and Abolition* 30 (2009), 41–66.

Marques, Joao Pedro, *Sounds of Silence: Nineteenth-Century Portugal and the Abolition of the Slave Trade*, trans. Richard Wall (New York: Bergahn Books, 2006).

Martinez, Jenny S., "Antislavery Courts and the Dawn of International Human Rights Law", *Yale Law Journal* 117 (2008), 550–641.

Mason, Matthew E., "Slavery Overshadowed: Congress Debates Prohibiting the Atlantic Slave Trade to the United States, 1806–7", *Journal of the Early Republic* 20 (2000), 59–81.

——, "Keeping Up Appearances: The International Politics of Slave Trade Abolition in the Nineteenth-Century World", *William and Mary Quarterly* 3rd ser. 66 (2009), 809–32.

McGowan, Winston, "African Resistance to the Atlantic Slave Trade in West Africa", *Slavery and Abolition* 11 (1990), 5–29.

McMillan, James, *The Final Victims: The Foreign Slave Trade to North America, 1783–1810* (Columbia: University of South Carolina Press, 2004).

Midgley, Clare, *Women Against Slavery: the British Campaigns, 1780–1870* (London: Routledge, 1992).

Miller, Christopher L., *The French Atlantic Triangle: Literature and Culture of the Slave Trade* (Durham, NC: Duke University Press, 2008).

Morgan, Philip D., "Ending the Slave Trade: A Caribbean and Atlantic Context", in Peterson, Derek, ed., *Abolitionism and Imperialism in Britain, Africa, and the Atlantic* (Athens: Ohio University Press, 2010), 101–28.

Murray, David, *Odious Commerce: Britain, Spain, and the Abolition of the Cuban Slave Trade* (Cambridge: Cambridge University Press, 1980).

Oldfield, J. R., *Popular Politics and British Anti-slavery: The Mobilization of Public Opinion against the Slave Trade, 1787–1807* (Manchester: Manchester University Press, 1995).

Paquette, Robert L., *Sugar is Made With Blood: The Conspiracy of La Escalera and the Conflict Between Empires over Slavery in Cuba*, (Middletown, CT: Wesleyan University Press, 1988).

Rawley, James, "London's Defense of the Slave Trade, 1787–1807", *Slavery and Abolition* 14 (1993), 48–69.

Rediker, Marcus, *The Slave Ship: A Human History* (New York: Viking, 2007).

Richardson, David, "The Ending of the British Slave Trade in 1807: The Economic Context", in Farrell, Stephen, Unwin, Melanie and Walvin, James, eds, *The British Slave Trade: Abolition, Parliament, and People* (Edinburgh: Edinburgh University Press, 2007), 127–40.

Roge, Pernille, "'La Clef de Commerce' – The Changing Role of Africa in France's Atlantic Empire, 1760–97", *Journal of the History of European Ideas* 34 (2008), 431–43.

Russell-Wood, A. J. R., "Iberian Expansion and the Issue of Black Slavery: Changing Portuguese Attitudes, 1440–1770", *American Historical Review* 83 (1978), 16–42.

Ryden, David Beck, ed., *The Abolitionist Struggle: The Promoters of the Slave Trade* (London: Pickering and Chatto, 2003).

——, *West Indian Slavery and British Abolition, 1783–1807* (New York: Cambridge University Press, 2009).

Sandiford, Keith A., *Measuring the Moment: Strategies of Protest in Eighteenth-Century Afro-English Writing* (Selinsgrove, PA: Susquehanna University Press, 1988).

Seeber, Edward Derbyshire, *Anti-Slavery Opinion in France during the Second Half of the Eighteenth Century* (Baltimore: Johns Hopkins University Press, 1937).

Taylor, Eric, *If We Must Die: Shipboard Insurrections in the Era of the Atlantic Slave Trade* (Baton Rouge: Louisiana State University Press, 2006).

Temperley, Howard, "Eric Williams and Abolition: The Birth of a New Orthodoxy", in Solow, Barbara Lewis and Engerman, Stanley L., eds, *British Capitalism and Caribbean Slavery: The Legacy of Eric Williams* (Cambridge: Cambridge University Press, 1987), 229–58.

——, *White Dreams, Black Africa: The Antislavery Expedition to the River Niger, 1841–1842* (New Haven, CT: Yale University Press, 1991).

Thompson, Alvin O., "African 'Recaptives' under Apprenticeship in the British West Indies, 1807–28", *Immigrants and Minorities* 9 (1990), 123–44.

Thornton, John, "Cannibals, Witches, and Slave Traders in the Atlantic World", *William and Mary Quarterly* 3rd ser. 60 (2003), 273–94.

——, "African Political Ethics and the Slave Trade", in Peterson, Derek, ed., *Abolitionism and Imperialism in Britain, Africa, and the Atlantic* (Athens: University of Ohio Press, 2010), 38–53.

Walton, Look Lai, *Indentured Labor, Caribbean Sugar: Chinese and Indian Migrants to the British West Indies, 1838–1918* (Baltimore: Johns Hopkins University Press, 1993).

Wax, Darold D., "'The Great Risque We Run:' The Aftermath of the Slave Rebellion at Stono, South Carolina, 1739–45", *Journal of Negro History* 67 (1982), 136–47.

Williams, Eric, *Capitalism and Slavery* (Chapel Hill: University of North Carolina Press, 1944).

Wood, Betty, *Slavery in Colonial Georgia, 1730–1775* (Athens: University of Georgia Press, 1984).

Wood, Marcus, *Blind Memory: Visual Representation of Slavery in England and America, 1780–1865* (Manchester: Manchester University Press, 1997).

18

FORGING FREEDOM

Steven Hahn

Introduction: struggling against slavery

From the moment the institution of slavery established its first toeholds in the Americas, the enslaved engaged in struggle against it. Their struggles were guided by personal and group histories, by their places of origin, their ages and genders, their work skills and regimens, their spiritual practices, the alliances they could fashion, the temperaments and resources of their owners, the geopolitical location of their captivity, and, of course, the wider historical context. The historian Hilary McD. Beckles can therefore write, in reference to the British West Indies, of the slaves' "two hundred year war" against slavery (Beckles, 1988).

Inevitably, struggles against slavery, wherever and whenever they took place, had as their aim the limiting, weakening, or destruction of the power of slaveholders. Thus some level of "freedom" always proved to be an objective for slaves struggling against enslavement. Slaves might flee individually from new or abusive owners, or might head in groups to less accessible terrain and try to establish fugitive settlements called maroon communities. More commonly, they would push back against the demands of their masters and the imperatives of enslavement, seeking to form relations of kinship and friendship, find time to provide for one another, create spaces to meet and worship together, and, of course, mitigate as best as possible the brutality of their daily lives. On occasion, when circumstances appeared most opportune, they might conspire to rebel against slavery as they knew it. At all events, they battled to constrain the reach of slaveholders, define relations and activities subject to some of their own control, and turn privileges that owners may have conceded into rights they could embrace and defend. Slaves looked, that is, to carve small spaces of freedom in a large world of slavery.

Waged with varying degrees of success across the hemisphere, these struggles contributed, by the last third of the eighteenth century, to a deepening crisis of slave regimes on both sides of the Atlantic. We know best about the growing moral doubts that slaveholding came to raise among Quakers and some Protestant evangelicals, as well as about the intellectual and economic challenges that the Enlightenment and the new political economists of England and France hurled at the hierarchies, coercions, and inefficiencies that slavery appeared to represent (see, for example, Davis, 1965; Brown, 2006; Drescher, 1987). But these may have come to little had they not been allied with the energies of slaves on the ground, which began to intensify during the 1770s and disrupted more and more of the Atlantic for at least the next six decades. In this sense, freedom was being "forged" well before it was officially proclaimed (Blackburn, 1988).

The forging of freedom, therefore, looked backward as well as forward, necessarily building upon the sensibilities and gains that had been developed and won under slavery, while imagining their deployments once slavery was no more. Maroon societies may initially have reflected notions of order and hierarchy derived from still-near African pasts, though eventually they reflected the plantation cultures from which they sprang. For most other slaves, freedom would not mean exchanging one way of life wholly for another, but rather meant enhancing what they had long battled to obtain. Even in the most explosive transitions, the weight of the past gave direction to the course of the future. In French Saint Domingue, the leaders of what would become the Haitian Revolution first looked to the amelioration of slavery (the end of whipping and an extra free day to work their provision grounds) instead of its abolition, and thought that the King of France supported their claims; only when those demands were rejected by colonial authorities did the slave rebels embrace emancipation as a goal, and only when the revolutionary assembly in Paris proclaimed abolition did most abandon royalism.[1]

Roads to emancipation

The case of Saint Domingue – the first large-scale emancipation in the Americas – is generally instructive because it suggests the complex dynamics that would ensnare the forging of freedom everywhere that slavery was undermined. The mass of slaves, overwhelmingly field hands and sugar mill workers, clearly wished to destroy the power of the island's master class and establish freeholds where they could labor under their own authority and provide for themselves. In this, they would turn their provision grounds and the exchange relations associated with them, which had emerged under slavery, into the centerpieces rather than the side-bars of a newly free society. But their vision of a post-emancipation Saint Domingue was not universally shared by their leaders and allies. The free people of color (*gens de couleur*), especially those who had prospered during the old regime, initially demanded expanded rights for themselves, not the abolition of slavery, and when brutally rebuffed by white planters, their growing commitment to anti-slavery was accompanied by a hope that "freedom" for the slaves and the revitalization of the plantation economy would go hand-in-glove. French republicans and radicals alike may have been brought around to the abolitionist cause, but they did not want to see the jewel of their colonial system taken out of the world sugar economy. Freedom, as they understood it, might bring former slaves into the folds of a new French citizenry but it would not absolve them from work on the plantations.

Even Toussaint Louverture, once a slave and then the leader of the rebellion-turned-revolution, feared the political consequences of a freedom that the mass of slaves looked to forge. Resolutely committed to emancipation, Toussaint nonetheless believed that it could be secured only if Saint Domingue were able to prosper and defend itself in a hostile world. Prosperity, to him, meant rebuilding the plantations and the staple economy, and, by extension, returning the ex-slaves to labor on the coffee and sugar estates – now for wages. It did not mean promoting small-scale peasant agriculture. So strongly did Toussaint embrace this view that he had to crush revolts in his own ranks by those who bridled at his economic policies.

Toussaint's plans for Saint Domingue died with him in a frigid cell in the mountains of France. After his death, the newly formed republic of Haiti was soon in a disastrous downward spiral, its freed population victimized by the economic and political isolation that American and European powers imposed, and by the political struggles of factions created by the revolution itself. But, in an important sense, Toussaint posed the question that all who pressed for the end of slavery would have to address: what would freedom mean in a world of imperial rivalries and capitalist markets and property relations?

There were no easy answers to this question, especially for those in positions of power and authority by virtue of their wealth, political placement, or white skin. To be sure, by the time of the Haitian Revolution a moral and economic indictment of slavery was being fashioned in Britain, France, and parts of the United States. Many people, especially in areas of the United States and Europe where slavery was not well established, were already regarding slaveholding as a sin. But the problems of emancipation and freedom proved immensely challenging, right from the start of abolitionist agitation. Slaves, after all, were valuable property, and it was not clear even to the most radical of abolitionists how freed people would be encouraged to work without the coercive mechanisms of enslavement. As a consequence, those who hoped for the day when slavery might be gone largely accepted the idea that owners would need to be compensated in some way for their economic losses and that slaves (perhaps slave owners too) would have to be "educated" in the new requirements and expectations of freedom. All of which meant that the ending of slavery and the forging of freedom – vaguely, at best, as the process was imagined – had to be gradual in their unfolding.

Gradualism expressed itself in two related ways. The first, and most indirect, was the growing attack on the Atlantic slave trade. For Europeans and Americans newly exposed to the iconography of the Middle Passage, the trade was especially horrific, emblematic of the savage disregard for human life that slavery promoted. It was not simply the images of shackled slaves in West African pens awaiting transport, or of ship cargo holds packed with suffering men, women, and children that outraged many viewers; it was also the recognition that the trade encouraged slave owners to work their slaves to death and replace them with newly purchased ones. Abolition of the trade would, it was therefore thought, end new enslavements in Africa and force masters to treat slaves more humanely, establishing a road of amelioration that would eventuate in the abolition of slavery itself.[2]

More directly, the gradualist orientation suggested that emancipation – when it occurred – must develop in a slow and ordered way, at once protecting important economic sectors from major disruptions, permitting slaves to learn about the new demands of freedom, and enabling slaveholders to minimize their losses. The new states of the American North provided (between 1780 and 1804) one model of how this might be done. Emancipation statutes there freed no slaves immediately. Rather, they freed the children of slaves, and only when they reached a certain age in their young adulthood: 21, 25 or 28, depending upon the state and the gender of the slave. Some statutes required slaveholders to educate their slaves and take some responsibility for them in their old age; others imposed no obligations on slaveholders, especially if they agreed to manumit their slaves early. In all cases, slaveholders had opportunities to replace slavery with indentures (some long-term), so that the road from slavery to freedom could be extremely protracted. Indeed, virtually every state that enacted emancipation in the late eighteenth and early nineteenth centuries had to pass additional legislation, decades later, that finally declared slavery officially dead: New York in 1827, New Jersey in 1846, Connecticut and Illinois in 1848, and New Hampshire in 1857. Indentures, on the other hand, continued to pass emancipationist scrutiny.[3]

The British constructed a different model in the 1830s. On the one hand, the government agreed to compensate colonial slaveholders directly and monetarily for the emancipation of their slaves; the bill would total £20,000,000. On the other hand, abolition was accompanied by a six-year period of "apprenticeship", during which former slaves would continue to labor for their former owners roughly 40 hours per week without pay, but could work for themselves in their free time thereafter. The flogging of men was to be regulated and that of women prohibited. A corps of "stipendiary magistrates", mostly from the ranks of the British Army, was assigned the task of adjudicating grievances that arose (Green, 1976; Holt, 1992: 3–112; Drescher, 2004).

During the 1870s and 1880s, both Cuba and Brazil followed approaches that combined features of the American North and the British colonies. In the middle of the anti-colonial struggle known as the Ten Years' War, Spanish authorities enacted the Moret Law (1870) which freed the children of slaves as well as all slaves who reached the age of 60; a decade later, the Spanish followed with the "*patronato*", effectively establishing an eight-year system of apprenticeship replete with oversight boards (Ferrer, 1999; Scott, 1985). In a similar sequence, the Brazilians responded to growing anti-slavery agitation and the abolition of the African slave trade first with the Rio Branco Law (1871 – known as the free womb law), eventually freeing the children of slave mothers, and then with the Sexagenarian Law (1885), freeing elderly slaves (da Costa, 1966; Toplin, 1972).

Even the American South, in the cauldron of Civil War, witnessed a truncated version of gradualism devised rather haphazardly by the Union government. Slaves who fled their plantations and farms and found their way to Union Army camps were initially designated in the summer of 1861 "contrabands of war" (their status as property, in other words, was preserved) and put to work on Union fortifications. Slavery was then outlawed in America's Western Territories and the District of Columbia (in spring 1862; in the latter case with substantial monetary compensation to slave owners). Abraham Lincoln issued a Preliminary Emancipation Proclamation in September 1862, which included plans for gradualism and compensation in the border states (states that remained in the Union but in which slavery was still legal) and colonization (forced exile) for freed slaves. The Emancipation Proclamation, signed several months later (January 1863), dropped proposals for gradualism but left the border states out of its reach. Only with the ratification of the Thirteenth Amendment to the United States Constitution (December 1865) was slavery finally destroyed – a nearly four-year process once it had commenced.[4]

The work of freedom

Nowhere did slaves share white people's sense that emancipation needed to be gradual in its implementation. Everywhere they moved to thwart the authorities' designs and to hasten slavery's complete demise. Where possible, both individually and collectively, they pressed owners to offer early manumission, sometimes through self-purchase and sometimes through special arrangements regarding labor and support. More generally, they frustrated slaveholders' efforts to maintain the coercions familiar to slavery, protested forms of punishment seen as inappropriate to freedom (such as the treadmill in the British West Indies), and sought redress for their grievances from newly designated officials. Together, they made a mockery of gradualist projects, and in most cases eventually forced their abandonment. As early as 1837, Caribbean island legislatures moved to terminate apprenticeship, and the British government formally acknowledged the writing on the wall on 1 August 1838, two years before apprenticeship had been scheduled to end. Faced with similar challenges, the Spanish government threw in the towel on the *patronato* system in Cuba in 1886 rather than wait until 1888 as the legislation had stipulated. By that time, the majority of *patrocinados* had already found their way to freedom. In Brazil, slaves' flight from the plantations, especially in the rapidly developing coffee areas of Rio de Janeiro and Sao Paulo, prodded the government into proclaiming emancipation in 1888 and helped usher in the first Brazilian republican a year later (Holt, 1992: 55–114; Scott, 1985: 127–97; da Costa, 2000: 125–233).

Still, the formal abolition of slavery, however it may have come about, hardly answered the question of what freedom would mean. Indeed, just as the problem of emancipation challenged even the strongest anti-slavery advocates, the problem of freedom challenged former slaves and their allies as well as former slaveholders and theirs. It would require the formulation of new policies by the state, complex negotiations between contending parties on the ground, and intensifying conflicts in various spheres of social and political life for the meanings of freedom to be established. What might appear to be a sharp set of goals and aspirations at one moment could be reconfigured in the next. In the end, no-one emerged as the unmistakable victor, and everyone had to adjust their expectations.

Former slaveholders, especially those who owned plantations oriented to staple-crop agriculture, hoped to keep their operations afloat in the uncharted seas of emancipation and, for the most part, they had important allies in metropolitan centers, central governments, and state houses. It is indeed difficult to find examples of any political or intellectual figures of stature who did not assume that staple-crop production would or should continue and expand in a post-slave world. Even in the United States, where abolition in the southern states was accompanied by the military defeat of the slaveholders, very few federal policy-makers – who were in an unrivaled position to dictate terms – thought that the plantation economy ought to go the way of slavery. Most, in fact, looked to prop up the plantation system and demonstrate the compatibility of free labor and commercial agriculture.

Where the emancipation process was especially protracted, as in Cuba and Brazil, slaveholders had chances to experiment with alternatives to slave labor, even while slavery remained in place and very much at the center of social and economic organization. By the middle of the nineteenth century, Cuban planters were mechanizing their sugar mills, hiring some wage laborers and, thanks to the support of the colonial state, importing Chinese contract laborers to help staff their estates. When slavery was ultimately abolished in the late 1880s, they had already been forging a road of freedom (as they understood it) and were poised to revamp the sugar sector on a more capital-intensive basis. In Brazil, the long-term unraveling of slavery and the sugar economy in the north-east saw the freed population grow at the expense of the slave, and a post-emancipation world develop within a larger context of labor dependency. Further south, in the newer and dynamic coffee districts, planters both shipped in surplus slaves from the north-east and, owing to state subsidies, began to import Italian contract laborers to work the coffee plantations. Like their Cuban and north-eastern Brazilian counterparts, they too looked to organize production around a free, but highly dependent, labor force (Scott, 1985: 3–41, 63–226; Northrup, 1995: 51–59, 106–48; Holloway, 1980: 13–110; Andrews, 1988).

Emancipation came more abruptly in the British colonies. Although ameliorative legislation enacted by Parliament in the aftermath of slave rebellions in Barbados (1816) and Demerara (1823) might have suggested that slavery's days were numbered, planters (absentee and resident) seemed determined to hold out until the bell tolled – or at least until the great Christmas Rebellion of 1831–32 in Jamaica (also known as the Baptist War) showed that the bell had to be tolled for their own safety and security. Apprenticeship offered a temporary structure of transition, but very soon the former slaveholders had to find ways of maintaining their sugar and coffee plantations without the coercive methods of enslavement. Almost everywhere, the assistance of the state – at local and metropolitan levels – proved crucial to their efforts, both in hedging in the economic alternatives available to former slaves and in affording access to new sources of labor (da Costa, 1994; Craton, 1982: 241–322; Foner, 1983, 2007: 8–38).

The challenges were greatest on large islands with extensive hinterlands, such as Jamaica, or in recently developing colonies, such as Trinidad and Guyana, because former slaves there had better opportunities to find subsistence off the estates, and thus to shift some of the balances of power in their favour. New vagrancy and police ordinances defined gainful employment and provided methods of punishing those who sought to avoid it. New taxes and land policies forced freed people to earn cash, and brought provision grounds and vacant land into the category of private property carrying prices well beyond their means. New rents imposed on housing previously occupied by slaves required that freed people work for wages on the plantations or be evicted. And a highly circumscribed franchise prevented freed people from holding the levers of formal political power. If all else failed, the planters could avail themselves of the benefits of global empire and the commercialization of agriculture: state-financed importation of contract laborers from East India. Nearly 400,000 of them eventually arrived, to be supplemented by migrants from Africa, China, and other West Indian islands.

Conversely, planters in the American South had to face emancipation and devise terms of freedom from positions of relative weakness. They had resisted gradualism as the crisis over slavery intensified in the United States. Although the Civil War-era emancipation had gradualist features, slavery ultimately collapsed in the middle of bloody and destructive warfare that involved the arming of thousands of slaves (similar, in fact, to what transpired in Saint Domingue). Southern planters, like their earlier counterparts in Saint Domingue, received no compensation for their financial "loss" when their slaves were freed. They also no longer had, after 1865, any political power in the nation. Indeed, their efforts to seize the initiative locally during the early phases of Reconstruction and, in the manner of their British counterparts, to legislate economic dependence (the "black codes" being notorious examples), were quickly overturned by the federal government (Hahn, 2009, 55–114; Foner, 1988: 199–209).

What former slaveholders did have going for them in the post-emancipation United States was an emerging community interest with northern elites in the defense of private property rights, the encouragement of commodity production, the maintenance of white supremacy, and the disciplining of labor. Although the demands of warfare had allowed the Union side to seize the property of rebellious Confederates and initiate land reform (most dramatically in William Sherman's Field Orders No. 15, which reserved 400,000 acres of valuable plantation land for exclusive black settlement), only a handful of federal officials were prepared to proceed very far along such a path. Most of the land under federal control (or which was being cultivated by freed people) was returned to white owners within months. Northerners generally wanted former slaves to remain in the South (many feared a massive influx of liberated slaves into the North) and work for wages growing cotton, tobacco, and other market crops that had long contributed to American economic growth. There was, in short, scant prospect that the planters would be displaced or that peasant agriculture would supplant the plantation sector. Moreover, within little more than a decade of the war's end, northerners were ready to concede home rule to their one-time enemies, and thereby dramatically narrow the road that freedom could travel (Hahn, 1997; Foner, 1988).

The land question

Whatever the challenges they faced, former slaves had developed ideas about the nature of freedom that would be of great consequence in the post-emancipation era. Those ideas had taken shape over many decades owing to their small-scale battles to limit the exploitation of slavery, to their changing spiritual sensibilities, and especially to their complex networks of communication that enabled them to learn of important political events near and far and to discuss the meaning of the events among themselves. At the very least, they could define freedom in direct opposition to what they experienced as enslavement. Since slavery meant that masters owned their persons, freedom should mean that they owned themselves. Since slavery meant that masters provided for them, freedom should mean that they provided for themselves. Since slavery meant that masters had nearly absolute power to govern them, freedom should mean that they would govern themselves. Since slavery meant that masters could determine their destinies, freedom should mean self-determination. And since slavery meant that masters and the masters' allies could visit violence on them at will, freedom should mean that they would defend themselves.

These objectives had little to do with maintaining the viability of the plantation system and facilitating the international flow of commodities and capital. They had to do, first and foremost, with organizing family and community life on freed people's own terms. This meant gaining access to means of production and subsistence, establishing new and different forms of authority, and escaping, as best as possible, the many brutalities, humiliations, and indignities that their former owners – and white people more generally – were accustomed to inflicting upon them.

Since former slaves, from the Brazilian south to the American border states, were overwhelmingly rural workers, they logically saw land as the foundation on which their aspirations for freedom might best be constructed. Besides offering them a vital source of economic independence, land could be a crucial site of family reconstitution and community building, not to mention a requirement for participation in the formal arenas of politics (since property qualifications for voting and office holding were the norm where some semblance of democratic procedures prevailed). Almost everywhere, moreover, freed people had some experience of tending land on their own, owing to the widespread allocation of provision grounds to slave households. For many slaves, the cultivation of provision grounds for subsistence and market purposes came to be regarded both as a "right" they had won and as a basis for claiming access to land once slavery had been abolished.[5]

Prospects for some sort of landed independence in the post-emancipation era were greatest in places where the end of slavery had been accompanied by slaveholders' loss of power. Haiti comes readily to mind. Even though Toussaint and, after him, Dessalines and Henri Christophe tried to restore the plantation sector, former slaves had sympathizers in the nation's leadership who, for various reasons, laid the groundwork for a landed peasantry that chiefly pursued semi-subsistence agriculture. It was an enormous change from the world of slavery, though one that would exact its own costs from the new peasantry.

Like Haiti, slavery was destroyed in the United States in the vortex of a revolution in which slaves played a central political and military role (this was true also in Cuba, though there the process was more protracted). Many American slaves learned of federal confiscation policies and the Sherman reserve, and they imagined that a program of land redistribution might be an accompaniment to their emancipation. In the spring and summer of 1865 it appeared that events might be moving in their direction. Lincoln had been assassinated and succeeded by Andrew Johnson (reputed to be a hard-liner intent on making treason "odious"), Congress had created the Freedmen's Bureau with provision for distributing confiscated and abandoned land, and many Freedmen's Bureau officials (including its top officer) sympathized with the project. But unlike Haiti, the slaves and former slaves in the United States were a distinct minority of the national population (they were even a minority in the former Confederate South – about 40 per cent), and their influence was decidedly limited. Before long, any hope of federally sponsored land reform had evaporated, and the freed people were left to their own devices in an unfavorable environment. Enclaves of black landownership remained where early land reform measures had been vigorously pursued (the coast of South Carolina and Georgia especially), and swathes of small, black-owned farms surfaced in association with agricultural diversification in parts of the border South. Otherwise, the only routes to landownership were rare grants of land from former masters or, far more likely, years of very hard work and slow individual and collective accumulation (Hahn, 2003: 116–59, 455–64).

Dramatic shifts in power at the level of the state were uncommon in the history of emancipation, and not always necessary to prospects for land acquisition by freed people. Jamaica was a prime example. Anti-slavery interests increasingly commanded public opinion in Britain and gained ever-stronger voices in Parliament. It is surely no accident that emancipation legislation and the great Reform Bill secured passage in close proximity. But the planters retained control of their estates, received monetary compensation, and won state support for overseeing the transition from slavery to freedom on the ground and for bringing in contract laborers. That contract laborers were needed, that a labor shortage loomed, speaks to the problems that the planting sector nonetheless faced: the freed population overwhelmingly outnumbered them, had accumulated resources because of their centrality to the island's marketing system under slavery (associated with the provision grounds), and looked out upon a landscape that included a great deal of uncultivated land outside the boundaries of the plantations. Despite local legislation designed to attach them to the estates, many freed people thereby managed to purchase small plots and establish "free villages". They could then supplement their subsistence by renting more land and working part-time on the plantations. The sugar economy suffered but the peasant sector grew until it encompassed a majority of the freed people (Holt, 1992: 143–76).

As the Jamaican case suggests, the land question was not a zero-sum game. It was part of a process whereby the social relations of slave society were reconfigured and new relations of freedom were contested. Combining small-scale peasant agriculture with wage labor (a mix seen in many rural societies of the nineteenth century) was one such outcome, and versions of it were to be found in virtually all post-slave societies. Former slaves might also look to squat upon unenclosed land or migrate to non-plantation districts where land was cheaper and easier to come by, as many did by moving east in Cuba. Yet, freeholds or other parcels of land were often impossible for freed people to obtain either through purchase or use-right, and so their aspirations for a life in freedom had to find different avenues of pursuit, most likely by means of labor on land owned by others.

Gender and power

Still, this was the beginning rather than the end of the battle. Whatever planters and other employers may have thought about the former slaves' "readiness" for freedom, they were not very well prepared either. Most planters wondered how freed people could be made to work without the threat of corporal punishment, and they surely did not relish the prospect of having to bargain with ex-slaves in some sort of labor market. At the very least, they hoped to preserve intact as much of the organization and supervisory authority of the slave plantation as possible. They expected the freed people to work as much as they did before, in the manner that they did before, and under the direction of themselves and their managers, as had happened before under slavery. They expected to regulate the freed people's family and community lives, limit their geographical mobility, and hold them accountable for their behavior during and after their work, imposing penalties when they deemed necessary.

Planters' expectations were, of course, easier to articulate than enforce, in good part because they clashed fundamentally with the objectives of the freed people. However much freed people might debate and disagree among themselves about the way freedom ought to be forged, they were unified in believing that freedom ought not to look like slavery with small wages thrown in. If they had to work in the fields, they wanted more control over the organization of their labor. If they had to live on someone else's land, they wanted to decide with whom and how they would reside. If they had to sell their labor in a market, they wanted employers to compete for their services. And if they had won certain concessions as slaves, such as the ability to cultivate provision grounds without paying extra rent for them, they wanted to hold onto them as freed people. Establishing these parameters through a contractual process was a tense and occasionally explosive process, as employers and workers alike tried to implement their understandings of the new world of freedom.[6]

In the battles to define the rules of the new game, gender relations were extremely important. In principle, slavery was no respecter of gender. Even if certain accommodations were made owing to issues of strength and child-bearing, men and women alike were owned by their masters as individuals and were expected to work at the master's command. Relations of family and kinship among the slaves were tolerated, but family relations were always just unofficial understandings in slave societies, with no formal backing under law. Power, as it was socially and legally recognized, linked master and slave, not slave and slave, whether or not the slaves were spouses or parents. What relations and understandings the slaves did devise emerged under great duress and with immense vulnerabilities.[7]

Thus, almost everywhere, one of the first things freed people did was to reconstruct gender and power by having freed women either leave the fields or, more commonly, perform substantially less field work than they did as slaves. White observers often interpreted this phenomenon as a manifestation of laziness or mimicry: black women taking the opportunity to lounge or to imitate the gender conventions of white ladies. In truth, freed people were struggling to redirect their labor time away from their employers and toward their families and communities. They also wanted to remove women from the threat of physical and sexual violence at the hands of white men. Freed women spent the time they would have been in the fields labouring for their families' sustenance, tending provision crops and livestock, making clothing, cooking food, and marketing surpluses. Among other things, what has been called the "withdrawal" of women from field work took a significant supply of labor from the disposal of employers and strengthened the bargaining position of freed people more generally. Not incidentally, it also established a foundation of reconstituted freed family life (Glymph, 2008: 137–226; Jones, 1985: 44–78; Schwalm, 1997: 147–268; Brereton, 2005; Stolcke, 1988).

Reorganizing the relations of gender and labor was part of a larger undertaking meant to afford freed workers more breathing room, more control over their labor, and better remuneration. Moreover, their prospects depended on the nature of the crop and the relative power of their employers. In cotton and tobacco economies, where the crop was not highly perishable and mechanization was limited, freed people had a good deal of success escaping the gang labor of their slave days. They were able to establish tenancy and sharecropping arrangements. Black households cultivated individual plots of land under their own direction, either paying rent or receiving a portion of the crop. In sugar economies, where the crop was highly perishable and capital-intensive in its processing, freed people had little opportunity to break free of the gangs or the intense mill work they had performed as slaves. Rather, they composed a wage-earning labor force until the advent of centralized mills, which fed off *colono* contracts with small producers who were often white or mixed race. In coffee economies, where the crop was perishable and its production labor-intensive, a mix of sharecropping, renting, and wage labor agreements developed (Hahn, 1990b: 71–88).

A new civil society

The irony was that, in the places where freed people helped to transform the labor organization of slavery (as in sharecropping), they were also most likely to be relatively isolated socially and vulnerable to the pressures brought against them by whites. In places where freed people worked under conditions most reminiscent of slavery, on the other hand, they had the best chance of protecting themselves against the exploitation of their employers. Sugar workers in southern Louisiana, for example, may have lived in the old slave barracks and cultivated the fields in gangs, but they also organized strikes and joined fledgling labor unions (Scott, 2005: 61–96; Rodrigue, 2001).

Efforts to reorganize relations of gender and labor remind us of the special challenges freed people faced in the aftermath of slavery. Even as they had struggled to build families, kinship networks, leadership structures, and communities as slaves, they would need to renegotiate many of these relationships and expectations in freedom. What sort of power would freed people bring into marriages and households, and would they embrace or resist the conventions and practices of European and American whites or of mixed race couples who had been free all along? What would happen to the petty property that freed people had accumulated by their own labor under slavery and to which different family groups had potential claims? What sort of hierarchies and divisions of labor would now prevail among them, and how would new responsibilities be prescribed and adjusted (how, for example, did the "withdrawal" of women from substantial field work unfold and what conflicting perspectives did it involve)? How would leaders who emerged under slavery retain their authority during the transition to freedom? Moreover, how would freed people conduct debates and enforce discipline in their ranks now that they would have some standing in civil and political society? Although the main axis of social and political conflict may have set freed people against their one-time owners, we must not forget the many conflicts that erupted and had to be settled among freed people themselves.

To some extent, freedom made public the relations and institutions that had long been effectively invisible in slavery, except to slaves. Religious congregations, community councils, forms of cultural transmission, strategies of coping with the loss of parents and mates, and networks of communication all took shape – with varying degrees of depth and density – under slave regimes, at times with the tacit acceptance of slave owners and other members of the ruling elite, and at times over the slave owners' objections. Necessarily, they were fragile in construction and mostly subterranean in their operations. Emancipation thus enabled freed people to provide firmer institutional footing to churches, schools, benevolent societies, and other forms of self-help and self-governance, though in most of the post-slave societies the financial burdens (the Reconstruction United States is an exception) fell onto the shoulders of the freed. Former slaveholders may have received state support for a number of their projects; former slaves were either left to their own meager resources or required to seek alliances with sympathetic whites and mixed race groups (Butler, 2000; Helg, 1995; Hahn, 2003: 163–464).

Economic reorganization

Freed peoples' efforts to renegotiate the terms of their living conditions after freedom affected not just them, but also their former masters. Masters generally faced challenging times after slave emancipation. Planters not only had to battle against the assertiveness of freed people; they also had to fend off challenges from merchants, manufacturers, and more humble folk in their own localities, as well as from competing social and economic groups at the national or metropolitan levels. The slaveholders who made the transition most smoothly (such as in Cuba and the Brazilian south) tended to be those who had begun to make appropriate accommodations with freed people before emancipation had occurred. Those planters who had long depended on mercantilist support, who were set in their ways, or who dug in their heels and fought to preserve the world of slavery that they knew, had a rougher time. They were buffeted by the vagaries of international commerce (as in the British possessions), were left mired in economic stagnation (as in north-eastern Brazil), or were driven from meaningful national power and outflanked by industrial and financial rivals (as in the United States). Before long, the plantation economies were reorganized around corporate ideals. Planters were displaced by new men with a business outlook (Scott, 1985: 84–124, 201–26; da Costa, 2000: 125–71; Hahn, 1990a: 75–98).

Black power and its limits

There is no obvious end point to the forging of freedom in the Americas, in part because slavery remained alive in Africa and other areas of the world into the twentieth century. An even more important reason why the forging of freedom does not have an end point is because freedom must be seen as a contested process, rather than as a clearly defined destination. Freedom struggles have been waged by descendants of slaves during the past century and undoubtedly will continue to be waged in the future. Yet there is a sense in which the forging of freedom reached certain limits by the end of the nineteenth century and, in so doing, produced a social and political reconstruction that would help organize the Atlantic for much of the twentieth.

Those limits were reached over the question of black empowerment. The discourse of antislavery, particularly where liberal theory was most prevalent, not only depicted slavery as retrograde but also imagined a world in which former slaves would respond to freedom in certain ways. They would respond as individuals and families rather than as groups. They would aspire to material betterment. In addition, they would work not because of coercive sanctions but in order to advance themselves. The compulsions and disciplines would be self-imposed, not externally imposed, and this would allow for new forms of social harmony and prosperity. Tutelage might be necessary; freed people would have to be divested of the old ways and prepared for the new. In the process, though, proper standards would be established and the right course would be charted. The problem with these plans for freedom was that liberal theory ignored the imbalances of power that liberal social relations embodied. Moreover, freedom was not something freed people just responded to; freedom was something they had a hand in making. And whatever their specific goals and aspirations, forging freedom demanded a redistribution of power: power to organize their lives, negotiate labor contracts, obtain greater resources, improve their living standards, and protect themselves against violence and harassment. Where political cultures emphasized representative government, they sought the franchise and a serious voice in policy deliberations. Where clientage was the norm, they sought greater bargaining leverage and power-sharing agreements.

Nothing troubled and terrified former slaveholders more than the idea of black empowerment. Reluctantly, they had come to accept emancipation. After all, they usually won some form of compensation after emancipation. They generally thought that the economic dependency of former slaves could be maintained and that their political rule would not be challenged. But black power was their "great fear", summoning as it always did the specter of "Saint Domingue", the massive and bloody slave revolution of the 1790s. The lesson of Haiti, as they saw it, was that freed people had to be kept in their place or all manner of destruction and social inversion would break loose, especially in those societies where blacks outnumbered whites by large margins. Since their counterparts in the industrial world also faced growing labor unrest during the nineteenth century, they were confident that they would not have to answer to new corporate elites about their iron-fisted retaliations.

Almost invariably, there were brutal reckonings as freed people pressed for rights and power, rallied to new leaders and movements, and pursued what they regarded as a meaningful freedom in a post-emancipation world; and as planters and their allies first stiffened their resistance and then struck back. The explosions detonated variously in Morant Bay, Jamaica (1865), Colfax, Louisiana (1873), the Brazilian *sertao* (1897), and the Cuban Oriente (1912). The immediate consequences were the tightening of discipline, the centralization of authority, the curtailment of democratic (or quasi-democratic) procedures, the repression of organized protest, the disempowering of freed people, and a resort to paramilitarism (see, for example, Heuman, 1994; Keith, 2009; Levine, 1988: 119–66; Helg, 1995: 193–226).

Constructions of race

In the longer term, however, new regimes of domination based on representations of race were constructed, and new languages of mobilization based on racial nationalism and pan-Africanism were fashioned. These regimes were by no means of a single type. They ranged from those espousing fictions of raceless nationalism (Cuba) and racial democracy (Brazil) to those developing highly repressive and institutionalized forms of white supremacy (United States). But in all cases, new hierarchies reflecting racial difference or racial categories found solid footings. With the exception of Haiti, European and Euro-American elites retained disproportionate power while former (black) slaves, regarded as backward, ignorant, and incapable of effective leadership, made up the lower and working classes. In Haiti, black people may have been in charge, but they faced immense difficulties in projecting that power in a world where statesmen refused to recognize Haiti's sovereign legitimacy. Where multi-caste systems had developed – largely owing to the absence of a white or European middle and service class – people of color could experience social and political mobility. In these places, the idea that "money whitened the skin" gained real traction. Where the "one-drop" rule prevailed, as in the United States (an assumption that anyone with any mixture of African descent would be classed as "black"), class stratification among people of African descent was far more limited, and exclusions from important arenas of social and political life would be easier to impose. Everywhere, as freedom replaced slavery, race came to be a central category of difference and domination.

Yet the construction of race was as much a political and cultural as a social and institutional phenomenon. The participants in these constructions included not only those who ruled, but also those who were ruled and who inhabited the categories that edifices of race supposedly prescribed. For as they forged new relations and solidarities in their struggles against slavery, the freed effectively used racial categories for their own purposes, establishing political identities in close association with them. Ideas of "blackness" or "Africanness" were possible only in the diaspora, and their political embrace by peoples of African descent served as a challenge to their discriminatory imposition by one-time masters.

Depending on the particular historical and cultural context, on racial demography and political projects, those ideas could find expression in what we have come to call both black nationalism and pan-Africanism, but either way, in a sense of peoplehood organized around race. W.E.B. DuBois was famously able to predict in 1903 that the twentieth century would be the century of the "color line", and his rival, the Jamaican Marcus Garvey, whose own roots were in slavery, was able to build an enormous international movement – one with important footholds in southern Africa, Brazil, Cuba, and Central America, as well as the United States – based on that very notion. These developments were a fitting apotheosis to the forging of freedom in the Atlantic world.

Notes

1 Among the important works on the Haitian Revolution are James (1963); Dubois (2004a); Fick (1990); Geggus (2002).
2 On the abolition of the slave trade, see W.E.B. DuBois, *The Suppression of the African Slave Trade to the United States* (Boston: Longman, Green, and Co., 1896); Carrington (2002); Anstey (1993); Eltis (1987); Bethell (1970); Murray (1980).
3 On the emancipations in the northern United States, see Hahn (2009: 1–54); Zilversmit (1967); Litwack (1961: 3–29).
4 The literature is enormous on the American Civil War-era emancipation, but for a very useful synopsis, see Berlin *et al.* (1992).
5 On the cultivation of provision grounds, see Berlin and Morgan (1991); Penningroth (2003: 45–78); McDonald (1993); Mintz (1974: 131–250).
6 On the complex negotiations and expectations in the immediate aftermath of emancipation, see Hahn *et al.* (2008).
7 For some interesting work along these lines, see Scully and Paton (2005).

Bibliography

Andrews, George Reid, "Black and White Workers: Sao Paulo, Brazil, 1888–1928", in Rebecca Scott *et al.*, eds, *The Abolition of Slavery and the Aftermath of Emancipation in Brazil* (Durham: Duke University Press, 1988), 87–114.
Anstey, Roger, *The Atlantic Slave Trade and British Abolition* (London: Ashgate Publishing, 1993).
Beckles, Hilary McD., "Caribbean Anti-Slavery: The Self-Liberation Ethos of Enslaved Blacks", *Journal of Caribbean History* 22 (1988), 1–19.
Berlin, Ira and Morgan, Philip D., eds, *The Slaves' Economy: Independent Production by Slaves in the Americas* (London: Frank Cass and Co., 1991).
Berlin, Ira, Fields, Barbara J., Miller, Steven F., Reidy, Joseph P. and Rowland, Leslie S., *Slaves No More: Three Essays on Emancipation and the Civil War* (New York: Cambridge University Press, 1992).
Bethell, Leslie, *The Abolition of the Brazilian Slave Trade* (Cambridge: Cambridge University Press, 1970).
Blackburn, Robin, *The Overthrow of Colonial Slavery, 1776–1848* (London: Verso Press, 1988).
Brereton, Bridget, "Family Strategies, Gender, and the Shift to Wage Labor in the British Caribbean", in Scully, Pamela and Paton, Diana, eds, *Gender and Slave Emancipation in the Atlantic World* (Durham: Duke University Press, 2005), 143–61.
Brown, Christopher, *Moral Capital: The Foundations of British Abolitionism* (Chapel Hill: University of North Carolina Press, 2006).
Butler, Kim D., *Freedoms Given, Freedoms Won: Afro-Brazilians in Post-Abolition Sao Paulo and Salvador* (New Brunswick: Rutgers University Press, 2000).
Carrington, Selwyn, *The Sugar Industry and the Abolition of the Slave Trade, 1770–1810* (Gainesville: University of Florida Press, 2002).
Craton, Michael, *Testing the Chains: Resistance to Slavery in the British West Indies* (Ithaca: Cornell University Press, 1982), 241–322.
da Costa, Emilia Viotti, *Da senzala a colonia* (Sao Paulo: Difusao Europeia do livro, 1966).
——, *Crowns of Glory, Tears of Blood: The Demerara Slave Revolt of 1823* (New York: Oxford University Press, 1994).
——, *The Brazilian Empire: Myths and Histories* (Chapel Hill: University of North Carolina Press, 2000).
Davis, David Brion, *The Problem of Slavery in Western Culture* (Ithaca: Cornel University Press, 1965).
Drescher, Seymour, *Capitalism and Antislavery: British Mobilization in Comparative Perspective* (New York: Oxford University Press, 1987).

——, *The Mighty Experiment: Free Labor Versus Slavery in British Emancipation* (New York: Oxford University Press, 2004).

Dubois, Laurent, *Avengers of the New World: The Story of the Haitian Revolution* (Cambridge, MA: Harvard University Press, 2004a).

——, *A Colony of Citizens: Revolution and Slave Emancipation in the French Caribbean, 1787–1804* (Chapel Hill: University of North Carolina Press, 2004b).

DuBois, W.E.B., *The Suppression of the African Slave Trade to the United States* (Boston: Longman, Green, and Co., 1896).

Eltis, David, *Economic Growth and the Ending of the Transatlantic Slave Trade* (New York: Oxford University Press, 1987).

Ferrer, Ada, *Insurgent Cuba: Race, Nation, and Revolution, 1868–1898* (Chapel Hill: University of North Carolina Press, 1999).

Fick, Carolyn E., *The Making of Haiti: The Saint Domingue Revolution from Below* (Knoxville: University of Tennessee Press, 1990).

Foner, Eric, *Reconstruction: America's Unfinished Revolution, 1863–1877* (New York: Harper and Row, 1988), 199–209.

——, *Nothing but Freedom: Emancipation and Its Legacy*, with new forward by Steven Hahn (Baton Rouge: Louisiana State University Press, 2007 [1982]).

Geggus, David P., *Haitian Revolutionary Studies* (Bloomington: Indiana University Press, 2002).

Genovese, Eugene D., *The World the Slaveholders Made: Two Essays in Interpretation* (New York: Pantheon, 1969).

——, *From Rebellion to Revolution: Afro-American Slave Revolts in the Making of the Modern World* (Baton Rouge: Louisiana State University Press, 1979).

Glymph, Thavolia, *Out of the House of Bondage: The Transformation of the Plantation Household* (New York: Cambridge University Press, 2008).

Green, William A., *British Slave Emancipation: The Sugar Colonies and the Great Experiment, 1830–1865*, (Oxford: Oxford University Press, 1976).

Hahn, Steven, "Class and State in Postemancipation Societies: Southern Planters in Comparative Perspective", *American Historical Review* 95 (1990a), 75–98.

——, "Emancipation and the Development of Capitalist Agriculture", in Kees Gispen, ed., *What Made the South Different?* (Jackson: University of Mississippi Press, 1990b), 71–88.

——, "'Extravagant Expectations' of Freedom: Rumour, Political Struggle, and the Christmas Insurrection Scare of 1865 in the American South", *Past and Present* 157 (1997), 122–58.

——, *A Nation Under Our Feet: Black Political Struggles in the Rural South from Slavery to the Great Migration* (Cambridge, MA: Harvard University Press, 2003).

——, *The Political Worlds of Slavery and Freedom* (Cambridge, MA: Harvard University Press, 2009).

Hahn, Steven, Miller, Steven F., O'Donovan, Susan E., Rodrigue, John C. and Rowland, Leslie S., eds, *Freedom: A Documentary History of Emancipation, 1861–1867, Series III, Vol. I, Land and Labor in 1865* (Chapel Hill: University of North Carolina Press, 2008).

Helg, Aline, *Our Rightful Share: The Afro-Cuban Struggle for Equality, 1886–1912* (Chapel Hill: University of North Carolina Press, 1995).

Heuman, Gad, *The Killing Time: The Morant Bay Rebellion in Jamaica* (Knoxville: University of Tennessee Press, 1994).

Holloway, Thomas H., *Immigrants on the Land: Coffee and Society in Sao Paulo, 1886–1934* (Chapel Hill: University of North Carolina Press, 1980).

Holt, Thomas, *The Problem of Freedom: Race, Labor, and Politics in Jamaica, 1832–1938* (Baltimore: Johns Hopkins University Press, 1992).

James, C.L.R., *The Black Jacobins: Toussaint L'Ouverture and the San Domingo Revolution* (New York: Vintage Books, 1963).

Jones, Jacqueline, *Labor of Love, Labor of Sorrow: Black Women, Work, and the Family from Slavery to the Present* (New York: Basic Books, 1985).

Keith, Leanna, *The Colfax Massacre: The Untold Story of Black Power, White Terror, and the Death of Reconstruction* (New York: Oxford University Press, 2009).

Kolchin, Peter, *A Sphinx on the Land: The Nineteenth Century South in Comparative Perspective* (Baton Rouge: Louisiana State University Press, 2003).

Levine, Robert M., "'Mud-Hut Jerusalem': Canudos Reconsidered", in Rebecca Scott *et al.*, eds, *The Abolition of Slavery and the Aftermath of Emancipation in Brazil* (Durham: Duke University Press, 1988), 119–66.

Litwack, Leon, *North of Slavery: The Negro in the Free States* (Chicago: University of Chicago Press, 1961).

McDonald, Roderick A., *The Economy and Material Culture of Slaves: Goods and Chattels on the Sugar Plantations of Jamaica and Louisiana* (Baton Rouge: Louisiana State University Press, 1993).

Mintz, Sidney, *Caribbean Transformations* (New York: Columbia University Press, 1974).

Murray, David R., *Odious Commerce: Britain, Spain, and the Abolition of the Cuban Slave Trade* (Cambridge: Cambridge University Press, 1980).

Northrup, David, *Indentured Labor in the Age of Imperialism, 1834–1922* (Cambridge: Cambridge University Press, 1995).

Paton, Diana, *No Bond but the Law: Punishment, Race, and Gender in Jamaican State Formation, 1780–1870* (Durham: Duke University Press, 2004).

Penningroth, Dylan C., *The Claims of Kinfolk: African American Property and Community in the Nineteenth-Century South* (Chapel Hill: University of North Carolina Press, 2003).

Rodney, Walter, *A History of the Guyanese Working People, 1881–1905* (Baltimore: Johns Hopkins University Press, 1981).

Rodrigue, John C., *Reconstruction in the Cane Fields: From Slavery to Free Labor in Louisiana's Sugar Parishes, 1862–1880* (Baton Rouge: Louisiana State University Press, 2001).

Schwalm, Leslie A., *A Hard Fight for We: Women's Transition from Slavery to Freedom in South Carolina* (Urbana: University of Illinois Press, 1997).

Scott, Rebecca, *Slave Emancipation in Cuba: The Transition to Free Labor* (Princeton, NJ: Princeton University Press, 1985).

——, *Degrees of Freedom: Louisiana and Cuba after Slavery* (Cambridge, MA: Harvard University Press, 2005).

Scott, Rebecca J., Andrews, George Reid, Castro, Hebe, Drescher, Seymour and Levine, Robert, eds, *The Abolition of Slavery and the Aftermath of Emancipation in Brazil* (Durham: Duke University Press, 1988).

Scully, Pamela and Paton, Diana, eds, *Gender and Slave Emancipation in the Atlantic World* (Durham: Duke University Press, 2005).

Stolcke, Verena, *Coffee Planters, Workers, and Wives: Class Conflict and Gender Relations on Sao Paulo Coffee Plantations, 1850–1980* (Basingstoke, UK: Macmillan, 1988).

Toplin, Robert Brent, *The Abolition of Slavery in Brazil* (New York: Atheneum, 1972).

Zilversmit, Arthur, *The First Emancipation: The Abolition of Slavery in the North* (Chicago: University of Chicago Press, 1967).

19

EMANCIPATION DAY TRADITIONS IN THE ANGLO-ATLANTIC WORLD

Edward B. Rugemer

Introduction

On 13 August 1834, the Marquess of Sligo, then Governor of Jamaica, reported to foreign Secretary Thomas Spring Rice on the happenings of the First of August – the first day of emancipation in the British West Indies. The Governor wrote that in most parts of the island, the day was devoted to worship in the sectarian chapels in special services arranged by the missionaries. In several towns there were "fancy balls" attended by the colonial authorities. Many planters distributed extra rations of rum and saltfish; others slaughtered a cow and had a feast for their former slaves on the estate. The feasts recalled the crop-over festivals that planters had traditionally held at the end of the sugar harvest. All of these events were planned by whites. Each ritual sought to define emancipation as a gift from them to the slaves. For the missionaries it was a gift from God; for the colonial authorities it was a gift from the state; and for the planters it was a gift from them.[1]

In the evening, after the missionary services and the planters' dinners, Sligo noted that the streets became "crowded with parties of John Cause Men and their usual noisy accompaniments". The Governor was fairly new to the island, and he referred to what modern scholars call the Jonkunnu, when troupes of outlandishly dressed dancers accompanied by drummers marched through the streets of Jamaican towns going house-to-house aggressively begging money from the residents. The Governor failed to observe that these performances were completely out of season. Traditionally, Jonkunnu was performed during the Christmas holidays, not in August. Yet black Jamaicans decided to perform Jonkunnu to mark emancipation. They sought to establish their own explanation for the passage of slavery. Black Jamaicans did not see emancipation as a gift (Dirks, 1987: 173–79).

The Jonkunnu troupes reminded Jamaican whites of the Christmas season they had long feared. Insurrections were always a threat during the holiday because rebel leaders often used the days off from work to plot rebellion. With the wild dancing, the drumming, and the aggressive seizure of public spaces, the Jonkunnu reminded white Jamaicans of insurrection. In 1800, for example, Lady Nugent described three days of "wild scenes" complete with singing and drums. A long-time Jamaica resident, John Stewart, wrote of the fear among whites "of the danger ... of riots, disorder, and even insurrection" during the Christmas holidays. In 1831 there had been an enormous insurrection that began on 27 December, the third day of revelry, in the hills above Montego Bay. That insurrection spread through half of the island, it took a month to suppress, and the rebellion led inexorably to the abolition of slavery three years later. When African Jamaicans celebrated emancipation with Jonkunnu, they reminded whites that emancipation had not been a gift; it had been a demand.[2]

The multiple celebrations of emancipation in Jamaica on 1 August 1834 illuminate the core elements of the Emancipation Day tradition that flourished in the English-speaking Atlantic World for most of the nineteenth century, and still persist in various forms today. Emancipation was a contested process involving numerous actors – slaves, slave-holders, and abolitionists – who held starkly different views on what emancipation meant, what slavery had meant, and how the abolition of slavery had been accomplished. Commemorations of emancipation became the events when slavery and its abolition were publicly defined in ritual form by those who had experienced emancipation and by their descendants. As we see in Jamaica in 1834, aspects of some Emancipation Day rituals often had roots in older celebrations that had developed during the era of slavery. But the Emancipation Day commemorations took on a variety of arrangements that allowed participants to grapple with the legacies of enslavement and emancipat-ion, as well as to pursue agendas for their own time. In the British West Indies, the United States, and Canada, peoples of African descent – often joined by white allies – commemorated a variety of emancipatory events. This chapter explores this tradition of commemorations from their roots in the slavery period throughout the nineteenth century.[3]

Slavery existed in every region of the Britain's Atlantic Empire, and all these societies shared the tradition of Emancipation Day celebrations. Yet there were significant differ-ences in the historical development of these societies that shaped distinctive styles of commemoration. The first Emancipation Day celebrations were in northern cities such as New York, Philadelphia, and Boston, beginning in 1808 in commemoration of the abo-lition of the transatlantic slave trade. In some northern black communities, such as the Finger Lakes region of New York, Emancipation Day commemorations persisted well into the twentieth century. In contrast, the region with the least vibrant Emancipation Day tradition has been the British West Indies, which in the eighteenth century included some of the most exploitative slave societies in the hemisphere. The first Emancipation Day celebrations in the West Indies took place on 1 August 1834, but by the late 1840s participation in commemorations had declined significantly. The US South lies in between. Enslaved people there made up a far smaller percentage of the southern popu-lation than in the West Indies. Whites were a small minority in islands such as Jamaica; in most of the US South, whites were numerically dominant. The Emancipation Day tradition in the US South started during the American Civil War, with the first celebra-tion taking place in Washington, DC, where Congress abolished slavery on 16 April 1862. Black southerners carried on the tradition until the end of the nineteenth century and the tradition revived in the later twentieth century. We can therefore speak of an Anglo-Atlantic tradition of Emancipation Day celebrations in that all of these celebra-tions commemorated the historic moment of black emancipation from New World slavery. But as the distinctive regional chronologies suggest, there were important differences in commemorative practice that reflected the multiple histories of Anglo-Atlantic emancipation.

Commemorations in the North

As the Anglo-Atlantic Emancipation Day tradition began in the northern United States, any detailed exploration of these celebrations must begin with the slave festivals of the northern colonies. Slaveholders were a minority group in the northern colonies. Most slave owners owned only a few enslaved Africans rather than large gangs of slaves. The nature of slave ownership meant that the northern black population was scattered throughout the countryside, yearning for companionship with other people of African descent. These desires were in part fulfilled by the festivals that developed over the course of the eighteenth century – the Pinkster celebrations of New York and New Jersey, and the Negro Elections of the New England colonies.

Festivals in the North during slavery were celebrations of a momentary freedom when masters relaxed the controls of enslavement – if only for a day – and Africans could celebrate among themselves in the manner they wished. Both the Negro Election and Pinkster began as days of festivity among the whites, celebrating the colonial elections in New England and Pentecost (seven weeks after Easter) among the Dutch of New York. Slaves accompanied their masters to both events, and the momentary sense of freedom developed first, as masters were too preoccupied by their own concerns to maintain the strict oversight of black behavior that predominated most of the year. Yet in New England by the 1750s, and in New York and New Jersey by the 1790s, Africans and their American descendants had seized upon these annual events and transformed them into African American celebrations. Negro Election took place on various days of the colonial calendar, but it was generally held one week after the "white" election; Pinkster retained its calendrical link to the Pentecost. While distinct events, Pinkster and Negro Election shared several components that would later be incorporated into the Emancipation Day celebrations of the nineteenth century. Most significantly, the festivities were planned and controlled by African Americans themselves (White, 1994: 16–18).

The process through which black communities chose their Governor or King differed by region; unfortunately, descriptions of elections have not survived from all regions. Yet the evidence suggests that men were always chosen as Governors or Kings. The consistent choice of men for these positions reflected the patriarchy that had already developed in northern black society, which was further evident in the parade that followed the election. Following his selection, the leader appointed lesser posts such as officers, sheriffs, and justices of the peace, and these men preceded their leader in a parade through the streets of the city or town, always accompanied by the drum and fife. Parades could include 100 participants, some mounted on horses loaned from their masters. If later parades are any indication, the formal parade of the Governor and his officers was followed by the entire black community in attendance. Black people dressed for the occasion in the finest clothes they could acquire, often borrowed from their masters. They arranged their clothes in styles that whites found "outlandish". The parade's destination varied, but it always included a party. In New England, most accounts describe the festivities taking place in a tavern or hall rented out for the occasion, while the Pinkster celebrations in New York and New Jersey ended at an outdoor space with booths constructed for the sellers of food and drinks. Dancing, drumming, singing, wrestling, sport, as well as drinking and feasting, were all a part of these celebrations. Whites participated in these festivities, but they were not in control of events. African American festivals turned the world of slavery upside-down, if only for a day (White, 1989: 197–98; Platt, 1900: 320–21, 331).[4]

Some modern historians have grouped these early black festivals together with the rituals of misrule that punctuated the lives of early modern peoples on either side of the Atlantic. In this interpretation, the temporary subversion of the power structure of a society actually reinforced the *status quo* by allowing the oppressed to blow off a little steam, to have one of their own play the public role of the master. But seen within a longer chronology, these early black celebrations were something more, as they laid the foundation for a black leadership that would foster abolitionism and ultimately help to bring about the permanent end of slavery. While the authority of the King of Pinkster seems to have ended with the festivities, the black Governor of New England had authority throughout the year. Significantly, this authority had meaning for the dominant white community. The New England black Governor had judicial power to resolve disputes concerning blacks, even when a charge was brought by a white. The Governor also had the power to exact punishment on those found guilty, usually through flogging. Similarly to the role played by black drivers on plantations, the authority of the Governor reinforced the power of slaveholders, but only through the empowerment of an enslaved individual (Reidy, 1978: 109–11; Piersen, 1988: 129–40).

The gradual end of slavery in the American North coincided with the development of a participatory politics in which public celebrations played an important role. The central public celebration in American society was the Fourth of July, commemorating the day the Declaration of Independence was presented to the Continental Congress for approval. There were parades with banners and marching bands that went through city streets, and there were public orations that gave definition to the "American freedom" being celebrated. The first celebrations took place during the Revolutionary War; in later decades, Fourth of July celebrations became major political affairs. The commemorations were partisan events, as many communities saw competing celebrations in which each political party claimed the mantle of the Revolutionary tradition. Tradesmen's associations and white ethnic associations also participated in these festivities, each using the commemoration to advance their own political agenda (Waldstreicher, 1997).

African Americans sometimes attended these events, but they were not welcome to participate. During the period between the Revolution and the abolition of the transatlantic slave trade in 1808, the black population in northern urban areas increased significantly, as those recently freed sought employment and community. At the same time, white racism intensified and blacks were increasingly excluded from the public sphere. Moreover, because slavery continued in the southern states, northern blacks still faced the threat of kidnapping and enslavement. The Emancipation Day tradition in the North had its genesis in the abolitionist movement among northern blacks that sought to end slavery where it remained, and to alleviate their own oppression. While Pinkster and the Negro elections continued into the 1810s, these older celebrations no longer suited the political needs of the black community. Black leaders embraced the concepts of "uplift" and "respectability" as the goals for the African American community. They believed white racism would diminish if blacks could lift themselves to economic independence and comport themselves in accordance with middle-class standards. The raucous festivities associated with the older celebrations were not in keeping with the vision of most black leaders, and the older festivals were discontinued. Replacing them were celebrations of the abolition of the transatlantic slave trade (White, 1994: 35).

In 1808, black communities in Boston, New York, and Philadelphia inaugurated the Freedom Day tradition by staging celebrations of the abolition of the transatlantic slave trade by Great Britain and the United States. In Boston, 14 July (Bastille Day) became the day of celebration, probably in recognition of the abolitionist contribution of the French Revolution. In New York and Philadelphia, black leaders chose 1 January, recognizing the day United States legislation banning the trade went into effect. New York blacks organized these celebrations for eight years; in Boston the celebrations ended in 1822; and in Philadelphia the event was commemorated as late as 1830, but only sporadically. The abolition of the transatlantic slave trade did not quickly inaugurate a period of liberation, as abolitionists had hoped. The slave trade with Africa continued illegally, and the expanding internal slave trade, from the upper South states of Maryland and Virginia to the upcountry of South Carolina and Georgia, made it clear that the abolition of the international slave trade would not end American slavery. Moreover, state legislatures in the North passed racist laws that barred the immigration of African Americans from some states and limited their civil rights in others. Clearly, the process of emancipation on the ground did not align with the narrative of progress hopefully put forth from the pulpits on Freedom Day (Gravely, 1982: 303).

Yet there was still cause for African Americans to hope. In 1827, the gradual emancipation laws of New York went into effect, making slavery illegal in the largest northern state. New York's legislature passed its gradual abolition legislation in 1799 and the day appointed for enactment was 4 July – Independence Day – a clear attempt to make emancipation a gift of the state. In 1827, four black communities held celebrations on 4 July: New York City; Baltimore; Cooperstown, New York; and Fredericksburgh, Virginia. But a significant portion of the black community thought it inappropriate to celebrate emancipation on 4 July. Independence Day had been established as a "white" holiday. Blacks were excluded from most of the celebrations and African Americans suffered from mob violence at some 4 July celebrations. Many blacks thus chose to celebrate emancipation on 5 July, and in 1827 there were celebrations in Albany and Rochester in upstate New York; in New Haven, Connecticut; and in New York City. The parades in New York attracted thousands of African Americans, who demonstrated by their actions that emancipation was a process in which rights had to be seized on the streets (ibid).

The 5 July tradition of commemoration became an important day for African American communities in New York State throughout the antebellum decades. While celebrations of emancipation in New York continued in some communities, they were ultimately replaced by celebrations of emancipation in the British West Indies. It must be remembered that there were significant links between the black communities of the United States and the British West Indies. Although specific numbers are not available, there were black West Indians living in the US North. After emancipation in the West Indies, some black Americans moved to the islands. The cultural and historic links between these two regions of the old British Empire made developments in the Caribbean and the mainland relevant to the people of each place (Rugemer, 2008: 102–4, 193–94).

In 1834, the black communities of Boston and New York celebrated West Indian emancipation on 1 August. The celebrations were quiet and small, reflecting awareness that the apprenticeship system and the compensation paid to slaveholders weakened the moral fiber of Parliament's abolition. But when apprenticeship was abolished in 1838, celebrations of the First of August expanded throughout the North and West. Thirty-six communities celebrated 1 August in 1838, in commemorations that ranged from quiet gatherings in churches to parades and public orations. In Cincinnati, for example, the black community held a "watch-night" ceremony in the Bethel Church that began in the evening of 31 July and re-created the moment of emancipation as it had been celebrated in Antigua. The next day, black Cincinnatians gathered again at the church and organized a parade through "a portion of the city". A more select dinner for members of the Cincinnati Union Society at the home of A.M. Sumner followed these events, where a series of toasts were offered in celebration of transatlantic abolitionism (*ibid.*: 2008: 228–35).[5]

The First of August celebrations brought together all the elements of former Emancipation Days, but they differed in one important way: significant numbers of whites began to participate, making many celebrations far more inter-racial than before. There had been a handful of whites involved in previous commemorations, but some of the celebrations took place in communities where the black population was too small to have organized the celebration. The *New York Emancipator* reported a celebration in Byron, New York, for example, but the census of 1830 recorded only one black adolescent living in the community. The involvement of whites in 1838 stemmed from the emergence of radical abolitionism. Radical abolitionism in the northern black community can be traced to at least the early nineteenth century, but antislavery among whites during this era was gradualist. In the early 1830s, a small but growing number of antislavery whites converted to radical abolitionism (which meant dedication to the immediate, uncompensated abolition of slavery). Radical abolitionism took on an institutional form with the formation of the American Antislavery Society in 1833, and in the following years local antislavery societies formed throughout the North. These local societies account for most of the geographic expansion of First of August celebrations in 1838.[6]

For the next 24 years, First of August celebrations in the northern United States were the most significant Emancipation Day celebrations in the Anglo-Atlantic world. Scholars have found newspaper accounts of more than 270 of these celebrations, and there were certainly more. In urban areas such as New York, Boston, Philadelphia, Rochester, and Cincinnati, the celebrations continued to be organized by black leaders and principally involved African Americans. The abolitionist societies, which were generally controlled by whites, organized First of August picnics in the countryside. While some blacks did attend, most participants were white. The antebellum celebrations could be quite large, with some newspaper accounts describing audiences of 5000 to 7000 people. Local railroad companies cooperated with the abolitionists, offering extra cars and reduced fares for those going to the celebrations. Abolitionist orators such as William Lloyd Garrison, Wendell Phillips, and Frederick Douglass were regular speakers. Most celebrations also featured a ceremonial reading of Parliament's Act of Emancipation and sometimes the Declaration of Independence was also read, with an emphasis on the lines: "all men are created equal ... endowed by their creator with certain unalienable rights". In the late 1850s, the white celebrations became increasingly connected to the growing popularity of the Republican Party. The Republicans were the first political party in the United States to take advantage of the growth of an antislavery constituency in the North, fostered in part by the abolitionist movement. At the black First of August celebrations, the oratory could become quite radical, as in 1857 when

Frederick Douglass recalled the rebellion in Jamaica that paved the road to abolition in 1834. First of August celebrations, then, contributed to the coming of the American Civil War by advancing antislavery in the North and by keeping alive the radicalism that would ultimately bring about the Emancipation Proclamation of 1 January 1863 (Rugemer, 2008: 249–53, 256–57).

Commemorations in the West Indies

In contrast to the Northern United States, the First of August 1834 in the British West Indies was highly contested. In the West Indies, the anger over the apprenticeship system was palpable and had consequences for Afro-Caribbean celebrations. We have seen in Jamaica that the missionary celebrations in the chapels by day were followed by the intimidating Jonkunnu dancers at night. Elsewhere in the island there were labor strikes to protest the apprenticeship, and some colonies saw riots. In St Kitts, the island that neighbored Antigua, when former slaves learned that their neighbors in Antigua were "full free" they refused to work unless they were paid wages, and many fled the estates to hide in the mountains. In Trinidad, former slaves from some of the French estates marched to the Government House in Port of Spain shouting "*point de six ans, point de six ans*" ("no six years, no six years"), protesting what seemed like six more years of slavery. The crowd did not disperse until 17 men were flogged and the leaders were imprisoned. The legal institution of slavery might have been abolished, but power still lay in the hands of colonial authorities and the planters (Kerr-Ritchie, 2007: 27).

As Barry Higman has observed, 1 August as Emancipation Day favored the interests of sugar planters because it coincided with the end of the sugar harvest when labor was most needed. The celebrations that did take place were organized and staged by whites. The Governors of several colonies – British Guiana, the Windward Islands, and Barbados – declared the day an official day of celebration and encouraged the missionaries to hold special religious services. We have described above the Methodist watch-night celebration held in Cincinnati that recreated Antigua's moment of emancipation; watch-nights were also held in several Jamaican towns where the Methodists had a presence, and missionaries of other denominations, such as the Baptists and the Moravians, also held special celebrations. Black West Indians attended these celebrations in large numbers and they were jubilant that slavery was soon coming to an end. However, the purpose of the celebrations was to cultivate gratitude for abolition. Emancipation had come through the beneficence of the planters, of the Empire, and of God. Nevertheless, the strikes and resentment offered on the same day revealed lasting antagonism toward those who were the enslavers, and a deep resentment at the partial nature of emancipation (Higman, 1979: 56; Kerr-Ritchie, 2007: 17–18).

Scholars have not explored emancipation commemorations in the West Indies during the apprenticeship period from 1835 to 1838, but it is clear that celebrations in 1838 were far more widespread and jovial, just as they were in the northern United States. Apprenticeship ended in part because the apprentices refused to cooperate in the unjust system; consequently, 1 August 1838 is now recognized as the true end of slavery in the British Caribbean. As in Jamaica in 1834, there were again two sets of celebrations – one organized by whites, followed by another organized by blacks. The Methodist missionaries again organized watch-night celebrations to begin on 31 July. In Kingston, the watch-night led to an all-night celebration in which black Methodists organized themselves into groups of 40 and paraded through the city singing psalms and crying "God Bless the Queen!". On the First of August, there were religious services throughout the colonies, and on many estates the planters organized crop-over festivals to try to maintain the loyalty of "their" people as the transition to freedom began (Kerr-Ritchie, 2007: 27–38).

The religious celebrations pervaded the colonies, but there were two more sets of celebrations that further complicated the public meaning of emancipation. Colonial officials in Jamaica and Barbados staged military parades and ceremonial readings of the Act of Emancipation. The colonial governments also put their militaries on alert on 1 August 1838, concerned that the rioting seen in 1834 would be repeated. Such actions conveyed the demand of the state that the emancipation transition should be orderly – there would not be *too much* freedom. Yet there were unofficial celebrations of emancipation that suggested an embrace of emancipation that disregarded order. In Cornwall, Jamaica, the Presbyterian missionary Hope Waddell reported that a former apprentice set up a booth in his yard and organized a series of dances during the week before 1 August. The dances attracted "a company of loose and disorderly people from all quarters, whose singing, and drumming, and dancing, disturbed the neighborhood". When Waddell went to the man's yard to complain, he was "furiously threatened" and told to leave. The man warned Waddell that when the First of August came, black and white would be equal, and he would "split his skull" if Waddell tried to enter his yard again. Waddell complained to the authorities, who went to the man's yard the next day. They destroyed the booth and imprisoned the man. If only we could see into the yard during that last week in July and see with eyes other than Waddell's, we might witness a culture in bloom, generations of desire for freedom constrained by a brutal slavery blossoming in anticipation.[7]

Of the three modes of celebration on 1 August 1838 – the official, the religious, and the folk – only the latter two persisted. Nowhere in the British West Indies did 1 August become an annual official holiday until late in the twentieth century. After 1838, we have detailed studies of the Emancipation Day tradition in only two colonies: Jamaica and Trinidad. The colonies had very different histories and very different populations in 1838. Jamaica was one of the older British West Indian colonies, and with about 350,000 people it was the largest colonial population in the Anglo-Atlantic. In 1838, about 90 per cent of the Jamaican population were of African descent. Only a small minority of this group were already free, and some were slaveholders who did not identify with African Jamaicans; rather, they considered themselves "browns". Originally a Spanish colony, Trinidad did not become British until 1797 during the wars of the French Revolution. The population of Trinidad was not even half that of Jamaica, and it was far more diverse. In 1797 Spanish speakers were already outnumbered by émigrés from the French Caribbean – white, black, and free colored – fleeing the tumult of the French and Haitian Revolutions described in this volume by Laurent Dubois (Chapter 16). The enslaved population in 1797 was about 10,000; free people numbered about 7300. Over the next decade, British slavers brought about 20,000 Africans across the Atlantic, yet on the eve of emancipation, free persons of color slightly outnumbered those enslaved (Heuman, 1981: 3–15; Pearse, 1956: 175–76).

The societal differences between Jamaica and Trinidad lent themselves toward very different traditions in commemorating emancipation. Beyond the outrage at the apprenticeship expressed in Port of Spain on 1 August 1834, little evidence has surfaced of any remembrance of 1 August as a significant day. The only Trinidadians to celebrate the First of August in the immediate post-emancipation period were members of the Trinidad Auxiliary Antislavery Society (TASS). The TASS was formed by educated young men mostly descended from free colored émigrés from the French Caribbean and a few white allies. They were politically ambitious and sought a greater role in colonial politics than was allowed them at the time. From 1839 through 1851, the TASS staged a series of dinners and meetings, mostly in Port of Spain but also in San Fernando, to commemorate the First of August. The planter class derided these events, but they found favourable coverage in the free colored press. Those who had been enslaved, however, were never involved in these events, nor were they encouraged to participate. Indeed, Bridget Brereton has found no evidence from 1838 through the 1860s of popular commemorations of the First of August. The only trace of a folk commemoration appears in the diary of a French Dominican priest who worked in Trinidad in the late 1870s. He reported that the descendants of slaves in Carenage, a fishing village to the west of Port of Spain, celebrated the First of August with a *"fête du diable"* complete with a Catholic mass, a procession, and three days of *"orgies san nom, souvenirs de la vie africaine"*. This brief account suggests a longer period of commemoration, perhaps a regional tradition kept among the descendants of French speakers. But the evidence is so scant and isolated that it does not suggest any island-wide tradition of commemoration.[8]

This does not mean that black Trinidadians did not commemorate emancipation; they simply did not do so on the First of August. Scholars agree that the Canboulay procession, which opens the Carnival celebration on the midnight before Carnival Sunday, clearly recalls slavery and celebrates the emancipatory moment. The word Canboulay descends from *cannes brullées*, which referred to the practice in the sugar districts, when in the event of a fire on one plantation, gangs of slaves from neighboring plantations would come to the aid of the victim of fire to prevent a general conflagration. In the early nineteenth century, the Canboulay was performed by white French planters, who dressed as field slaves, organized themselves into gangs, and marched down the street with torches, drums and horns blaring. It is not at all clear why whites began such a ritual, but in the post-emancipation period blacks took the lead in the Canboulay as a celebration of emancipation. Seen over 40 years of Trinidadian history, then, the transformation of the Canboulay can be seen as one of the rituals of misrule (similar to the Negro Elections in the northern United States) which transformed the meaning of a public ritual to convey a radically different meaning. Whites had appropriated to themselves the honor of starting the Carnival with this fantastic procession that mocked enslaved Africans. With emancipation, black Trinidadians re-appropriated the Canboulay as a commemoration of emancipation that heralded three days of festivities (Pearse, 1956: 181; Brereton, 1983: 73–74).

Further evidence from the nineteenth century clearly associates Carnival with the memory of slavery. According to the observances of the English traveler Charles Day, the Carnival procession in 1848 included a troupe that represented a scene from slavery. The dancers were made up with a black paint and one man "had a long chain and padlock attached to his leg", which was pulled by the others. Every so often those who held the chain would throw the representative bondman to the ground and thrash him with a "mock bastinadoing". The dancers (all of them black) in the procession wore a "white flesh-coloured mask" and covered their hair with handkerchiefs, a representation of whiteness that clearly illuminated responsibility for the crimes of slavery.[9]

In contrast with Trinidad, there is compelling evidence that black Jamaicans commemorated the end of slavery on the First of August with celebrations of their own creation. Furthering the distinct traditions between the islands, there is no evidence that the descendants of free coloreds employed the First of August for their political agenda, as this group did in Trinidad. We have seen the popular celebration in Cornwall recorded by Hope Waddell, and it is likely that such celebrations took place throughout the island. The First of August became the beginning of a fortnight's relief from plantation labour. As and as early as 1843, authorities in Kingston imposed fines for such celebratory activities as shell-blowing, drumming, kite-flying, or the use of fireworks. In 1847, *The Falmouth Post*, a newspaper published on the north coast, reported that on the First of August laborers marched "from one estate to another, drumming, fifing, dancing, and john-canooing, in the demi-savage spirit of the olden time". During the same year, the Reverend A.G. Hogg wrote from his mission in New Broughton (on the south coast) that on the First of August there were "dances and other scenes of amusement and temptation". Hogg worried about the souls of the members of his mission and believed the folk celebrations were "too prevalent".[10]

Missionaries such as Hogg had maintained the tradition of the First of August with special commemorations in their chapels. In 1847, Hogg reported an "immense assemblage" at his chapel for the commemoration of emancipation, where they listened to sermons by Hogg and other missionaries, as well as a "black elder" who recalled his own slavery and decried those who refused to remember slavery because of their shame. They were enslaved to sin, he argued, which in his opinion was worse. In 1854, the Reverend M. Strang held a commemoration on the First of August: it began with a prayer service and a short sermon by Strang, but then became an open forum in which members could speak their minds. Strang recorded the sentiments of eight speakers, most of them older men. Some recalled the days of slavery and, like the black elder in Hogg's mission, berated the next generation that declined to uphold its memory. Every speaker emphasized his conversion to Christ and spoke more about personal sin than about commemorating the end of slavery. Strang may well have recorded only the sentiments of which he approved, but he also noted his disappointment with the attendance; only two-thirds of the usual Sabbath congregation had come that year, and the "immense assemblage" of just seven years before had diminished.[11]

The shrinking audience for the commemorations at Strang's mission paralleled the decline in First of August observances throughout the island. Barry Higman found widespread evidence that First of August observances seemed to end in the 1850s. *The Falmouth Post* reported in 1853 that there had been no celebration that year, and the same paper noted in 1860 that as a "national festival" the First of August was no longer recognized. Higman identified two principal reasons for the decline. In 1846 the British Parliament equalized the sugar duties, ending the era of protection the British Caribbean had enjoyed since the eighteenth century. Economic depression followed and plantation laborers simply did not have as much money to spend on the celebrations. Of the two major festivals in the post-emancipation period – Christmas and the First of August – most black Jamaicans chose to celebrate Christmas. Few black Jamaicans could afford to celebrate both, and Christmas had deeper roots in Jamaican society than did the First of August (Higman, 1979: 60–61).

But we must also consider the declining attendance at Strang's chapel. The missionaries had worked very hard to convert the Jamaican people, and they associated themselves with the First of August and emancipation as part of this effort. But as myalism (a syncretic belief system rooted in Christianity and African worldviews) became ascendant in the 1840s and the 1850s, the missionaries could no longer meet the spiritual needs of the people. Jamaica had a young population looking to the future and, for many people, it may have seemed that the missionaries from Britain and their talk of redemption from slavery was a part of the past. Whatever it was, the prominent celebrations of the First of August fell out of practice. No doubt small rural communities still commemorated the day, but generally the First of August had come to an end.

Civil War commemorations and the post-bellum South

At the First of August celebrations in 1861, abolitionist orators throughout the North made it clear to President Abraham Lincoln that they expected the end of slavery to come out of the military conflict that had begun between the federal government and the Confederacy of the South. Enslaved people on plantations near the battle lines were the first to make a move toward emancipation. Slaves had heard about Abraham Lincoln. He was believed to be an abolitionist, the leader of the "Black Republican" party that their masters cursed during the election of 1860. When Lincoln was elected, black southerners waited in anticipation of what this development could mean. They did not know that Lincoln was not an abolitionist and that emancipation remained a contested question in the North. When the fighting began, the federal government promised to respect the "established institutions" of the southern states. But when a Union force of Massachusetts volunteers entered south-eastern Virginia under the command of General Benjamin Butler, daring young men made their escape from slavery and offered their labor to an army they saw as liberating. Like Lincoln, Butler was no abolitionist but he knew that Confederate armies were forcing slaves to labor in support of the army. He declared these fugitives from slavery the "contraband of war", legally confiscated by the Union army, which did not recognize the institution of slavery. Those young men were freed (Hahn, 2003: 65–70).

The actions of wartime fugitives from slavery slowly pushed the Lincoln administration and the federal Congress toward an emancipatory policy. On 16 April 1862, Congress abolished slavery in the District of Columbia, the only polity directly under federal power. Abolitionists had been petitioning for the abolition of slavery in the District since the 1830s, and there was a significant black community in Washington deeply involved with the abolitionist movement. But in the antebellum decades slaveholders controlled the city. There was a large slave market in the District and it was not uncommon to see coffles of enslaved men and women marching through the streets. Abolitionists in Washington, DC, then, could not celebrate the First of August as black communities did in the North. This changed in 1862 with the end of slavery in the capital. Black leaders set aside Sunday 13 April as a day of thanksgiving for emancipation in the District. While no parade was held, as would be the case in later years, it was the beginning of a tradition of 16 April celebrations that would continue into the twentieth century (Harrold, 2003; Kachun, 2003: 100–101).

Northern blacks established the First of August tradition in the mid-nineteenth century, but freedom of speech on the subject of slavery did not exist in the antebellum South, so the northern tradition could never have spread. The southernmost black community to participate in First of August celebrations was Baltimore, but Baltimore blacks had to travel north to Wilmington, Delaware in order to celebrate. Emancipation in Washington, DC changed that, and as the war progressed there were more momentous dates that lent themselves to commemorative traditions. On 22 September 1862, after the Union victory in the battle of Antietam, Lincoln declared that in 100 days those enslaved within the states of the Confederacy would be considered free by the United States government. The debate raged in the northern press as to whether Lincoln would actually sign an Emancipation Proclamation and what the results might be. But indicating a hopeful confidence, on 31 December 1862, African American communities across the country held "watch-night" celebrations in the West Indian tradition to await the news on the telegraph that the Proclamation had in fact been signed. Watch-nights were held in northern cities such as Boston and New York, in Washington, DC, and in parts of the South occupied by Union troops, such as Norfolk, Virginia, New Orleans, Louisiana, and the sea islands of South Carolina. Lincoln did, of course, sign the Emancipation Proclamation on 1 January 1863.[12]

The final wartime events to generate commemorative traditions illuminate the reality that emancipation did not come until after the abolition of slavery was enforced. Emancipation came gradually to the South. On 1 November 1864, the state of Maryland (which had remained part of the Union and thus was not affected by the Emancipation Proclamation) abolished slavery through a state constitutional convention. On 3 April 1865, Union troops entered Richmond, Virginia, the capital of the Confederacy, and on 9 April, General Robert E. Lee surrendered at Appomatox, Virginia. On 19 June 1865, Union troops arrived in Galveston, Texas and read aloud the Emancipation Proclamation. Because the Emancipation Proclamation radically altered the relationship between African Americans and the United States, the Civil War also transformed the meaning of Independence Day, 4 July. After the war, African Americans fiercely embraced their national identity. Independence Day became Emancipation Day (Kachun, 2003: 117–18).

The gradual unfolding of wartime emancipation created a calendar replete with days to commemorate. Emancipation Day celebrations on 1 January were by far the most common, taking place annually in large cities and in small black communities throughout the rural South.[13] Yet in the North, 1 January came in the middle of the winter, making it difficult to stage outdoor celebrations. Consequently, many black communities in the North continued to celebrate the First of August, although now orators focused on emancipation in the South and the struggles that still faced African Americans. In addition to celebrating 1 January, the black communities in Baltimore and Philadelphia celebrated abolition in the state of Maryland on 1 November. The black community in Washington, DC staged huge annual parades on 16 April: blacks marched through the streets of the city and were reviewed by the sitting president. Commemorations of Lincoln's preliminary Emancipation Proclamation on 22 September were held sporadically in the mid-west communities of Illinois and Indiana. The black community in Richmond celebrated 1 January, 3 April, and Surrender Day on 9 April. In Texas, 19 June became known as "Juneteenth". This event has become the most widespread commemoration of emancipation in the United States.

The organization and public display of the Emancipation Day celebrations in the postbellum South drew on two principal cultural sources: the funeral processions of free and enslaved blacks in the antebellum South, and the First of August tradition already established in the North. In 1860, free people were only about 6 per cent of the black population in the South, a number that had declined over the antebellum period. However, in urban centers throughout the South there were cohesive free black communities that established their own traditions. The funeral processions organized by free black communities were impressive affairs. In 1855, for example, the funeral procession for the deacon of the Third African Baptist Church included "three uniformed [black] fire companies", contingents from the Porter's Association, and at least two benevolent societies, 35 carriages, and many following the carriages on horseback. The correspondent to the *Savannah News* estimated that between 2000 and 5000 people participated in the procession. For a number this large, many from the enslaved community would have been following the horses, as was common in other funeral processions in the South.[14]

The slavery-era precedents for southern commemorations continued the pattern of influence already seen in the North and the British West Indies. Yet because of the established First of August tradition, and due to the activities of black and white abolitionists in the Union army and the Reconstruction South, the post-bellum commemorations in the South shared much with the northern First of August commemorations. Some of the earliest celebrations of 1 January reveal these influences. The sea islands of South Carolina were one of the first regions occupied by the Union army. In Port Royal, South Carolina, when the news arrived that the Emancipation Proclamation was imminent, General Rufus Saxton declared that 1 January 1863 would be "a day which is destined to be an everlasting beacon-light, marking a joyful era in the progress of the nation". Saxton was raised by abolitionist parents in Greenfield, Massachusetts, the site of an annual First of August celebration that Saxton likely attended as a young man. Moreover, the American Missionary Association (AMA) had sent missionaries to Port Royal earlier in the year, including Charlotte Forten, the daughter of James Forten, the wealthy black leader from Philadelphia who had been an organizer of New York Emancipation day celebrations in the 1820s and First of August celebrations thereafter. The AMA missionaries all had abolitionist backgrounds and would have participated in First of August celebrations for many years (Clark, 2005: 20, 23).

On 1 January 1863, people began to gather in Port Royal in the mid-morning sun, arriving on boats and on foot from villages in the area. Organizers had erected a speaker's platform in a grove of live oaks. The days events began with prayers and a ceremonial reading of the Emancipation Proclamation, followed by speeches and songs, including the abolitionist anthem *John Brown's Body*. Festivities continued into the evening with a barbecue, singing, and dancing. The next year's celebration in Beaufort continued the blend of northern and southern influences. Beaufort organizers staged a "civic and military procession" that included several regiments of black troops followed by skilled black workers such as the riverboat pilots. Next in line were the school-children and their teachers from the newly founded freedmen schools, followed by the freed people from the neighboring islands. Some observers noted that the entire black population in the vicinity came out for the celebration. The procession ended at a speaker's platform festooned with portraits of John Brown and Toussaint Louverture. In Beaufort, we clearly see the influence of the southern funeral procession, now parading to a platform with portraits of iconic abolitionists, as had long been done on the First of August (*ibid.*: 22–24; Kachun, 2003: 114).

The presence of black soldiers in the celebrations signified a militant determination among black southerners to assert their citizenship in the post-bellum South. The enthusiastic service of African American soldiers had been crucial to the Union victory, and the historical connections between military service and citizenship were not lost on Emancipation Day organizers. Fourth of July parades had been political vehicles for many groups in American society; now they served the same purpose for the freed people. As evident in the Carolina Sea islands, black southerners laid their claims for public citizenship as soon as they could. Emancipation came to Charleston two years later, when Union troops led by African American regiments entered the city in the spring of 1865. On 21 March, people began to assemble at the South Carolina Military Academy for a parade in celebration of emancipation. The meeting place was carefully chosen for its irony, as the Military Academy had been founded in 1842, in part to prepare young white Carolinians for the rigors of suppressing slave insurrections. Groups of skilled artisans and the black Union regiments led the parade: it included representative groups from the free black civic associations formed in the antebellum period, and a "car of liberty" with 15 young women, beautifully dressed and waving like celebrities to cheering spectators. The most vivid symbol of emancipation came at the end of the parade, where a mule-drawn cart with the sign "a number of negroes for sale" carried a group of men, women, and children. The pretended auctioneer harangued the crowd to buy his chattels, and following this spectacle came an open hearse with a coffin that bore the words "Slavery is dead". Fifty female mourners dressed in black walked slowly behind, completing the subversive scene with their "joyous faces" (Clark, 2005: 34–38).

By the late 1860s, Emancipation Day celebrations in the South had become the largest festive gatherings of former slaves in the Atlantic World. In cities such as Charleston, South Carolina, Atlanta, Georgia, and Richmond, Virginia, 10,000 people or more came out every year to celebrate their emancipation. Black soldiers led the parades through the city streets to platforms where black leaders recalled the triumph over slavery, decried the persistence of racial prejudices, and tried to project a world in which African Americans could actively participate in American society. While some white southerners shared these aspirations and participated in Emancipation Day celebrations, too many did not. As early as 1866, in Richmond, Virginia, angry whites burned down the church that had hosted the organizational meetings for that year's 3 April celebration. In 1867, the Norfolk *Virginian* described a threatening "great black serpent" entering the city on 1 January for the Emancipation Day parade (*ibid.*: 29, 54).

Nevertheless, Emancipation Day celebrations flourished in the South throughout the 1870s. The commemorations became Republican Party events, much as they had in the North in the late 1850s. White Republican officials often shared the rostrum with black leaders. But white Republicans were a minority in the South in the post-bellum decades, and most whites were hostile to black celebrations. In Georgia, for example, Kathleen Clark has documented the demise of African American Fourth of July celebrations during the 1870s, when terrorist organizations such as the Ku Klux Klan and the Knights of the White Camellia began to wage a war of lynching terror on the black population. By the 1880s, more and more people began to stay at home on what had been Emancipation Day. Some African Americans spoke with distaste about remembering slavery and argued for the discontinuation of the commemorations. But more important to the decline of the Emancipation Day tradition was the emergence of militant white supremacy. The abolition of slavery may have been permanent, but with the rise of lynch law and segregationist state governments, the avenues of black political participation gradually closed. After the contested national election of 1876, the federal government withdrew troops from the South and allowed white Democrats to control "their" state affairs. Violence against blacks escalated throughout the South, sometimes resulting in massacres and days of riotous carnage such as in Wilmington, North Carolina in 1898 and Atlanta, Georgia in 1906. State governments stripped African Americans of the right to form militia companies, meaning that Emancipation Day parades could no longer have the protection of black soldiers. The commemorations continued, but they were a lot smaller, and in most places the parades were discontinued. By the dawn of the twentieth century, the huge, public events of the late 1860s had withdrawn into churches where they sheathed their political edge, only to unleash it again in the 1950s (*ibid.*: 98, 190, 204; Kachun, 2003, 179–81).

Conclusion

The Emancipation Day tradition saw its peaks of strength in the northern United States in the 1850s, in the British West Indies in 1838, and in the southern United States in the 1870s. By the dawn of the twentieth century, however, whites had taken control. Throughout the Anglo-Atlantic, the public memory of a benign slavery of docile blacks and kindly white masters was predominant. There was little space in this historical vision for the triumph of emancipation, and Emancipation Day was largely confined to African American churches. Memories of slavery's brutal oppressions and the joy of emancipation lived on in these ceremonies and eventually they re-emerged to public view. During the Civil Rights movement of the 1950s and 1960s, the Juneteenth celebration spread beyond its roots in Texas, and today it remains one of the most widely celebrated Emancipation Days in the United States. 19 June is an official state holiday in Texas, and there are Juneteenth celebrations in every state. Jamaica and Trinidad became independent states in 1962, and for much of their modern history Independence Day has been the most important national holiday. But in 1985, Trinidad declared 1 August a national holiday. Jamaica followed suit in 1998. On 1 August 2002, for example, a parade of Rastafarians drummed their way through downtown Kingston; plays were performed at the Ward Theatre and at Devon House; and the William Knibb Memorial Baptist Church in Falmouth, Trelawney opened an exhibition on slavery and emancipation. On 31 December 2009, African American churches held watch-night celebrations in New York, Boston, Atlanta, and Los Angeles. With great anticipation for the dawn of the age of Obama, African Americans commemorated emancipation with great joy.[15]

Notes

1 Marquess of Sligo to Thomas Spring Rice, 13 August 1834, in *Parliamentary Papers* 1835 (177) L, "Papers in Explanation of Measures to give effect to Act for Abolition of Slavery. Part I. Jamaica, 1833–35", no. 17, 44.
2 Wright (1966: 49); J. Stewart, *An Account of Jamaica and Its Inhabitants* (London, 1808), 262.
3 The moment of emancipation was also celebrated in the former slave societies of the Iberian Atlantic and Emancipation Day traditions may have developed, but historians have not yet explored those traditions in detail. One exception is Andrews (1991: ch. 8).
4 Kathleen Clark (2005, ch. 2) explores the gendered quality of black celebrations for a later period.
5 African Americans learned of Antigua's watch-night celebration from James A. Thome and J. Horace Kimball, *Emancipation in the West Indies. A Six Months' Tour in Antigua,*

Barbadoes, and Jamaica, in the Year 1837 (New York, 1838), 36–37, which was reprinted in the *New York Colored American*, 12 April 1838. The "watchnight" celebration was first developed by John Wesley himself to inaugurate the New Year, and was a part of Methodist practice before African Americans became Methodists.

6 *New York Emancipator*, 16 August 1838; *Fifth Census*, 1830, Washington, DC, 1832, 51–74.

7 Hope Masterton Waddell, *Twenty-Nine Years in the West Indies and Central Africa* (London, 1863), 147.

8 Brereton (1983: 70–71, 76); M.B. Cothanay, *Trinidad: Journal d'un Missionaire Dominican des Antilles Auglaises* (Paris: Victor Retaux, 1893), 62–66.

9 Charles William Day, *Five Years Residence in the West Indies*, 2 vols (London, 1852), Vol. 1, 314.

10 Higman (1979: 59); *Missionary Record of the United Presbyterian Church*, December 1847: 195.

11 *Missionary Record of the United Presbyterian Church*, October 1854, 165–67.

12 *New York Anglo African*, 20 August 1859; Kachun (2003: 103–4).

13 Mitch Kachun has observed that the transformation of 1 January was even deeper than emancipation. In the antebellum South, 1 January had marked the end of the Christmas holidays and the day when slave-hiring contracts were set. This could mean the separation of friends and family for the entire next year, a mournful day (Kachun, 2003: 120).

14 *Savannah News*, quoted in *Louisville Daily Courier*, 6 March 1855, cited in Berlin (1974: 308).

15 www.juneteenth.com/worldwide.htm; G. Sinclair, "Thousands Mark Emancipation Day", *Jamaica Gleaner*, 2 August 2002; P. Vitello, "A Proud and Joyous Night for a Tradition Born in Hope", *New York Times*, 2 January 2009.

Bibliography

Andrews, George Reid, *Blacks and Whites in São Paulo, Brazil, 1888–1988* (Madison, University of Wisconsin Press, 1991).

Berlin, Ira, *Slaves Without Masters: The Free Negro in the Antebellum South* (New York: Vintage Books, 1974).

Brereton, Bridget, "The Birthday of Our Race: A Social History of Emancipation Day in Trinidad, 1838–88", in B.W. Higman, ed., *Trade, Government and Society in Caribbean History, 1700–1920: Essays Presented to Douglas Hall* (Kingston: Heinemann, 1983), 69–83.

——, "A Social History of Emancipation Day in the British Caribbean: The First Fifty Years", in Hilary McD. Beckles, ed., *Inside Slavery: Process and Legacy in the Caribbean Experience*, (Kingston: Canoe Press, 1996), 78–95.

Bryan, Patrick, ed., *August 1st A Celebration of Emancipation*, papers presented at a Symposium sponsored by Friedrich Ebert Stiftung and the Department of History, University of the West Indies, Mona (Kingston: University of the West Indies, 1995).

Campbell, S., "Carnival, Calypso, and Class Struggle in Nineteenth Century Trinidad", *History Workshop Journal* 26 (1988), 1–27.

Clark, Kathleen Ann, *Defining Moments: African American Commemoration and Political Culture in the South, 1863–1913* (Chapel Hill: University of North Carolina Press, 2005).

Dirks, Robert, *The Black Saturnalia: Conflict and its Ritual Expression on British West Indian Slave Plantations* (Gainesville: University of Florida Press, 1987).

Fabre, G., "African American Commemorative Celebrations in the Nineteenth Century", in G. Fabre and R. O'Meally, eds, *History and Memory in African American Culture* (New York: Oxford University Press, 1994), 72–88.

Gravely, W. B., "The Dialectic of Double-Consciousness in Black American Freedom Celebrations, 1808–63", *Journal of Negro History* 67 (1982), 302–17.

Hahn, Steven, *A Nation Under Our Feet: Black Political Struggles in the Rural South from Slavery to the Great Migration* (Cambridge, MA: Harvard University Press, 2003), 65–70.

Harrold, Stanley, *Subversives: Antislavery Community in Washington, D.C., 1828–1865* (Baton Rouge: Louisiana State University Press, 2003.

Heuman, Gad J., *Between Black and White: Race, Politics, and the Free Coloreds in Jamaica, 1792–1865* (Westport, CT: Greenwood Press, 1981).

Higman, B.W., "Slavery Remembered: The Celebration of Emancipation in Jamaica", *Journal of Caribbean History* 12 (1979), 55–74.

Horton, James Oliver and Horton, Lois E., *In Hope of Liberty: Culture, Community and Protest Among Northern Free Blacks, 1700–1860* (New York: Oxford University Press, 1997).

Kachun, Mitch, *Festivals of Freedom: Memory and Meaning in African American Emancipation Celebrations, 1808–1915* (Amherst: University of Massachusetts Press, 2003).

——, "Antebellum African Americans, Public Commemoration, and the Haitian Revolution: A Problem of Historical Mythmaking", *Journal of the Early Republic* 26 (2006), 249–73.

Kerr-Ritchie, J.R., "Rehearsal for War: Black Militias in the Atlantic World", *Slavery and Abolition* 26 (2005), 1–34.

——, *Rites of August First: Emancipation Day in the Black Atlantic World* (Baton Rouge: Louisiana State University Press, 2007).

McDaniel, W. C., "The Fourth and the First: Abolitionist Holidays, Respectability, and Radical Interracial Reform", *American Quarterly* 57 (2005), 129–51.

Pearse, Andrew, "Carnival in Nineteenth Century Trinidad", *Caribbean Quarterly* 4 (1956), 175–93.

Piersen, William D., *Black Yankees: The Development of an Afro-American Subculture in Eighteenth Century New England* (Amherst: University of Massachusetts Press, 1988).

Platt, O., "Negro Governors" (New Haven Colony Historical Society Papers 6, 1900), 315–35.

Quarles, Benjamin, *Black Abolitionists* (New York: Oxford University Press, 1969).

Reidy, J., "'Negro Election Day' 1860", *Marxist Perspectives* 1 (1978), 102–17.

Rugemer, Edward B., *The Problem of Emancipation: The Caribbean Roots of the American Civil War* (Baton Rouge: Louisiana State University Press, 2008).

Ryan, M., *Civic Wars: Democracy and Public Life in the American City during the Nineteenth Century* (Berkeley: University of California Press, 1997).

Stewart, James Brewer, *Holy Warriors: The Abolitionists and American Slavery*, revised edn (New York: Hill and Wang, 1997).

Waldstreicher, David, *In the Midst of Perpetual Fetes: The Making of American Nationalism, 1776–1820* (Chapel Hill: University of North Carolina Press, 1997).

White, S., "Pinkster in Albany, 1803: A Contemporary Description", *New York History* 70 (1989), 191–99.

——, "'It Was a Proud Day': African Americans, Festivals, and Parades in the North, 1741–1834", *Journal of American History* 81 (1994), 13–50.

Whitfield, Harvey Aamani, *Blacks on the Border: The Black Refugees in British North America, 1815–1860* (Burlington: University of Vermont Press, 2006).

Williams-Myers, A.J., "Pinkster Carnival: Africanisms in the Hudson River Valley", *Afro-Americans in New York Life and History* 9 (1985), 7–17.

Wright, Philip, ed., *Lady Nugent's Journal of Her Residence in Jamaica from 1801–1805* (Kingston: Institute of Jamaica, 1966).

20

MODERN SLAVERY

Joel Quirk

Introduction

Over the past decade, the problem of modern slavery has moved from being a marginal concern to a mainstream issue, with overall levels of public awareness, official engagement and specialised research all experiencing significant advances in recent times. The primary focal point of this renewed interest in human bondage has been trafficking in persons for the purposes of forced prostitution. Other key problem areas include bonded labour, the worst forms of child labour, "classical" slavery and descent-based discrimination, forced labour for the state, wartime enslavement, and the severe exploitation of migrants and domestic workers. This evolving agenda reflects contributions from human rights groups and international organizations such as Anti-Slavery International and the United Nations; a series of national, regional and global initiatives such as the annual Trafficking in Persons Reports published by the US government since 2001; and a number of high-profile court cases and popular exposés.

Efforts to understand and eradicate modern slavery face a number of distinctive challenges. The first and most obvious challenge involves determining where slavery begins and ends. With slavery now legally abolished throughout the globe, modern forms of slavery tend to be concentrated in social and economic settings that are not conducive to external scrutiny. While criminal prosecutions and other sources of information can offer some guidance, relatively few cases of human bondage find their way into the public domain, making it difficult to determine the scale and distribution of many contemporary problems. Attempts to classify modern slavery are also complicated by variations in individual experience, which can sometimes make it difficult to draw a clear-cut distinction between modern slavery and other types of exploitative activities. These variations in experience have proved especially challenging when it comes to contentious issues such as child labour and prostitution, where some human rights activists have sought to expand the boundaries of modern slavery to include nearly all forms of exploitation and abuse. In such cases, political rhetoric regularly takes the place of measured analysis.

While human rights activists regularly invoke the imagery of slavery in order to prioritise a variety of causes, many government officials continue to publicly insist that slavery is not a significant problem within their jurisdiction. These frequent denials represent the first of many obstacles that need to be overcome in order to eradicate modern slavery. On this front, there have recently been a number of promising developments, especially when it comes to legislative reforms, rehabilitation programmes, and the formation of specialised anti-slavery agencies. It is also clear, however, that a great deal remains to be accomplished. This is partially a reflection of ongoing failures by official agents, and partially a reflection of the entrenched nature of many of the problems involved. Much like political campaigns focusing upon global poverty and environmental degradation, recent efforts to combat modern slavery have tended to be geared towards cumulative reductions in the overall scale and severity of particular problem areas, rather than towards a single, decisive solution designed to bring modern slavery to an effective end.

The issues identified above can be approached in a variety of ways. In this chapter, I have organised my remarks into three main sections: modern slavery and international law; modern slavery by the numbers; and forms of modern slavery. The first section documents a gradual expansion of anti-slavery obligations under international law over the course of the twentieth century. This expansion has played a decisive role in shaping the terms of modern activism and analysis. The second section is concerned with a number of prominent estimates of the scale and distribution of modern slavery. These estimates are far from perfect, but they nonetheless offer a rough snapshot of the global dimensions of contemporary problems. The third and final section considers six themes, or problem areas, which represent the core of modern slavery. These are "classical" slavery and descent-based discrimination, bonded labour, forced prostitution, the exploitation of domestic workers, forced labour for the state, and wartime enslavement.

Modern slavery and international law

For thousands of years, the law was firmly on the side of slaveholders and slave-traders. In order to ensure that slave systems functioned effectively, legislators from various parts of the globe drafted elaborate legal codes which were designed to regulate both the conditions on which enslavement initially occurred, and the subsequent terms on which slaves were traded and treated. This longstanding relationship between law and slavery began to break down in the second half of the eighteenth century, with the emergence of an organised anti-slavery movement. These anti-slavery pioneers initially focused on the legal foundations of slave systems in the Americas, as political coalitions sought to first restrict and then abolish slavery and/or slave trading as legal institutions. With the passage of time, anti-slavery activism also extended to Africa, Asia and the Middle East, culminating in a state of affairs where every country in the world has now legally abolished slavery (Quirk, 2006; Miers, 2003).

The passage of laws prohibiting slavery can be best understood as an important first step, rather than a decisive endpoint. For most slave populations, the withdrawal of legal support for slavery translated into qualified yet still consequential improvements in overall levels of consumption, family integrity, economic remuneration and personal autonomy. It is also clear, however, that the legal abolition of slavery also left a great deal to be desired. Although most former slaves experienced some gains from legal reforms which prohibited slavery, they also continued to face widespread discrimination and exploitation. While laws against slavery were introduced, comparable forms of exploitation and abuse continued (Quirk, 2009: 93–98). This divide between legal injunctions and practical outcomes can partially be traced to ineffective enforcement of laws against slavery and servitude. In some cases, however, public officials have also continued actively to support related forms of servitude and exploitation, such as forced labour for the state. In response to these widespread problems, more recent anti-slavery activists have found it necessary to push for further reforms, making a concerted effort not only to close legal loopholes, but also to phase out government support for various forms of human bondage. This impulse has been especially prominent in the field of international law, where the parameters of slavery have steadily expanded over the past century. Having once been used to regulate slavery, the law now provides a key foundation for ongoing efforts to eradicate slavery in all its forms.

The modern relationship between slavery and international law dates back to 1926, and the drafting of the Slavery, Servitude, Forced Labour and Similar Institutions and Practices Convention. Negotiated under the auspices of the League of Nations, this Convention took the important step of defining slavery as "the status or condition of a person over whom any or all of the powers attaching to the right of ownership are exercised". Parties to the Convention (there were 95 in 2002) also undertook "to prevent and suppress the slave trade" and "[t]o bring about, progressively and as soon as possible, the complete abolition of slavery in all its forms". The Convention text does not define the nature of these "forms", but it does include a qualified call for "measures to prevent compulsory or forced labour from developing into conditions analogous to slavery", pointing to a cautious recognition of similarities between various forms of human bondage.[1] This lack of analytical precision regarding "slavery in all its forms" eventually contributed to a further round of deliberation following the Second World War, culminating in the 1956 United Nations Supplementary Convention on the Abolition of Slavery, the Slave Trade, and Institutions and Practices Similar to Slavery.[2]

Over the past half-century, the relationship between slavery and other forms of servitude has been gradually redefined. In this new formulation, chattel slavery no longer represents a separate, exceptional category, but is instead viewed as one of many forms of "contemporary" or "modern" slavery. The main catalyst for this more expansive approach has been the 1956 Supplementary Convention, which took the crucial step of legally equating four "practices and institutions" with chattel slavery. These were debt bondage, serfdom, servile marriage, and the transfer of children for the purpose of exploitation.[3] This formula not only represented a major expansion in anti-slavery obligations under international law, it also placed slavery at the centre of a family of human rights abuses. More recent international instruments have expanded upon this underlying formula. Two themes in particular deserve to be highlighted: human trafficking and child labour.

During the late nineteenth and early twentieth century, organised anti-slavery and human trafficking campaigns primarily moved along parallel, rather than overlapping paths. The main historical progenitor of modern conceptions of trafficking is not chattel slavery, but late nineteenth-century campaigns against prostitution and sexual servitude. This is not to say that there were no connections or associations with opposition to chattel slavery, but trafficking – or "white slavery" as it was then known – was chiefly defined by a political platform that gave limited consideration to either historical slave systems or other exploitative practices of a nonsexual nature. Early "white slavery" campaigns resulted in a series of largely ineffectual international agreements (1904, 1910, 1921, 1933), which were eventually supplanted by the 1949 Convention for the Suppression of the Traffic in Persons and of the Exploitation of the Prostitution of Others. This Convention introduced further provisions against prostitution, but did not explicitly define human trafficking. Since 1949, the issues associated with trafficking have been touched upon in many international instruments, but a universal definition has emerged only relatively recently. This codification occurred through the 2000 United Nations Protocol to Prevent, Suppress and Punish Trafficking in Persons Especially Women and Children (one of several supplements to the 2000 Convention Against Transnational Organized Crime), where trafficking in persons is defined as:

> the recruitment, transportation, transfer, harbouring or receipt of persons, by means of the threat or use of force or other forms of coercion, of abduction, of fraud, of deception, of the abuse of power or of a position of vulnerability … for the purpose of exploitation. Exploitation shall include, at a minimum, the exploitation of the prostitution of others or other forms of sexual exploitation, forced labour or services, slavery or practices similar to slavery, servitude or the removal of organs.[4]

This framework goes well beyond the issue of prostitution to legally incorporate most forms of modern slavery. This is in keeping with larger trends. While trafficking and sexual servitude continue to be closely linked, many practices have come to be analysed in terms of a trafficking framework.

The other key ingredient in recent discussion of modern slavery is child labour. A key starting point is the 1989 Convention on the Rights of the Child, which contains extensive provisions on many issues, including a call for protection against "economic exploitation and from performing any work that is likely to be hazardous or to interfere with the child's education, or to be harmful to the child's health or physical, mental, spiritual, moral or social development".[5] This call has recently been enhanced by the 1999 Convention Concerning the Prohibition and Immediate Action for the Elimination of the Worst Forms of Child Labour. Four main issues are identified here:

> all forms of slavery or practices similar to slavery, such as the sale and trafficking of children, debt bondage and serfdom and forced or compulsory labour, including forced or compulsory recruitment of children for use in armed conflict;
> the use, procuring or offering of a child for prostitution, for the production of pornography or for pornographic performances;
> the use, procuring or offering of a child for illicit activities, in particular for the production and trafficking of drugs as defined in the relevant international treaties;
> work which, by its nature or the circumstances in which it is carried out, is likely to harm the health, safety or morals of children.[6]

By prioritising these "worst" forms, the 1999 Convention divides child labour into different categories. This division is partially a response to a number of critics who have argued that not all examples of child labour involve grievous human rights abuses, but instead sometimes involve age-appropriate exertions for a variety of useful goals, such as training and family support. This line of argument has sometimes been abused by governments seeking to deflect criticism of their child labour records, but it nonetheless contains a grain of truth: not all child labourers endure the same sorts of burdens.

These individual variations in experience have important political and legal ramifications, as it can often be difficult to draw a distinction between slavery and other exploitative practices. Over the past decade, a number of courts have grappled with this question, but no clear consensus has emerged. In a 2002 Appeals Decision (*Kunarac*) before the International Criminal Tribunal for the former Yugoslavia, the court adopted an expansive approach, speaking of "differences of degree" amongst various forms of slavery. In a 2005 case (Siliadin v. France) before the European Court of Human Rights, a narrower interpretation was adopted, with the court ruling that the victim in the case was not held in slavery in "the proper sense", and that other relevant laws should instead apply.

When slavery was legal, identifying who was a slave was relatively straightforward, but with slavery now legally abolished, it is not always easy to say where slavery begins and ends (Quirk, 2009: 26–33). Some authors and organisations have embraced a very broad definition that includes tangential practices such as honour killings and incest, but this approach runs the risk of diluting the concept of slavery to little more than political theatre. Modern slavery may cover more ground than chattel slavery, but it should not be synonymous with all forms of exploitation and abuse. The issues at stake here are encapsulated in a recent judgement by the Australian High Court (Queen v. Tang), which ruled that:

> It is important not to debase the currency of language, or to banalise crimes against humanity, by giving slavery a meaning that extends beyond the limits set by the text, context, and purpose of the 1926 Slavery Convention ... Powers of control, in the context of an issue of slavery, are powers of the kind and degree that would attach to a right of ownership if such a right were legally possible, not powers of a kind that are no more than an incident of harsh employment, either generally or at a particular time or place.
>
> (Allain, 2009: 252)

This ruling represents a prominent challenge to advocates of a more expansive approach to defining slavery, but it is unlikely to represent the final word on this topic. The recent history of anti-slavery activism suggests that different actors will continue to define slavery in diverse ways, and to express different opinions about whether particular cases fit within their preferred criteria and agenda. In this environment, ambiguity and inconsistency can be difficult to avoid, notwithstanding the now extensive body of international law concerned with slavery and related practices and institutions.

Modern slavery by the numbers

The legal and political challenges involved in defining and demarcating modern slavery have also complicated efforts to determine its global scale, since not everyone involved in a particular industry, occupation or activity can be classified in the same way. Researchers attempting to assess the number of persons involved also tend to have limited and imperfect information to work with, since only a minority of cases find their way into the public domain. In this environment, recent figures on the scale and distribution of modern slavery need to be approached with a great deal of caution. Despite ongoing improvements in the use of sampling techniques, most estimates of modern slavery do not have a clearly articulated methodological foundation. Many of the figures that have featured in media reports and official documents, particularly in relation to human trafficking, are based upon "unexamined hypotheses, shoddy research, anecdotal information, or strong moralistic positions", yet they are nonetheless routinely presented as concrete facts (Sanghera, 2005: 5).

One prominent attempt to quantify the parameters of modern slavery comes from Kevin Bales, who has calculated that there are currently around 27 million slaves in the world today. Bales first made his estimate in the late 1990s, and his headline figure rapidly found its way into numerous media outlets, official reports and published works (Bales, 1999). The figure of 27 million slaves builds upon Bales' preferred definition of slavery, which comprises three main elements: "the use of violence to control the slave, the resulting loss of free will, and the economic exploitation that normally precludes the slave receiving any recompense for their work" (Bales, 2005: 91). This formula rejects more expansive approaches to modern slavery, and instead seeks to prioritise what Bales regards as genuine cases of real slavery. To demonstrate how he reached this overall total, he published a table in 2002 which estimates slave numbers across 101 countries, together with a tentative assessment of levels of human trafficking (*ibid.*: 183–86). In most countries, this survey speaks of tens of thousands of slaves. Larger figures are offered for Brazil (100,000–200,000), Burma (50,000–100,000), China (250,000–300,000), Haiti (75,000–150,000), Mauritania (250,000–300,000) and the United States (100,000–150,000). When it comes to these figures, it is important to take into account the overall population of the country in question. While China and Mauritania share the same overall totals, the much smaller size of the Mauritanian population indicates that slavery is a much more significant problem in Mauritania than in China.

There are two countries in Bales' survey which stand out. These are India, which is said to be home to between 18 and 22 million slaves, and Pakistan, which is said to be home to between 2.5 to 3.5 million slaves. According to these two lower estimates, these neighbouring countries account for around 75 per cent of the 27 million total enslaved population. The main issue here is bonded labour, which has been widely practised for centuries in Nepal, Sri Lanka, Bangladesh, India and Pakistan. As part of his 2002 survey, Bales estimated that there were between 250,000 and 300,000 slaves in Nepal (*ibid.*: 184–85). Five years later, he introduced a second much larger estimate, which suggested that "there are around 2.5 million slaves in Nepal today" (Bales, 2007: 98). These two very different estimates of the scale of slavery in Nepal provide a representative example of the imperfect nature of most recent attempts to quantify modern slavery. Unlike many of his peers, Bales has been remarkably candid about the limitations of his research methods. He has repeatedly expressed reservations about the "uncritical acceptance" of his calculations, and has welcomed "correction, new information, and the challenge of debate" (Bales, 2005: 103–4).

Over the past decade, new information about the size and distribution of modern slavery has emerged from a variety of different quarters. Especially prominent is the work of the International Labour Organization (ILO), which has recently devoted substantial resources to the study of modern slavery. In an influential 2005 report, the ILO determined that a minimum of 12.3 million people remained subject to forced labour. In this global survey, forced labour is defined in terms of two basic ingredients: work or services that are exacted under the menace of a penalty, and work or services that are undertaken involuntarily. This definition uses different language from Bales, yet covers very similar ground. The chief difference between Bales' and the ILO's estimates stems from their differing assessment of the scale of bonded labour in the Indian subcontinent. Instead of country-specific totals, the ILO report offers regional estimates.

From this standpoint, the three main regions with the largest concentrations of forced labour are said to be Asia and the Pacific (9,490,000), Latin America and the Caribbean (1,320,000), and sub-Saharan Africa (660,000). The figure for the Asia-Pacific represents around 77 per cent of the 12.3 million total, but is much lower in absolute terms than Bales' 2002 estimate of over 20 million for India and Pakistan alone.

In all three regions, the vast majority of cases of forced labour are said to involve private agents and economic exploitation, with forced prostitution accounting for between 8 and 10 per cent of cases. A somewhat different pattern emerges when it comes to wealthy industrialised countries, where forced prostitution is said to account for around 55 per cent of an overall total of 360,000 (ILO, 2005: 12–14). The report also offers specific information on human trafficking, calculating that the minimum number of persons in forced labour at a given moment as a result of trafficking is 2,450,000, or around 20 per cent of the overall total. Over the past decade, human trafficking has consistently enjoyed a much higher public profile than any other form of modern slavery, yet these findings suggest that a "large majority of forced labour globally is not linked to trafficking" (*ibid.*: 14).

Another key source of information comes from a related ILO report on child labour published in 2002. One of a series of global snapshots, this report suggests that around 211 million children aged between 5 and 14 were engaged in economic activity at the turn of the twenty-first century. The report also goes on to divide child labour into a series of sub-categories, with an estimated 171 million children said to be working in hazardous situations or conditions, and a minimum of 8.4 million children subject to the worst forms of child labour according to the terms of the 1999 Convention. This figure brings together human trafficking (1.2 million), forced and bonded labour (5.7 million), armed conflict (300,000), prostitution and pornography (1.8 million), and illicit activities such as the production and trafficking of drugs (600,000). From a regional standpoint, the largest concentration of child labour again comes from the Asia-Pacific, with bonded labour comprising most of the regional total. Human trafficking once again makes a modest contribution to the 8,400,000 total (14 per cent).[7]

Over the past decade, most efforts to quantify modern slavery have focused on questions of scale and distribution. As more detailed figures have emerged, researchers have begun to take the analysis one step further by attempting to quantify the economic foundations of modern slavery. One example of this larger trend comes from Siddarth Kara, who has recently published extensive data on the scale, regional distribution, growth rate, and economic contribution of various forms of modern slavery. Kara's primary focus is human trafficking for the purposes of forced prostitution, which he estimates to have grown at an annual global rate of 3.6 per cent during the 2007 calendar year, resulting in an overall increase from 1,200,000 to 1,243,050 trafficked sex slaves (Kara, 2009: 17–18). Kara has also produced detailed figures on global profits and revenues, leading him to conclude that:

> the commercial exploitation of trafficked sex slaves generated $51.3 billion in revenues in 2007, the result of millions of men purchasing sex from slaves everyday. After costs, the slaves' exploiters cleared $35.7 billion in profits, or a global average of $29,210 per slave ... the total revenue generated by all forms of contemporary slavery in 2007 was a staggering $152.3 billion, with profits of $91.2 billion.
>
> (*ibid.*: 19)

These figures echo the findings of other researchers, contributing to a general consensus that trafficking for the purposes of forced prostitution offers much greater returns than other forms of bondage. In Kara's model, trafficked sex slaves contribute 39.1 per cent of global profits, yet constitute only 4.2 per cent of the world's slaves (*ibid.*: 19–23). Like other attempts to quantify slavery these calculations rest on a limited methodological foundation. As the field continues to mature, new figures and more refined methods can be expected to emerge.

Forms of modern slavery

Over the past decade, efforts to understand and eradicate modern forms of slavery have primarily concentrated upon six core themes, or practices, which involve both adults and children. These are "classical" slavery and descent-based discrimination; bonded labour, or debt-bondage; forced prostitution, or sexual servitude; the exploitation of domestic workers; forced labour for the state; and wartime enslavement. Most of these themes involve substantial levels of migration, and therefore incorporate the various practices falling under the broader rubric of human trafficking.

Many of these themes are concentrated in specific countries or geographical regions. When it comes to "classical" or "traditional" slavery, the main focal point has been Saharan Africa, where various features of historical slave systems have persisted in a number of countries. Within the past ten years, the governments of both Mauritania (2007) and Niger (2003) have felt obliged to pass legislation (re)abolishing slavery in response to both domestic pressure and international exposure. For some citizens in both countries, slavery has been a fact of life for generations, with slaves enduring arduous work routines, cruel punishments, sexual abuse and family separations. While slave trading continues on a limited scale, the continued viability of these evolving slave systems chiefly depends on children born into slavery. Residual pockets of hereditary bondage (and related practices such as Trokosi "fetish" slavery) have also been recently reported in neighbouring countries, such as Burkina Faso, Cameroon, Chad, Ghana, Guinea, Mali, Nigeria and Western Sahara.[8]

Decades of official complicity in the continuation of slavery were recently highlighted by a high-profile court case in 2008, which saw the Community Court of Justice of the Economic Community of West African States (ECOWAS) determine that the government of Niger had failed to protect one of its citizens from slavery. The plaintiff in the case was Hadijatou Mani Koraou, who was born into slavery in 1984. At the age of 12, she was sold to a new owner for the sum of 240,000 Central African Francs (around $400). She subsequently endured years of systematic abuse and exploitation. Hadijatou's master, El Hadj Souleymane Naroua, had four wives and seven other *sadaka* (female slaves). In 2005, he decided to "liberate" Hadijatou in order to make her one of his wives. Having been issued with a formal liberation certificate, she refused to marry her master, triggering a series of legal proceedings that ended up in the Supreme Court, the highest court in Niger. The court acknowledged Hadijatou's slave status, yet failed to condemn this as unlawful. The judiciary and police not only repeatedly failed to support her bid for freedom, they also directly assisted her master. When Hadijatou later married another man, her former master had her successfully prosecuted for bigamy. She served two months of a six-month sentence for this "crime" before the ECOWAS regional court intervened. Rejecting government submissions that the case was a domestic matter, the court ruled in October 2008 that the government of Niger had failed to uphold its legal obligations, and should therefore pay 10,000,000 Central African Francs (around $20,000) in restitution, plus court costs (Duffy, 2009: 155).

The long-term ramifications of this landmark ruling are still being processed, but the pattern of widespread official complicity which Hadijatou's case has revealed strongly suggests that slavery remains firmly entrenched at both cultural and institutional levels in places such as Niger. In many parts of Saharan Africa, slavery is not an isolated problem, but is also connected to larger patterns of descent-based discrimination. In both Mauritania and Niger, there are hundreds of thousands of former slaves and the descendants of slaves who no longer owe extensive obligations to a specific master, yet nonetheless continue to experience various forms of social discrimination and subordination because of their slave heritage. This discrimination and subordination routinely shapes employment practices, marriage prospects and social relationships, and can also have a major influence upon ongoing failures by government officials to protect human rights.

This complementary relationship between slavery and social discrimination can also be found in other parts of globe besides Saharan Africa. In the Indian subcontinent, caste-based discrimination also facilitates and legitimates various forms of bonded labour. This relationship is especially prominent in the agricultural sector, where the vast majority of bonded labourers come from lower castes, who occupy the bottom rungs of a complex social hierarchy based upon notions of ritual purity. Bonded labour has been integral to agricultural production in places such as India and Pakistan for centuries, with whole villages of lower-caste peasant farmers being bonded to upper-caste landowners. In the worst cases, entire families labour under appalling conditions for their entire lives, with no real hope or expectation of release. It is also not unheard of for masters to sell those in bondage – through their debts – to third parties, inviting comparisons with slave trading. Since most bonded labourers come from "lower" castes, officials have regularly ignored their plight, or even actively supported their oppressors, in much the same way that officials from Niger favoured Hadijatou's master. Building upon earlier injunctions against slavery and forced labour, laws against bonded labour have been introduced in India (1976), Pakistan (1992/1995) and Nepal (2000), but the enforcement of these laws has proved to be sporadic at best, and totally ineffectual at worst (Upadhyaya, 2004).

In its most basic form, bonded labour involves a person promising their labour, or the labour of their family members, in exchange for cash advances which are designed to be very difficult (but not always impossible) to repay. These debts are usually enforced by the threat or use of physical violence, and they can involve either long-term relationships or more limited arrangements. In the traditional variant outlined above, bonded labour regularly spans generations, with children inheriting their parents' obligations. In other variants, victims endure shorter periods of arduous service for little reward before being discarded or discharged. Over the past half-century, bonded labour has become increasingly prominent in many economic sectors in South Asia, including mining, brick making and carpet weaving. In many cases, vulnerable and impoverished workers fall into debt when pursuing employment opportunities. This often begins with deceitful labour recruiters holding out the prospect of work on attractive terms. Faced with few appealing alternatives, those involved end up incurring significant debts as an advance upon future earnings, or to cover relocation costs, and when they subsequently discover that their work bears little resemblance to what was promised, they are told they cannot leave until their debts are repaid. Here, as elsewhere, bonded labour regularly overlaps with other forms of bondage such as child labour and forced prostitution.

Both child labour and prostitution are umbrella categories that can involve a range of experiences and varying degrees of coercion, consent and compensation. These variations in experience can be dissected in a number of ways. One way of distinguishing between modern slavery and other forms of exploitation is to focus on what happens when a person attempts to leave. There are tens of millions of workers throughout the globe who toil for marginal wages under poor working conditions. The majority of these workers have at least some capacity to leave their current job and pursue other opportunities. When they do leave, their employer looks for new recruits. In cases of modern slavery, individuals (and/or their families) usually face severe punishments for trying to leave, and are unable to quit. If they do manage to escape, their masters often expend considerable energy tracking them down. Since pursuing runaways can be expensive, slaveholders also use various means to deter slaves from leaving in the first place. This usually begins with the threat or use of violence, which is commonly associated with punishment for breaches of discipline, and as part of "seasoning" in the early stages of servitude. Not all violence is calculated; it can also reflect sadistic urges. The threat of violence also tends to reinforce other instruments of control such as debt-bondage. When slaveholders declare that debts must be honoured, their "employees" know they will be punished if they fail to uphold their obligations.

Severe restrictions on movement tend to go hand-in-hand with dreadful working conditions. By making it as difficult as possible for "workers" to depart, modern slaveholders can compel their victims to endure terms and conditions that they would not otherwise accept. In the case of forced prostitution, or sexual servitude, this typically involves a combination of high levels of coercion and physical abuse, cramped and unhygienic quarters, an inability to refuse demands for various sexual services, unusually large numbers of clients, high exposure to health risks and other hazards, and little or no financial returns. Modern slaveholders recognise that few individuals will voluntarily endure these inhuman conditions, so they resort to violence and other strategies in order to reduce wages paid to their "workers" to a minimum, while simultaneously enforcing arduous work schedules under unpleasant and unhealthy conditions. Any wages received as part of these arrangements usually go towards paying off debts (which can be manipulated through exorbitant interest rates and creative book-keeping) and living expenses (which tend to be charged above market rates), ensuring that those involved sometimes receive no financial returns from many years of systemic abuse.

While there is widespread recognition that sexual servitude is a serious issue, scholars and activists disagree profoundly over its overall dimensions and political ramifications. In recent years, a growing number of critics have charged that anti-trafficking campaigns have been defined by sensationalised moral panics that have provided justification for anti-immigration policies, reactionary models of sexuality, and the "rescue industry". One influential example from this now extensive literature comes from Ratna Kapur, who argues that a widespread conflation of migration and trafficking had tended to reinforce assumptions that "women and girls need constant male or state protection from harm, are incapable of decision making or consent and therefore must not be allowed to exercise their rights to movement or to earn a living in the manner they choose" (Kapur, 2008: 115). This line of argument also feeds into larger debates over the status of prostitution, which has long been a key bone of contention between those who view all forms of prostitution as an abuse of human rights that should be prohibited, and those who view sex work as a legitimate activity that needs to be regulated to prevent abuses. In this polarised environment, efforts to understand and eradicate sexual servitude frequently have been hijacked by larger ideological agendas and political interests.

Unlike "classical" slavery and traditional forms of bonded labour, forced prostitution is not concentrated in a specific geographical region, but instead can be found in most corners of the globe. It is clear, however, that there are important differences between a small number of wealthy industrialised (and some oil-producing) countries, and a much larger number of poor developing countries. When it comes to global differences between rich and poor, vulnerability to enslavement is often closely connected to citizenship status. Despite being chiefly determined by accident of birth, citizenship nonetheless has profound consequences for individual life-chances. While citizens of wealthy industrial countries are occasionally enslaved, these cases represent the exception, not the rule. Citizens of poorer countries tend to be much more vulnerable, and thus constitute the vast majority of slaves in the world today. This dynamic is not confined to their countries of origin, where vulnerable individuals can be trapped in bondage thanks to poverty, discrimination and desperation, but also extends to citizens from poorer countries who attempt to migrate to richer parts of the world. In such cases, their immigration status – or lack thereof – frequently increases their exposure to a range of highly exploitative situations. Most of these situations do not amount to modern slavery, but cases that fall short of this standard can still leave a great deal to be desired. While there is no question that migration can be rewarding, in far too many cases the search for a better life tends to be characterised by limited protections and high levels of vulnerability.

In most cases, modern slavery is largely defined by what happens after a person reaches his or her destination, rather than by a distinctive set of experiences in transit. This is especially relevant when it comes to international migration, where the pursuit of a better life can lead migrants down a range of paths of varying degrees of legality. Migrants who manage to overcome restrictive immigration controls (which tend to be targeted at citizens of poorer countries) are often regarded as unwelcome outsiders who pose a threat to social order. The vast majority of migrants do not end up in slavery, but a small minority end up in bondage once their journey is complete. There is not one path for migrants and one path for victims of modern slavery; there are many overlapping paths, with many overlapping destinations. While kidnapping and other forms of direct compulsion are not unheard of, most victims of modern slavery migrate voluntarily, albeit on the basis of imperfect or fraudulent information, only to find themselves in bondage once they reach their final destination.

This pattern applies to both undocumented migrants, and migrants who reside legally in another country yet are restricted by conditions of entry that leave them vulnerable to abuse. Since they are unable to work legally, undocumented migrants usually gravitate towards informal labour markets, which offer fertile ground for many forms of labour exploitation, since employers find it easy to ignore legal standards covering hours, wages and work conditions. Faced with the prospect of arrest and deportation, undocumented migrants are often reluctant to appeal to public officials for assistance, and thus have limited means of redress when they are mistreated. In the case of legal migration, the main issue to emerge in recent times has been migrant domestic labour. Over the past two decades, domestic labour has become a leading sector for female employment throughout the globe, building upon an evolving market for cleaners and carers in privileged households.

Global demand for domestic workers can involve both local and international recruitment. At an international level, elaborate networks have developed in order to recruit, place and police substantial flows of migrant domestic labourers from poor developing countries. These networks have led to a marked growth in unaccompanied female migration, which is said to be:

> particularly pronounced in the Philippines, Indonesia and Sri Lanka, where ... women comprise 60–75 percent of legal migrants. The vast majority of these are employed as domestic workers in the Middle East, Singapore, Malaysia and Hong Kong. Of the estimated 850,000 workers from Indonesia and Sri Lanka in Saudi Arabia, the majority are women and in some cases girls (using falsified travel documents) employed as domestic workers. There are approximately 160,000 migrant domestic workers in Singapore and 300,000 in Malaysia.
>
> (Sunderland and Varia, 2006: 3)

Since they are based in privileged households, both local and international domestic workers tend to be excluded from many legal rights and protections that govern labour relations more generally, building a widespread belief that private homes require more relaxed standards than other workplaces. Isolated within these private households, domestic workers routinely endure a host of physical and psychological abuses, long and irregular hours, demeaning treatment, arbitrary punishments, sexual advances, poor pay and conditions, and restrictions on movement. In wealthy countries such as Singapore and Saudi Arabia, migrant domestic workers are further constrained by restrictive work visas, which severely limit their ability to change jobs and access public services. In poorer countries, domestic workers can often start at a very young age. Child domestic labour is particularly notorious in Haiti, where tens of thousands of *restaveks* ("stay-with") children as young as five or six routinely endure appalling working conditions in the poorest country in the Americas.

Like forced prostitution, the abuse of domestic workers is a global problem. Until relatively recently, this was also true of forced labour for the state. During the first half of the twentieth century, tens of millions of people endured forced labour under both colonial and communist rule. By the 1990s, large-scale forced labour had come to an end in all but a handful of regimes, the most notable of which continue to be North Korea, Myanmar and China. The worst offender here is North Korea, where hundreds of thousands of victims are currently interned in penal labour camps, despite having never been formally arrested, informed of their specific offence, or subject to any sort of judicial procedure where they can offer a defence. One of the most egregious features of this system is the use of collective punishments, which sometimes span three generations, with mothers and fathers, sisters and brothers, children and grandchildren all being imprisoned. These political prisoners and their families are frequently subject to lifetime imprisonment, enduring gruelling work regimes, cruel punishments, abysmal food and living conditions, and high mortality. Family members are regularly separated, ending up in one of a series of isolated labour camps devoted to mining, logging, farming and industrial enterprises. These camps probably house between 150,000 and 200,000 prisoners (Hawk, 2003: 24).

Another parallel issue concerns the growth of illegal migration into northern China, where North Koreans caught crossing the border, or who end up being forcibly repatriated, are also condemned to forced labour. Most migrants have no strong political agenda, but instead seek refuge from desperate poverty, widespread famine and systematic repression. People who are caught seeking to escape this environment are usually handled through different channels, with prisoners being housed in short-term detention facilities, where they are once again subject to forced labour. This confinement usually lasts months, rather than years. For these migrants, the experience of forced labour is bound up in a larger pattern of vulnerability, desperation, corruption and other severe hardships. While forced labour camps date back to the mid-twentieth century, the growth of migration into northern China is largely a post-Cold War phenomenon, as the collapse of the Soviet Union ended generous subsidies for the already struggling economy North Korean economy.

The final theme to be considered here is wartime enslavement. Throughout human history, war and slavery have been closely related, with capture through violent conflict being a major source of "fresh" slaves in many historical settings. This relationship has been undermined by the success of organised anti-slavery, but it has not entirely come to an end. The main issue from a modern slavery perspective has been the wartime practice of kidnapping women and children as part of organised raiding parties. This practice is most prominently associated with decades of conflict in Sudan and Uganda, but has also been reported in other parallel conflicts in Africa. In the case of Sudan, persistent raids by government-backed militias between the early 1980s and 2001 resulted in tens of thousands of people from southern Sudan being forced into service as cattle-herders, domestic servants, sex slaves, and "wives". In order to secure the return of those taken in these raids, some local community leaders and – from 1995 onwards – international organisations developed extensive redemption programs, raising funds though high-profile public campaigns based around the idea of buying the freedom of enslaved captives. These proved to be extremely controversial, with critics charging that redemption programs encouraged further raids, that they unduly rewarded slaveholders, and that they were subject to fraud (Appiah and Bunzl, 2007). While the war between north and south formally came to an end in 2005, similar raiding parties have been reported as part of the ongoing campaign being waged by the Sudanese government against the people of Darfur.

Another dimension of wartime enslavement revolves around the forced recruitment and subsequent maltreatment of child soldiers. In recent and ongoing conflicts in countries such as Uganda, Sierra Leone, Liberia, Angola, Mozambique and the Democratic Republic of Congo, tens of thousands of children have been abducted and forced into military service by both rebel groups and government agents. These abductions often place children in situations where they are compelled to commit acts of violence against members of their own communities, leaving these children in the uncomfortable position of being both victims and perpetrators. While children of both sexes can serve as soldiers, girls often end up being both soldiers and sex slaves. Not all children are recruited through abductions, but instead come to serve through other paths; but in situations involving children below the age of 18 all forms of recruitment must be regarded as inherently problematic. Like other victims of modern slavery, child soldiers also tend to face severe restrictions on their movement, as attempts to escape tend to be severely punished as acts of desertion and betrayal. It is also clear, moreover, that the burden of being a child soldier tends to have long-term consequences, which can persist after military conflict comes to an end. Here, as elsewhere, former slaves consistently face profound psychological, social and economic challenges when it comes to adjusting to life after slavery, and thus require long-term assistance and support (Honwana, 2007).

Conclusion

Efforts to understand and eradicate modern slavery have come a long way in a short space of time. Until relatively recently, few people were even aware that modern slavery was a global problem. This perception began to change in the mid-1990s, when increasing concerns about illegal migration following the end of the Cold War played a decisive role in raising the profile of human trafficking and forced prostitution. As concerns about trafficking increased, other related forms of human bondage also came to be viewed in a new light. By the early twenty-first century, modern slavery had rapidly and unexpectedly emerged as a major human rights issue. This sea-change in public consciousness about the continuing importance of slavery in modern life has had far-reaching consequences, most notably when it comes to information, public awareness and political engagement. When it comes to information, researchers have recently made considerable progress documenting and analysing modern slavery. While silences and shortcomings persist, information on modern slavery is no longer in short supply. In the case of public awareness, sustained (and often sensationalised) media coverage of modern slavery in general, and human trafficking in particular, has now reached a point where few people are not aware that slavery is a problem. When it comes to political engagement, modern slavery is also now firmly established within the halls of power, leading to serious discussions at many different levels of government. Within the past decade, many nation-states have introduced new anti-slavery (mostly anti-trafficking) laws. Some have also established specialised anti-slavery agencies and taskforces. While the enforcement of these new laws sometimes leaves a great deal to be desired, it is nonetheless possible to point to significant improvements in overall levels of political engagement in many parts of the globe.

These recent advances offer a solid platform for future activism and analysis. It is also clear, however, that modern slavery will not be easy to eradicate. As we have seen, modern forms of slavery tend be closely linked to poverty, inequality, desperation and social discrimination. In order to combat slavery effectively, it is also necessary to address these underlying structural problems. This means confronting a number of complex and politically contentious issues. In countries such as India and Pakistan, combating slavery also means combating the centuries-old caste system at the heart of the prevailing social order. In richer countries, combating slavery also means confronting the privileges associated with citizenship, and the widespread exploitation and vulnerability of migrant workers. As we have seen, this dynamic not only applies to illegal migrants, but also extends to millions of individuals who migrate legally on terms that leave them extremely vulnerable to abuse. In countries such as North Korea, Myanmar and Sudan, challenging slavery also means confronting the complicity of political regimes that continue to enslave their own citizens. In all these examples, the challenge of ending slavery is likely to be a cumulative, long-term process, involving gradual reductions in the overall scale and severity of specific problem areas.

Notes

1 *Slavery Convention*, Office of the United Nations High Commissioner for Human Rights. www2.ohchr.org/english/law/slavery.htm
2 On the discussions surrounding the 1926 and 1956 Conventions, see Allain (2008).
3 *Supplementary Convention on the Abolition of Slavery, the Slave Trade, and Institutions and Practices Similar to Slavery*, Office of the United Nations High Commissioner for Human Rights. www2.ohchr.org/english/law/slavetrade.htm
4 *Protocol to Prevent, Suppress and Punish Trafficking in Persons Especially Women and Children, supplementing the United Nations Convention against Transnational Organized Crime*, Office of the United Nations High Commissioner for Human Rights. www2.ohchr.org/english/law/protocoltraffic.htm
5 *Convention on the Rights of the Child*, Office of the United Nations High Commissioner for Human Rights. www2.ohchr.org/english/law/crc.htm
6 *Worst Forms of Child Labour Convention, 1999* (No. 182), Office of the United Nations High Commissioner for Human Rights. www2.ohchr.org/english/law/childlabour.htm
7 ILO (2002: 14, 23–27). A more recent 2006 report does not provide specific information on the worst forms of labour.
8 On Trokosi "fetish" slavery, see Bales (1999: 21–22).

Bibliography

Allain, Jean, *The Slavery Conventions: The Travaux Préparatoires of the 1926 League of Nations Convention and the 1956 United Nations Convention* (Leiden: Martinus Nijhoff, 2008).
——, "Clarifying the Definition of 'Slavery' in International Law", *Melbourne Journal of International Law* 10 (2009), 246–57.
Anderson, Bridget, *Doing the Dirty Work: The Global Politics of Domestic Labour* (London: Zed Books, 2000).
Appiah, Kwame Anthony and Bunzl, Martin, eds, *Buying Freedom: The Ethics and Economics of Slave Redemption* (Princeton, NJ: Princeton University Press, 2007).
Bales, Kevin, *Disposable People: New Slavery in the Global Economy* (Berkeley: University of California Press, 1999).
——, *Understanding Global Slavery: A Reader* (Berkeley: University of California Press, 2005).
——, *Ending Slavery: How We Free Today's Slaves* (Berkeley: University of California Press, 2007).
Blagbrough, Jonathon, *"They Respect their Animals More": Voices of Child Domestic Workers* (London: Anti-Slavery International, 2008).
Davidson, Julia O'Connell, *Children and the Global Sex Trade* (Cambridge: Polity Press, 2005).
Duffy, Helen, "Hadijatou Mani Koraou v Niger: Slavery Unveiled by the ECOWAS Court", *Human Rights Law Review* 9 (2009), 151–70.
Hawk, David, *The Hidden Gulag: Exposing North Korea's Prison Camps, Prisoners' Testimonies and Satellite Photographs* (Washington, DC: US Committee for Human Rights in North Korea, 2003).
Honwana, Alcinda, *Child Soldiers in Africa* (Philadelphia: University of Pennsylvania Press, 2007).
ILO, *Every Child Counts: New Global Estimates on Child Labour* (Geneva: International Labour Office, 2002).
——, *A Global Alliance Against Forced Labour: Global Report Under the Follow-up to the ILO Declaration on Fundamental Principles and Rights at Work* (Geneva: International Labour Office, 2005).

Kara, Siddarth, *Sex Trafficking: Inside the Business of Modern Slavery* (New York: Columbia University Press, 2009).

Kapur, Ratna, "Migrant Women and the Legal Politics of Trafficking Interventions", in Sally Cameron and Edward Newman, eds, *Trafficking in Human Beings* (Tokyo: United Nations University Press, 2008), 111–25.

Miers, Suzanne, *Slavery in the Twentieth Century* (Walnut Creek, CA: Altamira Press, 2003).

Muico, Norma Kang, *Forced Labour in North Korean Prison Camps* (London: Anti-Slavery International, 2007).

Quirk, Joel, "The Anti-Slavery Project: Linking the Historical and Contemporary", *Human Rights Quarterly* 28 (2006), 565–98.

——, *Unfinished Business: A Comparative Survey of Historical and Contemporary Slavery* (Paris: UNESCO Publishing, 2009).

Ruf, Urs Peter, *Ending Slavery: Hierarchy, Dependency and Gender in Central Mauritania* (Bielefeld: Transcript Verlag, 1999).

Sanghera, Jyoti, "Unpacking the Trafficking Discourse", in Kamala Kempadoo, Jyoti Sanghera and Bandana Pattanaik, eds, *Trafficking and Prostitution Reconsidered: New Perspectives on Migration, Sex Work, and Human Rights* (Boulder, CO: Paradigm Publishers, 2005), 3–24.

Srivastava, Ravi, *Bonded Labour in India: Its Incidence and Pattern* (Geneva: International Labour Office, 2005).

Sunderland, Judith and Varia, Nisha, *Swept Under the Rug: Abuses against Domestic Workers Around the World* (New York: Human Rights Watch, 2006).

Upadhyaya, Krishna, "Bonded Labour in South Asia: India, Nepal and Pakistan", in Christien van den Anker, ed., *The Political Economy of the New Slavery* (Hampshire: Palgrave, 2004), 118–36.

INDEX

Aberdeen Act (1845), 292

abolition of slave trade, 91, 164; abolitionist publics, 284–87; British slave trade, 46, 91; Christmas Rebellion (1831), 12, 229, 230, 303; consequences, 292–93; explaining, 287–90; legacies, 292–93; origins of abolitionist opinion, 282–84; suppression of slave trade, 290–92; *see also* emancipation

Abu-Lughold, Janet, 61n2

Adams, John, 275

affranchisement, 236

Afonso, King, 155

Africa: famine in, 55–56; and Islamic slavery, 42–43; recreating in Americas, 180–83

African Atlantic religions *see* religions, African Atlantic

African Methodist Episcopal Church, 183

African people: attitudes to, 67, 69–70, 139–40; born into slavery, where, 37, 41; as "negroes," 89; as Sons of Ham, perceptions of, 70, 78

African slavery, 1, 35–49; and Atlantic slave trade, 83–84; colonial agriculture, contributions to, 107–8; and colonialism, 46–48; contemporary, 48, 49; and definitions of slavery, 35–38; demand for slaves by Europeans, 39, 205; English attitudes to slaves, 67, 69–70, 139–40; enslavement process in Africa, 173–77; European demand for African slaves, 39; gender factors, 141; insiders and outsiders, 37; and IOW slavery, 37, 44; and labour/work patterns, 39–41, 101–2, 106–8; methods of enslavement, 38–39; and Middle Passage, 87–90; pawnship, 42, 55; reasons for Atlantic slave trade, 83–84; slave trade, 43–46; slavery as one form of labour, 41–42; vs. slavery in Americas, 175–76; suppression of Atlantic slave trade, effects on, 293; violence by slaves, 88; *see also* Atlantic slave trade

African-led rebellions, 222–26

Age of Revolutions, 2, 5, 7, 267–79, 289; American Revolution, 106, 114–15, 162, 195, 272, 286; French Revolution, 193, 269, 272–73; Haitian Revolution *see* Haitian Revolution (1791–1803)

agriculture: colonial, African contributions to, 107–8; diversified, 108–9; intensification of work, 104–7; Roman slavery, 27; *see also* plantation societies; planter class; sugar production

Ahmad Baba, 42, 43

Akan slavery, 36, 45, 223

Allen, Richard, 183, 242

al-Maghili, 42

American Civil War (1861–65), 198, 200, 215, 245, 301, 315

American Missionary Association (AMA), 326

American Revolution (1775–83), 85, 106, 162, 195, 269–72; and abolition of slavery, 272, 286; trade disruptions, 114–15

American South, 105, 121, 125, 199, 303; Civil War commemorations, 324–28; *see also specific areas in American South*

Americas, 44, 64, 66, 171; Africa in, recreating, 180–83; importance of slavery in, 3–6; origins of slavery *see* Americas, origins of slavery in (1500–1700); Protestant slave societies, 182–83; slavery in vs slavery in Africa, 175–76; transmission of African Atlantic religions to (1519–1700), 156–61; *see also* Atlantic slave trade

Americas, origins of slavery in (1500–1700), 2, 64–78; consequences of transition to enslavement, 75–76; Iberian precedents, 65–66; labour relations in early seventeenth century, 66–73; mid-century transitions, 73–75; New England, seventeenth century, 76–78

Amis des noirs, 243

ancestral spirits, 153

anciens libres, 244

Haiti, 164, 310; *Vodun* (neo-African religion), 10, 164, 165, 207
Haitian Revolution (1791–1803), 220, 227, 240, 244, 272–76, 289; success of, 12, 214, 226; *see also* American Revolution (1775–83); French Revolution (1789–99); Louverture, Toussaint; Saint Domingue
Hakluyt, Richard, 138–39
Hall, Kim, 139
Hamlet, 1
Hammond, James Henry, 133–34, 199
Harris, Joseph, 270
Hartman, Saidiya, 95
Haskell, Thomas, 285
Hausa people, on children of slaves, 37
Hawkins, John, 68
Hawley, Henry, 72
Hegel, Georg Wilhelm Friedrich, 6
helots, ancient Greece, 20, 25
Herbert, Thomas, 140
Herskovits, Melville J., 9, 10, 171, 205–6
Heyward, Nathaniel, 191
Heywood, Linda, 155, 156, 176
Hidalgo rebellion (1810), Mexico, 278
Higman, B. W., 190, 192, 320, 323
Hispaniola, 11, 214
HIV/AIDS, risk of, 59
Hobbes, Thomas, 5
hoe, as universal implement of slavery, 149
Hogg, Rev. A. G., 323
Holton, Woody, 270
Homer, 20
Hopkins, Keith, 26
hoplites (Athenian farmers), 21, 22
horro (to free), 236
Howell, William, 255
Hughson, John, 254

Ibarra, José de, 242
Iberia/Iberian powers, 64, 65–66, 154
Iberian Peninsula, 154, 234
Igbo people, 40
Ikem dance, 226
Iliad (Homer), 20
illegal trading, 252–53
illnesses *see* diseases/conditions
immunity problems, 129
imperialism, and demand for labour, 58
indenture contract, 71
Indian Ocean World (IOW), 1, 2, 7, 44, 52–61; and Atlantic World, 52, 53; enslavement in, 54–56; global economy, 61; indebtedness as cause of enslavement, 54–55; meaning/historical significance, 52; monsoons, 53; natural disasters, as cause of enslavement,

55–56; servitude in, 59–61; slave trades over time, 56–59
Indians, enslavement of, 67–68
Indus Valley, 54
infections, 128, 129, 132, 259
infertility, 123, 141
influenza, 259
Inikori, Joseph, 35, 94
Inquisition, 159–60
institutions of marginality, 36
international law, and modern slavery, 332–35
inter-racial unions, 144, 255–57
IOW *see* Indian Ocean World (IOW)
irmandades (Brazilian brotherhoods), 164–65, 207
Isaacs, David, 256
Isabella of Castile, 65
Islam, 153–54, 166; Five Pillars of, 158
Islamic slavery, Africa, 41, 42–43

Jadin, L., 40
Jamaica, 115, 129, 163, 199, 212, 216, 221; 1831 slave rebellion, 229–31; and Atlantic slave trade, 87, 92, 93; demographic factors, 120, 121, 123, 125; emancipation of slaves/Emancipation Day traditions, 303, 305, 315, 321–22, 323; free coloureds in, 235, 240; ill-treatment of slaves, 132, 147; sugar cultivation and planter class, 190, 191; Tacky's Rebellion (1760), 197, 198, 212, 223–24, 226, 239; *see also* Worthy Park (Jamaican sugar plantation)
Jameson, Robert, 180
Jamestown, and origins of slavery in the Americas, 66, 67, 71
Jefferson, Thomas, 195, 196
jihad, 43, 46
Joaquim, Leandro, 242
John Brown's Body (abolitionist anthem), 326
John Cause Men, 314
Johnson, Andrew, 305
Johnson, Samuel, 195
Johnson, Walter, 216–17
Jones Creek Baptist Church, 258
Jonkunnu, 314
justification of slavery, ancient Greece, 25
Juvenal, 28

Kachun, Mitch, 329n13
Kansas-Nebraska Act (1854), 211
Kaufman, Chaim, 291
Kaye, Anthony, 216
Kemble, Frances, 149
Kempa Vita, Beatriz, 156
Kentucky, 112

warfare, and demand for labour, 58
Washington, George, 106
Wealth (Aristophanes), 23
weapons of the weak, 208
West, Nancy, 256
West Africa, 42, 46, 83, 154, 163, 176; and
    Atlantic slave trade, 92, 93; English
    voyages to, 68, 69
West Indies, Emancipation Day traditions,
    318, 320–24
Westmoreland Parish, Jamaica,
    132, 147
Wheatley, Phyllis, 242
"whipping posts," slaves as, 29
White, John, 67
white ancestry of slaves, 238
"white Atlantic," 81
Wilberforce, William, 228, 285
Wilkinson, Moses, 163
Williams, Eric, 94, 288–89
Williams, Raymond, 170
Wilson, David, 86–87
Windward Coast, 85
Windward Maroons, Jamaica, 212
Winthrop, John, 77
witch trials, 161, 162

"women's work," 149
work and slave economy, 8–9, 101–16;
    African contributions to colonial
    agriculture, 107–8; agricultural
    intensification, 104–7; changing work
    patterns, 108–9; diversified agriculture,
    108–9; early staple regimes, 101–4, 108;
    gender factors, 109; increase in available
    occupations to enslaved men, 108; intensity,
    duration and physical effects of work,
    109–11; internal slave economies, 113–15;
    productivity debates, 111–13; skeletal
    analysis, 110–11; slaves separated from
    servants, 102; *see also* labour
worms, 128, 132
Worthy Park (Jamaican sugar plantation),
    126, 130, 221
Wurdemann, John, 123
Wyatt-Brown, Bertram, 192

yaws, 128, 130
yellow fever, 223
Yoruba region, 38, 40, 41, 45, 166, 182
Yorubaland, 178

de Zurara, Gomes Eannes, 140–41, 235

Printed in the USA/Agawam, MA
August 29, 2011

560994.003